The Viṣṇu Purāṇa

ANCIENT ANNALS
OF THE GOD
WITH LOTUS EYES

The Viṣṇu Purāṇa

ANCIENT ANNALS
OF THE GOD
WITH LOTUS EYES

Translated from the Sanskrit
by McComas Taylor

PRESS

For my grandchildren

Published by ANU Press
The Australian National University
Acton ACT 2601, Australia
Email: anupress@anu.edu.au

Available to download for free at press.anu.edu.au

ISBN (print): 9781760464400
ISBN (online): 9781760464417

WorldCat (print): 1247155624
WorldCat (online): 1247154847

DOI: 10.22459/VP.2021

Cover design and layout by ANU Press

Cover image: Vishnu Reclining on Ananta. From Sage Markandeya's Ashram and the Milky Ocean, c. 1780–1790. Mehrangarh Museum Trust.

Contents

Book Four: The Royal Dynasties 275

Book Five: Kṛṣṇa 337

Preface

Viṣṇu is a central deity in the Hindu pantheon, especially in his manifestation as the seductive cattleherding youth, Kṛṣṇa. The purāṇas are a genre of sacred texts, which, as the Sanskrit name implies, are collections of narratives from 'long ago'. The *Viṣṇu Purāṇa* is thus an ancient account of the universe and a guide to life, which places Viṣṇu–Kṛṣṇa at the centre of creation, theology and reality itself.

This text, composed about 1,500 years ago, provides a comprehensive and accessible introduction to the most important themes and narratives that constitute the Hindu imagination: the cyclical creation and destruction of the universe, the origin of gods and mortals, the peopling of the world and the structure and conduct of ideal brahminical society.

The *Viṣṇu Purāṇa* describes the trials of exemplary devotees, the existential struggles between gods and demons and the exploits of legendary cultural heroes. It also contains many ecstatic songs of praise for the deity. The ever-popular accounts of Kṛṣṇa's love games with the cattle-herding girls of Vṛndāvana—which have proliferated in literature, dance, song and visual arts over the millennia—are found here in authoritative form.

This introduction provides background information to help non-specialist readers understand, appreciate and, most importantly, enjoy the *Viṣṇu Purāṇa*. It begins by describing the purāṇas as a genre, noting the difficulty of assigning specific dates and authors to individual texts. This is followed by an outline of the relationship between the *Viṣṇu Purāṇa* and other master texts of the Sanskritic archive.

I then outline the theology of the *Viṣṇu Purāṇa*, describing the place of the deity in the Hindu pantheon, along with his *avatāras*—his physical manifestations who have 'crossed down' into the world—including Kṛṣṇa.

To assist readers in navigating the purāṇic thought-world, the various classes of divine, semi-divine and mortal beings that inhabit these accounts are described.

I will briefly discuss the different elements that make up the text, beginning with the overall framing narrative, the verse and prose sections, the embedded subnarratives, the extensive genealogical lists and the all-important songs of praise.

The *Viṣṇu Purāṇa* is divided into six parts (*aṃśa*) or books, which I have labelled for convenience: 'Creation', 'The World', 'Society', 'The Dynasties', 'Kṛṣṇa' and 'Dissolution'. Each book is summarised to provide the reader with a convenient overview of the entire work. I conclude this introduction with a few notes on the various Sanskrit versions of the *Viṣṇu Purāṇa*, earlier translations and an explanation of how I approached some of the dilemmas faced by every translator, especially those working with Sanskrit texts.

Specialist readers, and indeed non-specialists who do not like reading introductions, may prefer to jump straight into the translation itself. For those encountering this style of narrative for the first time, there are several easy entry points. These include the story of the demon prince Prahlāda, who wins liberation (1.16–20); the story of Saubhari, a sage who lived underwater and used his magic powers to marry 50 sisters but ended up with more problems than he could handle (4.2); and the story of how Kṛṣṇa subdued the serpent Kāliya, who lived in the Yamunā River (5.7).[1]

1 References to the *Viṣṇu Purāṇa* are given in the form of book and chapter numbers or book, chapter and verse numbers.

Acknowledgements

Sweta Prajapati of the Oriental Institute at the Maharaja Sayajirao University of Baroda provided the original impetus for this project. Ulrich Timme Kragh generously hosted me at Adam Mickiewicz University in Poznan, Poland, as part of the Narrative Modes of Historical Discourse in Asia Project. During two sabbaticals, Tim taught me the true meaning of Danish *hygge*. Simon Brodbeck of the University of Cardiff generously shared the invaluable expertise he gained in the process of translating the *Harivaṃśa*. Peter Schreiner, whose German translation was always at my elbow during my labours, served as an absent guide and mentor. Mark Allon, Greg Bailey, Raj Balkaran, Adam Bowles, John and Mary Brockington, Beth Rohlman, Adheesh Sathaye and Christiane Weissbach-Berger have all shared this journey in various ways. I gratefully acknowledge the interest, guidance and encouragement provided by all these kind colleagues. I am especially grateful to the two anonymous referees engaged by ANU Press, whose meticulous and critical attention has saved me considerable embarrassment. Thanks also to Jan Borrie for her punctilious copyediting and proofreading. All remaining errors are, of course, my own.

Glossary

Ādityas	deities descended from Aditi
apsarases	semi-divine female beings
avatāras	the physical manifestations of a deity in this world
cāraṇas	a class of heavenly singers
Daityas	demons descended from Diti
Dānavas	demons descended from Danu
gandharvas	semi-divine male beings
guhyakas	demons, similar to rākṣasas
guṇas	the three constituent qualities of the universe
kiṃnaras	a class of semi-divine beings
kimpuruṣas	a class of semi-divine beings
kṣatriyas	the community of warriors
kūṣmāṇḍas	a class of demons
mahat	the fundamental element, 'greatness'
Manus	legendary rulers of the world
Maruts	wind gods
nāgas	semi-divine serpents
piśācas	flesh-eating demons
Pramathas	a class of demons in the service of Śiva
rākṣasas	night-ranging demons

saṃsāra	the cycle of life, death and rebirth
siddhas	highly accomplished seers with semi-divine powers
śrāddha	a ritual to sustain deceased relatives in the afterlife
śūdras	the community of servants
svayaṃvara	a tournament of warriors at which a noblewoman chooses a husband
vaiśyas	the community of merchants and farmers
Vasus	a class of deities
vidyādhara	a class of semi-divine musicians
Viśvas	a class of deities
yakṣas	a class of semi-divine beings

Introduction

The purāṇas

The purāṇas are an important genre of Hindu literature.[1] Together they constitute an authoritative archive—cosmogony and cosmology, theology and mythology as well as orthodoxy and orthopraxis—for Hindu traditions. Many important narratives relating to the deities Viṣṇu–Kṛṣṇa, Śiva and the great goddess Devī are found in their most authoritative form in purāṇic texts. These narratives—along with the two epics, the *Mahābhārata* and the *Rāmāyaṇa*—form the beating heart of Hindu identity and imagination. To be Hindu is to have internalised this purāṇic thought-world.

Traditionally, there are said to be eighteen great purāṇas and an equal number of lesser ones, although the membership of each category varies from one source to another. In addition, there are probably thousands of local purāṇas, ancient and modern, in Sanskrit and vernacular languages, which preserve accounts of specific sacred sites, communities and religious practices.

The great purāṇas are composed in Sanskrit—the elite language of scholarly and priestly discourse in premodern India. Ironically, the most authoritative forms of these narratives are preserved in a language inaccessible to the majority of the faith community, both then and now. Purāṇic narratives, though preserved in Sanskrit, are widely reproduced in popular vernaculars, not to mention the visual arts, drama, film and television and now, like everything else, online and through mobile apps.

1 The best general introduction to the purāṇas is Bailey (2018). See also Matchett (2005) and Rao (2007). For more detail on individual purāṇas, see Rocher (1986).

Most of the great purāṇas are thought to have reached their current state between 400 and 1500 CE or later. The most recent strata of the *Bhaviṣya Purāṇa*, for example, famously prophesises the existence of Queen Victoria's Calcutta, and must therefore have been either uncommonly prescient or completed during or after that monarch's reign (Hiltebeitel 1999: 277).

Most purāṇas are substantial bodies of literature, ranging from 10,000 to 20,000 verses. The outlier is the giant, sprawling *Skanda Purāṇa* at more than 80,000 verses. The *Viṣṇu Purāṇa*, which runs to about 5,600 verses or 15,000 lines, is among the more modest members of the genre. For comparison, Homer's *Odyssey* and *Iliad* are both about the same length as this text, as is a typical volume of *Harry Potter*.

By their own definition, purāṇas are supposed to exhibit five characteristics—the *pañca-lakṣaṇa*—and address five main themes:[2] the initial creation of the universe out of nothing (*sarga*), its subsequent re-creation after each cyclical destruction (*pratisarga*), the genealogies of the gods and patriarchs (*vaṃśa*), the reigns of fourteen mythical progenitors known as Manus (*manvantara*) and the history of two dynasties, the Solar and the Lunar (*vaṃśa-anucarita*).

There is great variation in the degree to which individual purāṇas adhere to this scheme. At one end of the spectrum is the *Agni Purāṇa*—an extensive encyclopedia of cultural, scientific and literary snippets—which dispenses with the *pañca-lakṣaṇa* in a few pages. The *Viṣṇu Purāṇa* is at the other end of the spectrum and, of all the major purāṇas, is most closely structured in accordance with this scheme.

These five topics constitute the bulk of the *Viṣṇu Purāṇa*'s content and are covered more or less systematically in its six books, but with devotional and other practical guidance for daily life included here and there. The description of the Lunar Dynasty balloons out to fill Books Four and Five, as these contain the account of Kṛṣṇa's forebears and the deeds of the deity himself. The final book, dealing with various forms of dissolution, rightly belongs to the second *lakṣaṇa*, which includes both the creation and the destruction of the universe, but the end of the book is perhaps a more appropriate place to describe the end of the world. This arrangement also reinforces the overall chronological structure of the *Viṣṇu Purāṇa*.

---

2 On the *pañca-lakṣaṇa*, see Schreiner (2002).

The *Viṣṇu Purāṇa*

In so far as the *Viṣṇu Purāṇa* has a single thrust or goal, it is to instil and heighten a sense of devotion to the deity in all his various forms. As the text says of itself: 'Lord Viṣṇu is mentioned at every stage, including the creation, re-creation, genealogies, Manvantaras and the rest without exception, best of brahmins' (3.6.26). It seeks to inspire devotion to the deity by continually emphasising his all-embracing and universal nature and by demonstrating that, by singing the deity's praises with devotion, gods, mortals and even demons get what they want—either earthly success or divine liberation.

This text is thought to have arisen at a time in Indian history when there was much competition in the spiritual marketplace among various traditions. Then, as now, traditions need to attract and retain devotees to survive. They can only maintain and perpetuate themselves with the energy and resources provided by the faithful. The *Viṣṇu Purāṇa* seeks to achieve this goal by confirming and constantly reconfirming the centrality of the deity in all creation. It describes the spiritual journey of exemplary devotees such as the young prince Dhruva and the demon boy Prahlāda, who escape the torments of existence through extreme devotion and piety. These model devotees eventually achieve a state of mystical union with Viṣṇu and thereby win liberation from *saṃsāra*—the otherwise endless cycle of birth, death and rebirth. This search for liberation or *mokṣa* is the ultimate goal, not only of Hindu traditions of which the *Viṣṇu Purāṇa* is a part, but also of the other Indic religions, Buddhism and Jainism. Liberation leads to a state of nonexistence or *nirvāṇa*.

The *Viṣṇu Purāṇa* has a socially conservative subtext. At every step, it asserts the superiority of the priestly community of brahmins at the expense of the other orders that constitute its idealised society: the warrior, merchant and serving classes—the *kṣatriyas*, *vaiśyas* and *śūdras*. Brahmins were placed by the Creator at the apex of the social hierarchy and are to be honoured, paid, fed and served by everyone else. The most heinous crime is brahminicide, and without brahmins to conduct the sacrifice that nourishes the gods, the world would perish.

The social conservatism of the *Viṣṇu Purāṇa* is also evident in terms of gender. This is a text composed by men and for men in a patriarchal society. Women are primarily wives and mothers whose role is to bear sons to perpetuate the male line. At one point, we read that children really belong to the father as he is the source of semen, while 'a mother is but a pouch of skin' (4.19.1). Fidelity to her husband is a woman's primary virtue. Nonhuman female characters, such as the Earth and cows, need to be uplifted, rescued and protected by males. The only other role for women is as the 'fair-hipped', 'almond-eyed' seductress who tempts pious men from the path of virtue.

One bright spot for female characters is found in the song of praise offered to the goddess Lakṣmī, Viṣṇu's consort (1.8.16–34). Here, the qualities of the divine couple are compared in relatively equal and complementary terms: Viṣṇu is 'meaning' and his partner is 'the word', and so on. Nevertheless, the *Viṣṇu Purāṇa* remains the product of the patriarchal system in which it is clearly invested.

Problems with dating

The dating of Sanskrit texts is always problematic, as they exist in multiple versions and have evolved over many centuries. Traditionally inscribed on palm leaves or birch bark, manuscripts perish in the hot and humid Indian climate. It has been said that the most enthusiastic consumer of Sanskrit manuscripts is 'His Majesty the Bookworm'. Even after paper was introduced in the thirteenth century, manuscripts had to be recopied every few generations. Each time a scribe sat down to write out an old worm-eaten manuscript, he or his sponsor might seek to 'improve' the text by adding a story here or inserting a discourse there. Purāṇas, like a premodern Sanskritic Wikipedia, thus evolved under many hands over many generations.[3] The result is that texts in their final form can seldom be assigned accurately to a single time, place or author.

Ironically, for the past two centuries or more, Western scholarship has tended to prioritise the oldest and therefore most 'original' version of a text. Scholars have regarded 'improvements' carried out by premodern scribes as corruptions or contaminations. Some Indological research is also criticised for being ahistorical—that is, for neglecting to address a text in its historical, political, social or economic context. But how is one to assign a text to a specific context when it has been in circulation across the length and breadth of the Indic world for a millennium or more? This problem remains unresolved.

3 I owe this simile to Wendy Doniger.

My particular approach has been to use current practice as an analogy. The modes in which texts are 'consumed' today may cast light on how they were used in the past. After all, the ideological context of these texts—the 'purāṇic thought-world'—remains intact alongside and within modernity, and the discourses conjured by texts like the *Viṣṇu Purāṇa* still resonate with audiences in the faith community today.

While it is impossible to assign an exact date to the *Viṣṇu Purāṇa*, we can position it relative to some of the other Sanskrit classics. We know, for example, that our text is later than the epics the *Mahābhārata* and the *Rāmāyaṇa*—which are thought to have reached their current form before the fourth or fifth centuries CE (van Buitenen 1973: xxv; Goldman 1984: 14)—as it makes many references to them. The *Viṣṇu Purāṇa* is probably older than the *Bhāgavata Purāṇa*, which dates from the eighth to tenth centuries at the latest (Holdrege 2013: 92; Hardy 1983), as our text is simpler in structure, less elaborate in diction and exhibits a less-developed sense of *bhakti*—the intense personal sentiment of devotion to the divine. It seems reasonable to guess—but little more than guess—that the *Viṣṇu Purāṇa* reached its current extent between the fourth and fifth centuries CE (Couture 2014; Schreiner 2013: 592).

The various dates mentioned above tend to align these important Sanskrit texts with the period of the Gupta Empire, one of India's 'Golden Ages', which flourished between 319 and 543 CE. This period witnessed a number of important changes in Indian society. Religious practices that had been the exclusive province of the brahmin elite now devolved towards individuals who were able to perform domestic and temple-based rituals themselves. There was rising competition for royal patronage and spiritual leadership among different traditions. These included Hindu schools centred on the deities Viṣṇu, Śiva and the great goddess Devī and 'heretical' schools including Jain, Buddhist and Tantric practitioners. All of these challenged the old Vedic order and are thought to have weakened the financial, social and ideological preeminence that the brahmins had enjoyed. Some scholars see the appearance of purāṇic literature as a brahminical response to these changing conditions. Brahmins wrote purāṇas to cement their place at the centre of the social order, and they were a means by which the authors sought to reclaim and maintain their social capital, which was increasingly under threat (Sathaye 2015: 111–112).

Authorship

Modern readers generally like to know who wrote the text they are reading, but the master works of the Sanskritic scriptural archive are all anonymous or, more accurately, pseudonymous. Not only are successive generations of individual originators, authors, editors and scribes unnamed, they also usually attempt to conceal all evidence of the human hand. The closest we come to a human author may be a legendary sage such as Vyāsa, but even then, he is often just an intermediary between gods and mortals. Most of the classics are ascribed to one or other deity. Texts like this one are said to have been passed down orally through glittering lineages of gods and semi-divine seers until they descended to the human realm.

A more prosaic account of authorship must acknowledge the fact that the *Viṣṇu Purāṇa* was composed in Sanskrit, so the creators, as we have seen, are likely to have been male members of the brahmin community, who were the literary elite. Not surprisingly, they are clearly exponents of the Vaiṣṇava tradition and have access to an encyclopedic archive of Sanskritic mythology and dogma.

While academics are concerned with the age and authorship of this and other Sanskrit texts, and the historical context in which they arose, these questions are largely irrelevant for traditional audiences and members of the faith community, for whom scriptures like these are of divine origin and are more or less eternally present and ageless.

The audience

We know little more about the audiences of these texts than we know about their authors. There are hints from the visual arts and, in both sculpture and painting, we sometimes see teachers, text in hand, apparently delivering a lecture or teaching a class of students seated before them. We also occasionally come across figures reading or possibly reciting texts on their own.

I have argued elsewhere that modern practice might be a useful guide to premodern habits (Taylor 2016). While researching the contemporary performance of the *Bhāgavata Purāṇa*—a close relative of the *Viṣṇu Purāṇa*—I identified three broad patterns of textual consumption. First, devout individuals literate in Sanskrit may read the text to themselves, either silently or in a low murmur, at the rate of a chapter or more a day. This is a means by which the reader may acquire religious merit and social capital. Second, a pious individual may engage a student or scholar to read the text on their behalf, in which case the sponsor earns the merit. Alternatively, a sponsor may dedicate the merit to someone else, such as a sick relative, an unmarried child or an aspiring student or professional.

The third way in which texts are experienced—and the one that reaches the largest audience—is through public oral performance. Again, a pious sponsor will engage a scholar to recite the text in part or in full before an audience. As Sanskrit has always been the language of an educated elite, these recitations are accompanied by an explanation in a local language that everyone can understand. The upshot of this is that the majority of people experience these texts aurally, through oral performance, rather than as text read privately, as in modern reading practice. All three modes of textual reproduction are believed to confer great merit on all concerned. While we do not have any direct evidence of how the *Viṣṇu Purāṇa* was consumed in premodern times, these three patterns provide a useful proxy in the absence of better evidence.

Relationship to other texts

From the point of view of literary analysis, a typical purāṇa can be said to exhibit

> a juxtaposition of mythic and didactic texts, a heavy dependence on earlier purāṇas as a source of content, the absolute predictability of the plots of its myths and its saturation with signifiers of a bhakti ideological referent. (Bailey 1995: 5)

This is certainly true of the *Viṣṇu Purāṇa*. The bulk of the text consists of *pañca-lakṣaṇa* material (the five generic themes mentioned above), which is primarily mythic. This is interspersed with didactic sections, particularly in the second half of Book Three, 'Society', which focuses on rituals and practices for daily life. Other important elements are the devotional passages, consisting mainly of songs in praise of the deity, and the genealogical sections, which will be discussed below.

In terms of the *Viṣṇu Purāṇa*'s reliance on earlier sources, it is obvious the text's creators were well acquainted with many narratives that go back to the Vedas, which themselves date at the very latest from the middle of the second millennium BCE. Episodes that are merely hinted at in those early sources are expanded and embellished here. The presence of Indra as king of gods and provider of rain and frequent references to the never-ending struggle between the gods and demigods are among the more common elements of Vedic mythology carried over to the *Viṣṇu Purāṇa*. The important Vedic myth about Viṣṇu pacing out the world in three strides is also alluded to in our text.

The creators of the *Viṣṇu Purāṇa* were well acquainted with the *Mahābhārata*. In a passage in praise of the epic's reputed author, the sage Vyāsa, we find the following: 'Understand that Vyāsa, Kṛṣṇa-Dvaipāyana, is Lord Nārāyaṇa himself, Maitreya. Who else on earth could compose the *Mahābhārata*?' (3.4.5).[4] The genealogy of the five Pāṇḍava brothers, the heroes of the epic, is given in Book Four (4.14.9–10), and the *Viṣṇu Purāṇa* also quotes verses directly from the *Mahābhārata* with reference to the king Bharata (4.19.1–2). Elsewhere the plots of the *Mahābhārata* and the *Viṣṇu Purāṇa* intertwine when Kṛṣṇa visits Hastināpura after Duryodhana attempted to incinerate the Pāṇḍavas in the house of lacquer (4.13.26).

The story of Kṛṣṇa as an *avatāra* of Viṣṇu is, of course, central to the latter part of the *Viṣṇu Purāṇa*, and his childhood, youth and adult life occupy more than one-quarter of its entire extent. Kṛṣṇa is also one of the central characters in the *Mahābhārata*, especially in his role as Arjuna's driver and confidant during the great eighteen-day war. The unique relationship between Kṛṣṇa and Arjuna, which lies at the heart of the *Mahābhārata* in general and the *Bhagavad Gītā* in particular, is foretold in Book Five of the *Viṣṇu Purāṇa*. Indra advises the young Kṛṣṇa that he, Indra, will manifest an aspect of himself on earth in the form of the warrior Arjuna, whom he will entrust to Kṛṣṇa's protection (5.12.15–18).

While Kṛṣṇa is central to both the *Mahābhārata* and the *Viṣṇu Purāṇa*, there is little overlap between their two accounts. The *Viṣṇu Purāṇa* focuses on Kṛṣṇa the boy, the amorous youth and his deeds as king of Dvārakā, but barely mentions the role he played in the Mahābhārata war, let alone his most famous discourse, the *Bhagavad Gītā*. Conversely, the *Mahābhārata* describes in great detail Kṛṣṇa's dealings with the Pāṇḍava family and his role in the war and does not record any of the events of his childhood or youth.

4 All references to the *Mahābhārata* are from the Critical Edition (Sukthankar 1933–66).

The *Harivaṃśa* (HV) describes itself as an appendix (*khila*) to the *Mahābhārata* (Brodbeck 2019; Vaidya 1969). It is almost certainly earlier than the *Viṣṇu Purāṇa* in its current form and may have been one of its sources. The *Harivaṃśa* includes many episodes of Kṛṣṇa's pastimes (*līlā*) and his battles with various demons. These accounts are also found in the *Viṣṇu Purāṇa*. Comparing the narratives in both sources, the versions in the *Harivaṃśa* are usually much longer, more detailed and closer in style to the martial cast of the *Mahābhārata*. The descriptions of some of Kṛṣṇa's encounters with various demons in the *Viṣṇu Purāṇa*, for example, are little more than caricatures when compared with earlier versions in the *Harivaṃśa*. The *Viṣṇu Purāṇa* seems to skip with almost indecent haste from one episode to the next. Many of the events of Kṛṣṇa's early life, which are fully fleshed out in rip-roaring detail in the *Harivaṃśa* (see, for example, the wrestling match and death of Kaṃsa, HV 72–76), are stripped to their bare narrative bones in the *Viṣṇu Purāṇa*. I wonder whether the authors of the *Viṣṇu Purāṇa* expected their audience to be so familiar with the specific episodes that there was no need to retell them in detail. On the other hand, they fill this narrative skeleton with songs of praise to elevate the sentiment of *bhakti*—an element conspicuously absent from the *Harivaṃśa*.

We cannot say with certainty whether the creators of the *Viṣṇu Purāṇa* drew directly from the *Harivaṃśa* or from some intermediate or common source. Nor can we be certain of the relationship between the *Viṣṇu Purāṇa* and the *Bhāgavata Purāṇa*. This later text attributes nearly double the number of miraculous feats to Kṛṣṇa and is saturated with the emotion of *bhakti*. Hardly a verse slips past without a sententious observation. These three sources occupy a continuum. The *Harivaṃśa* at one end is long on narrative and short on sentiment. In the middle is the *Viṣṇu Purāṇa*, which is moderately concerned with both aspects. At the other extreme is the *Bhāgatava Purāṇa*, which is less focused on narrative, but is strongly committed to devotion (Preciado-Solis 1984: 42).

The *Viṣṇu Purāṇa* may have been a direct source or inspiration for the *Bhāgavata Purāṇa*, but its relationship with another purāṇa, the *Brahma*, is also worth noting. For example, the narrative of the sage Kaṇḍu, who was distracted from his ascetic practice by the *apsaras* Pramlocā in the *Viṣṇu Purāṇa* (1.15.13–52), is found word for word with only trivial differences in the *Brahma Purāṇa* (69.69–106). Nearly one-quarter of the *Viṣṇu Purāṇa*, covering the whole of the Kṛṣṇa story, from his advent to his withdrawal from the world (5.1.22–5.38.93), is also found word for word in the *Brahma Purāṇa* (72.8–103.95). The only substantial change appears to be in the framing of the narrative. In the *Viṣṇu Purāṇa*, Parāśara is narrating the story to Maitreya, but in the *Brahma Purāṇa*, Vyāsa is instructing a community of sages. It is generally assumed that the *Viṣṇu Purāṇa* is the earlier of the two, so the creators of the *Brahma Purāṇa* appear to have copied the *Viṣṇu Purāṇa* or some similar source. This in itself reveals something interesting about purāṇic intertextuality and the process of textual creation in Sanskritic literary culture.

The nature of Viṣṇu

Viṣṇu is often depicted as a bluish four-armed deity holding the discus known as Sudarśana (the 'Splendid One'), a mace, a lotus and a conch whose sound robs enemies of their strength. His consort Lakṣmī (also known as Śrī), the goddess of prosperity, is sometimes standing by his side. Viṣṇu is also seen reclining on the cosmic ocean, sheltered by the fanned hoods of the many-headed serpent Śeṣa. The deity is usually wearing yellow robes, garlands and jewels. On his chest is a whorl of hair known as Śrīvatsa—a feature occasionally mentioned in the *Viṣṇu Purāṇa*. When travelling, he rides on Garuḍa, king of birds and arch enemy of all serpents.

Viṣṇu has been a member of the Hindu pantheon for a very long time, but he arose from humble beginnings. The *Ṛg Veda* (RV; see below) dates from, at the very latest, the second millennium before the current era. It contains just over 1,000 songs of praise to several dozen elemental deities, but only one song (ṚV 1.154) is dedicated exclusively to Viṣṇu—specifically, his pacing out of the universe. Five others (ṚV 1.155, 1.156, 6.69, 7.99, 7.100) mention him in company with Indra, the king of gods. Viṣṇu was certainly not one of the more prominent or significant deities at this early stage.

The *Upaniṣads* are a set of philosophical texts somewhat more recent than the Vedas. Here we see the emergence of the concept of *brahman*—an impersonal all-encompassing reality, of which all deities and the rest of creation are a part and which permeates everything. There is no suitable English equivalent for the term *brahman*, which I have reluctantly translated as 'the Absolute'. In the *Upaniṣads*, we start to see the idea that Viṣṇu himself is indeed *brahman*, the supreme reality—a concept that thoroughly pervades the *Viṣṇu Purāṇa*. To be fair, this same status is attributed to other deities as well. Within the Śaiva tradition, the deity Śiva is said to be the highest Absolute, and in the Śākta tradition, it is the great goddess Devī. In later traditions, Kṛṣṇa alone or with his consort Rādhā are equated with the Absolute at the heart of all reality.

Another important early thread of Hindu thought is the concept of the *trimūrti* or 'three bodies'. These include the original Vedic creator deity, Brahmā (not to be confused with *brahman*), Viṣṇu as the preserver and maintainer of the universe and Śiva, also known as Rudra (the 'Terrible One'), who destroys the world at the end of each era. We frequently encounter this Hindu trinity in our text, but always with the understanding that Viṣṇu is also the Absolute and highest overarching reality. Thus, Brahmā emerges from a lotus at Viṣṇu's navel and creates the world at his behest. Viṣṇu the Absolute awkwardly appears as Viṣṇu the preserver, and even Śiva-Rudra the destroyer is a manifestation of this deity.

Cyclical existence—also known as rebirth, *saṃsāra*, transmigration or reincarnation—lies at the heart of Hindu, Buddhist and Jain beliefs. With certain variations, these traditions share the idea that all beings possess an indestructible element—a soul, an *ātman* or a consciousness—which passes after death into another body. As a result of one's actions (*karma*) in this life, a being acquires merit or demerit and is consequently reborn in a more or less desirable womb. The hierarchy of lifeforms varies from tradition to tradition, but there is basic agreement that there are hell realms below us, then animals, we humans in the middle and gods above us. Lower lifeforms may move up the ladder if they are lucky, but even gods burn up their merit and eventually fall back to lower realms.

The cycle of birth, death and rebirth continues forever, unless one can escape. Different traditions have different roadmaps for this—known as liberation or *mokṣa*. Liberation, as presented in the *Viṣṇu Purāṇa*, is a merging with, or dissolution into, the Absolute, which is synonymous with the highest state of Viṣṇu. This is achieved by those who cultivate the deepest devotion to the Divine and those who realise that the universe and all it holds are ultimately no different to the deity and indeed oneself. This perhaps constitutes the central theological message of our text.

Thus, the *Viṣṇu Purāṇa* represents a joyous jumble of Vaiṣṇava theologies from different periods and traditions: Viṣṇu as the supreme deity, as the ineffable *brahman* or Absolute, as one of the 'purāṇic' trinity, the preserver of the universe and as the highest state of liberation from cyclical existence.

Viṣṇu and Kṛṣṇa

Viṣṇu also causes aspects (*aṃśa*) of himself to manifest in the universe. These are known as *avatāras*, as they have 'crossed down' into the world. The ten forms commonly listed are the fish, tortoise, boar, the demon-slaying man-lion, the dwarf who paced out the universe in three strides, the murderous brahmin Paraśurāma, Rāma, the hero of his own epic, Kṛṣṇa, who is arguably the hero of this epic, the Buddha (yes, *the* Buddha) and Kalki, the sword-wielding manifestation of the future, who will cleanse the world of evil. Earlier texts like the *Mahābhārata* list four, six or eight *avatāras*, while a later source, the *Bhāgavata Purāṇa*, which generally strives to outdo the *Viṣṇu Purāṇa*, gives twenty-two.

By far the most important manifestation of Viṣṇu in this purāṇa is Kṛṣṇa. Some scholarly authorities believe that Kṛṣṇa was originally a minor local deity of herding people who was subsequently incorporated into the mainstream Hindu pantheon. In fact, the *Viṣṇu Purāṇa* without Kṛṣṇa is unthinkable, but the relationship between Viṣṇu and Kṛṣṇa is more complicated than one simply being the manifestation of the other. There seem to be three different relationships. For much of our text, Kṛṣṇa simply *is* Viṣṇu. They are one and the same entity and their names and epithets are used interchangeably—sometimes even within the same or consecutive verses. Second, Kṛṣṇa appears as one among a number of manifestations of Viṣṇu, as mentioned above, but is less than Viṣṇu, being just a part or an aspect of the Divine. This is also a very common mode of representation in the *Viṣṇu Purāṇa*.

At the start of Book Five, we learn that Kṛṣṇa appeared in the world as 'an aspect of Viṣṇu's aspect' (*aṃśāṃśena*; 5.1.3). This may be a reference to the fact that Viṣṇu let two of his hairs, one black and one white, fall to earth, where they became Balarāma and Kṛṣṇa, respectively (5.1.61). Kṛṣṇa is an aspect of the hair, which is itself an aspect of Viṣṇu. We also discover that Kṛṣṇa's elder brother is an aspect of the divine serpent Śeṣa. As that being is itself an aspect of Viṣṇu, Balarāma is also said to be 'an aspect of an aspect' of the deity (5.1.73).

Book Five focuses almost exclusively on Kṛṣṇa and is, in many ways, the most accessible, ardent and significant part of the *Viṣṇu Purāṇa*. Why it would seek to downgrade its central character in the opening verses is unclear. It is interesting to reflect on the fact that in later Vaiṣṇava traditions, especially the Gauḍīya sects originating from Bengal, Kṛṣṇa totally eclipses Viṣṇu. It is he who is the ultimate being, and Viṣṇu is a mere manifestation of him, not vice versa, as in earlier sources.[5]

The irresistible cowherding youth, the adventurous lord of Dvārakā, as well as Arjuna's friend and confidant during the Mahābhārata war—these three different mythologies are tenuously linked with the name Kṛṣṇa, all of whom are the Divine incarnate. The academic impulse is to try to tease these skeins apart, but to a traditional audience and the faith community such an approach is irrelevant, as are the age and authorship of the text. Viṣṇu is everything, everything is Viṣṇu. The *Viṣṇu Purāṇa* is poetry, beauty and nectar to be imbibed and relished.[6]

The other *avatāras*

Apart from Kṛṣṇa, most of the other *avatāras* are not particularly significant in the *Viṣṇu Purāṇa*. We hear how, during creation, Viṣṇu in the form of the boar raised the world from the bottom of the cosmic ocean on the tip of his tusk. The deity also manifested as Rāma, the hero of the *Rāmāyaṇa*, who defeats the demon Rāvaṇa, abductor of Rāma's wife, Sītā. A potted version of the story of Rāma is included in the fourth book of the *Viṣṇu Purāṇa* (4.4.49–54). The fish *avatāra*, we know from other sources, saves humanity from a cataclysmic flood that closely resembles the Biblical event, right down to the ark. When the gods sought to churn the nectar of immortality from the Ocean of Milk, Viṣṇu manifested as a tortoise so the churning stick could rest on his back. In the form of a dwarf, he asked the demon king Bali for as much land as he could cover in three steps. Bali agreed, but the deity then assumed a giant cosmic form and 'paced out the threefold world with three heroic strides' (5.5.17). Viṣṇu manifested as Paraśurāma, the irascible brahmin who repeatedly exterminated the entire class of warriors, the *kṣatriyas*, as he believed they were abusing their power. The final *avatāra* is yet to come. He is named Kalki, and we are told he will be imbued with 'eight qualities and perfections, greatness and irresistible power'. Kalki will sweep away all barbarians to reestablish virtue in the world, and those who wake 'when this night has passed, will be stainless, clear and pure' (4.24.20).

5 See also Matchett (2001).

6 For more on the nature of Viṣṇu in the *Viṣṇu Purāṇa*, see Adluri (2019).

The role of the Buddha in the *Viṣṇu Purāṇa* is a curious one. Many other sources maintain that the Buddha was an *avatāra* of Viṣṇu. The Enlightened One appears in the *Viṣṇu Purāṇa* not in this form, but as a phantom brought forth by the deity to confuse the demigods. In Book Three, the deities are locked in one of their never-ending battles with the demons and, at this point in the narrative, they seem to be losing. To assist them, Viṣṇu creates a phantom (*māyāmoha*), who teaches the demons thinly disguised religious dogma that closely resembles the teachings of Jainism and Buddhism. The demigods are seduced by these heretical ideas and abandon the true religion of the Vedas. Once the demigods are weakened in this way, the gods are able to regain the upper hand and overcome them, at least for the short term (3.17–18).

The purāṇic thought-world

The *Viṣṇu Purāṇa* was created within a particular conceptual universe, its 'thought-world'. It reflects this universe and also serves to perpetuate it. The oldest stratum of the *Viṣṇu Purāṇa*'s thought-world are the Vedas. The word *veda* means 'knowledge' and is related to words like 'wit', 'witness' and 'wisdom' in English. The Vedas are anthologies of songs of praise, largely devoted to elemental deities, such as Agni, god of fire, Sūrya, the sun god, Uṣas, the goddess of dawn, and Vāyu, god of winds. The recurrent themes in the Vedas largely reflect the existential concerns of nomadic herding people: they need sun and rain to ensure good pasture, strong bulls to lead the herd, sons to perpetuate the family, victory in battle and protection from all sorts of night-ranging demons. No-one knows how old the Vedas are. The traditional view, such as that given in the *Viṣṇu Purāṇa*, is that they pre-date the universe. Current scholarly consensus holds that they date from at least 1,500 years before the current era. The evidence for this dating is wafer-thin and the Vedas could in fact be considerably older. In any case, they are the earliest surviving examples of Indo-European literature.

The most important Veda is the *Ṛg*, the 'Veda of Verses'. It consists of just over 1,000 songs (a total of about 10,000 verses) arranged in 10 books according to the priestly family said to preserve them.[7] The *Sāma Veda*,

7 The easiest points of access to the *Ṛg Veda* are Doniger (1981) and the Introduction to Jamison and Brereton (2014).

or 'Veda of Songs', has about 1,500 verses from the *Ṛg Veda* (one-sixth of the total), arranged either by the metre in which they are composed or by the deity to whom they are dedicated. Songs from the *Sāma Veda* are chanted during rituals. There are several references to the sound of the *Sāma Veda* in the *Viṣṇu Purāṇa*. The *Yajur Veda*, or 'Veda of Formulae', contains nearly 2,000 verses. These are largely sacred utterances or mantras used during rituals. Sometimes a fourth, the *Atharva Veda*, is mentioned in connection with the other three. This anthology of 700 songs contains about 6,000 mantras, including spells to ward off disease, snakes and other evils, as well as prayers for health and welfare.

For our purposes, and throughout much of Indian history, the literary content of the Vedas is not as important as their symbolic value. They were composed in an early dialect of Sanskrit that is often difficult, and in some cases impossible, to understand. In practice, their power lies in their sound and, in literature, their usefulness lies in their potency as a symbol of authority, validity and antiquity. We see this in the way the Vedas are employed in the *Viṣṇu Purāṇa*.

The Vedas were at the heart of a traditional brahminical education. A boy at the age of six was sent to live in the home of his guru—usually a male relative—and, as we see from the *Viṣṇu Purāṇa*, the student would be required to learn a certain number of Vedic and ancillary texts by heart. Even today, the family names Dvivedi, Trivedi and Chaturvedi indicate the number of Vedic texts—two, three or four—clan members are supposed to have mastered.

The Vedas have great creative potential. The creation of the universe is said to be ordained by these texts and carried out in accordance with their dictates. As the Vedas carry the highest possible symbolic value, the ultimate accolade is to call something 'the equal of the Vedas'. Thus, in the *Viṣṇu Purāṇa*, the deity Viṣṇu–Kṛṣṇa is said to embody these texts or, more simply, to *be* the Vedas (1.4.22). Authors of Sanskrit texts often appropriate Vedic prestige to elevate their own words. For example, the *Mahābhārata*, *Rāmāyaṇa* and the *Bhāgatava Purāṇas* all refer to themselves as 'the fifth Veda'. Towards the end of the *Viṣṇu Purāṇa*, the main narrator, Parāśara, claims that this text is also 'the equal of the Vedas' (6.8.12).

Conversely, the direst accusation one can make about a person is that he or she insults or disregards the Vedas. This is the most common accusation laid against 'heretics', which in the *Viṣṇu Purāṇa* usually indicates adherents of non-Hindu traditions such as Buddhists, Jains and possibly Tantric practitioners. Dishonouring or selling the Vedas leads to a hell realm called Lavaṇa, the 'Salty Hell' (2.6.13). As we have seen, to abandon the Vedic path of true religion will certainly lead to one's downfall.

The Vedas disappear from the world when it is destroyed at the end of each cosmic cycle. The deity then creates seven sages whose job it is to 'hear' the sound of the Vedas, which continue to reverberate and animate the cosmos, and to bring them down to earth again. Thus, Vedic texts are also known as *śruti*, 'that which is heard'. Each new age also has a Vyāsa, a sage who again divides the undifferentiated verses into their four anthologies.

These Vedic texts are used primarily in ritual, the most important of which is the sacrifice. There are two main kinds of sacrificial act. In one, the juice of an unidentified plant known as soma is offered into a fire or drunk. In the other, clarified butter or ghee is offered. As the oblations are made, relevant texts are recited and ritual cries of *vaṣat*, *svadhā*, *svāhā* and *oṃ* are made. There are several mentions of these cries in the *Viṣṇu Purāṇa*. In these rituals, the oblation is carried to the gods by fire personified as Agni. We also read of the deities being invited to the sacrifice, where, seated on mats of sacred grass known as *kuśa*, they receive their due portion of the offerings. The gods are nourished by the oblations and, if properly satisfied, provide rain. Rain of course enables all life to thrive and supplies the necessities for further sacrifices. Thus, the sacrifice, gods and humankind exist in a sort of circular symbiotic relationship.

The most extreme ritual is the *Aśvamedha* or horse-sacrifice. This is said to be undertaken by a king to proclaim and consolidate his sovereignty. A consecrated horse is allowed to wander freely for a year, accompanied by an armed force. Any territory the horse traverses is claimed by the king. After a year, the horse is brought back and killed. Were *Aśvamedhas* ever actually carried out or are they a literary fiction? While there are historical records of *Aśvamedhas* being performed, it is hard to imagine that every particular detail would be followed; the queen, for example, is required to have sexual intercourse with the horse after it has been sacrificed. Whether *Aśvamedhas* were real or not, they have a literary reality and are the ultimate source of religious merit. There are several references in the *Viṣṇu Purāṇa* to events or practices that generate 'as much merit as an *Aśvamedha*' or words to that effect.

The idealised society of the brahminical imagination consists of four communities or orders—a system that first appeared in the most recent layer of the Vedas. The Sanskrit term for these communities is *varṇa*, meaning 'colour', and has historically been translated as 'caste' or 'class'. This system may reflect some social reality prevalent in Vedic times, but its relationship to reality in later periods is less clear. What is clear, however, is that *varṇa* remains a powerful and pervasive concept in the *Viṣṇu Purāṇa* and, in various forms, continues to shape Hindu societies to this day.

The four orders are as follows: first, the brahmins or priestly community are chiefly responsible for ritual practice and performing the sacrifice. To do this, they must master the texts, and they live off the fees they receive for ritual practices they undertake on behalf of others. The *kṣatriyas* are the warrior community and, in this idealised world, they furnish kings to rule the state. It is the duty of *kṣatriyas* to wage war and to defend the realm and its population. The third community is that of the *vaiśyas*, whose occupations include animal husbandry, trade and agriculture. These three orders are known as the 'twice-born', because sons in these communities undergo a second, spiritual, rebirth when they are initiated into a school of Vedic study and receive their sacred thread. Although sacrifice and ritual practice are the special duties of brahmins, members of all three twice-born communities are entitled to study the Vedas and perform sacrifices.

The fourth community is that of the *śūdras*. This order is mentioned only briefly in the Vedas, and only in those sections thought to be more recent. By the time of the epics and purāṇas, the concept of an underclass of servants was firmly entrenched. The *Viṣṇu Purāṇa* also allows members of this class to practice a trade or craft. They may undertake rituals for their own ancestors, but for any other rites they must engage members of other communities on their behalf. The *Viṣṇu Purāṇa* declares not only that the system of four orders, the *cāturvarṇya*, is the natural structure of society in this world, but also that societies on the other six continents that make up the mythical purāṇic universe are all structured on similar lines.

Another important concept that is fundamental to traditional brahminical dogma is the four stages of life (*caturāśrama*), through which all pious individuals, especially brahmins, are theoretically expected to pass. The first stage is that of the celibate student or *brahmacārin*. As mentioned, between the ages of six and eighteen, a boy is expected to live with his guru to receive his education. This consists of learning Sanskrit and mastering one or more branches of Vedic recitation and practice. At the completion of this phase, the student recompenses his teacher with a fee, the *guru-dakṣiṇā*, and may then choose to marry. The young man then embarks on the second stage, the life of the householder (*gṛhastha*). In old age, the pious individual will leave his responsibilities with his sons and set out for the forest (*vanaprastha*). There he 'should live on leaves and roots and berries, his hair and beard and matted locks untended'. He is supposed to sleep on the ground and should welcome all comers as guests (3.9.19). During the fourth and final stage, that of the wandering ascetic (*saṃyāsin*), the devotee abandons the forest and lives with no fixed abode: 'He'll stay in a village for just one night, or in a city for five, lest he start to like or loathe them', begging food as he goes (3.9.28). Certainly, the first two stages were adhered to in premodern times and are still today. The third and fourth stages remain powerful ideals, even if rarely followed.

In addition to the stages of life, another important concept in the purāṇic thought-world are the goals of human existence (*puruṣārtha*). The first of these is love or desire (*kāma*), especially in a physical sense. The second is wealth or material wellbeing (*artha*), in the sense that human life has certain physical requirements that need to be met. The third is *dharma*, which I usually translate as virtue, but which also carries the sense of correct conduct, especially in relation to the responsibilities of one's community and stage of life. More broadly, it has the senses of religion or spiritual life and practice. These three are often spoken of, but sometimes a fourth—liberation from cyclical existence or *mokṣa*—is added.

The *Viṣṇu Purāṇa* contains an inherently conservative social message that seeks to preserve the community structure described above. Punishments are prescribed for individuals who neglect or stray from the duties of their community. On the other hand, sticking to one's communal role, as we are frequently reminded, is one of the ways a devout individual will be rewarded with heaven or liberation.

Divine and semi-divine beings

The purāṇic thought-world includes a rich ecosystem of supernatural beings. At the apex are the deities or gods known as *suras* or *devas*. These are in general the old Vedic deities led by their king, Indra, and include the creator, Brahmā, the 'grandsire of the world'; the generally destructive and unruly Śiva-Rudra; the heavenly twins known as the Aśvins; Varuṇa, god of oceans and waters; as well as the Agnis and Maruts, gods of fire and winds, respectively. A group of deities were the sons of a sage called Kaśyapa and his wife and are called Ādityas after her. Other frequently mentioned deities include the Sun, Moon and Earth and several undifferentiated hosts of gods known as the Viśvadevas, Vasus and Sādhyas. In the *Viṣṇu Purāṇa*, there are many mentions of the 'thirteen great deities' of whom Indra is the head, but the precise membership of this list varies. Many of these deities are said to have Indo-European precursors and may be 'related' to the gods of Greece and Rome.

The sage Kaśyapa, from whom the gods were descended, had another wife, Diti. She gave birth to the demonic demigods known as the Daityas. The Daityas are often mentioned in the same breath as the Dānavas, the offspring of Danu, another of Kaśyapa's wives. These two tribes of half-brothers—*asuras* or 'not-gods'—never got on with the *suras* and are locked in an eternal struggle with them for sovereignty over the universe. Usually the demigods seem to have the upper hand, and the gods are often reduced to seeking assistance from Viṣṇu. They supplicate the supreme being with effusive praise and he agrees to assist them. Granted some divine boon, the gods are thereby able to win the immediate battle, but the eternal war between good and evil drags on forever.

The demigods are in general much more interesting than their godly brothers. They are 'deceitful, ignorant, impatient and unrestrained' (3.17.18). They rage and fume, curse and swear, which makes their diction all the more lively. Demigods occasionally appear in the world of mortals. They all have supernatural powers, such as the ability to fly through the air and change shape at will. Most notable among the Daityas is the king Hiraṇyakaśipu, who had terrible trouble with his son Prahlāda. This demon lad betrayed his demonic roots and became enamoured of the divine ideology of Viṣṇu, his father's nemesis (1.15–20).

There are several other species of less-important semi-divine beings. *Siddhas* are highly accomplished saints or sages who have acquired supernatural powers. They do not have much to do in our text but turn up occasionally to sing the praises of Viṣṇu–Kṛṣṇa. *Gandharvas* are described in many sources as 'celestial musicians'. The *Viṣṇu Purāṇa* questionably claims that their name arises from the fact that they were born 'drinking speech' (1.5.46). They are handsome and, like the *siddhas*, their main function in our text is to sing the praises of the deity.

Apsarases are hosts of semi-divine female beings with supernatural powers and irresistible charms. If a deity ever needs to distract a sage from his meditation, he usually sends one of these beautiful females to do the job. Apart from seducing sages, the main role for *apsarases* in our text is to sing and dance in honour of the deities.

Nāgas are semi-divine serpent spirits that are neither particularly benevolent nor malevolent. We know from visual art that they resemble humans from the waist up, with a snake's body and tail from the waist down. Among the most famous *nāgas* are Śeṣa, the benign many-headed serpent who forms a couch for Viṣṇu to recline on, and venomous Kāliya, whom Kṛṣṇa defeats in battle. *Nāgas* reside either in the waters or in the lower realms, where, like other Indo-European dragons to whom they are probably related, they hoard treasure. In our text, *nāgas* are described as 'fork-tongued, resilient, cruel and bent on pleasure' (3.17.23).

Supernatural *yakṣas* are generally innocuous but somewhat shadowy in the *Viṣṇu Purāṇa*. They have frivolous hearts, lack discernment and hanker after sensual pleasures (3.17.19). Our text offers a fanciful etymology, claiming that they are named because of their desire for food (*jakṣaṇa*; 1.5.43). In other Sanskrit literature—notably Kālidāsa's courtly poem *Meghadūta*—they are the attendants of Kubera, god of wealth.

Among the more malevolent beings are *rākṣasas*, *guhyakas* and *paiśācas*—all hideous night-ranging demons who feed on human flesh. Parāśara, the narrator of the *Viṣṇu Purāṇa*, should know about these, as his own father was eaten by one. Described as 'cruel, deceptive, fierce and dark' (3.17.20), they continually strive to disrupt the sacrifices conducted by sages, in order to weaken the gods.

There are several other species of semi-divine being—some good and others bad—in the *Viṣṇu Purāṇa*, but they are usually mentioned only in lists and play no active role in the narrative. These include celestial musicians known as *cāraṇas* and *vidyādharas*, and *kiṃnaras* and *kimpuruṣas* (both of which literally mean 'What kind of person?!') and disease-causing spirits known as *kūṣmāṇḍas*.

Elements of the *Viṣṇu Purāṇa*

Overall frame

The *Viṣṇu Purāṇa* is framed simply as a dialogue between two legendary sages, Parāśara and his disciple Maitreya. This in itself distinguishes the *Viṣṇu Purāṇa* from most other purāṇas and the epics, which have much more complex framing structures. Typically, the primary storyteller is a wandering seer, such as Lomaharṣaṇa or Ugraśravas, who arrives at the Naimiṣa forest, where he narrates the story to the assembled sages led by Śaunaka. The narrator's story may be a direct account, but more often it is the repetition of another story told by a third or even a fourth party.

Parāśara explains to Maitreya that the *Viṣṇu Purāṇa* was first related by the original creator deity, Brahmā, grandsire of the world. From Brahmā, the narrative was passed orally from one listener to another. The lineage as recounted in the *Viṣṇu Purāṇa* consists of about twenty figures and includes divine sages, various semi-divine serpents, a river goddess and some residents of the underworld, before it finally reaches Parāśara, who relays the text in full to his inquisitive disciple.

Both Parāśara and Maitreya are prominent figures elsewhere in Sanskrit literature. Parāśara was the grandson of Vasiṣṭha, one of the original Seven Seers who are present at the beginning of every era, and domestic chaplain to Rāma and the Solar Dynasty. Parāśara is said to be the disciple of the great law-giver, Yājñavalkya, and was the Veda-vyāsa, or 'arranger of the Vedas', in a previous age. Parāśara's son Vyāsa, who arranged the Vedas in the 'current' age, was also the composer and transmitter of many seminal texts, including the *Mahābhārata* and many of the purāṇas. Parāśara himself appears as a character in the *Mahābhārata* as the great-grandfather of both the Kauravas and the Pāṇḍavas, the two warring families of cousins whose conflict lies at the heart of the epic. Another of Parāśara's grandsons (also through Vyāsa) was the naked sage Śuka, who recited the later Vaiṣṇava classic, the *Bhāgavata Purāṇa*. Thus, Parāśara and his lineage are associated with three of the most important genres of Sanskrit literature: Vedas, purāṇas and the epics.

Like his guru, Maitreya is a significant stock character in the intertextual network that unites many threads of the Sanskritic literary imagination. Maitreya appears as a fully fledged sage in the *Mahābhārata*, where he attempts to persuade the warring parties to make peace. After the cataclysmic war has finished, and while wandering the depopulated world, Maitreya comes upon Vidura, another prominent figure. Maitreya teaches Vidura about the world and the nature of reality. This discourse constitutes an important section of the *Bhāgavata Purāṇa* mentioned above.

The dialogue between Parāśara and Maitreya, which constitutes the *Viṣṇu Purāṇa*, takes place in deep mythological time. At one point, Parāśara mentions that the 'current' ruling monarch is the king named Parīkṣit (4.20.13). This character was the grandson of Arjuna, one of the five Pāṇḍava brothers, the heroes of the *Mahābhārata*, and one of the few to survive the war. We know that Parāśara delivered this discourse long after Arjuna's demise. This same king Parīkṣit is said to have listened to the *Bhāgavata Purāṇa* on his deathbed. Thus, the *Viṣṇu Purāṇa* is positioned in mythological time after the *Mahābhārata* and before the *Bhāgavata Purāṇa* and is fixed firmly between these two great classics of the Sanskrit archive.

Each of the *Viṣṇu Purāṇa*'s six books and many intermediate sections begin with Maitreya asking questions: What is the nature of the world? How did the gods and other beings arise? Who are the Manus? And so on. When his guru has answered in full, Maitreya usually replies, 'You have told me everything I asked about, now tell me about this', and initiates a fresh topic. This dialogic structure provides a clear framework for the narrative. It breaks the flow into manageable units and serves to focus the audience's attention on the matter in hand. It also provides some narrative tension that draws the account forward.

Parāśara includes many subnarratives in his answers to Maitreya's questions. As early as the second chapter of the first book, for example, he recounts a story that his grandfather, Vasiṣṭha, had once told him. The *Viṣṇu Purāṇa* is mercifully free of the complex, multiple embedded narratives that are common in other purāṇas and other genres. Texts such as the epics and fable literature (*kathā*) often have many levels of narrative framing: stories within stories within stories—up to five layers deep in the case of the *Pañcatantra* (Taylor 2007: 28). The overall structure of the *Viṣṇu Purāṇa* is relatively simple, reaching a maximum of three layers of narrative. At its most complex, Parāśara tells Maitreya the story of 'Foolish' Bharata, in which Bharata quotes the sage Ṛbhu lecturing Nidāgha on the subject of the highest truth (2.13–16). Elsewhere, Parāśara tells a story about how Bhīṣma recounted an episode he heard from a brahmin from Kaliṅga.

That brahmin heard the story from a certain sage who could remember his death at the end of a previous lifetime (3.7). All in all, the dialogic structure of the *Viṣṇu Purāṇa* remains relatively easy to follow.

About 80 per cent of the *Viṣṇu Purāṇa* is written in verse, and the great bulk of this is in a metre called Anuṣṭubh, consisting of four half-lines of eight syllables each. Within each half-line, the rhythm of short and long syllables is generally maintained. Anuṣṭubh is the 'vanilla' standard for Sanskrit narrative, epic and purāṇic literature. The fact that so much is composed in verse reminds us that it is to be chanted or, better still, sung. That is the reason I chose the medium of blank verse to translate the Sanskrit Anuṣṭubhs of the *Viṣṇu Purāṇa* and have tried to maintain a certain rhythm where appropriate in acknowledgement of the nature of the root text.

The remaining 20 per cent of the *Viṣṇu Purāṇa*—almost the whole of the fourth book—is written in prose. Why is this? This book, which describes the lineages and deeds of the legendary Solar and Lunar dynasties, contains many genealogical lists. There are similar lists in other parts of the text in verse, so it cannot be argued that prose is better suited to genealogy. Similarly, the narrative sections of Book Four, as opposed to the genealogical passages, are not essentially different from narratives in other parts of the *Viṣṇu Purāṇa*. Perhaps the answer lies in the fact that, to put it politely, the purāṇas are highly intertextual. Put less politely, some sections appear to have been cobbled together from other sources. Was Book Four included using a simple 'cut and paste' process from some other prose text? A quick search for passages similar to random samples from this book failed to reveal identical text elsewhere, but a systematic survey might provide more insights. I have translated the *Viṣṇu Purāṇa*'s Sanskrit prose passages into English prose.

If the form of the *Viṣṇu Purāṇa* is a combination of verse and prose, we can think of its content as being of four kinds: narratives, genealogies, songs of praise and didactic material. The narratives are the raison d'être for any purāṇa, because, as mentioned above, the word *purāṇa* itself suggests 'tales of ancient times' or, perhaps, 'ancient accounts'. Narratives form the backbone of the text and cover the five themes that define the genre: the creation of the world, its subsequent re-creation, the origin of the gods and sages, the Manus and their reigns as well as the deeds of the kings of the Solar and Lunar dynasties.

But what is the function of the long genealogical lists found throughout the *Viṣṇu Purāṇa*? For the reader of an English translation they may not be the most edifying or enjoyable reading experience, as they closely resemble the 'He begat ... He begat ...' passages of the Old Testament. I suggest they fulfil four functions. First, genealogies of both legendary 'human' lineages, the Solar and Lunar dynasties, begin with Brahmā, the original creator deity. This divine origin ultimately lends sanctity and authority to every member of the lineage. In this sense, the genealogical lists provide legitimacy. Second, the lists demonstrate, for anyone with sufficient detective skills, the relationship between every significant character in the purāṇic thought-world. Third, they provide the logical framework for the narratives. Much of the *Viṣṇu Purāṇa* is in mythical 'chronological' order. When a genealogical list reaches a significant character, the authors press 'pause' and insert narratives relevant to that individual. The fourth possible function of these passages is that they offer an opportunity for the accumulation of merit. This aspect is suggested in part by contemporary oral performance of purāṇic discourse. In these events, the simple act of hearing the words is regarded as meritorious (Taylor 2016). This idea is backed up by the *Viṣṇu Purāṇa* itself when Parāśara instructs his disciple:

> As the saying goes, 'The lineage of one who reflects each day on Manu's family, which descends from Brahmā, is never broken.' You should therefore listen to this lineage from start to finish, Maitreya, as it will wash away all sins. (4.1.4–5)

In addition to the narratives and genealogical material, the *Viṣṇu Purāṇa* includes more than twenty songs of praise of the deity. These are known as *stotra* or *stuti* in Sanskrit and are one of the most important features of the *Viṣṇu Purāṇa* and other works of Vaiṣṇava Bhakti literature. These *stutis* share a number of prominent themes: Viṣṇu is the creator, preserver and destroyer of the universe; he is without beginning or end; he is free from all qualities and pervades all creation. He is the Absolute, the highest state and *puruṣottama*, the supreme spirit. He abides within all beings, including gods, mortals, plants and animals. These songs are sung by a wide variety of characters, including the Earth herself, other deities, sages, humans and even the outstanding demon Prahlāda. In contemporary performance of the *Bhāgavata Purāṇa*, these songs of praise are regarded as the most important elements of the discourse (Taylor 2016: 85), and it is easy to imagine this was the case in oral performance of the *Viṣṇu Purāṇa* in premodern times.

The didactic material—largely confined to the third book, 'Society'—deals with the details and practicalities of day-to-day life, from birth to death and everything in between, dwelling in considerable detail on the performance of *śrāddha* offerings to nourish one's immediate ancestors. I will return to this in the summary of Book Three below.

As indicated above, the organisation of the *Viṣṇu Purāṇa* is largely 'chronological', beginning with the creation of the world, running through to the 'present', but also looking forward to the future when the world will come to an end. That is not to say the whole text flows smoothly, as there are several discontinuities in the narrative. Examples are Parāśara's praise of Lakṣmī (1.8.16–34), a hymn to the syllable *Oṃ* (3.3.22–31) and especially the story of how Kṛṣṇa won the Syamantaka jewel (4.13). Chapters Five to Seven in the sixth book, 'Dissolution', which present a debate about the relative benefits of yoga and sacrifice, seem to have been tacked on to the end of the text. It is impossible to say whether this is what some putative 'original' creator of the text intended or whether later scholars or scribes added these passages. In any case, from a stylistic and narrative point of view, these sections present noticeable discontinuities.

The six books

Book One: Creation

Book One describes the creation and peopling of the world. Parāśara first tells Maitreya how his own father was eaten by a *rākṣasa* and how he subsequently acquired knowledge of this purāṇa. He describes how Viṣṇu created the world out of emptiness by agitating spirit and matter, and how the elements and senses combine to form the cosmic egg that contains the whole universe. Chapter Two includes a difficult abstract passage on the interaction of the cosmogonic properties known as the Seen (*vyakta*) and Unseen (*avyakta*), Individuation (*ahaṃkāra*) and Greatness (*mahat*). Parāśara interrupts his account of creation to describe the units of time, which range from one *nimeṣa* or blink of the eye, to one *para*, the lifespan of the deity Brahmā. In the form of a boar, Viṣṇu catches the earth on the tip of his tusk and raises it from the floor of the cosmic ocean, to the delight of the onlooking sages. The earth is then divided into seven continents and is filled with plants, animals and humankind in four communities.

People build houses and raise crops, and the first patriarchs and a legendary ruler known as Manu populate the earth. The irascible sage Durvāsas curses the gods, who then churn the Ocean of Milk to win the nectar of immortality. The princeling Dhruva is elevated to become the Pole Star through his devotion to Viṣṇu. King Pṛthu is born from the hand of his dead father. Sages praise the deity from the bottom of the ocean. A stunning *apsaras* seduces an unsuspecting yogi and a girl is born from drops of sweat. Prahlāda, the son of the demon king, becomes a devotee of Viṣṇu and undergoes terrible tortures, but sticks to his beliefs and finally achieves liberation. We are reminded by Parāśara that Viṣṇu is *brahman*, the ineffable Absolute.

Book Two: The World

This book falls into two parts, the first of which deals with what we might call geography and astronomy. The world within the cosmic egg consists of the middle realm, which constitutes 'our' world, with lower realms below us and other realms above. This middle realm includes seven continents in the form of concentric rings, with each successive ring being twice as wide as the one within it. The seven continents are poetically named Rose-Apple, Pipal, Cottonwood, *Kuśa*-Grass, Crane, Teak and Banyan. They are separated by oceans of saltwater, syrup, wine, ghee, whey, milk and freshwater, respectively.

Each continent is divided into seven regions by seven mountain ranges and is watered by seven major rivers. Every land has one sovereign with seven sons, each of whom rules a region. A society of four communities—not coincidentally analogous to the four orders in 'our' world—inhabits each continent. The central continent, Rose-Apple or Jambūdvīpa, has the cosmic Mount Meru at its centre. One of Jambūdvīpa's regions, Bhārata—named after its regent, Bharata—is now known as India. The *Viṣṇu Purāṇa* says: 'More fortunate than the gods are those who live in Bhārata, the land that leads to heaven and beyond' (2.3.24), as this is the only region where sacrifice, the precursor to liberation, is possible.

Below us are seven realms inhabited by Dānavas, Daityas and *nāgas*, which are even more splendid than those above. But below them lie twenty-eight hell realms, each with its own exquisite tortures. All classes of sinners are catered for: those whose crimes range from killing their guru to starting dinner before their father, selling cochineal or feeding cats. Special hells are reserved for actors, fishermen and vandals who upset beehives. Students of religious studies who ejaculate while napping are in for a torrid time. Fortunately, meditation on Viṣṇu is prescribed as the atonement for all these crimes.

Above us are the upper realms, including the orbits of the sun, moon, planets and seven higher spheres. A challenging technical passage on the apparent annual movement of the sun and calendrical science is followed by a more readable chapter about rain.

The second half of this book, consisting of four chapters, contains a philosophical narrative delivered by the wise fool Bharata (no relation to the king of the same name above). This Bharata teaches the king of Sauvīra about the nature of reality, in which he recounts a snappy and amusing dialogue between two sages, Ṛbhu and Nidāgha.

Book Three: Society

This book is largely about the Vedas, their origin, arrangement, rituals and efficacy. The first few chapters describe the Manus, the legendary rulers who reign over vast intervals of cosmic time called Manvantaras or Manu-periods. Six Manus have already passed. We are in the period of the seventh, Vaivasvata, and there are seven more to come. In addition to its own Manu, each Manvantara has its own set of deities and seven sages who will 'hear' the Vedas anew. The fourteen Manus reign for a total of one thousand cycles of four ages—Kṛta, Tretā, Dvāpara and Kali—which together make one aeon or *kalpa*. In every Dvāpara age, a Veda-vyāsa (literally, a 'Veda-arranger') appears to divide the primeval and ever-existent Veda into four parts. Each of the four Vedas is further split into branches that are entrusted to various sages.

In Chapter Seven, Maitreya asks how one may escape hell. The answer is given in a lively dialogue in which Yama, the lord of death, instructs his servants to ignore the pious devotees of Viṣṇu when collecting souls for punishment. The rest of this book describes various Vedic life rituals pertaining to birth, marriage, daily practices, conduct in the bedroom, death and sacrifices for the ancestors known as *śrāddha*. Nine chapters (Eight to Sixteen) are in the form of an embedded dialogue between the sages Aurva and Sagara.

Book Three includes sections on how to choose a wife and name a son. Chapter Eleven describes a day in the life of a brahmin gentleman, and Chapter Twelve provides dos and don'ts for the wise, including such good advice as, 'Avoid animals with tusks and horns' and 'Don't blow your nose at mealtimes'.

This book ends with an episode in which Viṣṇu creates a phantom. This being closely resembles, first, a Jain ascetic and, then, a Buddhist monk, to trick the demigods into abandoning the Vedas. Once the demigods have strayed from the path of true religion, the gods easily defeat them. This last section offers a glimpse into the types of religious debates and tensions that may have been experienced during the period of the *Viṣṇu Purāṇa*'s development.

Book Four: The Royal Dynasties

The fourth book is largely 'historical', as it describes the kings of the Solar and Lunar dynasties. This topic, like the description of the Manvantaras in Book Three, is one of the five themes, or *pañca-lakṣaṇa*, that define a purāṇa. Book Four represents a significant change of pace as it is nearly all in prose, except for several embedded songs of praise and verses quoted from other sources. It is worth reading this book carefully, even the long genealogical lists, as doing so will 'wash away all misdeeds', we are assured.

After the creator deity Brahmā arose from the cosmic egg, the patriarch, Dakṣa, was born from his right thumb. Dakṣa's daughter was Aditi, who gave birth to the Sun. The Solar Dynasty begins with the son of the Sun, Manu Vaivasvata. This book detours through many subnarratives as it describes the Solar lineage, including many folk etymologies to explain the origins of various names. We read of King Yuvanāśva, the man who gave birth to a son. The sage Saubhari lived underwater, where he made friends with a fish but abandoned his vows to have children. Sagara's sixty thousand sons excavated the ocean while searching for a missing horse. A king named Kalmāṣapāda, like a modern vampire, turned into a *rākaṣasa* and dined on human flesh at night. This section includes the legend of King Nimi, which explains why all animals blink.

Included in the Solar Dynasty is Rāma, hero of the *Rāmāyaṇa*, whose story appears here in highly abbreviated form. Vālmīki's hegemonic version of the epic ends with Rāma's consort Sītā in miserable exile and her return to Mother Earth. The *Viṣṇu Purāṇa*'s potted version, by contrast, concludes on a happy note, with Sītā safely lodged in Ayodhyā. This raises the interesting possibility that this section of the *Viṣṇu Purāṇa* may have been composed before Vālmīki's orthodox and anticlimactic narrative swamped most other versions.

Like the Solar Dynasty, the Lunar Dynasty also originated with Brahmā. This deity had a son, Atri, whose son was Soma, the Moon personified. Soma's first son, Budha (no relation to the Buddha with two ds), was abandoned in a reedbed, just like Moses of the Old Testament. This section also contains dozens of iconic subnarratives: King Purūravas's ill-starred affair with an *apsaras* who kept two pet sheep in her bedroom; King Jahnu, who drank the Gaṅgā River dry; a mother-and-daughter pair who swapped bowls of magic porridge; King Raji, who did a deal with deities and won sovereignty over the gods; and Yayāti, who convinced his son to trade his youthfulness for his own old age. Chapter Thirteen includes the strange and somewhat inconsequential narrative of how Kṛṣṇa acquired the magnificent Syamantaka jewel. As mentioned above, this story seems out of place as it recounts this famous episode in the life of Kṛṣṇa, even though we do not reach his birth until a later chapter.

Book Four includes the ancestors of the Pāṇḍavas and Kauravas, the heroes of the *Mahābhārata*, and their descendants, including King Parīkṣit, 'who rules all the world today in accord with virtue' (4.20.13). Parāśara names the kings who will rule in future and foretells the existence of some of India's well-known early dynasties, including the Mauryas, Śuṅgas and Guptas. This is as close to verifiable history as the *Viṣṇu Purāṇa* gets. As the last-named dynasty ruled until the middle of the sixth century CE, we may assume that this passage of the *Viṣṇu Purāṇa* was composed during or after the Gupta Empire.

The age of Kali will come to an end with these lineages, and the *Viṣṇu Purāṇa* gives a damning description of this period of decadence. Parāśara closes the book with a pithy observation on the futility of human endeavour and the mercilessness of time: 'Bhagīratha, Sagara, Kakutstha and Rāvaṇa, Rāma, Lakṣmaṇa, Yudhiṣṭhira and the others—there's no doubt they all existed, but where are they now? We just don't know' (4.24.68).

Book Five: Kṛṣṇa

Book Five is really the heart of the *Viṣṇu Purāṇa*, as, in the broadest sense, the preceding four books have all been building towards this climax: the advent, exploits and eventual withdrawal of Viṣṇu's manifestation in the form of Kṛṣṇa. The book opens in the city of Mathurā with the wedding of Kṛṣṇa's parents, Vasudeva and Devakī. This happy event is spoiled when a disembodied voice from the heavens warns Kaṃsa, the king of Mathurā, that Devakī's eighth child will eventually destroy him. The king keeps the couple under lock and key for years and murders each infant as it is born. Vasudeva, with divine intervention, smuggles the eighth baby, Kṛṣṇa, out of the city and delivers him to the cattle-herders' camp across the river. There he places the baby in the bed of Yaśodā, the head herder's wife.

Kṛṣṇa and his elder brother Balarāma enjoy a bucolic childhood in the camp, and exhibit prodigies such as overturning a fully laden wagon and uprooting two huge *arjuna* trees. Kaṃsa sends a succession of demons to kill Kṛṣṇa, including the ogress Pūtanā, and others in the forms of a donkey, a bull and a horse. This book includes many other well-known episodes, such as the subjugation of the serpent Kāliya, the raising of Mount Govardhana and Kṛṣṇa's lovemaking with the cowherding girls. It includes a delightful episode in which the girls, playing detective, discover Kṛṣṇa's lovemaking by interpreting his footprints on the sandy forest floor (5.13).

Now a young adult, Kṛṣṇa leaves the cattle camp for the nearby city of Mathurā, where his adventures continue. He confronts and kills his nemesis, Kaṃsa, and becomes the leader of the Yādava clan. Kṛṣṇa leads his people across India to establish a new capital at Dvārakā in the west. He abducts and marries Rukmiṇī, and sires a vast tribe, the foremost of whom are his son Pradyumna and grandson Aniruddha, whose exploits are described. In accordance with a brahmin's curse, the Yādava clansmen eventually fall on one another in a murderous spree, leaving Kṛṣṇa alone alive. One day he is reclining in the forest when a passing hunter mistakes his foot for a deer and shoots him with an arrow. Thus, Viṣṇu's manifestation as Kṛṣṇa and Book Five draw to a close.

Book Six: Dissolution

Just as the *Viṣṇu Purāṇa* begins with the creation of the world, it now concludes with its multiple forms of dissolution. While the text states explicitly that there are three types of destruction—causal, elemental and final—it actually begins with another, the destruction that takes place at the end of each Kali age. It prefaces this with a description of this decadent time itself, some aspects of which may be disturbingly familiar. At the end of the age of Kali, the world is destroyed, only to be recreated in the Kṛta, and the cycle of four ages begins again.

The second type of cosmic destruction, causal dissolution, takes place at the end of each aeon or *kalpa*, which consists of one thousand cycles of four ages, or 4.32 billion years. The world is then consumed by fire, which is extinguished by a cosmic deluge leaving nothing but a vast ocean on which the deity rests until the universe is created again.

A *kalpa* is but a single day for the deity Brahmā, who is said to live for one hundred of his own years, after which the elemental dissolution of the world takes place. The very elements from which the universe is composed—earth, air, fire, water and space—are reabsorbed into the Absolute in this process.

The so-called final form of destruction is a hybrid of this concept of cosmic destruction and the idea of liberation from cyclical existence. Liberated beings achieve a state of union with the Divine and are never reborn. The *Viṣṇu Purāṇa* seeks to convince us of the desirability of this state with a gruelling description of the horrors of birth, life and death. The antidote to existential suffering and the means of achieving this final dissolution is total surrender to the deity, which, after all, is the *Viṣṇu Purāṇa*'s take-home message.

The latter part of Book Six offers a reflection on an age-old debate in Hindu traditions: is it better to seek perfection through ascetic practices such as yoga or social practices that include the Vedic sacrifice? This ill-fitting and anticlimactic appendix compares the twin paths known as *pravṛtti* and *nivṛtti*. The contest is put into the mouths of two kings, Khāṇḍikya and his cousin Keśidhvaja. With this, the *Viṣṇu Purāṇa* limps towards a conclusion.

Like many major Sanskrit texts, the *Viṣṇu Purāṇa* finishes with a section called the *phalaśruti*, the 'fruits of listening'. Anyone who hears this narrative with devotion, recites it or calls it to mind will be freed from all their sins, we are promised.

The Sanskrit text

The master list of Indian manuscripts, the *New Catalogus Catalogorum* of the University of Madras, lists about two hundred and seventy-five manuscripts of the *Viṣṇu Purāṇa* in public and private libraries all over India and elsewhere, which suggests that this was a relatively popular and widely dispersed text in premodern times (Pathak 1997–99: Vol.1, p.13).

Of the earlier printed editions of the *Viṣṇu Purāṇa*, the version edited by Rajendranatha Sharma and published by Nag Publishers in 1985 is relatively accessible (Sharma 1985). This version includes two commentaries, the Viṣṇucittīya of Viṣṇucitta (~twelfth century CE) and the Ātmaprakāśa of Śrīdhara (thirteenth to fourteenth century CE). These commentaries are said to be given from the perspectives of Viśiṣṭādvaita and Advaita Vedānta, respectively (Adluri 2019). Both are sometimes useful for unravelling otherwise obscure passages of the root text, but I am often reminded of the words of my colleague Barbara Nelson, who wryly observed that commentators tell you what you already know, but not what you want to know.

This is a translation of the critically reconstituted text of the *Viṣṇu Purāṇa* edited by M.M. Pathak of the Oriental Institute at the Maharaja Sayajirao University of Baroda in Vadodara, India. This edition was published by the university in two volumes (Pathak 1997–99). In Indological circles, a critical edition is usually taken to be the earliest version of a text from which all consulted manuscripts are ultimately derived. This is of course different from the 'original' text, if such a thing ever existed. A critical edition might also be regarded as a new version, based on selected manuscripts, subject to the personal preferences of the editorial team. The Baroda critical edition consists of the final edited text in Devanāgarī script at the top of each page, with the variations found in each manuscript (the 'critical apparatus') presented in fine print below. This allows an overview and comparison of all the manuscripts selected for the project.

Researchers preparing this critical edition consulted forty-three manuscripts, which they divided into two groups based on script. The northern group was written in Śāradā, Newārī, Maithilī, Beṅgālī and Devanāgarī, and the southern group in Telegu, Grantha and Malayālam scripts (Pathak 1997–99: Vol.1, pp.1–2). The team found considerable agreement among manuscripts from widely separated geographical areas. The broad range of manuscripts suggests that the *Viṣṇu Purāṇa* was known and valued through much of the Indic world, from Kashmir and Nepal in the north to Kerala and Tamil Nadu in the south. Most manuscripts are undated. The earliest is in Devanāgarī script and dates from about 1207 CE. The other five dated manuscripts are from the sixteenth to the eighteenth centuries CE (Pathak 1997–99: Vol.1, p.14).

Other translations

There are already several translations of the *Viṣṇu Purāṇa*, undertaken over the past two centuries. The first was by the pioneering British Orientalist Horace Hayman Wilson (1786–1860). This was originally published in 1840 in five volumes under the title *The Vishńu Puráńa: A System of Hindu Mythology and Tradition* (Wilson 1961). A second edition, which appeared in 1880, has since been reprinted in India a number of times. Wilson's was one of the first English translations of any purāṇic text, and it became an important source of information on Hindu traditions in the West at that time.

Wilson based his translation on 'a collection of various manuscripts in his possession'; a total of seven was consulted (Wilson 1961: lxxi). In general, it appears that the manuscripts he consulted differed only in minor details from the reconstituted Baroda text. Wilson's translation is generally accurate and his scholarly footnotes useful. His diction is lofty, chaste and antiquated. He omits most if not all of the epithets that Sanskrit authors use for metrical reasons, and he wrote before the current system of scholarly diacritics for Sanskrit words was established.[8]

Nearly twenty years after Wilson's second edition, M.N. Dutt, rector of the Keshub Academy, a high school in Calcutta, published a new version of the *Viṣṇu Purāṇa* (Dutt 1896). This version—simply a recasting of Wilson's translation—is in some senses more modern, as it uses many Sanskrit terms, which by that time would have been familiar to an Indian readership. In other ways, it is more archaic, as Dutt uses an anachronistic register filled with King James-isms, such as 'thee' and 'thy', in contrast with Wilson's 'you' and 'your'.

8 Madame H.P. Blavatsky, the co-founder of the Theosophical Society, made over a hundred references to Wilson's translation in her *Secret Doctrine*, a classic of high-Victorian occultism published in 1888 (Jansma 1999).

A bilingual Sanskrit–Hindi edition of the *Viṣṇu Purāṇa* was published in 1967 (Gupta 1967). The two languages are presented side by side on each page in columns, which facilitates comparison of the Hindi translation with the root text. I occasionally found this translation helpful for analysing complex compounds or clarifying certain points of grammar. It was less helpful when it came to understanding difficult Sanskrit terms, as the translator often simply repeated the original Sanskrit terms in grammatically correct Hindi sentences.

The only other recent translation of the *Viṣṇu Purāṇa* of which I am aware was undertaken by Peter Schreiner of the University of Zürich, under the title *Viṣṇupurāṇa: Althergebrachte Kunde über Viṣṇu* ('*Viṣṇu Purāṇa*: Traditional Lore about Viṣṇu') (Schreiner 2013). This reliable and scholarly German prose translation makes good, clear sense of difficult passages in the original and was of great assistance to me. Schreiner includes a comprehensive commentary and a complete index of proper names. Some Sanskritists will be perplexed by the fact that Schreiner elected to translate some Sanskrit names into German—thus, the well-known demon king Hiraṇyakaśipu appears as 'Goldpolster' or 'Golden Cushion' in English.

About this translation

My friend and colleague Simon Brodbeck of the University of Cardiff has recently published a translation of the *Harivaṃśa*, entitled *Krishna's Lineage* (Brodbeck 2019). Dipping into early drafts of Simon's book, I suddenly felt that I was reading for the first time a truly modern translation of a Sanskrit text. As another colleague noted, it was easy to forget that one was actually reading a translation at all. The author has achieved a laudable balance between clear contemporary diction and a timeless dignity that has inspired and informed my own approach to the *Viṣṇu Purāṇa*. I have attempted to balance the requirements of creating a contemporary translation that is readily accessible to modern readers with the need to retain something of the gravity that befits a text like the *Viṣṇu Purāṇa*, which is, after all, 1,500 years old.

'Poetry is what gets lost in translation': this useful definition applies of course to the *Viṣṇu Purāṇa*, as well as to any other text. The greater part of the *Viṣṇu Purāṇa*—five out of its six books—is written in verse and is meant to be recited, chanted or sung. How, then, can one best render Sanskrit poetry into a suitable form of English for a general readership?

Here, I would like to acknowledge Carole Satyamurti's *Mahabharata: A Modern Retelling* (2015). As it is a free transcreation of the epic in blank verse, rather than a translation in the conventional sense, the author was not tied by strict fidelity to the root text, but enjoyed the freedom to create beautiful, natural and rhythmic iambic pentameter.

Although necessarily constrained by the demands of translation, I have tried to create a text with some poetic sensibility in English, one that honours and respects both the sense and the rhythmic properties of the root text, without doing violence to the meaning of the original or to English syntax. I hope—perhaps vainly—that just as the Sanskrit verses of the *Viṣṇu Purāṇa* are pleasant to the ear when read aloud, readers might also find pleasure in the sonic and rhythmic properties of this translation.

While poetic, the *Viṣṇu Purāṇa* is written in workaday purāṇic Sanskrit—a literary style it shares with the epics, the *Mahābhārata* and the *Rāmāyaṇa*. This is quite distinct from the elaborate courtly style of the later *Bhāgavata Purāṇa* or other poetic works known as *kāvya*. As the Sanskrit diction of the *Viṣṇu Purāṇa* is relatively simple, I have tried to avoid translations that sound bombastic, overly classical, archaic or Jacobean, in general favouring a simple Anglo-Saxon register over a Latinate one. This became more difficult when translating the effusive songs of praise, the *stutis*, in which devotees pour out unbroken streams of emotion at an almost ecstatic fever pitch.

The *Viṣṇu Purāṇa* is not without internal contradictions and confusion. To provide clarity, I have used two approaches. In some cases, I have added a few words to the translation. To improve clarity in the genealogical passages, I have occasionally added explanations to assist the reader in determining who is who. I have ignored the usual scholarly practice of putting these interpolations in square brackets, to minimise visual 'noise' in the text. In cases where an explanation is too long or complex to be inserted in the text neatly and unobtrusively, my second approach is to provide additional information in footnotes. Again, I have tried to keep these to a minimum for the convenience of the reader.

This translation of the *Viṣṇu Purāṇa* was undertaken with the inquisitive non-specialist reader in mind. No prior knowledge of Sanskrit or Hindu traditions is assumed, and I have tried to keep the number of Sanskrit terms to a minimum. There are some words for which no suitable English equivalent exists, especially philosophical terms and the names of various species of divine and semi-divine beings. These I have left untranslated.

Where I have translated selected Sanskrit terms, some specialists will not be pleased. For example, some will disapprove of my translation of *brahman* as the Absolute, or of the very common phrase *namas te* as 'I bow to you'. Specialists will have further legitimate quibbles with most if not all of the following: I have rendered the very common epithet *mahātman* simply as 'great', *mahābhāga* as 'fortunate' or 'blessed' and *prakṛti* as 'primal nature'. I have translated *varṇa* as 'community' or 'order', as the usual rendering of 'caste' is inadequate and deeply value-laden. The common epithet *puruṣottama* I have given as 'supreme spirit' or 'highest spirit', and *bhagavant* as 'Lord' or 'lord', the former for Viṣṇu–Kṛṣṇa as the supreme deity and the latter for other less-significant characters, such as 'lord of demons', 'lord of men', and so on. *Dharma* is a notoriously difficult term, as no single English word can account for its range of meanings. Accordingly, I have in some places left it untranslated, but in others, have rendered it as 'virtue', 'tradition' or 'religion', depending on the context. I am not very apologetic for these translations, as this text is aimed at the general reader and specialists can always consult the original at sites such as the *Göttingen Register of Electronic Texts in Indian Languages* (*GRETIL*) or the *Digital Corpus of Sanskrit*.

Frequent repetition of a word in close proximity is not a sin in Sanskrit composition, but it is irritating for the reader of English. For this reason, I have often substituted pronouns for proper names and vice versa. The Sanskrit text gives the name of the speaker of each passage in the form 'Parāśara said:' (*parāśara uvāca*), but I have dropped the word 'said' to reduce the tedium of repetition.

Most verses in the *Viṣṇu Purāṇa* are complete, freestanding syntactical units, but occasionally two or three verses form a single sentence governed by a single verb. In such cases, I have moved words around to ensure the clarity of the translation. Bearing all this in mind, mine is not a word-for-word rendering. Some forms in the root text will not be found in the English and some in the translation have no equivalent in the Sanskrit. Nevertheless, the overall sense of the root text has been preserved as accurately and parsimoniously as possible.

I have already mentioned that the names Viṣṇu and Kṛṣṇa are used interchangeably in our text as, according to this tradition, the two deities are one and the same entity. There are also several common epithets that are used more or less interchangeably for Viṣṇu–Kṛṣṇa. Kṛṣṇa's father was named Vasudeva, and Vāsudeva with a long *ā* is a patronymic. This very common epithet of Kṛṣṇa applies equally to Viṣṇu himself. Nārāyaṇa is an epithet used somewhat more frequently for Viṣṇu in the sense of the universal creator. Viṣṇu–Kṛṣṇa is also referred to as Madhusūdana, meaning 'Subduer of Madhu'. This is a reference to an event that is only hinted at in the *Viṣṇu Purāṇa*, in which the deity killed a demon of that name. This epithet, with its connotations of conquest, is used more frequently in contexts where a martial tone is called for, such as when Kṛṣṇa is battling various demons. Three common epithets are applied equally to both aspects of the deity and without reference to any particular context. Hari is said to be derived from the verb *hṛ* ('take away'), as the deity is the remover of evils. Acyuta means 'unfallen' and hence infallible or eternal, and Keśava, puzzlingly, means 'hairy', or perhaps 'slayer of Keśin', as is suggested in the *Viṣṇu Purāṇa*.

Kṛṣṇa's elder brother is called Balarāma, Baladeva and Balabhadra with equal frequency, but also Rāma and Saṃkarṣaṇa. For simplicity, I have standardised on the first name, Balarāma, even where the root text uses one of the other forms.[9]

Many of the deities of the *Viṣṇu Purāṇa* are also referred to by their epithets. To relieve the burden of remembering multiple names and titles, I have often given the deity's name along with the epithet—for example, for Hiraṇyagarbha, I use 'Brahmā born of the golden egg'; for Śakra, 'mighty Indra'. You will also find Varuṇa, lord of waters, Yama, lord of death, and many others. The forms Sun, Moon and Earth with capital letters are used for the respective deities in their embodied forms, and sun, moon and earth (without capitals) for these entities in the usual sense of their mundane physical equivalents.

In English, the passive voice is usually avoided, yet Sanskrit authors delight in this construction. I have consistently recast passives, which are very common in the root text, in the active voice.

9 For a detailed study of the names of Balarāma, see Bigger (1998).

The overriding concern of Sanskrit authors when composing verses is to preserve the integrity of the metre. If they are short of a syllable here or two syllables there, they have recourse to a range of inconsequential 'fillers'—particles that carry little semantic weight. These include words such as *eva*, *hi*, *vai*, *atha*, *tataḥ*, *ca* and *tu*. Given that they contribute so little to the overall meaning of a verse, I have usually chosen to ignore them in the translation.

In addition to these particles, Sanskrit authors often use vocatives (direct forms of address or invocations of individuals by name—for example, 'O Viṣṇu', 'O Kṛṣṇa') to pad out a verse to satisfy the metre. As mentioned, Wilson omitted these vocatives and epithets entirely from his translation, but I feel that this significantly detracts from the overall flavour of the text. I have opted to retain them (without the anachronistic 'O'), but generally shifted them to the caesura between two hemistichs—that is, the break between two lines in the middle of each verse—which seems the most natural place for them in English. As Sanskrit authors used vocatives largely for euphonic effect, I have sought to do something similar.

In conclusion, I can do no better than quote directly from Wilson's elegant preface, which, while written nearly two hundred years ago, is again eerily appropriate for our own age of turbulence:

> I trust, however ... that the translation of the Vishṇu Puráṇa will be of service and of interest to the few, who in these times of utilitarian selfishness, conflicting opinion, party virulence, and political agitation, can find a resting place for their thoughts in the tranquil contemplation of those yet living pictures of the ancient world which are exhibited by the literature and mythology of the Hindus. (Wilson 1961: lxxii)

References

Adluri, S. (2019). Who is the Viṣṇu of the Viṣṇu Purāṇa? *Purāṇic Studies: Proceedings of the Purāṇa Section of the 17th World Sanskrit Conference, July 9–13, 2018* (pp. 47–78). Vancouver: University of British Columbia.

Austin, C. (2011). The mystery of the Syamantaka jewel: The intersection of genealogy and biography in the Harivaṃśa. *Religions of South Asia*, 5(1–2): 153–169. doi.org/10.1558/rosa.v5i1/2.153.

Austin, C. (2014). The abduction of Śrī-Rukmiṇī: Politics, genealogy and theology in Harivaṁśa 87-90. *Religious Studies and Theology*, 33(1): 23–46. doi.org/10.1558/rsth.v33i1.23.

Austin, C. (2019). *Pradyumna: Lover, Magician and Scion of the Avatāra*. New York: Oxford University Press. doi.org/10.1093/oso/9780190054113.001.0001.

Bailey, G. (1995). *Gaṇeśapurāṇa: Introduction, Translation, Notes and Index*. Wiesbaden, Germany: Harrassowitz.

Bailey, G. (2018). Purāṇas. In K. Jacobsen, H. Basu, A. Malinar and V. Narayanan (eds), *Brill's Encyclopedia of Hinduism Online*. Leiden: Brill. doi.org/10.1163/2212-5019_beh_COM_2020070.

Bigger, A. (1998). *Balarāma im Mahābhārata: Seine Darstellung im Rahmen des Textes und Seiner Entwicklung* [*Balarāma in Mahābhārata: His Presentation in the Context of the Text and its Development*]. Wiesbaden, Germany: Harrassowitz Verlag.

Brodbeck, S. (2019). *Krishna's Lineage: The Harivamsha of Vyāsa's Mahābhārata*. New York: Oxford University Press.

Couture, A. (2014). Viṣṇu. In K. Jacobsen, H. Basu, A. Malinar and V. Narayanan (eds), *Brill's Encyclopedia of Hinduism Online*. Leiden: Brill. doi.org/10.1163/2212-5019_beh_COM_1030070.

Doniger, W. (1981). *The Rig Veda: An Anthology—One Hundred and Eight Hymns*. New York: Penguin.

Dutt, M. (1896). *A Prose English Translation of Vishnupuranam*. Calcutta: Elysium Press.

Fleet, J. (1915). The ancient Indian water-clock. *The Journal of the Royal Asiatic Society of Great Britain and Ireland*, (April): 213–230. Available from: www.jstor.org/stable/25189309.

Goldman, R. (1984). *The Rāmāyaṇa of Vālmīki: An Epic of Ancient India. Volume 1: Bālakāṇḍa*. Princeton, NJ: Princeton University Press. doi.org/10.1515/9781400884551.

Goswami, C. (2005). *Śrīmad Bhāgavata Mahāpurāṇa*. Gorakhpur, India: Gita Press.

Gupta, M. (1967). *Śrīśrīviṣṇupurāṇa: mūla śloka aur hiṃdī anuvādasahita*. Gorakhpur, India: Gita Press.

Gupta, R. and Valpey, K. (2013). *The Bhāgavata Purāṇa: Sacred Text and Living Tradition*. New York: Columbia University Press.

Hardy, F. (1983). *Viraha-bhakti: The Early History of Kṛṣṇa Devotion in South India*. Delhi: Oxford University Press.

Hiltebeitel, A. (1999). *Rethinking India's Oral and Classical Epics: Draupadī among Raputs, Muslims and Dalits*. Chicago: University of Chicago Press. doi.org/10.7208/chicago/9780226340555.001.0001.

Holdrege, B. (2013). Sacred geography: Vraja-dhāman—Krishna embodied in geographic place and transcendent space. In R. Gupta and K. Valpey (eds), *The Bhāgavata Purāṇa: Sacred Text and Living Tradition* (pp. 91–116). New York: Columbia University Press.

Jamison, S. and Brereton, J. (2014). *The Rigveda: The Earliest Religious Poetry of India*. New York: Oxford University Press.

Jansma, R. (1999). Evolution in the Vishnu Purana. *Sunrise Magazine*, April/May [n.p]. Available from: www.theosophy-nw.org/theosnw/world/asia/as-rudi.htm.

Matchett, F. (2001). *Kṛṣṇa, Lord or Avatāra? The Relationship between Kṛṣṇa and Viṣṇu in the Context of the Avatāra Myth as Presented by the Harivaṃśa, the Viṣṇupurāṇa and the Bhāgavatapurāṇa*. Richmond, UK: Curzon.

Matchett, F. (2005). The purāṇas. In G. Flood (ed.), *The Blackwell Companion to Hinduism* (pp. 129–143). Oxford: Blackwell Publishers.

Monier-Williams, M. (1899). *A Sanskrit-English Dictionary Etymologically and Philologically Arranged with Special Reference to Cognate Indo-European Languages*. Oxford: Clarendon Press.

Pathak, M. (1997–99). *The Critical Edition of the Viṣṇupurāṇam*. 2 vols. Vadodara, India: Oriental Institute.

Preciado-Solis, B. (1984). *The Kṛṣṇa Cycle in the Purāṇas: Themes and Motifs in a Heroic Saga*. New Delhi: Motilal Banarsidass.

Rao, V. (2007). Purāṇa. In S. Mittal and G. Thursby (eds), *The Hindu World* (pp. 97–115). New York: Routledge.

Rocher, L. (1986). *The Purāṇas*. Wiesbaden, Germany: Harrassowitz.

Sathaye, A. (2015). *Crossing the Lines of Caste: Viśvāmitra and the Construction of Brahmin Power in Hindu Mythology*. New York: Oxford University Press. doi.org/10.1093/acprof:oso/9780199341108.001.0001.

Satyamurti, C. (2015). *Mahabharata: A Modern Retelling*. New York: W.W. Norton.

Schreiner, P. (2002). Five topics, three functions, one god: On the interrelatedness of purāṇapañcalakṣaṇa-material and trimūrti concept in the Viṣṇupurāṇa. In M. Brockington (ed.), *Stages and Transitions: Temporal and Historical Frameworks in Epic and Purāṇic Literature* (pp. 261–286). Zagreb: Croatian Academy of Sciences and Arts.

Schreiner, P. (2013). *Viṣṇupurāṇa: Althergebrachte Kunde über Viṣṇu* [*Viṣṇu Purāṇa: Traditional Lore about Viṣṇu*]. Berlin: Verlag der Weltreligionen.

Sharma, R. (1985). *The Viṣṇumahāpurāṇam*. Delhi: Nag Publishers.

Sukthankar, V. (1933–66). *The Mahābhārata*. 19 vols. Poona, India: Bhandarkar Oriental Research Institute.

Taylor, M. (2007). *The Fall of the Indigo Jackal: The Discourse of Division and Pūrṇabhadra's Pañcatantra*. Albany, NY: State University of New York Press.

Taylor, M. (2016). *Seven Days of Nectar: Contemporary Oral Performance of the Bhāgavatapurāṇa*. New York: Oxford University Press. doi.org/10.1093/acprof:oso/9780190611910.001.0001.

Vaidya, L. (1969). *The Harivaṃśa: Being the Khila or Supplement to the Mahābhārata*. Poona, India: Bhandarkar Oriental Research Institute.

van Buitenen, J. (1973). *The Mahābhārata: The Book of the Beginning*. Chicago: University of Chicago Press.

Wilson, H. (1961 [1840]). *The Vishńu Puráńa: A System of Hindu Mythology and Tradition*. 5 vols. Calcutta: Punthi Pustak.

Book One: Creation

1. Maitreya asks Parāśara about the world

When Parāśara, that best of sages, had finished his morning rites, Maitreya bowed, saluted him and asked: *1*

'I've studied all the Vedas with you, master, and all the legal texts and supplements in due order. *2*

Thanks to your generosity, none could say that I'm remiss in any of these works, great sage, not even my adversaries. *3*

You know virtue, fortunate seer, and now I'd like to hear about the origin of the world and how it will fare in future. *4*

What's it made of, brahmin, and whence did all things, moving and unmoving, arise? How did the world end in earlier times and how will it end hereafter? *5*

What's the nature of the elements? What's the origin of gods and other beings? What's the state of the oceans, earth and mountains? *6*

What's the size and nature of the sun and other luminaries, best of sages? What about the families of gods and other beings, the Manus and Manvantaras? *7*

What about the aeons, how are they divided and apportioned into ages? How does each aeon end, and what traditions mark each age? I'd like to hear all this. *8*

What about the deeds of kings and heavenly seers, great sage? How did the branches of Vedic learning come about when Vyāsa had arranged them? *9*

What are the duties of the brahmins, the other orders and various life stages? I'd like to hear all this from you who pleased your father, Vasiṣṭha's son. *10*

Turn your gracious mind to me, brahmin, so that I may learn this through your kindness, you great sage.' *11*

How Parāśara acquired the *Viṣṇu Purāṇa*

Parāśara:

You've spoken well, Maitreya, and you know virtue. I recall an old account my grandsire, holy Vasiṣṭha, once told me. *12*

When I learned my father had been eaten by a rākṣasa sent by Viśvāmitra, Maitreya, my fury knew no bounds. *13*

I then began a major sacrifice to exterminate those demons, and hundreds of those night-ranging creatures were reduced to ashes. *14*

But while I was destroying them, my grandsire, eminent Vasiṣṭha, counselled me: *15*

'Don't be angry, my dear boy. Set aside your fury. The rākṣasas haven't wronged your father. It was his destiny. *16*

Only fools get angry, not the wise. Who is killed, dear boy, and who's the killer, when a person merely suffers the outcomes of his actions? *17*

Anger is the prime undoing of fame and penance, my dear, that people strive so hard to win. *18*

Great seers always eschew anger, dear boy, as it blocks the way to heaven and to liberation. Don't give in to fury. *19*

Don't burn these miserable night-ranging demons; they've done no harm. Call off this sacrifice of yours. Good people should be merciful.' *20*

Thus chastised by that great sage, my grandsire, I stopped the sacrifice at once, as I respected his opinion. *21*

This pleased that best of sages, holy Vasiṣṭha. Just then, Pulastya, Brahmā's son, appeared. *22*

My grandsire welcomed him and offered him a seat. That noble being, Pulaha's elder brother, spoke to me, Maitreya. *23*

Pulastya:

'Because you heed your grandsire's words and show forbearance in the midst of great hostility, you'll comprehend all sacred texts. *24*

Even though you were enraged, you lucky man, you refrained from killing all my clan. I therefore grant you this great boon. *25*

You'll be the creator of a purāṇa, dear boy, and understand precisely the nature of divinity. *26*

Whether you lead a life of sacrifice or renunciation, blessed by me, your mind will be pure and unconfused, my dear.' *27*

Then my grandsire, holy Vasiṣṭha, confirmed that everything would happen just as Pulastya had foretold. *28*

Such was the conversation long ago with Vasiṣṭha and wise Pulastya that came to mind when you questioned me. *29*

I'll relate this whole purāṇa for you, Maitreya, seeing as you ask, so listen carefully. *30*

The world arose from Viṣṇu and depends on him. He maintains it, he destroys it—he *is* the world. *31*

So ends Chapter One in Book One of the glorious Viṣṇu Purāṇa.

2. Parāśara praises Viṣṇu; Creation

Parāśara:

I bow to Viṣṇu, unchanging, pure, eternal, supreme, always in universal form, all-conquering, *1*

Who is also Brahmā, Hari, Śiva, Vāsudeva, saviour and cause of creation, preservation and destruction of the world. *2*

I bow to Viṣṇu whose form is one and many, gross and subtle, unseen and seen, the cause of liberation. *3*

I bow to Viṣṇu, who is the world, its creator, keeper and destroyer, its root and highest spirit. *4*

Having bowed to Viṣṇu, who is the base of everything, smaller than the smallest, yet abiding in all beings, imperishable, the highest spirit, *5*

Who in the truest sense is unsullied wisdom, yet is falsely seen as having concrete form, *6*

Who consumes the world, but is also lord of creation and preservation, master of the threefold realms, unborn, unageing and unchanging, *7*

I'll tell you what was said in former times by Brahmā, my blessed lotus-born grandsire, when asked by Dakṣa and other leading sages. *8*

They passed this tale to King Purukutsa by the river Narmadā. He related it to Sārasvata, who passed it on to me. *9*

The highest, who is higher than the highest, the supreme spirit who abides in all, transcending colour, form, description and distinction, *10*

Unfettered by decline, destruction, change, development or birth; of whom alone it can be said that he exists, *11*

As he dwells (*vasati*) in all locations and everything abides in him, the wise refer to him as Vāsudeva. *12*

He is the Absolute, supreme, eternal, unborn, undecaying, unchanging and universal being. Never to be abandoned, he is pure. *13*

He is this whole world, Unseen (*avyakta*) and Seen (*vyakta*), existing in the form of Time (*kāla*) and Spirit (*puruṣa*). *14*

The primary form of the highest Absolute is Spirit, brahmin, next are Seen and Unseen, with Time as the fourth. *15*

The learned know the pure and highest state of Viṣṇu is superior to primal Matter (*pradhāna*), Spirit, the Seen and Time. *16*

Matter, Spirit, the Seen and Time are in due proportion the cause of the existence of creation, preservation and destruction. *17*

Viṣṇu is the Seen and Unseen, Time and Spirit. Understand his deeds are like the play of children. *18*

The best of sages say that Matter makes the Unseen possible. This primordial stuff is subtle, eternal, existent and nonexistent. *19*

It's durable, needs no other basis, is boundless, ageless, firm, beyond the reach of sound and touch and has no form attainable by these or other senses. *20*

Consisting of three qualities—purity, passion and dullness—it is the origin of the world, but has no beginning, end or middle. Between each creation and dissolution, it is all-pervading. *21*

The world is created

Those self-restrained individuals who understand the Vedas' words, wise sage, and who discourse on sacred topics, recite this verse about the origin of Matter: *22*

'There was neither day nor night, sky nor earth, light nor darkness or any other quality. There was just a single entity: the Absolute, beyond hearing, thought and other senses, composed of Matter and of Spirit.'[1] *23*

Those two forms exist apart from Viṣṇu's own state, brahmin. He has another that's known as Time, by which these two are joined or parted, brahmin. *24*

Because the Seen returns to primal elements at the dissolution of the world, that reabsorption is known as 'elemental'. *25*

In the form of Time, the lord lacks start or finish, brahmin, so these rounds of creation, preservation and dissolution never cease. *26*

At the time of dissolution, these three qualities are in balance, Spirit abides alone in Matter, Maitreya, and Viṣṇu exists in the form of Time. *27*

The highest Absolute, the supreme spirit in whom the world abides, all-pervading master of creation, supreme lord at the heart of all, *28*

Hari, having entered Matter and Spirit, then willingly agitates these changing and unchanging elements when the moment of creation is at hand. *29*

Just as scent excites the mind by proximity alone in the absence of all contact, in that same way, the supreme lord stirs the elements in his role as benefactor. *30*

The highest being is indeed the agitator, brahmin, and that which is agitated subsisting in the state of matter during its contraction and expansion. *31*

Viṣṇu, highest lord of lords, is manifest in the form of things composed of atoms, and in the form of Brahmā and other beings. *32*

Then, at the moment of creation, from that equilibrium of qualities, overseen by Viṣṇu as a sentient being, sage, comes the property known as Greatness (*mahat*), which is produced by the appearance of those qualities, best of brahmins. *33*

1 *Ṛg Veda* (RV, 10.129.1–2).

Matter then surrounds the Greatness that arises. This Greatness is threefold—pure, passionate and dark—and is swathed in Matter, just as seeds are covered by a husk. *34*

From Greatness, threefold individuation arises: pure, passionate and elemental. *35*

It's the cause of elements and the senses as it consists of threefold qualities, great sage. Just as Greatness is enclosed by Matter, so Matter is enclosed by Greatness. *36*

Elemental individuation becomes productive and brings forth the subtle element of sound. From that arises space, characterised by that sensation. *37*

Elemental individuation envelops space, which has sound as its element. Space then becomes productive and gives rise to the element of touch. *38*

From that is born a mighty wind whose property is touch; and space, whose element is sound, envelops the element of touch. *39*

Wind then becomes productive and brings forth the element of form, and light, whose quality is form, arises from the wind. *40*

Then wind, whose element is touch, envelops light, whose element is form, and light then becomes productive, bringing forth the element of taste. *41*

Next arise the waters, which are the source of taste, and the waters, whose element is taste, envelop light, whose element is form. *42*

The waters then become productive, bringing forth the element of scent. From that arises solid earth, whose quality is that sensation. *43*

As each of these phenomena has its own subtle element, they are considered in terms of their elemental natures, but the subtle elements, lacking distinctive qualities, are known as 'indistinct'. *44*

Being indistinct, they lack qualities such as terror, peace or dullness. This is the elemental creation that arises from individuation and is marked itself by dullness. *45*

They say the organs of the senses arise from individuation marked by passion, and the ten senses themselves, with mind as the eleventh, arise from individuation marked by purity. Accordingly, the senses are thought to be pure. *46*

The skin, eye, nose and tongue, with ear as the fifth, brahmin, combine with the intellect to experience sound and other sensations. *47*

The functions of the organs of excretion and reproduction, the hands, the feet and voice, Maitreya, are said to be evacuation, production, movement and communication. *48*

Space, wind, light, water and earth combine with each of their respective qualities of sound and so on, brahmin. *49*

These now exhibit terror, peace or dullness, so are said to be 'distinct'. *50*

Possessing energy of different kinds, but existing independently and not combining, these are incapable of creation unless completely unified. *51*

Having combined with one another, blending together, they become a single mass and achieve a perfect unity. *52*

Overseen by Spirit, with the Unseen element's assent, the factors beginning with Greatness and ending with the distinctive elements form an egg. *53*

This egg increases slowly like a bubble on the water. Consisting of the elements, wise sage, and resting on the waters, it is the natural and excellent abode of Viṣṇu when he takes the form of Brahmā. *54*

There, Viṣṇu, universal lord, whose form is unmanifest, abides in the manifest form of Brahmā. *55*

Meru and the other mountain ranges are the inner and outer membranes of the egg, and the waters inside it are the oceans. *56*

The mountains, lands and oceans, heavenly bodies, the threefold worlds, gods and demigods and humankind, brahmin, are all inside that egg. *57*

The egg is wrapped in water, fire, wind and space and other elements, and by the individuation that is their source. Each layer is ten times greater than the one within, and the whole is covered by Greatness, the origin of the elements. *58*

The Greatness, together with the others, is enveloped by the Unseen, brahmin. The egg is covered by these seven natural layers, like a coconut with an inner kernel and an outer husk. *59*

Delighting in the quality of activity, the lord of all, Hari himself, becoming Brahmā, sets about creation of the world. *60*

Lord Viṣṇu, imbued with purity, whose prowess is immeasurable, preserves the world through every age until each aeon ends. *61*

Filled with the quality of dullness, at the end of every aeon, Janārdana takes the wrathful form of Rudra, Maitreya, and devours the universe. *62*

When he has consumed it all and reduced the world to a single ocean, the highest lord reclines on his couch, the serpent's lap. *63*

When he wakes, in Brahmā's form, he creates the world once more. *64*

The one Lord Janārdana is known as Brahmā, Viṣṇu and Śiva when carrying out creation, preservation and destruction of the world. *65*

Lord Viṣṇu, the creator, creates himself. He is both protector and protected. He is the destroyer who destroys himself at the aeon's end. *66*

Earth, water, light, wind and space, all the senses and the mind that together make the world: these are known as Spirit. *67*

Since this alone is the universal, eternal governor of all creation, it's also the agent that abides in all the elements, from which arise the creation, preservation and destruction of the world. *68*

He alone is creation and creator. He alone is preserver and preserved. In the form of Brahmā and the others, Viṣṇu, whose forms are endless, is the foremost, desirable bestower of desires. *69*

So ends Chapter Two in Book One of the glorious Viṣṇu Purāṇa.

3. The divisions of time

Maitreya:

How are we to understand that Brahmā is the agent of creation and the rest when he's free from qualities, measureless, pure and perfect? *1*

Parāśara:

Not all essential powers of beings are in the realm of comprehension. Powers including creativity are aspects of Brahmā's essential nature, just as heat is fire's aspect, best of sages. *2*

You must therefore understand the function of the lord at the moment of creation. He manifests as Brahmā, also known as Nārāyaṇa, the grandsire of the world. *3*

By convention, Brahmā is said to be arisen, wise one, even though he is eternal. *4*

He's thought to live a hundred of his own years, a period called a *para*, half of which is one *parārdha*. *5*

As I told you, blameless one, time is a form of Viṣṇu. Now understand how time applies to the measurement of Brahmā's lifespan, *6*

And to those of other beings, moving and unmoving, best of sages, and to the earth and mountains, seas and all the rest. *7*

Fifteen *nimeṣas* or blinks of the eye are said to make a *kāṣṭhā,* best of sages. Thirty *kāṣṭhās* make one *kalā*, and thirty *kalās* make a *muhūrta*, as a rule. *8*

Thirty *muhūrtas* make one day and night for mortals. A month has thirty days and nights, divided into fortnights. *9*

Six months make an *ayana*, and two *ayanas*, south and north, comprise a year.[2] The southern one is the deities' night-time; the northern one, their day. *10*

Each cycle of four ages—the Kṛta, Tretā and the others—lasts twelve thousand divine years. Now hear from me how they're divided. *11*

Those who understand the past have said the Kṛta and other ages last for four, three, two and one thousand divine years, respectively. *12*

The period before each age is called a 'dawn'. Each dawn lasts as many centuries as the following age has millennia. The time that follows every age is called a 'dusk' and is of the same duration. *13*

The time between each dawn and dusk is called an age or *yuga*, known by the names of Kṛta, Tretā and the others, best of sages. *14*

The Kṛta, Tretā, Dvāpara and Kali together make one fourfold cycle, sage. They say a thousand cycles make just one day for Brahmā. *15*

In each of Brahmā's days, brahmin, fourteen Manus reign. Now you'll hear about the length of each of these. *16*

In the reign of every Manu, seven seers, deities, their king, a Manu himself and the sovereigns who are his progeny are created and absorbed again. *17*

Each period is somewhat longer than seventy-one times the total years in each cycle of four ages. Called a Manvantara, it lasts for the duration of the Manu, gods and others, best of sages. *18*

It's thought to be as long as eight hundred and fifty-two thousand divine years. *19*

2 The two *ayanas* are periods during which the sun is south or north of the celestial equator.

This, brahmin, is a total of three hundred and sixty-seven million and twenty thousand years for mortals, best of sages. *20*

That's exactly the length of time, brahmin, for which each Manvantara endures. *21*

Fourteen Manvantaras are thought to be the length of one of Brahmā's days, from which its name, one *brahma*, is derived. At the conclusion of each day, the universe is destroyed. *22*

At that time, the threefold worlds—earth, space and all the rest—are consumed by fire. The inhabitants of the realm of Maharloka, oppressed by heat, retreat to Janaloka. *23*

When all three worlds have been reduced to a single ocean, Brahmā, none other than Nārāyaṇa himself, reclines upon his serpent-couch, having grown in strength by consuming the universe. *24*

Ascetics who dwell in Janaloka meditate on Brahmā all through the night, which lasts as long as a *brahma* day. When the night is done, he creates the world again. *25*

In the same way that Brahmā has his years, he has one hundred of his years. One hundred make a *para*, the lifespan of that great deity. *26*

One-half of Brahmā's *para*—a *parārdha*—has passed already, purest sage. The final aeon of that *parārdha* was the period known as Padma. *27*

This aeon called Vārāha, brahmin, is the first of the second *parārdha*, which has now begun. *28*

So ends Chapter Three in Book One of the glorious Viṣṇu Purāṇa.

4. Brahmā creates the world anew

Maitreya:

Tell me, great sage, how Lord Brahmā, known as Nārāyaṇa, created all the beings when the aeon first began. *1*

Parāśara:

Hear from me how Brahmā, Lord Nārāyaṇa himself and heavenly master of all progenitors, made the world. *2*

At the end of the previous aeon, Lord Brahmā, filled with purity, having slept all through the night, awoke and saw the world, bereft of living things, was empty. *3*

Nārāyaṇa—supreme, unimaginable, universal master—is the beginningless lord and all-creator in the form of Brahmā. *4*

In this regard, they sing a verse about Nārāyaṇa in the heavenly form of Brahmā, the creation and destruction of the world: *5*

'The waters were known as Nāra, as they were Nara's sons. As these were the deity's first abode (*ayana*), he is known as Nārāyaṇa, "whose home was water".'[3] *6*

When the world still lay below the single ocean, the progenitor and lord, knowing that the earth was in its waters, after consideration, desired to raise it. *7*

Just as he had taken the forms of tortoise, fish and others in earlier ages, he now took another form: the boar. *8*

The changeless, universal, supreme progenitor took that form, which embodied all the Vedas and the sacrifice, for the preservation of the world. *9*

Praised by Sanaka and other perfect sages who sheltered in Janaloka, he entered the waters, being the foundation of the spiritual and material worlds. *10*

When the goddess Earth saw that he had reached the lower realm of Pātāla, bowing with deep devotion, she praised him. *11*

The Earth:

I bow to you who are everything, and who bear the conch and discus. Lift me up from here right now as you've done before. *12*

You raised me in the past, and I consist of you, Janārdana, as does the sky and all that is. *13*

I bow to you, the essence of the highest Spirit. Spirit's essence, to you I bow. I bow to you, primal Matter, the Seen and Time itself. *14*

You are creator of every being, you are protector and destroyer of creation and the other phases, Lord, when you take the forms of Brahmā, Viṣṇu and of Rudra. *15*

3 This quotation is found in *Manu Smṛti* (1.10).

When you've consumed the world and it lies beneath the single ocean, you sleep, Govinda, while the wise ones contemplate you. *16*

As no-one knows your ultimate form, the deities worship whichever form you take. *17*

Revering you as the highest Absolute, those who yearn for liberation reach it. Who will reach perfection if they do not worship Vāsudeva? *18*

All that can be grasped by mind, by eye or other senses and all that can be known by mind are surely forms of you. *19*

I'm made of you, you are my foundation and creator, I depend on you. That's why the whole world calls me Mādhavī.[4] *20*

Be victorious! You are all knowledge. Be victorious! You are unchanging and enduring. Be victorious! You are unending. Be victorious! You are Unseen. Be victorious! You are the Seen, Lord. You are the highest supreme, you are everything. Be victorious! You are the purest lord of sacrifices. *21*

You *are* the sacrifice. You are the cry of *vaṣaṭ*. You are the syllable *Oṃ*. You are the sacrificial fires. You are the Vedas and their supplements. Hari, you are the spirit of the sacrifice. *22*

You are the sun and other heavenly bodies, the planets, stars and all the constellations, the formed and formless, the visible and invisible, the highest spirit. *23*

You are all that I have said, highest Lord, and all that I've left unsaid just now. I bow to you again. To you I bow again and again. *24*

Varāha the Boar raises the Earth and the ascetics praise him

Parāśara:

While the Earth was praising him like this, the glorious bearer of the world, whose voice resounded like the chanting of the *Sāma Veda*, bellowed loudly. *25*

The mighty boar then raised the earth with just one tusk. His eyes like full-blown lotuses and his body dark as lily leaves, he rose from the lower regions, towering like Mount Nīla. *26*

4 The female counterpart of Mādhava, a patronymic of Kṛṣṇa.

The water from his dive, driven by the breath he breathed as he emerged, washed away the sins of Sanandana and the other sages sheltering in Janaloka, leaving them in a purer state. *27*

Thundering unceasingly, the waters rushed down to the lower realm, trampled by his hooves. The accomplished seers in Janaloka, blasted by the wind whipped up by his breath, were scattered in all directions. *28*

The sages, who landed in the bristles on the back of that mighty boar, praised him as he rose, bearing the earth aloft, his belly wet, as he shook his body, which was the very Vedas. *29*

Sanandana and the others in Janaloka, their hearts all filled with joy, bowing with humility, praised that bearer of the earth, whose gaze was steady: *30*

'Be victorious, Keśava, highest lord of lords! You, Lord, are the bearer of the mace and conch, sword and discus. You, Lord, are the cause of creation, preservation and destruction of the world. There is no state superior to yours. *31*

Your legs are the form of the Vedas, your tusks the sacrificial post, your teeth the offerings, your mouth the altar, your tongue the fire, the hairs on your body the blades of sacrificial grass. You, Lord, are indeed the spirit of the sacrifice. *32*

Your two eyes are day and night, your head the highest Absolute, the universal state, great being. The bristles of your mane are all the Vedic hymns, Lord, your nose the offerings, *33*

Your snout the ladle, your deep grunt the chanting of the *Sāma Veda*, your body the pavilion, your joints the rituals and your two ears the *iṣṭa* and *pūrta* rites conducted for oneself and others, God. Favour us, eternal Lord. *34*

We know you paced the world in just three strides, and that you are endless, but are present at the origin. You are imperishable and your form is universal. We know that you are the highest lord of all. Favour us, protector of all moving and unmoving things. *35*

This whole world rests on the tip of your tusk, protector, like a muddy lotus leaf that sticks to you when diving in a lily pond. *36*

Your might is unequalled, your body fills the space between earth and heaven and your light pervades the world. Lord, abide for the good of every being. *37*

You are indeed the single highest goal, there is no other, universal Lord. Your greatness fills the universe of moving and unmoving things. *38*

This visible world is your body when you take the form of knowledge, but those who aren't ascetics cannot see the world correctly. *39*

Those unwise beings who see this world, which is in nature knowledge, as an object with reality sink in an ocean of delusion. *40*

But pure-hearted beings who understand true knowledge, highest Lord, see this world as your own form comprising knowledge itself. *41*

Favour us! You are all and at the heart of all. Raise the earth to make the worlds! You are beyond all measure. Lotus-eyed deity, gratify us! *42*

You are filled with goodness, Lord. Raise up this earth, Lord Govinda, to make the worlds. Lotus-eyed deity, gratify us! *43*

May your act of creation benefit the worlds. We bow to you. Lotus-eyed deity, gratify us!' *44*

Parāśara:

While the sages were praising him with these words, the highest spirit, bearer of the earth, raised the world and set it down at once amid that mighty ocean. *45*

The earth floated on the surface of the water like some great vessel, and because it was so broad it didn't sink. *46*

Then the lord, who has no start but is the origin of all, spread the earth and heaped up mountains on its surface place by place. *47*

He whose wishes are never thwarted used his unfailing power to create again on the surface of the earth all the mountains burned at the end of the previous aeon. *48*

He divided the earth into regions, remade the seven continents in the same manner, and laid out four spheres, beginning with the land, as he had before.[5] *49*

Divine Lord Hari, in the form of four-faced Brahmā, swathed in energy, then created all other things. *50*

5 The four spheres are the earth, sky, heaven and Maharloka, the sphere of the sages.

Brahmā is, however, just the instrumental cause in the creation of that which is created, since all this arises from primal matter. *51*

Apart from this single instrumental cause, no other cause is needed. One substance becomes another from its own inherent tendency, excellent ascetic. *52*

So ends Chapter Four in Book One of the glorious Viṣṇu Purāṇa.

5. Brahmā creates living beings

Maitreya:

How did that divine being create the gods, sages, ancestral spirits, Dānavas, humankind, animals, plants and all the rest that live on land, in air or water? *1*

What are the qualities, form and nature of the world that Brahmā made at the beginning of creation? Describe all this in detail, brahmin. *2*

Parāśara:

Listen carefully, Maitreya, and I'll tell you how the divine lord created the gods and all. *3*

While contemplating creation, as at the start of every previous aeon, there appeared a creation preceded by ignorance and consisting of darkness. *4*

Fivefold ignorance—darkness, error, delusion, gloom and blindness—arose from that great being. *5*

This creation, which sprang from his meditation, is the fivefold world of plants, in which there is no perception.[6] Outer sensations and inner emotions are absent, and objects are veiled and static. *6*

Because immobile things were created first, this is called foundational creation. *7*

Seeing this was not enough, Brahmā thought about creating more. *8*

While he was contemplating, the creation of animals took place. This is known as the Tiryaksrotas creation, because animals have horizontal (*tiryak*) digestive tracts (*srotas*). *9*

6 The five kinds of plants are trees, shrubs, vines, herbs and grasses.

They're called beasts and other names, are generally dull by nature, unwitting, have bad habits and mistake ignorance for knowledge. *10*

Self-centred, proud and subject to twenty-eight faults, yet all have feelings and interact with one another. *11*

Brahmā thought that this was insufficient and, while contemplating, a further creation took place: the third, Ūrdhvasrotas, blessed with goodness, appeared above (*ūrdhva*) in the heavenly sphere. *12*

Those born of the Ūrdhvasrotas creation are said to know much happiness and joy; they're not immune from outer sensations or inner emotions, but are awake to both. *13*

Filled with contentment, this third creation is called divine, and Brahmā was pleased with all the work that he had done. *14*

Knowing that the first and following creative acts were not enough, he then thought another feat of excellent creation would suffice. *15*

While contemplating, as his mind was set on truth, the creation known as Arvāksrotas appeared from the Unseen element, and this he thought sufficient. *16*

Because these creatures have vertical (*arvāk*) digestive tracts, they're called Arvāksrotas. Although they are most gifted, they're still subject to dullness and excessive energy. *17*

They therefore suffer from much pain and are always forced to act. They also have sensations and emotions. This, then, is humanity and Brahmā thought this was sufficient. *18*

Six stages of creation have been explained here, best of sages. The first was the creation from the element of Greatness, that of Brahmā. *19*

The second was the elemental creation of rudimentary factors. The third was the subsequent creation of the senses. *20*

These are the primary creations and are preceded by intellect. The foundational creation was the fourth, so called because unmoving things provide a basis. *21*

The fifth is called Tiryaksrotas or animal creation. Next came divine creation, the sixth, or Urdhvasrotas. *22*

Then came Arvāksrotas, the creation of humanity, the seventh. *23*

The eighth is Anugraha, marked by purity and dullness. These are the five secondary creations. The primary ones are three in number. *24*

The primary and secondary events, with Kaumāra as the ninth, are known as the nine creations of Brahmā, the creative lord. *25*

These primary and secondary creations, proceeding from the universal lord, are the root cause of the universe. What further do you wish to hear? *26*

Maitreya:

You've described in brief the creation of the deities and the rest, master, but I'd like to hear more details from you, best of sages. *27*

Parāśara:

Beings are shaped by their previous actions, good and bad. They can't escape this fact, even when they're burned at the end of time. *28*

When Brahmā made the world, there arose four kinds of creatures, from static things to deities and others, brahmin—all products of his mind. *29*

Desiring to produce the fourfold creation of gods, demigods, ancestral spirits and humankind, he combined these four within himself. *30*

Thus, merged within his mind, Brahmā, lord of creation, became completely filled with dullness. Then, desiring to begin creation, from his thighs the demigods arose at first. *31*

Brahmā cast off that body of dullness, Maitreya, and, once abandoned, it became the night. *32*

Still filled with that creative urge and taking on another body, Brahmā was pleased, brahmin, and the deities, imbued with purity, appeared from his mouth. *33*

That body was also shed by Brahmā and became the day that's filled with light. That's why demigods are strong by night and deities are strong by day. *34*

Brahmā then took another body imbued with purity and, thinking of himself as sire, the ancestors of humankind appeared. *35*

After the lord had made the ancestors, he cast off that body as well and, being abandoned, it became the dusk. *36*

He then took another form imbued with energy, best of brahmins, and humankind, which abounds in vigour, was born. *37*

At that very moment, the creative lord cast off that form, and it became the glimmer known as dawn. *38*

That's why folk are more active at the break of day and the ancestors more powerful at dusk, Maitreya. *39*

Night and day, dawn and dusk—these four are bodies of Lord Brahmā imbued with threefold qualities of dullness, purity and energy. *40*

Brahmā then took another form infused with energy, and hunger was born from him, with the anger it engenders. *41*

Then in darkness filled with hunger, Lord Brahmā created beings, hairy monsters, who rushed towards him. *42*

Those who cried, 'Don't do this, Lord. Protect us! (*rakṣyatām*)', became the demons known as rākṣasas. Others cried, 'We want to eat!', and they became the yakṣas because they needed food (*jakṣaṇa*). *43*

When Brahmā beheld these awful beings, the hairs dropped from his head, but having fallen, they climbed up again. *44*

Because they slipped (*sarpaṇa*) from his scalp, they became the serpents (*sarpa*), and because they left (*hīna*) his head behind, they're also known as snakes (*ahi*). The enraged creator of the world then brought forth flesh-eating *bhūta*-spirits, red in colour, furious and terrifying. *45*

While he meditated, the gandharvas arose from his body at that time, brahmin, so-called as they were born while drinking speech (*gandharva*). *46*

After Lord Brahmā had made these beings, spurred by the energy of that endeavour, he then produced other beings at will, and with that energy made the birds. *47*

The lord of creation made sheep from his chest, goats from his mouth and cattle from his belly and flanks. *48*

From his feet came elephants and horses, donkeys, wild oxen, deer, camels, mules, antelopes and beasts of other kinds. *49*

Those plants that bring forth fruit and roots arose from the hairs of his head. Having made all the plants and animals at the onset of the aeon, best of brahmins, Brahmā employed them in sacrifices at the beginning of the Tretā age. *50*

Cattle, goats, buffalo,[7] sheep, horses, mules and donkeys—these they call domestic animals. Now learn about wild animals from me: *51*

Those with claws or cloven hooves, elephants, monkeys, birds are fifth, those that live in water sixth, and those that creep and crawl are the seventh kind. *52*

The Gāyatrī metre, the *Ṛg Veda*, the Trivṛtsāma, the Rathantara and, of the sacrifices, the Agniṣṭoma, arose from Brahmā's eastern mouth. *53*

The *Yajur Veda*, the Triṣṭubh metre, the Pañcadaśa hymns, the Bṛhatsāman and the Uktha issued from his southern mouth. *54*

The *Sāma Veda*, the Jagatī metre, the Saptadaśa hymns, the Vairūpa and the Atirātra sacrifice issued from his western mouth. *55*

The Ekaviṃśa hymns, the *Atharva Veda*, the Āptoryāma, the Anuṣṭubh metre and the Vairāja issued from his northern mouth. *56*

Creatures great and small arose from his limbs after the lord of creation made the gods, demigods, ancestors and humankind. *57*

At the beginning of the aeon, the universal grandsire made the yakṣas, piśācas, gandharvas and hosts of apsarases, *58*

Naras, kiṃnaras and rākṣasas, birds, animals of village and forest, snakes—everything in the world, changing and unchanging, moving and unmoving. *59*

Lord Brahmā, original creator, made all this. The roles all these beings had filled in previous aeons, they undertook once more, being made again. *60*

Cruel and kind, harsh and gentle, right and wrong, true and false—beings undertook and delighted in the roles they were assigned. *61*

The lord creator made the differences among the objects of the senses, beings, bodies and their functions. *62*

He gave names and forms to all the creatures and fixed the range of tasks for gods and other beings in the beginning, following the Vedas' words. *63*

He provided names and fitting roles to all the sages in accordance with the Vedas. *64*

---

7 Most manuscripts clearly give *puruṣa* ('people') at this point, a word that does not fit well. I have diverged from the Critical Edition and used *mahiṣa* ('buffalo'), as attested by several other manuscripts. Wilson has 'hog'.

Just as varied signs of every season appear in turn, so, too, are the characteristics of each age. *65*

Thus, Brahmā undertakes creation once more at the start of every aeon, filled with the power of creative urges and driven by the energies of those to be created. *66*

So ends Chapter Five in Book One of the glorious Viṣṇu Purāṇa.

6. Human society

Maitreya:

You've mentioned the Arvāksrotas creation, the origin of humankind, brahmin, but tell me in more detail how Brahmā accomplished this. *1*

Tell me how he made the four communities, the *varṇas*, with their respective qualities, great sage, as well as the duties of the brahmins and the others. *2*

Parāśara:

When Brahmā wished to create the world, while contemplating purity, best of brahmins, beings invested with that quality first issued from his mouth. *3*

From Brahmā's chest came others filled with energy, and from his thighs came beings with both energy and dullness. *4*

Brahmā brought forth others from his feet, best of brahmins, all overcome by dullness. These comprise the four communities. *5*

Brahmins, kṣatriyas, vaiśyas and śūdras arose from his mouth, chest, thighs and feet, best of brahmins. *6*

Brahmā did this so that sacrifices could be undertaken, blessed sage, and these four orders are the perfect means for doing so. *7*

Deities are sustained by sacrifices, and folk are nourished when the gods send rain. Sacrifices are the source of welfare—you understand this, dharma. *8*

Sacrifice is carried out by pious men delighting in their duties and pure in their behaviour as they walk the path of virtue. *9*

By means of sacrifice, men reach heaven or liberation by adhering to their duties, sage, or else they'll reach a realm where they'll be happy, brahmin. *10*

People blessed with perfect faith and filled with virtue were made in four communities by Brahmā, best of sages. *11*

Residing happily where they wished, they were free from troubles, pure of heart, blameless and virtuous in all their actions. *12*

When Hari in pure form dwelled within them, perfect knowledge filled their stainless minds and, on this account, they saw that state called Viṣṇu. *13*

Then Hari's aspect known as Time caused wickedness to come among them. It was frightening but petty, of little substance, *14*

Misconduct's seed, born of greed and darkness. It took the form of anger and other negative emotions and impeded their success. *15*

Then innate perfection, consisting of eight accomplishments, spontaneous satisfaction and the others, arose no more to the same extent among them. *16*

While all were weakened and evil grew apace, they were beset by strife, defeat and suffering. *17*

Seeking refuge in the forests, in the mountains and on water, there they built their strongholds, towns and cities. *18*

They duly made their dwellings in those cities and elsewhere, wise sage, to shelter from the cold, the heat and other troubles. *19*

Warding off the cold and other elements, folk adopted manual labour as their livelihood. *20*

Rice, barley, wheat, millet, sesame, foxtail millet, sorghum, ditch millet, peas, *21*

Beans, black and brown lentils, cowpeas, horse gram, pigeon peas, chickpeas and hemp—these are the seventeen crops they grew, sage. *22*

Fourteen plants, both cultivated and wild, are suitable for sacrifice: *23*

Rice, barley, beans, wheat, millet, sesame, with foxtail millet as the seventh and horse gram as the eighth, barnyard millet, *24*

Wild rice, wild sesame, mallow and bamboo seeds are mentioned, sage, along with corn. *25*

These fourteen, wild and cultivated, are used in the performance of the sacrifice, and yet it is the sacrifice that enables them to grow. *26*

These plants and sacrifice are humanity's first foundation. That's why the wise who understand both causes and effects perform these rites. *27*

Daily performance of the sacrifice benefits humanity, best of sages, and cleanses all impurities from those who do so. *28*

The seed of evil sown by Time grew in some men's hearts, wise sage, and their thoughts began to wander from the sacrifice. *29*

Making light of Vedic discourse, the Vedas and the rites, they opposed the sacrificial act. *30*

These wicked, devious miscreants mocked the Vedas and blocked the path of sacrificial action. *31*

After the lord of creation had established people in the livelihoods prepared for them, he laid down limits suited to the status and the qualities *32*

Of each order and stage of life, best guardian of duty, and also their responsibilities. He also made the heavenly realms for each community who adhered perfectly to their obligations. *33*

The realm for brahmins who carry out the sacrifice is that of Brahmā. The realm for kṣatriyas who never retreat in battle is Indra's. *34*

The realm for vaiśyas who delight in duty is the Maruts', while that for śūdras who rejoice in service is the gandharvas'. *35*

The realm for those who lived in their guru's home is that of the eighty-one thousand sages who never shed their semen. *36*

The realm for those who retire to the forest is that of the Seven Sages. The progenitors' realm is for householders, and Brahmā's is for renunciants. *37*

The immortal realm for ascetics is the highest state of Viṣṇu. *38*

Those ascetics who always contemplate the Absolute alone achieve this, the highest realm perceived by the wise. *39*

After every dissolution, the moon, the sun and planets are all re-created, but those who contemplate the mantra of twelve syllables, even now, need never be reborn.[8] *40*

The hell realms of Tāmistra, Andhatāmisra, Mahāraurava, Raurava, Asipatravana, Ghora, Kālasūtra and Avīci *41*

Are said to wait for those who insult the Vedas, obstruct the sacrifice or shirk their communal duties. *42*

So ends Chapter Six in Book One of the glorious Viṣṇu Purāṇa.

8 The 12-syllable mantra *oṃ namo bhagavate vāsudevāya.*

7. The first patriarchs

Parāśara:

While Brahmā was engaged in contemplation, his mind-born progeny arose. These conscious beings, whose forms and senses came from Brahmā's body, appeared from the limbs of that wise deity. *1*

All the creatures I've described, from gods to static objects, occupy a world infused with threefold qualities. *2*

All creatures, moving and unmoving, were created in this way. *3*

But as these beings, arising from that wise deity, failed to multiply, he then brought forth more sons from his own mind in the image of himself: *4*

Bhṛgu, Pulastya, Pulaha, Kratu, Aṅgiras, Marīci, Dakṣa, Atri and Vasiṣṭha. *5*

These are the nine mind-born sons of Brahmā named in the purāṇas. *6*

Sanandana and the others whom Brahmā brought forth earlier had neither worldly ties nor an urge for procreation. *7*

All had perfect knowledge and were therefore free from envy and desire, but as they showed indifference to the creation of the world, a terrible fury, able to burn the universe, arose in that great deity. *8*

All three worlds were set ablaze in a ring of fire sparked by Brahmā's anger, sage. *9*

From his forehead, furrowed with burning fury, sprang wrathful Rudra, blazing like the midday sun, his vast form half-man, half-woman. *10*

Brahmā ordered Rudra to divide himself, then withdrew from sight. *11*

Thus, addressed by Brahmā, Rudra split his male and female halves apart, then divided his male half eleven ways. *12*

Some forms were pleasant, some hideous, some mild and others fierce. That lordly being then split his female half in many forms, both black and white. *13*

Brahmā then manifested himself as Manu, Lord Svāyaṃbhuva, brahmin, the patriarch of humanity. *14*

That divine and lordly Manu took to wife the woman Śatarupā, who was purified of sins through penance. *15*

With him, divine Śatarūpa bore two sons, Priyavrata and Uttānapāda, and two daughters, named Prasūti and Ākūti, endowed with beauty, nobility and virtue—you know this, dharma. *16*

Svāyaṃbhuva gave Prasūti to Dakṣa and Ākūti to Ruci in those far-off times. The patriarch Ruci accepted Ākūti, and they had a son called Sacrifice and a daughter, Recompense, who became a couple, blessed sage.[9] *17*

Sacrifice and Recompense had twelve sons, known as the divine Yāmas in the age of Manu Svāyaṃbhuva. *18*

Similarly, Dakṣa had twenty-four daughters with Prasūti. Listen carefully to their names: *19*

Faith, Fortune, Constance, Contentment, Comfort, Prudence, Ritual, Intellect, Modesty, Beauty, Peace and Felicity, with Fame as the thirteenth. *20*

The lord Virtue took these daughters of Dakṣa as his wives.[10] The eleven remaining younger fair-eyed daughters were: *21*

Renown, Truth, Increase, Memory, Joy, Patience, Humility, Kindness, Energy, Svāhā and Svadhā.[11] *22*

Bhṛgu, Bhava, Marīci, the sage Aṅgiras, Pulastya, Pulaha, the excellent seer Kratu, *23*

Atri, Vasiṣṭha, Vahni and Pitara—these seers duly wedded Renown and her sisters, best of sages. *24*

The sons of Virtue were as follows: Faith bore Desire, Fortune Pride, Constance a son, Restraint. Contentment bore Satisfaction and Comfort Greed, *25*

Prudence bore Knowledge and Ritual bore Correction, Conduct and Decency. Intellect bore Understanding, Modesty Propriety, the son of Beauty was Resolve, Peace bore Security, *26*

Felicity bore Happiness and Fame Glory. Such were the sons of Virtue. With Desire, Love gave birth to Rapture, the grandson of Virtue. *27*

---

9 In the following passage, I have diverged from the usual practice of leaving proper names in the original Sanskrit and have translated them into English, as I believe the author wanted them to be understood at a semantic level.

10 The relationships of Virtue and Vice (see below) are not immediately clear in the *Viṣṇu Purāṇa*. Other sources suggest they are sons of Brahmā. Whatever the case, in this context, they play the role of patriarchs of humankind.

11 *Svāhā* and *svadhā* are auspicious syllables uttered during a sacrifice.

Vice's wife was Violence. They gave birth to a son, Falsehood, and a daughter, Deceit, who became a couple and bore two sons, Fear and the hell realm Naraka. *28*

Their two daughters, Delusion and Pain, became their brothers' wives. Fear and Delusion gave birth to Death, who carries off all beings. *29*

Pain and Fear had a son, Suffering. The children of Death were Disease, Decrepitude, Sorrow, Avidity and Anger. *30*

These all knew pain and were marked by vice. None had a wife, a son or retained his semen. *31*

Such are the terrible forms of Viṣṇu, best sage's son. They went forth as the eternal causes of destruction in this world. *32*

Dakṣa, Marīci, Atri, Bhṛgu and the other patriarchs, blessed sage, are the eternal causes of creation here. *33*

The Manus and their sons, brave protectors of the earth, are heroes who rejoice in the path of truth and are the ever-present causes of the preservation of the world. *34*

Maitreya:

Tell me, brahmin, what is the nature of this perpetual process of creation, preservation and destruction? *35*

Parāśara:

Lord Madhusūdana, who is beyond conception, in all three varied forms, brings about the never-ending cycle of creation, preservation and destruction. *36*

The destruction of all beings is fourfold, brahmin: occasional, foundational, continual and perpetual. *37*

Occasional or Brāhmic destruction takes place when the universal lord is sleeping. In foundational destruction, the world is broken into fundamental elements. *38*

Continual destruction is said to be that of the ascetic who, through spiritual knowledge, abides in the Supreme. Perpetual destruction is the unrelenting death, day and night, of every being ever born. *39*

The production of fundamental elements is thought to be foundational creation. The creation that follows the intermediate destruction of the world is called ephemeral. *40*

The creation in which beings are born each day is called perpetual creation by those who understand the meaning of purāṇas, best of sages. *41*

That's how Lord Viṣṇu, creator of beings abiding in all bodies, undertakes creation, preservation and destruction. *42*

The powers of Viṣṇu to create, preserve and to destroy, Maitreya, are always present in all bodies, day and night. *43*

One who transcends this great threefold power consisting of all qualities, brahmin, proceeds to the highest state, never to return. *44*

So ends Chapter Seven in Book One of the glorious Viṣṇu Purāṇa.

8. The eight forms of Rudra

Parāśara:

I've described for you the creation undertaken by Brahmā that has the quality of dullness, great sage. Now I'll speak about the creation of Rudra. Listen while I explain. *1*

While Brahmā was meditating at the beginning of the aeon, a son, his equal, manifested in his lap, a boy of ruddy complexion. *2*

He ran about while wailing loudly (*rudan*), best of brahmins. When Brahmā asked the weeping child why he wept, 'I want a name!' was his reply. *3*

The lord of creation answered, 'Deity, your name is Rudra, but do not cry. Be firm!' But even after Brahmā had spoken, the child cried out another seven times. *4*

Each time the lord gave him another name. To each of these eight aspects the lord assigned stations, wives and sons. *5*

The universal grandsire gave him all these names, brahmin: Bhava, Śarva, Īśāna, Paśupati, Bhīma, Ugra and Mahādeva. *6*

He gave these names, then fixed a place for each: the sun, water, earth, wind, fire, air, the consecrated brahmin and the moon—these are the eight stations in order. *7*

Suvarcalā, Uṣā, Vikeśī, Śivā, Svāhā and Diśas, Dīkṣā and Rohiṇī— *8*

These are the respective wives of the sun and other forms, which are known by the names of Rudra and the others, best of men. Next, you'll hear from me about their offspring, blessed sage. *9*

Their descendants filled this world: *10*

The sons in order were tardy Saturn, brilliant Venus, ruddy Mars, Manojava, Skanda, Svarga, Saṃtāna and wise Mercury. *11*

In the form of Rudra, he took Satī as his wife. She later sacrificed her body when enraged by Dakṣa. *12*

Satī was reborn the daughter of the mountain-deity Himālaya and Menā, best of brahmins, and, as peerless Umā, Lord Śiva married her again. *13*

The divine sons Dhātṛ and Vidhātṛ were born to the sage Bhṛgu and Renown, as was Śrī, the consort of Nārāyaṇa, god of gods. *14*

Maitreya:

It's said that glorious Śrī arose from the waters at the churning of the nectar of immortality. How can you now say that she was born to Bhṛgu and Renown? *15*

Parāśara praises Lakṣmī

Parāśara:

Śrī, the mother of the universe, is eternal and never leaves the side of Viṣṇu, best of brahmins. Just as Viṣṇu is everywhere, so indeed is she. *16*

Viṣṇu is meaning and she is word. She is policy and Hari is principle. Viṣṇu is perception and she is intellect. He is virtue and she is conduct. *17*

Viṣṇu is creator and she is creation. Śrī is earth and Hari is support. The lord is satisfaction and Lakṣmī is eternal contentment, Maitreya. *18*

Śrī is inclination and the lord is desire. He is sacrifice and she, the fee. The goddess is the oblation of clarified butter and Janārdana, the prayer that accompanies it. *19*

Lakṣmī is the pavilion for the sacrificer's wives, sage, and Madhusūdana, the pavilion for the men of the family. Lakṣmī is the altar and Hari is the sacrificial post. Śrī is the kindling and the lord is the sacred grass. *20*

The lord takes the form of the Sāma Veda and the lotus-throned goddess is the chanting. Lakṣmī is the invocation *svāhā*, and Vāsudeva, master of the universe, is the fire that consumes the offering. *21*

Lord Viṣṇu is Śiva and Lakṣmī is Gaurī, his wife, best of brahmins. Keśava is the sun and lotus-throned Śrī its brilliance, Maitreya. *22*

Viṣṇu is the host of ancestral spirits and Padmā is the invocation *svadhā*, which provides their eternal sustenance. Śrī is heaven and Viṣṇu, the universal lord, is boundless space. *23*

Śrī's husband is the hare-marked moon and Śrī its ever-present loveliness. Lakṣmī is the firmness that girds the world and Hari is the all-pervading wind. *24*

Govinda is the ocean and Śrī its shore, wise brahmin. Indrāṇī, wife of Indra, is a form of Lakṣmī, and the king of gods is Madhusūdana. *25*

Viṣṇu who bears the discus is Yama himself, the lord of the underworld, and the lotus-throned Śrī is Yama's wife, Dhūmorṇā. Śrī is wealth and her husband is the deity Kubera, lord of riches. *26*

Fortunate Lakṣmī is Gaurī and Keśava is Varuṇa, god of oceans. Śrī is the army of the gods and Hari its commander, best of brahmins. *27*

Viṣṇu who wields the mace is support and Lakṣmī is power, best of brahmins. Lakṣmī is the unit of time known as *kāṣṭhā* and he is the *nimeṣa*. He is the *muhūrta* and she the *kalā*.[12] *28*

Lakṣmī is light and Hari, lord of all, the shining sun. Śrī, the mother of the world, takes the form of a vine and Viṣṇu, the tree it clings to. *29*

Śrī is night and the god who bears the mace and discus is the day. Wish-granting Viṣṇu is the groom and she who dwells in the lotus grove his bride. *30*

The lord takes the form of all masculine rivers and Śrī the feminine ones. Lotus-eyed Viṣṇu is the banner and lotus-throned Śrī the pennant. *31*

Lakṣmī is yearning and supreme Nārāyaṇa, master of the world, is greed. Lakṣmī is love and Govinda is sex—you understand this, dharma. *32*

Why say more when it can be said so simply? *33*

All things masculine among the animals, gods and humankind are Lord Hari, while everything feminine is Lakṣmī, Maitreya. There is nothing apart from them. *34*

So ends Chapter Eight in Book One of the glorious Viṣṇu Purāṇa.

12 See *Viṣṇu Purāṇa*, 1.3.8.

9. The sage Durvāsas curses Indra; Churning of the ocean

Parāśara:

Now listen to this account of Śrī, about whom you asked me, Maitreya, as I heard it from the seer Marīci. *1*

The sage Durvāsas, a partial manifestation of Śiva, was wandering this world when he saw a female vidyādhara holding a divine garland. *2*

The perfume of the garland's *santānaka* flowers filled the forest, brahmin, and the scent brought great delight to those who roamed there. *3*

That brahmin, who held vows of holy craziness, saw the splendid garland and asked the fair-hipped vidyādhara woman to give it to him. *4*

At his request, the slender, wide-eyed vidyādharī bowed graciously and handed him the flowers. *5*

That wild brahmin took the garland and placed it on his head, Maitreya, as he wandered through the world. *6*

One day, Durvāsas beheld the deity Indra, overlord of the threefold worlds, Śacī's husband, approaching on his raging elephant Airāvata, accompanied by the other gods. *7*

The sage took the garland, along with its frenzied bees, from his head and, like a madman, tossed it to the king of gods. *8*

Indra caught the garland and placed it on the elephant's brow, where it shone like the river Gaṅgā, Jahnu's daughter, on the summit of Mount Kailāsa. *9*

The elephant, whose eyes were blinded by intoxication, was attracted by the scent and sniffed the garland with its trunk but tossed it to the ground. *10*

The best of sages, holy Durvāsas, was enraged, Maitreya, and angrily addressed the king of gods: *11*

Durvāsas:

Your heart has been corrupted by the intoxication of your power. You're worse than arrogant, Indra. The garland that I gave you is the dwelling place of Śrī, but you didn't really like it. *12*

You didn't thank me with a bow. You didn't place it on your head, your cheeks aglow with pleasure. *13*

Because you shunned the garland that I offered you, fool, you'll lose your sovereignty over all three worlds. *14*

You clearly think that I'm like other brahmins, Indra, and in doing so, you arrogantly insult me. *15*

Because you tossed the garland that I gave you to the ground, the threefold worlds will lose their splendour. *16*

This whole world of moving and unmoving things fears me when I'm angry, but you, king of gods, full of pride, disrespect me. *17*

Parāśara:

Mighty Indra quickly climbed down from the elephant's back and apologised to the unstained seer Durvāsas. *18*

Being appeased, that best of sages then replied to the god of a thousand eyes, who bowed respectfully before him: *19*

Durvāsas:

Unlike other sages, I'm neither kind nor patient, mighty Indra. Remember that I'm Durvāsas! *20*

You've been flattered by sages such as Gautama for no good reason. Remember that I'm Durvāsas, the very essence of impatience! *21*

Because Vasiṣṭha and other sweet-natured seers loudly sang your praises, you've grown proud and disrespect me. *22*

My matted locks are a blazing mass and my brow is deeply furrowed. Seeing me, who in all three worlds isn't fearful? *23*

Why waste words, god of a hundred sacrifices? I won't accept any further semblance of respect you try to show me. *24*

Parāśara:

So saying, the brahmin left, and Indra, king of gods, mounted on Airāvata, returned to his city of Amarāvatī. *25*

From that moment, brahmin, all three worlds, along with mighty Indra, lost their splendour, Maitreya, and grew wretched. Herbs and other plant life withered, *26*

Sacrifices ceased, ascetics gave up penance and folk no longer turned their minds to charity or other virtues. *27*

All the people suffered, their senses overcome by greed, best of brahmins, and they began to covet trifles. *28*

Where vitality exists, one also finds prosperity, as they follow one another. Where is vitality for those who lose prosperity? Without vitality, where are virtues? *29*

Without virtues, where are people's strength, courage and other noble sentiments? Bereft of strength and courage, a person will be shunned by everyone, and a man rejected will lose his mind. *30*

When all three worlds thus lost prosperity and vitality, the Daityas and the Dānavas made war against the deities. *31*

Overcome by greed, and without wellbeing and energy themselves, the Daityas fought against the gods who also lacked those qualities. *32*

After they'd been worsted by the demons, Indra and the thirteen deities led by Agni sought protection from Brahmā, the fortunate grandsire of the world. *33*

The gods relayed all this to Brahmā. 'Go to Viṣṇu for protection, lord of high and low,' he said, 'for he's the scourge of demigods. *34*

He's the lord who has no cause, and origin of creation, preservation and destruction of the world. Viṣṇu is lord of all progenitors, unending and unconquerable. *35*

He's the cause of unborn primal matter and of spirit, which are transformed by his energy. Viṣṇu, who eases the pain of those who bow before him, will restore your splendour.' *36*

Brahmā praises Viṣṇu

Parāśara:

Having thus addressed them, Brahmā, universal grandsire, set off with all the gods for the Milky Ocean's northern shore. *37*

Arriving with the thirteen deities, Brahmā gratified Hari, lord of high and low, with these words that pleased him: *38*

Brahmā:

I bow to the universal lord of all, unending, unarising, unchanging, the abode and foundation of the world, invisible, indivisible, *39*

Nārāyaṇa, smallest of the small, largest of the large, including all the world and all things in it, *40*

In whom all things abide, from whom all things including me arise, the deity who is all things, higher than the highest, *41*

Who is beyond the highest spirit, who takes the form of the Supreme itself, and on whom ascetics who yearn for liberation meditate as the source of freedom. *42*

May the lord beyond vitality and other basic qualities, purest of the pure, primal spirit, favour us. *43*

May that pure being, Hari, whose power lies beyond the passage of time that's made of *kalās*, *kāṣṭhās*, *nimeṣas* and so on, favour us. *44*

May Viṣṇu, known as the pure supreme lord because of his favours, and who is at the heart of all embodied beings, favour us. *45*

May Hari, the cause and the effect, the cause of the cause itself, and the effect of the effect itself, favour us. *46*

Who himself is also the effect, which is the effect of the effect of the effect, and who has become the effect of that effect, I bow to him.[13] *47*

Who is the cause of the cause, and the cause of the cause of that cause, and is the cause of all these causes—I bow to that lord of gods. *48*

The enjoyer and the enjoyed, the creator and the creation, the deed and the doer—I bow to that highest state. *49*

That highest state of Viṣṇu consists of purest understanding and is unending, unborn, undying, undecaying, unmanifest and unchanging. *50*

I bow to that highest state of Viṣṇu, which is neither gross nor subtle, but lies beyond description and is forever pure. *51*

The power to create all things abides in one ten-thousandth part of one ten-thousandth part of that being in the form of the Absolute supreme. I bow to that undecaying entity. *52*

Neither gods, nor sages, nor I, nor Śiva know that state that is the ultimate condition of the highest lord, Viṣṇu. *53*

---

13 The solution to this riddle is as follows: according to the commentator, the six effects referred to here in order are primal substance (*prakṛti*), Greatness (*mahat*), individuation (*ahaṃkāra*), the primal elements (*bhūta*), the cosmic egg and progenitors Brahmā, Dakṣa and the others. The idea is that Viṣṇu is all these.

That indestructible state, which ever-striving ascetics perceive in the syllable *Oṃ*, and which is the destroyer of both merit and demerit, is the highest state of Viṣṇu that should be contemplated. *54*

That is the highest state of Viṣṇu, the deity whose powers are at the heart of Brahmā, Viṣṇu and Śiva, and before whom nothing else existed. *55*

Universal Lord who is at the heart of everything, who is everything, the everlasting refuge of everything—favour us, your devotees, Viṣṇu, and reveal yourself. *56*

Parāśara:

Hearing Brahmā's supplication, the thirteen deities also bowed and said, 'Favour us and reveal yourself. *57*

We bow down to that highest state of yours, which even Brahmā cannot comprehend. You are the domicile of the world, all-pervasive and imperishable.' *58*

After Brahmā and the gods had spoken, all the heavenly sages, led by Bṛhaspati, said: *59*

'The primal sacrifice, primal and praiseworthy spirit, born before the first of beings: we bow to him, creator of the world's creator, beyond description. *60*

Lord, you are the master of all that's been and all that is to be, you embody the sacrifice and are undying; favour all those who bow to you and show yourself to us. *61*

Here is Brahmā, and here is three-eyed Śiva accompanied by the Rudras. Pūṣan is here with all the Ādityas, as is Agni and the fire gods. *62*

These are the Aśvins and Vasus, and these, the hosts of Maruts. All the Sādhyas are here as well. These are the gods and this, their sovereign, Indra. *63*

Routed by the Daitya army, they bow deeply, protector. All these hosts of gods have come for your protection.' *64*

Parāśara:

Thus praised, Maitreya, the holy bearer of conch and discus, the highest lord, appeared before them. *65*

Beholding the bearer of these weapons of incomparable appearance, a mass of splendour and magnificence, *66*

Having first bowed down, the reverent deities' eyes were filled with anxious tears and, led by Brahmā, grandsire of the world, they praised lotus-eyed Viṣṇu. *67*

The deities:

We bow to you again and again, lord of all. You are Brahmā and Śiva, who wields the bow Pinākа. You are Indra, Agni, purifying Wind, Varuṇa, Savitṛ and Yama. You are the Vasus, Maruts, Sādhyas and the hosts of Viśvedevas. *68*

You, Lord, are indeed this host of deities that has come before you, creator of the world, because you are everywhere. *69*

You are the sacrifice, the cry of *vaṣaṭ*, the syllable *Oṃ*, lord of creation, knowledge and knower. You are at the heart of everything, and all the world consists of you. *70*

Defeated by the Daityas, we're miserable and come to you for refuge, Viṣṇu, so favour us. You are at the heart of everything. Please defend us with your might. *71*

Until a being comes to you for refuge, dispeller of all impurities, they'll have pain and longing, delusion and unhappiness. *72*

You are grace itself, so be gracious to us, your devotees. With power arising from all your energy, protector, protect us. *73*

Churning of the Ocean of Milk

Parāśara:

Thus praised by the reverent immortals, Lord Hari, creator of the universe, whose eyes were filled with grace, addressed them: *74*

The Lord:

I'll restore your energy, deities, and tell you what to do. *75*

In collaboration with the Daityas, cast every kind of healing herb into the Milky Ocean, take the sacred mountain Mandara as your churning-stick and the nāga Vāsuki as the cord with which to turn it. Then, with my help, you deities will churn forth the nectar of immortality. *76*

First speak kindly to the Daityas in this regard, and tell them they'll receive an equal portion from this shared labour. *77*

By drinking nectar from the churning of the ocean, they'll gain power and immortality. *78*

But I'll ensure your enemies, you thirteen deathless gods, receive no nectar and gain nothing from their efforts. *79*

Parāśara:

Thus addressed by Viṣṇu, god of gods, all the deities made a compact with the Daityas and set about the churning of the nectar. *80*

The deities, Daityas and Dānavas gathered varied herbs and cast them on the waters of the Milky Ocean, pure and splendid like the clouds in autumn. *81*

Taking Mount Mandara as their churning-stick and using Vāsuki as the cord, they then began to churn the nectar vigorously, Maitreya. *82*

Viṣṇu sent the assembled gods to the tail of Vāsuki, and the Daityas to the fore part of that serpent's body. *83*

Scorched by fiery blasts from Vāsuki's hood, best of sages, all the Daityas lost their vigour and grew weak. *84*

But the deities at the serpent's tail were refreshed by rain that fell from clouds whipped up by gusts of breath from Vāsuki's maw. *85*

In the middle of the Milky Ocean, Lord Hari himself in the form of a tortoise served as a support for Mount Mandara as it turned, great sage. *86*

Taking a second form among the gods, the bearer of the mace and discus drew on that serpent king and, in yet another form, he did the same among the Daityas. *87*

Keśava ascended to the mountain top in third gigantic form, Maitreya, invisible to both gods and Daityas. *88*

With one portion of his energy, Hari sustained the serpent king and, with another, reinforced the deities. *89*

As the gods and Dānavas churned the ocean, there first arose the sacred cow Surabhi, source of all milk, worshipped by the deities. *90*

Both gods and Dānavas were delighted, sage, their minds held captive and their eyes agleam. *91*

When next the goddess of wine, Vāruṇī, arose, her eyes rolling with drunkenness, the siddhas in the heavens asked themselves, 'What's this?!' *92*

From the Milky Ocean as it turned, there then appeared the Pārijāta tree, filling all the worlds with perfume and delighting the deities' womenfolk. *93*

And next a marvellous host of apsarases, endowed with beauty, nobility and virtue, Maitreya, emerged from the Milky Ocean. *94*

The cool-rayed moon that next came forth was seized by Śiva, and the nāgas took the poison arising from the ocean. *95*

Finally, the gods' physician, the white-clad deity Dhanvantari himself, appeared with a jar of nectar. *96*

The hearts of all those Daityas and Dānavas were filled at once with joy and they exulted, Maitreya, along with all the sages. *97*

From the milk then arose the goddess Śrī, radiant with beauty, standing on an open lotus, with another in her hand. *98*

Great sages filled with joy then praised her with the paean called *Śrī-sūkta*. *99*

Gandharvas with Viśvāvasu at their head sang before her, brahmin, as hosts of *apsarases* led by Ghṛtācī danced. *100*

Gaṅgā and the other rivers came forward to bathe her with their waters. The guardian elephants of four quarters brought pure water in golden vessels and poured it on the goddess, sovereign of all the worlds. *101*

The Milky Ocean, appearing as a deity, offered her a garland of fresh waterlilies, and the gods' own artificer, Viśvakarman, crafted jewellery to adorn her. *102*

Clad in heavenly wreathes and garments, bathed and wearing jewels, Śrī pressed herself to Hari's bosom while all the gods looked on. *103*

The deities, observed by Lakṣmī as she clung to Hari's bosom, Maitreya, attained at once the highest state of bliss. *104*

But the Daityas led by Vipracitti, shunned by Viṣṇu and ignored by Lakṣmī, blessed sage, descended into deep despair. *105*

Those mighty Daityas, brahmin, then seized the pitcher with the nectar from the hands of Dhanvantari. *106*

But Viṣṇu, appearing in a female form, tricked them with an apparition. Seizing back the pitcher from the demons, he returned it to the gods. *107*

Indra and the hosts of gods then drank that nectar, but the Daityas, wielding weapons, assailed them without mercy. *108*

As the mighty gods had drunk the draft, they destroyed the demon army, which was scattered in all directions and fled to the lower realm of Pātāla. *109*

Then the deities, filled with joy, bowed to Viṣṇu, bearer of the discus, conch and mace, and ruled once more the realm of Triviṣṭapa. *110*

The sun of shining brilliance resumed his usual course, best of sages, and the other luminaries proceeded on their proper paths. *111*

The lovely light of sacred fires blazed brightly, and the minds of every being turned once more to virtue. *112*

All three worlds now prospered, best of brahmins, and mighty Indra, chief of thirteen deities, regained his splendour. *113*

Seated on his lion throne, Indra, having gained again the threefold worlds and ruling over the gods once more, praised the goddess who holds a lotus in her hand. *114*

Indra praises Lakṣmī

Indra:

I bow to you, Śrī, mother of the world, born from a lotus, with eyes like wakeful waterlilies, pressed to Viṣṇu's bosom. *115*

You are success personified. You are the cries of *svadhā* and *svāhā*. You are the nectar that purifies the world. You are the twilight at dawn and dusk, prosperity, faith and wisdom. You are Sarasvatī, the deity of speech. *116*

You are knowledge of the sacrifice, knowledge that is great and secret, fairest goddess, and the knowledge of the self that yields the prize of liberation. *117*

You are logic, the threefold Vedas, the professions and the art of governance. This world is filled with all your forms, both mild and wrathful, goddess. *118*

Who, apart from you, goddess, dwells in the bosom of the god of gods, the embodiment of all the sacrifice, the object of ascetics' meditation, the bearer of the mace? *119*

Bereft of you, all three worlds were on the brink of ruin, goddess, but now you've rescued them. *120*

Whenever you are looking on, goddess of good fortune, men will always have a wife, sons, a house, companions, sustenance, money and all the rest. *121*

Health, power, victory and happiness, goddess, aren't hard to find for those on whom you cast your gaze. *122*

You are the mother of every being and Hari god of gods their sire. You and Viṣṇu, mother, pervade this world of moving and unmoving things. *123*

Don't forsake our storehouse, byre, our home, our goods, our bodies or our wives—you, who confers purity on everything. *124*

Don't forsake my sons, my circle of companions, my cattle or adornments—you, whose place is in the bosom of lordly Viṣṇu. *125*

Those whom you reject, stainless goddess, are bereft at once of goodness, truth and purity and of the virtues like morality and the rest. *126*

Under your gaze, even the wicked are filled at once with every wished-for quality, including morality, and their kinsfolk prosper. *127*

Under your gaze, goddess, a person becomes praiseworthy, virtuous, wealthy, noble, wise, courageous and victorious. *128*

But when you, supporter of the world, beloved of Viṣṇu, turn your face away, a person's entire store of virtues starting with morality is lost at once. *129*

Even the tongue of Brahmā can't describe your virtues. Favour us, lotus-eyed goddess, and never forsake us. *130*

Parāśara:

Śrī, abiding in all beings, thus praised, was perfectly delighted, brahmin, and replied to Indra, deity of a hundred sacrifices, while all the other gods attended. *131*

Śrī:

Indra, king of gods, your song has pleased me. Ask for anything you desire, for I am here to grant your wish. *132*

Indra:

If you'll grant my wish, goddess, and if I'm worthy of such a favour, then never forsake this threefold world. Let this be my first request. *133*

Never forsake the person who lauds you with this song, ocean-born goddess. Let this be my second wish. *134*

Śrī:

I'll not forsake the threefold worlds, Indra, chief of thirteen gods. I grant this favour as I'm pleased with the adoration of your song. *135*

Likewise, I'll never turn my back on one who lauds me with this paean at dawn and dusk. *136*

Parāśara:

That's how the blessed goddess Śrī, pleased with Indra's song of praise, Maitreya, granted two wishes to the king of gods in former times. *137*

Śrī was originally born the daughter of Bhṛgu and Khyāti and arose again from the ocean when the gods and demons churned the nectar. *138*

When Janārdana, master of the world and god of gods, manifests on earth, Śrī arises as his consort. *139*

Later, when Hari was born the son of Aditi in the form of a dwarf, Śrī was born as Padmā, and when he was born as Paraśurāma, Bhṛgu's scion, she was born as Dharaṇī. *140*

When he appeared as Rāma, scion of Raghu, she was Sītā. When he was Kṛṣṇa, she was Rukmiṇī, and during the other manifestations of Viṣṇu, she was always his companion. *141*

When he appears as a deity, she also takes a heavenly form, and when he appears in mortal form, she always does the same; Śrī adopts a form to complement that of Viṣṇu. *142*

Prosperity will never wane for three generations in the house of one who hears or recites this account of Lakṣmī's birth. *143*

Misfortune, the source of woe, sage, never falls on homes in which this song of Śrī is sung. *144*

This is the answer to your question, brahmin, as to how Śrī, previously born as Bhṛgu's daughter Satī, arose from the Milky Ocean. *145*

Calamity will never visit those who recite this song in praise of Lakṣmī daily, as it's the key to all good fortune, and originated with the deities led by Indra. *146*

So ends Chapter Nine in Book One of the glorious Viṣṇu Purāṇa.

10. Descendants of the first patriarchs and Dakṣa's daughters

Maitreya:

You've told me everything I asked about, great sage, but tell me more about creation. How did Bhṛgu beget offspring, for a start? *1*

Parāśara:

Just as Viṣṇu's consort Lakṣmī was born to Bhṛgu and Khyāti, they also had two sons, Dhātṛ and Vidhārtṛ.[14] *2*

Two daughters of great Mount Meru, Āyati and Niyati, became the wives of Dhātṛ and Vidhārtṛ, and each one bore a son, *3*

Prāṇa and Mṛkaṇḍu, respectively. The sage Mārkaṇḍeya was descended from the latter. Mṛkaṇḍu also had a son named Vedaśiras, but now you'll hear about the son of Prāṇa: *4*

Prāṇa's son was Dyutimant, and his son was Rājavant, fortunate sage. The lengthy lineage of Bhārgavas were his descendants. *5*

Marīci's wife, Saṃbhūti, bore Paurṇamāsa, and Virajas and Parvata were that great being's two sons. *6*

I'll tell you more about them when I describe this lineage in more detail, brahmin. Aṅgiras's wife, Smṛti, bore daughters, Sinīvālī, Kuhū, Rākā and Anumati.[15] *7*

Atri's wife, Anasūyā, had three pure sons, Soma, Durvāsas and the ascetic Dattātreya. *8*

Pulastya's wife, Prīti, had a son Dattoli, who, in Svāyaṃbhuva's reign, was previously born as Agastya. *9*

Kardama, Arvarīvant and Sahiṣṇu were the three sons born to Kṣamā, wife of the patriarch Pulaha. *10*

Kratu's wife, Sannati, gave birth to sixty thousand Vālakhilya sages who retained their semen, and were no bigger than your thumb, but each had the energy of the blazing sun. *11*

---

14 Bhṛgu, Marīci, Aṅgiras, Atri, Pulastya, Pulaha and Kratu, mentioned in these following verses, are all the 'mind-born' sons of Brahmā.

15 These are phases of the moon.

Vasiṣṭha's seven sons were born to Ūrjā: *12*

Rajas, Gotra, Ūrdhvabāhu, Savana, Anagha, Sutapas and Śukra, all of whom were stainless sages. *13*

Brahmā's first-born son, the fire god Agni, also known as Abhimānin, had three sons of brilliant energy with Svāhā, brahmin: *14*

Pāvaka, Pavamāna and Śuci who lived on water. *15*

Together they had another forty-five descendants. Along with their father and his three sons, they were known together as the Vahnaya fire gods. *16*

They say the Vahnayas are forty-nine in all. *17*

These patriarchs whom I've described to you, brought forth by Brahmā, include both Agniṣvāttas who maintained no sacrificial fires, and the Barhiṣads, who did. *18*

Svadhā bore the Vahnayas two daughters, Menā and Dhāriṇī, brahmin, both ascetics who expounded on the Vedas. *19*

These two were blessed with highest knowledge and every noble virtue. *20*

Recalling this account of Dakṣa's daughters' offspring, a faithful person never remains childless. *21*

So ends Chapter Ten in Book One of the glorious Viṣṇu Purāṇa.

11. The birth of Dhruva

Parāśara:

I've spoken of Priyavrata and Uttānapāda, Manu Svāyaṃbhuva's noble and heroic sons. *1*

One of these, Uttānapāda, had a favourite wife, Suruci, who had a son, Uttama, on whom his father doted, brahmin. *2*

King Uttānapāda had a second wife, Sunīti, whom he didn't love so deeply, but she also bore a son, named Dhruva. *3*

The king was seated on his throne one day when Dhruva saw his brother Uttama nestled in his father's lap and tried to climb up too. *4*

Because Uttama's mother, Suruci, was watching, the king discouraged Dhruva, although the lad had come to him so eagerly. *5*

When Suruci saw her rival's son clambering on his father's lap where Uttama was sitting, she spoke these words to him: *6*

'Why hanker after things you cannot have, dear child? Don't you know that you were born from another mother, not from me? You want a thing that's just for Uttama, who's special. *7*

It's true that you're a prince also, but you are not my child. *8*

This throne is just for princes like Uttama, my son. Don't trouble yourself on its account. *9*

Why have such hopes for things that cannot be, as if you were my boy? Don't you understand Sunīti is your mother?' *10*

Parāśara:

After Dhruva heard what Uttama's mother said, brahmin, the angry child then left his father and retreated to his mother's chambers. *11*

When Sunīti saw her furious son, his lower lip atremble, Maitreya, she placed him on her lap and spoke these words to him: *12*

Sunīti:

Who's made you angry, darling boy? Who's upset you? Who offends your father by hurting your feelings so? *13*

Parāśara:

Hearing this, Dhruva told his mother all that proud Suruci had said in the presence of the king. *14*

When her son relayed all this, heavy-hearted Sunīti groaned, her eyes ablaze with angry sighs. The miserable woman made this reply: *15*

Sunīti:

What Suruci said is true. You're not so privileged, my son. The rivals of more fortunate folk would never speak like that, dear boy. *16*

Don't be upset, my love. Who can undo the deeds of previous lives, and who can hold you to account for deeds as yet undone? *17*

One who's blessed with a royal throne and umbrella, excellent horses and fine elephants—these are his alone. Remember this and calm yourself, my boy. *18*

On account of merit earned in former lifetimes, the king takes great delight (*suruci*) in Suruci, but others like me who are not so lucky are his wives in name alone. *19*

Her son Uttama is blessed with heaps of merit, but you, my son, Dhruva, were not born to privilege. *20*

But don't be sad, my boy. The wise are always happy with their lot. *21*

If you're really pained by what Suruci said, then try to win some merit, which will bring you all rewards. *22*

Be polite, virtuous, friendly and kind to animals, for just as water flows downhill, good fortune comes to those who earn it. *23*

Dhruva:

Mother, the words you've spoken to comfort me find no place within my heart, which was broken by her insults. *24*

I'll strive to reach that highest, peerless state, honoured by all the worlds. *25*

Suruci is the royal favourite and, although I'm not her son, you'll see my glory, mother, even though I lay inside your womb. *26*

She bore my brother Uttama in her belly, so let him have the throne our father gave him. That's how matters ought to be. *27*

I don't desire a place that's promised to another. Through my efforts, mother, I want a state that even father hasn't reached. *28*

Dhruva is instructed by the sages

Parāśara:

So saying, Dhruva left his mother's rooms and left the city for a grove beyond the walls. *29*

There he saw the Seven Sages, who'd arrived before him, seated on their deer-skin cloaks spread upon the ground. *30*

The prince duly greeted them, bowed respectfully and, while stooping with humility, addressed them. *31*

Dhruva:

Best of sages, know me to be Uttānapāda's son, born to Sunīti. I've come to you because I'm disenchanted with the world. *32*

The sages:

Prince, you're just a boy of four or five. There cannot yet be any reason for your disillusion. *33*

You've no cause for worry while your royal father lives. We can't foresee that you will want for anything, dear boy. *34*

You don't look sick. What's causing your unhappiness? If there's a problem, you should tell us. *35*

Parāśara:

Dhruva then repeated Surūci's words and, hearing this, the sages said to one another, *36*

'Aha! Even though he's just a child, he's got real warrior spirit. His irritation at his mother's rival's words hasn't left his heart. *37*

Come, come, you warrior's son. Tell us, if you like, what you plan to do on account of disenchantment. *38*

Tell us what we can do to help. You're clearly very bright, and we see you have something that you want to say.' *39*

Dhruva:

I don't want riches or a kingdom, best of brahmins. I only want to know that state that none has reached before. *40*

Tell me, best of sages, what I must do to reach that situation, which is superior to all others. *41*

Marīci:

That foremost state cannot be reached by those who do not praise Govinda. You must therefore venerate the everlasting one. *42*

Atri:

One with whom Janārdana, highest of the high, the primal spirit, is pleased, will reach the everlasting state. I speak the truth. *43*

Aṅgiras:

Worship eternal, changeless Govinda, within whom all this world abides, if you wish to reach that highest situation. *44*

Pulastya:

A person who has venerated Hari, the highest Absolute, the supreme abode, who is both supreme and Absolute, reaches liberation, even though it's difficult to attain. *45*

Kratu:

Janārdana is the spirit of the sacrifice when a ritual is performed, and the highest spirit reached through yoga practice. When he is pleased, what is unattainable? *46*

Pulaha:

After Indra praised the universal lord, he attained the highest state of sovereignty. You must also worship Viṣṇu, lord of sacrifices, you who are loyal to your vows. *47*

Vasiṣṭha:

When Viṣṇu is venerated, you'll obtain your heart's desires, dear boy, even that state that is higher than the highest in all three worlds. *48*

Dhruva:

As I bow before you, you've told me that the deity must be worshipped. Now tell me which prayer I should offer to gratify that being, *49*

And tell me how to venerate the greatest lord, kind and gracious sages. *50*

The sages:

Prince, you deserve to hear from us exactly how the praise of Viṣṇu is undertaken by those who are devoted to it. *51*

First, you should rid your mind of all external worries. Next, you should fix your thoughts on the god in whom the world abides. *52*

When your mind is focused on that single entity, conscious of the fact that you consist of the deity and holding yourself firm, prince, you should then recite this mantra that you'll hear from us: *53*

'*Oṃ*. I bow to Vāsudeva, who takes the forms of Brahmā born from the golden egg, Spirit, Matter and the Unseen element, and whose essential nature is pure knowledge.' *54*

Because Manu, Lord Svāyaṃbhuva, your grandsire, recited this mantra in former times, Janārdana was gratified by him. *55*

The deity granted him all the wealth that he desired, unequalled in all three worlds. You should also please Govinda with continual recitation of this mantra. *56*

So ends Chapter Eleven in Book One of the glorious Viṣṇu Purāṇa.

12. The trials of Dhruva

Parāśara:

Hearing this, Maitreya, the prince bowed deeply to the sages and departed from the forest. *1*

Thinking what he had to do, brahmin, Dhruva proceeded to the sacred ford called Madhu on the Yamunā River's banks. *2*

It's known in all the world as Madhu's Forest, because a Daitya of that name had once resided there. *3*

It's where Śatrughna slew Madhu's son, the mighty rākṣasa Lavaṇa, and built the city known as Madhurā. *4*

At that sacred ford, which removes all sins, Dhruva undertook austerities in Hari's presence, god of gods. *5*

As instructed by Marīci and the other sages, Dhruva contemplated Viṣṇu, lord of all the deities, abiding in his heart. *6*

While Dhruva set his mind on nothing else, brahmin, Lord Hari, who occupies all creation, pervaded Dhruva's being. *7*

With Viṣṇu dwelling in his ascetic heart, Maitreya, the earth, support of all creation, could no longer bear its burden. *8*

When Dhruva stood on his left foot, half the world sank beneath him, and when he stood on his right foot, the other half then sank as well. *9*

When he stood on just one toe, brahmin, the whole world with all its mountains shook. *10*

The rivers and oceans trembled, great sage, and the gods were deeply troubled. *11*

The deities known as Yāmas were most alarmed, Maitreya, and, having consulted Indra, set out to disrupt Dhruva's meditation. *12*

The anxious Kūṣmāṇḍa demigods, taking various forms and accompanied by their king, great sage, also tried to break his concentration. *13*

They created an illusion of Sunīti Dhruva's mother, who stood in tears before him, weeping piteously, *14*

'Son, son, stop this cruel penance at the cost of your body. I only conceived you by persevering with much hope. *15*

Don't forsake me—miserable, alone and vulnerable—because of something that my rival said, my dear. You're my refuge and I have no other. *16*

You're only five years old, and these are terrible austerities. Turn your mind away from this foolish, fruitless whim. *17*

Now's the time for toys, and later you can go to school. Then comes the age for lots of fun. Only after that comes penance. *18*

Now's the time for toys for a child like you, son, but you're wasting it in austerities. How could you enjoy such self-destruction? *19*

Your first duty is to be nice to me. Life's a series of stages and of duties. Don't follow this delusion. Stop this nonsense. *20*

If you don't give up austerities now, my dear, I'll kill myself before your very eyes!' *21*

Parāśara:

But Dhruva's mind was fixed on Viṣṇu, and, even though his eyes were open, he didn't see her tearful lamentations. *22*

'Son, son! Frightful demons wielding weapons are gathering in this awful forest. We must flee at once!' *23*

With these words, she ran away and, at that very moment, rākṣasas appeared, holding frightful weapons and belching wreaths of flame. *24*

Those night-ranging demons roared their terrible roars before the prince and waved their glinting weapons. *25*

Jackals by the hundred with flaming maws howled to terrify the boy, but he remained most perfectly absorbed in yoga. *26*

'Kill him, kill him! Chop him up, chop him up! Eat him, eat him!' cried those demons of the night. *27*

Rākṣasas with heads of lions, camels and crocodiles made all sorts of cries to frighten that young prince. *28*

But neither demons, roars, nor jackals, nor the weapons impinged on Dhruva's senses, as his mind was fixed on Govinda alone. *29*

With singular concentration, the prince perceived nothing other than Viṣṇu himself abiding in his heart. *30*

When all these phantoms disappeared, the deities, alarmed by failure, grew even more concerned. *31*

Worried by Dhruva's austerities, they went in a group to Hari, the beginningless and endless origin of the world and refuge of all tormented beings who seek it. *32*

The deities:

God of gods, protector of the world, highest lord and ultimate spirit: we're worried by Dhruva's austerities and have come for your protection. *33*

Just as the hare-marked moon waxes day by day, so do his austerities increase his power, Lord. *34*

We fear the practices of Uttānapāda's son and come to you for refuge, Janārdana. Please make him stop. *35*

We do not understand his purpose—to be like Indra or the sun? Does he want to be the equal of the god of wealth, the lord of oceans or the moon? *36*

Favour us, Lord, take this thorn from our hearts and cause Uttānapāda's son to abandon his austerities. *37*

The Lord:

Dhruva has no desire to be like Indra, the sun, Kubera or Varuṇa, gods, and I'll grant his wish in full. *38*

Return to your own realms at leisure, gods, but do not worry, as I'll cause that boy whose heart is set on austerities to desist. *39*

Parāśara:

Thus addressed by the god of gods, the thirteen deities bowed and set out for their respective realms, led by Indra, deity of a hundred sacrifices. *40*

Then Lord Hari, heart of all, pleased that Dhruva was absorbed in him, appearing to the boy in four-armed form, spoke these words: *41*

The Glorious Lord:

Well done, son of Uttānapāda! I'm pleased with your austerities, and I've come to grant your wish. Ask for anything you desire, as you've upheld your vows. *42*

I'm pleased with you because your mind is set on me alone, excluding other matters. You may therefore ask your dearest wish. *43*

Dhruva praises Viṣṇu

Parāśara:

Hearing these words spoken by the god of gods, the boy opened his eyes and beheld Hari before him, just as he'd perceived him in his meditation. *44*

Seeing the imperishable being with discus, conch, mace, bow and brilliant sword, and wearing a diadem on his head, Dhruva pressed his forehead to the ground. *45*

The hairs on the prince's limbs arose at once and, filled with awe, he set his heart on praising the god of gods. *46*

'What should I say to praise him? What words can express my adoration?' Such thoughts filled Dhruva's mind as he took refuge in the deity. *47*

Dhruva:

Lord, if you're truly pleased with my austerities, then grant my wish: I only want to praise you. *48*

But how can a child like me adore you, Lord, whose state is unknown even to Brahmā and to those who comprehend the Vedas? *49*

This heart of mine is filled with faith in you, highest Lord, and is ready to worship at your feet; only grant me wisdom to do so. *50*

Parāśara:

With the tip of his conch shell, the universal Lord Govinda touched the son of Uttānapāda, best of brahmins, whose palms were joined respectfully. *51*

The prince's face began at once to shine and, bowing with devotion, he praised the eternal basis of all creation. *52*

Dhruva:

I bow to him who takes the form of earth, water, fire, wind, sky, mind, intellect, primal elements and matter. *53*

I bow to him whose form is pure, subtle and all-pervading; the spirit which transcends elemental substance; the spirit at the heart of every quality; *54*

The eternal one who lies beyond creation, starting with the earth, the sense-objects starting with scent, the senses starting with intellect and spirit as well as matter. *55*

I take refuge in that pure form of yours, which is the Absolute, creation itself, supreme Lord, and master of the universe. *56*

I bow to that changeless form contemplated by ascetics and known as the Absolute because of its greatness and because it shapes the world—you who are at the heart of everything. *57*

The all-pervasive being with a thousand heads, a thousand eyes and a thousand feet extends ten inches beyond the furthest limit of the universe. *58*

You, supreme spirit, are all that was and all that is to be. From you arise Virāj, Svarāj, Samrāj, and from you arises Adhipūruṣa.[16] *59*

You extend above, below and beyond the universe. All this is born from you, as is all that has existed and all that's still to come. *60*

This whole world is in you when you take this form. The sacrifice with all the offerings, the clarified butter spotted with curds and both kinds of sacrificial animals arose from you. *61*

The *Ṛg* and *Sāma Vedas* arose from you, the Vedic metres were born from you, and from you the *Yajur Veda* came. From you arose the horses and those animals which have no teeth in their upper jaw.[17] *62*

Cattle arose from you, and from you arose the goats, the sheep and deer. From your mouth arose the brahmins, and from your arms the kṣatriyas. *63*

16 Authorities vary on the meaning of these four aspects of Viṣṇu. Wilson glosses them as follows: 1) Brahmāṇda, the material universe; 2) Brahmā the creator; 3) Manu, the ruler of the period; and 4) the supreme or abiding period (Wilson 1961: 78, fn. 3).

17 The front part of the upper jaw of cows, sheep, goats, camels, buffalo and deer is a modified dental pad.

The vaiśyas were born from your thighs, and the śūdras from your feet. The sun arose from your eyes, the wind from your breath and the moon from your mind. *64*

Breath was born from your inner channel and fire arose from your mouth. From your navel came the sky, and heaven was born from your head. The ten directions arose from your ears, the earth was born of your feet. All this arose from you! *65*

Just as a mighty banyan tree is inherent in a tiny seed, at the time of its destruction, all the world inheres in you in that same way. *66*

Just as a banyan sprouts from that seed and grows both tall and wide, so, too, does the world that you emit. *67*

Just as a banana palm has no reality distinct from its trunk and leaves, in the same way, protector, Lord, you are no different from the universe that is seen to abide in you. *68*

Unified consciousness, the source of joy, dwells as one with all within you, but the individual origins of pain and pleasure do not exist in you, as you are free from all these qualities. *69*

I bow to you, both one and many, the essence of all beings. I bow to you, the cause of primary elements and the heart of all creation. *70*

You are the Seen, Matter and Spirit. You are perceived as indestructible and as Virāj, Samrāj and Svarāj in the hearts of men. *71*

You consist of all and exist in all. You *are* all. All this is a form of you and comes from you yet is separate from you. I bow to you at the heart of all. *72*

You form the nature of everything, Lord of all, because you abide in all creation. But what's the use of saying this, when you know all that's in my heart? *73*

You who are at the heart of everything, Lord of all creation, origin of all beings, you consist of everything and know the desire of every heart. *74*

My heart's desire has been fulfilled by you, protector, as the austerities I undertook succeeded when I saw you, universal Lord. *75*

Dhruva's wish

The Glorious Lord:

Your austerities have succeeded as you've beheld me, Dhruva, and the sight of me is never fruitless, prince. *76*

Make a wish, therefore, in accord with your heart's desire, as everything is possible for those to whom I manifest. *77*

Dhruva:

Lord, master of all creation, you abide in the heart of everything. Lord, how could my heart's desire remain unknown to you? *78*

Nevertheless, Lord of gods, I'll describe to you the single thing, most difficult to attain, that my stubborn heart desires. *79*

What, on the other hand, is difficult to attain when you are pleased, creator of the universe? With your blessing even mighty Indra enjoys the threefold worlds. *80*

On account of her arrogance, my mother's rival shouted that the royal throne was unsuited to a child born from another woman's womb. *81*

By your grace, I ask you, Lord, for that state, supporter of the world, higher than the highest of all, which endures forever. *82*

The Glorious Lord:

You will attain the state that you requested as you pleased me previously in another life, my boy. *83*

In former times, you were a brahmin whose mind was ever set on me alone. You served your mother and your father and did your duty. *84*

In time, you befriended a certain prince who partook in all those youthful pastimes and cut a dashing, handsome figure. *85*

Through your friendship with him, you saw his rare wealth and formed a wish to be a prince yourself. *86*

Then, in accordance with that desire, Dhruva, you were duly born a royal son in the lofty house of Uttānapāda. *87*

But birth in the lineage of Svāyaṃbhuva, which for others is a blessing, *88*

Was not so good for you, my boy, which pleases me, as those who worship me will win liberation without delay. *89*

What's a place in heaven to one whose heart is set on me, my son? In a place above the threefold worlds, with my blessing, you will surely be the pivot of all the stars and planets, *90*

Beyond the sun and moon, Mars, Mercury, Jupiter, Venus and the other luminaries, the stars, *91*

And the Seven Sages without exception, as well as the deities in their celestial carriages. I'll give you, Dhruva, a station above all these.[18] *92*

Some gods endure for all four ages, some for a Manvantara, but I'll give you the lifespan of one whole aeon. *93*

Your mother, Sunīti, will also become a brilliant star always dwelling in a mansion by your side. *94*

All those who praise you with deep devotion at dawn and dusk will win great merit. *95*

Parāśara:

So it was in former times that Janārdana, protector of the world and god of gods, granted Dhruva's wish, and this wise sage is now forever fixed (*dhruvam*) in that position. *96*

Seeing Dhruva's greatness, pride and wealth, Uśanas, preceptor of gods and demigods, sang these verses: *97*

'Ah! Such was the power of his austerities. Ah! Such was the reward of his great penance, that Dhruva stands above the Seven Sages. *98*

And this is Dhruva's mother, Sunīti, also called Sūnṛtā. Who on earth can describe her majesty? *99*

She who carried Dhruva in her womb now occupies a lofty station, resort of all three worlds, and attains the highest state of Viṣṇu.' *100*

Those who always honour Dhruva's rise to heaven will be free from all misdeeds, while dwelling with joy in paradise. *101*

Such a being will never slip from his place in heaven or on earth and, filled with every happiness, will lead a long and joyous life. *102*

So ends Chapter Twelve in Book One of the glorious Viṣṇu Purāṇa.

18 The Seven Sages are the stars of Ursa Major. Dhruva, whose name means 'fixed' or 'stationary', became the Pole Star.

13. Dhruva's descendants

Parāśara:

Dhruva had two sons, Śiṣṭi and Bhavya. Bhavya's son was Śaṃbhu. Śiṣṭi had five pure sons with his wife, Succhā: *1*

Ripu, Ripuñjaya, Vipra, Vṛkala and Vṛkatejas. Ripu's son with his wife, Bṛhatī, was the glorious Cākṣusa. *2*

Cākṣusa had a son, Manu, with his wife, Puṣkariṇī, a descendant of Varuṇa and daughter of the great patriarch Vīraṇa. *3*

Manu had ten mighty sons with his wife, Naḍvalā, peerless ascetic, daughter of the patriarch Vairāja. *4*

Kuru, Puru, Śatadyumna, Tapasvin, Satyavant, Śuci, Agniṣṭut, Atirātra and Sudyumna—these nine, with mighty Abhimanyu as the tenth, were born to Naḍvalā. *5*

Kuru's wife, Āgneyī, had six brilliant sons: Aṅga, Sumanas, Khyāti, Kratu, Aṅgiras and Śibi. *6*

Aṅga's wife, Sunīthā, had one son, Vena, whose right hand was massaged by the sages to bring forth a son. *7*

When Vena's hand was massaged, sage, a son named Vainya arose from it, and became the king called Pṛthu. *8*

It was he, in former times, who milked the earth for the benefit of his subjects. *9*

Maitreya:

Why did seers massage Vena's hand, best of sages, leading to heroic Pṛthu's birth? *10*

Parāśara:

A girl named Sunīthā, first-born daughter of Mṛtyu ('Death'), was given in marriage to Aṅga and then gave birth to Vena. *11*

This son of Mṛtyu's daughter, Maitreya, born under his grandsire's evil sway, was wicked by his nature. *12*

When Vena was anointed king by the best of sages, he proclaimed to the all world, *13*

'There shall be neither sacrifice, nor offerings, nor sacrificial gifts, for who apart from me, lord of the sacrifice and king, is fit to enjoy these rituals?' *14*

The sages came before the king, Maitreya, and, having paid respects, tried to soothe him with these words: *15*

The sages:

Come, come, your majesty, listen to what we say to you for the benefit of your kingdom, your own wellbeing and for the greatest good of all your subjects. *16*

We will worship Hari, the lord of gods and master of all sacrifices, with a ritual of long duration. May you enjoy good fortune! A portion of the fruit of that event will come to you. *17*

Viṣṇu, spirit of the sacrifice, will be gratified by the ritual we conduct, sire, and will grant your every wish. *18*

In those kingdoms where Hari, lord of sacrifices, is honoured with oblations, he grants those kings fulfillment of all desires, your majesty. *19*

Vena:

Who is superior to me, and who is honoured apart from me? Who is this being known as Hari, whom you regard as lord of rites? *20*

Brahmā, Janārdana, Śiva, Indra, Vāyu, Yama, the Sun, Agni, consumer of the offerings, Varuṇa, Dhātṛ, Pūṣan, the Earth and the Moon, who brings the night; *21*

These and other deities, who both curse and bless, all abide in the person of the king. The king embodies all these gods. *22*

Knowing this, you'll do as I command. There shall be no sacrifice, brahmins, no gifts or offerings. *23*

Just as women's highest duty is to serve their husbands, brahmins, your duty is to carry out my wishes. *24*

The sages:

Great king, command us to continue with the sacrifice so virtue won't decline, as all the world depends on sacrificial offerings. *25*

Parāśara:

Even though the best of sages gave Vena this advice and implored him many times, the wicked king ignored them. *26*

Then all the seers, filled with anger and indignation, said to one another, 'This wicked ruler must be killed. He must be killed. *27*

Any wretch who denigrates the spirit of the sacrifice, the lord divine, who has no start or end, is unfit to rule the earth.' *28*

So saying, the host of sages beat the king to death with *kuśa*-grass that had been purified with mantras, but as he'd insulted Viṣṇu, he was dead already. *29*

The sages later saw great clouds of dust billowing in all directions, brahmin. 'What's that?' they asked the folk nearby. *30*

'Now the kingdom has no king,' they said, 'those who suffer have turned to theft and are seizing others' goods. *31*

The clouds of dust you see, good sages, are raised by thieves who rush about while stealing people's things.' *32*

After consulting one another, all the sages tightly squeezed the dead king's thigh to bring forth progeny, as he had died without a son. *33*

As they did so, a dwarfish man with flattened features, looking like a blackened stump, appeared from it.[19] *34*

This being then asked the brahmins what he should do, to which they said, 'Sit down—*niṣīda*.' That's why he's called Niṣāda. *35*

His descendants are Niṣādas who inhabit the Vindhya mountains and are noted for their deeds of cruelty, tiger of a sage.[20] *36*

By these means, King Vena's misdeeds were expunged, as Niṣādas came to shoulder them. *37*

Pṛthu saves the world

Those best of sages then began to squeeze the king's right hand. *38*

19 I am following Wilson (1961) here. The word *kharvāṭa* ('flattened') has presented great difficulties for commentators and scribes throughout the centuries. Wilson's translation seems logical but is unattested.

20 Notably hunting, which is considered cruel.

And as they did so, Vena's son, the mighty ruler known as Pṛthu, appeared. His body blazed with its own light, shining like a second Agni. *39*

At that moment, the primeval bow called Ājagava descended from the sky, along with heavenly shafts and armour. *40*

Beings everywhere rejoiced at Pṛthu's birth. *41*

Because Vena brought forth such a noble son, he was rescued from the hell realm known as Put by mighty Pṛthu and rose to heaven.[21] *42*

The Oceans and the Rivers came from all directions, bringing jewels and water for Pṛthu's consecration. *43*

Lord Brahmā, grandsire of the world, the deities accompanied by Aṅgiras's descendants and beings mobile and immobile gathered from all sides for Vena's son's anointing. *44*

When Brahmā saw that Pṛthu's right hand bore the discus mark, he recognised him as Viṣṇu's partial manifestation and was overjoyed. *45*

(This sign of Viṣṇu marks the hand of every universal sovereign. Even the thirteen deities cannot thwart the rule of such a being.) *46*

Pṛthu, Vena's mighty shining son, was anointed universal ruler in a rite performed by experts. *47*

He gratified the subjects who'd been slighted by his father and, because of their affection (*anurāga*), the title 'king' (*rājan*) came into use. *48*

The waters solidified for him when he went to cross the ocean, the mountains opened paths for him and his banner was never torn. *49*

The earth untouched by ploughs bore crops, food appeared with just a thought, cows fulfilled each wish and honey dripped from every hollow. *50*

As soon as Pṛthu was born, at the glorious sacrifice held by Brahmā, grandsire of the world, a wise bard (*sūta*) arose at the pressing (*sūti*) of the soma on the day that rite was held.[22] *51*

At that same great sacrifice, a gifted panegyrist was born, and the best of sages then addressed him and that bard: *52*

21 This playful etymology suggests that the word for son, *putra*, means 'one who rescues (his father) from hell' (*put-trā*).

22 The *sūta* is the bard by whom, according to tradition, many works of Sanskrit literature are narrated. This etymology seeks to derive his name from the pressing of soma.

'Praise this king, Pṛthu, the mighty son of Vena, for it's your special role and he's a worthy subject for your acclaim.' *53*

With folded palms, they then replied to all those brahmins, 'The king was only born today, and his exploits are as yet unknown. *54*

We haven't witnessed his qualities, and his fame is yet to spread. Say which virtues should be eulogised.' *55*

The sages:

Praise this mighty universal sovereign for the deeds he will perform, and for his future qualities. *56*

Parāśara:

Hearing this, King Pṛthu, filled with joy, exclaimed, 'Because a person is commended for good qualities, the bard and the panegyrist will acclaim my virtues. *57*

I shall therefore diligently practise all those virtues commended in their paean, *58*

And I'll avoid those things they say are best avoided.' Such was the resolution of the king. *59*

Then the sweet-voiced bard and panegyrist composed this paean in praise of Pṛthu's future deeds, Vena's sagacious son: *60*

'Truthful, generous and honest, this prudent king is patient with his allies, but remains the doughty bane of foe. *61*

He knows virtue and is grateful, kind and gently spoken, bestowing honour where it's due and undertaking sacrifices. He's devout and cherishes the good. *62*

This king fairly metes out justice to friend and foe alike.' *63*

Pṛthu then held in his heart the virtues thus praised by the bard and the panegyrist, and always acted in accordance with their words. *64*

He then performed various major sacrifices, accompanied by generous donations, while protecting all the world. *65*

In the absence of a ruler, plant life had perished, and the people, beset by hunger, approached the king. Asked by Pṛthu why they came, they replied as follows: *66*

The subjects:

Your most excellent majesty, without a king, the Earth withheld all vegetation and, as a result, the entire population is heading to destruction, Lord of men. *67*

You provide subsistence and are our support; you are regarded as protector of the people. Give us, your famine-stricken subjects, some vegetables to live on. *68*

Parāśara:

The furious king took up the heavenly bow called Ājagava and some arrows, and set off searching for the Earth. *69*

But the Earth took the appearance of a cow and, filled with fear, she fled to Brahmā's heaven and other divine realms. *70*

Wherever that heavenly support of all creation went, there she saw the son of Vena with his weapon at the ready. *71*

The trembling Earth cried out to Pṛthu of great prowess, hoping to be spared his arrows. *72*

The Earth:

You're endeavouring to slay me, sire, but don't you know it's a dire sin to kill a female? *73*

Pṛthu:

When the death of a single evildoer yields security for many, then that death is meritorious. *74*

The Earth:

If you kill me for your subjects' sake, who'll support them, best of sovereigns? *75*

Pṛthu:

Having slain you with these arrows, Earth, who turned your back on my commands, I'll support my subjects through the power of my yoga. *76*

Parāśara:

At this, the Earth grew even more afraid, her every limb atremble, and, bowing down, she made the king this offer. *77*

The Earth:

All undertakings will succeed if proper steps are taken. I'll therefore tell you what to do, if only you are willing. *78*

If your majesty desires, with my milk, I shall restore the vegetation that I'd allowed to wither. *79*

For the welfare of your subjects, virtue's best defender, bestow on me a calf so I, affectionate mother that I am, may bring forth milk for him. *80*

Level the surface of the world so I may cause my milk, which will become the source of finest vegetation, to flow in all directions. *81*

Parāśara:

With his bow-tip, Vena's son then dragged the mountains by the hundreds and the thousands into massive heaps. *82*

(Before he did so, the surface of the world was rough and undivided into villages or towns. *83*

There were no crops of grain, nor cattle-rearing, nor ploughing, nor paths for merchants. All these began with Vena's son, Maitreya.) *84*

The king deemed all the level places of the world fit for his subjects' habitations. *85*

Before this time, people lived on roots and berries, but life grew hard when all the vegetation died. *86*

Pṛthu gave the Earth a calf, which was in fact Lord Manu Svāyaṃbhuva. From his desire to benefit his subjects, King Pṛthu then milked all kinds of grain from the Earth into his own two hands. *87*

The people thrived on that nutrition, my dear, as they do today and always will. *88*

Pṛthu gave the Earth the gift of life, and so became her father. That's why the Earth, support of every living thing, is known as Pṛthivī, 'Pṛthu's daughter'. *89*

The deities, sages, Daityas, rākṣasas, mountains, gandharvas, nāgas, yakṣas, ancestral spirits and trees *90*

All took a bowl and received some milk, sage. Each had their own specific calf and milker, the source of their vitality.[23] *91*

This Earth—supporter, creator, bearer and nurturer of the world—was born from Viṣṇu's sole. *92*

Such was Pṛthu's prowess, Vena's mighty son, born to rule the world in former times, and who was known as *rājā* because he pleased (*rañjana*) his subjects. *93*

One who tells this tale of Pṛthu's birth will never endure the consequence of any sin. *94*

This account of Pṛthu's noble origin and prowess will always drive away the evil dreams of all who hear it. *95*

So ends Chapter Thirteen in Book One of the glorious Viṣṇu Purāṇa.

14. Pṛthu's descendants

Parāśara:

Pṛthu had two heroic sons, Antardhi and Vādin. Antardhana's wife, Śikhaṇḍinī, had a son, Havirdhāna. *1*

Havirdhāna had six sons with his wife, Dhiṣaṇā, a descendant of Agni. They were Prācīnabarhis, Śukra, Gaya, Kṛṣṇa, Vṛja and Ajina. *2*

Havirdhāna's son holy Prācīnabarhis was an important patriarch and mighty ruler who caused the human race to multiply. *3*

It was said that he placed sacrificial *kuśa*-grass (*barhis*) on the ground with its tips pointing east (*prācīna*), sage, and that's why that mighty king was known in the world as Prācīnabarhis. *4*

At the conclusion of severe austerities, Prācīnabarhis married Savarṇā, the daughter of the Ocean. *5*

The Ocean's daughter, Savarṇā, bore the king ten sons known as the Pracetases, who mastered the science of archery. *6*

Together they practised virtue and undertook great austerities, living in the waters of the ocean for ten thousand years. *7*

23 As the original text is opaque here, I am guided by the commentary.

Maitreya:

Please explain, great sage, why the noble Pracetases undertook austerities below the ocean's waters. *8*

Parāśara:

Respecting the command of the lord of creation, Brahmā, their noble-minded father, Prācīnabarhis, told the Pracetases that they needed progeny. *9*

Prācīnabarhis:

Brahmā, god of gods, commanded me to raise the population, sons, and I've agreed to do so. *10*

Therefore, to please me, sons, spare no effort in this regard and duly follow Brahmā's orders, which deserve respect. *11*

Parāśara:

Hearing their father's words, those princes all agreed, sage, but asked a further question. *12*

The Pracetases:

Father, tell us exactly what we must do to raise the population. *13*

Their father:

By worshipping Viṣṇu, who grants all wishes, a mortal will surely attain his goal. As there is no other way, what else can I tell you? *14*

To raise the population, you must therefore worship Hari, Govinda, lord of all creation, if you want success. *15*

The beginningless lord, the highest spirit, should always be revered by one who yearns for virtue, wealth, love or liberation. *16*

In the beginning, Brahmā worshipped Hari, then made the world. When you've praised the everlasting lord, you'll raise the population. *17*

Parāśara:

After Prācīnabarhis spoke, his ten sons, the Pracetases, dived into the Milky Ocean, where they resolutely undertook austerities. *18*

For ten thousand years, their minds were set on Nārāyaṇa, best of sages, the universal lord and refuge of the world. *19*

There they remained, meditating solely on the deity and praising Hari, who grants the wishes of all who worship him. *20*

Maitreya:

Repeat for me the wondrous song of praise the Pracetases sang for Viṣṇu while they lived in the ocean's waters, best of sages. *21*

Parāśara:

Now listen to the paean sung by the Pracetases, Maitreya, who were in truth composed of Govinda, while living underwater long ago. *22*

The Pracetases praise Viṣṇu

The Pracetases:

We bow to him whose eternal glory is the subject of all speech, the start and finish, the highest universal lord, *23*

Who is primal light, incomparable, indivisible, unending and unlimited; the origin of all that moves and all that's static. *24*

We bow to the formless one whose initial form is day, then night and twilight; the highest lord, who is Time itself. *25*

We bow to him who, as the moon, is imbibed each day by gods and ancestors in the form of nectar, and is the life of all. *26*

We bow to him who, as the sun, dispels the dark, burns bright, illuminates the sky with his own rays and is the source of heat and cold and rain. *27*

We bow to him who, as the earth, is imbued with firmness, supports the world, is the realm of sound and all sensations and is all-pervading. *28*

We bow with joy to blessed Hari in the form of water, which is the universal womb and seed of every living being. *29*

We bow to Viṣṇu in the form of fire, which is the mouth of all the gods and ancestors, and which consumes the *havya* and *kavya* offerings. *30*

We bow to the lord in the form of wind, existing in the body in five different modes, constant source of motion, whose origin is the sky. *31*

We bow to him in the form of air, which constitutes the space between all beings and is endless, pure and formless. *32*

We bow to the creator Kṛṣṇa, in the form of sensations such as sound, who is always the ultimate object of all the senses. *33*

We bow to Hari, who in the form of senses always apprehends their objects, changing and unchanging, the root of understanding. *34*

We bow to him in the form of intellect, at the heart of all, who carries to the mind that which the senses apprehend. *35*

We bow to the endless being in whom all things abide, from whom all things arise, in whom all things dissolve, who is marked by primal nature. *36*

We bow to that deity whose own form is the highest primal spirit, who is pure and has no qualities, but is misperceived to have them. *37*

We bow to that supreme state of Viṣṇu, the highest Absolute, changeless, unborn, pure, unqualified and unsullied. *38*

That state has neither length, coarseness, fineness, peer, affection, splendour, shape, passion nor movement. *39*

It lies beyond space, touch, smell, taste, eyes and ears. It's unmoving, having neither voice, nor hands, nor mind. *40*

It has neither name, lineage, comfort, glory, cause, fear, doubt, sleep nor waking. *41*

Without passion, sound, death, decline or limit, nothing exists before or after Viṣṇu's highest state. *42*

We bow to that state which has the quality of highest supremacy, which is in all beings but depends on none, and which exists beyond the range of tongue and eye. *43*

Parāśara:

Thus praising Viṣṇu while contemplating him, the Pracetases undertook austerities on the ocean floor for ten thousand years. *44*

Lord Hari, complexioned like a fully opened azure lotus petal, was gratified and appeared before them underwater. *45*

Seeing Viṣṇu mounted on Garuḍa, king of birds, the Pracetases fell down before him, bowing their heads in reverence. *46*

The lord then said to them, 'Ask for anything you desire, as I'm inclined to favour you and have come to grant your wish.' *47*

The Pracetases, bowing before the wish-granting lord, reported that their father had instructed them to raise the population. *48*

The deity allowed the boon they requested, then withdrew from sight. The Pracetases then left behind the waters of the ocean. *49*

So ends Chapter Fourteen in Book One of the glorious Viṣṇu Purāṇa.

15. The Pracetases, Māriṣā, the Ādityas and Prahlāda

Parāśara:

While the Pracetases were undertaking their austerities, the unprotected earth was overgrown with vegetation and the people suffered. *1*

The winds had ceased to blow, the sky was filled with clouds and for ten thousand years folk could do no work. *2*

The Pracetases, emerging from the ocean, saw all this and were enraged. From their mouths blew wind and fire born of their anger. *3*

The wind uprooted trees and dried them out. The terrible fire then burned them, consuming all the vegetation. *4*

Seeing the ruin of the forests with so little left behind, Soma, the regal deity of the moon, approached the patriarchs and said, *5*

'Don't be angry, your majesties, and listen to my words. I'll make a deal with you about these trees. *6*

Because I'm able to foresee the future, with my light I raised this precious girl, the fair-faced daughter of the forest. *7*

Māriṣā by name, she is indeed the offspring of the trees. Why don't you marry this lucky girl, as she will doubtless bring about the increase of your race? *8*

Māriṣā will bear a son with half your splendour and half of mine, and he'll become the prudent patriarch known as Dakṣa. *9*

Endowed with a part of me and blessed with your energy, he'll blaze like fire, causing humanity to thrive. *10*

Kaṇḍu and Pramlocā

In former times, there was a sage named Kaṇḍu, an outstanding Vedic expert, who undertook extreme austerities on the Gomatī River's pleasant banks. *11*

To distract him, Indra, king of gods, engaged a lovely apsaras named Pramlocā, and the sweetly smiling woman succeeded in diverting that sagacious man. *12*

Distracted by Pramlocā, Kaṇḍu lived with her for a hundred years or more in a valley on Mount Mandara's slopes, his heart engrossed in sensual pleasures. *13*

One day, Pramlocā said to that fortunate sage, 'I want to return to heaven. Look kindly on me, brahmin, and grant that I may leave.' *14*

After she had spoken, the sage, whose heart was ever set on her, replied, 'Just stay a few more days, my dear.' *15*

Thus addressed by that great sage, the slender girl spent another century enjoying herself with him. *16*

'Please permit me, master, to return to the realm of the thirteen gods,' she begged the sage, but again he begged her to remain. *17*

When another hundred years had passed, that fair-faced girl said with a bright and loving smile, 'Brahmin, I'm going back to heaven.' *18*

Hearing this, the sage embraced the apsaras with almond eyes. 'Stay a while,' said he, 'as you'll be gone so long, and your eyebrows are so lovely.' *19*

Fearing the sage's curse, fair-hipped Pramlocā stayed with him for another two hundred years or so. *20*

Again and again, the slender girl told the lucky sage that she was leaving for the home of Indra, king of gods, but he always talked her out of it. *21*

Still fearing the sage's curse, the respectful woman spoke sweetly and stayed with him, because she understood the pain of separation that lovers feel. *22*

While the best of sages enjoyed himself with Pramlocā by day and night, his love for her was constantly renewed and his heart was filled with passion. *23*

One day, the sage was hurrying from his hut and, as he did so, the splendid woman asked where he was going. *24*

'The day is done, my dear, so I must perform my twilight rituals,' he replied, 'otherwise an essential rite will be neglected.' *25*

With a laugh, the cheerful girl replied to him, 'You know all about virtue, but is just one day really done for you? *26*

One day for you appears to last for many years, brahmin. Who wouldn't be amazed by this? Please explain your meaning.' *27*

The sage:

This morning you came to this lovely riverbank, my dear. I saw you there, so slender, and you came back to my ashram. *28*

Now it's dusk and the day is done. Why are you laughing? Tell me truly. *29*

Pramlocā:

It's true I came at dawn, brahmin—there is no doubt of that. But many hundred years have passed since then! *30*

Soma:

Then the brahmin, filled with consternation, asked the girl with almond eyes, 'Tell me, timid one, how long have we been enjoying ourselves together?' *31*

Pramlocā:

Nine hundred and seven years, six months and three days. *32*

The sage:

Is this the truth or some kind of joke, you lovely timid girl? I thought we'd spent a single day together. *33*

Pramlocā:

How could I mislead you, brahmin, especially as you, a sage on virtue's path, inquired of me. *34*

Soma:

When the sage heard her explanation, princes, he cursed himself and cried, 'Shame on me! Shame on me!' *35*

The sage:

'My austerities have been wasted, my store of Vedic knowledge lost, and my judgement's been impaired. Someone must have sent this woman to distract me. *36*

I'd conquered my own impulses and was about to grasp the Absolute, which lies beyond the sixfold waves of pain. Curse that greatest evil, desire, which robbed me of my resolution! *37*

All my vows, which would have yielded Vedic knowledge, have been stolen by a tryst that leads to hell.' *38*

Uttering these curses, the sage, who apprehended virtue, shouted at the apsaras, who sat nearby: *39*

'Get out, you wicked woman. You distracted me by making love, just as the king of gods intended. *40*

I should burn you to ashes with the fire of my anger. On the other hand, like virtuous people, we took the seven steps of marriage and lived together as a couple. *41*

You've done no wrong. Why should I be angry with you? It's my own fault because I couldn't curb my senses. *42*

You wanted Indra's favour and disrupted my austerities. Shame on you! You're a bundle of distractions best avoided!' *43*

Soma:

While that sagacious brahmin abused the girl with the lovely waist, she began to sweat and tremble. *44*

The poor lass shook as sweat rolled down her slender limbs. 'Get out! Get out!' the best of sages shouted angrily. *45*

Thus abused by Kaṇḍu, the sky-going apsaras fled the ashram and, as she flew, the forest's tender branches brushed away her perspiration. *46*

As she passed from tree to tree, the delicate shoots that grew on each brushed against her sweaty limbs. *47*

The child within her womb, which she'd conceived with Kaṇḍu, emerged from her limbs in the form of droplets, such as attend excitement. *48*

The trees collected all the drops, and the wind combined them in a single body. I nurtured that body with my rays, and in this way the infant slowly grew. *49*

That baby, begotten among the branches, became this fair-faced girl, Māriṣā. The trees now offer her to you, so set aside your anger. *50*

Māriṣā, child of Kaṇḍu, brought forth by trees, is also daughter of the wind, of Pramlocā and of me, the Moon. *51*

When holy Kaṇḍu's austerities had been reduced to nothing, best of princes, he retired to the lofty mountain known as Puruṣottama, abode of Viṣṇu. *52*

There, the great ascetic stood, his arms above his head, praising Hari and reciting a prayer that encompasses the furthest reaches of the Absolute, princes, his heart set on the deity alone. *53*

The Pracetases:

We'd like to hear that sage's brilliant song of praise, which reached the Absolute's outer limits, which Kaṇḍu sang to worship heavenly Keśava. *54*

Soma:

Viṣṇu is beyond the furthest limit, further than the furthest, higher than the highest and is the form of the utmost destination. He is the furthest reach of the Absolute, he is beyond the furthest limit, highest of the high, furthest of the far. *55*

He is the cause of the universe and that cause's cause. He is that cause's cause, and the cause of the highest cause. Thus, in every act, in every form of action and of agent, he protects the universe. *56*

He is the Absolute, the lord and the Absolute that is everything. He is the Absolute, Acyuta, unfailing father of creation. He is the changeless Absolute, Viṣṇu, eternal and unborn, free from all beginnings and all endings. *57*

Just as the highest spirit, the Absolute, is imperishable, unborn and everlasting, so may all my passions and other faults be overcome. *58*

Māriṣā's former life

Soma:

Reciting this excellent song of praise, known as the 'Prayer of the Supreme Absolute', Kaṇḍu worshipped Keśava and reached the highest goal. *59*

Now I'll tell you who Māriṣā was in her previous life, because the significance of her deeds in this account will benefit you. *60*

In earlier times, outstanding princes, she was a fortunate queen. After her husband's death and being childless, she gratified Lord Viṣṇu with her devotion. *61*

Worshipped by her, Viṣṇu, appearing to that splendid woman, said, 'Make a wish.' She then revealed her heart's desire: *62*

'Widowed at a tender age, Lord, my birth has been in vain. Father of creation, I was born amid misfortune and futility. *63*

May I therefore have a worthy husband in every birth. Similarly, by your mercy, may I have a son who's equal to the patriarchs. *64*

May I have both wealth and beauty, may I be agreeable in the sight of all, Viṣṇu, and may I not be issued from a womb.' *65*

Soma:

After she had spoken, Hṛṣīkeśa, chief of gods, highest lord and wish-bestower, lifted up the deeply bowing woman and addressed these words to her: *66*

The Lord:

'In a single lifetime, you will have ten husbands, heroic and renowned for noble deeds. *67*

And you, splendid woman, will have a mighty son, courageous, strong and blessed with the qualities of a patriarch. *68*

He will be the founder of many lineages on this earth, and his progeny will fill the threefold worlds. *69*

You will not be issued from a womb, but will be a virtuous woman endowed with beauty, nobility and other wished-for qualities, and, by my grace, you'll delight the hearts of men.' *70*

Having spoken to that girl with almond eyes, the lord withdrew from sight and she was born Māriṣā and will be a helpmeet for you, royal princes. *71*

Parāśara:

In accord with Soma's orders, the Pracetases shed their anger and accepted Māriṣā from the forest as their spouse. *72*

With the ten Pracetases, Māriṣā gave birth to Dakṣa, that mighty patriarch, who was born as Brahmā's son in a previous life. *73*

This fortunate Dakṣa brought forth sons for the peopling of the world, wise sage, and to provide himself with offspring. *74*

Obeying Brahmā's orders, Dakṣa established moving and unmoving things, creatures with two feet and those with four, to further procreation. *75*

Dakṣa brought forth fifty women with his mental power, gave ten to Dharma, thirteen to Kaśyapa and twenty-seven to the Moon, all of whom were charged with regulating time.[24] *76*

These women then gave rise to gods, Daityas, nāgas, cattle, birds, gandharvas, apsarases, Dānavas and the rest. *77*

Since then, Maitreya, all creatures have been born of sexual union. The offspring of beings who arose before that time were born of willpower, sight or touch, or were brought forth by the various extreme austerities of those who undertook them. *78*

Maitreya:

I'd heard before that Dakṣa had been born from the thumb of Brahmā's right hand, sage. How could he be born a second time as the son of the Pracetases? *79*

This grave doubt weighs on my mind, brahmin, because Dakṣa was Soma's grandson, but at the same time was his father-in-law! *80*

Parāśara:

Beings are always subject to both birth and death, you best of sages. The wise are not confused by this, nor are those endowed with special insight. *81*

Dakṣa and the other patriarchs exist in every era, foremost seer, and they also cease to be. This should not perplex the wise. *82*

24 These are the 27 lunar mansions through which the moon passes each year.

In former times, there was no concept of young or old among them, best of brahmins. The severity of their austerities and their power were the only standards of comparison. *83*

Maitreya:

Brahmin, describe to me in detail the origin of the deities, Dānavas, gandharvas, nāgas and rākṣasas. *84*

Parāśara:

In former times, Brahmā, the self-arisen deity, commanded Dakṣa to bring forth living things, wise sage. Listen to how he did so. *85*

Dakṣa created living beings before—including deities, sages, gandharvas, demigods and nāgas—with his mental energy. *86*

But the beings that creative lord brought forth did not increase in number, and, after much reflection, *87*

Desiring the procreation of varied kinds of offspring, he determined sexual union should become the normal means of reproduction. Accordingly, he wedded Asiknī, the daughter of the patriarch Vīraṇa, who had undertaken dire austerities and was a great supporter of the world. *88*

Following this, the mighty patriarch Dakṣa had five thousand sons with her to raise the population. *89*

Seeing these sons were keen on procreation, brahmin, Nārada, that heavenly sage, appeared to them and spoke these honeyed words. *90*

Nārada:

You mighty Haryaśvas will have progeny—your wishes have been noted—but hear what I have to say: *91*

It's a pity that you're so naive and do not know the limits of the earth—above, below or on all sides. How will you populate it otherwise? *92*

Only when the upper, lower and sideward paths have all been cleared will you innocents behold the limits of the world. *93*

Parāśara:

Hearing this, the Haryaśvas set off in all directions, but to this day they've not returned, just as rivers don't flow backwards from the sea. *94*

After they had disappeared, holy Dakṣa, son of the Pracetases, had another thousand sons with Vīraṇa's daughter. *95*

These, the Śabalāśvas, also intent on procreation, brahmin, were dispatched by Nārada with the same instructions as before. *96*

'This sage has spoken truly,' they said to one another. 'We should doubtless take the paths our brothers took. *97*

Once we know the limits of the world, we'll be able to populate it.' *98*

Off they went in all directions along those very paths, but to this day they've not returned, just as rivers don't flow backwards from the sea. *99*

Ever since that time, one brother who searches for another is lost, brahmin, and that's why a prudent brother never does so. *100*

When the great patriarch Dakṣa learned those sons had disappeared as well, he was furious and cursed Nārada. *101*

But still wishing to populate the earth, Maitreya, Dakṣa had sixty daughters with Vīraṇa's daughter, so we heard. *102*

He gave ten girls to Dharma, thirteen to Kaśyapa, twenty-seven to Soma and four to Ariṣṭanemi, *103*

Two to Bahuputra, two to Aṅgiras and two to wise Kṛśāśva. Listen while I tell you all their names: *104*

Arundhatī, Vasu, Jāmī, Lambā, Bhānu, Marutvatī, Saṃkalpā, Muhūrtā, Sādhyā and Viśvā: these ten were the wives of Dharma. Now listen while I tell you of their progeny. *105*

Viśvā gave birth to the divine Viśvedevas, Sādhyā bore the Sādhyas, Marutvatī bore the Maruts, the Vasus are regarded as the progeny of Vasu.[25] *106*

Bhānu bore the Bhānus (the Suns), and Muhūrtā bore the Muhūrtas (the Moments). Lambā bore Ghoṣa (Sound), and Nāgavīthī was born of Jāmī. *107*

All the region of the earth was born from Arundhatī. Saṃkalpā gave birth to Saṃkalpa (Resolve), which is at the heart of everything. *108*

I'll now describe in detail the deities called the Eight Vasus, led by Jyotis (Light), filled with radiance and energy: *109*

---

25 The Vasus are a class of elemental deities and divine personifications of various natural phenomena. In the following verses, I have given their names in English where appropriate.

Āpa (Water), Dhruva (Pole Star), Soma (Moon), Dhara (Earth), Anila (Wind), Anala (Fire), Pratyūṣa (Dawn) and Prabhāsa (Splendour): this is how the Vasus are recalled by name. *110*

Āpa's sons were Vaitaṇḍa, Śrama (Toil), Śrānta (Fatigue) and Adhuni. Dhruva's son was holy Kāla (Time), who impels the world. *111*

Soma's son was holy Varcas (Power), whose son was Varcasvin (Energy). *112*

Dhara's sons with his wife, Manoharā (Attraction), were Draviṇas (Offerings), Hutahavyavaha (Sacrificial Fire), Śiśira (Cold), Prāṇa (Breath) and Ramaṇa (Pleasure). *113*

Anila's wife was Śivā. Her sons were Purojava and Avijñātagati. These were the sons she bore with Anila. *114*

Agni's son Kumāra was born in a clump of reeds. Śākha, Viśākha and Naigameya were his younger brothers. *115*

The son of the Kṛttikās (the Pleiades) was Kārttikeya, the god of war. *116*

They called Pratyuṣa's son the sage Devala. Devala had two wise and patient sons. *117*

Bṛhaspati's sister, the brilliant celibate woman Yogasiddhā, traversed the whole world without attachment, and became the wife of Prabhāsa, the eighth Vasu. *118*

Yogasiddhā gave birth to the fortunate patriarch Viśvakarman, the inventor of a thousand arts and craftsman of the thirteen gods. *119*

He was creator of every ornament and foremost artisan who made the carriages for all the gods. Humankind depends on skills perfected by that great being. *120*

His sons were Ajaikapād, Ahirbudhnya, Tvaṣṭṛ and wise Rudra. Tvaṣṭṛ's own son was the great ascetic Viśvarūpa. *121*

Hara, Bahurūpa, Tryambaka, Aparājita, Vṛṣākapi, Śaṃbhu, Kapardin, Raivata, *122*

Mṛgavyādha, Śarva and Kapālin: these, great sage, are said to be the eleven Rudras, lords of the threefold worlds. *123*

A total of one hundred Rudras of immeasurable energy are mentioned. *124*

The origin of the Āditya deities

I'll now tell you, knower of virtue, about the offspring of Aditi, Diti, Danu, Ariṣṭā, Surasā, Svasā, Surabhi, Vinatā, Tāmrā, Krodhavaśā, Irā, Kadru and Muni.[26] *125*

In the previous Manvantara, there were twelve excellent celestial beings known as the Tuṣitas. When the beginning of the Vaivasvata Manvantara was approaching, *126*

And the period of the previous glorious Manu, Cākṣuṣa, was drawing to a close, having come together, the assembled Tuṣitas conferred with one another: *127*

'Come quickly, fellow deities. If we enter Aditi's womb and are born in the next Manvantara, it will be to our advantage.' *128*

So saying, they were born in the period of Manu Vaivasvata as the sons of Mārīca Kaśyapa and Aditi, Dakṣa's daughter. *129*

As such, Viṣṇu, mighty Indra, Āryaman, Dhātṛ, Tvaṣṭṛ, Pūṣan, *130*

Vivasvat, Savitṛ, Mitra, Varuṇa, Aṃśa and Bhaga are recognised as the twelve magnificent sons of Aditi, the Ādityas. *131*

Those who had previously been the divine Tuṣitas in the Cākṣuṣa Manvantara are the twelve Ādityas in the current Vaivasvata period. *132*

The twenty-seven daughters of Dakṣa who are described as the faithful wives of Soma, and whose energy was beyond measure, also brought forth brilliant offspring. *133*

The wives of Ariṣṭanemi bore sixteen children. *134*

The daughters of prudent Bahuputra are remembered as the four lightning deities, the Vidyuts. *135*

The patron deities of Vedic verses, the excellent Ṛces, honoured by brahminical sages, were born to Aṅgiras. *136*

The sons of the godly sage Kṛśāśva were the Devapraharaṇas, patron gods of heavenly weapons. *137*

26 These are Dakṣa's thirteen daughters, who married Kaśyapa.

These thirty-three divine hosts are born again of their own volition at the end of a thousand ages, my dear, but even they are said to be ever subject to birth and death. *138*

Just as the sun rises and sets in this world, Maitreya, these hosts of deities are born again in every aeon. *139*

The origin of the Daitya Prahlāda

We've heard that Kaśyapa had two sons with Diti, Hiraṇyakaśipu and Hiraṇyākṣa. *140*

Diti also had a daughter, Siṃhikā, who married Vipracitti. *141*

Hiraṇyakaśipu had four outstanding sons, Anuhlāda, Hlāda, virtuous Prahlāda and brave Saṃhlāda, who increased the lineage of the Daityas, Diti's offspring. *142*

Among them, great Prahlāda looked on all things with equanimity and was perfectly devoted to Janārdana. *143*

In former times, the Daitya king lit a fire and heaped it round Prahlāda, brahmin, but the flames did him no harm, as Vāsudeva dwelt in his heart. *144*

When that wise child, bound up with ropes, shivered at the bottom of the sea, the whole world trembled. *145*

The Daitya king hurled several weapons at Prahlāda, but he was never harmed, his body firm as a mountain and his heart set on eternal Viṣṇu. *146*

Mighty serpent-lords, sent by the Daitya king, their jaws ablaze with flames and venom, couldn't kill him. *147*

Even mountain ranges were piled upon his body, but, recalling the highest spirit, he didn't die, protected by the thought of Viṣṇu. *148*

The Daitya king, the denizen of heaven, cast that prudent boy down from a lofty palace, but the Earth embraced him before he hit the ground. *149*

The king of Daityas sent a wind to scorch his body, but it was baffled as Prahlāda's heart was always set on Madhusūdana. *150*

The raging guardian elephants of the quarters sent by the Daitya king broke their tusks on Prahlāda's broad chest, which robbed them of their arrogance. *151*

With all their spells the king's own priests could not destroy Prahlāda then, as his heart was fixed on Govinda. *152*

The thousand phantoms set on him by Śambara the sorcerer were rendered harmless by Kṛṣṇa's discus. *153*

The poison known as *hālāhala* administered by the chefs of the Daitya king had no effect on wise and selfless Prahlāda. *154*

His mind was equally well-disposed to every creature in this world, he treated others as he would himself, filled with the virtue of benevolence. *155*

He was the soul of virtue, a brilliant font of purity, truth and other qualities, ever standing as a paragon for all good people. *156*

So ends Chapter Fifteen in Book One of the glorious Viṣṇu Purāṇa.

16. Maitreya asks about Prahlāda

Maitreya:

You've described the origin of humanity, great sage, and everlasting Viṣṇu, the universal cause. *1*

But who's this excellent Daitya, Prahlāda, whom you mentioned and who didn't die when burned with fire or struck by weapons? *2*

The whole earth shook when he lay beneath the ocean, even though he was tied with bonds, and the firm ground trembled when he moved his limbs. *3*

Buried under mountains in former times, he didn't die. You've said so much about the greatness of this prudent being. *4*

I want to hear about the peerless power of that devotee of Viṣṇu, sage, and about the deeds of this being of immeasurable energy. *5*

Why did the sons of Diti attack him with weapons, sage, and why was he, intent on virtue, cast into the sea? *6*

Why was he crushed by mountains and bitten by great serpents? Why cast from heights and thrown into a fire? *7*

Why was he made a target for the tusks of guardian elephants, and why did great demons send a wind to scorch him? *8*

Why did the Daitya's gurus perform those rituals, sage, and why did Śambara loose a thousand phantoms at him? *9*

Why did the Daitya's chefs administer the virulent poison *hālāhala* to dispatch that great and prudent being, which he rendered harmless? *10*

I want to hear all about the deeds of noble Prahlāda, blessed sage, which demonstrate his special virtue. *11*

No wonder the Daityas didn't kill him, for who can harm a person whose heart is set on Viṣṇu? *12*

He was bent on virtue and always lauded Keśava, but Daityas, his own kinsfolk, showed him extreme antipathy. *13*

A pious, fortunate and selfless devotee of Viṣṇu—why was he attacked by Diti's sons? You must explain all this to me. *14*

Noble beings would never strike a virtuous foe like him, filled as he was with goodness, let alone a person born among one's allies. *15*

You must therefore describe all this in detail, best of sages, as I want to hear about the deeds of this Daitya prince. *16*

So ends Chapter Sixteen in Book One of the glorious Viṣṇu Purāṇa.

17. Prahlāda instructs the Daitya boys

Parāśara:

Listen carefully, Maitreya, to the deeds of the great and prudent Prahlāda, whose actions were always noble. *1*

In former days, Diti's son, brave Hiraṇyakaśipu, received a boon from Brahmā and brought all three worlds under his control. *2*

The Daitya usurped the authority of Indra, and then assumed the functions of the Sun, Wind, Fire, Varuṇa, lord of waters, the Moon, *3*

Kubera, lord of riches, and Yama, ruler of the underworld. That demon then partook of every portion of the sacrifice. *4*

The gods fled heaven, fearing him, best of sages, and wandered the world in human form. *5*

After the Daitya conquered all three worlds, he grew arrogant because of his universal sovereignty, and, while gandharvas sang his praises, he indulged his favourite senses. *6*

All the siddhas, gandharvas and nāgas waited on mighty Hiraṇyakaśipu, who loved to drink. *7*

In the presence of the Daitya lord, joyful siddhas provided music, some sang, while others cried, 'Be victorious!' *8*

Apsarases danced in that delightful crystal palace in the clouds, where the demon, filled with pleasure, spent time drinking. *9*

Hiraṇyakaśipu had a gifted son, Prahlāda by name, a lad who studied subjects suited to young children in his guru's home. *10*

One day, that pious youth, accompanied by his teacher, came before the Daitya lord, his drunken father. *11*

When Prahlāda bowed to touch Hiraṇyakaśipu's feet, his father lifted up this child of boundless energy and spoke these words. *12*

Hiraṇyakaśipu:

Recite for me, dear boy, your favourite verse that you've carefully learned to date. *13*

Prahlāda:

Listen well, dear father, and as you command, I'll diligently recite the most important thing that occupies my heart: *14*

'I bow to him who has no start, no middle and no ending; who is unborn, unageing, undying and unchanging; destroyer and maintainer of the universe; the cause of every cause.' *15*

Parāśara:

Hearing this, the eyes of the Daitya king grew red with fury. He glared at his son's guru and berated him, his bud-like lower lip alive with rage. *16*

Hiraṇyakaśipu:

Brahmin, what insulting nonsense in praise of my arch rival have you taught this boy, you fool? *17*

The guru:

Your anger is misplaced, my lord, as your son didn't learn this from me. *18*

Hiraṇyakaśipu:

Who taught you this, Prahlāda? Tell me, boy, because your guru says it wasn't him. *19*

Prahlāda:

Viṣṇu, teacher of all the world, is fixed within my heart, father. Apart from him, the highest spirit, what remains to be taught by anyone? *20*

Hiraṇyakaśipu:

Who's this Viṣṇu you prattle on about before me, silly boy? I'm the lord of the threefold worlds! *21*

Prahlāda:

Ascetics may contemplate his highest state, but it cannot be described. From him arises everything, and he *is* everything. He is Viṣṇu, the highest lord. *22*

Hiraṇyakaśipu:

How can anyone be called the 'highest lord' while I am here, you foolish boy? If you want to die, just mention him again. *23*

Prahlāda:

Viṣṇu, the Absolute, is creator, disposer and highest lord, not just of me and all the world, but of you as well, father. Be merciful to me. What use is anger? *24*

Hiraṇyakaśipu:

Which evil being has occupied the heart of this foolish child? He's talking nonsense as if possessed. *25*

Prahlāda:

Viṣṇu not only occupies my heart but fills all three worlds. He's the universal being who enjoins me, you, father, and other beings to undertake all actions. *26*

Hiraṇyakaśipu:

Take this wicked boy away and punish him in his teacher's home. Who's encouraged this stupid child to falsely praise my enemy? *27*

Parāśara:

After the king had spoken thus, the Daityas took Prahlāda to his teacher's home, where he kept up his schooling, while serving his guru diligently. *28*

Some time later, the demon king summoned Prahlāda again. 'Sing something for me, son,' he said to him. *29*

Prahlāda:

May Viṣṇu, from whom both matter and spirit arise, from whom this world of moving and unmoving things ensues, and who is the cause of everything, show mercy to us all. *30*

Prahlāda's torments begin

Hiraṇyakaśipu:

Kill this wicked child—his life is worthless! Because he'll bring ruin on his family, he's like a glowing ember in a house. *31*

Parāśara:

At the king's command, hundreds of thousands of Daityas, weapons in hand, prepared to kill the boy. *32*

Prahlāda:

Just as Viṣṇu occupies your swords, as well as you and me, you Daityas, by this same truth, may all your weapons be rendered harmless! *33*

Parāśara:

Even though the Daityas in their hundreds struck him with their awful weapons, Prahlāda felt not the slightest pain and was continually restored. *34*

Hiraṇyakaśipu:

You foolish child, don't praise our rivals! You'll have nought to fear from me if you renounce these stupid thoughts. *35*

Prahlāda:

When the everlasting lord, who dispels all anxiety, abides within my heart, what fear have I? Calling him to mind, father, all concerns of birth, old age and death are gone. *36*

Hiraṇyakaśipu:

Come, serpents! With your jaws that spew those venomous flames, dispatch at once this ill-mannered wretch. *37*

Parāśara:

At the king's command, Takṣaka and other sly poisonous snakes struck Prahlāda's every limb. *38*

But his mind was fixed on Kṛṣṇa, and even when those mighty snakes assailed him, unaware of his own body and filled with bliss, he recalled the deity. *39*

The serpents:

Our fangs have snapped and our crest jewels cracked, our hoods are sore and our hearts all tremble, but we've made not the slightest mark on this child's skin. Assign some other task to us, your majesty. *40*

Hiraṇyakaśipu:

Come, you guardian elephants of the quarters with your massive tusks. Strike down this boy who's been seduced by enemies. One's progeny can cause one's own destruction, just like a fire that burns the forest where it was kindled. *41*

Parāśara:

The elephants of the quarters, towering like great mountain peaks, threw Prahlāda to the ground and gored him with their tusks. *42*

Because his mind was set on Govinda, their tusks broke into a thousand pieces when they touched his chest. The boy then addressed his father: *43*

Prahlāda:

These elephants' tusks with tips as hard as diamonds snapped, not because of my own strength, but because I remembered Janārdana, the great destroyer of death and sin. *44*

Hiraṇyakaśipu:

Get those elephants out of here! Light a fire, you demons, and Vāyu, fan the flames to burn this wretch! *45*

Parāśara:

At their lord's command, the Dānavas covered the son of the demon king with a towering pile of kindling and lit a fire to burn him. *46*

Prahlāda:

Father, this wind-fanned fire can do no harm, as all around on every side I see cooling prospects spread with lotuses. *47*

Parāśara:

The brahmin sons of Bhārgava, those wise and eloquent priests, praised their patron, the Daitya king, with soothing words: *48*

The priests:

Sire, don't be angry with this boy, your son, because your fury will bear fruit among the gathered hosts of gods. *49*

We'll be your son's instructors, and we'll teach him to destroy your rivals. *50*

Childhood is a time of many errors, Daitya king. Don't be angry with the boy. *51*

If, after our instruction, he still cleaves to Hari's cause, we'll then take steps to bring about his downfall. In this we will not fail. *52*

Parāśara:

After the priests of the Daitya king petitioned him with these words, he ordered the demons to pull his son out of the fire. *53*

Later, residing in his guru's home, during breaks between his teacher's lessons, Prahlāda often gave instruction to the other demon boys. *54*

Prahlāda:

Listen, Daityas, Diti's grandsons, while I speak about the highest goal. Nothing else is worthy of consideration or desire. *55*

Every living being experiences birth, childhood and youth, and then in time old age will surely come. *56*

After that, you sons of the Daitya lord, a creature faces death, as you and I all clearly see. *57*

Each being who dies will be reborn, and according to our sacred texts it must be thus, but there is no existence without a cause. *58*

As long as pregnancy results in birth, the pain of every new existence will be felt. *59*

People foolishly believe that the end of thirst and hunger, and the absence of cold and other irritations, will lead to happiness, but these are in truth merely further forms of pain. *60*

Just as those with aching limbs seek comfort when they stretch, even a slap enlivens those whose minds have wandered. *61*

How ill-matched are the physical body, a mass of phlegm and other humours, and sought-for qualities such as beauty and a pleasant scent. *62*

The fool who delights in a body composed of blood and muscle, pus and faeces, urine, sinews, bones and marrow will surely go to hell. *63*

Fire gives comfort when one is cold, water when thirsty and food when hungry, but in other circumstances, they have the opposite effect. *64*

As long as you persist with marriage, sons of Daityas, such miseries will weigh upon your hearts. *65*

As many relatives as a being holds dear, so many painful arrows will pierce his heart. *66*

Wherever a person journeys, he always worries that his goods at home are lost or burned or stolen. *67*

Birth is attended by great pain and, for the dying, there are the awful torments under Yama's rod. Then comes the pain of passing through another womb. *68*

If you conclude there's little pleasure in the embryonic state, then you must admit that this whole world consists of woe. *69*

I'll therefore speak truthfully to you: here in the abode of suffering, the ocean of existence, Viṣṇu is your only refuge. *70*

Do not think: 'We're only boys, and the embodied being that inhabits our physical form is everlasting. Birth, youth and old age are the way of the body, not the soul.' *71*

Or: 'While I'm a boy, I'll do as I wish, but when I become a youth I'll strive for some improvement.' Or: 'I'm a young man now, but I'll do something to benefit my soul when I'm older.' *72*

Or: 'Now I'm old, those things I should have done are out of reach. I didn't do them then when I was able; how can I do them now I'm slowing down?' *73*

One whose mind is always filled with such vain thoughts will not improve himself, even though he yearns to do so. *74*

Children love their toys; young people seek out sensual pleasures, but before they know it, relentless age creeps up on them. *75*

A discerning being should always strive to improve himself while young, without regard to boyhood, youth, old age or other states. *76*

This, then, is what I have to tell you. If you believe that it is true, then out of your affection for me, remember Viṣṇu, who will free you from the bonds of life. *77*

What's so hard about remembering him? When called to mind, he blesses you, so think about him day and night and all your sins will be forgiven. *78*

Let your love and thoughts both day and night be on him who dwells within all creatures, and in doing so you'll leave your woes behind. *79*

As threefold suffering afflicts the world, which wise person would be angry with other creatures deserving of our pity? *80*

If other beings enjoy good fortune, but I'm powerless to enjoy it too, I should be as happy as they, since my misfortune results from anger I expressed before. *81*

As beings bound by hatred feel anger in their hearts, the wise should pity them because they're filled with great delusion. *82*

I've described the ideas of those who perceive the deity and creation as distinct from one another. Now listen, if you demon boys are willing, to a summary of the other view. *83*

This whole world is but an aspect of universal Viṣṇu. The wise see everything as one and as no different from themselves. *84*

Casting off our demonic natures, let us—you and I together—strive to gain the highest bliss. *85*

This bliss will never be undone by fire, the sun, the moon, Vāyu, Parjanya, Varuṇa, the siddhas, rākṣasas, *86*

Yakṣas, Daitya kings, nāgas, kiṃnaras, humans, animals, afflictions born of our own natures, *87*

Fevers, eye diseases, dysentery, diseases of the spleen and other illnesses, anger, envy, greed, passion, avarice or any other thing. *88*

Nothing can rob us of this joy, as it's the everlasting, purest state attained by one who sets his heart on stainless Keśava. *89*

I beseech you, Daityas, to give up satisfaction. Be equally disposed in every situation, because equanimity is a form of worship of unfailing Viṣṇu. *90*

When Viṣṇu is gratified, what in this world is out of reach? Virtue, wealth and pleasure will all mean nought to you. *91*

Great is the reward you'll surely win if you seek refuge beneath the everlasting tree of knowledge. *92*

So ends Chapter Seventeen in Book One of the glorious Viṣṇu Purāṇa.

18. Prahlāda instructs his gurus

Parāśara:

When the Dānavas saw what Prahlāda was doing, fearing the Daitya lord, they informed Hiraṇyakaṣipu, who called his cooks at once and addressed them thus. *1*

Hiraṇyakaśipu:

Come, cooks. Because this perverse and wicked son of mine is leading other boys astray, you must poison him at once. *2*

Without his knowledge, poison his food with *hālāhala*. This wretch must die as soon as possible! *3*

Parāśara:

Just as his mighty father ordered, the cooks administered that poison to noble Prahlāda. *4*

But Prahlāda sanctified the virulent *hālāhala* by reciting the name of imperishable Viṣṇu, Maitreya, as he swallowed it with his food. *5*

Prahlāda consumed that poison with no ill effects and, remaining calm, he digested the terrible dose rendered harmless by Viṣṇu's name. *6*

Seeing that Prahlāda had consumed it, the fearful cooks came before the Daitya lord and, falling at his feet, reported what had happened. *7*

The cooks:

Daitya king, your son, Prahlāda, was able to digest the terrible poison that we fed him with his other food. *8*

Hiraṇyakaśipu:

Hurry! Hurry! Come at once, you Daitya priests. Create an apparition to destroy him without delay! *9*

Parāśara:

But the household priests then came to Prahlāda, spoke soothingly to him and gave him this advice: *10*

The priests:

You were born in Brahmā's lineage, renowned in all three worlds, as the son of the Daitya king, Hiraṇyakaśipu. May you live long! *11*

What good to you are other gods? What good is this so-called imperishable being or anyone else, when your father is the refuge of all the worlds, as you will be one day? *12*

Don't venerate our enemy. One's father is the highest guru, so they say. *13*

Prahlāda:

'What you lucky priests have said is true: this great lineage of Marīci is praised in all three worlds, and no-one would say otherwise. *14*

My father has performed prodigious feats throughout the universe. I understand all this and certainly it is true. *15*

One's father is indeed the highest guru. I've not the slightest doubt about your words. *16*

One's father is indeed a guru to be honoured with devotion. I know in my heart that I must never offend against this principle. *17*

But when you ask things like, "What good is this imperishable being?", who can say that you're correct? Your questions make no sense.' *18*

So saying, Prahlāda fell silent in deference to the priests, but added with a laugh, 'What good is this imperishable being? An excellent question indeed! *19*

I repeat: an excellent question! I salute you! What good is this imperishable being? Again: an excellent question! I salute you, gurus. Hear what this everlasting being means to me. I hope this won't upset you. *20*

Virtue, wealth, love and liberation are said to be the goals of life. Your questions about the deity from whom these four arise make no sense to me. *21*

Marīci, Dakṣa and the other sages learned virtue from this eternal being. Similarly, others acquired wealth, yet others, love. *22*

Some, understanding his true nature through spiritual insight, meditation or realisation, won liberation once their bonds to life were all undone. *23*

Worship of Hari is the singular root cause of prosperity, influence, greatness, knowledge, progeny, activity and liberation. *24*

Since virtue, wealth, love and liberation all result from praising him, brahmins, how could you doubt the good of this imperishable being? *25*

Why say more, respected gurus? Tell me if I'm right or not, as my ability to discriminate is weak.' *26*

The priests:

We saved you from being burnt alive, you foolish child, thinking that you'd stop this nonsense, but we failed to see how unwise you were. *27*

If you do not follow our advice and free yourself from the grip of folly, ignorant boy, we'll conjure up an apparition to destroy you. *28*

Prahlāda:

Who is saved or killed by whom? This whole world of moving and unmoving things destroys and saves itself. *29*

Parāśara:

After Prahlāda had spoken thus, the priests of the Daitya king were furious and conjured up an awful apparition. Her mouth ablaze with rings of fire, *30*

She scorched the earth with the touch of her feet. With her spear, that raging phantom struck Prahlāda on the chest. *31*

But when the flaming weapon reached the young boy's heart, it burst into a hundred shards and fell upon the ground. *32*

The heart in which unfailing Hari dwells could resist the thunderbolt of Indra, to say nothing of a spear. *33*

The apparition set upon the sinless boy by the wicked Daitya priests now struck out at them and vanished in an instant. *34*

Seeing the priests scorched by the ghoul, the noble child ran towards them crying, 'Eternal Kṛṣṇa, save them!' *35*

Prahlāda:

You pervade most everything, Janārdana, and are the form and author of the world. Save these priests from this spell-born fire, so difficult to endure. *36*

Since you are Viṣṇu, guru of the world who abides in all, spare these priests. *37*

As I meditate on you, universal and eternal Viṣṇu, and even though I think they've sided with my enemy, spare these brahmins' lives. *38*

If I regard as friendly those who came to kill me, fed me poison, tried to burn me, sent elephants to crush me and snakes to bite me, *39*

And if I'm free from sin, then, by that same truth, spare the lives of these demon priests today. *40*

Parāśara:

After Prahlāda spoke these words, all the afflicted brahmins rose unharmed and addressed him with respect. *41*

The priests:

May you lead a long and stainless life, dear boy, imbued with strength and courage, and be blessed with sons and grandsons, wealth and power. *42*

Parāśara:

So saying, the priests approached the Daitya king to tell him what had happened, sage. *43*

So ends Chapter Eighteen in Book One of the glorious Viṣṇu Purāṇa.

19. Prahlāda's torments continue

Parāśara:

When Hiraṇyakaśipu heard that the phantom had been foiled, he summoned his son to ask about the origin of his strength. *1*

Hiraṇyakaśipu:

Your endurance is amazing, Prahlāda. How do you do it? Is it the result of some mantra or were you born with it? *2*

Parāśara:

Questioned by Hiraṇyakaśipu, the Daitya boy Prahlāda fell at his father's feet and gave him this reply: *3*

'My strength does not arise from a mantra or anything else, father, nor was I born with it, but it's common to all who hold in their hearts the everlasting deity. *4*

A being who wishes no harm on others, as he wouldn't wish it on himself, father, will undergo no harm, as harm will have no cause. *5*

The harm one brings upon another by word or thought or deed becomes the seed of one's next birth and will result in pain. *6*

I wish no harm on anyone, nor do I act or speak unkindly, thinking Keśava exists in every being, as he does in me. *7*

As my mind is well disposed to everything, how can I experience bodily or mental suffering sent by heaven or by earth? *8*

Knowing that Hari is at the heart of all, the wise should show unwavering devotion towards all beings.' *9*

Parāśara:

Hearing his son say this, the face of the Daitya king, who was standing on the palace roof, grew black with fury as he cried out to his demon minions: *10*

'Throw this wicked child off the roof—it's a hundred leagues above the ground! Drop him on that mountain so his body's smashed upon the rocks.' *11*

The Daitya servants threw the boy from the palace roof, but after they had done so and even as he fell, Prahlāda still held Hari in his heart. *12*

As he reached the ground, the Earth, supporter of the world, caught him as he fell, filled as he was with devotion to Keśava, protector of the universe. *13*

Seeing Prahlāda unharmed and without a single broken bone, Hiraṇyakaśipu spoke to Śambara, his most powerful sorcerer: *14*

'We can't kill this wretched child, but you know magic, so you can do it!' *15*

Śambara:

I'll kill him, Daitya king. Just watch the power of my spells. Behold these thousand apparitions, and here are another million! *16*

Parāśara:

Then the wicked demon Śambara, desiring Prahlāda's ruin, loosed the apparitions upon the child who was equally kind to all. *17*

But Prahlāda mastered his thoughts, Maitreya, and, free from anger even towards the sorcerer, he contemplated Viṣṇu, Madhu's nemesis. *18*

The brilliant discus, Sudarśana, wreathed in flames and summoned by the lord, appeared to save the boy. *19*

The speeding weapon destroyed each and every one of the thousand apparitions raised by Śambara, to defend the child. *20*

The Daitya king then addressed the drying wind, 'I order you to kill this wicked child at once.' *21*

'So be it,' replied the raging wind as it filled the boy. Cold and harsh, the undaunted wind strove to dry his body. *22*

The Daitya lad, knowing he'd been beset by wind, set his heart on mighty Viṣṇu, foundation of the world. *23*

Furious Janārdana, abiding in Prahlāda's heart, imbibed the wind and caused it to be still. *24*

When all the apparitions had departed and the wind was overcome, wise Prahlāda then returned to his guru's home. *25*

Each day, his teacher taught the boy good governance as devised for rulers by the sage Uśanas, so that they might govern well. *26*

When Prahlāda's guru judged that he had mastered all these texts, he informed Hiraṇyakaśipu that his son was now well-schooled. *27*

The master:

I've taught your son, Prahlāda, the science of governance, Daitya king, and now he truly understands the principles of Uśanas, Bhṛgu's scion. *28*

Hiraṇyakaśipu:

How should a king behave towards his friends and foe, Prahlāda? What should he do in the three times of decrease, increase and stability? How should he treat those neutral parties? *29*

How should he behave towards his councillors and ministers, those responsible for affairs inside the palace and outside it, informants and his citizens, those whom he suspects and those he trusts? *30*

Relationships that one should seek or shun, the means of handling strongholds, forest tribes and thorny issues—describe in detail ways to manage each of these, Prahlāda. *31*

Tell me this and other things you've learned, as I'd like to hear your thoughts. *32*

Parāśara:

Prahlāda bowed at his father's feet, wearing respect like an ornament, and, standing before the Daitya king, he spoke with folded palms. *33*

Prahlāda instructs his father

Prahlāda:

My guru taught all this to me, no doubt, and I've taken it all in, but I do not think that it's correct. *34*

He described conciliation, generosity, subversion and aggression as strategies for dealing with one's allies and with others. *35*

But I see neither friend nor foe—don't be angry, father—you're a strong-armed warrior yourself, but if there's nothing to be achieved, why bother with the means? *36*

As Govinda is at the heart of all creation, the universal lord and highest being who incorporates the world, father, why speak of friend and enemy? *37*

Because Lord Viṣṇu is in you, in me and every other thing, what's the difference between my friend and him I call my enemy? *38*

What use are boring talks on dubious subjects based on ignorance, father, when we should strive for virtue? *39*

The idea of what forms knowledge arises from our ignorance, father, and a lack of understanding, demon king. Does not a child mistake a firefly for a fire? *40*

Action that doesn't lead to bondage is true knowledge that sets us free. All other action is wasted effort; all other knowledge merely artful cleverness. *41*

I therefore hold that all of this is vain. Now listen to the highest goal. Bowing at your feet, blessed monarch, I'll describe it. *42*

Who doesn't worry about sovereignty? Who doesn't hanker after wealth? People may have both in the life that follows this. *43*

Everyone strives for greatness, fortunate king, but fate, not effort, will determine their success. *44*

Even fools, cowards, the undiscerning and those who know nought of governance, lord, win kingdoms because of fate. *45*

One who desires the greatest glory should therefore strive for virtue, and one who yearns for liberation should aspire to equanimity. *46*

Deities, mortals, animals, birds, plants and creeping creatures are all forms of everlasting Viṣṇu, yet all seem to stand apart from him. *47*

One who understands all this perceives the world of moving and unmoving things as no different from himself, and as one with Viṣṇu, whose form is universal. *48*

When this is understood, the beginningless lord, the imperishable supreme master, is pleased and, when he's pleased, all afflictions cease. *49*

Parāśara:

Hearing this, Hiraṇyakaśipu leapt from his throne in a rage and kicked his son in the chest. *50*

The impetuous king seemed to blaze with anger and wrung his hands together as if he intended to destroy the entire world as he spoke. *51*

Hiraṇyakaśipu:

Come, Vipracitti! Come, Rāhu! Come, Bali! Bind this boy with serpent-ropes and throw him in the ocean. Don't delay! *52*

If not, all this world, including Dānavas and Daityas, will start to follow this stubborn fool's ideas. *53*

We've tried everything to stop him, but the wicked child keeps singing praises of our foe. Getting rid of evildoers is a social service! *54*

Parāśara:

The Daityas then quickly bound Prahlāda with serpent-ropes and, with their master's orders foremost in their minds, they cast him in the sea. *55*

But when Prahlāda hit the water, the ocean was set in motion and threw up a towering wave, causing floods in all directions. *56*

Seeing the whole world inundated, great sage, Hiraṇyakaśipu addressed the Daityas. *57*

Hiraṇyakaśipu:

'Cover this wicked child in the ocean, Varuṇa's realm, with all the rocks you Daityas find. Don't leave a single gap. *58*

Fire didn't burn him; weapons, serpents, poison, wind and magic all failed to harm him. *59*

Neither apparitions, nor falling from a height, nor elephants of the quarters could destroy this evil-minded child, but there's no point in allowing him to live. *60*

Let's keep him in the water under heaps of rocks for a thousand years—that should finish off the wretch!' *61*

The Daityas and the Dānavas then piled mountains on Prahlāda underwater, raising a heap that soared a thousand leagues. *62*

But at the time of his daily rites, from below the heap of rocks on the ocean floor, wise Prahlāda intently worshipped Viṣṇu who never fails. *63*

Prahlāda praises Viṣṇu

Prahlāda:

I bow to you, lotus-eyed deity. I bow to you, supreme being. I bow to you, heart of the world. I bow to you, wielder of the flaming discus. *64*

I bow to the deity of the pious, patron of the cattle and of brahmins, benefactor of the world. To Kṛṣṇa and to Govinda, I bow and bow again. *65*

In the form of Brahmā, you create the world. While it endures, you keep it. At the aeon's end, you take the form of Rudra. I bow to you, deity of threefold forms. *66*

Gods, yakṣas, demigods, siddhas, nāgas, gandharvas, kiṃnaras, piśācas, rākṣasas, humans and animals, *67*

Birds, inanimate things, ants and crawling creatures, earth, water, fire, sky, wind, sound, touch, taste, *68*

Form, smell, mind, intellect, ego, time and the qualities known as *guṇas*—you are the highest sense of these, as well as being all of these, eternal Viṣṇu. *69*

You are knowledge and you are ignorance, truth and falsehood, poison and nectar, the practice of rites and contemplation. You are the rituals determined by the Vedas. *70*

You are the beneficiary of all these acts and the means of their achievement. You are all this, Viṣṇu, and the result of every ritual. *71*

Your presence, Lord, which manifests power and virtue, is in me, in others, in all beings and all the worlds. *72*

Ascetics contemplate you, and those who offer sacrifices sacrifice to you. You alone enjoy oblations intended for gods and spirits, as you are one with them. *73*

Everything's encompassed in your great form, imperishable Lord, from which is born your subtle form, this world and other subtle forms, the fundamental elements and that which is known as the subtlest essence of them all. *74*

The form that is the highest goal beyond description of gross or subtle, something that surpasses thought, is also a form of yours. I bow to you in the form of the highest spirit. *75*

You who are at the heart of everything, I bow to your other form, the universal power in every being, abode of threefold *guṇas*, Lord of gods. *76*

I praise that supreme and heavenly power that lies beyond the reach of words and is not encompassed by the mind, but is perceptible to the wisdom of the wise. *77*

Oṃ! May I always bow to Vāsudeva, Lord. Nothing is distinct from him, but he's distinct from everything. *78*

I bow to him. I bow to him. I bow to that great being who has neither name nor form, and who alone is understood by the fact of his existence. *79*

I bow to that great being whose earthly forms are worshipped by the denizens of heaven, being blind to his supreme form. *80*

I bow to him who dwells in all, the lord who sees both good and evil, Viṣṇu, the universal witness and supreme master. *81*

Let us all bow down to Viṣṇu, who is no different from this world. May we all regard him as the first in every realm. May that imperishable being be favourable to me. *82*

May Hari, the universe's warp and weft, known as the everlasting deity and support of all creation, be favourable to me. *83*

Oṃ! I bow to Viṣṇu. I bow again and again to him in whom all this exists, from whom all this arises, who is all this, yet stands apart from it. *84*

Because that eternal being pervades all things, I am him. All this is born from me, I am all this, all this is in me, the everlasting being. *85*

I myself am indestructible and eternal, I'm the abode of the heart of the heart of everything. I'm the one called *brahman*, the Absolute, the highest being at the start and at the end. *86*

So ends Chapter Nineteen in Book One of the glorious Viṣṇu Purāṇa.

20. Prahlāda achieves liberation

Parāśara:

Thus contemplating Viṣṇu as unified with himself, brahmin, Prahlāda felt that he'd achieved the highest state of oneness with that eternal being. *1*

He forgot himself and knew of nothing else while thinking, 'I am indeed the unchanging, unending, highest spirit.' *2*

As the result of Prahlāda's practice of cultivating the deity and being cleansed in time of all his sins, eternal Viṣṇu, knowledge itself, filled his unsullied heart. *3*

When the Daitya Prahlāda, now one with Viṣṇu through the power of his practice, moved his limbs, Maitreya, those serpent-bonds all snapped at once. *4*

The boundless undulating ocean, with its surging hosts of monsters, was agitated, and all the world with mountains, groves and forests began to quake. *5*

Casting off the rocks the Daityas heaped on him, wise Prahlāda rose from the ocean depths. *6*

Beholding the world, the sky and everything else, he remembered who he was once more. *7*

Wise Prahlāda, firm and focused, sang further praises of the highest being who has no start, his body, voice and mind restrained. *8*

Prahlāda:

Oṃ! I bow to you, highest of all goals, gross and subtle, perishable and imperishable, visible and invisible, who transcends division, lord of all, free from faults, *9*

Bestower of qualities, source of qualities, free from qualities, abiding in qualities, formed and formless, gross and subtle, distinct and indistinct. *10*

You are fearsome and benign, knowledge and ignorance, eternal Lord, you are existence and nonexistence, and the cause of both, *11*

Permanent and impermanent, you are manifold elements and the unstained dwelling place of elements non-manifold. You are one and you are many. I bow to you, Vāsudeva, the primary cause of everything, *12*

Gross and subtle, evident and manifest. You are all creation and yet distinct from it. Everything arises from you, yet you are distinct from the cause of everything. I bow to you, the highest being. *13*

Parāśara:

While Prahlāda sang this praise, his mind on Viṣṇu, Lord Hari appeared before him, clad in yellow robes. *14*

Seeing him, Prahlāda was thrown into confusion, brahmin. He stood up and stammered repeatedly, 'I bow to Viṣṇu!' *15*

Prahlāda:

Lord, you take away the pain we feel. Be merciful to me, Keśava. Purify me further, eternal god, by looking down on me. *16*

The Lord:

I'm pleased with your unwavering devotion, Prahlāda. You may ask for anything you desire. *17*

Prahlāda:

Master, in whichever of myriad wombs I am reborn, may I always have undying faith in you. *18*

May that constant joy the undiscerning find in objects of the senses never leave my heart while contemplating you. *19*

The Lord:

You are indeed my devotee, Prahlāda, and will be so in future. Now ask for something else that you desire. *20*

Prahlāda:

As I was intent on praising you, my father was enraged. Lord, forgive the sins that he's committed. *21*

Weapons struck my body, I was thrown into a fire, I was bitten by his serpents and my food was laced with poison, *22*

I was bound and cast into the ocean where mountains were heaped upon me. These and other wicked deeds my father has committed. *23*

All this he did as I, your devotee, had angered him, so by your mercy, Lord, set my father free at once. *24*

The Lord:

By my mercy all will be as you desire, Prahlāda. I grant you yet another boon, so make a wish, you demon boy. *25*

Prahlāda:

Now you've granted me my wishes, I've done all I had to do, Lord. By your mercy, may my devotion never waver. *26*

What are virtue, wealth or love to one with freedom in his hands and whose faith in you, the root of all the worlds, is firm? *27*

The Lord:

Since your steady heart is filled with faith in me, you'll reach final liberation with my blessing. *28*

Parāśara:

So saying, Viṣṇu withdrew from sight before Prahlāda's eyes, Maitreya. The lad then approached his sire and paid homage at his feet. *29*

Hiraṇyakaśipu kissed Prahlāda's forehead and embraced the boy who had endured so much. 'You're alive, my son!' he cried as tears were glistening in his eyes, brahmin. *30*

That great demon, now regretful, showed affection to his son, and Prahlāda, who knew virtue, duly served his guru and his father. *31*

After Hiraṇyakaśipu was destroyed by Viṣṇu in the form of Narasiṃha, Maitreya, Prahlāda became the Daityas' lord. *32*

Having attained the glory of sovereignty through his pure deeds, brahmin, he had many sons and grandsons, and enjoyed great supremacy. *33*

When Prahlāda shed his worldly duties and transcended notions of good and evil, while contemplating the lord intently, he finally accomplished liberation. *34*

Such was the power of the prudent Daitya, Prahlāda, devotee of the lord, Maitreya, about whom you questioned me. *35*

The sins of one who hears the deeds of this great being are washed away at once. *36*

Hearing or narrating this account will free a man from misdeeds done by day or night, Maitreya. *37*

Reciting it when the moon is full or new, or on the eighth or twelfth day of the lunar month, brahmin, confers the same reward as the donation of a cow. *38*

Just as Hari shielded Prahlāda in his trials, he'll protect a person who listens to this tale. *39*

So ends Chapter Twenty in Book One of the glorious Viṣṇu Purāṇa.

21. Kaśyapa's descendants and the origin of the Maruts

Parāśara:

The sons of Prahlāda's brother Saṃhlāda were Āyuṣmant, Śibi and Bāṣkala. Prahlāda's son was Virocana, and Virocana's son was Bali.[27] *1*

Bali had one hundred sons, great sage, of whom Bāṇa was the eldest. The sons of Hiraṇyakaśipu's brother Hiraṇyākṣa were all mighty beings: *2*

Jharjhara, Śakuni, Bhūtasaṃtāpana, strong-armed Mahānābha and also Kālanābha. *3*

27 This chapter returns to the account of the sage Kaśyapa's descendants. The Daityas Hiraṇyakaśipu and Hiraṇyākṣa were Kaśyapa's sons with his second wife, Diti. The offspring of Kaśyapa's other wives are given below. I have added some names to improve clarity.

The sons of Kaśyapa's third wife, Danu, were Dvimūrdhan, Śaṃkara, Ayomukha, Śaṅkuśiras, Kapila, Śambara, *4*

Strong-armed Ekacakra, mighty Tāraka, Svarbhānu, Vṛṣaparvan and powerful Puloma. *5*

These, along with heroic Vipracitti, were the famous sons of Danu. *6*

Prabhā was the daughter of Svarbhānu. Śarmiṣṭhā was the daughter of Vṛṣaparvan, as were Upadānavī and Hayaśiras—all renowned and brilliant women. *7*

Danu's son Vaiśvānara had two daughters, Pulomā and Kālakā, both of whom were highly fortunate and married Mārīci. *8*

These two had sixty thousand sons with Mārīci, the excellent Dānavas known as the Paulomas and Kālakeyas. *9*

Other mighty, fearsome and pitiless sons were born to Vipracitti and Siṃhikā: *10*

Tryaṃśa, powerful Śalya, Nabha the strong, Vātāpi, Namuci, Ilvala, Khasṛma, *11*

Andhaka, Naraka, Kālanābha, heroic Svarbhānu and the great demon Vaktrayodhin. *12*

These were the best of the Dānavas who swelled the lineage of Danu and whose sons and grandsons numbered in the hundreds and thousands. *13*

The Nivātakavacas, purified through austere penances, also arose in the family of the Daitya Prahlāda. *14*

The six daughters of Kaśyapa's fourth wife, Tāmrā, renowned as mighty beings, were Śukī, Śyenī, Bhāsī, Sugrīvī, Śuci and Gṛdhrikā. *15*

Śukī gave rise to parrots, Ulūkī to crows, the natural enemies of owls, while Śyeni gave rise to hawks, Bhāsī to kites and Gṛdhrī to vultures. *16*

Śuci brought forth waterbirds, and Sugrīvī gave rise to horses, camels and donkeys. All these are known as the lineage of Tāmrā. *17*

Kaśyapa's fifth wife, Vinatā, bore two sons, famed Garuḍa and Aruṇa. Fair-winged Garuḍa, foremost of flying creatures, was the merciless devourer of serpents. *18*

His sixth wife, Surasā, gave rise to a thousand great many-headed snakes of boundless energy, brahmin, which coursed the sky. *19*

His seventh wife, Kadru, gave rise to the Kādravas, another thousand mighty serpents subject to fair-winged Garuḍa, brahmin, similarly many-headed. *20*

Chief among these were Śeṣa, Vāsuki, Takṣaka, Śaṅkaśveta, Mahāpadma and both Kambala and Aśvatara, *21*

Elāputra, Nāga, Karkoṭaka and Dhanaṃjaya—these and many other serpents full of venom. *22*

You also need to know about the host descended from Kaśyapa's eighth wife, Krodhavaśā: whether born on land, flying on the wing or living in water, all were pitiless carnivores with sharp teeth. *23*

His ninth wife, Surabhi, gave rise to cattle and buffalo, and Irā to varieties of trees and vines, grass and creepers everywhere. *24*

His tenth wife brought forth yakṣas and rākṣasas; his eleventh, Muni, bore apsarases; and his twelfth, Ariṣṭā, gave birth to the great gandharvas. *25*

These, then, are the renowned descendants of Kaśyapa, both moving and unmoving, whose sons and grandsons number in the hundreds of thousands. *26*

This creation took place in the second Manvantara, known as Svārociṣa, brahmin. In the present Manvantara, the Vaivasvata, while Brahmā was engaged in the great sacrifice initiated by Varuṇa, *27*

The so-called Prajāsarga or 'progeny creation' took place. In the age before this, Brahmā brought forth the Seven Sages from his mind. *28*

Now he brought them to the world as his own sons, and he himself became the grandsire of the gandharvas, serpents, deities and Dānavas, best of sages. *29*

Diti, who later lost her sons,[28] pleased Kaśyapa, and that foremost of ascetics, being fully gratified, then granted her a wish. *30*

She asked him for a son of boundless power, one capable of slaying Indra. *31*

That foremost sage allowed his wife her wish, and, having done so, Kaśyapa calmly said to her, *32*

---

28 Diti's sons were the demons known as Daityas, who were annihilated by the deities. Diti now sought revenge.

'Your son will conquer Indra if you're pure and steadfast and bear the infant in your womb for a hundred years with perfect love.' *33*

Having addressed that heavenly woman, sagacious Kaśyapa departed, and Diti, filled with faultless purity, then conceived a child. *34*

Mighty Indra, king of gods, knowing that the child was destined to destroy him, respectfully approached the woman to wait upon her. *35*

Indra, chastiser of the demon Pāka, remained in Diti's presence while waiting for a chance to thwart her, and, in the ninety-ninth year, the self-possessed deity saw an opportunity. *36*

Diti lay down to sleep one day, but forgot to wash her feet, and Indra entered her womb. *37*

With his vajra in his hand, he cut the mighty foetus into seven pieces. Sliced by Indra's weapon, the infant wailed most piteously. *38*

'Don't cry! *Mā rodīḥ*!' Indra said repeatedly, and, even though the foetus was already cut in seven, the deity's anger grew. *39*

Indra, scourge of enemies, then used his vajra to cut each piece into seven more. These became in time the speeding deities of the wind. *40*

Because mighty Indra said *mā rodīḥ*, they were called the Maruts, forty-nine in all, deity-companions to the bearer of the vajra. *41*

So ends Chapter Twenty-One in Book One of the glorious Viṣṇu Purāṇa.

22. Brahmā appoints sovereigns; Nature of the Absolute

Parāśara:

When Pṛthu had been anointed sovereign of the earth by the foremost sages, Brahmā, grandsire of the world, bestowed the other sovereignties in order. *1*

To Soma he gave sovereignty over the stars, planets, brahmins, all plant life, as well as sacrifices and austerities. *2*

He gave Vaiśravaṇa sovereignty over kings, and Varuṇa over waters. He made Viṣṇu lord of Ādityas and shining Agni lord of Vasus. *3*

He made Dakṣa lord of patriarchs, Indra lord of Maruts and Prahlāda lord of Daityas and Dānavas. *4*

He caused Yama, king of justice, to be anointed lord of *pitṛs*, the ancestral spirits, and made Airāvata lord of all the elephant kings. *5*

He made Garuḍa king of birds, Indra king of gods, Uccaiḥśravas lord of horses and Vṛṣabha king of cattle. *6*

He made Śeṣa lord of serpent kings, the lion the king of beasts and caused the sacred fig to be anointed king of forest trees. *7*

Having thus shared out sovereignties, Brahmā, lord of patriarchs, immediately appointed guardians for each direction. *8*

He caused the king Sudhanvan, son of the patriarch Vairāja, to be anointed guardian-king of the east. *9*

The son of the patriarch Kardama, Śaṅkhapada by name, was anointed king of the south. *10*

He had the great immortal Ketumant, son of Rajas, anointed king of the west. *11*

Hiraṇyaroman, son of the patriarch Parjanya, was anointed doughty king of the north. *12*

Even today, this whole world with its forests and seven continents is protected by these beings, realm by realm, in accord with virtue. *13*

All these and other sovereigns, invested with authority for the preservation of the world by mighty Viṣṇu, best of sages, *14*

As well as those to come in future and lords of creation in times gone by, are aspects of Viṣṇu, who himself is all creation, best of brahmins. *15*

Kings of gods and kings of Daityas, lords of Dānavas and flesh-eating demons, *16*

Lords of beasts and winged creatures, and lords of humankind and snakes and nāgas, *17*

Lords of trees and mountains and planets, those of the present, past and future—all these arise as aspects of Viṣṇu, who is all creation. *18*

None other than Hari, lord of all, wise sage, has the power to preserve the world. *19*

He creates this universe and, once it's made, he is the everlasting being who preserves it. In the form of the destroyer, he destroys it, filled in turn with energy, purity and the other quality, darkness. *20*

Four aspects of Viṣṇu

Janārdana appears in four aspects during the creation of the world, another four during its preservation and yet another four during final dissolution. *21*

During creation, one aspect is Brahmā, the manifest form of the unmanifest being. The second is the patriarch Marīci and the others. *22*

Time is the third aspect, and all other creatures are the fourth. Thus, he exists in four aspects during the creation of the world, having the quality of energy. *23*

In one aspect, Viṣṇu preserves creation; in another, he manifests as Manu and the patriarchs; and in yet another takes the form of Time. *24*

Manifesting in yet another aspect within all creatures, he comprises all the world. Taking on the quality of purity, he becomes *puruṣottama*, the highest spirit of the universe. *25*

Assuming the quality of darkness at the time of dissolution, the birthless lord manifests one aspect in the form of Rudra. *26*

Another aspect of Viṣṇu exists in the forms of Agni, Yama and the other gods. The third appears in the form of Time, and yet another is all creatures. *27*

Thus, this great deity exists in four aspects during the destruction of the world. This set of four aspects is called *sārvakālikī*, 'universal dissolution', brahmin. *28*

Brahmā, Dakṣa and the other patriarchs, Time and other creatures—these are manifestations of Hari's power and are the cause of the creation of the world. *29*

Viṣṇu is Manu and the progenitors, Time and other beings, brahmin. These are also manifestations of his power, and he himself is the cause of the preservation of the world. *30*

Rudra, Time, Yama, the other deities and all creatures are the fourfold manifestations of Janārdana's power for the destruction of the universe. *31*

At the beginning of the world, in the middle period and until its final dissolution, brahmin, the processes of creation are undertaken by the arranger Viṣṇu through the agency of Marīci, the patriarchs and other living creatures. *32*

In the beginning, Brahmā creates the world, then Marīci and the foremost patriarchs bring forth progeny unhindered, as do other creatures. *33*

But Brahmā cannot undertake creation without Time, brahmin, nor can the patriarchs or any other beings. *34*

Thus, these four aspects of Viṣṇu, god of gods, Maitreya, are essential for creation and destruction of the world. *35*

Anything brought forth by a living being, brahmin, is entirely Hari's body. *36*

Whatever destroys a creature, whether moving or unmoving, anywhere, Maitreya, is the destructive form of Janārdana, who brings an end to all. *37*

Janārdana is creator of the world, preserver, the world itself, its destroyer and universal lord. *38*

He exists in threefold forms during its creation, preservation and destruction, acting in accord with each of these three qualities, but his ultimate state is a higher one beyond all these. *39*

That fourfold form of the highest spirit consists of true knowledge, is all-pervading, unequalled and is comprehended by Viṣṇu himself alone. *40*

The nature of the Absolute

Maitreya:

Sage, duly describe for me the four forms of the Absolute, which is called the highest state. *41*

Parāśara:

The way to reach a goal is called the means, Maitreya, and that which one desires to reach is the goal itself. *42*

For an ascetic who yearns for liberation, breath control and other practices are the means, and his goal is the highest Absolute, from which there's no return. *43*

The knowledge on which ascetics rely for achieving liberation is discrimination. This, sage, is the first aspect of the Absolute as knowledge. *44*

The second aspect of the Absolute is the knowledge of causes, great sage, as it pertains to ascetics whose goal is liberation from all suffering. *45*

Knowledge of the inseparability and non-duality of both goal and means I call the third aspect. *46*

Knowledge that overcomes distinctions between the first three aspects, great sage, and reveals the true form of the Self, *47*

Which is free from action, inexpressible, omnipresent, unequalled, has self-understanding as its object and simply exists without characteristics, *48*

Which is tranquil, fearless, pure, difficult to comprehend and independent—that is called the highest state of Viṣṇu in the form of knowledge. *49*

Those ascetics who achieve absorption in that state by dispelling ignorance will never take root in worldly existence, brahmin, unlike seeds sown in a ploughed field. *50*

Such is the nature of the pure, eternal, universal, undecaying, faultless supreme state called Viṣṇu. *51*

The ascetic who reaches that highest Absolute knows no return. Transcending concepts of vice and virtue, he is free from suffering and is completely pure. *52*

Two states of the Absolute abide in all creation: one with form and the other without. One may perish, the other is eternal. *53*

The eternal is the highest Absolute, while the perishable form is all this world. Just as moonlight spreads in all directions though the moon itself stands still, so, too, does the power of the highest Absolute fill all the world. *54*

In that same regard, just as the intensity of light depends on distance from its source, Maitreya, the power of the Absolute is likewise. *55*

Brahmā, Viṣṇu and Śiva are the primary forms of the Absolute and are imbued with its power. Next come the lesser deities, Maitreya, and then Dakṣa and the other patriarchs, *56*

After these come humankind, cattle, wild beasts, birds and things that creep, each inferior to the one before, finally followed by trees and shrubs and all the others. *57*

Thus, this whole world, although imperishable and eternal, best of sages, appears and disappears as if subject to birth and death. *58*

Viṣṇu, who comprises all power, is the highest form of the Absolute. This is the form on which ascetics first meditate at the beginning of their practices. *59*

Perfect identity with the deity arises in an untroubled heart, fully one with the divine, which itself is dependent on the divine, sage, and which is endowed with the seed of the divine. *60*

Viṣṇu is superior to all those with power. He is identical with the Absolute and is the Absolute in form. Hari consists entirely of the Absolute, blessed sage. *61*

This whole world without exception is imbued with him, sage. It arises from him, abides in him and is indeed identical with him. *62*

Viṣṇu comprises all that's perishable and imperishable. He is the lord who bears this whole world of spirit and matter in the form of his ornaments and his weapons. *63*

Maitreya:

Kindly explain how Lord Viṣṇu thus upholds the world. *64*

Parāśara:

Having bowed down to mighty Viṣṇu, who's beyond all measure, I'll relate to you what the sage Vasiṣṭha once told me. *65*

Lord Hari wears the unblemished essence of the world, free from stains and qualities, as the Kaustubha jewel on his breast. *66*

Eternal Viṣṇu wears all primal matter in the whorl of hair, Śrīvatsa, on his chest. Primal intellect abides in Mādhava as his mace. *67*

The lord bears twofold individuation, consisting of the elements and the senses, in the form of his conch and bow. *68*

Viṣṇu carries primal mind, fickle and swifter than the wind, in the form of the discus he holds in his hand. *69*

The garland of fundamental elements, consisting of the elements themselves and their causes, is the fivefold wreath of victory, Vaijayantī, worn by the mace-bearing deity, brahmin. *70*

Janārdana bears all the faculties of perception and action in the form of his many arrows. *71*

The excellent sword of surpassing brilliance borne by the unfailing deity is knowledge: this is wisdom that may be sheathed in ignorance. *72*

In this way, primal spirit, matter, intellect, individuation, the elements, mind, all the senses, knowledge, ignorance and all the world, Maitreya, abide in Hṛṣīkeśa. *73*

Hari, who is formless and consists of illusion, adopts this form with weapons and adornments for the benefit of all living beings. *74*

The supreme lotus-eyed deity carries primal matter with its permutations, spirit and the universe. *75*

That which is knowledge and that which is ignorance, that which exists and that which does not—all this abides in eternal Madhusūdana, lord of all creation, Maitreya. *76*

The lord, boundless and eternal Hari, appears in the form of time consisting of subseconds, seconds, minutes, days, seasons, half-years and years. *77*

The lord upholds the seven realms of earth, sky, heaven, Mahar, Jana, Tapas and Satya, best of sages. *78*

Hari's form is the essence of the world, he is firstborn of all firstborn, foundation of all knowledge and stands alone. *79*

The lord, master of all, who has neither end nor body, abides in the manifold forms of creation as gods, mortals, beasts and others. *80*

The *Ṛg*, *Yajur*, *Sāma* and *Atharva Vedas*, the histories, the lesser Vedic texts and the declarations of the *Upaniṣads*, *81*

The Vedic supplements, *Manu* and other legal texts, lyrics, treatises, narratives, any texts for recital, *82*

Poetry, speech and song are all the body of great Viṣṇu in the form of sound. *83*

All things with and without form, here and elsewhere, are his body. *84*

'I am Hari. All this is Janārdana. There is no cause or effect other than him'—one whose mind is set on this will never be subjected to repeated rebirths. *85*

Such is the first part of this purāṇa, brahmin, which I've accurately recalled for you. Hearing this, you'll be freed from all misdeeds. *86*

A person acquires as much merit from listening to this, Maitreya, as from bathing in Puṣkara Lake on the full-moon day in the month of Kārttika for twelve consecutive years. *87*

To a person who hears this, the wish-granting gods bestow the status of a deity, sage, ancestral spirit, gandharva, yakṣa and the rest. *88*

So ends Chapter Twenty-Two in Book One of the glorious Viṣṇu Purāṇa.

End of Book One.

Book Two: The World

1. Priyavrata distributes the continents

Maitreya:

You've told me all about the creation of the universe in answer to my question, holy guru. *1*

But there's an aspect of creation you've recounted, best of sages, about which I'd like to hear some more. *2*

Svāyaṃbhuva had two sons, Priyavrata and Uttānapāda. Regarding these, you mentioned that Uttānapāda's son was Dhruva, *3*

But you've said nothing about Priyavrata's descendants, brahmin. I'd like to hear about them, if it pleases you to tell me. *4*

Parāśara:

Priyavrata married the daughter of Kardama. They had ten sons and two daughters, Samrāj and Kukṣi. *5*

The sons of Priyavrata were said to be wise, brave, gracious and dear to their father. Listen while I tell you the names by which they're known: *6*

Āgnīdhra, Agnibāhu, Vapuṣmant, Dyutimant, Medhas, Medhātithi, Bhavya, Savana and Putra. *7*

Jyotiṣmant, the 'Shining One', was tenth among them and was as brilliant as his name suggests, but all of Priyavrata's sons were famed for strength and courage. *8*

Three—namely, Medhas, Agnibāhu and Putra—were devoted to yoga. Remembering their former lives, these fortunate men didn't set their hearts on sovereignty. *9*

They remained ever selfless in all matters, sage, and performed sacrifices in accordance with propriety, not thinking of reward. *10*

Priyavrata divided the world into seven continents, best of sages, and gave one to each of his other seven great sons, Maitreya. *11*

Āgnīdhra received Jambūdvīpa from his father, fortunate seer. To Medhātithi, he gave another continent, Plakṣadvīpa. *12*

Vapuṣmant was anointed king of Śālmala, and holy Priyavrata made Jyotiṣmant king of Kuśadvīpa. *13*

Priyavrata also appointed Dyutimant as king of Krauñcadvīpa and made Bhavya lord over Śākadvīpa. *14*

That holy one made Savana king of Puṣkara. Āgnīdhra, who was king of Jambūdvīpa, best of sages, had nine sons, equal to the patriarchs: *15*

Nābhi, Kimpuruṣa, Harivarṣa, Ilāvṛta, Ramya, Hiraṇvant was the sixth, along with Kuru and Bhadrāśva. The other was Ketumāla, a king of virtuous conduct. *16*

Āgnīdhra divides Jambūdvīpa

Hear how Āgnīdhra divided Jambūdvīpa among his sons, brahmin: Nābhi was given the southern region of Himāhva by his father. *17*

Āgnīdhra gave Hemakūṭa to Kimpuruṣa. The third region, Naiṣadha, he gave to Harivarṣa. *18*

He gave the region centred on Mount Meru to Ilāvṛta, and the lands around Mount Nīla his father gave to Ramya. *19*

Hiraṇvant was given the region to the north of that, known as Śveta. *20*

The lands to the north of Śṛṅgavant he gave to Kuru, and he gave the region that lies east of Meru to Bhadrāśva. *21*

The region of Gandhamādana he gave to Ketumāla. This is how that king divided the regions among his sons. *22*

After that sovereign had enthroned his sons in each of these, Maitreya, he retired to the most auspicious site of Śālagrāma to undertake austerities. *23*

In the eight regions given to Kimpuruṣa and the others, great sage, achievement was spontaneous and happiness was effortless. *24*

They were free from misfortune and the woes of age and death. There was no distinction between vice and virtue, or between best, worst and middling. *25*

These eight regions never knew the cycle of ages. The region of Himāhvaya was ruled by the great Nābhi. With his queen, Merudevī, he had a brilliant son, Ṛṣabha. *26*

Ṛṣabha himself had a hundred sons, of whom Bharata was the eldest. Having ruled wisely and performed varied sacrifices, *27*

King Ṛṣabha placed his son heroic Bharata upon the throne, then that fortunate man retired to the ashram of Pulaha to undertake austerities. *28*

Following the prescription for those who retire to the forest, that resolute king duly performed austerities and instituted sacrifices. *29*

Wasted by his practices, he grew thin, his veins distended. Naked Ṛṣabha placed a pebble in his mouth and took the path of heroes. *30*

The kings of Bhārata

Because this region was given to Bharata by his father when he retired to the forest, it's known throughout the threefold worlds as Bhārata. *31*

Bharata had a most virtuous son, Sumati. After Bharata had successfully completed the required sacrifices, he bestowed the kingdom on his son. *32*

King Bharata, who delighted in the practice of yoga, sage, passed responsibility to his son and drew his final breath at Śālagrāma. *33*

In time, he was reborn a brahmin in a brilliant line of ascetics. I'll recount his exploits for you later, Maitreya. *34*

Brilliant Sumati had a son, Indradyumna. His son was Parameṣṭhin, and his son was Pratihāra. *35*

He had a son named Pratiharta. His son was Bhuva. Next came Udgītha. King Prastāva was his son. *36*

Then came Pṛthu, followed by Nakta. Nakta's son was Gaya. Nara was the son of Gaya. He had a son, Virāj. *37*

His son was heroic Dhīmant. Then came Mahānta, whose son was Manasyu. *38*

Then came Tvaṣṭṛ. Tvaṣṭṛ's son was Viraja, and his son was Raja. His son was Śatajit, who had a hundred sons, sage. *39*

Of these, Viśvagjyoti was the eldest. They all contributed to the growth of the population and shone like ornaments in the ninefold region of Bhārata. *40*

In former times, their descendants had possession of the land of Bhārata for seventy-one cycles of the ages, each consisting of the Kṛta, Tretā and the others. *41*

This was the period of creation under Manu Svāyaṃbhuva, who presided over the first Manvantara in the era known as Vārāha, sage, when this whole world was populated. *42*

So ends Chapter One in Book Two of the glorious Viṣṇu Purāṇa.

2. Jambūdvīpa, 'Land of the Rose-Apple Tree'

Maitreya:

Brahmin, you've told me about creation during the period of Svāyaṃbhuva. Now I'd like to hear from you about the entire circle of the earth, *1*

Including oceans, lands, regions, mountains, forests, lakes and the cities of the gods and other beings, sage, *2*

As well as the dimensions, support, nature and state of each. It befits you, sage, to describe all this. *3*

Parāśara:

Listen while I explain it all in brief, Maitreya, because I couldn't give you all the details even in a hundred years. *4*

Jambū, Plakṣa, Śālma, Kuśa, Krauñca and Śāka, with Puṣkara as the seventh, brahmin: *5*

These are the continents surrounded by seven oceans, of saltwater, syrup, wine, ghee, whey, milk and water, respectively. *6*

Jambūdvīpa is in the middle of these, and the golden mountain, Meru, is at the centre of that continent, Maitreya. *7*

Mount Meru stands eighty-four thousand leagues in height. *8*

It descends below the surface of the earth for a further sixteen thousand leagues, its summit is thirty-two thousand leagues across and the base of the mountain is fully sixteen thousand leagues wide. *9*

The world resembles a lotus flower with Mount Meru as the seed head at its heart. *10*

The mountain ranges Himavant, Hemakūṭa and Niṣadha are to the south of Meru, while Nīla, Śveta and Śṛṅgin lie northward. *11*

The two ranges closest to the centre are one hundred thousand leagues in length, while each of the others is successively ten thousand leagues shorter. They are all two thousand leagues high and two thousand wide. *12*

To the south of Meru, the first region is Bhārata, Kimpuruṣa is next, then comes another, Harivarṣa, brahmin. *13*

To the north of Meru is the region Ramya, followed by Hiraṇmaya and the Northern Kurus, whose position mirrors that of Bhārata. *14*

Each of these regions is nine thousand leagues wide, excellent brahmin, including Ilāvṛta, which has the towering golden mountain, Meru, at its centre. *15*

From the four sides of Meru, Ilāvṛta extends nine thousand leagues in each direction, fortunate brahmin, and there are four mountains in this region. *16*

Arranged like pillars around Mount Meru, each stands ten thousand leagues high. To the east is Mandara by name, to the south Gandhamādana, Vipula is on the western side and Supārśva is to the north. *17*

On each of these stands a tree, eleven hundred leagues across—a *kadamba*, a *jambū*, a *pippala* and a *vaṭa*, respectively—like banners on a mountain top. *18*

Jambūdvīpa is named for this *jambū*, a rose-apple tree, great sage, the fruits of which are as large as elephants. *19*

When they fall down upon the mountain, they split open and their juices form a river, the Jambūnadī, from which the residents of that region drink. *20*

As a result of drinking from the river, the people never sweat, smell bad, grow old or lose their senses, and their minds are always sharp. *21*

When the mud on the riverbank, coming into contact with the juice, is dried by pleasant breezes, it becomes the kind of gold that's known as *jāmbūnada* and is used in making jewellery for the siddhas. *22*

The region of Bhadrāśva lies east of Meru, Ketumāla is to the west, best of sages, and Ilāvṛta lies between them. *23*

The Caitraratha forest is also east of Meru, and the forest of Gandhamādana is to the south. Similarly, Vaibhrāja is to the west and Nandana to the north. *24*

The four lakes of Aruṇoda, Mahābhadra, Asitoda and Mānasa are always enjoyed by deities. *25*

The mountain ranges Śītāmbha, Kumanda, Kurarin, Mālyavant, with Vaikaṅka as the foremost, extend eastwards from Meru. *26*

The Trikūṭa, Śiśira, Pataṅga, Rucaka, Niṣadha and other ranges lie south. *27*

Śikhivāsas, Savaiḍūya, Kapila, Gandhamādana, with Jārudhi as the main one, are to the west. *28*

Śaṅkhakūṭa, Ṛṣabha, Haṃsa, Nāga, Kālañjana and others lie northward. These are situated in the regions around Mount Meru, including Jaṭhara. *29*

On the summit of Mount Meru is Brahmā's wondrous city, fourteen thousand leagues across, Maitreya, and renowned throughout the heavens. *30*

On all sides of that city, at the four cardinal points and the four intermediate ones, are the famed and excellent cities of Indra and other world-protecting deities. *31*

Here, the River Gaṅgā, which flows across the foot of Viṣṇu, having first bathed the face of the moon, cascades from the heavens on every side of Brahmā's city. *32*

After it has descended there, it flows in four directions as the Sītā, Alakanandā, Cakṣu and Bhadrā rivers, respectively. *33*

The Sītā flows eastwards through the sky from mountain to mountain, then crosses the eastern region of Bhadrāśva to the ocean. *34*

Similarly, the Alakanandā flows south to Bhārata, before dividing into seven streams and entering the ocean, great sage. *35*

The Cakṣu flows west past all the mountain ranges and, having reached the western region of Ketumāla, there joins the ocean. *36*

Likewise, the Bhadrā crosses the northern mountain ranges and the land of Northern Kurus to reach the ocean in that direction, great sage. *37*

Meru stands amid the Nīla, Niṣadha, Mālyavant and Gandhamādana mountains, like the seed head at the centre of a lotus. *38*

The Bhāratas, Ketumālas, Bhadrāśvas and the Kurus, like the petals of the lotus-world, lie beyond the limits of the mountains. *39*

Jaṭhara and Devakūṭa are two ranges that form a barrier extending north to south, meeting the Nīla and Niṣadha mountains. *40*

Gandhamādana and Kailāsa stretch east and west, eighty leagues in width, from sea to sea. *41*

The two ranges Niṣadha and Pāriyātra also form barriers to the west of Meru, as do those on the east. *42*

Triśṛṅga and Jārudhi, two regional ranges in the north, also extend east and west from sea to sea. *43*

Thus, I've described for you, best of sages, the mountain ranges of Jaṭhara and the rest, which, in pairs, form barriers on the sides of Meru. *44*

The chains of mountains on each side of Meru that I've mentioned, such as Śītā, are exceedingly delightful, sage. The valleys found between these ranges, inhabited by siddhas and cāraṇas, are pleasant, as are the forests and the cities. *45*

There the excellent sanctuaries of Lakṣmī, Viṣṇu, Agni, Sūrya and other deities, best of sages, are frequented by the foremost kiṃnaras. *46*

Gandharvas, yakṣas, rākṣasas, Daityas and Dānavas disport themselves both day and night in those splendid valleys. *47*

These regions are like heaven on earth and are the abode of the righteous, sage. Evildoers may not approach them, even after a hundred rebirths. *48*

In the region of Bhadrāśva, Lord Viṣṇu dwells in the form of horse-headed Hayaśiras, brahmin. He takes the form of a boar in Ketumāla and a tortoise in Bhārata. *49*

Govinda takes the form of a fish in the land of Kurus, but Janārdana of universal form is in fact everywhere, and Hari, the universal being, is master of all. *50*

He is the foundation of everything, Maitreya, and lies at the heart of all. *51*

The other eight regions beginning with Kimpuruṣa are free from pain, fatigue, anxiety, hunger, calamities and other woes, great sage. *52*

Their inhabitants are healthy, fearless, free from suffering and live for ten or twelve millennia. *53*

The rain god Indra has no need to provide showers in those regions as there is sufficient water on the ground, nor are they subject to the cycles of the ages, Kṛta, Tretā and the others. *54*

In each of these regions are seven mountain ranges, best of brahmins, where hundreds upon hundreds of rivers rise. *55*

So ends Chapter Two in Book Two of the glorious Viṣṇu Purāṇa.

3. The land of Bhārata

Parāśara:

The region north of the ocean and south of the Himālaya, known as Bhārata, is inhabited by Bharata's descendants. *1*

Nine thousand leagues across, great sage, it's where those who reach heaven or liberation do their deeds. *2*

Mahendra, Malaya, Sahya, Śuktimant, Ṛkṣparvata, Vindhya and Pāriyātra are the seven mountain ranges. *3*

From this region one may ascend to heaven or win liberation, sage, but folk are also born as animals or descend to hell. *4*

From Bhārata, heaven, liberation, somewhere in between or an end are possible. No other region is given to the deeds of mortals. *5*

Listen to the nine divisions of the land of Bhārata: Indradvīpa, Kaśeru, Tāmraparṇa, Gabhastimant, *6*

Nāgadvīpa, Saumya, Gāndharva and Vāruṇa. The ninth of these is Dvīpa, surrounded by the ocean. *7*

Dvīpa is a thousand leagues from north to south. At the eastern edge of Bhārata are the Kirātas and in the west the Yavanas. *8*

In the centre are brahmins, kṣatriyas, vaiśyas and śūdras, engaged in their respective occupations of sacrifice, warfare, commerce and service. *9*

The Śatadrū, Candrabhāga and other rivers flow from the foot of the Himalāya. Others, most importantly the Vedasmṛti, arise in the Pāriyātra ranges, sage. *10*

The Narmadā, Surasā and others flow from the Vindhya mountains, while the Tāpī, Payoṣṇī and Nirvindhyā are the major rivers issuing from the Ṛkṣa ranges. *11*

The Godāvarī, Bhīmarathī, Kṛṣṇaveṇī and other streams that arise at the foot of the Sahya mountains assuage the sins of people and their fears. *12*

The Kṛtamālā and Tāmraparṇī are the largest rivers flowing from the Malaya ranges. The Trisāmā, Cāryakulyā and others arise in the Mahendra mountains. *13*

The Ṛṣikulyā, Kumārā and others flow from the foot of the Śaktimant ranges.[1] There are thousands of other streams besides, both great and small. *14*

The Kuru, Pāñcāla and other peoples inhabit the central districts. The easterners include the residents of Kāmarūpa. *15*

Puṇḍras, Kaliṅgas, Magadhas and others live in the southern reaches. To the west are the Saurāṣṭras, Śūras, Bhīras and Arbudas. *16*

The Kārūṣas and Mālavas inhabit the Pāriyātra mountains. The Sauvīras, Saindhavas, Hūṇas, Sālvas and the inhabitants of Śākala, *17*

The Madras, Rāmas, Ambaṣṭhas, Pārasīkas and others drink the waters of these rivers and reside permanently in their vicinity, enjoying great prosperity. These rivers are populated by peoples, affluent and happy. *18*

Here in the region of Bhārata, the fourfold ages of Kṛta, Tretā, Dvāpara and Kali are experienced, great sage, but nowhere else. *19*

Ascetics perform austerities, the devout conduct sacrifices and make donations with piety, all for the sake of the next world. *20*

In Jambūdvīpa, people always worship Viṣṇu, the spirit of the sacrifice and practice itself, with such rituals, but on other continents, he's revered in other ways. *21*

Furthermore, in all of Jambūdvīpa, Bhārata is the perfect region, great sage, because it alone is fit for sacrificial action, the others being set on pleasure. *22*

A being is reborn in Jambūdvīpa in human form, best of sages, from merit won in a thousand thousand lifetimes. *23*

1 The critical edition lists the river Ṛṣikulyā twice. I have followed the Gītā Press edition, which gives 'Cāryakulyā' in the place of the first occurrence of Ṛṣikulyā.

The deities themselves have sung this song: 'More fortunate than the gods are those who live in Bhārata, the land that leads to heaven and beyond. *24*

Dedicating all their practice, never thinking of reward, to Viṣṇu, the highest spirit, and having reached that land of sacrificial action, they go forth unstained to liberation. *25*

We do not know where we'll be born when the karma that gave us heaven has expired. Fortunate indeed are those who are born in Bhārata with all their senses sharp.' *26*

I've described in brief to you, Maitreya, the land of Jambūdvīpa, with its nine regions, one hundred thousand leagues across. *27*

Jambūdvīpa is ringed by an ocean of salty water, Maitreya, as wide as the land it girds. *28*

So ends Chapter Three in Book Two of the glorious Viṣṇu Purāṇa.

4. Plakṣadvīpa and the other continents

Parāśara:

Just as the land called Jambūdvīpa is ringed by an ocean of salty water, that ocean is surrounded by the land of Plakṣadvīpa, the 'Land of the Pipal Tree'. *1*

Jambūdvīpa is one hundred thousand leagues across, brahmin, and Plakṣadvīpa is said to be twice as wide again. *2*

Medhātithi, lord of Plakṣadvīpa, had seven sons, the eldest of whom was Śāntabhaya, followed by Śiśira, *3*

Sukhodaya, Ānanda, Śiva and Kṣemaka, with Dhruva as the seventh among them. All became rulers of Plakṣadvīpa. *4*

The region named for its sovereign Śāntabhaya is the first, followed by Śiśira, Sukhada, Ānanda, Śiva, Kṣemaka and Dhruva. *5*

The borders of each region are formed by seven ranges. Listen to their names, best of sages: *6*

Gomeda, Candra, Nārada, Dundubhi, Somaka and Sumanas, with Mount Vaibhāja as the seventh. *7*

In these pleasant ranges and the regions dwell blameless inhabitants, always in the company of deities and *gandharvas*. *8*

In these locales are auspicious settlements whose residents enjoy long lives, free from pain and illness, always living happily. *9*

The seven regions each have a river flowing to the sea. I'll tell you all their names, as hearing them will wash away your sins: *10*

Anutaptā, Śikhī, Vipāśā, Tridivā, Kramu and Amṛtā, with Sukṛtā as the seventh—such are the rivers found there. *11*

I've told you about the mountains and the major rivers, but there are thousands of lesser chains and streams from which the inhabitants always delight in drinking. *12*

In those seven regions, lifespans never shrink or grow, brahmin, as the cycle of four ages is unknown. *13*

There, it's always like the Tretā age, great sage. The inhabitants of the five continents between Plakṣadvīpa and Śākadvīpa, brahmin, *14*

Live healthy lives for five millennia. On these five continents, occupations are determined by one's community and stage of life. *15*

There are four orders in Plakṣadvīpa; listen while I name them for you: *16*

The Āryakas, Kuraras, Viviṃśas and Bhāvins are like our brahmins, kṣatriyas, vaiśyas and śūdras. *17*

There's one huge tree in the middle of Plakṣadvīpa, best of sages, as big as the *jambū*, called the *plakṣa* or pipal, hence its name. *18*

All the communities there, beginning with the Āryakas, worship Lord Hari, the universal creator of the world and master of all, in the form of Soma the Moon. *19*

Plakṣadvīpa is girt by a circular sea of syrup, as wide as the continent itself. *20*

Śālmaladvīpa, 'Land of the Cottonwood Tree'

I've briefly described the land of Plakṣadvīpa for you, Maitreya. Now you'll hear about Śālmala from me. *21*

The lord of Śālmala is the hero Vapuṣmant. Listen to the names of his sons, which are also the names of the seven regions: *22*

Śveta, Harita, Jīmūta, Rohita, Vaidyuta, Mānasa and Suprabha, great sage. *23*

The sea of syrup is ringed by the land of Śālmala, twice as wide as the sea itself. *24*

This continent also has seven ranges, the source of jewels, which divide the regions, in addition to seven rivers: *25*

Kumuda, Unnata, Balāhaka is the third, Mount Droṇa the great source of healing plants is fourth, *26*

Kaṅka is the fifth, Mahiṣa the sixth and Kukudmant the seventh splendid mountain. Now you'll hear the rivers' names from me: *27*

Yonī, Toyā, Vitṛṣṇā, Candrā, Śuklā and Vimocanī, with Nivṛtti as the seventh—all of which are thought to wash away one's sins. *28*

Śveta, Harita, Jīmūta, Rohita, Vaidyuta, Mānasa and especially the lovely Suprabha are the seven regions. There are also four communities. *29*

Those who inhabit Śālmala, great sage, are the Kapilas, Aruṇas, Pītās and Kṛṣṇas,[2] like our brahmins, kṣatriyas, vaiśyas and śūdras. *30*

The pious population worships everlasting Viṣṇu, heart of all who constitutes the sacrifice, in the form of Vāyu, god of winds, with finest sacrifices. *31*

Here in this very pleasant land, whose denizens enjoy the company of gods, there is a great *śālmali*, a cottonwood tree, bestowing perfect bliss. *32*

Śālmala is ringed by a sea of wine as wide as the land itself. *33*

This sea of wine is ringed by the land of Kuśadvīpa, twice as wide as Śālmala. *34*

Kuśadvīpa, 'Land of *Kuśa*-Grass'

In Kuśadvīpa, King Jyotiṣmant had seven sons. Listen to their names: *35*

Udbhida, Veṇumant, Svairatha, Lambana, Dhṛti, Prabhākara and Kapila. These are also the names of the seven regions there. *36*

In that land, people dwell with deities, Daityas, Dānavas, gandharvas, yakṣas, kimpuruṣas and the rest. *37*

Here are also four communities, each devoted to their duties: Damins, Śuṣmins, Snehas and Mandehas, great sage, *38*

2 The names of the four communities of Śālmala literally mean 'brown', 'red', 'yellow' and 'black'.

Corresponding to our brahmins, kṣatriyas, vaiśyas and śūdras. *39*

Because they undertake prescribed responsibilities, and in order to escape their earthly tasks, there on Kuśadvīpa, while worshipping Janārdana in the form of Brahmā, they abandon deeds that would otherwise result in further tedious duties.[3] *40*

Vidruma, Hemaśaila, Dyutimant, Puṣpavant, Kuśeśaya and Hari, with Mount Mandata as the seventh— *41*

These are the seven ranges that divide the regions of that land, great sage. Now listen to the names of the seven streams in turn: *42*

Dhūtapāpā, Śivā, Pavitrā, Saṃmati, Vidyudambhā, Mahī and Sarvapāpaharā, *43*

In addition, there are thousands of lesser streams and mountains. Kuśadvīpa is thought to be named for a clump of *kuśa*-grass that grows there. *44*

It's ringed by a sea of ghee as wide as the land itself. That sea is then enclosed within the land of Krauñcadvīpa. *45*

Krauñcadvīpa, 'Land of Cranes'

Now you'll hear about that other continent, Krauñcadvīpa, fortunate sage, twice as wide as Kuśadvīpa. *46*

On Krauñcadvīpa, King Dyutimant had seven great sons, after whom he named its regions: *47*

Kuśala, Manuga, Uṣṇa, Pīvara, Andhakāraka, Muni and Dundubhi—such were his seven sons, sage. *48*

There are also pleasant mountain ranges between each region, inhabited by gods and gandharvas. Listen to their names: *49*

Krauñca, Vāmana, Andhakāraka is the third, the fourth is jewel-bearing Svāhinī, which resembles a horse, Divāvṛt is the fifth, then comes Puṇḍarīkavant, *50*

And then the great mountain Dundubhi. Just as each land is twice as wide as the one before it, each of these mountains is twice as high as the preceding one. *51*

3 That is, they are released from further rebirths.

In all these pleasant regions, and in the ranges that divide them, dwell communities free from worry and attended by hosts of deities. *52*

Their Puṣkaras, Puṣkalas, Dhanyas and Tiṣyas, great sage, are like our brahmins, kṣatriyas, vaiśyas and śūdras. *53*

Now, Maitreya, you'll hear about the seven major rivers from which they drink, but there are also smaller rivers by the hundred: *54*

Gaurī, Kumudvatī, Saṃdhyā, Rātri, Manojavā, Khyāti and Puṇḍarīkā are the seven rivers of those regions. *55*

Here, too, Lord Janārdana is worshipped by the Puṣkaras and other orders in the form of Rūdra, with offerings made in sacrifices. *56*

Krauñcadvīpa is ringed all round by a sea of whey as wide as the land itself. *57*

This sea is surrounded by Śākadvīpa, sage, which is twice as wide as Krauñcadvīpa. *58*

Śākadvīpa, 'Land of the Teak Tree'

Bhavya, the overlord of Śākadvīpa, had seven sons, to whom he gave the regions of his land: *59*

Jalada, Kumāra, Sukumāra, Maṇīcaka, Kusumoda and Sumodāki, with Mahādruma as the seventh. *60*

The seven regions, all named after these seven sons, are divided by seven ranges: *61*

The first is Udayagiri, then Jaladhāra, Raivataka, Śyāma, Ambhogiri, Āmbikeya and delightful Kesarī, that excellent mountain, brahmin. *62*

On that continent is a giant *śāka*—teak—enjoyed by siddhas and gandharvas. The touch of the breeze that passes through its leaves yields excellent refreshment. *63*

There are pleasant settlements wherein dwell the four communities, and auspicious rivers that wash away all sins: *64*

Sukumārī, Kumārī, Nalinī, Veṇukā, Ikṣu and Dhenukā, with Gabhastī as the seventh. *65*

There are also tens of thousands of lesser streams, great sage, and myriad mountains. *66*

The residents of Jalada and other regions descend from heaven to the earth to drink from these very rivers and, having done so, are refreshed. *67*

Virtue is never lacking in these seven lands, nor are the inhabitants jealous of one another, nor do they transgress the boundaries of propriety. *68*

The Magas, Māgadhas, Mānasas and Mandagas are the four communities. The Magas are in general like our brahmins, the Māgadhas our kṣatriyas, the Mānasas our vaiśyas and the Mandagas śūdras. *69*

In Śākadvīpa, the communities I mentioned worship Viṣṇu in the form of Sūrya the Sun, sage, with perfect rituals, while holding themselves in check. *70*

Śākadvīpa is ringed by a sea of milk as wide as the land itself, Maitreya, as if by a bracelet. *71*

Puṣkara, 'Land of the Banyan Tree'

The sea of milk is girt by the land called Puṣkara, brahmin, which is twice as wide as Śākadvīpa. *72*

On Puṣkara, King Savana had but a pair of sons, Mahāvīra and Dhātika, and he named the regions of the continent after them: one Mahāvīra, the other Dhātakī. *73*

The land has a single range of mountains dividing the regions, known as Mānasottara, blessed sage, which rings the centre of the continent like a bangle. *74*

This circular range, fifty thousand leagues in height and fifty thousand wide, *75*

Forms a ring in the middle of Puṣkara and divides the island down its centre, sage, being located in such a way that it separates the regions. *76*

Thus, each region, as well as the range itself, is shaped like a bracelet. *77*

This continent's inhabitants live for ten millennia, free from sorrow and disease, knowing neither enmity nor passion. *78*

They have no concept of worse or better, nor are there killers or killed, brahmin, nor is there jealousy, envy, anger, greed or malice. *79*

The region of Mahāvīra lies beyond the Mānasottara range, while the Dhātakī region, inhabited by deities, Daityas and the rest, lies within it. *80*

Ideas of right and wrong remain unknown in the land called Puṣkara, nor are there rivers or other ranges in this land of just two regions. *81*

All its people resemble deities, *82*

And need not follow the codes of practice otherwise prescribed for every order and stage of life, but are free from the need to practise virtue. The threefold Vedas, governance, trade and servitude are equally unknown. *83*

These two regions are like the highest heaven on earth, Maitreya, and seasons are always pleasant, sage, as Puṣkara, Dhātakī and Mahāvīra are free from the woes of age and sickness. *84*

The banyan tree that grows on Puṣkara is the preferred abode of Brahmā. There he dwells while worshipped by gods and demigods alike. *85*

Puṣkara is ringed by a sea of fresh water as wide as the land itself. *86*

Each of the seven continents is thus surrounded by an ocean, and each continent and ocean is twice as wide as the one that it encloses. *87*

The volume of all these oceans is unchanging, and is never more or less, *88*

But just as water in a cauldron seems to rise when it begins to seethe, best of sages, so, too, the waters of the oceans rise with the waxing of the moon. *89*

The waters rise and fall without changing in their volume, in response to the rising and setting of the moon during the light and darker fortnights. *90*

A tidal range of five hundred and ten inches has been observed in these oceans, great sage.[4] *91*

On the continent of Puṣkara, all inhabitants partake of food of sixfold flavours, brahmin, which arises of its own accord. *92*

Beyond the ocean of fresh water is the land at the end of the world. It's twice as wide as the ocean within it, but this realm, made of gold, is quite bereft of life. *93*

The Lokāloka mountain range is ten thousand leagues in length and ten thousand high. *94*

The space beyond the range is cloaked in utter darkness, and beyond the darkness everything lies within the shell of the cosmic egg. *95*

4 Wilson notes drily: 'Although the Hindus seem to have had a notion of the cause of the tides, they were not very accurate observers of the effect' (1961: 166).

This universe, including the outer shell, the lands, the seas and ranges, sage, is five hundred million leagues across. *96*

It's the mother and the nursemaid of every host of beings, Maitreya, and foundation of all the worlds. *97*

So ends Chapter Four in Book Two of the glorious Viṣṇu Purāṇa.

5. The lower realms; The serpent Śeṣa

Parāśara:

I've described the upper realms for you, brahmin, which rise for seventy thousand leagues, they say. *1*

Each of the lower realms descends ten thousand leagues: Atala, Vitala, Nitala, Gabhastimat, Mahākhya and Sutala, best of sages, with the foremost one, Pātāla, as the seventh. *2*

Those realms, whose surfaces are white, black, brown, yellow, sand, stone and gold, are beautified with gracious mansions. *3*

Clans of Dānavas and Daityas dwell there in the hundreds, great sage, as well as tribes of mighty nāgas. *4*

Nārada, who had visited the lower realms, declared amid the gods' assembly that the underworlds were even more magnificent than those above: *5*

'What can compare with Pātāla, where the nāgas wear jewellery made with lovely gems that shine so brightly? *6*

Who wouldn't delight in Pātāla, ornamented here and there by Dānava and Daitya girls? Even a liberated being would revel in it.' *7*

The rays of the sun shed light, not heat, by day, and at night the moon is bright yet isn't cool.[5] *8*

Danu's offspring never notice time is passing, addicted as they are to entertainments, delighting there in food and drink and other pleasures. *9*

There are forests, rivers, lovely lakes and lily-pools where the pleasant air resounds with calls of koel cocks. *10*

5 Just as the rays of the sun are hot, the rays of the moon are said to be cooling.

There are brilliant decorations, rarest scents and lotions, brahmin, and the sounds of lute and pipe, clarion and tabour. *11*

These and other noble pleasures are enjoyed by Dānavas, Daityas and nāgas who inhabit Pātāla. *12*

The serpent Śeṣa

Below the lower realms lies the darker form of Viṣṇu known as Śeṣa, whose qualities even Dānavas and Daityas can't describe. *13*

The siddhas call him Ananta ('Endless'), and the gods and heavenly sages worship him. He has a thousand heads and bears the swastika, the purest transcendental mark. *14*

On his hood myriad jewels shine forth in all directions as he robs the demons of their power, to benefit the world. *15*

His eyes are always glowing with excitement, he sports a single earring, a diadem and a garland, and blazes like a hill of silver flames. *16*

Clad in blue and wild with bliss, Śeṣa wears a pearly necklace and rears up like cloud-capped Kailāsa with the river Gaṅgā flowing down its flanks. *17*

Wielding mace and ploughshare in his hands, he's attended by the goddess Vāruṇī, who embodies his own splendour. *18*

At the end of every aeon, Rudra, who's one with Saṃkarṣaṇa,[6] ablaze with fire and venom, emerges from the mouths of Śeṣa to devour the threefold worlds. *19*

Wearing this whole universe as a crown upon his head, Śeṣa rests beneath Pātāla while all the deities worship him. *20*

Even the thirteen gods themselves cannot describe or grasp his splendour, strength, form or nature. *21*

Who can speak of the might of one who wears the universe, glowing in the brilliance of his jewelled hood, as if it were a garland? *22*

When Ananta yawns and flashes his eyes with fury, the earth, mountains, waters and forests tremble. *23*

---

6 Saṃkarṣaṇa is Kṛṣṇa's elder brother, also known as Baladeva, Balarāma and Balabhadra. Elsewhere, Śeṣa himself, as opposed to Rudra, is said to be a form of Baladeva (see 5.18.36).

Gandharvas, apsarases, siddhas, kiṃnaras, nāgas and cāraṇas never reach the end of praising his qualities. That's why he's called imperishable endless one. *24*

Sandal powder, ground at the hands of nāga women, is always carried by his breath and scents the air in all directions. *25*

Having worshipped Śeṣa, the ancient sage named Garga gained true knowledge of astrology and all the benefits to be gained from understanding omens. *26*

With his serpent strength, he bears the world upon his head, while wearing realms of gods and demigods and mortals like a garland. *27*

So ends Chapter Five in Book Two of the glorious Viṣṇu Purāṇa.

6. The hell realms

Parāśara:

Now hear about the hell realms, brahmin, which lie beneath the earth and oceans, and into which the wicked fall, great sage. *1*

Raurava, Sūkara, Rodha, Tāla, Viśasana, Mahājvāla, Taptakumbha, Lavaṇa, Vilohita, *2*

Rudhirāmbhas, Vaitaraṇī, Kṛmiśa, Kṛmibhojana, Asipatravana, Kṛṣṇa, Lālābhakṣa, Dāruṇa, *3*

Pūyavaha, Pāpa, Vahnijvāla, Adhaḥśiras, Saṃdaṃśa, Kṛṣṇasūtra, Tamas, Avīci, *4*

Śvabhojana, Apratiṣṭha and another called Avīci—these are just the first few hells of dreadful suffering, but there are others. *5*

Those who delight in wickedness fall into Yama's realm, filled with fearsome fires and weapons. *6*

A dishonest witness who lies because of partiality and one who utters any other falsehood goes to Raurava, 'Fearful'. *7*

One who performs abortions, best of sages, or kills his guru or a cow goes to the hell of Rodha, 'Suppression', as does the strangler. *8*

One who drinks liquor, kills a brahmin or steals another's gold goes to Sūraka, 'Swine', along with his accomplices. *9*

One who kills a kṣatriya or a vaiśya goes to Tāla, the 'Palm Tree', as does one who violates his guru's marriage bed. One who molests his sister or kills a royal emissary goes to Taptakumbha, the 'Heated Cauldron'. *10*

Purveyors of virtuous women, prison guards and horsetraders fall into Taptaloha, 'Red-Hot Iron', as does one who forsakes his devotees. *11*

A man who violates his daughter or daughter-in-law is cast into Mahājvāla, the 'Great Inferno', as is the lowly wretch who disrespects or scorns his gurus. *12*

One who reviles or sells the Vedas, brahmin, or has improper sexual contacts goes to Lavaṇa, the 'Salty Hell'. *13*

The thief and he who crosses moral boundaries fall into Vimoha, 'Confusion'. *14*

One who despises deities, brahmins or his father and one who damages any gemstone go to Kṛmibhakṣa, 'Worms-for-Food'. The practitioner of black magic goes to Kṛmiśa, 'Insect Hell'. *15*

The wretch who eats before his father, deities or guests goes to frightful Lālābhakṣa, 'Saliva-for-Food', while arrow-makers go to Vedhaka, 'Piercing'. *16*

Those who manufacture missiles with barbs, swords or other weapons fall into the terrible hell of Viśasana, 'Vivisection'. *17*

One who accepts improper gifts goes to Adhomukha, 'Upside-Down', as do those who sacrifice to unworthy beings or point at constellations. *18*

Headstrong men and those who gorge on delicacies alone end up in Pūyavaha, 'River of Pus'. *19*

A brahmin selling cochineal, or meat, or wine, or sesame or salt goes to that same hell realm, brahmin. *20*

Those who feed cats, chickens, goats, horses, pigs or birds, best of brahmins, also go to the 'River of Pus'. *21*

Actors, fishermen, those who marry bastards, poisoners, informers, men who prostitute their wives, brahmins who have sex on days of abstinence, *22*

Arsonists, those who murder friends, fortune tellers and those who sacrifice for rustics fall into Rudhirāndha, the 'Well of Blood', as do those purveying soma. *23*

All those who destroy a beehive or a village go to Vaitaraṇī, 'Hard-to-Cross'. *24*

Trespassers and those obsessed by wealth or youth go to Kṛṣṇa, the 'Black Hell', as do debauchees and liars. *25*

Those who cut down trees for no good purpose go to Asipatravana, the 'Sword-Leaf Forest', while shepherds and deer-hunters fall into Vahnijvāla, the 'Blazing Fire'. *26*

The potter who fires a kiln, brahmin, goes to that same end. *27*

One who breaks his vows descends to torment in Saṃdaṃśa, the 'Hell of Pincers', as does one who shirks the duties of his stage of life. *28*

Students of religion who ejaculate while napping and those who learn the scriptures from their children fall into Śvabhojana, 'Dogs-for-Food'. *29*

These and others are among the hundreds and thousands of hell realms where evildoers are cooked and otherwise tormented. *30*

Just as these and other misdeeds number in the myriad, there are myriad hell realms to be suffered by the guilty. *31*

Those who perform actions contrary to the duties of their order or their stage of life, whether in thought or word or deed, all go to hell. *32*

Those condemned to hell look up at gods in heaven, then hang their heads, while gods look down on all those suffering beings. *33*

Immobile things, insects, fish, birds, animals, humans, sages, the thirteen great deities and liberated beings— *34*

Each successive stage is a thousand times as good as the one before, fortunate sage. All beings must pass through these until attaining liberation. *35*

There are as many beings in heaven as there are in hell, and the evildoer who neglects atonement will surely finish there. *36*

Meditation on Viṣṇu as atonement

After consideration, the greatest sages pronounced atonements fit for every sin. *37*

Svāyaṃbhava and other experts in such matters proclaimed dire punishments for major crimes and lesser ones for minor sins. *38*

But setting one's heart on Kṛṣṇa is superior to every other penitence, including austerity and sacrifice. *39*

For one who rues a deed he's done, remembering Hari is alone the best atonement. *40*

One who sets his heart on Nārāyaṇa morning, noon and night, and at dawn and dusk, is at once absolved of all his sins. *41*

Recalling Viṣṇu, all accumulated sins are shed and one reaches liberation. For such a person, even heaven is accounted an impediment. *42*

For one whose heart is set on Vāsudeva while praying, sacrificing or worshipping, Maitreya, even rewards including sovereignty over gods become an obstacle. *43*

'On one hand is ascent to highest heaven whence one must fall to earth again; on the other, one may pray to Vāsudeva'—such is the excellent seed that leads to liberation. *44*

Hence, a person recalling Viṣṇu day and night avoids the realms of hell, sage, and is pure, as all his sins are swept away. *45*

Heaven is that which delights the mind, and hell its opposite, best of brahmins, and deeds both good and bad are simply forms of those two realms. *46*

Because a single thing may cause both pain and pleasure, rage and envy, where is its essential nature? *47*

That which renders pleasure now gives rise to future pain. That which makes us angry now may later bring us peace. *48*

Nothing is in essence painful or enjoyable; only responses in our minds are marked by such sensations. *49*

Knowledge alone is the highest Absolute, but knowledge also binds us. This whole world consists of that, to which nothing is superior. *50*

Understand that knowing and not knowing are both aspects of knowledge, Maitreya. *51*

I've thus described the universe for you, brahmin, with its lower realms and hells. *52*

The oceans, mountains, regions, lands and rivers have all been described in brief. What would you like to hear of next? *53*

So ends Chapter Six in Book Two of the glorious Viṣṇu Purāṇa.

7. The upper spheres; The power of Viṣṇu

Maitreya:

You have indeed described all this to me, brahmin, but now I wish to hear about Bhuvarloka, sage, and the other upper realms. *1*

I'd also like to hear in detail about the nature of the planets and their dimensions, blessed seer. Kindly answer these questions of mine. *2*

Parāśara:

The region touched by rays of sun and moon is the earthly realm, with its rivers, seas and mountains. *3*

The realm of the sky is the same shape and size as that of the earth, brahmin. *4*

The sun is a hundred thousand leagues above the earth, Maitreya, and the moon is an equal distance above the sun. *5*

All the lunar mansions lie a hundred thousand leagues beyond the moon. *6*

Prudent Mercury lies two hundred thousand leagues above the lunar mansions, brahmin, and hasty Venus is that same distance beyond Mercury. *7*

Glowering Mars lies just as far beyond Venus, and Jupiter, the deities' own ministrant, is two hundred thousand leagues beyond that planet. *8*

Saturn, the Sun's own son, is two hundred thousand leagues beyond Jupiter, and the Seven Sages are another hundred thousand beyond that.[7] *9*

One hundred thousand leagues above the Seven Sages is Dhruva, the Pole Star, the hub around which the wheel of heavenly bodies turns. *10*

I've described the threefold spheres in terms of elevation, sage. This earthly sphere is the Bhūrloka, where rewards of sacrifice are won, as this is where the rituals are performed. *11*

Ten million leagues above Dhruva is Maharloka, where sages live for an aeon—that's why it's called 'Unmoving'. *12*

Twenty million leagues higher is Janaloka, Maitreya, where Sanandana and Brahmā's other pure-minded sons are said to live. *13*

Four times higher than Janaloka is Tapoloka, the sphere of austerities, inhabited by the Vairāja gods, whom fire cannot burn. *14*

---

7 The Seven Sages are major stars of Ursa Major.

Six times higher than Tapoloka is Satyaloka, the sphere of truth, whose denizens never die again. This is thought to be the realm of Brahmā. *15*

Anywhere that can be reached on foot is defined as earth, or Bhūrloka, whose dimensions I described before. *16*

The region between the earth and sun, inhabited by siddhas and other sages, is the Bhuvarloka, the second sphere that I described, best of sages. *17*

The space between the sun and Dhruva, fourteen hundred thousand leagues across, is called Svarloka by those who contemplate these realms. *18*

These three spheres are transitory, Maitreya, but the outer ones of Janaloka, Tapaloka and Satyaloka are enduring. *19*

Between the transitory and enduring spheres lies Maharloka. At the end of every aeon it's vacated, but not entirely destroyed. *20*

I've told you about these seven spheres, Maitreya, the seven lower realms and the dimensions of the universe. *21*

These are enclosed above, below and on all sides by the shell of the cosmic egg, just as the wood-apple's outer rind conceals the seed within. *22*

The cosmic egg is surrounded by water ten times as wide as the egg itself, and the water is ringed by fire. *23*

The fire is surrounded by wind, Maitreya, and the wind by space. Space is surrounded by the fundamental elements, and they are enclosed within *mahat*, the elemental principle of Greatness. Each of these seven layers is ten times larger than the one within, Maitreya. *24*

Mahat is enclosed within primal Matter, which is infinite, endless and immeasurable. *25*

Because it's thus, it's the underlying cause of all phenomena. This, sage, is supreme *prakṛti*, primal Substance. *26*

There are millions and tens of millions and quadrillions of cosmic eggs identical to this one. *27*

Just as fire is latent in wood, and oil is latent in a sesame seed, so, too, all-pervasive *puṃs*, elemental Spirit, is inherent in Matter in the form of self-manifesting consciousness. *28*

The power of Viṣṇu

Both Matter and Spirit are mutually dependent, wise sage, and are enveloped by the power of Viṣṇu, which is at the heart of all creation. *29*

That power is the cause of their separation and their interdependence, sage. It's also the cause of their initial stirring at the moment of creation. *30*

Just as wind raises ripples by the hundred on the surface of the water, in that same way the power of Viṣṇu agitates both Matter and Spirit. *31*

A tree, consisting of roots, trunk, branches and so on, grows from a seed in the beginning, which releases other seeds. *32*

These grow into further trees, which share its character, nature and ultimate origin, sage. *33*

In the same way, *mahat* and the other elemental phenomena arise in the beginning from this Unseen principle. These phenomena then give rise to gods and other beings, who have sons, and those sons have offspring of their own. *34*

Just as the growth of a new tree from a seed does not diminish the parent plant, in the same way, the creation of beings has no effect on the primal elements. *35*

As a combination of space, time and other factors influences a tree's growth, Lord Hari, though himself unchanging, is the cause of everything. *36*

The root, stalk, leaf, shoot, stem, bud, flower, sap, ear, *37*

Chaff and further grains are all latent in a single grain of rice, best of sages, and appear when the conditions for growth arise. *38*

Similarly, the gods and other beings, engaged in their own activities, arise when they encounter Viṣṇu's energy. *39*

Viṣṇu is the supreme Absolute from whom all this arises. The world abides in him and is absorbed in him. *40*

The Absolute is the supreme abode of Viṣṇu, a state beyond existence and nonexistence. Viṣṇu is one with this whole world of moving and unmoving things. *41*

He is the manifest form of both the root and the nature of the world. He *is* the world. In him the world concludes, on him the world relies. *42*

He performs the sacrifice. He is the sacrifice that's offered. He is the sacrificial outcome. He is the ladle and utensils with which it's carried out. Nothing is apart from Hari! *43*

So ends Chapter Seven in Book Two of the glorious Viṣṇu Purāṇa.

8. The movement of the sun; Time; The heavenly paths

Parāśara:

I've described the nature of the cosmic egg to you, sage of rigid vows. Now hear about the size and nature of the sun and other bodies.[8] *1*

The carriage of the sun is nine thousand leagues in length, best of sages, and its shaft is twice as long again. *2*

The axle is more than fifteen million and seven hundred thousand leagues in length, to which a wheel is fixed. *3*

This eternal wheel, with three hubs, six fellies and five spokes, forms a year, and on it rests the entire cycle of time. *4*

The carriage's second axle is forty-five thousand and five hundred leagues in length, wise sage. *5*

The two halves of the yoke are the same length as the two axles, respectively. The carriage's shorter axle and the shorter half of the yoke rest on the Pole Star. The longer axle, to which the wheel is fixed, rests on Mount Mānasa.[9] *6*

The carriage's seven horses are the Vedic metres. Listen to their names: Gāyatrī, Bṛhatī, Uṣṇih, Jagatī, Triṣṭubh, Anuṣṭubh and Paṅkti. These are said to be the horses of the sun. *7*

Indra's city lies on the eastern side of Mount Mānasottara, Yama's city lies southward, Varuṇa's to the west and Soma's to the north. Listen to their names: *8*

8 This chapter presents several unique challenges. Beautiful and fanciful imagery (four-sided Mount Meru, the daylight filling the ocean, and so on) is intermixed with verifiable astronomical observation, but even much of that is expressed in mythological terms. Some verses simply remain obscure.

9 In a long footnote, Wilson states: 'The contrivance is commonly compared to an oil mill, and was probably suggested by that machine as constructed in India' (1961: 179, n.5). See also: commons.wikimedia.org/wiki/File:Oil_Mill_India.jpg.

Mighty Indra's city is called Vasvokasārā, Yama's is Saṃyamanī, that of Varunā, lord of waters, is Sukhā and Soma's is Vibhāvarī. *9*

During its southern passage, the lordly sun flies like an arrow, Maitreya, attended by the wheel of stars. *10*

The sun is the cause of the difference between day and night. This divine vehicle is the highest resort for ascetics who've transcended worldly woes. *11*

The sun is always overhead at midday on one continent, Maitreya, while on the others, it is midnight. *12*

It always rises and sets at opposing cardinal and intermediate points on the horizon, Maitreya. *13*

Those who see the sun appear think that it is rising, and when it disappears from sight, they believe that it is setting. *14*

In fact, it doesn't rise or set, and what we call its rising and its setting are merely its appearance and disappearance. *15*

When the sun is directly over mighty Indra's city, for example, it illuminates three cities and two intermediate points of the compass. When it's located above one of the intermediate points, it shines on three other points and two cities. *16*

When the sun has risen, its rays, growing ever stronger, become hotter until midday, after which they weaken as it nears its setting place. *17*

The directions of east (*pūrva*, 'before') and west (*apara*, 'after') are named for the rising and the setting of the sun. The distance it shines towards the east is the same as the distance it shines westwards and on both sides. *18*

(The only exception is the palace of Brahmā on the summit of divine Mount Meru, where the rays of the sun that reach that edifice are outshone by the city's brilliance and are driven back.) *19*

As a result, there's always a distinction between day and night in northern parts, since Meru stands northward of the continents and other regions. *20*

In the evening when the sun has set, its brilliance enters fire, and that's why fire is brighter in the night. *21*

During the day, one-quarter of fire's brilliance joins the sun, brahmin, and, resulting from this union, the sun shines even brighter. *22*

These two forms of brightness, the light and heat of the sun and fire, are strengthened during day and night, respectively, as they merge with one another. *23*

When the sun is above the horizon, night enters the waters, filling them with darkness, and, after it has set, daylight fills the waters, imbuing them with light. *24*

The ocean appears dark by day because it absorbs the night. Daylight imbues the waters when the sun goes down, and that's why the ocean is brighter at night: it's filled with light. *25*

When the sun is in the middle of Puṣkara, the time taken to transit for one lunar mansion—one-thirtieth part of the circumference of the celestial globe—is one *muhūrta*. *26*

Turning as if on the edge of a potter's wheel, the sun brings day, brahmin, freeing the world from night. *27*

During its passage to the north of the celestial equator, the sun first traverses Capricorn, then Aquarius and Pisces, brahmin, moving from one house to the next. *28*

After it has passed through these three, the sun reaches the point of the equinox, making day and night of equal length. *29*

The nights become thereafter shorter as the days grow longer. *30*

Then when the sun reaches the end of Gemini, it takes a different course, and, reaching the sign of Cancer, begins its southern passage. *31*

Just as the outer edge of the potter's wheel moves more quickly, the sun hastens during this passage. *32*

On account of its speed, it proceeds as quickly as the wind and traverses a great distance in but little time. *33*

Because of its haste, while on its southern passage, the sun takes twelve *muhūrtas* to traverse an extent equivalent to thirteen and a half lunar mansions during the day, brahmin, but during the night it takes eighteen *muhūrtas* to travel the same distance. *34*

Just as a point near the centre of a potter's wheel moves more slowly, so does the sun during its northern passage. *35*

For this reason, it traverses less space in longer time. When the sun reaches the end of its northern path, the length of the days is again eighteen *muhūrtas*. *36*

Here, too, the sun is in the sky for a longer time. *37*

Its path is as long as thirteen and a half mansions during the day, and the same distance is traversed in twelve *muhūrtas* at night. *38*

Just as a lump of clay at the centre of a potter's wheel turns more slowly still, this is the case with Dhruva, which stands at the celestial pole. *39*

And just as the hub of a potter's wheel turns on the spot, Maitreya, so it is with that star. *40*

The relative length of day and night is a function of the length of the arc traversed by the sun between the points at which it rises and sets—that is, the length of time it appears in the sky. *41*

When, during its journey, the daytime passage of the sun is long, the nights are short, and when its passage is long at night, the days are short. *42*

The actual course of the sun is the same in either case, brahmin, because all signs of the zodiac appear to pass overhead in one day and night. *43*

Six signs pass at night and the other six by day. *44*

The length or shortness of a day is the result of the variation in the width of the signs of the zodiac, and, similarly, the length or shortness of the night is determined by the measure of the signs during that time. *45*

The long and short durations of day and night are the result of the width of the signs. During its northern passage, the sun moves more quickly at night and slower by day. *46*

During its southern passage, the opposite is the case. *47*

The night is called *uṣā*, and the day is known as *vyuṣṭi*. The interval between day and night is called *sandhyā*, 'twilight'. *48*

When the cruel and pitiless twilit hours arrive, terrible rākṣasas known as *mandehas* attempt to swallow the sun. *49*

Brahmā, lord of creation, pronounced a curse on these rākṣasas, Maitreya, such that they must die each day, but their bodies aren't destroyed. *50*

As a result, there's a frightful daily struggle between the sun and them. That's why eminent brahmins sprinkle water at such times, great sage, *51*

While chanting the syllable *Oṃ*, consecrated with the Gāyatrī mantra. This water becomes thunderbolts and destroys those wicked beings. *52*

The first offering, accompanied by mantras, made into the sacred fire each morning causes the brilliant light-giving sun of a thousand rays to shine. *53*

The syllable *Oṃ* is Lord Viṣṇu, essence of the threefold Vedas and sovereign of each form of speech. By reciting it, those rākṣasas meet their doom. *54*

The sun is the highest aspect of Viṣṇu, whose brilliance never fades. The syllable *Oṃ* is expressive of the sun and causes it to move. *55*

The light brought forth by *Oṃ* begins to blaze and incinerates all those wicked *mandehas*. *56*

That's why the *sandhyā* twilight rituals must never be neglected. One who fails to perform them at that time is guilty of murdering the sun. *57*

Protected by the brahmins and the Vālakhilya sages, the lordly sun then journeys on its way for the welfare of the world. *58*

Divisions of time

Fifteen *nimeṣas* or 'blinks of the eye' make one *kāṣṭhā*. Thirty *kāṣṭhās* make one *kalā*. Thirty *kalās* make a *muhūrta*, and thirty *muhūrtas*, one day and night. *59*

The periods into which a day is divided may be longer or shorter, as the days progress, but twilight always lasts one *muhūrta*. Even though the days are long or short, its duration stays the same. *60*

The first three *muhūrtas* after sunrise are called morning, one-fifth part of the day. *61*

The three *muhūrtas* after morning are the forenoon, and the three *murhūrtas* after forenoon are midday. *62*

Following midday comes the afternoon. The wise consider that this also lasts for three *muhūrtas*. *63*

When the afternoon is over, the next period is called the evening. In this manner, a day lasts for fifteen *muhūrtas* and consists of periods of three *muhūrtas* each. *64*

But only at the equinox does the day actually last for fifteen *muhūrtas*. *65*

The days grow longer or shorter according to the sun's southern or northern passage, when the day swallows part of the night or the night swallows part of the day. *66*

The equinoxes occur in mid-autumn and mid-spring, and, when the sun reaches Libra and Aries, then night and day are equal. *67*

When the sun enters Cancer, it begins its southern passage. Its northern passage starts when it enters Capricorn. *68*

As I said, thirty *muhūrtas* make one day and night. Fifteen days and nights are called a half-month, brahmin. *69*

Two half-months make a month and two months make a season. There are three seasons during each passage or *ayana* and two passages a year. *70*

There are five kinds of years, made up of four kinds of months. The aggregate of all these divisions of time is called a *yuga* or a cycle. *71*

The first year is the *saṃvatsara*, the second is *parivatsara*, *idvatsara* is the third and the fourth is the *anuvatsara*, with *vatsara* as the fifth. These five make one cycle. *72*

The mountain to the north of Śveta is known as Śṛṅgavant, so called as it has three peaks (*śṛṅga*): *73*

A southern, a northern and a central one. The central peak is also called the equinoctial summit, because the sun reaches this point at the equinoxes in the middle of autumn and spring, when it first enters Aries and Libra, Maitreya. *74*

At such times, the sun, dispeller of the darkness, makes day and night of equal length, both being fifteen *muhūrtas*. *75*

When the sun is in the first segment of the lunar mansion of Kṛttikā, and the moon stands in the fourth segment of Viśākhā, sage, *76*

Or when the sun is in the third segment of Viśākhā and the moon is at the head of Kṛttikā, *77*

It's known as the time of the auspicious equinox, when self-restrained individuals make offerings to the deities, *78*

Brahmins and ancestors, for at this time, donations give rise to an opening to the gods. One fulfils one's obligations by making offerings at the equinox and at the following times: *79*

During the day, night, half-month, *kalā*, *kāṣṭhā* and *kṣaṇa* of the full moon, new moon, the day of its first appearance, the first day of the first quarter, the actual day of full moon and one day before that. *80*

The sun's northern passage occupies the months of Tapas, Tapasya, Madhu, Mādhava, Śukra and Śuci. Nabhas, Nabhasya, Iṣa, Ūrja, Sahas and Sahasya constitute its southern passage. *81*

I've already told you about Mount Lokāloka, where the four guardians of the world, firm in their vows, reside: *82*

Kardama's two sons Sudhāman and Śaṅkhapād, brahmin, as well as Hiraṇyaroman, with Ketumant as the fourth. *83*

Indifferent to extremes, free from pride, vigilant and unencumbered, these global guardians dwell on that mountain, facing the four directions. *84*

The path of the ancestors

North of Canopus and south of Aries, beyond the path of Vaiśvānara, lies Pitṛyāna, the path of ancestral spirits. *85*

There reside great sages who maintain the sacred fires and eulogise the Vedas that began the process of creation, intent upon their priestly duties. The path of sages who cause the creation of the world lies southward. *86*

In every age, they reestablish Vedic tradition, which has been interrupted, with its lineages, austerities, social limits and oral teachings. *87*

The sages of the east are born in residences of the west, and the sages of the west are born in eastern mansions. *88*

Alternating in this way, they remain upon this path until the destruction of the world. Their path lies southward of the sun and will endure as long as the moon and stars. *89*

The path of gods

North of Aries and Taurus, south of the Great Bear and north of the sun lies the path of gods. *90*

There reside the chaste and stainless siddhas, who have no thought of progeny, and have therefore conquered death. *91*

Eighty-eight thousand ascetics, retaining their semen, reside on the northern path of the sun until the world is destroyed. *92*

Because they're free of greed and have renounced all sexual union, and because they abjure the creation of life, which is characterised by love and hate, *93*

And further, because they're free from desire and misapprehension of sound and other sensations—for all these reasons, they're purified and immortal. *94*

This deathless state persists until the destruction of the world, and they're said to be free from death while the threefold worlds endure. *95*

The results of wicked acts like brahminicide, brahmin, and of auspicious ones like the Aśvamedha sacrifice, will endure until universal dissolution. *96*

At such a time, Maitreya, all that lies between the Pole Star and the earth will be destroyed. *97*

The realm of Viṣṇu

North of the Great Bear and extending as far as the Pole Star is the third division of the sky, Viṣṇu's brilliant, heavenly realm. *98*

This is the highest state for self-controlled ascetics who've washed away the stains of sin, brahmin, and for whom vice and virtue are no more. *99*

When ideas of 'good' and 'evil' cease and the cause of further birth is gone—when they attain all this, they grieve no more; that's Viṣṇu's highest state. *100*

Where Dharma, Dhruva and other witnesses of the world abide, blazing in their union with the majesty that imbues the god—that's Viṣṇu's highest state. *101*

The warp and weft of all creation, of all moving and unmoving things and of all that will arise in future, Maitreya—that's Viṣṇu's highest state. *102*

That which the wise regard as the great heavenly eye and that which appear as knowledge and discernment—that's Viṣṇu's highest state. *103*

Brilliant Dhruva himself, serving as the axis of the heavens, is located there. All the heavenly luminaries depend on him, brahmin, as do water-yielding clouds. *104*

Rain is born in them, and all creation, including deities and the other beings, great sage, are nourished and refreshed by rain. *105*

The gods who consume the offerings are sustained by oblations of butter, and they send rain for the further sustenance of the world. *106*

Such is the third portion of the sky, the pure abode of Viṣṇu, foundation of the threefold worlds and source of rain. *107*

The origin of the Gaṅgā

Hence arises the river Gaṅgā, brahmin, which removes all sins and is itself suffused with lotions washed from the limbs of the deities' wives. *108*

Her torrents, which flow from the nail of the big toe of Viṣṇu's lotus-like left foot, are devoutly borne by Dhruva on his head by day and night. *109*

Downstream, the Seven Sages, intent on breath control, their matted locks swept along by her wreath-like waves, stand amid her waters. *110*

The disk of the hare-marked moon, washed by her spreading currents, acquires still greater loveliness as her waters remove its stain. *111*

Descending from the moon, she cascades upon Mount Meru's summit, and, to purify the world, flows forth in four directions. *112*

In the forms of Sītā, Alakanandā, Cakṣu and Bhadrā, she's a fourfold stream in one, according to the path she takes. *113*

Śiva kindly bore the southern branch of Alakanandā on his head for more than a hundred years. *114*

Emerging from the deity's mass of matted locks, she bathed the shattered bones of Sagara's wicked sons and raised them up to heaven. *115*

The sins of those who bathe in her are instantly expunged, and they taste good fortune as they never have before. *116*

Ancestors, offered her waters by faithful sons, are nourished for three years, Maitreya—a feat of no mean achievement. *117*

Worshipping Viṣṇu, lord of sacrifice and highest spirit, with great rituals on her banks, kings and brahmins reap supreme rewards in this world and the next. *118*

Cleansed of sin by bathing in her waters, ascetics and those whose minds are set on Keśava reach ultimate extinction. *119*

When heard, desired, seen or touched, imbibed or bathed in, or praised each day, she purifies all beings. *120*

Those who summon her by name—'Gaṅgā! Gaṅgā!'—even at a distance of a hundred leagues, are cleansed of all the deeds they've done in three previous lives. *121*

The place whence Gaṅgā flows to purify the worlds is the third division of the sky, the supreme abode of Viṣṇu. *122*

So ends Chapter Eight in Book Two of the glorious Viṣṇu Purāṇa.

9. The source of rain

Parāśara:

Lord Hari takes the astral form of a dolphin, Śiśumāra, in the heavens, with Dhruva standing on his tail. *1*

Dhruva, turning, sets the moon, the sun and planets in motion. The constellations follow them, spinning like a wheel. *2*

The sun, moon, stars, constellations and planets are all tied to Dhruva with bonds of wind. *3*

Nārāyaṇa, refuge of the worlds, who exists in the heavens in astral form, is Śiśumāra's foundation and is himself located at its heart. *4*

Dhruva, son of Uttānapāda, worshipping the universal lord, won a place on Śiśumāra's tail. *5*

Janārdana, witness of the world, is Śiśumāra's support. Śiśumāra supports Dhruva, and Dhruva supports the sun. *6*

The sun supports the universe, including gods and demigods and mortals. *7*

Listen carefully how this happens, brahmin. Eight months each year, the sun draws up water, the essence of existence. Falling showers then nourish crops on which the world relies. *8*

The sun takes water from the earth with drying rays and releases it to the moon. The moon directs this water through aerial channels to the clouds composed of smoke and fire and wind. *9*

Because the rains don't fall (*bhraśyanti*) at once, clouds are known as *abhra*. Water held in clouds descends when stirred by wind, unsullied and purified by passing time, Maitreya. *10*

The lordly sun draws water from four sources, sage: from rivers, oceans, earth and living things. *11*

Taking water from the Gaṅgā flowing through the sky, the sun bears it immediately to earth by means of rays, without the need for clouds. *12*

A mortal touched by water of this kind is cleansed of the stain of his misdeeds, best of brahmins, and doesn't go to hell, as it's thought to be divine ablution. *13*

Rain that falls while the sun appears in a cloudless sky is the water of aerial Gaṅgā, and is borne to earth on sunbeams. *14*

That which falls when the sun is seen in Kṛttikā or other odd-numbered lunar mansions is also from the Gaṅgā, but is scattered by the elephants that guard the four directions. *15*

That which falls when the sun is in the even-numbered mansions is dispersed by the sun itself, borne at once to earth by rays. *16*

In all these cases, rain is highly auspicious and cleanses people of their sins, brahmin, as the waters of airborne Gaṅgā provide divine ablution, sage. *17*

Rain falling from the clouds nourishes every kind of plant, brahmin, and is nectar for living beings. *18*

Rain leads plants to full maturity, brahmin, thanks to which, ripe crops appear for humankind. *19*

Relying on these, men who have regard for scripture perform the proper rites each day, and nourish the gods thereby. *20*

In this way, the sacrifices, the Vedas, the communities with brahmins as the first, all the assembled deities and herds of beasts all depend on rain. *21*

Rain brings food, best of brahmins, and the sun gives rise to rain. *22*

Dhruva is the sun's support, best of brahmins, as Śiśumāra is of Dhruva, while Śiśumāra depends on Nārāyaṇa. *23*

At Śiśumāra's heart is Nārāyaṇa, support of every being, primal and eternal. *24*

So ends Chapter Nine in Book Two of the glorious Viṣṇu Purāṇa.

10. The carriage of the sun

Parāśara:

The sun proceeds through one hundred and eighty degrees on its passage between its ascending and descending nodes. *1*

Deities, Ādityas and sages ride the carriage of the sun, along with gandharvas, apsarases, yakṣas, nāgas and rākṣasas.[10] *2*

Dhātṛ, Kṛtasthalā, Pulastya, Vāsuki, the yakṣa Rathakṛt and Heti, with Tumburu as the seventh— *3*

These seven always ride on the sun's carriage during Caitra, also known as Madhu, Maitreya, and preside over this month. *4*

Aryaman, Pulaha, Rathaujas, Puñjikasthalā, Praheti, Kacchanīra and Nārada ride the sun's carriage during Mādhava. *5*

Now hear about the month of Śuci: *6*

Mitra, Atri, Takṣaka, the rākṣasa Pauruṣeya, Menakā, Hāhā and Rathasvana ride the carriage at that time, Maitreya. *7*

In the month of Śukra, also known as Āṣāḍha, Varuṇa, Vasiṣṭha, Rambhā, Sahajanyā, Huhū, Ratha and Rathacitra ride it. *8*

Indra, Viśvāvasu, Srotas, Elāpatra, Aṅgiras, Pramlocā and Sarpa ride the sun's carriage in the month of Nabhas. *9*

During Bhādrapada, it's the turn of Vivasvat, Ugrasena, Bhṛgu, Āpūraṇa, Umlocā, Śaṅkhapāla and Vyāghra. *10*

In the month of Āśvin, Pūṣan, Suruci, Vāta, Gautama, Dhanaṃjaya, Suṣeṇa and Ghṛtācī ride it. *11*

Viśvāvasu, Bharadvāja, Parjanya, Airāvata, Viśvācī, Senajit and Cāpi preside over the month of Kārttika. *12*

Aṃśu, Kaśyapa, Tārkṣya, Mahāpadma, Urvaśī, Citrasena and Vidyut preside over Mārgaśīrṣa. *13*

10 Each month, seven beings—roughly one from each category—take up residence on the disk or carriage of the sun. In the following passage, the poet gives the names of each set of beings in an order determined by the metre. Their identities can be found in the index or any standard reference work, such as Monier-Williams (1899).

Kratu, Bhaga, Urṇāyu, Sphūrja, Karkoṭaka, Ariṣṭanemi and the excellent apsaras Pūrvacitti— *14*

These seven ride the solar disk in the month of Pauṣa to ensure the world is properly lit, and they are its outstanding overseers. *15*

Tvaṣṭṛ, Jamadagni, Kambala, Tilottamā, Brahmāpeta and Ṛtajit, with Dhṛtarāṣṭra as the seventh— *16*

In the month of Māgha, these seven ride the sun, Maitreya. Now you'll hear about those who ride its carriage in the month of Phālguna: *17*

Viṣṇu, Aśvatara, Rambhā, Sūryavarcas, Satyajit, Viśvāmitra and the rākṣasa Yañjopeta, great sage. *18*

During these months, Maitreya, these groups of seven beings occupy the solar disk, brahmin, strengthened by the power of Viṣṇu. *19*

The sages praise the sun, gandharvas sing before it, apsarases dance while rākṣasas attend it. *20*

The nāgas guide the carriage and yakṣas hold the reins. *21*

The Vālakhilya sages surround it on all sides. *22*

Each cohort residing on the solar disk, great sage, brings heat and cold and showers of rain in season. *23*

So ends Chapter Ten in Book Two of the glorious Viṣṇu Purāṇa.

11. The sun's energy

Maitreya:

Master, I've listened to your description of the groups of seven beings who occupy the solar disk, bringing heat and cold and so on. *1*

You've spoken of the role of gandharvas, nāgas, rākṣasas, sages, Vālakhilyas and apsarases, guru, *2*

As well as yakṣas on the carriage of the sun, all of whom are held by Viṣṇu's power. But you've said nothing, sage, of the function of the sun itself. *3*

If these seven beings cause heat and cold and rain, then what role has the sun in this regard? I thought you said it sends down showers. *4*

Why do folk contend the sun first rises, passes overhead, then sets, if these are but the work of seven beings? *5*

Parāśara:

Listen, Maitreya, and I'll answer your question as to how the sun alone is superior to the seven. *6*

Viṣṇu's threefold power, known as the *Ṛg*, *Yajur* and *Sāma Vedas*, warms the world and dispels its sins. *7*

This power is Viṣṇu and is actively engaged in the upkeep of the world. In the form of the threefold Veda, brahmin, it dwells within the sun. *8*

Month by month, wherever the sun abides, Viṣṇu's peerless threefold energy determines its condition. *9*

Ṛg Vedic verses light the world each morning, the *Yajur* does at noon and the *Sāma Veda*, including the Bṛhadrathantara, illuminates the world at sunset. *10*

These three Vedas are all aspects of the lord. His energy always dwells within the sun and determines its condition. *11*

This threefold energy of the Divine is not confined to the sun alone, as Brahmā, the highest spirit, and Rudra also share its nature. *12*

At the onset of creation, this energy is Brahmā in the form of the *Ṛg Veda*. While the world endures, it's Viṣṇu as the *Yajur* and, at its dissolution, it's Rudra as the *Sāma Veda*. That's why the recitation of the latter is considered inauspicious. *13*

Thus, Viṣṇu's pure and threefold power invests the sun, even while the seven beings occupy it. *14*

Filled with power, the sun shines brightly, and with its rays it banishes the darkness from all the worlds. *15*

The sages praise the sun, the gandharvas sing before it and apsarases dance while rākṣasas attend it. *16*

The nāgas guide its carriage, yakṣas hold the reins and Vālakhilya seers surround it on all sides.[11] *17*

11 The two verses, 2.11.16–17, are repeated in slightly different form from the previous chapter, 2.10.20–22.

The sun itself neither sets nor rises, but is ever filled with Viṣṇu's power. The seven beings are all Viṣṇu, but are at once distinct from him. *18*

Just like a man who nears a mirror perceives his own reflection in it, *19*

In that same way, the power of Viṣṇu never leaves the sun, but month by month abides there, brahmin. *20*

The lordly sun brings night and day and, ever moving, brahmin, wheels above the ancestors and gods and men. *21*

The solar ray called Suṣumṇa nourishes the moon, but when it wanes, the deities imbibe its nectarine disk. *22*

Finally, the ancestors drink up the last two slivers of the moon, and thus both gods and ancestors are nurtured by the sun. *23*

With its rays, the sun draws moisture from the earth, which falls as rain to prosper beings and nourish crops. *24*

Thus, the lordly sun delights all beings and gives new strength to ancestors, gods and humankind. *25*

Satisfying the gods each fortnight and the ancestors each month, the sun provides perpetual nourishment for mortals, Maitreya. *26*

So ends Chapter Eleven in Book Two of the glorious Viṣṇu Purāṇa.

12. The moon and planets

Parāśara:

The three-wheeled carriage of the moon is drawn by horses, ten in number, white as jasmine, harnessed left and right. *1*

With that swift carriage, it traverses lunar mansions on the way, ruled by Dhruva, when the reins are loosed or drawn back, just like the sun. *2*

As with the horses of the sun, the moon's own steeds, born of water, are harnessed together and draw its chariot for an aeon, best of sages. *3*

When the moon, drunk up by gods, has been reduced to just one sliver, the blazing sun replenishes it with a ray, Maitreya. *4*

The deities reduce the moon, who makes the night, by stages as it wanes, but the water-stealing sun restores it day by day. *5*

The deities drink nectar, which gathers while it waxes, Maitreya, and with this nectar as their sustenance, they, too, become immortal. *6*

All thirty-six thousand, three hundred and thirty-three gods drink from the night-making moon. *7*

When two slivers alone remain, the moon draws near the sun and abides (*vasati*) in a ray of light called Amā, hence this phase is known as Amāvāsyā. *8*

During that day and night, the moon first enters the waters and, after dwelling among the plants, draws closer to the sun. *9*

One who cuts a plant while the moon is in that state, or causes a single leaf to fall, is guilty of brahminicide. *10*

When just one-fifteenth of the moon remains, a host of ancestors attend it in the afternoon. *11*

And from this moon of two mere slivers, sage, they drink the auspicious nectar of immortality until just one remains. *12*

Having drunk the finest nectar shed by the moon's own rays at the phase of Amāvāsyā, the ancestors—these Saumyas, Barhiṣads and Agniṣvāttas—are sustained all month and are satisfied. *13*

Thus, the waxing moon sustains the gods and, when it wanes, it succours ancestors and plants with cooling drops of nectar. *14*

By bringing forth both plants and herbs, the cool-rayed moon quickens man and beast and creeping things, refreshing them with light. *15*

The planets and stars

The chariot of Mercury, the moon's own son, composed of wind and fire, is drawn by eight bay horses, swift as wind itself. *16*

The great chariot of pure Venus, with fender, floor, bench and banner, is drawn by horses born of earth. *17*

Eight golden horses, ruby-red and fire-born, draw the chariot of Mars, glorious and huge. *18*

Jupiter rides throughout the year from one star sign to another in a chariot made of gold, drawn by eight steeds, swift and white. *19*

Sluggish Saturn moves at leisure on a chariot yoked to dappled horses born of air. *20*

Eight steeds, black as bees and hitched together, draw the dusky carriage of Svarbhānu, demon of eclipses; they never rest, Maitreya. *21*

At times, this demon, also known as Rāhu, leaves the sun to hide the moon, then from the moon he blocks the sun again to bring eclipses. *22*

Likewise, the carriage of the shadow-planet Ketu is drawn by horses, eight in number, swift as wind and dark as the smoke of burning straw, or red as cochineal. *23*

I've described to you the chariots of nine planets, lucky sage, all bound to Dhruva by bonds of air. *24*

The planets, mansions and constellations, all tied to Dhruva, circle in their proper orbits, restricted by these ties, Maitreya. *25*

For every star, there is a bond and, as they move, the Pole Star rotates with them. *26*

Just as workers pressing oil turn the wheel by pacing round it, similarly, the stars revolve, all bound with aerial bonds. *27*

The stars turn like a disk of fire driven by a wheel of wind. Because it carries (*vahati*) the stars, this force is called Pravaha. *28*

The constellation where Dhruva stands is Śiśumāra, as I mentioned. Now I'll tell you, best of sages, about its stars as well. *29*

If you see it in the evening, you're freed from misdeeds done by day. As many stars are seen in Śiśumāra in the heavens, that's how many years you'll live, or maybe more. *30*

Uttānapāda is thought to be its upper jaw, the lower one is Yajña, while Dharma is standing at its head. *31*

At its heart sits Nārāyaṇa, the Aśvins are its two front feet, with Varuṇa and Āryaman behind them. *32*

Saṃvatsara is at Śiśumāra's penis, with Mitra at its anus. *33*

At its tail are Agni, Mahendra, Kaśyapa and Dhruva—Śiśumāra's quartet of stars, which never set. *34*

The universal nature of Viṣṇu

I've described the nature of the earth, the planets, continents, seas and mountains, *35*

And lands and rivers, as well as those who dwell there. Now listen while I summarise all this once more. *36*

From the waters, Viṣṇu's body, arose the world in lotus form, brahmin, replete with seas and ranges. *37*

The stars are Viṣṇu, as are the worlds, the forests, lands and mountains, as are streams and oceans. He is all that is and all that isn't, best of brahmins. *38*

Because the lord is knowledge, and is all forms but has no substance, understand that distinctive forms of mountains, oceans, earth and so on give rise to a misconception. *39*

When knowledge is pure, natural, complete, independent of action and free from faults, then the distinction between manifold substances, which are the fruits of the tree of longing, is no more. *40*

What is substance? Where is an entity without beginning, middle or end, and eternally uniform? Where is the reality of that which proceeds again to a state of otherness and doesn't stay the same, brahmin? *41*

Clay is shaped into a pot; the pot is broken into pieces; the pieces ground to dust; the dust reduced to atoms. This is clearly seen by folk whose notions are informed by personal experience. But tell me, what is substance? *42*

Therefore, except for truest knowledge, there is never anything anywhere, brahmin, that arises from such substances. This knowledge is uniform but appears manifold to those who perceive it as differentiated, as the result of the varied nature of their own actions. *43*

Knowledge is pure, unblemished, painless, free from the influence of greed and other faults. It's uniform, ever one, supreme, the highest lord. It's Vāsudeva, other than whom no thing exists. *44*

I've explained this verity to you: this knowledge is truth, all else is false and I've spoken of the mundane aspects of the world. *45*

I've shown the sacrifice to you, the beasts, the fire, the ministrants, the soma, sacrificial liquor and the wish for heaven—all these and other aspects related to the rites—and all the worlds and pleasures that arise therefrom. *46*

Driven by one's actions, a being moves alone among the worlds that I've described to you. Knowing Vāsudeva to be firm, unmoving and unchanging, one may still do his duty and, doing so, may enter the divine. *47*

So ends Chapter Twelve in Book Two of the glorious Viṣṇu Purāṇa.

13. 'Foolish' Bharata

Maitreya:

Master, you've given me the perfect answer to my question on the nature of the earth, the oceans, rivers and the planets, *1*

And the system of the threefold worlds, with Viṣṇu as their foundation. You've described to me the highest goal of life and knowledge, because of their significance. *2*

As you said you'd speak about the deeds of Bharata the king, please do so now. *3*

King Bharata dwelled at Sālagrāma, intent on yoga, his heart ever set on Vāsudeva. *4*

With the power of that sacred place and his unbroken thoughts of Hari, why was he not liberated, but reborn a brahmin? *5*

Please tell me what that illustrious being achieved when, driven by his previous karma, he was born again in that community. *6*

Parāśara:

In Sālagrāma, that pious king reposed for many long years, Maitreya, his heart fixed on the lord. *7*

He was the best of worthy men. While shunning harm, he clung to virtue, having reached perfection in the mastery of his mind. *8*

The names 'Viṣṇu', 'Yajñeśa', 'Acyuta', 'Govinda', 'Mādhava', 'Ananta', 'Keśava', 'Kṛṣṇa' and 'Hṛṣīkeśa' were the only words he ever uttered. *9*

He spoke no others, Maitreya, even in his dreams, and thought of nothing but these names and their significance. *10*

Accepting gifts of kindling, flowers and *kuśa*-grass so he could worship the divine, he shunned all other action, unattached, intent on his austerities and yoga. *11*

One day, he reached a mighty river to purify himself and, having bathed, undertook the rites that follow such ablutions. *12*

And to that sacred bathing place there came from the woods a pregnant doe, thirsting for some water, brahmin. *13*

But while she drank, she heard the roaring of a lion, which frightens every living thing. *14*

The startled doe leapt from the water to the shore, but the violence of her movement forced the infant from her womb, and it fell into the river. *15*

Carried by the current and sinking beneath the waves, the miscarried fawn was fetched up by the king. *16*

With the pain of her miscarriage and the violence of her leap, Maitreya, the doe fell down and died. *17*

Seeing that its dam had perished, the ascetic king took up the fawn and bore it to his ashram. *18*

Every day he fed that fawn, sage, and, nurtured by the king, it grew and grew. *19*

The young deer grazed on grass in thickets near the ashram, but even when it strayed afar, the fear of tigers drove it back. *20*

Having wandered out at dawn and returning in the dusk, it could be found as usual in the thatched byre of Bharata's retreat. *21*

The king was always worried when the deer strayed near and far, brahmin, and thought of nothing else. *22*

Free from his kingdom and his sons and free from all his kinsfolk, he now became possessive of that fawn in high degree. *23*

'Perhaps it's fallen prey to wolves or tigers or been taken by a lion'—such were his worries when the deer was gone for long. *24*

'This fawn, dotting the earth with hoofprints, *25*

Has brought me joy since the day that he arrived. But where is he now? He loves to scratch my arm with his antler tip. I'll be so happy when he's safely home from roaming in the forest. *26*

With his young teeth, he's nibbled off the tips of *kuśa*-grass so they resemble brahmin boys who chant the *Sāma Veda*.' *27*

Such worries filled the sage's mind when the fawn was overdue, but his face would shine with pleasure whenever it was near. *28*

The king, who shunned his kingdom, pleasures, wealth and kin, now lost his peace of mind as his heart was filled with worry. *29*

That mind, once firm, began to wander and grew distant when the fawn strayed far from home. *30*

In time, the sovereign's death drew near, and that young deer watched over him, just like a tearful son who sees his sire's demise. *31*

As he drew his final breath, the king beheld the deer and, being still obsessed with it, he thought of nothing else. *32*

In that state of mind when the time of death arrived, the king was born a deer in the expansive forest of Jambūmārga, but he could still recall his former life. *33*

Because of this ability and troubled by saṃsāra, best of brahmins, the fawn now left his mother and returned to Sālagrāma. *34*

Living on dry grass and leaves, he atoned for deeds that caused his birth in the body of a deer. *35*

He perished there but was born a brahmin in a pure and lofty family of virtuous ascetics, yet still recalled his previous existence. *36*

Having mastered every branch of learning and knowing the true purport of all the sacred texts, he saw that *ātman*, the Self, Maitreya, lay beyond *prakṛti*, matter. *37*

Knowing well the nature of the Self, that wise man viewed all creatures, deities and the rest as essentially the same, great sage. *38*

But once invested with the sacred thread, he took no part in Vedic recitation as instructed by his elders, nor witnessed any sacrifice, nor studied any text. *39*

Whenever he was spoken to, he'd answer with some foolish quip and, like some country bumpkin, his speech was un-Sanskritic. *40*

This brahmin failed to groom himself, his clothes were vile, saliva dribbled down his chin and all the townsfolk shunned him. *41*

'Praise does great harm to those of self-restraint whose wealth is yoga. Such ascetics, despised by folk, should seek success through practice. *42*

Ascetics must therefore train without offending the virtue of the wise. Whenever folk abuse them, let them walk away.' *43*

Recalling these words of Brahmā, born of the golden egg, that prudent being appeared to others to be a foolish madman. *44*

He ate half-ripe barley, raw beans and other greens, as well as forest seeds and berries—whatever came to his fair hand at any time. *45*

When his father passed away, his brothers, cousins and other kin sent him to the fields to work, with little food to succour him. *46*

Though he seemed a simpleton, his limbs proved tough while labouring, and so he helped out other folk, receiving food as wages. *47*

Now, the chamberlain of the king of Sauvīra thought this man a fool who just effected the appearance of a brahmin, but who could provide free labour. *48*

The king, riding in his palanquin, wished to visit Kapila's retreat, that best of sages, on the banks of the Ikṣumatī River, brahmin. *49*

He sought to ask that learned sage, who understood the dharma of liberation, about the best course for humankind in this world of suffering. *50*

The brahmin, along with others who, at the chamberlain's command, had been pressed into service, now bore the royal carriage. *51*

Forced to work, the brahmin, who alone had grasped all understanding, recalled his previous existence and bore the palanquin, desiring to atone for past misdeeds. *52*

His eyes fixed solely on the pole, the wisest of the wise just stumbled on, while all the others walked in step. *53*

Seeing that the palanquin was moving so unevenly, the king called out, 'What's going on? You bearers should all walk in step!' *54*

But noting no improvement, the king then laughed and cried aloud, 'What now? You're still all out of kilter!' *55*

Hearing the sovereign's new complaint, the carriers replied, 'There's a fellow here who's much too slow.' *56*

The king:

How can you be tired? You haven't borne my palanquin that far. Can't you take the weight? You look strong enough to me. *57*

The brahmin:

It isn't me who's weak, nor me who bears your palanquin. It isn't me who is fatigued, nor me who takes its weight, your majesty. *58*

The king:

I see myself that you are strong, and even now you bear my carriage. Everyone is subject to fatigue when shouldering a burden. *59*

The brahmin:

Please state exactly what you see in me, your majesty, as only then is it possible to speak of strong and weak. *60*

You just said I'm carrying your palanquin, but that is not the case. Please listen while I explain. *61*

My feet are on the ground, and they support my shins. My shins uphold my thighs, and they in turn hold up my belly. *62*

My belly supports my chest, my arms and shoulders. As my shoulders bear this palanquin, how can you say the load is mine alone? *63*

The body sitting on the chair is defined as 'you', but it's not right to say that you are there and I am here. *64*

Both you and I and all the others are composed of elements, your majesty, and this mass of elements becomes a body, determined by the *guṇas*, the stream of qualities. *65*

These qualities—namely, purity and the others—are subject to one's karma, sire. And karma, accumulated in ignorance, affects all beings without exception. *66*

The Self—the *ātman*—is pure and indestructible, tranquil, lacking qualities and transcends materiality. It does not wax or wane but is the same in every being. *67*

Since it's beyond decay and growth, your majesty, on what grounds say you that I am strong? *68*

This palanquin is borne on shoulders that depend on earth and feet, on shins and thighs, on hips and bellies and the rest, and so this weight is shared by all, including you. *69*

Similarly, sire, it's not just other entities that bear your carriage, as mountains, trees and houses all rest upon the earth as well. *70*

If people's natures were unalike or differed for given reasons, your majesty, then I'd agree this load was borne by one or other person. *71*

But the stuff that forms this chair comprises you and me and other things and is composed of elements that are moulded by a sense of self. *72*

Parāśara:

Having spoken, the brahmin bore the palanquin in silence, but the king climbed down and hastened to touch his feet. *73*

The king:

I salute you, brahmin! Forget about the palanquin. I have a favour to ask of you. Pray tell me who you really are, appearing here in such disreputable form? *74*

Why are you like this and why have you come? Tell me all, wise man. I wish to hear the reason. *75*

The brahmin:

Listen well, your majesty, but I cannot tell you who I am. The act of going anywhere is for the sake of some experience. *76*

Pain and pleasure are the source of everybody and all else. A living thing assumes a body to undergo the karmic fruit of vice and virtue. *77*

Since vice and virtue are the cause of everything for every being, sire, why ask about the reason that I'm here? *78*

The king:

Vice and virtue are indeed the cause of all events, and beings appear in place to suffer their effects. *79*

But this is what I'd like to hear: Why claim you cannot tell me who you are? *80*

How can it be impossible for one to describe himself? The word 'I' can't harm you, brahmin. *81*

The brahmin:

It's true the word can do no harm, but the very term betrays the fault of seeing a 'self' in something that is without it. *82*

The tongue, the teeth, the lips and palate utter this word 'I', your majesty. Yet none of these is 'I', as they are just the means by which the sound is made. *83*

If speech itself just forms this word by means of these same organs, it's wrong to claim that speech is 'I'. *84*

Since a person's body is made of many parts—the head, the hands and all the rest—to which of these does 'I' apply, your majesty? *85*

If another man is different from me, best of kings, then it may be said that 'I am this' and 'He's the other'. *86*

But when a single primal spirit—*puṃs*—pervades all bodies, it's vain to ask the questions, 'Who are you?' and 'Who am I?' *87*

You're the king and this the palanquin. We're the bearers who attend you and this your realm—but none of this is really true, your majesty. *88*

The palanquin on which you ride was made of wood from certain trees. To which does 'tree' apply, your majesty, or is it 'wood'? *89*

When you're seated on the palanquin, none would say the king is riding on a tree or on a piece of timber. *90*

The palanquin is an assembly of wood, created in the process of manufacture. Can you see a distinction between the wood and the palanquin, best of kings? *91*

Similarly, consider now the separate existence of an umbrella's ribs. Whence does the umbrella arise? With this in mind, the same idea applies to you and me. *92*

Man, woman, cow, horse, elephant, bird and tree—such names are commonly assigned to things, which, we must understand, arise because of karma. *93*

The primal spirit is neither god, nor man, nor beast, nor tree. These differences are merely in the shape of forms, your majesty, caused by prior actions. *94*

That entity which folk call 'king', that which is the 'soldier of the king' and similarly all else, sire, lack their own reality, yet arise in our conceptions. *95*

What entity, subject to varied changes, isn't known by other names in time, your majesty? *96*

You're the king of all your realm, your father's son, your rival's foe, the husband of your wife and father of your son, sire. Who should I say you truly are? *97*

Are you this head, or does this head belong to you? What about your belly? Are you your feet and so on, sire, or are they yours? *98*

You seem to be apart from all these component limbs. Now that you are better informed, sire, please contemplate the question 'Who am I?' *99*

Seeing the truth has been established in this way, how can I speak of 'I', sire, which is the mere result of a process of differentiation? *100*

So ends Chapter Thirteen in Book Two of the glorious Viṣṇu Purāṇa.

14. Bharata teaches the highest goal

Parāśara:

Hearing the brahmin's words imbued with such significance, the king bowed down with deep respect and spoke to him as follows. *1*

The king:

The words you've uttered, sir, contain the highest truth, but hearing them, the patterns of my mind are troubled. *2*

This understanding of discrimination, present in all beings, as you've shown, brahmin, is the greatest principle that transcends the mundane world. *3*

'I don't carry the palanquin.' 'The palanquin doesn't rest on me.' 'The body that supports it is different from me.' *4*

'The actions of all beings are determined by their karma as driven by the *guṇas*.' 'The *guṇas* are preeminent.' What do such statements mean to me? *5*

You understand the highest truth, but when I heard what you have said, my mind, though yearning for such knowledge, is perplexed. *6*

I've just set out to meet that sage of greatest fortune, Kapila, fully prepared to ask him what is best. *7*

But in the meantime, because of words that you have spoken, my mind, which hankers after highest truth, is drawn to you. *8*

The sage Kapila is an aspect of Lord Viṣṇu, the universal being, manifesting in the world to free it from delusion. *9*

Surely, it's the lord himself who came here as you spoke, from his desire for our wellbeing. *10*

As I bow before you, brahmin, teach me about the highest good, for you're an ocean filled with waves of wisdom. *11*

The brahmin:

Your majesty, you ask what's best, but not about the highest goal. Something may be one, great king, but may not be the other. *12*

Having worshipped all the gods, a man may wish for wealth, prosperity, sons or sovereignty. Fulfilling that desire then counts as 'best' for him. *13*

Some think that acts of sacrifice are best, because they lead to heavenly realms. But 'best' is often found when no specific goal is wanted. *14*

Those disciplined in yoga, sire, should always contemplate the Self, as that is best for them. This union is best for one who holds as ultimate the highest spirit. *15*

Things by hundreds and by thousands may be considered 'best', but they are not the highest goal in life, so listen to me now: *16*

How can wealth be the highest goal if sacrificed for virtue? Why spend money just to satisfy desire? *17*

While a son is said to be the highest goal, the term may be applied to something else, your majesty. A son may be another person's highest goal, as his father was once *his* father's deepest wish. *18*

Thus, in this world of moving and unmoving things, there's no single highest goal, as all these goals have causes. *19*

If winning a kingdom was said to be the highest, then such goals would exist at times and at others cease to be. *20*

If you think the highest goal is sacrifice effected by the *Ṛg*, *Yajur* and *Sāma Vedas*, then listen to what I say. *21*

If a thing is formed from clay as its raw material, the finished product, following the nature of that substance, is also made of clay, your majesty. *22*

Similarly, a rite performed with perishable materials, like kindling, butter and *kuśa*-grass, will only yield impermanent results. *23*

The wise understand that the highest goal is permanent, but this would certainly not be true if it depended on impermanent materials. *24*

You may think the highest goal is ritual action, from which no reward is wanted, as it leads to liberation, but the highest goal is no mere means of achieving things. *25*

Meditation on the Self is said to be the meaning of the highest goal, your majesty, but this divides the Self from others. The highest goal yields no such divisions. *26*

The highest goal is said to be the union of the spirit and oneself, but this is also false because one kind of substance cannot become another. *27*

All these are said to be 'the best', sire, but now I'll briefly tell you, a guardian of the world, what truly is the highest goal. *28*

It is the Self: unitary, pervading, constant, pure, unqualified, immaterial, free from birth and ageing and the rest, universal and unchanging, *29*

Comprising highest wisdom and unyoked to falsehood, name or lineage in the past, the present or the future, your majesty. *30*

The form of knowledge that exists as one in each and every body is the highest goal; the dualists' view is incorrect. *31*

Just as a single current of air is divided into notes on passing through the body of a flute, *32*

The unity of this great spirit is divided into varied forms under the sway of external factors. When the difference between the deities and the rest is removed, no distinction between high and low remains. *33*

So ends Chapter Fourteen in Book Two of the glorious Viṣṇu Purāṇa.

15. Ṛbhu's discourse on the highest truth

Parāśara:

After he had spoken, the brahmin then imparted to the silent king, still deep in thought, this account of nonduality. *1*

The brahmin:

Listen, tiger of a king, to what was sung in former times by Ṛbhu, who led the brahmin Nidāgha to enlightenment. *2*

Ṛbhu by name, Lord Brahmā's son, understood the nature of reality, sire, on account of his noble origin. *3*

In former times, Ṛbhu had a disciple, Pulastya's scion Nidāgha, to whom he taught all knowledge with greatest joy. *4*

When Nidāgha grasped reality, sire, Ṛbhu thought that he was free from false notions of dichotomy. *5*

Pulastya lived in the rich and pleasant city known as Vīranagara on the banks of the Devikā River. *6*

Ṛbhu's disciple Nidāgha, now a yoga expert, sire, resided in a grove outside the city long ago. *7*

One thousand divine years later, Ṛbhu approached that city to visit him. *8*

After the midday rituals, Ṛbhu came to Nidāgha's door unrecognised, where his disciple welcomed him hospitably and showed him in. *9*

Ṛbhu washed his hands and feet and accepted a place to sit. That best of brahmins Nidāgha then invited his guest to dine. *10*

Ṛbhu:

Tell me, best of brahmins, what food you have at home, because I find no pleasure in inferior cuisine. *11*

Nidāgha:

We have cakes of *saktu*, *yāvaka* and *vāṭya* barley in the house. You're welcome to have whichever of these appeals to you, best of brahmins, as you wish. *12*

Ṛbhu:

These are all inferior foods, brahmin. Bring me something sweet, like *saṃyāva* cakes, rice pudding or dishes made with curds and treacle. *13*

Nidāgha:

Hey, wife! Use the best we have at home to make something sweet to please our visitor's palate. *14*

The brahmin:

Thus addressed by Nidāgha, his wife, in deference to her husband's words, made some sweets for Ṛbhu. *15*

Nidāgha, bowing politely, then addressed the sage, your majesty, while the latter ate the sweets that he'd requested. *16*

Nidāgha:

Are you really satisfied? Do you like the food? Is your mind well-pleased with it, brahmin? *17*

Where are you residing, and where do you plan to travel? Tell me the reason for your visit, brahmin. *18*

Ṛbhu:

A hungry person knows satisfaction once he's eaten, brahmin. As I've finished, why ask if I am satisfied? *19*

Hunger arises when the element of earth has been digested. When the body loses moisture, folk get thirsty. *20*

Because I'm not subject to thirst or hunger, even though they're said to be the natural condition of the body, brahmin, and because I'm free from the cause of hunger, I'm always satisfied. *21*

Mental wellbeing and contentment are both natural states of mind, brahmin, but the spirit—*puṃs*—is untouched by these. Ask your questions of one whose mind is prone to them. *22*

You asked me where I live, where I'm going and why I've come. Listen to my answers to these three questions. *23*

Since this spirit is everywhere and pervasive like the sky, how can questions such as 'Why?' and 'Whence?' and 'Whither?' be meaningful? *24*

I neither come nor go, nor do I reside in a particular place. You're not you, others are not themselves and I'm not me. *25*

If you want to know why I chose between sweet and unsweet food, then listen to my explanation, best of brahmins. *26*

What is sweet or bland to one who eats the food, best of brahmins? Sweet food loses its appeal when you don't desire it. *27*

Tasteless food is still delicious to a man who's hungry, but what food tastes as good at first, halfway through and at the end? *28*

Just as houses made from mud are strengthened when plastered with the same material, similarly, this body, composed of earthy elements, is strengthened with particles of the same. *29*

Barley, wheat, lentils, butter, oil, milk, yoghurt, sugar, fruit and the others all consist of atoms. *30*

When you've therefore understood this false distinction between bland and tasty, then your mind will be impartial, and impartiality leads to liberation. *31*

The brahmin:

Hearing these words of great import, your majesty, fortunate Nidāgha threw himself to the floor and said, *32*

'Please have mercy! Tell me who you really are, now that you've come to help me, brahmin. Hearing what you've said, my confusion is dispelled.' *33*

Ṛbhu:

I'm your teacher, Ṛbhu, and I came to teach you, brahmin, but now I've imparted the highest truth, I'll set out again. *34*

Understand that all this world is one and undivided and is just a form of the highest spirit known as Vāsudeva. *35*

The brahmin:

After Ṛbhu had spoken thus, Nidāgha bowed with reverence and worshipped him with deepest faith. Then the sage departed and wandered of his own accord. *36*

So ends Chapter Fifteen in Book Two of the glorious Viṣṇu Purāṇa.

16. Ṛbhu's discourse continues

The brahmin:

When another thousand years had passed, your majesty, Ṛbhu returned to that same place to teach Nidāgha again. *1*

The sage beheld Nidāgha outside the city as the king was entering with a mighty army. *2*

Fortunate Nidāgha, returning from the forest with firewood and *kuśa*-grass, stood apart from the pressing crowd, wracked by pangs of hunger. *3*

Seeing Nidāgha, Ṛbhu approached unrecognised and greeted him: 'Brahmin, why are you standing here alone?' *4*

Nidāgha:

Greetings, brahmin! This crowd is here to see the king return to our fair city. That's why I'm here as well. *5*

Ṛbhu:

Which is the king and which are his attendants? Tell me, best of brahmins, because I think you must be wise. *6*

Nidāgha:

The king is mounted on that sacred raging elephant, towering like a mountain peak, and the others are his attendants. *7*

Ṛbhu:

You've shown me the elephant and the king together but haven't said which features may distinguish them. *8*

Therefore, fortunate brahmin, describe for me the difference between these two, because I wish to know which one is which. *9*

Nidāgha:

The elephant is the one below, brahmin, and the one on top is king. One is being carried by the other. Who doesn't understand this, brahmin? *10*

Ṛbhu:

Kindly tell me, brahmin, so I can comprehend: what's meant by the word 'below', and what's the meaning of 'on top'? *11*

The brahmin:

Hearing this, Nidāgha suddenly leapt on Ṛbhu's back and cried, 'Listen and I'll tell you. *12*

I'm on top of you, just like the king, and, like the elephant, you're below. I'm giving you this demonstration, brahmin, to help you understand.' *13*

Ṛbhu:

If you are like the king and I am like the elephant, kindly tell me, best of brahmins, which of us am I and which is you? *14*

The brahmin:

Hearing this, Nidāgha reverently clasped the sage's feet and said, 'You must be Ṛbhu, my holy teacher! *15*

None other than my master has a mind so perfectly impressed by the unity of all things. That's why I guess that you're my guru, finally returned.' *16*

Ṛbhu:

I am indeed your guru, Nidāgha, and Ṛbhu is my name. Having received your homage in former times, I've returned to teach you further. *17*

I therefore give you this instruction, wise brahmin, which in brief consists of the essence of the highest truth: all this is one. *18*

The brahmin:

After that wise guru Ṛbhu had spoken thus to Nidāgha, he set out and, following his instruction, Nidāgha also came to realise the unity of everything. *19*

He saw no distinction between himself and other creatures, brahmin, and so that twice-born sage reached final liberation. *20*

Similarly, you, understanding virtue, should look upon yourself, your friends and foe as one, your majesty, while realising that the Self—the *ātman*—is all-pervading. *21*

Just as the sky looks white or blue or another colour, the single Self appears divided to those whose perception is imperfect. *22*

That single entity, all that's in this world, is unfailing Viṣṇu. Aside from him, there's nothing. He is me, and he is you, and he is all of this. Abandon the delusion that the Self is still divided! *23*

Parāśara:

Thus addressed by the brahmin, that excellent king, perceiving the highest truth, now cast off all distinctions and the brahmin who recalled his former lives won freedom from rebirth. *24*

A pure-minded individual who tells or hears this pithy tale of Bharata and the king while filled with true devotion will not mistake the nature of the Self, and will be fit for freedom from *saṃsāra*. *25*

So ends Chapter Sixteen in Book Two of the glorious Viṣṇu Purāṇa.

End of Book Two.

Book Three: Society

1. The past and present Manvantaras

Maitreya:

Master, you've given me an excellent and detailed description of the earth, the oceans and the rest, as well as the nature of the sun, the stars and other luminaries. *1*

Similarly, you've explained the creation of the gods and sages, and the origin of the four communities and the realm of animals. *2*

You've also described in detail the feats of Dhruva and Prahlāda. Now I wish to hear about each Manvantara in order. *3*

I'd like to hear you speak of each age's overlord, my guru, with mighty Indra at their head. *4*

Parāśara:

I'll now give you a full and orderly account of the past and future Manvantaras. *5*

The initial Manu was Svāyaṃbhuva, then came Svārociṣa, Uttama, Tāmasa, Raivata and Cākṣuṣa. *6*

These six Manus have already passed. The current one is Vaivasvata, the Sun's own son, and his Manvantara is the seventh. *7*

I've already spoken of the Manvantara of Svāyaṃbhuva at the beginning of the age, and I've told you all about the gods and sages of that period. *8*

Now I'll list the overlords, the deities, the seers and their progeny, who lived in the Manvantara of the Manu Svārociṣa. *9*

During that period, the deities were the Pārāvatas and Satuṣitas, and mighty Vipaścit was the king of gods, Maitreya. *10*

Ūrja, Stambha, Prāṇa, Dattoli, Ṛṣabha, Niścara and Arvarīvant were the seven sages. *11*

Caitra, Kimpuruṣa and others were the sons of Svārociṣa. I've described the second Manvantara. Now listen to the one that followed. *12*

In the third Manvantara, brahmin, the Manu was named Uttama and the regal deity Suśānti was the king of gods, Maitreya. *13*

There were five hosts of deities, the Sudhāmans, Satyas, Śivas, Pratardanas and Vaśavartins, each of which comprised twelve gods. *14*

The seven sons of Vasiṣṭha were the seven sages, and Aja, Paraśu, Divya and the others were the sons of Manu Uttama. *15*

During the Manvantara of Tāmasa, the deities were Surūpas, Haris, Satyas and Sudhis. Each host had twenty-seven gods. *16*

Śibi, also known as Śatakratu or 'Hundred Sacrifices', was their king. Now hear from me the names of the seven sages at that time: *17*

Jyotirdhāman, Pṛthu, Kāvya, Caitra, Agni, Vanaka and Pīvara were the sages then. *18*

The mighty kings named Nara, Khyāti, Śāntahaya, Jānujaṅgha and others were the sons of Tāmasa. *19*

In the fifth Manvantara, the Manu was known as Raivata by name, and Vibhu was the king of gods, Maitreya. Now listen to the names of the deities of that period: *20*

The Amitābhas, Bhūtarayas, Vaikuṇṭhas and Sumedhases. Each host had fourteen gods. *21*

Hiraṇyaroman, Vedaśrī, Ūrdhvabāhu, Vedabāhu, Sudhāman, Parjanya and Mahāmuni were the seven sages during the Manvantara of Raivata, brahmin. *22*

The valiant kings Balabandhu, Susaṃbhāvya and Satyaka, among others, were his sons, best of sages. *23*

The four Manus Svārociṣa, Uttama, Tāmasa and Raivata are thought to be Priyavrata's offspring. *24*

Having propitiated Viṣṇu with his austerities, the sage-king Priyavrata was granted these Manvantara overlords as his descendants. *25*

In the sixth Manvantara, the Manu was known as Cākṣuṣa, and Manojava was the king of gods. Now hear about the deities: *26*

The Āpyas, Prasūtas, Bhavyas, the divine Pṛthugas and the resolute Lekhas were the five hosts, each of which comprised eight deities. *27*

Sumedhas, Virajas, Haviṣmant, Uttama, Madhu, Atināman and Suhiṣṇu were the seven sages. *28*

The sons of the Manu Cākṣuṣa—mighty Ūru and Pūru, with Śatadyumna as the foremost—were the kings. *29*

The son of Vivasvat, brahmin, that brilliant god presiding over funerary rites, is the wise Manu who oversees the present Manvantara, the seventh. *30*

The Ādityas, Vasus, Rudras and others are the deities of this period, great sage, and Indra, conqueror of cities, is the lord of thirteen gods, Maitreya. *31*

Vasiṣṭha, Kāśyapa, Atri, Jamadagni, Gautama, Viśvāmitra and Bharadvāja are the seven sages of this period. *32*

Ikṣvāku, Nṛga, Dhṛṣṭa, Śaryāti, famed Nariṣyanta, Nābhāga, Diṣṭa, *33*

Karūṣa and Pṛṣadhra, rich and famous—these are the nine good sons of Manu Vaivasvata. *34*

The unequalled energy of Viṣṇu, abounding in vitality, infuses all creation and presides over every Manvantara in the form of a deity. *35*

A portion of that energy appeared as Yajña during the period of Svāyaṃbhuva. This divine being arose from Svāyaṃbhuva's mind and was born to his daughter Ākūtī in the first Manvantara. *36*

Later, that same deity was born to Tuṣitā as Ajita during the period of Svārociṣa, along with the other Tuṣita gods. *37*

In the period of Uttama, Tuṣita was born again to Satyā as Satya, together with the peerless Satya deities. *38*

And when the period of Tāmasa began, he was born again to Harī as Hari, along with the Hari gods. *39*

During the period of Raivata, the most excellent deity Hari was born as Saṃbhūta, mind-begotten son of Saṃbhūtī, along with the Rājasa deities. *40*

In the period of Cākṣuṣa, the highest divine spirit was born as Vaikuṇṭha to Vikuṇṭhā, together with the Vaikuṇṭha gods. *41*

In the present Vaivasvata Manvantara, brahmin, Viṣṇu was born as Vāmana, the divine dwarf, the son of Kaśyapa and Aditi. *42*

That great being conquered the threefold worlds in just three strides and entrusted them to Indra, vanquisher of cities, having freed them from all obstacles. *43*

Such are the seven forms of Viṣṇu, brahmin, arising in each of the seven Manvantaras for the preservation of all creatures. *44*

Because the whole world is infused (*viṣṭam*) with the energy of that great being, he is called Viṣṇu, from the root *viś*, meaning 'enter'. *45*

All the gods, the Manus, the seven sages, the Manus' sons, and whoever is Indra, lord of thirteen deities, are all just forms of Viṣṇu's might. *46*

So ends Chapter One in Book Three of the glorious Viṣṇu Purāṇa.

2. The future Manvantaras

Maitreya:

You've described these seven Manvantaras, brahmin sage, please tell me now about the periods yet to come. *1*

Parāśara:

Viśvakarman's daughter Saṃjñā was married to the Sun, and their offspring were the Manu Vaivasvata, Yama and Yamī, sage. *2*

Unable to endure her husband's energy, Saṃjñā engaged Chāyā to serve him, and she herself retired to the forest to undertake austerities. *3*

Thinking Chāyā to be Saṃjñā, the Sun had three more children with her: sluggish Saturn, another Manu named Sāvarṇi, as well as Tapatī. *4*

One day, Chāyā, enraged with Yama, cursed him. Only then did Yama and the Sun realise that she wasn't Saṃjñā. *5*

When Chāyā admitted to the Sun that Saṃjñā was in the forest, he perceived through his yogic power that she was practising austerities in the form of a mare. *6*

Appearing as a stallion, the Sun mounted Saṃjñā and sired the heavenly twins the Aśvins, as well as Revanta. *7*

The lordly Sun then led Saṃjñā to his own abode, where Viśvakarman pared back his energy. *8*

Turning the Sun upon his lathe, the heavenly craftsman reduced his brilliance by just one-eighth, without impairing his eternal light. *9*

The blazing energy of the Sun shaved off by Viśvakarman fell back to earth, best of sages. *10*

There, the heavenly artisan Tvaṣṭṛ used that energy to fashion Viṣṇu's discus, Śiva's trident and a palanquin for wealth-giving Kubera. *11*

Viśvakarman then used the rest to make Kārttikeya's lance and all the other deities' weapons. *12*

Chāyā's second son was also called a Manu and, because he had the same complexion (*savarṇa*) as his elder brother, he was called Sāvarṇi. *13*

His Manvantara, the Sāvarṇi period, will be the eighth. Listen, blessed sage, while I describe it for you. *14*

Sāvarṇi will be the following Manu, Maitreya, and the Sutapas, Amitābhas and Mukhyas will be the gods. *15*

Each host will include twenty deities. Now I'll name the seven sages, best of seers: *16*

Dīptimant, Gālava, Rāma, Kṛpa, Drauṇi and my son Vyāsa, with Ṛśyaśṛṅga as the seventh. *17*

By the grace of Viṣṇu, Bali, blameless son of Virocana, whose realm is the underworld of Pātāla, will be the king of gods. *18*

The kings Virajas, Arvarīvant, Nirmoha and others will be Manu Sāvarṇi's sons. *19*

The ninth Manu will be Dakṣasāvarṇi, Maitreya. *20*

The Pāras, Marīcigarbhas and Sudharmans will be the threefold hosts of gods then, each with a dozen deities. *21*

Their king will be mighty Adbhuta, brahmin. *22*

Savana, Dyutimant, Bhavya, Vasu, Medhātithi and Jyotiṣmant, with Satya as the seventh—these will be the seven great sages. *23*

Dhṛtaketu, Dīptiketu, Pañcahasta, Nirāmaya, Pṛthuśravas and others will be Dakṣasāvarṇi's sons. *24*

The tenth Manu will be Brahmasāvarṇi, sage. The gods will be Sudhāmans, Viruddhas and Śatasaṃkhyas. *25*

Mighty Śānti by name will be their king. Now hear about the seven sages of that period: *26*

Haviṣmant, Sukṛti, Satya, Apāṃmūrti, Nābhāga, Apratimaujas and Satyaketu. *27*

The ten sons of Brahmasāvarṇi—Sukṣetra, Uttamaujas, Bhūriṣeṇa and the rest—will protect the earth. *28*

The eleventh Manu will be Dharmasāvarṇika. *29*

The Vihaṃgamas, Kāmagamas and Nirmāṇarucis will be the principal hosts of deities then, each comprising thirty gods, with Vṛṣa as their king. *30*

Niścara, Agnitejas, Vapuṣmant, Viṣṇu, Āruṇi, Haviṣmant and Anagha will be the seven sages. *31*

The kings Sarvaga, Sarvadharman, Devānīka and others will be that Manu's sons. *32*

The twelfth Manu will be Sāvarṇi, son of Rudra, with Ṛtudhāman as king of gods. Now hear about the deities from me. *33*

The Haritas, divine Lohitas, Sumanases, Sukarmans and Supāras will be the hosts of gods, each with fifteen deities, brahmin. *34*

Tapasvin, Sutapas, Tapomūrti, Taporati, Tapodhṛti, with Dyuti as another and Tapodhana as the seventh will be the sages. *35*

The kings Devavant, Upadeva, Devaśreṣṭha and others will be that Manu's mighty sons. *36*

The thirteenth Manu will be known as Raucya, sage. *37*

The Sutrāmans, Sukarmans and Sudharmans will be the various hosts of gods, each with thirty-three deities. *38*

Mighty Divaspati will be their king. *39*

The seven sages will be Nirmoha, Tattvadarśin, Niṣprakampa, Nirutsuka, Dhṛtimant and Avyaya, with Sutapas as the seventh. *40*

The kings will be Citrasena, Vicitra and others. *41*

Bhautya will be the fourteenth Manu, Maitreya. Śuci will be the king of gods and there'll be five heavenly hosts. Listen to their names: *42*

The Cākṣuṣas, Pavitras, Kaniṣṭhas, Bhrājiras and Vācāvṛddhas will be the deities. Now hear from me the seven sages: *43*

Agnibāhu, Śuci, Śukra, Māgadha, Agrīdhra and Yukta, with Jita as the other. Listen to the Manu's sons: *45*

The kings Ūru, Gambhīra, Budhna and others will be the sons of Manu. Those whom I've named will protect the earth, you tiger of a sage. *45*

The cycle of ages

At the end of every cycle of four ages, the Vedas disappear, but seven sages descend from heaven to the world to propound them once again. *46*

In each Kṛta age, a Manu arises to promulgate *smṛti*, the sacred texts recalled by men, brahmin. The deities enjoy the sacrifices during each Manvantara. *47*

The Manu's sons and their descendants also rule the world for the duration of that period. *48*

A Manu, seven sages, the deities, the Manu's sons who rule the earth and one king of gods preside over every period. *49*

When fourteen Manvantaras have passed, an aeon or *kalpa* of one thousand cycles of four ages is said to be complete. *50*

Then comes a night of the same duration, best of sages, during which Viṣṇu, who also takes the form of Brahmā, reposes on the serpent Śeṣa in the middle of the ocean. *51*

After consuming all three worlds, the lord, creator and universal Janārdana, rests amid his own illusory power, brahmin. *52*

Following which, the eternal lord awakes, and, taking on the quality of energy, creates the world again at the onset of each new aeon as before. *53*

Viṣṇu's stainless aspect—which manifests as Manus, sovereigns, seven sages, deities and their kings—maintains the universe, best of brahmins. *54*

Now you'll hear how Viṣṇu, in the character of the maintainer of the world, undertakes its preservation during every age, Maitreya. *55*

In the Kṛta, Viṣṇu, at the heart of all creation, delighting in the welfare of the world, takes the form of Kapila and other sages, and teaches highest knowledge. *56*

In the Tretā, in the form of a universal monarch, the lord protects the threefold worlds while destroying wicked beings. *57*

In the form of Veda-vyāsa, having split the single Veda into four, the lord arranges these in lesser branches by the hundreds. *58*

Once he's arranged the Vedas in the Dvāpara, Lord Hari takes the form of Kalki at the end of the Kali *yuga*, setting sinners on the path of virtue. *59*

In this way, the infinite being creates, protects and, in the end, destroys the world. There's nothing more beside him. *60*

I've described to you the past, the present and the future of creation, brahmin, and mighty Viṣṇu's actual nature in this world and elsewhere. *61*

I've also told you all about the Manvantaras and those who oversee them. What else would you like to hear? *62*

So ends Chapter Two in Book Three of the glorious Viṣṇu Purāṇa.

3. The Vyāsas arrange the Vedas; The syllable *Oṃ*

Maitreya:

I've learned from you how this world is Viṣṇu, is in Viṣṇu, is from Viṣṇu and how there's nothing else beside him. *1*

But I'd like to hear how the Vedas are arranged by that great being in the form of a Veda-vyāsa, or 'arranger of the Vedas', in each successive age. *2*

Tell me of the varied forms of Vyāsa that appear in every aeon, sage and master, and how the Vedic branches are divided. *3*

Parāśara:

As the Veda-tree is divided into branches by the thousand, Maitreya, it's impossible to describe them one by one, so listen to this summary. *4*

In each Dvāpara age, Viṣṇu takes the form of Vyāsa, sage, and divides the single Veda into several parts to benefit the world. *5*

Seeing humankind lacks courage, strength and energy, he divides the Veda for the good of every being. *6*

The form that Viṣṇu takes, that enemy of Madhu, when he divides the Veda, is known as 'Veda-vyāsa'. *7*

Now you'll learn about the varied Vyāsas who appear in this Manvantara, sage, and how the division into branches is undertaken. *8*

The Vedas have been divided on twenty-eight occasions by great sages during each successive Dvāpara age in this Vaivasvata Manvantara. *9*

Twenty-eight Veda-vyāsas, who arranged the Vedas into four in each Dvāpara age, best of sages, have already gone by. *10*

In the first Dvāpara, the Vedas were arranged by the self-existent deity Brahmā. In the second, the Veda-vyāsa was the patriarch Manu. *11*

In the third, the arranger was Uśanas, and in the fourth Bṛhaspati. Savitṛ was the arranger in the fifth, and in the sixth was Mṛtyu, Lord of Death. *12*

In the seventh it was Indra, and Vasiṣṭha in the eighth, Sārasvata in the ninth and Tridhāman in the tenth. *13*

In the eleventh it was Trivṛṣan, and Bhāradvāja followed him. In the thirteenth it was Antarikṣa, and Varṇin in the fourteenth, *14*

Trayyāruṇa in the fifteenth, in the sixteenth Dhanaṃjaya, Kṛtaṃjaya in the seventeenth and Ṛṇjaya in the eighteenth. *15*

The next Vyāsa was Bharadvāja, and after him came Gautama. After Gautama the Vyāsa was Uttama, also known as Haryātman. *16*

After Haryātman was Vena or Vājaśravas, then Soma Śuṣmāyaṇa or Tṛṇabindu. *17*

Then came Ṛkṣa, scion of Bhṛgu, also known as Vālmīki. After him was my father, Śakti, sage, and I was the Vyāsa after him. *18*

Jātukarṇa followed me, then Kṛṣṇa Dvaipāyana. These are the twenty-eight Veda-vyāsas of ancient times. *19*

They split the single Veda into four in each Dvāpara age. *20*

In the next Dvāpara period, Droṇa's son Drauṇi will be the Vyāsa after my son, the sage Kṛṣṇa Dvaipāyana, has passed. *21*

The syllable Oṃ and the Absolute

Oṃ is defined as the Absolute (*brahman*) in the form of one eternal syllable. It's so called on account of its greatness (*bṛhatvāt*) and its capacity to strengthen (*bṛṃhaṇatvāt*). *22*

I bow to the Absolute in the form of the everlasting syllable, *Oṃ*, invoked as 'earth, sky and heaven' (*bhūr, bhuvas, svaḥ*) in the *Ṛg*, *Yajur*, *Sāma* and *Atharva Vedas*. *23*

I bow to the Absolute, known as the cause of creation and destruction of the world, the deepest secret of *mahat*, the principle of Greatness. *24*

Unfathomable, unbound and undecaying, it's the source of illusion in the world. With brilliance and efficacy, it's the cause by which the purpose of the highest spirit is accomplished. *25*

The Absolute is the crown for those who know the Sāṃkhya teachings, and the goal for those who pacify and regulate themselves. It's unmanifest, undying efficacy. *26*

It's also called the essence, the origin of the Self, the heart of all reality. It's indivisible, pure, imperishable and manifold. *27*

I bow again and again to that eternal, highest Absolute, a form of Vāsudeva, who is himself a form of the highest spirit. *28*

This Absolute is the threefold lord, yet also one. That undivided being is thought to be divided among all creation by those who regard him as divisible. *29*

This universal being, composed of the *Ṛg*, *Sāma* and *Yajur Vedas*, is their essence. He is indeed the heart of all embodied beings. *30*

Consisting of the Vedas, he is divided, but he made these texts and splits them into many. The eternal lord is author of their branches, and takes the form of knowledge of them all. *31*

So ends Chapter Three in Book Three of the glorious Viṣṇu Purāṇa.

4. The origin of the four Vedas

Parāśara:

The ancient four-limbed Veda had a hundred thousand verses, and all ten kinds of sacrifice, like a wish-fulfilling cow, are derived from it. *1*

In this, the twenty-eighth Dvāpara age, my holy scion Vyāsa arranged that single four-limbed text. *2*

Just as wise Veda-vyāsa arranged it, so was it divided by all the former Vyāsas and by me as well. *3*

You should know that the division into branches that he undertook, best of brahmins, is likewise done in every fourfold era. *4*

Understand that Vyāsa, Kṛṣṇa-Dvaipāyana, is Lord Nārāyaṇa himself, Maitreya. Who else on earth could compose the *Mahābhārata*? *5*

Listen now, Maitreya, while I explain how my great son arranged the Vedas during this Dvāpara age. *6*

Urged by Brahmā, he began to organise the texts, and first accepted four disciples, all well-steeped in Vedic lore. *7*

That great sage adopted Paila as disciple for the *Ṛg*, and Vaiśampāyana for the *Yajur Veda*. *8*

For the *Sāma*, Veda-vyāsa took on Jaimini. Sumantu, who understood the *Atharva Veda*, became a student of that prudent sage. *9*

Vyāsa accepted Romaharṣaṇa, a wise disciple, as narrator for the histories and purāṇas. *10*

The *Yajur Veda* was a single text, but he divided it in four, and, in doing so, he brought about the fourfold *cāturhotra* sacrifice. *11*

The sage assigned the *yajus* prayers to the director of the sacrifice, the *adhvaryu*; the *ṛc* verses to the sacrificing priest or *hotṛ*; the *sāman* hymns to the cantor or *udgātṛ*; and the *atharva* incantations to the brahmin. *12*

Vyāsa compiled the *ṛc* verses as the *Ṛg Veda*, *yajus* prayers as the *Yajur Veda* and the *sāman* hymns as the *Sāma Veda*. *13*

With the *atharva* incantations, that master created all the rituals for the kings and for the office of the brahmins, as per usage. *14*

He split in four that single spreading Veda-tree and so began a Veda forest. *15*

The branches of the *Ṛg Veda*

First, Paila split the *Ṛg* in two, and gave one part to Indrapramati and one to Bāṣkala. *16*

Wise Bāṣkala split his part in four, and gave each one to his disciples, Baudhya and the others. *17*

Baudhya, Agnimāṭhara, Yājñavalkya and Parāśara, sage, adopted these subsections of that branch.[1] *18*

Indrapramati taught one collection to his son, great Māṇḍukeya, Maitreya. *19*

This was then passed down in turn from his disciples and their disciples to their sons and *their* disciples. *20*

Vedamitra, also known as Śākalya, studied that collection. He divided it in five and gave each part to his disciples. *21*

Now hear their names from me: Mudgala, Gālava, Vātsya and Śālīya, with the great sage Śiśira as the fifth, Maitreya. *22*

Śākapūṇi split that same collection differently by dividing it in three and adding an appendix as the fourth division, best of sages. *23*

Krauñca, Vaitālaki and Balāka, that great sage, were his disciples, and Nirukta, master of the Vedas and their supplements, was the fourth. *24*

This is how the later branches grew from all these subbranches, best of brahmins. Bāṣkala made three other compilations, brahmin. Kālāyani was his disciple, as was Gārgya, with Java as the third. *25*

It is they who spread abroad these sets of Vedic verses. *26*

So ends Chapter Four in Book Three of the glorious Viṣṇu Purāṇa.

5. The branches of the *Yajur Veda*

Parāśara:

Vyāsa's wise disciple Vaiśampāyana split the tree-like *Yajur Veda* into twenty-seven.[2] *1*

He then conferred each branch upon his disciples, who accepted them in turn. *2*

His disciple Yājñavalkya, Brahmarāta's son, understood the highest virtues and was always dedicated to the service of his master, brahmin. *3*

1 Is this the same Parāśara who narrates the *Viṣṇu Purāṇa*?

2 The verse breaks in this chapter are very messy and I have not followed them strictly.

'One who fails to join our gathering on Mount Meru for seven nights will be guilty of brahminicide.'[3] *4*

Such was the first agreement of the gathered sages, brahmin, but Vaiśampāyana was the only one to break it. *5*

He later tripped over his sister's son and caused the infant's death. *6*

The sage called on his disciples to do penance to absolve him of his crime, yet none of them was willing. *7*

Yājñavalkya then addressed his guru, 'Master, how can I do penance with these lazy, mediocre brahmins?' *8*

His wise guru, enraged by this, replied to him, 'Forget all that you have learned from me. You're a failure as a brahmin! *9*

You say these other brilliant men are mediocre, but what good are you, a follower who disobeys my words?' *10*

Yājñavalkya said, 'I told you this in good faith, brahmin, but now I've had enough. This is what I've learned from you!' *11*

Parāśara:

So saying, the sage vomited the blood-stained *yajus* prayers in physical form, handed them to his guru and walked away. *12*

The other disciples all turned into partridges (*tittira*), brahmin, and gobbled up the prayers that Yājñavalkya had disgorged. That's why these texts are known as Taittirīyas. *13*

Those who performed penance for brahminicide at the urging of their guru became known as Caraka priests, on account of their undertaking (*caraṇa*), best of sages. *14*

But Yājñavalkya, who knew the art of breath control, Maitreya, wanted to win back the *yajus* prayers and devoutly worshipped Sūrya. *15*

3 The Critical Edition reads *samājenāgamiṣyati*. I have interpreted this as *samāje nāgamiṣyati*, which makes better sense.

Prayer to the Sun

Yājñavalkya:

I bow to you, Savitṛ, door to liberation, whose brilliance has no measure. The *Ṛg*, *Yajur* and *Sāma Vedas* are your three abodes; I bow to you. *16*

In the form of fire and moon, you are the origin of the world, light-giving sun, pure energy and origin of the ray Sauṣumṇa. *17*

I bow to you, one with the notion of time, consisting of *kalā*, *kāṣṭhā*, *nimeṣa* and other measures. You should be contemplated as a form of Viṣṇu; you are the syllable *Oṃ*. *18*

You support the hosts of deities, having sustained the moon with your own rays, and the ancestral spirits with sweet nectarine libations. I bow to you, the essence of nourishment. *19*

You bring cold and water, heat and rain, Lord, then take them away again. I bow to you who are three seasons, sun and arranger of all things. *20*

You dispel darkness from the world and are its lord. You are the deity who is the abode of goodness. I bow to you, the brilliant sun. *21*

Before you've risen, people are unfit for virtuous acts, nor does water purify. I bow to you, resplendent god. *22*

Touched by your rays, the world is fit for rituals. I bow to you, the cause of purity. You are purity itself. *23*

I bow to Savitṛ, the sun, light-bringer, the shining one. To Aditi's offspring, first of beings including gods and all the rest, I bow and bow again. *24*

Your chariot is golden, your banners bestow nectar. I bow to you, the universal eye. *25*

Parāśara:

After Yājñavalkya had praised the Sun with these and other words, the deity took the form of a stallion. 'Make a wish,' he said. *26*

Falling to the ground, Yājñavalkya besought the Sun, maker of the day, 'Give me those *yajus* prayers that even my guru doesn't know.' *27*

Parāśara:

Hearing this, the lordly Sun bestowed on him the *yajus* prayers known as *Ayātayāma*, unknown even to his guru. *28*

Because the Sun in equine form revealed these prayers, brahmins who learn them are called Vājins, 'horse-possessors', best of brahmins. *29*

The Vājins are divided into fifteen branches, all stemming from Yājñavalkya, Kaṇva and other blessed sages. *30*

So ends Chapter Five in Book Three of the glorious Viṣṇu Purāṇa.

6. The branches of the *Sāma* and *Atharva Vedas*; The purāṇas

Parāśara:

Now hear of Vyāsa's student Jaimini, Maitreya, who duly arranged the branches of the tree-like *Sāma Veda*. *1*

Jaimini's son was Sumantu and his son was Sukarman. These two wise men each mastered one compilation. *2*

Sumantu's son Sukarman created the *Sāhasra Saṃhitā*, a compilation with a thousand verses. This was taken up by his two disciples, both adherents of great vows: *3*

Hiraṇyanābha Kausalya and Pauṣpiñji, best of brahmins. The latter had fifteen disciples known as the northern singers of the *Sāma Veda*. *4*

The brilliant brahmins who received the fifteen compilations from Hiraṇyanābha are known by the wise as the eastern singers of that tradition. *5*

Lokākṣi, Kuthumi, Kuṣīdin and Lāṅgali were Pauṣpiñji's disciples. Their followers and their followers' disciples further raised the number of compilations. *6*

Hiraṇyanābha's wise disciple, Kṛti by name, taught twenty-four compilations to his disciples. *7*

They, too, split the *Sāma Veda* into many branches. I'll now describe the compilations of the *Atharva Veda*. Sumantu was a brilliant sage. *8*

He taught the *Atharva Veda* to his disciple Kabandha, who divided it in two and gave these to Devadarśa and Pathya. *9*

Devadarśa's disciples included Maudga, Brahmabali, Śaulkāyani and Pippalāda, best of sages. *10*

Pathya had three disciples who also made compilations, brahmin: Jājali, Kumudādi, with Śaunaka as the third, brahmin. *11*

Śaunaka split his part in two and gave half to Babhru, and the second he gave to his follower named Saindhava. *12*

Mañjakeśa further divided the Veda he received from Saindhava into two. Sections dealing with astrology, rules governing the sacrifice, mantras, *13*

With incantations as the fourth and spells for dispelling evil as the fifth—these are the major divisions of the *Atharva Veda*. *14*

The purāṇas

Vyāsa, skilled in the import of the purāṇas, compiled these texts from myths and legends, verses and historical accounts. *15*

The great sage then conferred this purāṇic compilation on his famous disciple, Romaharṣaṇa the bard. *16*

Romaharṣaṇa had six disciples: Sumati, Agnivarcas, Mitrāyu, Śāṃśapāyana, Akṛtavraṇa and Sāvarṇi. *17*

Akṛtavraṇa, scion of Kaśyapa, Sāvarṇi and Śāṃśapāyana were the creators of three root compilations, and Romaharṣaṇa's was the fourth. *18*

This, the *Viṣṇu Purāṇa*, is based on these four compilations, sage. *19*

The first of all the purāṇas is said to be the *Brahma*, but eighteen are enumerated by experts in the field: *20*

The *Brahma*, *Padma*, *Viṣṇu*, *Śiva* and the *Bhāgavata*. The *Nārada* is another, with the *Mārkaṇḍeya* as the seventh, *21*

The *Agni* is eighth, *Bhaviṣya* the ninth, the tenth is the *Brahmavaivarta* and the *Liṅga* is eleventh. *22*

The *Varāha* is the twelfth and the *Skanda* is thirteenth. The fourteenth is the *Vāmana*, and the *Kūrma* is the fifteenth. These are followed by the *Matsya*, *Garuḍa* and *Brahmāṇḍa purāṇas*. *23*

The first creation of the world, the subsequent re-creations, the genealogies of the patriarchs, the Manvantaras and accounts of royal dynasties are found in all these texts. *24*

The purāṇa that I'm teaching you, Maitreya, is known as the *Viṣṇu* and is listed after *Padma*. *25*

Lord Viṣṇu is mentioned at every stage, including the creation, re-creation, genealogies, Manvantaras and the rest without exception, best of brahmins. *26*

The four Vedas, the six Vedāṅgas, Mīmāṃsā, Nyāya, the purāṇas and Dharma Śāstras make up the fourteen branches of knowledge. *27*

The *Āyur*, *Dhanur* and *Gāndharva Vedas*, with the *Artha Śāstra* as the fourth, make eighteen in all.[4] *28*

You should know that sages are of three descriptions: first are brahmin sages, then come divine sages and after them are royal seers. *29*

Thus, I've described the branches of the Vedas and their subbranches, the creators of each and the reason they're divided. *30*

The same division into branches is carried out in every Manvantara. *31*

As the primal Veda is eternal, these branches are merely differences in appearance, brahmin. *32*

I've told you all you asked about the Vedas. What else shall I tell you now, Maitreya? *33*

So ends Chapter Six in Book Three of the glorious Viṣṇu Purāṇa.

7. How to escape death: Yama's song

Maitreya:

You've told me precisely all I asked about, my guru, but please tell me one more thing I'd like to hear. *1*

Seven continents, great sage, the underworlds and seven realms all lie within the egg of Brahmā. *2*

This whole world is filled with living things: small, smaller and the smallest, as well as large, larger and the largest. *3*

There's not one-eighth of an inch where living creatures, tied by bonds of karma, are not found, great sage. *4*

4 The Vedāṅgas are supplements to the Vedas that cover phonetics, metre, grammar, vocabulary, astrology and recitation. Mīmāṃsā and Nyāya deal with critical investigation of the Vedas and with logic. The Dharma Śāstras are legal texts, while the last four treat health, archery, performative arts and governance, respectively.

Yet all fall prey to Yama, Lord of Death, and when their lives are at an end, master, he drags them off for torture. *5*

And when they've been released from hell, they're born again among the gods or some other class of being, or so the scriptures say. *6*

I'd like to hear about pure conduct by which we may escape from Yama's grip. Pray speak on this. *7*

Parāśara:

Big-hearted Nakula once asked the same of his grandsire, so now you'll hear what Bhīṣma said to him.[5] *8*

Bhīṣma:

Long ago, a friend of mine, a brahmin from Kaliṅga, had come to visit me, dear boy. He said that he'd once asked this very question of a sage who knew his former lives. *9*

That sage described the current state, and how things would be in future, and everything took place exactly as he foretold. *10*

Filled with faith, I asked the brahmin more about it, and I've seen nothing anywhere that contradicts his words. *11*

This is what he told me when I asked him long ago, recalling what that sage had said to him. *12*

This man who recalled his former lives revealed to him a secret most profound. It was this dialogue between Lord Yama and his minion that I'll now repeat for you. *13*

The Kaliṅgan:

Seeing his minion with noose in hand, Yama whispered in his ear, 'Leave the devotees of Madhusūdana alone, for I'm the lord of all, except the Vaiṣṇavas. *14*

I was told by Brahmā, the disposer revered by hosts of gods, to govern (*yam*) every being in this world according to their deeds, both good and bad. But I myself am subject to my guru, Hari, and cannot act alone. When it comes to governance, Viṣṇu is my superior. *15*

5 Nakula is one of the five Pāṇḍava brothers.

Just as gold is all one kind, but may be crafted into bracelets, bands and earrings, in that same way, Hari is present in all the deities, animals, mortals and the rest. *16*

Just as drops of water, drawn from earth by wind, return to earth when the wind subsides, in that same way, deities, animals, mortals and the rest, separated on account of their impure qualities, are in the end united with that eternal being. *17*

A mortal who understands this highest truth and bows to Hari, whose lotus-like feet are worshipped by the hosts of gods, is freed from all the bonds of sin. Avoid such persons, as you would a fire that's fed with oil, and continue on your way.' *18*

When Yama's servant, noose in hand, heard his master's words, he asked the king of justice, 'Tell me, master, how shall I know a devotee of Hari, the arranger of the universe?' *19*

Yama:

One who never strays from traditions of his community, who is equally disposed to friend and foe, who takes nothing, harms no-one and is pure of mind—know him to be a devotee of Viṣṇu. *20*

One whose self remains unstained by filth and folly in the age of Kali, whose thoughts are pure, always holding Janārdana in his heart when delusion ends—know him to be a faithful devotee of Hari. *21*

One who finds another's hidden gold yet thinks it no better than a straw, and one whose heart is always set on the lord alone—know that fine being to be a devotee of Viṣṇu. *22*

Where, on the one hand, is Viṣṇu, a mountain of purest crystal, and on the other, the selfishness and sundry faults that fill the hearts of men? The heat produced by blazing fires will not be found in webs of cooling moonbeams. *23*

Vāsudeva always occupies the heart of one whose mind is pure, selfless, tranquil, of unblemished conduct, a friend to all, whose words are kind and beneficial and who resists the lure of fame. *24*

When eternal Viṣṇu dwells within a person's heart, he seems to all the world to be resplendent, as a *śāla* sapling's beauty betrays the splendid essence of the earth beneath it. *25*

Keep well away, my servant, from those whose sins have been assuaged by obligatory and voluntary acts of penance, whose hearts are daily fixed on Viṣṇu and who are free from folly, selfishness and pride. *26*

If Lord Hari, beginningless and eternal, bearer of the sword, the conch and mace, abides in a person's heart, his sins are destroyed by Viṣṇu, conqueror of all misdeeds, for how can darkness reign when the sun is shining? *27*

The eternal lord will not be found in the heart of one who steals another's wealth, who harms a living thing, whose speech is false or harsh, who's proud of shameful deeds or harbours impure thoughts. *28*

Janārdana dwells not in the heart of the rogue who eyes another's wealth, the wicked man who vilifies the good, he who neglects the sacrifice or gives nothing to the worthy. *29*

A deceitful man who begs a loan from his bosom friend, kinsman, spouse, son, daughter, father, mother or servant—recognise that such a lowly wretch is not a devotee of Viṣṇu. *30*

Of impure thought, attached to vice, ever smitten by the company of the vulgar and influential and who daily exerts himself in wicked ways—this bestial being isn't Vāsudeva's devotee. *31*

'This whole world, including me, is Vāsudeva, the ultimate being, the highest lord, the One'—when such pure thoughts as these reach eternal Viṣṇu in their hearts, let those people be and pass them by. *32*

Keep well away, my servant, from sinless men who say, 'Lotus-eyed Vāsudeva, Viṣṇu, supporter of the world, eternal bearer of the conch and discus, be my refuge!' *33*

Don't go near that worthy man in whose heart the everlasting being abides, for he is destined for a realm that's different from mine, as my power is checked by Viṣṇu's discus. *34*

The Kaliṅgan:

Such was the command that the god of death, the Sun's own son and lord of justice, made to his emissary. This is what the sage told me, and I've told you, best of Kurus, exactly what he said. *35*

Bhīṣma:

Thus spoke my friend in former times, Nakula, the kind-hearted brahmin from Kaliṅga. *36*

I've relayed the whole account to you, dear boy, as is fitting, since Viṣṇu is the only means of rescue from the ocean of *saṃsāra*. *37*

The minions with their staves and ropes, Yama himself and the torments he inflicts, hold no fear for those whose inner self is always fixed on Keśava. *38*

Parāśara:

In answer to your question, sage, I've retold in full this song of Yama, the Sun's own son. What further would you like to hear? *39*

So ends Chapter Seven in Book Three of the glorious Viṣṇu Purāṇa.

8. The four communities

Maitreya:

Tell me, master, how those who wish to flee *saṃsāra* worship the divine lord, the ruler of the world. *1*

I'd also like to hear about the fruits of praising Govinda, sage, won by those intent upon such practices. *2*

Parāśara:

The question you've just asked was also put to Aurva by Sagara, that great sage. Listen and I'll tell you what he said. *3*

Bowing deeply, Sagara questioned Aurva, the scion of Bhṛgu, about the perfect way to worship Viṣṇu, best of sages, *4*

And the benefits that people gain by doing so. Now listen to his reply, Maitreya. *5*

Aurva:

When Viṣṇu is praised, one gains one's wishes in this world, and then in heaven as sought by blessed ones, and finally supreme nirvāṇa. *6*

One receives whatever reward of any size, great or small, that one desires, your majesty, when one worships everlasting Viṣṇu. *7*

Since you ask, ruler of the earth, I'll tell you how he's worshipped and the rewards that result therefrom, so listen: *8*

Viṣṇu, the highest being, is worshipped by a person who practises the traditions of his community; there's no other path that pleases him. *9*

The sacrificer worships him, as does one who offers prayers, sire. But harming others injures Hari, too, because he's everything. *10*

Janārdana is therefore worshipped by any person of good conduct who follows the traditions and the practices set down for his community. *11*

A brahmin, kṣatriya, vaiśya or śūdra, sire, who's intent upon his duties worships Viṣṇu; there is no other way. *12*

Keśava is pleased by one who doesn't curse or lie or slander, which might upset another being. *13*

He is pleased by one who doesn't covet another's wife or goods, and never thinks of doing harm, your majesty. *14*

Keśava's pleased by one who doesn't strike or kill a living thing, sire. *15*

Govinda's pleased by one who's always keen to serve the gods, the brahmins and his guru, sire. *16*

Hari's ever gratified by one who wants the welfare of all beings, as for his son or for himself. *17*

Viṣṇu's always pleased by one whose mind is free from faults like anger, and whose thoughts are without stain, your majesty. *18*

One who undertakes the duties of his community and stage of life, as ordained by scripture, sire, worships Viṣṇu; there is no other way. *19*

The practices of the four communities

Sagara:

As this is so, I wish to hear about the duties of each community and stage of life. So, tell me all, you brahmin hero. *20*

Aurva:

Listen well while I explain the duties of the brahmins, kṣatriyas, vaiśyas and śūdras in that order. *21*

A brahmin, intent upon the study of the Vedas, should practise generosity and worship gods with sacrifices. He should always be supplied with water and maintain the sacred fires. *22*

To earn a living, he may perform a sacrifice for others or do some teaching. He may accept donations as befits a brahmin because he is respected. *23*

He should act to benefit all beings and disadvantage none, because his greatest treasure is benevolence to everything. *24*

A brahmin should be equally disposed towards a rock and to a jewel belonging to another man. It's also been prescribed that he approach his wife at the proper season, sire. *25*

A kṣatriya should willingly make donations to the brahmins, and such a king should offer various sacrifices and undertake the study of the Vedas. *26*

Military life and defence of the realm are his principal occupations, but his primary duty is the protection of the world. *27*

A king fulfils his duty by defending his dominion and, on that account, a portion of the merit of the sacrifice and other rituals accrue to him. *28*

By punishing the wicked and protecting virtuous people, a king who keeps each order in its place attains the place in heaven that he desires. *29*

Brahmā, universal grandsire, gave the occupations of animal husbandry, trade and agriculture to the vaiśya, sire. *30*

Study, sacrifice and generosity are also duties ordained for him, as well as the performance of regular and occasional rites. *31*

The śūdra's intended duty is to serve the twice-born orders, and sustain himself thereby, or with income raised from trading or practising a craft. *32*

The śūdra makes donations and offerings of cooked food, and performs each ritual for his forebears, or hires another to perform them for him. *33*

Acquisition of wealth for the support of their dependants, approaching wives at the proper season, sire, *34*

Compassion towards all creatures, patience, humility, truth, purity, resilience, cheerfulness, eloquence, *35*

Friendliness, generosity and kindness are said to be the virtues for every order, sire. *36*

These are also features common to every stage of life. Now hear about the virtues and the practices to be followed by brahmins and the others in times of strife. *37*

It's said a brahmin may adopt the practices of a kṣatriya or a vaiśya in a crisis, and a vaiśya may adopt a kṣatriya's ways, but neither a kṣatriya nor a vaiśya may adopt the practices of a śūdra if it's possible to avoid them, sire. *38*

If they must adopt another's ways in times of crisis, then they shouldn't mix the practices of different orders. *39*

I've told you all about the duties of each community. Now listen while I describe the duties for each stage of life. *40*

So ends Chapter Eight in Book Three of the glorious Viṣṇu Purāṇa.

9. The four stages of life

Aurva:

Once he's been invested with the sacred thread, sire, a boy should live in his guru's home as a devout *brahmacārin*, a celibate student, intent on mastering the Vedas. *1*

Pure in conduct, he should serve his master, observe the vows and study with all his heart. *2*

At dawn and dusk, he should devoutly venerate the sun, attend the sacred fire, your majesty, and pay homage to his guru. *3*

He should stand when his guru stands, walk when he walks and sit below his guru when he sits. The disciple should do nothing to upset his master, best of kings. *4*

When directed, he should chant the Veda before his teacher, with his mind on nothing else. With permission, he may eat the food received as alms. *5*

He should bathe in water that his teacher used for washing, then bring him firewood, water and other requisites each morning. *6*

When he's finally mastered the appropriate Veda and received his guru's blessing, having recompensed him fully, that learned man may then become a householder. *7*

He should take a wife with proper rites and, having earned some money through his efforts, he should diligently fulfil the duties of that station, sire. *8*

He should honour his ancestral spirits with oblations, the deities with sacrifices, guests with food, sages with recitation, the progenitor Brahmā with offspring, *9*

All living creatures with offerings and all the world with kindness. Such a person reaches those heavenly realms that are won through one's own actions. *10*

Some wandering *brahmacārins* live on alms, after which they establish their own households. *11*

These brahmins journey widely in accord with Vedic teaching, to bathe at sacred fords, master, and to see the world. *12*

For those who roam with neither home nor food, finding shelter where they can at dusk, the householder offers sustenance and refuge. *13*

To his home he welcomes guests with kindly words, sire, offering a bed, a seat and food to eat. *14*

When a traveller turns with disappointment from a person's door, he leaves his misdeeds with the householder and takes that person's good luck with him. *15*

In the homes of virtuous people, one meets neither disrespect, pride, deceit, regret, harm nor insult. *16*

A householder who follows these noble precepts to the letter will be released from all his bonds and ascend to the highest realms. *17*

In ripe old age, your majesty, a householder who has done his duty should venture to the forest, leaving his wife in the care of his sons, or he may take her with him. *18*

There, that sage should live on leaves and roots and berries, his hair and beard and matted locks untended. He'll sleep directly on the ground, sire, welcoming all comers as his guests. *19*

He'll fashion upper and lower garments from skins, or *kāsa* and *kuśa*-grass, your majesty. It's ordained that he should bathe three times a day. *20*

It's prescribed that he should worship deities with fire sacrifices, sire, honour all who come as guests and offer food to mendicants. *21*

It's ordained that he should rub his limbs with forest oils and, during his austerities, your majesty, he must endure the heat and cold and other trials. *22*

The forest-dwelling sage who takes this course with self-restraint burns away his misdeeds like a fire, and wins the everlasting realms. *23*

The fourth stage, that of mendicant, is mentioned by the wise, your majesty. Listen while I describe it. *24*

One who sheds affection for his sons, possessions and his wife, sire, should begin the final stage of life, freed from all his selfishness. *25*

He should forsake the threefold goals—love, wealth and virtue—and other undertakings, your majesty, and be just as well disposed to friends and foe and other living things. *26*

Restrained in voice and thought and deed, he'll not harm a womb-born being, or one that's hatched or any other, while renouncing all attachments. *27*

He'll stay in a village for just one night, or in a city for five, lest he start to like or loathe them. *28*

To support himself, he'll visit the homes of the first three orders to ask for food when the fires are out and the people fed. *29*

Having cast off desire, anger, pride, delusion, greed and every other fault, he'll become a selfless mendicant. *30*

A sage who roams without a threat to any creature is not threatened by them in turn. *31*

The brahmin lights a sacrificial fire within his body and makes oblations to it through his mouth with any food that he has come by. With this body, a mass of fire, he proceeds to heavenly realms. *32*

A stainless brahmin who attains the state of liberation that I've described, fixed on the thought of his own resolution, will reach the tranquil realm of Brahmā, which shines like a light that needs no fuel. *33*

So ends Chapter Nine in Book Three of the glorious Viṣṇu Purāṇa.

10. Birth and marriage

Sagara:

You've described the fourfold stages and the duties of each community, best of brahmins. Now I'd like to hear about the rituals folk perform. *1*

Tell me all about the regular and occasional rites and those performed by people with a special need, outstanding Bhṛgu, as you know it all, or so it seems to me. *2*

Aurva:

I'll now describe the regular and occasional rites you've asked about, your majesty, so listen carefully. *3*

A father should perform the entire cycle of birth rituals, as well as a joyous *śrāddha*, when a son is born. *4*

He should offer food to pairs of brahmins facing east, sire, and, according to his means, sacrifice to the gods and ancestral spirits, as befits the twice-born orders. *5*

Filled with joy, he should offer riceballs mixed with yoghurt, dates and barley to the Nāndīmukha spirits, sire, with the tips of those fingers sacred to the gods, *6*

or with the root of his little finger, sacrosanct to Brahmā. He should then perform all the rites and circumambulations to ensure the child will come of age, your majesty. *7*

Following that, on the tenth day, the father should name the child. The first part should be a deity's name, and the second should befit a person, such as *śarman* or *varman*, 'prosperity' or 'defence'. *8*

Śarman is said to be for brahmins and *varman* for kṣatriyas, while *gupta* and *dāsa*, 'protected' and 'servant', are best for vaiśyas and for śūdras. *9*

He shouldn't choose a name that has no meaning, is unattested, vulgar, unlucky or unsuitable, and it should have an even number of syllables. *10*

He should choose a name that's not too long or short. It shouldn't have too many long vowels but be easy to pronounce and end in a short vowel. *11*

Following this, after the child has been blessed with successive rites, he should start his education in his guru's home in accordance with tradition, as I've described. *12*

Marriage

Once his education is complete and he has recompensed his guru, your majesty, if he wants to be a householder, he should marry. *13*

Alternatively, he may remain a *brahmacārin*, having taken fitting vows, and serve his guru, his guru's sons and dependants. *14*

He may decide to be an ascetic in the forest or a mendicant. Whichever path he takes, sire, he should abide by his decision. *15*

He should wed a girl one-third his own age, who's neither bald nor hairy, dark nor pale. *16*

He shouldn't wed a girl who was born a cripple, has extra limbs or is impure, hirsute, low-born or sickly, *17*

Or wicked, rude or who inherited deformity from her father or her mother, *18*

Who has signs of a beard or a mannish appearance or who mumbles, shrieks or whispers. Nor should he wed a girl who blinks too much or whose eyes are bulging. *19*

Nor should he wed a girl with hairy legs, thick ankles or dimples in her cheeks when laughing. *20*

A wise man should never wed a girl with rough skin, white fingernails, red eyes, pudgy hands or fat feet. *21*

Nor should he wed a girl who's too short or tall, whose eyebrows meet, whose teeth protrude or have gaps between them. *22*

In accordance with tradition, your majesty, a householder should wed a girl five degrees removed on his mother's side and seven on his father's. *23*

Different forms of marriage are attributed to Brahmā, the deities, sages, patriarchs, demigods, gandharvas and rākṣasas, with paiśācas as the eighth and vilest form. *24*

One should marry according to whichever form great sages recommend for one's community, avoiding all the others. *25*

When a man becomes a householder, he should wed a girl who practises virtue at his side. This custom, closely followed, yields magnificent rewards. *26*

So ends Chapter Ten in Book Three of the glorious Viṣṇu Purāṇa.

11. Rituals of the householder

Sagara:

I'd like to hear about the proper conduct of a householder, sage, adhering to which he'll never be excluded from this world or the next. *1*

Aurva:

Listen, your majesty, to the marks of proper conduct. Anyone who follows these will conquer both the worlds. *2*

Sādhus are faultless, holy men. *Sat* is another word for *sādhu*, and the behaviour, *ācāra*, of such beings is called *sat-ācāra*, 'good conduct'. *3*

The seven sages, Manus and patriarchs, sire, both taught and practised such behaviour. *4*

The wise person wakes at the *Brāhma-muhūrta*, 'the hour of Brahmā', ninety minutes before the dawn, when his mind is clear, your majesty. When he's wide awake, he should meditate on virtue, prosperity and the obstacles to both. *5*

He should also meditate on love in forms that don't conflict with other goals and should regard these threefold aims of life as equally important to overcome all obstacles, both visible and invisible. *6*

He should abandon wealth and love if they conflict with virtue, sire, but may depart from virtue if it leads to misery or offends against society. *7*

Following this, after rising in the morning, your majesty, he should venerate the sun. *8*

Leaving the village in a south-westerly direction, he should relieve himself at a distance further than an arrow flies. *9*

After washing hiṣ two feet, he should discard the dirty water in the courtyard of his house. *10*

A wise man never urinates on his shadow or that of a tree or in the direction of a cow, the sun, a fire, the wind, his guru or a member of the twice-born orders. *11*

Nor should he defecate or urinate on cultivated land, in a field of corn, a cow-pen, in an assembly, on a road, in a river or at a sacred ford, you bull among men, *12*

Nor should he defecate or urinate in water, on a riverbank or cremation ground. *13*

During the day, a wise man should urinate facing north, and at night the opposite direction, except in an emergency, your majesty. *14*

Spreading grass on the ground and placing his clothes on his head, he shouldn't tarry or engage in conversation. *15*

He shouldn't use earth from an anthill, or dug up by rats, or taken from water, or used by someone else for cleaning, or left over from plastering a house, *16*

Or cast up by worms or turned by a plough, sire, but should avoid these types of earth to clean himself. *17*

He should use one handful of earth to clean his penis, three for his anus, ten for his left hand and seven for both hands, your majesty. *18*

He should rinse his mouth with clear, odourless water, free from froth and bubbles. With a steadied mind, he should use more earth again. *19*

When he's cleaned his feet and rinsed them, he should take three sips of water and wash his face twice over. *20*

Next, he should splash water on the orifices of his head—the eyes, ears and nostrils—and on his crown, arms, chest and navel, sire. *21*

When he's finished washing, he should tidy up his hair and place a *tilak* on his forehead before a mirror with a stalk of *dūrvā*-grass or something similar. *22*

Daytime rituals

In accordance with the practices of his community, sire, he should start to earn some money to support himself and carry out the sacrifices, filled with faith. *23*

Since these rituals, based on offerings of soma, foods and butter, are undertaken to bring folk wealth, he may try to earn a living from them. *24*

Before conducting regular sacrifices, he should bathe in the water of a river great or small, a pool or mountain stream. *25*

He may wash himself on land with water from a well, or with water brought for bathing from a nearby source. *26*

After he has washed, donned fresh clothes and calmed his mind, he should make libations to the gods, the sages and ancestral spirits with those parts of his hand sacred to each. *27*

He should make three libations of water to please the gods, the same for the sages according to propriety and one for Brahmā the progenitor. *28*

He should also make three offerings of water to please his ancestral spirits, sire, including his grandfathers and great-grandfathers. *29*

With his mind still focused, he should make offerings to his paternal grandmother, her father and *his* father with the forefinger sacred to each, and, if he so desires—listen to me— *30*

To his mother, maternal grandmother, her mother, his guru's wife, his guru, his maternal uncles and other kin, to his dearest friends and to the king, your majesty. *31*

Once he has propitiated the deities and the rest, if he wishes, sire, he may recite this prayer and offer water for the benefit of all beings: *32*

'Gods, demigods, yakṣas, nāgas, gandharvas, rākṣasas, paiśācas, guhyakas, siddhas, kūṣmāṇḍas, trees, birds, *33*

Those animals that live in water, on land or in the air—may all these beings be satisfied at once by this water that I offer. *34*

This I do to benefit all those beings enduring torment in the hells. *35*

Those who are my kin and those who aren't, those who were my kin in previous lives and any beings who desire an offering of water from me—may they all be satisfied! *36*

May these drops of water that I offer relieve those beings beset by thirst and hunger wherever they may be.' *37*

A person may propitiate this whole world with the voluntary libations I've described, your majesty, and, having done so, may acquire the merit that arises from benefiting the world, blameless monarch. *38*

Having duly made these offerings, filled with faith and taking water for himself, he should cup his hands and offer it to the sun: *39*

'I bow to the shining one, the Absolute, the brilliant sun whose energy comes from Viṣṇu, who enlivens the world, the pure stimulator who grants the reward of sacrifices.' *40*

Following this, he should perform a domestic ritual, worshipping his tutelary deity with offerings of water, flowers, incense and the rest. *41*

Before all else, he should perform a fire sacrifice for Brahmā. *42*

He should reverently offer an oblation to the progenitor, the household deities, Kāśyapa and Anumati in succession. *43*

He should then pour the remaining water as a libation to the Maṇika and Parjanya rain gods, at the door of his house to Dhātṛ and Vidhātṛ and at its centre to Brahmā. *44*

Now, tiger among men, you'll hear about the household deities of the four directions. *45*

A prudent man should offer food left over from the sacrifice to Indra, Yama, king of justice, Varuṇa and Indu the Moon in the east and other directions in succession. *46*

In the north-east corner, a wise person should scatter an offering of food for Dhanvantari, the heavenly physician, then offer some to Viśvadeva. *47*

In the north-west corner, he should offer food to Vāyu, god of winds, then to each direction, to Brahmā, the sky and sun, which is the source of everything. *48*

He should offer food to all the deities and other beings, the universal lords, ancestral spirits and Yakṣman, god of tuberculosis, your majesty. *49*

Bringing other foodstuffs, a wise person may make an offering with a focused mind to all the other beings on a clean patch of ground if he so desires. *50*

'Deities, humankind, animals, birds, siddhas, hosts of yakṣas, nāgas and Daityas, spirits of the dead, paiśācas, trees and all those who desire the food I offer, *51*

Ants, worms, moths and other insects—hungry and bound by bonds of karma—may they all be sustained by this and may they all be happy. *52*

I place this food upon the ground to nourish those who have no mother, father, family, sustenance or the means of preparing it, and may they all be satisfied and gladdened! *53*

Since all creatures, this food, Viṣṇu and I are one, I make this offering, a form of every being, to benefit them all. *54*

Here I scatter food to nourish living beings of fourteen kinds and all the gathered hosts of creatures. May they all rejoice!' *55*

Reciting this prayer, a person filled with faith should cast some food upon the ground to benefit each living thing, because the householder is the refuge of them all. *56*

Following this, one may place some food upon the ground for dogs, birds, untouchables and other fallen and unworthy people. *57*

Hospitality

After this, he should stand in the courtyard of his house for as long as it takes to milk a cow, or longer if he so desires, to wait for any visitors. *58*

He should warmly welcome any guest who comes, offer him a seat and allow him to wash his feet. *59*

He should sincerely offer food and ask and answer questions in a civil manner. When the visitor departs, the householder should show respect by seeing him on his way. *60*

He should also duly welcome any guest whose clan and name he does not know, who comes from far away or who lives in another village. *61*

One who feeds himself but doesn't honour hungry guests who have no kin or come from a distant region goes to hell. *62*

Without asking which branch of the Veda he recites, or about his lineage, religious practice or family, a householder should regard a guest as Brahmā, the deity born of the golden egg. *63*

To benefit his ancestors, sire, he should accommodate one additional brahmin from the same locality as himself, whose conduct and lineage are known, in order to perform the five required sacrifices. *64*

Taking a serve of grain, he should cry 'Come!', your majesty, and offer it to a brahmin who is expert in the Vedas. *65*

He should also give three serves to mendicants and *brahmacārins*. The prudent man should give generously, in accordance with his wishes, if he can afford to do so. *66*

One should honour these four as guests, including the mendicants mentioned earlier. By doing so, he acquits his debt to humanity and the sacrifice. *67*

A guest who turns from a house to go elsewhere, his hopes frustrated, leaves his sins with the householder and takes that person's good luck with him.[6] *68*

Brahmā the progenitor, mighty Indra, Agni, god of fire, the host of Vasus and the Sun are all present in the person of a guest, sire, and eat the food he eats. *69*

That's why you should always do your best to honour guests. One who eats without offering food to guests will feed on suffering alone. *70*

6 This is similar to verse 3.9.15.

The householder should next give sanctified food to those daughters who still live with him, the afflicted, pregnant, elderly and the young, while he himself eats last. *71*

One who dines before these others commits a grave misdeed and, when he dies, he'll go to hell and live on nothing but phlegm. *72*

One who eats without bathing first will feed on filth; without a prayer, on pus and blood. One who eats unsanctified foods will drink urine, and one who eats before the young and others will swallow excrement. *73*

Listen therefore, your majesty, to how a householder should eat, and how, when eating, he may avoid the bonds of sin. *74*

And how in this life he may enjoy unequalled health, increased vigour, an end to strife and his enemies' demise, your majesty. *75*

The midday meal

After he has duly bathed and propitiated the gods, the ancestors and sages, the prudent householder, wearing an appropriate gemstone on his finger, may eat, *76*

But only after he's said his prayers, made an offering to the fire, changed his clothes, your majesty, and offered food to guests and brahmins, elders and dependants. He should wear some pleasant scent and a fitting garland, sire. *77*

He shouldn't eat while wearing just a single robe,[7] or while his hands or feet are wet, your majesty. With a clean and cheerful visage, he should face one cardinal point or other: *78*

East or north are best. Let his mind not dwell on other matters, and let his food be fitting, wholesome and prepared with purest water. *79*

Food should not be accepted from those of loose morality, be unattractive or unconsecrated. The householder should offer food to hungry students. *80*

He may then dine cheerfully from vessels clean and suitable, your majesty. *81*

He shouldn't eat from dishes on a stool, in an improper place, sire, or at improper times, or with a troubled mind, first having offered the best part to the fire. *82*

7 A single garment would be something like a lungi, dhoti or sarong, while the upper garment would be shawl. The implication is, I think, that he should cover his chest.

His food should be sanctified with mantras, be suitable and be fresh on the day, your majesty, except for fruit and meat and varieties of dried vegetables. *83*

Dates and thickened treacle are also excepted, sire. He should never eat anything from which the essence has been extracted. *84*

A discerning person should eat without leaving anything over, sire, except for honey, water, yoghurt, butter or barley grits. *85*

With his mind on what he's eating, he should first take something sweet, then eat something sour or salty as the middle course, followed by pungent or astringent foods. *86*

One who begins and ends a meal with liquids, taking solid food between, will never be deprived of health or strength. *87*

One should take five mouthfuls of wholesome food like this, in silence, without complaint or conversation, in order to sustain himself. *88*

When he's finished eating and rinsed his mouth, facing east or north, he should duly rinse his mouth a second time and wash his hands below the wrist. *89*

Content, his mind at rest and seated comfortably, he should turn his thoughts to his tutelary deities. *90*

'May fire, stirred by wind, reduce this food to earthy elements, and in the space that air provides, digest it, and may I be satisfied. *91*

May this food, when digested, replenish the elements of earth, water, fire and wind within me, and may I enjoy unbroken happiness. *92*

May this food vivify the five vital airs, *prāṇa*, *apāna*, *samāna*, *udāna* and *vyāna*, and may I enjoy unbroken happiness. *93*

May the fires known as Agasti, Agni and Vaḍavā digest all the food I've eaten.[8] May they grant me the happiness that arises from the digestion of that food, and may I be free from physical afflictions. *94*

Viṣṇu, primary being and universal lord, is embodied in all the senses and in everybody. By this truth, may all the health-giving food I've eaten be digested. *95*

---

8 Vaḍavā or 'Mare's Fire' is found underwater or in the lower regions and is said to emerge from a cavity called the 'Mare's Mouth' in the southern ocean (from Monier-Williams 1899).

Viṣṇu is consumer, food and digestion. By this truth also, may all the food I've eaten be digested.' *96*

Having made this prayer, one should rub his stomach with his hand, then eagerly devote himself to relaxation. *97*

Dusk: The *sandhyā* rituals

One should spend the remainder of the day engaged in pastimes endorsed by proper scriptural authority and which don't conflict with the path of virtue, after which one should perform the *sandhyā* rituals with devotion. *98*

At day's end, a wise person should duly undertake these rites as the sun goes down, and in the morning before the stars have faded, having properly rinsed his mouth, your majesty. *99*

The two *sandhyā* rituals should always be performed, sire, except when a baby is being born or at a time of impurity, anxiety, illness or danger. *100*

One who rises after the sun, or retires before it sets, is obliged to perform some penance, unless he is unwell. *101*

Having risen before the sun, sire, one should perform the *sandhyā* ritual, and, before he sleeps, the ritual suited to the dusk. *102*

Wicked folk who fail to offer these at dawn and dusk go to Tāmisra, the hell of darkness, sire. *103*

In the evening, furthermore, a householder's wife should offer food to the Viśvadevas without a mantra, sire. *104*

At that same time, she should scatter food for dog-eating *śvapacas* and other untouchables. *105*

A wise person should hospitably honour a guest who arrives at that hour, to the best of his ability, with water for washing his feet, a seat, a polite bow and words of welcome. He should then offer him food and a bed, your majesty. *106*

The sin of turning back a guest arriving after sunset is eight times greater than that of refusing one who comes in daylight, sire. *107*

One should therefore honour guests who come at night with every effort, sire, as when such guests are welcomed, all the gods are honoured. *108*

One should try to please a guest as much as possible by offering rice, vegetables, water, a bed, a mattress or just a place on the floor. *109*

Night: Marital relations

In the evening, when he has washed his feet and all his body, and has finished dinner, sire, the householder should retire to a sturdy wooden bed. *110*

He shouldn't sleep on one that's narrow, broken, uneven, dirty, bug-infested or lacks a bedspread. *111*

They recommend that he should sleep with his head to the east or south, sire, as any other direction is unhealthy. *112*

It's also recommended that a man approach his wife at the proper season, sire, under an asterism with a masculine name, at an auspicious hour and on even nights. *113*

One should not approach a woman who hasn't washed or is unwell, menstruating, unattractive, angry, unsuitable, pregnant, *114*

Unskilled, has another lover, is not affectionate, is the wife of another man, is hungry or has overeaten. He himself should have these qualities: *115*

Having bathed, and wearing garlands and some fragrance, he should show affection, being neither full nor hungry, and approach intercourse with love and passion. *116*

On the eighth and fourteenth days of the lunar month, and on days of the new and full moon, sire, and when the sun first enters a sign of the zodiac— *117*

A person who enjoys oil, women or meat on these days proceeds after death to a hell realm where he'll feed on excrement and urine. *118*

On all such days, therefore, wise, self-restrained men devote themselves to holy scripture, divine sacrifice, meditation and prayer. *119*

There should be no intercourse in a vagina other than a woman's, or in an orifice other than a vagina, or under the influence of drugs, or in the home of a deity, brahmin or guru, *120*

Or at sacred sites, public squares, riverbanks, assembly rooms, crossroads, cremation grounds or in groves or water, sire. *121*

A wise person should avoid intercourse during all the days I mentioned and during twilight, sire, or he'll be punished with urine and faeces in the next world. *122*

Intercourse at any of these times is unproductive, and during the day it's simply wrong, your majesty. Sex on the ground makes people sick, and sex in the water is not recommended either. *123*

One should never approach another man's wife for intercourse, or even contemplate it, let alone discuss it with her, as this will weaken his bones and joints. *124*

One who has enjoyed the wife of another man will be punished in both worlds: in this, his life is short, and in the next, he'll go to hell. *125*

Bearing all this in mind, a wise man may approach his wife in season, when she is free from all the states I've mentioned and if she's in the mood, even if the timing is not exactly right. *126*

So ends Chapter Eleven in Book Three of the glorious Viṣṇu Purāṇa.

12. The conduct of the wise

Aurva:

The householder should worship gods, cattle, brahmins, holy men, the elderly and his teachers. Twice a day he should perform the *sandhyā* rituals and fire sacrifices. *1*

A prudent person should always wear garments that have no holes, take medicine as recommended and carry gemstones for protection. *2*

With clean and freshly pomaded hair, a man should always wear a pleasant scent and dress in tasteful garments with attractive garlands of white flowers. *3*

He should never take another's property, or make the slightest harsh remark, but should speak politely and truthfully, without mentioning another person's faults. *4*

He shouldn't covet another man's wife, nor seek enmity with him, sire, nor should he ride in an unsafe vehicle or rest in the shade of an overhanging cliff. *5*

Those who are odious, wicked, drunk, aggressive or louse-infested, prostitutes and their clients, the lowly, liars, wastrels, slanderers and cheats— *6*

A wise person should befriend none of these, nor should he travel with them alone. *7*

He should never dive into a fast-flowing river, sire, or enter a burning house or climb to the top of a tree. *8*

He shouldn't grind his teeth, pick his nose or yawn without covering his mouth, and he should try not to sigh or cough. *9*

A wise person shouldn't laugh raucously, break wind loudly, bite his nails, snap off stalks of grass or scratch the ground. *10*

A wise man doesn't chew his beard or crumble clods of earth. He doesn't look at auspicious heavenly bodies when he's impure, master, *11*

Or at another man's wife when she is naked, or at the setting sun. He shouldn't express disgust when he sees a corpse, because the odour of the dead arises from the moon. *12*

At night, he should always avoid crossroads, sacred trees, groves near cremation grounds and the company of immoral women. *13*

A wise man never oversteps the shadow of a sacred object, a deity, a brahmin or a heavenly body, nor should he enter a lonely forest by himself or sleep in a vacant house. *14*

He should avoid hair, bones, thorns, filth, food offerings, ashes, chaff and places splashed with other people's bathwater. *15*

A wise person should never seek refuge with unworthy folk or amuse himself with rogues. He shouldn't approach wild animals, nor should he dawdle when he rises in the morning. *16*

A prudent person wastes no time when waking up or turning in, or when standing, sitting, lying down or working, sire. *17*

He should keep clear of animals with tusks and horns, your majesty, and avoid frosts, thunderstorms and heat. *18*

A wise man never bathes or sleeps or drinks water while he's naked, nor should he drink anything or worship deities if the top of his lower garment is loose. *19*

He shouldn't perform a fire sacrifice, worship the deities, undertake any other ritual, rinse his mouth, make a speech or recite a prayer while wearing just a single garment. *20*

He should never sit with those who misbehave; decent people shouldn't spend as much as half a moment in such company. *21*

A wise man never quarrels with superiors or inferiors, sire—marriages and arguments are best conducted between equals. *22*

A wise man shouldn't start an argument but avoid pointless hostility; a little loss may be endured, but the wise reject the wealth that's won with aggravation. *23*

After bathing, a person shouldn't wipe his limbs with a towel or with his hands or shake his hair or rinse his mouth before he's standing. *24*

He shouldn't sit cross-legged in the presence of important people or stretch his legs towards them. He should kneel with modesty when he's with his guru. *25*

He shouldn't pass auspicious or holy places or crossroads on the left, nor should he pass inauspicious ones on the right. *26*

An educated person does not spit, defecate or urinate while facing the moon, fire, the sun, water, the wind or important people. *27*

He shouldn't urinate while standing on a road, nor should he ever step over mucus, excrement, blood or urine. *28*

Clearing the throat and blowing the nose are not recommended at mealtimes, when making food offerings, during other auspicious rituals, prayers or fire sacrifices or in the presence of important people. *29*

A prudent man should never disrespect women, but neither should he trust them. He shouldn't be impatient with them, but neither should he grant them authority. *30*

A wise person who is attentive to correct conduct shouldn't leave his house, your majesty, without respectfully acknowledging the sacred images, flowers, gems, sacrificial butter and venerable persons inside it. *31*

He should be circumspect at crossroads and attentive towards sacrifices at the proper season. He should assist virtuous people in distress and seek the company of the learned. *32*

One who venerates the deities and sages with devotion, who offers food and water to the spirits, and who welcomes guests hospitably, may reach the highest realms. *33*

A restrained individual whose speech is beneficial, measured, kind and timely, sire, will reach those worlds that are the source of everlasting happiness. *34*

One who is intelligent, modest, patient, devout and polite, and who respects wisdom, worthy people and his elders, will proceed to peerless realms. *35*

A wise man shouldn't study Vedas when there is unseasonal thunder or anything inauspicious, or on days when he's impure or during an eclipse. *36*

Heaven is the least reward for that good man who calms the angry, who treats each person as his kin, who is selfless and who reassures the timid. *37*

One concerned for his own welfare should carry an umbrella in rain or shine, a stick at night or in a forest and should always wear sandals. *38*

A wise man shouldn't look up, to either side or in the distance when walking, but should keep his eyes on the ground two paces in front of him.[9] *39*

The restrained man who shuns each cause of wickedness will never know the slightest diminution of virtue, wealth or love. *40*

Sinless in the presence of the sinful, a kindly word upon his lips, a heart that's filled with benevolence—such a man holds liberation in the palm of his hand. *41*

The world is upheld by the dignity of those who are always free from passion, beyond the reach of lust and greed and anger and firmly set on perfect conduct. *42*

A wise person, therefore, speaks the truth when it's pleasing to another, but when the truth is painful, he stays silent. *43*

He shouldn't speak if he thinks his words are merely pleasant but unhelpful. It's better to offer something beneficial even if it's hard to hear. *44*

A wise man strives with body, voice and mind for the benefit of living beings in this world and the next. *45*

So ends Chapter Twelve in Book Three of the glorious Viṣṇu Purāṇa.

9 The text says 'the length of a yoke' in front of him.

13. Rituals relating to birth and death

Aurva:

When a son is born, it's recommended that a father bathe himself fully clothed, after which he should undertake those rituals pertaining to the birth and a *śrāddha* befitting the occasion. *1*

After he has respectfully circumambulated the deities associated with even days and the ancestral spirits, he should honour brahmins and offer food with his mind on this and nothing else. *2*

Facing east or north, he should offer food such as yoghurt, whole grains of barley and dates with that part of his hand or body sacred to each deity, your majesty. *3*

As the host of ancestral spirits known as the Nāndīmukhas are propitiated by this *śrāddha*, sire, it should be performed by people at all such happy times. *4*

At the marriage of a son or daughter, on entering a new house, at the naming ceremony of a child, at the first cutting of the hair and so on, *5*

At the parting of a pregnant woman's hair and at the first showing of a baby's face, the faithful householder should venerate the host of Nāndīmukhas. *6*

I've described in brief a set of rituals for the ancestors to be conducted on occasions marked by joy. Now you'll hear about the rules for undertaking funerals, your majesty. *7*

After the corpse has been washed with fresh water and garlanded with flowers, it's cremated outside the village. The relatives of the deceased should immerse themselves in water fully dressed. *8*

Facing south, they offer water in cupped hands, saying, 'This is for you, wherever you are.' *9*

Entering the village with the cows when the stars begin to shine, they should sleep on straw mats spread on the floor. *10*

Every day, they should place food on the ground as an offering for the deceased, your majesty. They may eat boiled rice during the day, but no meat, you bull among men. *11*

Brahmins are to be fed for as many days as the mourner sees fit, for the deceased person is also nourished when his kin are dining. *12*

On the first, third, seventh and ninth days, having changed his clothes and washed himself outdoors, he should make an offering of sesame seeds and water. *13*

On the fourth day, the bones and ashes should be gathered, sire, after which the bodies of those who make offerings of food may be touched again. *14*

Those who made offerings of water are also able to resume all their usual activities, but should refrain from luxuries, such as garlands and body lotions, sire. *15*

Those who made food offerings are permitted to use beds and seats after the deceased's ashes and bones have been gathered, but sexual intercourse with women is forbidden. *16*

If the deceased is a child, or in another place, or is a fallen person or a sage, purity returns more quickly, and the rituals involving water, fire and so on are discretionary. *17*

The food of a family whose relative has died may not be eaten for ten days, and the giving and receiving of gifts, sacrifice and Vedic studies are suspended. *18*

Such are the rules when the deceased is a brahmin. For a kṣatriya, impurity persists for twelve days; for a vaiśya, two weeks; but for a śūdra, purity returns only one month later. *19*

One might choose to feed the brahmins on odd days, and on each following day, one should place an offering of food on a bed of *kuśa*-grass for the spirit of the deceased, along with any leftovers. *20*

As soon as a man has fed the brahmins, he should touch some water, a weapon, a goad or stick, depending on his community, as he'll be purified by doing so. *21*

After this, a man may resume his occupation as befits the brahmin order and the others, so he might live on earnings from a fitting source. *22*

In every month that follows, the *ekodiṣṭa* ceremony should be undertaken on the date of death, but rituals such as invocation of the deities are unnecessary. *23*

A single offering of water should be made on these occasions to purify one person. A food offering should be made for the deceased, while brahmins take a meal. *24*

The brahmins who perform the sacrifice are to be asked if they are satisfied, and, if they are, then the words, 'May he also be eternally so', should be addressed to the deceased. *25*

The practice known as *ekodiṣṭa* takes place for one year after death, and an offering of food is made on such occasions. Now you'll hear some more about this, sire. *26*

In the performance of this ritual, a set of four vessels filled with sesame seeds, fragrances and water is used, your majesty. *27*

One is for the deceased, while the others are for the ancestors. The contents of the first are poured into the other three. *28*

When the deceased has reached the status of an ancestor by this process, sire, one should venerate the old ancestral spirits with all the *śrāddha* rituals. *29*

A son, grandson, great-grandson, other relative, a brother's descendant or a descendant related through participation in a food-offering ritual are all entitled to perform these funerary rites, your majesty. *30*

In the absence of all these, a descendant related through shared participation in a water offering, or a relative connected through a food or water offering on the mother's side, may officiate. *31*

If the male line is extinct on both sides, these rituals may be performed by women, sire. The rites may even be performed by the deceased's acquaintances. Further, the king himself may cause the rites to be performed with wealth left by a person without heirs. *32*

Funerary rites are of three kinds: initial, medial and final. Now you'll hear from me about the differences among them. *33*

The initial rites are those performed after the cremation and the touching of water, a weapon and so on. The *ekodiṣṭa* rituals performed in months that follow are known as medial rites. *34*

The rituals after the food offering for the deceased, during which he acquires the status of an ancestral spirit, are called the final rites, your majesty. *35*

The initial rites should be performed by those connected through a food or water offering on the father's or mother's side, or by the deceased's acquaintances or by the king when he has taken over the property of the deceased. *36*

The final rites are performed by the deceased's son or his descendants, the deceased's daughter's sons or by their descendants, sire. *37*

The final rite of *ekodiṣṭa* should also be performed each year by women on the anniversary of the death, your majesty. *38*

For this reason, you should hear about these final rites, sire, the times at which they are performed and the procedure to be followed, flawless monarch. *39*

So ends Chapter Thirteen in Book Three of the glorious Viṣṇu Purāṇa.

14. The *śrāddha* ritual for the ancestral spirits

Aurva:

Brahmā, Indra, Rudra, the Aśvins, Sūrya, Agni, the Vasus, Maruts and Viśvadevas, the hosts of sages, humankind, beasts and birds, *1*

Things that creep and crawl, ancestral spirits and all other beings—a faithful individual who performs a *śrāddha* nourishes this whole world. *2*

A man should undertake a *śrāddha* on the fifteenth day of the dark fortnight each month, your majesty, and on the eighth day, or at any other time he wishes. Listen to me: *3*

A householder should perform this ritual when he feels that an occasion worthy of a *śrāddha* has arisen, or when a distinguished brahmin arrives. On the day of the new moon, or when the sun crosses the celestial equator, *4*

At the equinox, at an eclipse of the sun or moon, when the sun first enters a sign of the zodiac, your majesty, *5*

When an asterism or planet becomes inauspicious, when he has a nightmare or when the grain harvest begins, he may perform a discretionary *śrāddha*. *6*

The hosts of ancestral spirits are nourished for eight years by a *śrāddha* performed on the day of the new moon in the lunar mansions of Anurādhā, Viśākhā and Svāti. *7*

When the ancestors are honoured on the new-moon day in the mansions of Puṣya, Raudra or Punarvasu, they are sustained for twelve years. *8*

On the day of the new moon in Dhaniṣṭhā, Pūrvabhādrapadā or Śatabhiśak, the ancestral spirits, desiring nourishment, receive as much as even deities rarely do. *9*

Now hear more about the *śrāddhas* conducted on new-moon days in these nine mansions, and which afford such satisfaction to the ancestors, sire. *10*

Brahmā's son Sanatkumāra sang this song to great Purūravas, son of Ilā, who, bowing with respect, had asked about the *śrāddhas*, and who was devoted to his ancestors: *11*

Sanatkumāra:

The third day of Vaiśākha, the ninth in the bright fortnight of Kārttika, the thirteenth in the dark fortnight of Nabhas and the fifteenth day of Māgha— *12*

These four, the Yugādya, or 'first days of the age', are said to be endlessly auspicious, your majesty. Eclipses of the sun and moon, the eighth day of the three months of Agrahāyana, Māgha and Phālguna and the two days on which the sun crosses the celestial equator— *13*

On these occasions, a dutiful man should offer water mixed with sesame to the ancestors. This is equal to a *śrāddha* of a thousand years, and the ancestors declare this rite is secret. *14*

Whenever the fifteenth day of the dark fortnight of Māgha comes into conjunction with the constellation Śatabhiṣaj, presided over by Varuṇa, this is the best time for a *śrāddha*, sire, as the benefit for the ancestors is not inconsiderable. *15*

Food and water offered by individuals born at the time of a conjunction with the constellation Dhaniṣṭhā, sire, will satisfy the ancestors of their families for ten thousand years. *16*

If a *śrāddha* is performed when the conjunction occurs in the Former Bhādrapadas, the ancestors experience deepest satisfaction, and will be able to repose for an entire age. *17*

A person who venerates the ancestors with respect, having first bathed in the Gaṅgā, Śatadrū, Vipāśā, Sarasvatī or the Gomatī at Naimiṣa, casts off all his sins. *18*

The ancestors always sing this song: 'Having enjoyed a year of unalloyed satisfaction from water offered by our descendants at the end of the dark fortnight in the month of Māgha at a sacred ford, let us be satisfied again.' *19*

The abovementioned rites undertaken at an appropriate time with pure devotion on behalf of a suitable recipient will enable everyone to achieve their wishes, unbroken prosperity and all else they might desire. *20*

Now you'll hear from me the verses sung by the ancestors. Listen carefully and all this will come to pass. *21*

'The prudent man who undertakes food offerings for us, and doesn't try to hide his wealth, may be reborn a fortunate being in our own lineage. *22*

If a man, when rich, gives wealth in the form of jewels, garments, lands, carriages or other great luxuries to brahmins for our benefit, *23*

Or gives food according to his capacity at such a time with his heart filled with faith and devotion, and if he entertains the foremost brahmins, then he'll receive such wealth in equal measure. *24*

If he cannot offer food, let him give to eminent brahmins as much uncooked grain as he is able, or even a little sacrificial fee. *25*

If even that lies beyond his means, your majesty, he should bow down before a brahmin and offer him as many sesame seeds as he can hold on the tip of one finger. *26*

Or, bowing with devotion, he may offer us seven or eight sesame seeds on the ground, along with water from his cupped hands. *27*

If even that's not possible, the devotee may gather enough fodder for just one day from somewhere, and, bowing to us, filled with piety, he should feed it to a cow. *28*

If none of these is possible, he must go to the forest and, raising his arms to salute the sun and the guardians of the four directions, he should recite this verse aloud: *29*

"I have no possessions, wealth or anything else with which to express my faith. I bow down to my ancestors. May they be satisfied with these two arms, which I've raised with devotion in the path of the wind."' *30*

Aurva:

Such is the song the ancestral spirits sang, and which befits times of both wealth and poverty. One who undertakes a *śrāddha* should follow this prescription, sire. *31*

So ends Chapter Fourteen in Book Three of the glorious Viṣṇu Purāṇa.

15. Conducting a *śrāddha*

Aurva:

Now you'll hear about the ranks of brahmins to be offered food when a *śrāddha* is conducted: *1*

One who knows the three Nāciketas, three Madhus or three Suparṇas,[10] the six Vedic supplements or the Vedas themselves; a scholar; an ascetic; one who chants the Jyeṣṭhasāman; *2*

An officiating priest; the householder's sister's son, daughter's son, son-in-law, father-in-law or maternal uncle; one who practises austerities or maintains five sacred fires; the householder's students or relatives; and one who is devoted to his mother and father. *3*

The householder should first engage the brahmins mentioned above in a *śrāddha*, sire, in order to nourish his ancestral spirits, while others may be employed for less important rituals. *4*

A false friend, a person with bad fingernails, one who is impotent, a brahmin with discoloured teeth, one who has sexually assaulted young women, one who has abandoned his sacred fires or Vedic studies, one who sells soma, *5*

A person accused of a crime, a thief, a slanderer, one who performs sacrifices for villagers, one who teaches sacred texts to his servants or learns such texts from them, *6*

The husband of a woman who was previously married, one who has abandoned his mother and father, one who supports the children of a śūdra or who is married to one, *7*

One who lives off offerings made to an idol—none of these is worthy of an invitation to a *śrāddha*. *8*

On the first day, the prudent man should welcome outstanding scholars and other dignitaries and should explain to them his intention with regard to his ancestors and the deities. *9*

After this, the initiator of the sacrifice, together with the brahmins, should refrain from anger, sexual intercourse and other business, as these are major obstacles to the ritual. *10*

If a man who holds a *śrāddha*, having begun to eat or having fed the brahmins whom he tasked with the ritual, then has sexual intercourse, he will cause his own ancestors to drown in a pool of semen. *11*

First inviting eminent brahmins, as I mentioned, he should also offer food to any pious members of that order who arrive at his home unexpectedly. *12*

10 Nāciketa, Madhu and Suparṇa appear to be different parts of the *Ṛg Vedic* corpus. Authorities differ as to the precise details.

He should welcome all such individuals who come to his door with water for their feet and so on. *13*

With blades of *kuśa*-grass in his hands, he should offer them water to drink and invite them to be seated—an odd number of brahmins for an ancestral *śrāddha*, and an even number for rituals for the deities, or as he wishes. *14*

He may also engage a single brahmin for both the deities and his ancestors. *15*

Filled with devotion, he should perform a *śrāddha* for his maternal grandfather, which incorporates the worship of the Viśvadevas, or he may perform a ritual specifically for them. *16*

He should offer food to those brahmins engaged for the deities, or those engaged for both paternal and maternal ancestors, while they are facing east, and to those engaged solely for his paternal ancestors, while facing north. *17*

Some say that *śrāddhas* for paternal and maternal ancestors should be undertaken separately, sire, while other famous sages say they may be held together and with the same offerings of food. *18*

After spreading *kuśa*-grass upon the ground and duly welcoming brahmins with hospitality, the wise man should, with the brahmins' permission, call upon the deities. *19*

He should welcome them with grains of barley and some water, having offered garlands, perfumes, incense, lamps and other things, in accordance with tradition. *20*

He should also offer these, placed on the left, to his ancestors, having first obtained permission from the brahmins and after spreading two layers of *darbha*-grass. *21*

The wise man should then invoke the deities, preceded by mantras, sire, and on the lefthand side should make an offering to them with sesame and water. *22*

At that time, again with the permission of the brahmins, sire, he should willingly offer food to any hungry traveller who arrives. *23*

Ascetics, who appear in various forms to do folk favours, wander about the world disguised. *24*

For this reason, a prudent man should always welcome visitors when a *śrāddha* is conducted, sire, for when a guest is deprived of hospitality, the outcome of the ritual is imperilled. *25*

With permission from the brahmins, the householder should then offer three handfuls of plain, unsalted food into the fire, you bull among men. *26*

He should first say, '*Svāhā* to the fire, bearer of the offering!' Thereupon, your majesty, he should make an offering to Soma, the Moon, who nourishes ancestral spirits. *27*

The householder should then make a third offering to Vaivasvata, the Sun's own son, after which he places a portion of the remnant food in the brahmins' bowls. *28*

He should then offer the brahmins some delicious, highly desirable, carefully prepared food, with the polite invitation, 'Please enjoy this at your leisure.' *29*

The brahmins should happily partake of this meal attentively, in silence and with cheerful smiles. It should be served without anger or haste, but rather with devotion. *30*

Having uttered mantras to ward off rākṣasas and scattered sesame on the ground, the householder should then regard the leading brahmins as his own forebears. *31*

'May my father, grandfather and great-grandfather, in the form of these brahmins, be satisfied today. *32*

May my father, grandfather and great-grandfather be satisfied, their bodies nourished by this offering made into the fire. *33*

May my father, grandfather and great-grandfather be satisfied with the food I've scattered on the ground. *34*

May my father, grandfather and great-grandfather be satisfied by this offering I've made here with devotion. *35*

May my maternal grandfather, his father, his father and his father be satisfied. May all the deities achieve highest satisfaction, and may all evil spirits be dispelled. *36*

May the master of the sacrifice, Hari, the everlasting lord, enjoy all the offerings I've made here. May all rākṣasas and demons be gone at once from the vicinity of this sacrifice.' *37*

When the brahmins have been satisfied, the householder should scatter leftover food upon the ground and offer every brahmin some water to rinse his mouth. *38*

With the permission of the well-fed brahmins, and with careful attention, he should place an offering of food mixed with sesame seeds on the ground. *39*

With the part of his hand sacred to the ancestors, he should offer water in his cupped hands to his maternal forefathers, and with the same part of his hand, make an offering of food. *40*

On a mat of *darbha*-grass with its tips pointing south, he should place the first food offering for his own father, consecrated with flowers, incense and so on, next to the leftover foods. *41*

He should then make a second offering to his grandfather, and another to his great-grandfather. He should then satisfy his distant ancestors by scattering remnants of food wiped from his fingers on to the roots of the grass. *42*

Having honoured his maternal ancestors in the same manner with offerings of food accompanied by incense and garlands, the householder should again give the leading brahmins water with which to rinse their mouths. *43*

Thinking of them alone, sire, he should first make offerings to the ancestors with devotion, and then, requesting their benediction, while uttering '*susvadhā*', he should give gifts such as he can afford to the brahmins. *44*

After he has given gifts to the Viśvadevas, he should address these words to them: 'May those who are Viśvadevas be pleased with this offering.' *45*

When the brahmins have replied 'So be it', the householder should request their benediction, wise sovereign, after which he should first dismiss the ancestral spirits and then the deities. *46*

The offering of food, the giving of gifts in accordance with one's capacity and the dismissal—all these follow the same order for both maternal ancestors and the deities. *47*

From the initial washing of the feet to the dismissal of the gods and brahmins, the householder should make offerings first to his paternal and then to his maternal ancestors. *48*

He should send the brahmins off with kind words, having paid them due respect, and then accompany them to the gate, after which, with their permission, he may return. *49*

The wise man should then perform the usual ritual, the so-called *vaiśvadeva* rite, for all the deities. He may then enjoy a meal together with respected individuals, his dependants and relations. *50*

In this way, a wise man should conduct *śrāddha* rituals for his paternal and maternal ancestors. Nourished by such *śrāddhas*, his ancestors will grant his every wish. *51*

Three things have purifying power at a *śrāddha*: one's daughter's son, a cashmere blanket and sesame seeds. There is also the giving, naming and displaying of silver. *52*

A person offering a *śrāddha* should eschew anger, wandering and haste, sire, as these three are not recommended for those who take part in this ritual. *53*

The Viśvadevas, the paternal and maternal ancestors and the entire family of those who perform a *śrāddha* are nourished, sire. *54*

The host of ancestors is supported by the moon, and the moon is supported by ascetic practices. That's why, your majesty, it's recommended that ascetics be engaged to undertake a *śrāddha*. *55*

If just one ascetic stands before a thousand brahmins, sire, he will lead all participants, including the initiator, to the further shore. *56*

So ends Chapter Fifteen in Book Three of the glorious Viṣṇu Purāṇa.

16. *Śrāddha* offerings

Aurva:

An offering of fish or the flesh of a hare, bird, pig, goat, black antelope, deer, wild ox, *1*

Sheep or cow—each of these nourishes the ancestors for one month longer than the offering named before it, but they will be satisfied forever with the flesh of the leather-billed bird, the *vādhrīṇasa*. *2*

The flesh of a rhinoceros, sacred basil and honey are highly recommended for these offerings, sire, as they, too, provide eternal nourishment. *3*

The life of one who undertakes a *śrāddha* at Gayā is fulfilled, sire, because it nourishes his ancestors. *4*

Small-grained rice, wild rice, sorghum of both kinds and forest herbs are all fit for a *śrāddha*, you bull among men. *5*

Barley, foxtail millet, black lentils, wheat, rice, sesame, cowpeas, kodo millet and mustard seeds are also suitable. *6*

The householder should not use grain unconsecrated at the time of the first harvest, sire, or black-eyed peas, proso millet or garlic. *7*

Bottle gourds, red or brown onions, wild carrots, *gandhāraka*, groats, sea salt, rock salt, *8*

Any reddish gums and other substances resembling salt—these are best avoided for a *śrāddha*, along with other substances that have not been recommended. *9*

Water that was drawn at night, or isn't fresh, sire, or is insufficient to satisfy a cow, or smells unpleasant or is frothy is unsuitable for a *śrāddha*. *10*

During the performance of a *śrāddha*, one should avoid the milk of animals whose hooves are not cloven, including camels, sheep, deer and buffalo. *11*

A eunuch, outcaste, untouchable, heretic, drunk, invalid, rooster, dog, naked person, monkey, village pig, *12*

Menstruating woman or a woman who has recently given birth—neither deities nor ancestors will accept a *śrāddha* observed by any of these. *13*

The devout individual should therefore conduct a *śrāddha* in an enclosed space and should drive off evil spirits by strewing sesame on the ground. *14*

Food should not be rotten, contaminated with hairs, insects or anything else, sire, or be mixed with substances that lead to fermentation, but must be fresh. *15*

Food offered by the faithful to the ancestors, while intoning their names and lineages, is sustenance for those very beings. *16*

The following song was sung by ancestors long ago, your majesty, and was heard by Manu's son Ikṣvāku in the grove of Kalāpa: *17*

'May those who come to Gayā to make food offerings, out of respect for us, be reborn in our lineage as followers of the true path. *18*

May one who offers us rice pudding with honey and butter on the thirteenth day of Bhādrapada or Maghā be reborn in our lineage, *19*

Or when he marries a fair girl, or liberates a black bull or performs a horse-sacrifice in accordance with the rules and with the proper recompense.' *20*

So ends Chapter Sixteen in Book Three of the glorious Viṣṇu Purāṇa.

17. The protection afforded by the Vedas; Viṣṇu's phantom

Parāśara:

This is precisely what holy Aurva told the great sage Sagara, Maitreya, when he asked about good conduct long ago. *1*

Now I've told you everything, brahmin. One who strays from this will never win success. *2*

Maitreya:

I know about the eunuchs, outcastes, menstruating women and the others, master, but I'd like to hear some more about the naked ones. *3*

Who goes naked, and what acts lead to a person being called this? I'd like you to describe exactly what is meant by nakedness. *4*

Parāśara:

The *Ṛg*, *Yajur* and *Sāma Vedas* are a threefold garment for the various communities, brahmin, but a deluded individual who casts off this mantle is regarded as both sinful and naked. *5*

Because the three Vedas clad each community, when they're cast aside, an individual is surely rendered naked. *6*

Listen to what our ancestor Vasiṣṭha, who understood tradition, said to mighty Bhīṣma. *7*

This is what I heard that great-souled individual say with regard to nakedness, and which you asked about just now. *8*

Long ago, the deities waged a war against the demigods, brahmin. During that confrontation, which continued for one divine year, they were routed by the Daityas led by Hrāda. *9*

The deities then retreated to the Milky Ocean's northern shore, where they undertook austerities to propitiate Lord Viṣṇu, and they sang this song of praise: *10*

The gods praise Viṣṇu

The deities:

May Lord Viṣṇu, first among beings and master of the worlds, be pleased with this song we sing to worship him. *11*

Who can sing the praises of that great being, the origin of all creation, into whom it dissolves again? *12*

Although our power was thwarted in this battle, desiring our own felicity, we still praise you, even though your actual nature is beyond the reach of words. *13*

You are earth, water, fire, wind, space, mind, primal matter and the highest spirit beyond them all. *14*

You are at the heart of all creation. This whole world, from Brahmā to a tuft of grass, both formed and formless, is your single body, only split by time and place. *15*

We bow to you, Lord, in the form of Brahmā, who first arose from the lotus at your navel to create the world. *16*

We bow to your divine form, divided among ourselves as mighty Indra, the Sun, Rudra, the Vasus, Aśvins, Maruts, the Moon and others. *17*

We bow to you, Govinda, in the form of Daityas: deceitful, ignorant, impatient and unrestrained. *18*

We bow to you in the form of yakṣas, whose frivolous hearts lack discernment and who hanker for sensations such as sound. *19*

We bow to you, highest spirit, in the form of night-ranging rākṣasas: cruel, deceptive, fierce and dark. *20*

We bow to you, Janārdana, in the form called dharma, which yields rewards of truest virtue for pious beings who dwell in heaven. *21*

We bow to you, success embodied, in the form of siddhas, those perfected beings consisting of unalloyed bliss, the goal of all departures. *22*

We bow to you, Hari, in the form of nāgas: fork-tongued, resilient, cruel and bent on pleasure. *23*

We bow to you, Viṣṇu, in the form of sages: knowledgeable, tranquil, pure and faultless. *24*

We bow to you, lotus-eyed deity, in the form of Time, which, unstoppable, consumes all creatures when each aeon ends. *25*

We bow to you in the form of Rudra, who, having swallowed all creation including gods, dances at the destruction of the world. *26*

We bow to you, Janārdana, in the form of humankind, the motive force of acts that are carried out with energy. *27*

We bow to you, the universal being, in the form of animal life, which ends in twenty-eight modes of death and, marked by stupidity, often goes astray. *28*

We bow to you, the foremost one, the diverse being differentiated into trees and other kinds of plants, which provide the basis for the sacrifice, and which in turn allow perfection of the world. *29*

We bow to you, universal being, whose initial form is the elements including space and sensations such as sound, all of which are experienced by animals, humans, deities and the rest. *30*

We bow to you, the highest being, cause of every cause, whose ultimate form is distinct from us and all that consists of matter, intelligence and so on, and has no equal. *31*

We bow, Lord, to that form that has no colour such as white, no dimension such as length and no quality such as density, which is beyond the range of descriptions, which is the purest of the pure and is perceptible only to the highest sages. *32*

We bow to that form of the Absolute that is in our bodies, and in others, and in all things, unborn, unchanging and beyond which there is nothing. *33*

We bow to the stainless Lord Vāsudeva, the highest state, the everlasting unborn being whose form is all the universe, who has no end and is the seed of all creation. *34*

Viṣṇu creates a phantom

Parāśara:

At the conclusion of this paean, the deities beheld the supreme Lord Hari, holding the conch, sword and discus, mounted on Garuḍa. *35*

Falling to the ground, the host of deities, seeking his protection, beseeched him: 'Be merciful to us, Lord, and save us from these Daityas. *36*

Led by Hrāda, the demons have deprived us of all three worlds and our portion of the sacrifice, highest Lord, ignoring the injunctions of the Vedas. *37*

Even though we deities and Daityas are merely aspects of you, the universal being, we still perceive the world to be divided, such differences appearing as the result of ignorance. *38*

Adhering to the traditions of our own community, following the Vedic path and filled with ascetic energy, we still cannot destroy our enemies. *39*

Give us, please, the means, universal Lord, by which we may defeat the demigods.' *40*

Parāśara:

Thus addressed by the deities, Lord Viṣṇu produced a phantom from his body, which he presented to the best of gods with this explanation: *41*

The Lord:

When this phantom has confused the Daityas, you'll be able to kill them all, as they will have left the Vedic path. *42*

I'm inherent in all creation, and any who offend the Vedas will be destroyed by me. All divine beings, including gods and Daityas and the rest, are subject to Vedic authority. *43*

Go, therefore, and do not fear. Proceed with the phantom before you, gods—it will serve you well this very day. *44*

Parāśara:

Hearing this, the deities bowed again to Viṣṇu and returned as they had come, accompanied by the phantom, to confront the mighty demigods. *45*

So ends Chapter Seventeen in Book Three of the glorious Viṣṇu Purāṇa.

18. The phantom confounds the demigods

Parāśara:

When the phantom reached the banks of the Narmadā River, Maitreya, he saw the mighty demigods engaged in ascetic practice. *1*

Taking the form of a naked holy man, shaven-headed and carrying a peacock feather, brahmin, the phantom addressed the demigods with gentle words.[11] *2*

The phantom:

Greetings, Daitya lords! Tell me, why do you practise these austerities? Do you desire a reward in this world or the next? *3*

The demigods:

We undertake these practices because we want rewards hereafter. Why do you ask, wise sage? *4*

The phantom:

You must follow my instructions if you wish for liberation. You must be worthy of my religion, as it's the door to freedom that never closes. *5*

This noble religion of liberation is the best. Once established in this tradition, you'll proceed to heaven or to freedom from existence. *6*

But you mighty beings must first prove worthy! *7*

Parāśara:

With many such cunning words to inculcate his views, the phantom led those Daityas from the Vedic path. *8*

He taught that vice is virtue, truth is falsehood and that which leads to liberation does not do so, *9*

That which is absolute highest truth is not so; *10*

That which is to be done is not so; that this is wrong and that is right; that this is the religion of naked ascetics, and that is the religion of those who dress. *11*

Such were the endlessly repeated blandishments, brahmin, by which the phantom induced the Daityas to shun their own religion. *12*

Since the apparition told them they were worthy (*arhatha*) of his great tradition, they trusted him, converted to Jainism and became Arhats. *13*

After the phantom caused the demigods to abandon the traditions of the threefold Vedas, they began to instruct others. *14*

11 This is a thinly veiled reference to the naked Jain ascetics of the Digambara tradition. The feather was used to brush living things safely out of their path.

These others taught others again, and they in turn taught even more, so that within a few days every Daitya left the Vedic path. *15*

Some time later, wearing monkish saffron robes, the phantom, whose gaze was irresistible, approached another group of Daityas and spoke to them with simple words, both soft and sweet:[12] *16*

The phantom:

If you want to go to heaven or reach nirvāṇa, you demigods must give up this false religion, including the animal sacrifice. Listen! *17*

Understand that this whole world consists of knowledge. Understand my words in full, as they were uttered by the wise. *18*

All the world has no foundation, but is ever bent on chasing baseless knowledge. Plagued by passion and other such emotions, it's caused to wander through the straits of being. *19*

Parāśara:

When the phantom said, 'Understand! Understand!', the Daityas said, 'We understand', and thus he led them from their own traditions. *20*

Precisely in accord with these varied false instructions, which the phantom thrust upon them, the Daityas then abandoned true religion. *21*

They also taught this doctrine to others, and those others taught others again, Maitreya, and they all forsook the true religion prescribed by the Vedas and sacred law. *22*

The phantom, that great purveyor of delusion, brahmin, also confounded other Daityas with many varied heresies. *23*

In little time, the demigods, led astray by him, no longer spoke of the threefold Vedic path. *24*

Some disparaged the Vedas, others insulted the deities, brahmin, and some belittled the totality of sacrifice, ritual action and even the brahmin order: *25*

'Violence towards animals for a sacrifice has no part in true religion. Such a necessity is mistaken. To say that butter burnt in fire can yield rewards is childish nonsense. *26*

---

12 The following verses refer to Buddhism. In verses 18 and 20, the words *budhaiḥ*, *budhyata*, *budhyadhvam* and *budhyate* ('understand', and so on) are all cognate with the word 'Buddha'.

If Indra, having reached the status of a god through many sacrifices, is fed with wood from *śamī*-trees or similar, then he's no better than wild beasts which eat the leaves. *27*

If the beast that's sacrificed then goes to heaven, why doesn't the sacrificer kill his father? *28*

If food that's eaten by someone at a *śrāddha* nourishes another, then those who live afar could offer it wherever they are and need not faithfully bring it to the ceremony. *29*

Once you understand what people may reasonably believe, then you'll see the benefits expected from the words I've spoken. *30*

Wise words don't simply fall from heaven, mighty demigods, and reasonable instruction should be acceptable to me and others of your kind.' *31*

Parāśara explains 'nakedness'

Parāśara:

The phantom misled the Daityas with so many notions that not one continued to accept the authority of the threefold Vedas. *32*

When the Daityas strayed along these paths of falsehood in this manner, the deities prepared for war and advanced upon their foe. *33*

The battle of the gods and demigods resumed, brahmin, but on this occasion, the demons were overcome by those who took the path of truth. *34*

As the Daityas had forsaken the armour of true religion that protected them before, brahmin, they were overcome. *35*

That's why, Maitreya, those who took the path of truth, but vainly shed the safety of the threefold Vedas, are called 'naked'. *36*

Student, householder and forest-dweller, with wandering mendicant as the fourth—these are the stages of life. There is no fifth. *37*

The wicked man who abandons married life but doesn't retire to the forest or become a mendicant, Maitreya, is also naked. *38*

One who fails to perform an obligatory ritual, brahmin, even though he's able, spoils his obligatory rites for an entire day and night, and on that very day, is fallen. *39*

One who neglects his regular rites, except in an emergency, Maitreya, only regains his state of purity after a fortnight of sincere atonement. *40*

Seeing a man who has neglected his rituals for a year, virtuous people must turn their gaze upon the sun. *41*

If they touch that man, they purify themselves by bathing fully clothed, great sage, but no expatiation is prescribed for the evildoer himself. *42*

There is no baser person in the world than one in whose house the deities, sages, ancestors and spirits, being neglected, heave a sigh and go away. *43*

One should avoid the house, the seat or property of a person whose body or residence has felt the sighs of gods and other beings. *44*

One who converses with, inquires after or socialises with such a person, brahmin, incurs the same portion of guilt, which endures for one whole year. *45*

If one eats with such a person, sits in his house or lies on a couch with him, he immediately becomes the equal of the sinner. *46*

One who eats without honouring the deities, ancestors, spirits or guests is guilty of a misdeed. How great is his negligence! *47*

Brahmins and members of other orders who turn their backs on their own traditions are also described as 'naked' and are ranked with those who neglect their rites. *48*

Living in a place where there's excessive contact among the orders is harmful to those of virtuous conduct. *49*

Those who speak with a person who eats before honouring sages, deities, ancestors, spirits and guests will go to hell. *50*

A wise man should therefore always avoid conversation or any other contact with these 'naked' individuals, who are defiled by rejection of the threefold Vedas. *51*

A *śrāddha* diligently performed by pious individuals brings no satisfaction to gods or spirits if 'naked' people see it. *52*

King Śatadhanu is born as a dog

Long ago, it's said, a king called Śatadhanu had a pious wife named Śaibyā. *53*

Faithful, fortunate, truthful, pure and kind, Śaibyā was blessed with decorum and every other virtue. *54*

The royal couple worshipped Lord Janārdana, god of gods, with deep devotion. *55*

Day after day, they devoutly undertook oblations, prayers, donations, fasts and rituals with their hearts on him alone. *56*

One day, the royal couple, who were fasting on the full-moon day of the month of Kārttika, emerged from the waters of the Bhāgīrathī River in which they'd bathed together, brahmin, and saw a heretic drawing near. *57*

Because the heretic was a friend of the monarch's archery instructor, the king, out of respect for his teacher, engaged the man in conversation. *58*

But his wife, the queen, observant of her vow, said nothing and, because she was fasting, raised her eyes to the sun when she saw the stranger. *59*

On returning to the palace, the king and queen duly completed their worship of Viṣṇu and other deities as prescribed, best of brahmins. *60*

In time, the once victorious king expired, and the queen ascended his pyre to join her husband where he lay. *61*

Because of his transgression of speaking to a heretic in a time of fasting, the king was born as a dog. *62*

The queen, however, was born as the brilliant daughter of the king of Kāśī and could recall her previous lives. She possessed all forms of knowledge and wore each desirable quality as an ornament. *63*

Her royal father sought a husband for her, but that slender girl dissuaded him and so she never married. *64*

Sometime later, the princess, who possessed divine insight, beheld the dog, her former husband. She journeyed to the city known as Vaidiśa, where she found him. *65*

The fortunate girl, recognising her husband in that form, gave him nice things to eat and treated him with kindness. *66*

Eating the tasty and desirable food she gave him, and playing about as dogs are wont to do, he repeatedly showed her his affection. *67*

The young girl, however, was embarrassed by his friendliness and, bowing deeply, addressed her beloved husband, who had suffered such a lowly birth. *68*

The wife:

Try to remember the kindly greeting you gave the heretic, your majesty, on account of which you were born as this dog, now showing me such friendship. *69*

You addressed that man after we bathed together at the sacred ford, and now you've had this deplorable rebirth. Do you not remember, lord? *70*

Parāśara:

Reminded of his former life, he reflected for a while and was filled with dreadful pain. *71*

Broken-hearted, the dog set out from the city and died in the desert, where he was born as a jackal. *72*

The following year, the princess, using her divine insight, perceived all this and journeyed to Mount Kolāhala to see him. *73*

Beholding him there, the delicate princess addressed her husband born from a jackal's womb. *74*

The wife:

Don't you remember, your majesty, what I told you when you were born as a dog, about the time you addressed that heretic? *75*

Parāśara:

Realising she had spoken truly, and being the best of those who understand such words, the jackal in the wilderness then starved himself to death. *76*

Once more, the blameless princess found him, reborn this time as a wolf in a lonely forest, and reminded him of his prior fault: *77*

'You're not a wolf, you fortunate being, but King Śatadhanu. You were born as a dog, a jackal and now this creature.' *78*

Parāśara:

Reminded of his true identity, the king was born as a vulture. Once more, the sinless beauty informed him of his past: *79*

'Your majesty, remember what you used to be. Give up this vulture's life! You're in this state because you erred in talking to a heretic.' *80*

As a result, he was born as a crow in his next life. Using her special powers, that slender girl located him and said: *81*

'All the sovereigns on the earth paid tribute to you formerly, but now you're born as a crow that scavenges food oblations, lord.'[13] *82*

Parāśara:

The king in corvine form was thus reminded of his past, and, having drawn his final breath, was born as a peacock. *83*

The splendid girl pursued that bird and always fed it things that peacocks like to eat. *84*

A little later, her royal father performed a great horse-sacrifice, at the end of which the peacock received a ritual bath. *85*

The girl with slender limbs then bathed herself and reminded the former king how he'd been born as a dog, a jackal and the others. *86*

Remembering this string of births, he left his body and was born as the son of a man of exemplary standing. *87*

When the slim girl pressed her father on the matter of her wedding, he arranged a *svayaṃvara* for her.[14] *88*

On the day of that event, her former husband was the man the splendid princess chose. *89*

The prince partook of many pleasures together with his wife, and, when her royal father died, the realm of Videha passed to him. *90*

He performed many great sacrifices, made donations to the poor, fathered many sons and vanquished all his enemies. *91*

Having duly ruled his realm and defended all the earth, the king, following tradition, died in battle. *92*

Once more that fair-eyed woman, filled with joy, duly climbed her husband's pyre as she had done so long ago. *93*

Together with the princess, the king now passed beyond the heavenly realms of Indra to reach eternal regions where all wishes are fulfilled: *94*

13 This verse contains a pun on the word *bali*, which means both the tribute paid by kings and the food offerings made to the ancestral spirits, which are later eaten by the birds.

14 An assembly of suitors from which a princess may choose a husband—along the lines of 'The Bachelorette', as one of my students suggested.

That unequalled, unending paradise, which is the rarely won reward for merit earned in marriage, best of brahmins. There he reached a state of perfect purity. *95*

Such is the sin of speaking with a heretic that I've described, brahmin, and the efficacy of a ritual bath at the conclusion of a horse-sacrifice. *96*

That's why one should never speak with wicked apostates or contact them, especially during rituals or when initiated for a sacrifice. *97*

If a prudent person is required to look up to the sun when he's seen a man whose rituals have been neglected for a month, *98*

How much greater the expatiation when one has contact with a sinner who whole-heartedly forsakes the threefold Vedas, eats food prepared by members of the lower orders or opposes Vedic teachings? *99*

One should never honour heretics, those who act unlawfully, false saints like the cat in the famous story, charlatans, sceptics or hypocrites like the fabled heron, or even speak with them.[15] *100*

One should keep one's distance from the wicked, heretics and those of doubtful conduct, and avoid their company. It's therefore best to stay away from them. *101*

I've described to you the people known as 'naked', the sight of whom will spoil a *śrāddha*. By speaking to such apostates, a full day's merit will be lost. *102*

As these heretics are evil, a wise man shouldn't speak with them, but if he does, all the merit earned that day is lost. *103*

Men will go to hell for speaking with those who wear their hair in matted locks, or shave their heads, or vainly eat before others do, or disregard the rules of purity, or are forbidden to offer food or water to the ancestors. *104*

So ends Chapter Eighteen in Book Three of the glorious Viṣṇu Purāṇa.

End of Book Three.

15 The cat and heron are well-known hypocritical characters in fable collections such as the *Pañcatantra* and *Hitopadeśa*.

Book Four: The Royal Dynasties

1. The Solar Dynasty: The lineage of Manu

Maitreya:

Master, as my guru, you've told me what regular and occasional rites must be performed by those committed to good conduct. *1*

You've also described the duties of the four communities and life stages. Now I'd like to hear about the historical lineages, guru. Please tell me all about them. *2*

Parāśara:

Maitreya, you'll now hear about the lineage of Manu, which begins with Brahmā, and which boasts many sacrificers, heroes, warriors and kings. *3* As the saying goes, 'The lineage of one who reflects each day on Manu's family, which descends from Brahmā, is never broken.' *4* You should therefore listen to this lineage from start to finish, Maitreya, as it will wash away all sins. *5*

It is as follows: in the beginning, Lord Brahmā, Hiraṇyagarbha, appeared from the cosmic egg, the incarnate form of the Absolute, which consists of Lord Viṣṇu, beginningless in all the worlds, the primeval cause, embodying the *Ṛg*, *Yajur* and *Sāma Vedas*. *6* The patriarch Dakṣa arose from Brahmā's right thumb. Dakṣa's daughter was Aditi. Aditi's son was the Sun. The son of the Sun was Manu. *7* Manu had ten sons, named Ikṣvāku, Nṛga, Dhṛṣṭa, Śaryāti, Nariṣyanta, Prāṃśu, Nābhāga, Nediṣṭa, Karūṣa and Pṛṣadhra. *8*

Desiring yet another son, Manu performed a sacrifice to Mitra and Varuṇa. *9* Because the invocatory priest erred during that corrupted rite, a daughter by the name of Ilā was born. *10* By the grace of the two deities, Maitreya, she was transformed into a son for Manu, named Sudyumna. *11* Later, as a result of Śiva's anger, Sudyumna became a woman once more, and wandered into the vicinity of the ashram of Budha, son of the Moon. *12* Budha fell in love with her and they had a son, Purūravas. *13* After the baby was born, the great sages of immeasurable energy, desiring to turn Sudyumna back into a man, performed a sacrifice for Lord Viṣṇu, who embodies the *Ṛg*, *Yajur*, *Sāma* and *Atharva Vedas*, mind and knowledge, everything and nothingness, and who takes the form of the spirit of the sacrifice. Through the mercy of the deity, Ilā became Sudyumna once more. *14* He had three sons, named Utkala, Gaya and Vinata. *15* Because he'd previously been a woman, Sudyumna received no share of his father's kingdom. *16* His father, however, at the suggestion of Vasiṣṭha, gave him the city named Pratiṣṭhāna, which he later bestowed on Purūravas. *17*

Manu's son Pṛṣadhra was reduced to the status of a śūdra because he killed his guru's cow. *18* From Karūṣa were descended the kṣatriyas known as Kārūṣas, possessed of peerless strength and courage. *19* Nediṣṭa's son Nābhāga became a vaiśya and had a son, Bhalandana.[1] *20* Bhalandana's son was the renowned Vatsapri. *21* Vatsupri's son was Prāṃśu. *22* Prāṃśu's only son was Prajāni. *23* His son was Khanitra, and his son was Cakṣupa. From Cakṣupa was descended Viṃśa, mighty and courageous. *24* His son was Viviṃśa, and his son was Khaninetra. His son was Ativibhūti. *25* Ativibhūti's son was Karandhama, who was even stronger and more courageous than his father. His son was Avikṣi. Avikṣi's mighty son was Marutta, about whom these two verses are sung today: *26*

'Who in this world has held a sacrifice like Marutta's, in which all utensils were made of shining gold? *27*

Indra got drunk on soma and the brahmins got drunk on their fees. The Maruts served the food, and all the gods were there.' *28*

The universal monarch Marutta had a son named Nariṣyanta. *29* His son was Dama, and Dama had a son, Rājyavardhana. *30* Rājyavardhana's son was Sudhṛti. His son was Nara, and his son was Kevala. Kevala's son was Bandhumant. Bandhumant's son was Vegavant. Vegavant's son was Budha. His son was Tṛṇabindu. *31* He had one daughter, Ilavilā by name. *32* An excellent apsaras named Alambuṣā fell in love with Tṛṇabindu, *33* and they had a son, Viśāla, who founded the city known as Vaiśālī. *34* Viśāla's son was Hemacandra. *35* His son was Sucandra. His son was Dhūmrāśva, and his son was Sṛñjaya. *36* Sṛñjaya's son was Sahadeva. He had a son called

1 At 4.1.8, Nābhāga and Nediṣṭa are said to be brothers.

Kṛśāśva. *37* Kṛśāśva's son Somadatta performed ten horse-sacrifices. *38* His son was Janamejaya. Janamejaya's son was Sumati. These were the kings of Vaiśālī, *39* about whom this verse is sung:

'By the grace of Tṛṇabindu, all the kings of Vaiśālī were long-lived, generous, brave and good.' *40*

Manu's son Śaryāti had a daughter by the name of Sukanyā, whom Cyavana married. *41* Śaryāti had a virtuous son called Ānarta. *42* Ānarta's son, Revata, ruled a kingdom named after his father and resided in the city of Kuśasthalī. *43*

Brahmā suggests that Revatī marry Balarāma

Revata's son was Raivata, also known as Kakudmin. He was the eldest of one hundred brothers and was a man of virtue. *44* Raivata had a daughter named Revatī. Raivata took his daughter with him to the realm of Brahmā, in order to ask the lotus-born deity for a husband worthy of the girl. *45* Just as he arrived, two gandharvas, Hāhā and Hūhū by name, were singing a heavenly song called 'Atitāna' in the presence of the deity. *46* Even though Raivata waited for many entire cycles of ages, it seemed that he'd only been listening for a moment. *47* At the end of the song, Raivata bowed to Brahmā, the lotus-born deity, and asked about a suitable husband for his daughter. *48*

The lord replied, 'Tell me, who would you like to marry her?' *49* Raivata bowed again to the lord and mentioned the names of potential husbands of whom he approved, adding, 'I'll give my daughter to whichever of these the lord thinks suitable.' *50* The lotus-born deity gave a little nod and said with a smile, *51* 'Even the great-grandchildren of those you think fit are no longer living. *52* Many cycles of ages passed while you listened to that song. *53* At this moment, the twenty-eighth cycle of the present Manu is nearly over, and the age of Kali is about to begin on earth. *54* Give this gem of a girl to someone else. You're now on your own, *55* as your friends, ministers, servants, wives, kinsfolk, armies and treasuries have all been swept away by the passage of time.' *56* The astonished king bowed to Brahmā again and asked, *57* 'In that case, Lord, to whom should I give her?' *58* The holy lotus-born preceptor of all the worlds then replied to the king, whose head was slightly bowed and whose hands were joined in supplication: *59*

'The unborn universal arranger, the supreme lord whose beginning, middle, end, form, highest state and essence are unknown to us, *60*

Is beyond time, which, composed of minutes, hours and other units, brings an end to all creation. He is free from birth and death, embodies everything, has neither name nor form, and is eternal. *61*

By the grace of that imperishable being, I became the creator of the world and, through his anger, Rudra brings it to an end. In the interim, *puruṣa*, the Spirit, arises from him to preserve it. *62*

The unborn deity takes my form to create the world, maintains it in the form of Spirit and consumes all this in Rudra's form. That divine being, whose forms are endless, disposes everything. *63*

In the form of mighty Indra and the gods, he guards the world; in the form of sun and moon, he dispels the gloom. He takes the form of fire to bring us warmth; in the form of earth, he supports the world, yet his essence is unchanging. *64*

In the form of breath, he enables all activity; in the form of food and water, he nourishes the world. He occupies all creation and, in the form of ether, provides the space wherein all things abide. *65*

He is both creation and creator, the object of protection and the deity who protects it, destroyer and destroyed, but as the changeless universal being he remains distinct from these. *66*

The world abides in him, he *is* the world, the primary being, the self-arising one abiding in all things, yet is superior to all creation. Now, your majesty, Viṣṇu has manifested an aspect of himself on earth. *67*

The city of Kuśasthalī, as lovely as Indra's Amarāvatī and previously your majesty's capital, is now known as Dvārakā. There resides one Balarāma by name, an aspect of Lord Keśava.[2] *68*

Give this girl to him in marriage, your majesty. He is divine illusion in human form, and is a husband worthy of the girl, a fitting partner for that gem of womanhood.' *69*

Parāśara:

Thus addressed by lotus-born Brahmā, the king returned to earth, where he noticed all the people were now shorter and less vigorous, discerning and courageous than they were before. *70*

2 The text actually gives the name of Kṛṣṇa's elder brother as Baladeva at this point. For clarity, I have standardised on Balarāma throughout, as mentioned in the Introduction.

On reaching the city of Kuśasthalī, which now looked somewhat different, the wise king gave his daughter to Balarāma, whose weapon was a plough and whose broad chest gleamed like a crystal mountain. *71*

Balarāma, who bore a palm tree on his standard, saw the princess and, considering her unnecessarily tall, pressed her down with his ploughshare. She was reduced at once to the height of other women. *72*

That plough-wielding warrior duly married King Raivata's daughter, Revatī. After giving the girl away, Raivata retired to the Himālaya to undertake austerities. *73*

So ends Chapter One in Book Four of the glorious Viṣṇu Purāṇa.

2. Manu's sons Dhṛṣta, Nābhāga and Ikṣvāku

Parāśara:

Before Kukudmin Raivata returned from Brahmā's realm, rākṣasas known as Puṇyajanas attacked his capital, Kuśasthalī. *1* His one hundred brothers, fearing the Puṇyajanas, fled in all directions. *2* As a result, kṣatriya lineages sprang up everywhere. *3* From Manu's son Dhṛṣṭa arose the warrior lineage of Dhārṣṭakas. *4* Nābhāga's son was Nabhaga.[3] His son was Ambarīṣa. Ambarīṣa's son was Virūpa. *5* Virūpa's son was Pṛṣadaśva. After him came Rathītara. *6* There is a verse about these kings:

'Born as kṣatriyas, they're known as Aṅgirases, Aṅgiras's offspring. The families of Rathītara's descendants include both kṣatriyas and brahmins.' *7*

Ikṣvāku was born from Manu's nose when he sneezed, '*ikṣvāku*!' *8* He had a hundred sons, the foremost of whom were the three named Vikukṣi, Nimi and Daṇḍa. Fifty of his sons led by Śakuni became protectors of the northern lands, and the other forty-eight were sovereigns of the south. *9*

On the eighth day after the full moon, Ikṣvāku told his son Vikukṣi to fetch some meat suitable for a *śrāddha*. Vikukṣi agreed and, following his father's instructions, entered the forest, where he slew many wild animals. Tired and hungry, Vikukṣi helped himself to a single hare, but took the rest and presented it to his father. *10*

---

3 I have reversed the order of these two names, because Manu's son was Nābhāga, not Nabhaga. Some manuscripts indicate that both father and son share the name Nābhāga.

Ikṣvāku's family preceptor, Vasiṣṭha, who had been invited to consecrate the offering, shouted, 'Get rid of this meat! It's unfit for sacrifice, as your wicked son has spoiled it by eating a hare.'[4] *11* As a result, Vikukṣi became known as Śaśāda, 'Hare-Eater', and, because of his guru's condemnation, he was rejected by his father. *12* After the monarch died, however, Śaśāda became the virtuous ruler of all the world. *13* He had a son known as Puraṃjaya. *14* But this son also had another name. *14*

Long ago, in the age of Tretā, the gods and demigods fought an awful war. The gods, overcome by their mighty foe, paid homage to Lord Viṣṇu. *15* Nārāyaṇa, who has neither start nor finish and is the refuge of all the world, was gratified by them and said: 'I know already what you want, so listen to what you must do. The sage-king Śaśāda has a son called Puraṃjaya, a warrior of renown. An aspect of myself will descend into his body, and I'll strike down your enemies. You must therefore engage Puraṃjaya to destroy them.' Hearing this, the immortals bowed to Lord Viṣṇu and appeared before Puraṃjaya. *16*

The deities spoke to him as follows: 'Greetings, mighty warrior! In accordance with our request, we trust that you will help us kill our enemies. Don't disappoint the hopes of those assembled here before you.' Hearing this, Puraṃjaya replied, 'If I'm able to ride on the shoulders of your leader, Indra, master of all three worlds and deity of a hundred sacrifices, then I'll fight as your ally against your enemies.' Hearing this, all the deities including Indra agreed, saying, 'So be it.' *17* The god of a hundred sacrifices then took the form of a bull and Puraṃjaya, filled with enthusiasm, climbed upon his back. Blessed with the energy of the eternal lord, master of every moving and unmoving thing, Puraṃjaya fought beside the gods in their battle with the demigods and destroyed their enemies. *18* Because he overcame the demon army while riding on the back of a bull (*kakut-stha*), Kakutstha became his name. *19*

Kakutstha's son was Anenas. Anenas's son was Pṛthu. Pṛthu's son was Viśvagaśva. His son was Cāndra. Cāndra's son was Yuvanāśva. Yuvanāśva's son was Śrāvasta, who founded the city of Śrāvastī. *20* Śrāvasta's son was Bṛhadaśva. His son was Kuvalayāśva, who, filled with the power of Viṣṇu and surrounded by twenty-one thousand sons, killed the demon called Dhundhu, molester of the great sage Uttaṅka, and thereby became known as Dhundhumāra, 'Dhundhu's Slayer'. *21* All his sons were consumed

4 By eating the hare, Vikukṣi caused the rest of the food to become a mere remnant and therefore unfit for sacrifice.

by the fire that Dhundhu breathed on them, *22* leaving only three alive: Dṛḍhāśva, Candrāśva and Kapilāśva. *23* Dṛḍhāśva's son was Haryaśva. His son was Nikumbha. Nikumbha's son was Saṃhitāśva. His son was Kṛśāśva, and his son was Prasenajit. His son was another Yuvanāśva. *24*

This Yuvanāśva always worried that he was childless. While residing in the vicinity of the ashrams of certain sages, those holy men took pity on him and undertook a sacrifice so he might have his wish. One night during the event, before they went to bed, the sages placed a pitcher of water, consecrated with mantras, on the altar. *25* While they slept, the king, overcome by terrible thirst, entered the ashram. *26* Without waking the slumbering sages, he found the consecrated water, which had incredible powers, and drank it. *27* When the sages woke, they asked who'd drunk the water. *28* Were it King Yuvanāśva's wife, they said, she would bear a mighty and courageous son. Hearing this, the king admitted it was he who had unwittingly drunk the draught. *29* Accordingly, an infant arose in Yuvanāśva's belly and began to grow. *30* When the time arrived, the king's right flank split open and a child was born. In spite of this, the king survived. *31* 'Now this baby's been delivered, to whom will he entrust it?' asked the sages. *32* At that moment, Indra, king of gods, appeared and said, 'He'll entrust it to me (*mām dhāsyati*)', *33* and so the child was called Māṃdhātṛ. The king of gods put his finger in the baby's mouth and the child began to suck. Having tasted the nectar of immortality that flowed from the deity's hand, the child achieved maturity in just one day. *34* Māṃdhātṛ became a universal monarch who ruled the earth with all its seven continents. *35* There is a verse about him:

'As long as the sun will rise, and as long as it keeps on shining, this whole world is said to be the realm of Yuvanāśva's son, Māṃdhātṛ.' *36*

Māṃdhātṛ's daughters, the sage and the fish

Māṃdhātṛ married Bindumatī, the daughter of Śaśabindu, and together they had three sons, Purukutsa, Ambarīṣa and Mucukunda, *37* as well as fifty daughters. *38* A well-versed sage by the name of Saubhari spent twelve years living underwater. *39* He shared the pool with the king of fish, Saṃmada by name, who was of immense size and had innumerable offspring. Saṃmada's sons and grandsons frolicked by his side, behind him, in front of him and on his chest, tail and head, by day and night, while playing happily in his presence. *40* Saṃmada found great pleasure in this endless contact with his sons, grandsons and other offspring and, while the sage looked on, he enjoyed all sorts of games with them each day. *41*

Now, Saubhari, living underwater and seeing the daily joy this fish experienced while capering with his family, couldn't concentrate on his meditation. 'This fish is very lucky,' he said to himself. 'Even though he's had a lowly rebirth, he can play with his children and grandchildren. This has stirred a strong desire in me. Now, just like him, I want to play with children of my own.' With this thought, the sage left the water and, wishing to settle down, approached King Māṃdhātṛ to ask for one of his daughters in marriage. *42* As soon as the king heard that the sage was coming, he rose and duly welcomed him with hospitality. Accepting the seat that had been offered, Saubhari spoke: *43*

Saubhari:

I want to start a family, sire, so kindly give me one of your daughters. Please don't disappoint me. Those who, compelled by circumstance, approach the family of Kakutstha with a special wish are never turned away dissatisfied. *44*

In this world are other kings to whom daughters have been born, your majesty, but your family is famous for its vow to grant the wishes of all who ask. *45*

Give me one of your fifty girls, your majesty. I fear I'll suffer greatly if my petition is refused, best of monarchs. *46*

Parāśara:

Hearing this, the king looked at the sage's body, wizened with age, and was about to refuse his request, but, fearing the sage's curse, lowered his gaze and pondered a while. *47*

Saubhari:

What's the problem, your majesty? What I ask is not impossible. Nothing will be beyond your reach if I'm satisfied with the girl, who must be given to me in any case. *48*

Parāśara:

Still fearing the sage's curse, the king made this humble reply: *49*

The king:

'It's the custom of our family, sir, that a girl be given to a suitor of noble descent who pleases her. Your request is beyond the realm of my imagination, yet has arisen somehow. I was just wondering what to do in this situation.'

When the king had spoken, the sage said to himself, 'Well, this is just another way of refusing my request. He said this because he thinks that an old man like me is unattractive to mature women, let alone young girls. So be it! I'll do what's necessary.' With this thought, he said to Māṃdhātṛ, *50* 'This being the case, tell the palace guard to admit me to the women's quarters. If any of the girls desire me, I'll marry her. If not, I'll give up this endeavour as a waste of time.' So saying, he fell silent. *51*

Parāśara:

Then Māṃdhātṛ, still fearing the sage's curse, ordered the palace guard to admit him to the women's quarters. *52* As that holy sage went in, he took a form more handsome than that of any siddha, gandharva or any mortal man. *53* The guard admitted him and told the girls the king, their father, had issued this instruction: *54* 'This holy sage has come to ask us for a girl in marriage. I promised him that if any of my daughters chose to marry him, I would not refuse her wishes.' Hearing this, each of the girls, filled with love and passion, asserted her own superiority to win the sage, just like she-elephants in the presence of the head of the herd. *55*

The girls:

'Enough, sisters! I've chosen him!' 'He was chosen by me!' 'He doesn't suit you!' 'He was created by Brahmā to be my husband!' 'I was made for him!' 'Shut up!' *56* 'I chose him first!' 'I chose him as soon as he came in.' 'What's your problem?' 'He's mine!' 'No, he's mine!'

Such was the awful fuss the princesses raised over the sage. *57* While Saubhari, whose reputation was impeccable, was surrounded by all these most affectionate girls, the guard bowed his head and informed the king of exactly what had happened. *58*

Parāśara:

Learning of the situation, the king was thrown into a flurry and cried, 'Why, why has this befallen me? Tell me what to do. What have I said?', but in spite of his wishes, he eventually gave in to the sage. *59* After the great ascetic had duly married all the girls, he led them to his ashram. *60*

There, he summoned Viśvakarman, the deities' artificer and master of every craft, a second Creator, and instructed him to build a palace for each girl, complete with gardens, lawns, comfortable couches and pleasant pools filled with flowering lotuses, and which resounded with the cries of wild geese, ducks and other birds. *61* When Viśvakarman, the original teacher of every practical art, had built the palaces, he showed them to Saubhari. *62* Next, at the command of that brilliant sage, he placed in every residence an inexhaustible heavenly treasure known as Nanda. *63* In each palace the princesses entertained their guests, retinues and dependants by night and day with amusements including endless supplies of food of all descriptions. *64*

One day, the king, whose heart was troubled by affection for his daughters, wondered whether they were happy. On approaching the great sage's ashram, he beheld a row of crystal palaces, shining like the sun and set among the pleasant groves and lakes. *65* The king entered one such palace, hugged his daughter and took a seat. His eyes were brimming with tears of deep affection as he asked, *66* 'Are you happy here, my darling? Does anything trouble you? Is the great sage kind to you? Are you ever homesick?'

Hearing this, the girl replied to her father, *67* 'This palace is lovely, father. We have a beautiful garden and a swimming pool filled with lotuses, and the birds are always singing. The food is great, and we have the best entertainment, including massages, clothes and jewellery, plus the beds are really comfortable. Now I'm married, I have every luxury. All the same, who doesn't think fondly of the home where they were born? *68* Because of your kindness, everything has turned out splendidly. *69* There's just one thing that bothers me. This great sage, my husband, never leaves my house. Because he really likes me, he's always here, and never visits any of my sisters. *70* That must upset them, and that's my only worry.'

After she had spoken, the king went to the next palace, where he hugged the daughter who lived there, took a seat and asked her the same question. *71* Her reply was identical: she also enjoyed the luxuries of the palace and the rest, but because the sage doted on her, he never left her side or visited the others. Hearing this, the king visited each palace in turn and questioned his other daughters. *72* As they all gave the same reply, the king's satisfaction and amazement relieved the burden of his heart. Approaching holy Saubhari at a quiet moment, the king paid his respects and said, *73* 'We've seen your miraculous power, sir, but we've never observed anyone perform such a prodigious feat before. How great is the reward of your austerities!' Having honoured him with these words, the king tarried there a while, enjoying the best of entertainments with that great sage, and eventually returned to his own capital. *74*

As time passed, the princesses bore the sage one hundred and fifty sons. *75* But as the rush of love he felt grew stronger every day, the sage's heart was dragged down by worries. *76* 'Will my sons learn to talk nicely? Will they begin to walk? Will they grow up? Perhaps I'll see them marry. Maybe they'll have children of their own. Perhaps I'll even see my great-grandchildren.' But when he realised that such fancies ran far ahead of the day-to-day passage of time, he realised that he'd been utterly deluded: *77*

The sage Saubhari surrenders to Viṣṇu

'There's no end to my desires. Even if all the wishes made in ten thousand years or a hundred thousand years are satisfied, further desires will still arise. *78*

My children will learn to walk, grow up, get married and have children of their own. I've seen my own sons, but now my heart yearns to see my grandsons. *79*

Even if I see the birth of my grandchildren, some other desire will still arise. And even when that desire has been satisfied, what can stop the advent of the next desire? *80*

I realise now that, short of death, there'll be no end to these fantasies. The heart of one attached to desire will never experience union with the highest truth. *81*

My peace of mind was suddenly destroyed when I became attached to that friendly fish who shared the pool with me. As a result of that attachment I was married and, because of marriage, I have all these desires. *82*

The suffering engendered by birth in a single body, and that which arises in fifty others, will be multiplied by the many sons born of the princesses whom I've married. *83*

The cause of this great suffering will keep on growing with the marriages of my grandchildren, great-grandchildren and every generation after that. Marriage is indeed the source of individual anxiety. *84*

The magic power resulting from the austerities I performed while living underwater was the undoing of that practice. I was swept away by my affection for my sons and all the others, and this came about because of my friendship with the fish. *85*

Freedom from attachment is the basis of liberation for ascetics. Attachment is the source of all my problems. Even an ascetic riding high on yoga falls to earth because of this, to say nothing of a less-accomplished person. *86*

My heart was caught in the grip of marriage, but now I'll strive for my own welfare to escape from further troubles and avoid the suffering caused by others. *87*

With my penance, I'll honour Viṣṇu, creator of the world, whose form is beyond imagination, smaller than the smallest, larger than the largest, both light and dark, the lord of lords. *88*

May my mind be steady, free from faults and ever set on almighty Viṣṇu, who assumes all forms, whose eternal body is unmanifest and manifest, so that I may be free from future rebirths. *89*

I take refuge in Viṣṇu, who is all creation, purest lord of everything, who has neither start, nor end, nor middle, apart from whom no thing exists, the ultimate guru of every guru.' *90*

Parāśara:

With these words, Saubhari surrendered himself, and, having abandoned his
children, home, furnishings, goods, chattels and all his other possessions,
accompanied by his wives, he entered the forest. *91* There, he daily
undertook each practice befitting forest-dwelling sages and was cleansed
of all his misdeeds. His stream of thought was purified and, having devoted
himself to tending sacred fires, he became a wandering mendicant. *92*
Relinquishing all actions to the lord, he attained the unborn, unchanging
eternal state beyond the reach of life and death, higher than the highest. *93*

Such is the story of the marriage of Māṃdhātṛ's daughters. *94* Anyone who
recalls, recites, hears or understands the story of Saubhari's deeds, or causes
it to be written out, will not be disrespected, or stray from perfect virtue,
or take the path of error, but will be free from individual anxieties amid all
distractions for the next eight lives. *95*

So ends Chapter Two in Book Four of the glorious Viṣṇu Purāṇa.

3. The descendants of Ambarīṣa

Parāśara:

I'll now describe the descendants of Māṃdhātṛ's sons. *1* His first son, Ambarīṣa, had a son, Yuvanāśva. *2* His son was Harīta, from whom the Aṅgirases known as Hārītas were descended. *3* In the lower realm of Rasātala lived gandharvas known as Mauneyas, who numbered sixty million. They plundered all the nāga clans of their most precious treasures, not to mention their sovereignty. *4* The nāga kings, deprived of power by these beings, roused Viṣṇu from his slumber while he was reclining on the waters. The lord opened his eyes, which were like flowering lotuses, as he listened to the praises of all those regal deities. Bowing down before him, the nāgas asked: 'Lord, will we ever overcome our fear of these gandharvas?' The lord, the spirit without beginning, the supreme being, replied, 'The son of Māṃdhātṛ's son Yuvanāśva has a son named Purukutsa. I'll take possession of his person and subdue these wicked gandharvas.' *5* Hearing this, the nāga kings bowed to the lord and returned to their own dominion.

The nāgas then dispatched Narmadā to summon Purukutsa *6* and bring him back to Rasātala. *7* Arriving in the lower realm, his own prowess augmented with the might of Viṣṇu, Purukutsa overcame the gandharvas, then returned to his residence. *8* As a result, all the nāga kings granted Narmadā a boon that anyone who invoked her name, while calling her to mind, would have nought to fear from venomous snakes. *9* Here is the verse:

'I bow to Narmadā in the morning. I bow to Narmadā at night. Narmadā, I bow to you. Protect me from all poisonous snakes!' *10*

One who recites this prayer will never be bitten by a snake by day or night, in the dark or on entering a room, and anyone who recalls Narmadā while eating will never be harmed by poison. *11* The nāga kings also blessed Purukutsa so that his lineage would never be disrupted. *12*

Purukutsa and Narmadā had a son, Trasadasyu. *13* Trasadasyu's son was Saṃbhūta. His son Anaraṇya was slain by Rāvaṇa during the latter's war of global conquest. Anaraṇya's son was Pṛṣadaśva. Pṛṣadaśva's son was Haryaśva. His son was Vasumanas, and his son was Tridhanvan. Tridhanvan's son was Trayyāruṇa. His son was Satyavrata, who was given the name of Triśaṅku and was relegated to the status of an untouchable. *14*

Every day, during a twelve-year drought, Triśaṅku hung some venison in a banyan tree on the banks of the Gaṅgā River as food for Viśvāmitra, his wife and children, so that they need never accept a gift directly from an outcaste. *15* The sage was well pleased by this and raised Triśaṅku to heaven in bodily form. *16*

Triśaṅku's son was Hariścandra. His son was Rohitāśva. His son was Harita. Harita's son was Cañcu. Cañcu had two sons, Vijaya and Sudeva. Vijaya's son was Ruruka. Ruruka's son was Vṛka. *17* His son was Bāhu. It was he who, conquered by the Haihayas, Tālajaṅghas and other tribes, fled to the forest, accompanied by his pregnant wife. *18* One of her co-wives gave her poison to induce an abortion, *19* but as a result of the dose, the foetus remained in her womb for seven years. Bāhu died of old age in the vicinity of Aurva's ashram. *20* His wife prepared a funeral pyre and mounted it, determined to follow him in death. *21* But holy Aurva, who knew the past, present and future, rushed out of his ashram, crying, 'Abandon your foolish plan! In your womb is a future universal sovereign of great courage and prowess. He'll rule the world, perform many sacrifices and overcome his enemies. *22* Don't do this! Don't be so rash!' Hearing this, the widow abandoned her intention to follow her husband in death. *23*

The birth of Sagara

That holy sage led her back to his ashram and, a few days later, she gave birth to a splendid boy, along with the poison (*sa gareṇa*) she had swallowed. Aurva performed the natal rituals for the baby and named him Sagara. *24* He later invested the boy with the sacred thread, instructed him in the Vedas and other scriptures and taught him how to wield the fiery weapons named for Bhārgava. *25*

One day, this gifted child asked his mother, 'Why are we living here? Where's my father?' In reply to these and other questions, his mother explained everything. *26* Later, being anxious to win back his father's kingdom, he vowed to destroy the Haihayas, Tālajaṅghas and the rest. First, he killed most of the Haihayas, *27* but as he was attacking the Śakas, Yavanas, Kāmbojas, Pāradas and Pahlavas, they sought refuge with Vasiṣṭha, Sagara's own family guru. *28* Even though they were still alive, Vasiṣṭha thought them as good as dead. 'My dear boy,' said the sage to Sagara, 'Have done with these, the living dead, who are about to meet their doom. *29* So that your vow may be fulfilled, I've caused these nations to abandon their traditions and lose contact with the brahmins.' *30*

Respecting his guru's words, Sagara agreed, but forced each tribe to adopt a different appearance. He caused the Yavanas to shave their heads, the Śakas to shave half their heads, the Pāradas to wear long hair and the Pahlavas to grow beards. He forbade these and other kṣatriyas to study the Vedas or perform sacrifices with the cry of *vaṣaṭ*. *31* Because they abandoned their traditions and were shunned by brahmins, they were reduced to the status of barbarians. *32* Sagara went back to his kingdom and ruled all seven continents of the world with uncontested authority. *33*

So ends Chapter Three in Book Four of the glorious Viṣṇu Purāṇa.

4. Sagara's sons excavate the ocean; The story of Rāma

Parāśara:

Sagara had two wives, Kaśyapa's daughter Sumati and the king of Vidarbha's daughter Keśinī. *1* Desiring children, the two women propitiated Aurva with all their hearts, and the sage granted them the boon that *2* one wife would have a single son, who would continue the lineage, while the other would have sixty thousand sons, saying, 'Choose whichever destiny you desire.' Keśinī chose to have a single child, and Sumati chose sixty thousand. *3* The sage agreed, and a few days later Keśinī bore a son named Asamañjas, who would continue the lineage. Vinatā's daughter Sumati had sixty thousand sons. *4* Asamañjas had a son named Aṃśumant. *5* From the time he was a baby, Asamañjas was ill-behaved, but his father hoped he would improve as he grew older. *6* But leaving childhood behind, his behaviour was no better, and his father gave up on him. *7* Even Sumati's sixty thousand sons followed Asamañjas's bad example. *8*

Because these sons of Sagara, all aping Asamañjas's poor behaviour, left the worthy path of sacrifice in this world, the gods bowed down to Kapila, the sage who embodied every branch of knowledge, who was untouched by any fault and who was an aspect of the lord, the highest spirit. The deities explained the problem: *9* 'Lord, these sons of Sagara are copying Asamañjas's bad behaviour. What will become of the world with followers like these? We beseech you to take bodily form to save the troubled universe.' Hearing this, the sage replied, 'In a few short days, they will be no more.' *10*

At about this time, Sagara began a horse-sacrifice, but during the ritual, someone stole the steed that had been guarded by his sons and hid it in a cavern beneath the earth. *12* The king sent the boys to find the beast and, following its hoofprints, each of them dug down, with great persistence, one league into the earth. *13* They finally found the horse wandering in the underworld of Pātāla. *14* They also saw the sage Kapila nearby, ceaselessly illuminating all directions with his splendour, like the lordly sun in a cloudless autumn sky. *15* Wielding their weapons, they cried, 'Here's the wretch who wronged us, the horse thief who spoiled our sacrifice! Kill him, kill him!' The sage then turned his gaze upon them for just an instant, reducing them all to ashes with fire that sprang from his own body. *16*

Realising that all his sons who followed the horse had been consumed by the fiery energy of the supreme sage Kapila, Sagara dispatched Asamañjas's son Aṃśumant to retrieve the steed. *17* Aṃśumant reached Kapila by following the path dug by his uncles, and, bowing respectfully, he praised the sage. Holy Kapila said to him, 'Go and take this horse to your grandsire. You may ask this boon of me: that your sons and grandsons may lead the Gaṅgā down to earth from the heavens above.' *18* But Aṃśumant replied to the sage, 'Grant me a boon that my uncles who've been struck down by divine punishment, even though unworthy of heaven, may be admitted to that realm regardless.' *19* Holy Kapila replied, 'I've already spoken. Your descendants will conduct the Gaṅgā down from heaven to earth. When your uncles' bones and ashes are touched by the water of that sacred stream, they'll ascend to heaven. Such is the efficacy of the water that flows across the toes of blessed Viṣṇu. *20* It not only yields all happiness for those who bathe there purposely, but even one whose bones, skin, sinews, hair or other body parts fall by chance to the ground in its vicinity will immediately go to heaven when they die.' Hearing this, Aṃśumant bowed to the holy sage, and returned the horse to his grandsire's sacrifice. *21* Once Sagara had retrieved the beast, he was able to complete the ritual. *22* Out of affection for the boys, he raised the chasm that they had dug, now named Sāgara in their honour, to the status of his own son.[5] *23*

Aṃśumant's son was Dilīpa. *24* It was Dilīpa's son Bhagīratha who led the Gaṅgā to earth from heaven and named it Bhāgīrathī. *25* Bhagīratha's son was Śruta. His son was Nābhāga. His son was Ambarīṣa. His son was Sindhudvīpa. Sindhudvīpa's son was Ayutāyu. His son was Ṛtuparṇa, the

5 I have had to add some words of explanation to this translation. Later, this chasm filled with water and formed an ocean, known as *sāgara* in Sanskrit.

companion of Nala and expert in the game of dice.[6] *26* Ṛtuparṇa's son was Sarvakāma. His son was Sudāsa. Sudāsa's son, Saudāsa, was also known as Mitrasaha. *27*

Saudāsa becomes a rākṣasa

One day, Saudāsa was hunting in the forest when he saw two tigers. *28* These beasts had killed all the deer in the vicinity, so Saudāsa shot one with an arrow, *29* but, as it lay dying, it turned into a rākṣasa of terrible appearance with a hideous expression. *30* The surviving tiger–rakṣasa roared, 'I'll have revenge on you!', and vanished from sight. *31* Some time later, this Saudāsa was performing a sacrifice. When the great sage and sacrificial expert Vasiṣṭha had stepped away for a moment, the tiger–rākṣasa disguised himself as the sage and said to the king, 'When the sacrifice is over, all the food, including the meat, should be given to me to eat. Have it cooked for me, and I'll be back in just a minute.' So saying, he departed. *32*

This same rākṣasa then disguised himself as a cook and, instructed by the king, prepared a dish of human flesh, which he presented to the sovereign. *33* Saudāsa accepted the flesh served on a golden platter and waited for Vasiṣṭha to return. When the real sage came back, the king offered him the platter. *34* But the sage said to himself, 'How rude of the king to give this meat to me. What is it, anyway?' Vasiṣṭha began to meditate and, realising it was human flesh, his mind spun round with fury. He cursed the king, saying, 'You know that we ascetics can't eat human flesh, but you gave it to me anyway! Now your heart will crave such food!' *35* But the king snapped back, 'It was you who ordered me to cook it!'

Wondering how he could have said such things, the sage began to meditate again. *36* With the insight gained through contemplation, he discovered the truth of the matter and took pity on the king: 'You won't have to eat this food for ever,' he said, 'Just twelve years.' *37* The king, holding water in his cupped hands, was about to curse the sage when his consort Madayantī soothed him with these words, 'The holy sage is our guru! You can't curse a preceptor who is like our personal deity!' The king couldn't throw the cursed water on the ground for fear of damaging the crops, nor could he throw it into the air, as he worried it might disperse the clouds, so he poured it on to his own feet. *38* The water, imbued with all the king's own anger, burned his feet so badly that they were blotched with black and white. As a

6 Nala is a famous character in the *Mahābhārata*.

result, he became known as Kalmāṣapāda, 'Blotch-Foot'. *39* In accordance with Vasiṣṭha's curse, every day at the sixth watch, the king became a rākṣasa and, prowling in the forest, devoured multitudes of people. *40*

One day, the rākṣasa spied a sage enjoying intercourse with his wife, as became the season. The frightened couple saw the dreadful creature and tried to flee, but the rākṣasa seized the brahmin. *41* His wife pleaded with the demon repeatedly, 'Have mercy on us! You're the great king Mitrasaha, crown-jewel of Ikṣvāku's lineage, not a rākṣasa at all. You understand women's pleasure. Please don't eat my husband before my desire has been satisfied!' But even as she made these varied pleas, he ate the brahmin anyway, just as tigers devour their prey. *42* The brahmin's wife, filled with rage, cursed the king, saying, 'Because you ate my husband before I was satisfied, your end will come while you're making love!' With this, she entered the flames. *43*

Twelve years later, the king was freed from the sage's curse, but when he yearned for the company of a woman, Madayantī reminded him what the brahmin's wife had said. *44* The king thereafter avoided intercourse and, being childless, asked Vasiṣṭha for a son, and the sage himself conceived a son with Madayantī. Another seven years passed by, but as the infant remained unborn, the queen struck her belly with a stone (*aśman*). This finally induced the child's birth, and they called him Aśmaka. *45*

Aśmaka's descendants

Aśmaka had a son called Mūlaka. When the earth was being cleansed of kṣatriyas, Mūlaka survived by protecting (*kavaca*) himself with naked women (*nārī*). That's why he's also known as Nārīkavaca. *46* Mūlaka's son was Daśaratha. His son was Ilivila. His son was Viśvasaha. His son was Khaṭvāṅga, also known as Dilīpa. It was he who, petitioned by the deities, destroyed their enemies in their war in heaven against the demigods. As he'd done this favour for the gods, they urged him to request a boon. Khaṭvāṅga said, 'If I must accept your offer, tell me how long I'll live.' The deities replied at once, 'You'll only live for one more minute.' Thus addressed, and imbued with the quality of lightness, he was carried down to the world of men on a comfortable sky-going chariot. On arrival, Khaḍvāṅga said, 'My own self is no dearer to me than being in the presence of brahmins. I've never strayed from the traditions of my order. I've always seen the eternal, indivisible unity in all creation, embracing gods, mortals, animals, plants and the rest. May I, therefore, with unfaltering steps, reach the lord, the very deity on whom sages set their hearts.' So saying, he merged into the most senior of all the gods, the lord whose form is beyond description and who is all existence, the highest spirit known as Vāsudeva, and there Khaṭvāṅga achieved absorption. *47*

People hear this verse about King Khaṭvāṅga sung by the Seven Sages long ago:

'There'll never be another in the world like Khaṭvāṅga, who came from heaven down to earth to live for just one minute. With his intellect and generosity, he was one with all three worlds.' *48*

The story of Rāma

Khaṭvāṅga's son was Dīrghabāhu. His son was Raghu. His son was Aja. His son was also called Daśaratha. For the preservation of the world, Lord Viṣṇu, who has a lotus at his navel, manifested aspects of himself as the four sons of Daśaratha in the forms of Rāma, Lakṣmaṇa, Bharata and Śatrughna. When Rāma was just a boy, while journeying to protect Viśvāmitra's sacrifice, he slew the demoness called Tāṭakā. *49* At the sacrifice itself, he drove off the rākṣasa Mārīca with a shower of arrows. He killed the other rākṣasas led by Subāhu, and cleansed Ahalyā of her sins with just a glance. In the palace of Janaka, he lifted Śiva's bow, snapped it easily and won King Janaka's daughter Sītā, born of Earth, as reward for his prowess. *50* He stripped the courage, strength and pride from Paraśurāma, who destroyed the kṣatriyas, and consumed the clan of Haihayas like a fire. *51* On his father's orders, Rāma entered the forest with his wife and brother, giving not a thought to the sovereignty he'd relinquished. *52* There he slew Virādha, Kharadūṣaṇa, Kabandha and other rākṣasas, as well as Vālin, king of monkeys. *53* Rāma built a bridge across the sea and destroyed the race of rākṣasas. He then returned to Ayodhyā with King Janaka's daughter Sītā, who'd been seized by ten-headed Rāvaṇa and whose blemish was removed after that rākṣasa's demise. Sītā's purity was confirmed when she passed unharmed through fire, while all the deities sang her praises. *54*

Bharata, too, slew thirty million fearsome gandharvas in order to subdue their realm. Śatrughna killed the brave and powerful rākṣasa lord named Lavaṇa, son of Madhu, and occupied his capital, Madhurā. *55* By these and other feats of unequalled strength and courage, Rāma, Lakṣmaṇa, Bharata and Śatrughna destroyed those wicked beings and guaranteed security for all the world. Having done so, they ascended again to heaven. *56*

The inhabitants of Rāma's kingdom, Kosala, loved all four brothers, each an aspect of Viṣṇu, and, with their hearts devoted to the lord, they, too, achieved that heavenly state. *57*

Rāma's descendants

Rāma had two sons, Kuśa and Lava. Lakṣmaṇa's sons were Aṅgada and Candraketu. Takṣa and Puṣkara were Bharata's sons. Subāhu and Śūrasena were the sons of Śatrughna. Kuśa's son was Atithi. Atithi's son was Niṣadha. Niṣadha's son was Nala. His son was Nabhas. Nabhas's son was Puṇḍarīka. His son was Kṣemadhanvan. His son was Devānīka. His son was Ahīnagu. His son was Ruru. His son was Pāriyātra. Pāriyātra's son was Dala. Dala's son was Chala. His son was Uktha. Uktha's son was Vajranābha. His son was Śaṅkhanābha. His son was Vyutthitāśva. He had a son, Viśvasaha. *58* His son was Hiraṇyanābha, the great ascetic master and disciple of the sage Jaimini, from whom Yājñavalkya learned the art of yoga. *59* Hiraṇyanābha's son was Puṣya. His son was Dhruvasaṃdhi. His son was Sudarśana. His son was Agnivarṇa. His son was Śīghraga. His son was Maru, who, having established his ascetic practice, dwells in the village of Kalāpa to this very day. In some future age, he will reestablish the kṣatriya order in the Solar Dynasty. His son was Prasuśruta. His son was Susandhi. His son was Amarṣa. His son was Mahasvant. His son was Viśrutavant. His son was Bṛhadbala, who was slain by Abhimanyu, son of Arjuna, in the Bhārata war. *60*

I've given you a summary of the kings of Ikṣvāku's lineage. By hearing their accomplishments, you'll be freed from all misdeeds. *61*

So ends Chapter Four in Book Four of the glorious Viṣṇu Purāṇa.

5. The legend of Nimi: Why we blink

Parāśara:

Ikṣvāku's son Nimi selected Vasiṣṭha as the priest to officiate at a thousand-year-long sacrifice. *1* But Vasiṣṭha said to him, 'I've already been engaged by Indra to conduct a sacrifice of five hundred years for him. You must wait, but I'll come to be your priest as soon as it is finished.' After Vasiṣṭha had spoken, King Nimi said nothing. *2* Believing that he had Nimi's agreement, the sage Vasiṣṭha performed the sacrifice for Indra, king of the immortals. *3* Nimi, however, invited other sages including Gautama to conduct his

ritual. When Indra's sacrifice had been completed, Visiṣṭha hastened back,
believing he would conduct the sacrifice for Nimi. When he saw that the
position of officiating priest had been given to Gautama, he cursed the king,
who was asleep at the time: 'Because you gave this task to Gautama without
informing me, you'll exist no more in bodily form!' *4* On waking, the king
said, 'As this irascible guru has cursed me without warning while I slept,
and I knew nothing of the matter, may he also cease to exist in physical
form!' Uttering this counter-curse, the monarch left his body. *5* As a result
of Nimi's imprecation, Vasiṣṭha's life force merged with that of the deities
Mitra and Varuṇa. One day, while spying on the apsaras Urvaśī, the two
deities experienced an ejaculation of semen and, as a result, Vasiṣṭha gained
at once another body. *6* Nimi's remains, treated with the finest oils and
fragrances, showed no sign of putrefaction or decay, and looked as though
he'd only just departed.

At the conclusion of the sacrifice that Nimi had undertaken, the priests said
to the deities who arrived to collect their share, 'You should grant a wish to
the person who initiated this ritual.' The deities agreed, and Nimi's voice
was heard to say, *7* 'You can end the torrent of suffering endured by all the
world. There is no greater pain on earth than the parting of body and soul.
I therefore wish to remain in the eyes of all living things, but never again
shall I take a physical form.' Hearing this, the deities caused Nimi to appear
in the eyes of every living creature, *8* and that's why they all blink (*nimeṣa*).

Nimi's descendants

As Nimi had no son, the sages feared the absence of a king. They therefore
rubbed his body with a firestick *9* and thus brought forth a baby boy.
Because the child was generated (*janana*) in this manner, he was called
Janaka, *10* and because his father was without a body (*videha*), the boy was
known as Vaideha. He also had another name, Mithi, as he'd been brought
forth by rubbing (*mathana*) with a stick. Janaka's son was Udāvasu.
Udāvasu's son was Nandivardhana. His son was Suketu. His son was
Devarāta. His son was Bṛhaduktha. His son was Mahāvīrya. His son
was Satyadhṛti. His son was Dhṛṣṭaketu. Dhṛṣṭaketu's son was Haryaśva.
His son was Maru. Maru's son was Pratibandhaka. His son was Kṛtaratha.
His son was Kṛti. His son was Vibudha. His son was Mahādhṛti. His son
was Kṛtirāta. His son was Mahāroman. His son was Suvarṇaroman. His
son was Hrasvaroman. His son was Sīradhvaja. When Sīradhvaja was
ploughing the sacrificial ground to obtain a son, a daughter, Sītā, appeared
at the tip of his ploughshare.

Sīradhvaja's brother, the king of Sāṃkāśī, was called Kuśadhvaja. Sīradhvaja's descendant was Bhānumant. Bhānumant's son was Śatadyumna. His son was Śuci. He had a son named Ūrjavaha. *11* His son was Satyadhvaja. His son was Kuṇi. Kuṇi's son was Añjana. His son was Ṛtujit. His son was Ariṣṭanemi. His son was Śrutāyus. Śrutāyus's son was Supārśva. His son was Saṃjaya. His son was Kṣemāri. His son was Anenas. His son was Mīnaratha. His son was Satyaratha. His son was Sātyarathi. Sātyarathi's son was Upagu. His son was Śāśvata. His son was Sudhanvan. His son was Subhāṣa. His son was Suśruta. His son was Jaya. The son of Jaya was Vijaya. His son was called Ṛta. Ṛta's son was Sunaya. His son was Vītahavya. His son was Dhṛti. Dhṛti's son was Bahulāśva. His son was Kṛti and, with Kṛti, the lineage of Janaka came to an end. *12*

Such were the kings of Mithilā, known as the Maithilas, most of whom were sovereigns who had recourse to the knowledge of the Self. *13*

So ends Chapter Five in Book Four of the glorious Viṣṇu Purāṇa.

6. The Lunar Dynasty

Maitreya:

Master, you've described the Solar Dynasty to me, but I'd like to hear in detail about the monarchs in the lineage of the Moon. *1*

The offspring of these famous men are celebrated to this day, so it would befit you, kind and gracious brahmin, to describe them all to me. *2*

Parāśara:

Listen, you tiger of a sage, to the lineage of the beaming Moon in which successive famous kings arose. *3*

This dynasty is resplendent with sovereigns such as Nahuṣa, Yayāti and Kārtavīrya Arjuna, who were richly blessed with qualities of great strength, courage, dignity, integrity and endeavour. Listen and I'll describe them for you. *4*

Brahmā, creator of the universe, born from the lotus at the lily-like navel of Lord Nārāyaṇa, had a son, Atri. Atri's son was Soma the Moon. *5* Lotus-born Lord Brahmā consecrated Soma as sovereign over all plant life, the brahmins and constellations. *6*

Soma abducts Tārā

Soma conducted a *rājasūya*—a royal coronation sacrifice—and, with the power he gained thereby and because he ruled a vast domain, he grew arrogant. *7* Proud and haughty, Soma abducted Tārā, wife of Bṛhaspati, preceptor of all the deities. *8* Even though he was urged repeatedly by Bṛhaspati, chastised by Lord Brahmā and implored by all the heavenly sages, he refused to give her back. *9* Because of his enmity towards Bṛhaspati, the sage Uśanas took Soma's side. *10* Lord Rudra, who had acquired his knowledge of the Vedas from Aṅgiras, allied himself with Bṛhaspati. *11* Jambha, Kumbha and all the other Dānava and Daitya hordes, following Uśanas, made great efforts in Soma's cause. Indra, with the backing of all the divine armies, supported Bṛhaspati. *12* Thus, two sides fought a terrible battle over Tārā known as the Tārakā War. The deities led by Rudra loosed all their weapons against the demigods, as did the Dānavas in return. *13*

This whole world, with hearts atremble at the shock of the battle between the gods and demigods, sought refuge with Brahmā. *14* The lord commanded Uśanas, the demigods, Rudra and the deities to desist and returned Tārā to Bṛhaspati. Seeing she was pregnant, Bṛhaspati said, *15* 'You, my own wife, shall not bear the son of another man. Get rid of it! I've had enough of your audacity!' *16* Thus addressed by her husband, and even though she'd been faithful to him, she obeyed his orders and gave birth to the infant in a bed of reeds. *17*

As soon as the child was born, his splendour outshone the brilliance of the deities. *18* Seeing both Bṛhaspati and Soma overcome with affection for the child because of his magnificence, the gods became suspicious and questioned Tārā: *19* 'Tell us truly, lucky woman. Whose son is he, Soma's or Bṛhaspati's?' Tārā, hearing this, was too ashamed to answer. She said nothing to the gods, even though they questioned her repeatedly. The child himself desired to curse her, saying, 'Wicked woman! Why don't you tell them who my father is? This very day, I'll inflict such punishment on you, filled with this false modesty, that no woman will ever be so slow to speak again.' *20* But Lord Brahmā, grandsire of the world, stopped the boy and questioned Tārā himself, 'Tell me, my dear, whose child it is, Soma's or Bṛhaspati's?' Hearing this, and frozen with embarrassment, she confessed the child was Soma's. *21* The blessed Moon, lord of constellations, heaved a sigh of relief and his cheeks shone again with loveliness. He hugged the boy and cried aloud, 'Well done, well done, my son. How wise you are!' and named him Budha, 'clever'. *22*

Purūravas's affair with the apsaras Urvaśī

I previously described how Budha had a son named Purūravas with Ilā, who was generous, devout and energetic.[7] Now, the apsaras Urvaśī, cursed by Mitra and Varuṇa, chose to live in the world of men, where she beheld this truthful, handsome Purūravas. *23* At first sight, she shed her pride and lost all interest in the pleasures of heaven. Setting her heart on this mortal man, she approached him. *24* When Purūravas saw Urvaśī imbued with qualities such as tenderness and loveliness, which outshone every woman in the world, her charming way of walking and her sweetest smile, he lost his heart to her. *25* They fell in love, had eyes for no-one else and abandoned all other interests. *26* Summoning his courage, King Purūravas said to Urvaśī, *27* 'You have such lovely eyebrows that I'm completely rapt in you! Take pity on me and love me in return.' Hearing this, Urvaśī shyly stammered her reply, *28* 'We'll be lovers, but you must first accept my terms.' *29* 'State them!' said the king. 'First, I keep two pet sheep beside my bed,' Urvaśī explained, 'They're like my sons, and must never be removed. Second, I must never see you naked and, third, butter is the only thing I eat.' 'Agreed!' replied the king.

In the region of Alakā, in Caitraratha and other forests and in lakes ablaze with freshest lotuses, the king enjoyed himself with Urvaśī for sixty-one years, his pleasure increasing daily. *30* Urvaśī shared these delights with him and, as she loved him more each day, she had no desire to return to the immortals' realm. *31*

In her absence, however, heaven lost its charm for the other apsarases, siddhas and gandharvas. *32* Accordingly, one night, Viśvāvasu, who knew of Urvaśī and Purūravas's agreement, accompanied by some gandharvas, stole a sheep from Urvaśī's bedside. *33* As it was carried through the air, Urvaśī heard it bleating and cried aloud, 'Someone's stealing one of my boys! Who'll protect me, a helpless woman?' The king heard her cries, but fearing she would see him naked, didn't go to her assistance.

Sometime later, the gandharvas stole her other sheep, and again Urvaśī heard it bleating as it was carried off. 'A helpless woman who has no husband, I have to rely on cowards!' Such were her anguished cries. *34* The king, unable to restrain himself and thinking he'd be safe in the darkness, seized his sword and charged in, shouting 'Stop, thief! Stop! I'll kill you!' *35* At that moment, the gandharvas caused a blinding flash of light and in the

7 See *Viṣṇu Purāṇa*, 4.1.12.

glare Urvaśī beheld the naked king. As their pact had now been broken, she vanished in an instant. *36* The gandharvas then dropped the sheep and flew back up to heaven. *37* The king caught both animals and, feeling pleased with himself, went back to bed. It was only then that he discovered Urvaśī had vanished. *38* Unable to see her, the frenzied king, still naked, rushed about in search of her.

At last he found Urvaśī in Kurukṣetra, swimming in a lotus pool with four other apsarases. 'Hey! That's my wife!' he shouted in great excitement, 'Wait, you hard-hearted woman. Wait! Speak to me!', and so on. *39* But Urvaśī merely replied, 'That's enough of your ill-considered actions. I'm pregnant, sire. Come back next year and you'll have a son. We'll then spend one last night together.' Hearing this, the joyful king returned to his dominion. *40* Urvaśī then explained to the other apsarases that she'd been in love with him and stayed with him for many years. 'You're right about his handsome looks,' the apsarases said, 'We'd gladly live with him forever!'

One year later, the king returned and Urvaśī presented him with a son, Āyus. *41* They spent that night together and Urvaśī conceived five more boys. *42* 'Because all the gandharvas favour me,' she said to the king, 'they'll grant your majesty a boon. Just ask for anything you want.' *43* 'I've conquered all my enemies,' the king replied, 'My five senses are still sharp, I've a family of my own, with wealth and power beyond all measure. I wish for nothing other than to share a realm with Urvaśī. I only want to be with her.' *44*

Hearing this, the gandharvas gave him a brazier in which a fire was burning, *45* with this instruction, 'In accordance with sacred tradition, divide this fire in three. Perform a perfect sacrifice to accomplish your desire of sharing a realm with Urvaśī. Then your wish will certainly be fulfilled.' Hearing this, the king took the brazier with the fire and went into the forest, but when he got there, he thought, 'How stupid of me! I've brought the brazier, but I should have brought Urvaśī as well.' With this, he left the fire and returned to the city. *46*

In the middle of the night, the king woke up with this thought, 'The gandharvas gave me the brazier so I could share a realm with Urvaśī, but I left it in the forest. I should go back and get it.' With this, he got up, but when he reached the forest, the brazier was nowhere to be seen. In its place, however, stood two trees, an *aśvatthama* with a *śamī* growing up its middle. Seeing this, the king said to himself, 'This is where I left the brazier, but it's turned into these two trees. They must be fire in another form, so

I'll take them back to the city and make a firestick out of them. I'll then use the stick to start a fire and make oblations into that.' With this thought, he returned to the capital once more and set to work. *47*

Measuring with his thumb as he chanted the Gāyatrī mantra, he made a firestick twenty-four inches long, as that's the number of syllables in the verse. He then used the stick to start a fire. The king divided the fire in three as required by scripture, and made oblations into each, stating that his goal was to share a realm with Urvaśī. *48* By undertaking the fire sacrifice many times in accordance with tradition, he finally reached the dominions of the gandharvas, and was never parted from Urvaśī again. *49* That's why they say, 'In the beginning there was but a single fire, but during the current Manvantara, Ilā's son divided it in three.' *50*

So ends Chapter Six in Book Four of the glorious Viṣṇu Purāṇa.

7. King Jahnu drinks the Gaṅgā dry

Parāśara:

Purūravas had six sons, Āyus, Dhīmant, Amāvasu, Viśvāvasu, Śatāyus and Śrutāyus by name. *1* Amāvasu had a son called Bhīma. *2* Bhīma's son was Kāñcana. Kāñcana's son was Suhotra. His son was Jahnu. Seeing that his entire sacrificial enclosure had been flooded with water from the Gaṅgā River, Jahnu, his eyes red with fury, deployed his supreme powers of concentration to draw the holy spirit of the sacrifice to himself. He then drank the Gaṅgā dry. *3* The divine sages placated him, giving him the river as his daughter. *4*

Jahnu also had a son, called Sumantu. His son was Ajaka. His son was Balākāśva. His son was Kuśa. Kuśa had four sons: Kuśāmba, Kuśanābha, Amūrtaraya and Amāvasu. *5* Of these, Kuśāmba undertook austerities, hoping for a son who would be Indra's equal. Seeing his awesome practices and thinking there could never be another being with prowess equal to his own, Indra appeared himself as Kuśāmba's son. *6* He was born as Gādhi, also known as Kauśaki.

Mother and daughter swap gruel

Gādhi had a daughter named Satyavatī, whom Ṛcīka, Bhṛgu's scion, wished to marry. *7* Gādhi, however, unwilling to give the girl to a cantankerous old brahmin, demanded a bride-price of one thousand fleet-footed horses, each as white as the moon and each with one black ear. *8* The sage Ṛcīka acquired a thousand such steeds from Varuṇa at the sacred ford of Aśvatīrtha, presented them to Gādhi and so married his daughter. In order that Satyavatī might conceive a son, Ṛcīka prepared some gruel for her. *9* Satyavatī pleased the sage, so he made a second bowl of gruel for her mother, so that she, too, might have a son who would become a peerless warrior. *10* 'This gruel is yours, and the other is for your mother. Don't mix them up.' So saying, the sage set out for the forest. *11*

When it was time to eat, Satyavatī's mother said, 'Daughter, every father wants his son to be outstanding, and no son should be outdone by his mother's brother. Give me your gruel and you eat mine. *12* My son is destined to rule the world, while yours will be a brahmin. How much strength, courage or glory would such a son possess?' Hearing this, Satyavatī gave her gruel to her mother. *13*

When the sage returned from the forest, he looked at Satyavatī *14* and said, 'You wicked girl! Why have you done wrong? You look terrible. You must've eaten the gruel I made for your mother. You shouldn't have done that! *15* I imbued her gruel with glory, strength and courage. In yours I put tranquillity, knowledge, patience and all the other virtues of a brahmin. Because you ate the wrong one, your son will lead a fearsome warrior's life, obsessed with war and death. Your mother's son will be a brahmin who delights in peace.' Hearing this, Satyavatī clutched her husband's feet, *16* and in that abject position, implored him, 'Husband, I didn't know what I was doing. Have pity on me. Don't let my own son be like that. Kindly let it be my grandson.' Hearing this, that wise man acceded to her request. *17*

In due course, Satyavatī gave birth to Jamadagni, and her mother bore Viśvāmitra. Satyavatī became the river known as Kauśakī. Jamadagni married Reṇukā, the daughter of Reṇu, born in the lineage of Ikṣvāku. Jamadagni and Reṇukā had a son named Paraśurāma, who wiped out all the kṣatriyas and was an aspect of Lord Nārāyaṇa, preceptor of the universe. *18* The gods gave Viśvāmitra a son, Śunaḥśepa, in the lineage of Bhṛgu. His son was called Devarāta. Later, Viśvāmitra had other sons, named Madhucchanda, Jayakṛta, Devāṣṭaka, Kacchapa and Hārītaka. *19* From these descended many branches of the line of Kauśika, linked by marriage to families of other sages. *20*

So ends Chapter Seven in Book Four of the glorious Viṣṇu Purāṇa.

8. The descendants of Purūravas's son Āyus

Parāśara:

Purūravas's eldest son, Āyus, married the daughter of Rāhu. *1* Āyus had five sons with her: Nahuṣa, Kṣatravṛddha, Rambha and Raji, with Anenas as the fifth. Kṣatravṛddha's son was Suhotra. *2* He had three sons, Kāśya, Leśa and Gṛtsamadās. Gṛtsamadās's son, Śaunaka, established the system of four communities. *3* Kāśya's son was the king of Kāśī. His son was Dīrghatamas. Dīrghatamas's son was Dhanvantari, who achieved great things and in every subsequent rebirth mastered each branch of knowledge. Lord Nārāyaṇa granted him a boon *4* that, in this life, he would be born in the clan of Kāśirāja, would compose the complete eightfold Āyurveda and would enjoy a portion of the sacrifice. *5*

Dhanvantari's son was Ketumant. Ketumant's son was Bhīmaratha. His son was Divodāsa. His son was Pratardana. After the destruction of the Bhadraśreṇya clan, he vanquished all his foes and hence was called Śatrujit, 'Enemy-Conqueror'. *6* His father affectionately called him *vatsa* or 'darling', so he was also known by that name. Because he was dedicated to truth, he was called Ṛtadhvaja, 'Whose Banner is Honesty'. Further, as he acquired a horse (*aśva*) named Kuvalaya, he was known around the world as Kuvalayāśva. *7* This Vatsa had a son called Alarka, about whom people still sing this verse:

'For sixty thousand years, and six thousand more, none other than young Alarka ruled the world.' *8*

This Alarka had a son called Sannati. His son was Sunītha. His son was Suketu. His son was Dharmaketu. His son was Satyaketu. His son was Vibhu. His son was Suvibhu. His son was Sukumāra. His son was Dhṛṣṭaketu. His son was Vainahotra. His son was Bhārga. Bhārga's son was Bhārgabhūmi, who further developed the system of four communities.

I've told you about the kings of Kāśi. Now you'll hear of Raji's offspring. *9*

So ends Chapter Eight in Book Four of the glorious Viṣṇu Purāṇa.

9. Āyus's son Raji usurps Indra

Parāśara:

Raji, son of Āyus, had five hundred sons of peerless strength and courage. *1*
At the outbreak of the war between the gods and demigods, each side strove
to overcome the other. Both questioned Brahmā, saying, *2* 'Lord, which
side will be victorious in this war between us?' *3* Lord Brahmā replied, 'The
side for which Raji takes up arms and fights.' The Daityas therefore went to
Raji and requested his assistance. 'I'll fight for you if, when we overcome the
gods, I become your king,' he replied. Hearing this, they said, 'We cannot
say one thing and do another. Prahlāda is our king and we fight for him.'
With this, the demigods departed. After they had left, the gods then put the
same question to the king. Raji promised to help them and they agreed to
accept him as their sovereign. *4*

Supported by the army of the gods and wielding many powerful weapons,
Raji vanquished all the forces of the demigods. *5* When his rivals had been
overcome, Indra pressed his forehead to Raji's feet and said, 'Because you
saved us from calamity, you're like a father to us. You're unexcelled in all the
worlds. I, sovereign of all three realms, am but your son!' *6* The king said
with a laugh, 'So be it! Such a respectful salutation, filled with varied words
of flattery, cannot be disregarded, even when it's spoken by an enemy.'
So saying, he returned to his own capital *7* and Indra, deity of a hundred
sacrifices, conferred sovereignty on him there. *8*

After Raji died and went to heaven, the sage Nārada encouraged Raji's
sons to petition Indra, who ranked as one of their own brothers, to confer
sovereignty on them in accordance with tradition. *9* As Indra refused
their request, those mighty beings defeated him, usurping his position for
themselves. *10*

Some days later, Indra, now deprived of sovereignty over the threefold
worlds and no longer receiving his portion of the sacrifice, met Bṛhaspati
in a secluded place and said to him, *11* 'It would be nice if you could give
me some of the leftover oblations to keep me going—something the size of a dried date would do.' Hearing this, Bṛhaspati replied, 'If that's the case, you should've told me earlier. There's nothing I wouldn't do for you. I can get your position back in a couple of days.' So saying, Bṛhaspati performed a sacrifice each day to sow confusion in the brothers' minds and to restore Indra's ardour. When the five brothers were overcome by mental turmoil, they became the brahmins' rivals, rejected true religion and turned away

from the teachings of the Vedas. *12* As soon as they abandoned dharma, Indra was able to destroy them. With the energy that his preceptor, Bṛhaspati, had restored to him, he bestrode the threefold world once more.

Anyone who hears how Indra lost, then won his status back again, will never suffer anguish should he lose his own position. *13*

Āyus's third son, Rambha, had no offspring. His second son, Kṣatravṛddha, had a son, Pratikṣatra. His son was Saṃjaya. His son was Jaya. His son was Vijaya, and his son was Kṛta. His son was Harṣavardhana. Harṣavardhana's son was Sahadeva. His son was Adīna. His son was Jayatsena. His son was Saṃkṛti. His son was Kṣatradharman. These were the descendants of Kṣatravṛddha. Next I'll describe the lineage of Nahuṣa. *14*

So ends Chapter Nine in Book Four of the glorious Viṣṇu Purāṇa.

10. Āyus's grandson Yayāti exchanges old age for youth

Parāśara:

Yati, Yayāti, Saṃyāti, Āyāti, Viyāti and Kṛti were Nahuṣa's six brave and powerful sons. *1* As Yati had no desire for sovereignty, Yayāti became the king. *2* He married Uśanas's daughter Devayānī and Śarmiṣṭhā, the daughter of Vṛṣaparvan. There is a verse about their offspring: *3* 'Devayānī had two sons, Yadu and Turvasu. Vṛṣaparvan's daughter Śarmiṣṭhā had three, Druhyu, Anu and Puru.'[8] *4*

Yayāti was cursed by the poet Uśanas to grow old before his time. *5* With the intervention of mighty Indra, whom he had propitiated, Yayāti was able to transfer his old age to another person. Accordingly, he said to his eldest son, Yadu, *6* 'Your maternal grandfather has cursed me to grow old prematurely, but with Indra's permission, I can transfer my old age to you for a thousand years. I'm not yet sated with the pleasures of life and want to enjoy myself by taking on your youthfulness. You can't refuse me!' Hearing this, Yadu had no desire to accept Yayāti's old age, so his father cursed him, saying, 'Your descendants will never be fit to rule.' *7* The king then asked Turvasu, Druhyu and Anu to exchange their youth for his old age, but they all refused, so he cursed them as well. *8*

8 See *Mahābhārata*, 1.90.9.

Yayāti then made the same request to Śarmiṣṭhā's youngest son, Puru. Having a generous disposition, Puru bowed to his father and said with respect, 'You're doing me a great favour.' So saying, Puru accepted Yayāti's old age and gave his father his youth. *9* Having acquired Puru's youthfulness and without offending against virtue, Yayāti indulged in the pleasures of life as suited to his desire, age and energy, while properly defending his subjects. *10*

Enjoying himself with the apsaras Viśvācī and with his own wife, Devayānī, he daily thought his desires would eventually cease. *11* Every day, however, pursuing these pleasures, his mind turned again to his exquisite yearning. *12* People sing these verses in this regard:

'Desires cannot be satisfied when you indulge them. A fire flares up with every offering of butter. *13*

All the rice, barley, gold, cattle and women in the world cannot satisfy a man. He must therefore cast off desire. *14*

If a man rejects a dim view of the world, then, seeing everything as equal, he'll find pleasure all around. *15*

The feeble-minded person finds it hard to shun desires; they don't grow old with age. The wise abjure such yearning, as then they're filled with happiness. *16*

Hair grows white with age, and with age the teeth decay. But love of money and love of life never wither, even as one grows old. *17*

I've spent a thousand years, my heart obsessed with pleasure, But every day desire for more still grows in me. *18*

I'll therefore abandon these desires and set my mind on the Absolute. Free from dualities and selfishness, I'll roam with wild animals.' *19*

Parāśara:

Yayāti eventually retrieved his old age from Puru and returned his son's youthfulness. He then anointed Puru as king and retired to the forest to undertake austerities. *20*

He invested Turvasu as regent over the south-east, Druhyu over the west and Yadu over the south. *21*

He made Anu regent of the north and, having consecrated Puru as king of all the world, retreated to the wilderness. *22*

So ends Chapter Ten in Book Four of the glorious Viṣṇu Purāṇa.

11. Yayāti's son Yadu

Parāśara:

I'll now describe the lineage of Yayāti's first son, Yadu, in which Lord Viṣṇu revealed an aspect of himself, who has no start or finish and whose immeasurable greatness is always praised in order to obtain each possible reward by all the inhabitants of the universe, including humankind, siddhas, gandharvas, yakṣas, rākṣasas, guhyakas, kimpuruṣas, apsarases, serpents, birds, Daityas, Dānavas, Rudras, Vasus, the Aśvins, Maruts and divine and brahminical sages, who yearn to escape from cyclical existence and who wish for virtue, wealth, love and liberation. *1* There is a verse in this regard:

'One who hears about the lineage of Yadu, in which the formless highest Absolute known as Viṣṇu appeared, will be freed from all misdeeds.' *2*

The four sons of Yadu were called Sahasrajit, Kroṣṭu, Nala and Raghu. Sahasrajit's son was Śatajit. His three sons were Haihaya, Hehaya and Veṇuhaya. Haihaya's son was Dharma. His son was Dharmanetra. His son was Kunti. Kunti's son was Sāhaṃji. His son was Mahiṣmant. *3* His son was Bhadraśreṇya. His son was Durdama. His son was Dhanaka. Dhanaka's four sons were Kṛtavīrya, Kṛtāgni, Kṛtadharma and Kṛtaujas. Kṛtavīrya's son was thousand-armed Arjuna, lord of seven continents. It was he who, having worshipped Dattātreya, an aspect of the lord born in the lineage of Atri, requested and received these boons from him: a thousand arms, the constant practice of virtue, victory over all the world by means of truth, talent to rule with justice, invincibility in the face of enemies and death only at the hands of a person with global fame. *4* He ruled the whole world superbly, including all the continents, and performed ten thousand sacrifices. *5* Even today, this verse is sung about him:

'Surely no king on earth will follow in Arjuna Kārtavīrya's footsteps, in terms of sacrifices, generosity, austerity, learning or demeanour.' *6*

During his reign, nothing ever decayed and he ruled for eighty-five thousand years with undiminished health, prosperity, energy and courage. *7* One day, Arjuna Kārttavīrya, having had too much to drink, was swimming and relaxing in the waters of the Narmadā River near the city of Māhiṣmatī. Yet he still managed, without effort, to bind Rāvaṇa like a sacrificial animal, and made him stand in a corner of the city, even though Rāvaṇa had begun his conquest of the world and was filled with arrogance after defeating all the deities, Daityas and gandharva lords. *8*

At the end of his reign of eighty-five thousand years, Arjuna Kārttavīrya was slain by Paraśurāma, an aspect of Lord Nārāyaṇa. Of his hundred sons, the five most eminent were Śūra, Śūrasena, Vṛṣaṇa, Madhu and Jayadhvaja. *9* Jayadhvaja's son was Tālajaṅgha. Tālajaṅgha had a hundred sons who were known as the Tālajaṅghas after him. The eldest one was Vītahotra. Another was Bharata. Bharata had two sons, Vṛṣa and Sujāta. Vṛṣa's son was Madhu. He had one hundred sons of whom Vṛṣṇi was the foremost and after whom the Vṛṣṇi clan is named. *10* They are also known as Madhus after their ancestor of that name, and Yādavas after Yadu. *11*

So ends Chapter Eleven in Book Four of the glorious Viṣṇu Purāṇa.

12. Yadu's descendant Jyāmagha rescues a princess

Parāśara:

Yadu's son Kroṣṭu had a son, Vṛjinīvant. His son was Svāhi. His son was Ruṣaṅku. Ruṣaṅku's son was Citraratha. His son, Śaśabindu, became supreme lord of fourteen great gems.[9] He had a hundred thousand wives and a million sons, *1* among whom the foremost six were Pṛthuyaśas, Pṛthukarman, Pṛthujaya, Pṛthukīrti, Pṛthudāna and Pṛthuśravas. *2* Pṛthuśravas's son was Tamas. His son was Uśanas, who performed a hundred horse-sacrifices. His son was called Śitapu. His son was Rukmakavaca. His son was Parāvṛt. Parāvṛt had five sons, named Rukmeṣu, Pṛthu, Jyāmagha, Pālita and Harita. *3* These verses about Jyāmagha are still sung today:

'Of all husbands, past or future, who are dominated by their wives, the premier example is King Jyāmagha, Śaibyā's husband. *4*

9 According to the commentary, these are the best discus, chariot, jewel, sword, armour, banner, treasure, wife, family priest, general, charioteer, foot soldiers, horse and elephant.

Neither he nor Śaibyā had a son, and even though he wanted one, he
couldn't take another wife because he feared Śaibyā.' *5*

On one occasion, Jyāmagha fought a terrible battle in which hosts of
elephants, horses and chariots clashed together. He conquered all his
enemy's forces and, abandoning sons, wives, kinsfolk, arms, treasure and
territory, they fled in all directions. *6* After they had disappeared, the king
beheld a jewel of a royal princess, her almond eyes rolling with fear as she
wailed piteously, 'Save me! Save me, Father! Mother! Brother!' *7* As soon as
he saw her, the king's heart was filled with affection. 'How excellent is this!'
he said to himself, 'I have no children and I'm the husband of a childless
wife. Now Fate has provided me with this gem of a girl that I may have
progeny. I'll marry her, but first I'll lift her into my chariot and take her
to the palace. *8* With Queen Śaibyā's permission, she'll become my second
wife.' So saying, the king lifted the girl into his chariot and bore her to
the capital. *9*

Śaibyā came to the palace gate to welcome the victorious king accompanied
by all the townsfolk, servants, ministers and attendants. *10* Seeing the girl
standing at her husband's left hand, the queen's bud-like lower lip trembled
with jealousy. 'You fickle-hearted man!' she said to him, 'Who's this girl
riding in your chariot?' The king had no time to consider his reply and,
being terrified of his wife, he blurted out, 'She's my daughter-in-law.' *11*
Śaibyā replied,

'I've never had a son, and you have no other wife. Which of your sons did
this girl marry?' *12*

Parāśara:

Deprived of his better judgement by the queen's harsh words, which were
born of jealousy and rage, the king made this reply to avoid any further
argument: 'She'll marry the son that you will have one day.' Hearing this,
the queen said with a little smile, 'That's all right then', and accompanied
the king into the palace. *13*

A few days later, at a highly auspicious minute, hour, day and season, as a
result of their conversation regarding the birth of a son, and even though
she was past childbearing age, Śaibyā conceived an infant. *14* When the time
arrived, she was delivered of a boy. His father named him Vidarbha, and he
eventually married the girl whom the king had called his daughter-in-law. *15*

Vidarbha had two sons, Kratha and Kaiśika, and later, a third, named Romapāda. Romapāda's son was Babhru. Babhru's son was Dhṛti. Dhṛti's son was another Kaiśika. Kaiśika's son was Cedi, whose descendants are known as the Caidya kings. Kratha, the son of Jyāmagha's daughter-in-law, had a son, Kunti. *16* Kunti's son was Vṛṣṇi. Vṛṣṇi's son was Nirvṛti. Nirvṛti's son was Daśārha. His son was Vyoma. His son was Jīmūta. His son was Vikṛti. His son was Bhīmaratha. His son was Navaratha. His son was Daśaratha. His son was Śakuni. His son was Karambhi. Karambhi's son was Devarāta. His son was Devakṣatra. Devakṣatra's son was Madhu. Madhu's son was Anavaratha. Anavaratha's son was Kuruvatsa. His son was Anuratha. His son was Puruhotra. His son was Aṃśu. His son was Satvata. Satvata's descendants are known as the Sātvatas.

One who hears this lineage of Jyāmagha while filled with perfect faith is freed from all misdeeds. *17*

So ends Chapter Twelve in Book Four of the glorious Viṣṇu Purāṇa.

13. Kṛṣṇa and the Syamantaka jewel

Parāśara:

Satvata's sons were Bhajana, Bhajamāna, Divya, Andhaka, Devāvṛdha, Mahābhoja and Vṛṣṇi. *1* Bhajamāna's sons with his first wife were Nimi, Kṛkaṇa and another Vṛṣṇi, and, with his second wife, Śatajit, Sahasrajit and Ayutajit. *2* Devāvṛdha's son was Babhru. These two verses are sung about them:

'We hear about them when far away and see for ourselves when close at hand: Babhru was first among mankind, and Devāvṛdha was the equal of the gods. *3*

One had sixty-six followers, the other six thousand and eight, All of whom won immortality on account of those two alone.' *4*

Mahābhoja was deeply religious. His descendants were the Mārtikāvata Bhojas. *5* Vṛṣṇi had two sons, Sumitra and Yudhajit. Sumitra's sons were Anamitra and Śinī. Anamitra's son was Nighna. Nighna's sons were Prasena and Satrājita. Lord Āditya, the Sun, was Satrājita's friend. One day, Satrājita was singing the Sun's praises by the ocean, his heart set on that deity alone. While doing so, the Sun appeared before him. Beholding the deity's indistinct form, Satrājita said to him, 'I've seen you resembling a ball of fire in the sky, but now you've appeared before me, you haven't blessed me by manifesting clearly.' Hearing this, the lordly Sun took the great jewel known as Syamantaka from around his neck and placed it to one side. *6* Then Satrājita beheld the Sun in a less effulgent form, with reddish eyes that blazed like burnished copper. Satrājita threw himself to the ground and praised the deity, whereupon the Sun offered to grant him anything he desired. Satrājita requested the jewel, the Sun gave it to him and then returned to his station in the heavens. *7*

Now the owner of that perfect gem, which he wore around his neck, Satrājita, shining in every direction like the Sun himself, entered Dvārakā. *8* When the residents of the city saw Satrājita approaching, they bowed deeply to Lord Kṛṣṇa, the original being and highest spirit, who had manifested an aspect of himself in human form to relieve the burden of the earth.[10] 'Lord, surely the Sun has come to see you!' they said. Hearing this, Kṛṣṇa replied with a laugh, 'This isn't the blessed Sun. It's Satrājita approaching with the great jewel known as Syamantaka, bestowed on him by the deity. You may look upon him fearlessly.' Hearing this, the townsfolk withdrew.

Satrājita kept the great jewel Syamantaka in his own home. *9* Every day, that most magnificent of gems produced eight measures of gold. The power of the jewel also prevented natural disasters throughout the kingdom, including droughts, pests, fires, floods and famines. *10* Infallible Kṛṣṇa formed the opinion that the jewel would befit his grandfather, King Ugrasena, but fearing this would cause division in his family, he didn't requisition it, even though he could have done so. *11* Satrājita understood that Kṛṣṇa desired the jewel and worried that he might request it, so he gave it to his brother Prasena.

Whenever the gem was worn by a man of virtue it brought forth every desirable quality, including rivers of gold, but if the wearer was unvirtuous, the gem would lead to death. This Prasena, wearing the Syamantaka around his neck, went hunting on horseback in the forest, where he was killed by a lion. Having slain both man and horse, the lion then took that perfect gem in his jaws and was about to set off with it, when he was observed by Jāmbavant, the king of bears. Jāmbavant then slew the lion and took the peerless jewel to his cave as a plaything for his son Sukumāra. *12*

---

10 In this chapter, the narrative gets ahead of itself, as here we meet Kṛṣṇa as a mature chieftain in the city of Dvārakā. We will not come to his birth until Chapter 15. For a comprehensive account of the Syamantaka narratives, see Austin (2011).

When Prasena failed to return, all the Yādavas whispered among themselves, 'Kṛṣṇa wants the jewel and Prasena has disappeared. This must be Kṛṣṇa's doing.' *13* When Lord Kṛṣṇa heard these rumours, he set off with the Yādava army. Following the track left by Prasena's horse, he eventually discovered that both horse and rider had been killed by a lion. At the sight of the lion's pawprints, Kṛṣṇa was cleared of suspicion by everyone, and continued in search of the culprit. *14* A short distance further he saw where Jāmbavant had killed the lion. Because of the great attraction of the jewel, he now followed the tracks left by the bear. He left the Yādava soldiers at the foot of the mountain, as he traced Jāmbavant to his lair. Kṛṣṇa was halfway into the cavern when he heard the crooning tones of the bear cub's nurse:

'A lion killed Prasena, and Jāmbavant killed the lion. Don't cry little Sukumāra, this Syamantaka is yours.' *15*

Hearing this and realising that his goal was within reach, Kṛṣṇa entered the cave. There he beheld the Syamantaka, blazing with energy and dangling from the nurse's hand like a bauble for a child. *16* When the nurse saw the stranger approaching with his eager eye on the jewel, she cried, 'Save me! Save me!' *17* Jāmbavant heard her anguished cries and rushed in, his heart filled with fury, whereupon the bear and Kṛṣṇa fought a battle for twenty-one days.

The Yādava soldiers waited for seven or eight days at the foot of the mountain for Kṛṣṇa to return. When Madhu's adversary failed to reappear, they thought he must have met his match in the cave. How otherwise could it have taken so long for him to overcome his adversary? Returning to Dvārakā, they reported that Kṛṣṇa had been killed. *18* His kinsfolk performed all the proper funerary rites and, while Kṛṣṇa kept fighting, the food, water and other substances they offered him in special vessels during the *śrāddha* ritual sustained his strength and vitality. *19* His adversary, Jāmbavant, assailed by that mighty being, his every limb smitten by cruel blows and having nothing to eat, grew weaker by the day.

In the end, the bear surrendered to Lord Kṛṣṇa and, bowing deeply, said to him, 'You cannot be defeated by gods, demigods, yakṣas, gandharvas, rākṣasas or any other being, to say nothing of men who walk upon the surface of the earth, who lack courage and have only human limbs to fight with. How much less by an animal like me! You were surely created by our master, Lord Nārāyaṇa, refuge of all the world, as an aspect of himself.'

Thus addressed by Jāmbavant, Lord Kṛṣṇa explained to him in detail that he had appeared to relieve the burden of the earth. Merely with the touch of his hands, Kṛṣṇa affectionately dispelled the pain that Jāmbavant suffered during the battle. *20* The bear fell to the ground and, praising Kṛṣṇa again and again, presented his daughter, Jāmbavatī by name, as a gift worthy of such a guest. *21* Bowing deeply, Jāmbavant also gave him the Syamantaka jewel. Eternal Kṛṣṇa accepted the gem from the prostrate beast just to clear his name, even though he had no need to do so. *22* Accompanied by Jāmbavatī, he then returned to Dvārakā.

The residents of the city were filled with joy when Kṛṣṇa returned and, seeing him, even those who were stooped with age grew young once more. All the Yādavas, both men and women, congratulated Kṛṣṇa's father, Vasudeva, with the words, 'How fortunate you are! How fortunate!' The lord then explained to all the gathered Yādavas exactly what had happened. Kṛṣṇa returned the Syamantaka to Satrājita and was exonerated of the false accusations that had been made against him. *23* He then conducted Jāmbavatī to the inner chambers.

Satrājita, fearing he had caused a stain on Kṛṣṇa's reputation, gave his own daughter Satyabhāmā to him in marriage. She, however, had already been sought by some of the other leading Yādavas, including Akrūra, Kṛtavarman and Śatadhanvan. Because Satyabhāmā had been given to another, they felt slighted and therefore formed an alliance against Satrājita. *24* Akrūra, Kṛtavarman and the other leaders said to Śatadhanvan, 'This Satrājita is very wicked. We requested his daughter, as did you, but he ignored us all and gave her to Kṛṣṇa. Satrājita's life is worthless. Why don't you kill him and take the jewel? If Kṛṣṇa allies himself with Satrājita, we'll come to your defence.' *25* Hearing this, Śatadhanvan accepted their proposal.

Lord Kṛṣṇa, who knew the truth about the five sons of Pāṇḍu and the burning house of lacquer, went to Hastināpura, the City of Elephants, in order to placate Duryodhana and to dissuade him from further attempts on the Pāṇḍavas's lives.[11] *26* In Kṛṣṇa's absence, Śatadhanvan murdered Satrājita while he slept and seized the jewel. Filled with anger at her father's death, Satyabhāmā mounted a chariot and travelled at once to Hastināpura.

11 In the *Mahābhārata* (1.148), Duryodhana attempted to murder his five Pāṇḍava cousins by incinerating them in a house made from flammable lacquer.

There she said to Kṛṣṇa, 'Śatadhanvan can't accept that I was given to you in marriage. He has killed my father and taken the Syamantaka. Now he's become a laughing stock. Consider this, then do what must be done.' *27*

After Satyabhāmā had spoken, Kṛṣṇa, although usually kind-hearted, replied to her, his eyes like burnished copper blazed with fury, 'My dear girl, this makes *me* a laughing stock. I won't stand for this behaviour from that wretch. If you don't fell the tree, you can't kill the birds that nest in it. You've spoken enough of these weighty words, stirred up by grief.' So saying, Kṛṣṇa returned to Dvārakā, where he said to Balarāma in secret, 'Prasena was killed by a lion while hunting in the forest. Now Satrājita has been murdered by Śatadhanvan. Because both of them are dead, the jewel should become our property. *28* Get up, mount your chariot and try to kill him.' Balarāma agreed at once and set out in pursuit.

When Śatadhanvan learned that Kṛṣṇa and Balarāma had taken up arms against him, he went to Kṛtavarman and pressed him for support, but Kṛtavarman replied that he couldn't fight those two warriors. Hearing this, Śatadhanvan then approached Akrūra, but he gave this reply: 'No-one, even the best of gods who are praised by all the world, would be able to fight Lord Kṛṣṇa. His footsteps make the three worlds tremble, he makes widows of the women in the cities of the demigods and he's the discus warrior whose weapon can't be thwarted, even by those of his mightiest foes. Balarāma, the plough-wielding fighter, wild-eyed with drunkenness, destroys his enemy's forces with just a glance. The manifest power of his mighty weapon checks and abolishes even the strongest enemy. What chance have I? Ask someone else to help you.' *29* Hearing this, Śatadhanvan replied, 'If you, knowing your own limits, can't save me, then at least take this jewel and treasure it.' Thus addressed, Akrūra agreed, but added, 'Even under the direst circumstances, you must tell no-one that I have it.' Śatadhanvan agreed and Akrūra accepted the jewel. *30*

Śatadhanvan then set off on a mare of unmatched speed that could gallop a hundred leagues a day. But Balarāma and Kṛṣṇa followed him in a chariot drawn by four steeds, Śaibya, Sugrīva, Meghapuṣpa and Balāhaka. *31* Śatadhanvan's mare carried him for a hundred leagues, but when they reached the forest regions of Mithilā, the steed expired, so Śatadhanvan abandoned it and set off on foot. *32* Kṛṣṇa said to Balarāma, 'You wait in the chariot while I chase this wretch and kill him. The ground here looks too rough for the horses. You won't be able to drive across it.' *33* Balarāma agreed and waited with the chariot, while Kṛṣṇa chased Śatadhanvan for two furlongs. Kṛṣṇa hurled his discus at his quarry, who was still some way off, and struck off his head. Kṛṣṇa made a thorough search of his victim's body, clothes and possessions but failed to find the Syamantaka. Returning to Balarāma, he said, 'We've killed Śatadhanvan for nothing, as I still haven't found the jewel, the essence of the world.'

Hearing this, furious Balarāma cursed Vāsudeva, 'Damn you! You hanker after wealth so much, I can't bear to be your brother! My path lies here, you can go where you like. I'll have nothing more to do with Dvārakā or the rest of the family. I've had enough of the deceitful curses you've made in my presence.' Even though Kṛṣṇa had been reviled with these words, he tried to placate Balarāma, but his brother, refusing to stay, took refuge in the city of Videha. *34* There, King Janaka welcomed him hospitably and showed him to the palace, where he remained. Vāsudeva, however, returned to Dvārakā. While Balarāma lived in King Janaka's domain, he personally instructed Dhṛtarāṣṭra's son Duryodhana in how to wield the mace. Three years later, Babhru, Ugrasena and other Yādava clansmen, realising that Kṛṣṇa hadn't seized the gem, went to Videha to convince Balarāma to return with them to Dvārakā. *35*

Akrūra, however, was obsessed with the thought of the gold brought forth by that extraordinary jewel. He undertook many sacrifices because he knew that killing a kṣatriya or a vaiśya who is engaged in such a rite is tantamount to brahminicide. He was therefore able to protect himself by maintaining his sacrificial initiation. For sixty-two years, owing to the power of the jewel, the kingdom was free from calamity, famine and epidemics. *36* Later, when Sātvata's great-grandson Śatrughna was killed by the Bhojas allied with Akrūra, they all abandoned Dvārakā and fled together. *37* From the very day they departed, disasters, wild animals, drought, plague and other troubles struck. Lord Kṛṣṇa, who has Garuḍa, the enemy of serpents, on his banner, then summoned the Yādavas along with Balarāma and Ugrasena to ask them why so many calamities had befallen at the same time. *38* After Kṛṣṇa had spoken, a Yādava elder named Andhaka gave this explanation:

'Wherever Akrūra's father, Śvaphalka, ventured, such places were free from famine, plague, drought and other woes. *39* Śvaphalka was invited to the king of Kāśī's realm during a particularly long drought, and at once the rains began to fall from heaven. The consort of the king had earlier conceived a baby girl, *40* but on the date it was due, no infant was delivered. Indeed, twelve years passed and still the child remained unborn. The king of Kāśī then addressed his daughter in the womb, "Why aren't

you born? Come out! I want to see your face. Why do you make your
mother suffer so?" Hearing this, the infant in the womb replied, "Father,
if you give the brahmins one cow every day, I'll surely leave this womb in
three years' time." Hearing this, the king did as she suggested, and the baby
girl was duly born three years later. Her father named her Gāndinī, and
later bestowed her on Śvaphalka as a gift befitting a guest who'd shown the
king such kindness. 41 Śvaphalka and Gāndinī had a son, Akrūra. As such,
Akrūra's birth was the result of the union of excellent qualities. 42 Now that
he has gone, how could there be no pestilence, famine or other calamities?
You must therefore beg him to return. What's the use of finding fault in
a person of such virtues?' 43

Hearing this report from the Yadu elder Andhaka, the Yādavas, led by Keśava, Ugrasena and Balarāma, gave Śvaphalka's son Akrūra a guarantee that they would overlook the offences he'd committed and invited him to return to the city. As soon as Akrūra came back, drought, plague, famine, pests and other troubles all abated owing to the power of the gem he wore.

'The fact that Akrūra was born to Gāndinī and Śvaphalka is irrelevant,'
thought Kṛṣṇa. 'Only a greater power could prevent such troubles. 44
He surely has the mighty Syamantaka about his person, as people say it has
the power to do such things. Akrūra has been undertaking one sacrifice
after another, but I doubt he can afford to do so. It's clear he has the jewel.'

Reaching this conclusion, Kṛṣṇa found a pretext to call a meeting of all
the Yādavas in his residence. 45 When they were seated, Janārdana revealed
his true intent and, having done so, gave an amusing speech for Akrūra,
befitting the occasion, in which he said to him, 46 'You're a wealthy man,
and we know that Śatadhanvan gave Syamantaka, the essence of all the
world, to you. This jewel, which profits the entire kingdom, is in your
possession. Leave it with us, so we may all benefit from its power. Balarāma,
however, suspects that I have it, so do us all a favour and reveal it.'

Hearing this, Akrūra, who did indeed possess the gem, said to himself, 47
'What's to be done now? If I deny I have the jewel, they'll search for it and,
as it's hidden in my clothes, they'll certainly discover it.' With this thought,
Akrūra decided to avoid a search and said to Kṛṣṇa–Nārāyaṇa, cause of
all the universe, 'Lord, Śatadhanvan gave me this Syamantaka jewel. 48
Ever since he left, I always thought that you'd ask me for it—if not today,
then tomorrow or the following day. Because of the burden of wearing it,
I've lost all interest in pleasures, nor do I have a moment's happiness. 49

All this time, I've feared you'd think I couldn't bear the jewel that benefits this whole realm, so I said nothing. *50* Take the Syamantaka and give it to whomsoever you desire.'

Akrūra then produced a tiny golden casket from beneath his dhoti; *51* taking out the Syamantaka, he set it before the Yādava assembly. As soon as he had done so, a lovely light spread in all directions. *52* Akrūra continued, 'Here's the jewel that Śatadhanvan gave me. Let its rightful owner take it.' Seeing the gemstone, all the astonished Yādavas cried out, 'Marvellous! Marvellous!' When Balarāma beheld the stone, he was filled with greed and said to himself, 'It's mine! Never-failing Kṛṣṇa and I searched for it together.' *53* Satyabhāmā also wanted it, as she considered it the property of her father, Satrājita.

Seeing Balarāma's and Satyabhāmā's faces, Kṛṣṇa felt like an ox yoked to two wagons. In the presence of all the Yādavas, he said to Akrūra, 'By showing this jewel in the presence of the assembly, my name's been cleared. It's owned in common by me and Balarāma, but it's also part of Satyabhāmā's patrimony. It belongs to no-one else. *54* When the jewel is carried at all times by a person, pure and chaste, who adheres to virtue, it benefits the realm, but if it's carried by an unchaste man, the jewel will be his downfall. *55* I have sixteen thousand wives, so I'm not qualified to carry it. How could Satyabhāmā accept it either? Noble Balarāma has succumbed to drink and other pleasures, so he can't have it. For these reasons, this whole Yadu clan, including Balarāma, Satyabhāmā and myself, beseech you, Akrūra, a wealthy man, as you alone are fit to bear the jewel. In your possession, it will benefit the entire realm. You, therefore, should carry it as before, since it brings prosperity to the land. Please don't try to argue with us!' Hearing this, munificent Akrūra agreed to accept the mighty gem and, from that day, he wore it openly and moved about like the light-wreathed sun, shining with the extraordinary brilliance of the jewel that hung about his neck. *56*

Anyone who recalls how Lord Kṛṣṇa was absolved of this false accusation will not suffer even the slightest allegation himself, his senses will never be impaired and he'll be absolved of all his sins. *57*

So ends Chapter Thirteen in Book Four of the glorious Viṣṇu Purāṇa.

14. The ancestry of Kṛṣṇa's father, Vasudeva, and his nemesis, Śiśupāla

Parāśara:

Anamitra's son was Śini.[12] His son was Satyaka. Satyaka's son was Sātyaki, also known as Yuyudhāna. His son was Asaṅga. His son was Tūṇi. Tūṇi's son was Yugaṃdhara. These were known collectively as the Śaineyas. *1* Vṛṣṇi was born in the lineage of Anamitra. His son was Śvaphalka, whose prowess has already been described. Śvaphalka's younger brother was called Citraka. Śvaphalka and Gāndinī's son was Akrūra. Their other son was Upamadgu. Upamadgu's sons were Mṛdura, Viśāri, Mejaya, Girikṣatra, Upakṣatra, Śatrughna, Arimardana, Dharmadṛk, Dṛṣṭavarman, Gandhamojavāha and Prativāha. They also had a daughter named Sutārā. Akrūra had two sons, Devavant and Upadeva.

Citraka had many sons, among whom Pṛthu and Vipṛthu were the foremost. *2* Andhaka had four sons, Kukura, Bhajamāna, Śuci and Kambalabarhis. *3* Kukura's son was Dhṛṣṭa. His son was Kapotaroman. His son was Viloman. His son was Bhava, also known as Candanodaka Dundubhi, a friend of the gandharva Tumburu. His son was Abhijit. His son was Punarvasu. He had a son, Āhuka, and a daughter, Āhukī. *4* Āhuka had two sons, Devaka and Ugrasena. Devaka had four sons, Devavant, Upadeva, Sudeva and Devarakṣita. They had seven sisters, Vṛkadevā, Upadevā, Devarakṣitā, Śrīdevā, Śāntidevā, Sahadevā and Devakī—all of whom were married to Vasudeva.

Ugrasena's sons were called Kaṃsa, Nyagrodha, Sunāman, Kaṅka, Śaṅku, Subhūmi, Rāṣṭrapāla, Yuddhamuṣṭi and Tuṣṭimant. Ugrasena's daughters were Kaṃsā, Kaṃsavatī, Sutanu, Rāṣṭrapālī and Kaṅkī. Bhajamāna's son was Vidūratha. Vidūratha's son was Śūra. Śūra's son was Śamin. Śamin's son was Pratikṣatra. His son was Svayaṃbhoja. His son was Hṛdika. *5* His sons were called Kṛtavarman, Śatadhanu and Devamīḍhuṣa. *6* Devamīḍhuṣa's son, Śūra, had a wife named Māriṣā. *7* They had ten sons, of whom Vasudeva was the first. As soon as Vasudeva was born, the deities, who could see the future clearly, realised that he was an aspect of Lord Viṣṇu manifesting in the world, and caused divine *ānaka* and *dundubhi* drums to be beaten throughout the royal residence. That's why he was given the

12 Elsewhere, Śini (or Śinī) is said to be Anamitra's younger brother (4.13.6 above). In any case, Anamitra was the grandfather of Satrājita, who featured in the Syamantaka narrative above.

name Ānakadundubhi at the time. Vasudeva had nine brothers: Devabhāga, Devaśravas, Anādhṛṣṭi, Karundhaka, Vatsabālaka, Sṛñjaya, Śyāma, Śamīka and Gaṇḍūṣa. His five sisters were Pṛthā, Śrutadevā, Śrutakīrti, Śrutaśravas and Rājādhidevī. *8*

Śūra had a friend by the name of Kunti who had no children, so he duly gave Kunti his own daughter, Pṛthā. She was married to Pāṇḍu. Pṛthā conceived three sons, Yudhiṣṭhira, Bhīma and Arjuna, with the deities Dharma, Vāyu and mighty Indra, respectively. Earlier, as a young, unmarried woman, she had a son by the name of Karṇa with the lordly Sun. *9* Pṛthā's co-wife Mādrī bore two more sons for Pāṇḍu, Nakula and Sahadeva, with the divine Aśvins, Nāsatya and Dasra.[13]

Vasudeva's sister Śrutadevā was married to Vṛddhaśarman, a prince of the Kārūṣas. Their son was the great demigod Dantavakra. Śrutakīrti was married to the king of the Kaikeyas. They had five sons, including Saṃtardana, who were also known as Kaikeyas. Rājādhidevī bore the two Avantis, Vinda and Anuvinda. Śrutaśravas was married to Damaghoṣa, the king of the Cedis. She bore Śiśupāla.

In a previous life, Śiśupāla had been the unruly but courageous Daitya king Hiraṇyakaśipu, *10* who was slain by Lord Viṣṇu, preceptor of all the world. Hiraṇyakaśipu was reborn as the ten-headed Rāvaṇa, whose qualities of energy, valour, accomplishment and prowess were unrivalled, and who conquered the three worlds with his regal might. *11* Because Rāvaṇa had been in the presence of the lord so long, and as a result of the merit he acquired in bodily form, he was killed by Lord Viṣṇu in the person of Rāma, descendant of Raghu. Rāvaṇa was then reborn as the overlord of the Cedis, Śiśupāla by name, the son of the Cedi king Damaghoṣa. *12* Appearing in this form, he was even more hostile towards Lord Viṣṇu, who had manifested an aspect of himself in the world as lotus-eyed Kṛṣṇa to ease the burden of the earth. Śiśupāla was slain by the lord, but even so, as his mind had been fully focused on the supreme spirit, he achieved a state of union with the divine. *13* When the lord is pleased, he grants all wishes. Even when displeased, to the extent of striking down an enemy, he may still bestow peerless divinity upon that being. *14*

So ends Chapter Fourteen in Book Four of the glorious Viṣṇu Purāṇa.

13 These five sons of Pāṇḍu, the Pāṇḍavas, are the heroes of the *Mahābhārata*.

15. Hiraṇyakaśipu, Rāvaṇa and Śiśupāla

Maitreya:

In the persons of Hiraṇyakaśipu and Rāvaṇa, that being, slain by Viṣṇu, achieved an everlasting state of bliss that lies even beyond the reach of gods. *1* How, then, did he achieve this state of union with eternal Hari when slain again in the person of Śiśupāla? *2* I wish to hear about this, as you're preeminent among those who uphold virtue. I ask because I'm filled with curiosity, and it befits you to explain all this to me. *3*

Parāśara:

In former times, the lord, who is the cause of creation, preservation and destruction of the world, manifested in physical form as the man–lion Nṛsiṃha to kill the Daitya king. Hiraṇyakaśipu, however, had no inkling that his adversary was Viṣṇu. *4* A single thought arising from excessive passion occupied his mind: that his state of excellence was born of the peerless merit that he acquired. As a result of this conception, after he was slain by Viṣṇu, he achieved unchallenged sovereignty in all three worlds in the person of ten-headed Rāvaṇa, winning leisure and prosperity. *5*

Even then, his mind did not achieve absorption with Lord Viṣṇu, the highest Absolute, who has neither start nor finish and needs no other support. Again, in the person of Rāvaṇa, obsessed with the thought of love, he set his heart on Janaka's daughter Sītā. When he saw Viṣṇu, who'd taken the form of Rāma, the son of Daśaratha, he failed again to recognise the eternal lord. Even at the moment of his death, he mistook his slayer for a mortal. *6* Just by being slain by Viṣṇu, he won rebirth and sovereignty in the world-renowned line of Cedi kings in the person of Śiśupāla. *7* His heart constricted by an enmity that grew stronger over many lifetimes, when mocking or abusing Viṣṇu, Śiśupāla constantly uttered every name of the everlasting deity, all of which affected him. *8* As a consequence of his deep hostility, whether walking, eating, bathing, sitting, reclining or anything else, the image of Viṣṇu never left his mind: eyes like the unstained petals of a full-blown lotus, clad in radiant golden garments, resplendent with gleaming diadem, armbands and bracelets, and sporting four long, strong arms that held the discus, conch and mace. *9*

Calling his name, and holding him ever in his thoughts, Śiśupāla beheld Lord Kṛṣṇa in the form of indestructible energy, the supreme Absolute, blazing with rays of light that shone from his heavenly discus, which was destined for his demise. Śiśupāla was freed from passion, anger and every other fault. *10* The instant that the lordly discus struck him, recalling the Divine, all his sins were burned away and, even though he was slain by Kṛṣṇa, he achieved absorption into him.

Now I've explained it all to you: when the lord is called by name or contemplated, even by a person bound by hatred, he bestows rewards that even gods or demigods or any other being find hard to win. How much greater the reward, then, for those who are filled with perfect faith?

The descendants of Vasudeva and Kṛṣṇa

Kṛṣṇa's natural father, Vasudeva, also known as Ānakadundubhi, had many wives, the foremost being Pauravī, Rohiṇī, Madirā, Bhadrā and Devakī. *11* Ānakadundubhi's sons with Rohiṇī included Balarāma, Sāraṇa, Śaṭha and Durmada. Balarāma had two sons with Revatī, Niśaṭha and Ulmuka. The foremost sons of Sāraṇa were Mārṣṭi, Mārṣimant, Śiśi, Śiśu and Satyadhṛti. Bhadrāśva, Bhadrabāhu, Durdama, Bhūta and others were also born in the family of Rohiṇī. *12* Vasudeva's sons with Madirā included Nanda, Upananda and Kṛtaka. With Bhadrā, he fathered Upanidhi, Gada and others. With Vaiśālī, he had one son, Kauśika. Ānakadundubhi had six sons with Devakī, named Kīrtimant, Suṣeṇa, Udāyin, Bhadrasena, Ṛjudāsa and Bhadradeva, *13* all of whom were killed by Kaṃsa. Following this, the lord sent Yoganidrā to take the seventh infant from Devakī's womb in the middle of the night and place it in Rohiṇī's. *14* Because he'd been pulled (*karṣaṇāt*) from the womb, this child, Balarāma, was also known as Saṃkarṣaṇa. *15*

Next, Lord Vāsudeva—root of the spreading universal tree; who lies beyond the conception of all the gods, demigods, sages and humans of the past, the present and future; who is worshipped by reverent deities led by lotus-born Brahmā and by the elements led by Fire; and who has neither start nor middle—descended to the womb of Devakī to ease the burden of the earth. *16* Yoganidrā, whose pride and love had burgeoned through the blessings of the lord, carried the infant Vāsudeva to the womb of Yaśodā, wife of cattle-herding Nanda. *17*

When lotus-eyed Kṛṣṇa was born, the sun, moon and planets shone more brightly, fear of wild animals subsided, minds were eased and in every corner of the world immoral conduct was set aside. *18* At his birth, all the world was led to the path of righteousness. The lord, having descended to the mortal world, took sixteen thousand, one hundred wives. Among these, eight consorts were foremost, including Rukmiṇī, Satyabhāmā, Jāmbavatī and

Cāruhāsinī. With these women, the lord, whose form is universal and has no beginning, sired one hundred and eighty thousand sons. *19* The thirteen most important included Pradyumna, Cārudeṣṇa, Sāmba and others. Pradyumna married Rukmin's daughter Kakudvatī, and they had a son, Aniruddha. Aniruddha married Rukmin's granddaughter Subhadrā, and they had a son, Vajra. Vajra's son was Pratibāhu, and his son was Sucāru.

It would be impossible, even in many centuries, to know all the members of the Yadu clan, who numbered in the hundreds of thousands. Two songs in praise of them are current: *20*

'Thirty-eight million inhouse instructors happily taught archery to the youths of the mighty Yādava clan. *21* Who, then, could put an exact number to the family of ten thousand times ten thousand times one hundred thousand souls, among whom the king, Āhuka, is always present?' *22*

'The mighty Daityas, struck down in battle with the gods, were born again as tyrants among mankind. *23* The deities appeared on earth to vanquish them, brahmin, as the one hundred and one branches of the Yadu clan.' *24*

Viṣṇu was established as their paragon and overlord, and the Yādavas all obeyed his word. *25*

Anyone who listens repeatedly to the origins of the Vṛṣṇi heroes is freed from all misdeeds and will reach the realm of Viṣṇu. *26*

So ends Chapter Fifteen in Book Four of the glorious Viṣṇu Purāṇa.

16. Yayāti's son Turvasu

Parāśara:

I've described in brief the lineage of Yadu. Now you'll hear about Turvasu's descendants. His son was Vahni. Vahni's son was Gobhānu. His son was Traiśānu. His son was Karaṃdhama. His son was Marutta. Marutta had no sons of his own, so he adopted Duṣyanta, the Puru's descendant. In this way, as the result of Yayāti's curse, the lineage of Turvasu had to merge with that of Puru.[14] *1*

So ends Chapter Sixteen in Book Four of the glorious Viṣṇu Purāṇa.

14 Turvasu refused to exchange his youthfulness for Yayāti's old age, so Yayāti cursed him so that he would never wield sovereignty. See above, 4.10.8. In this passage, the text uses Pūru for Puru. I have standardised on the latter.

17. Yayāti's son Druhyu

Parāśara:

Druhyu's son was Babhru. *1* His son was Setu. His son was called Āradvant. His son was Gāndhāra. His son was Dharma. His son was Dhṛta. Dhṛta's son was Durdama. His son was Pracetas. Pracetas had one hundred sons who became overlords of the heretical barbarians of the north. *2*

So ends Chapter Seventeen in Book Four of the glorious Viṣṇu Purāṇa.

18. Yayāti's son Anu

Parāśara:

Yayāti's fourth son, Anu, had three sons: Sabhānara, Cakṣu and Paramekṣu. Sabhānara's son was Kālānara. Kālānara's son was Sṛñjaya. Sṛñjaya's son was Puraṃjaya. His son was Janamejaya. His son was Mahāśāla, and his son was Mahāmanas. His two sons were Uśīnara and Titikṣu. Uśīnara had five sons: Śibi, Nṛga, Nara, Kṛmi and Darva. Śibi had four sons: Vṛṣadarbha, Suvīra, Kaikeya and Madraka. Titikṣu's son was Ruṣadratha. His son was Hema. Hema's son was Sutapas. His son was Bali. With Bali's wife, Dīrghatamas had Aṅga, Vaṅga, Kaliṅga, Suhya and Pauṇḍra—the Bāleya warriors. *1* Each of their lineages was named after them, as were their five kingdoms. Aṅga's son was Anapāna. His son was Diviratha. His son was Dharmaratha. His son was Citraratha, also known as Romapāda. His son was Daśaratha. As this Daśaratha was childless, Aja's son, also named Daśaratha, gave him his daughter Śāntā. *2* Romapāda's son was Caturaṅga. His son was Pṛthulākṣa. His son was Campa, who founded the city of Campā. *3* Campa's son was Haryaṅga. His son was Bhadraratha. His son was Bṛhadratha. His son was Bṛhatkarman. Bṛhatkarman's son was Bṛhadbhānu. His son was Bṛhanmanas. His son was Jayadratha, who married the daughter of a brahmin mother and a kṣatriya father. Together they had a son named Vijaya. *4* Vijaya's son was Dhṛti. His son was Dhṛtivrata. Dhṛtivrata's son was Satyakarman. Satyakarman's son was Adhiratha. It was he who, wandering along the banks of the Gaṅgā, found Karṇa in a basket where he had been abandoned by his mother, Pṛthā. Adhiratha adopted Karṇa as his own son.[15] Karṇa's son was Vṛṣasena. These were the descendants of Aṅga. *5* Next you'll hear about the lineage of Puru. *6*

So ends Chapter Eighteen in Book Four of the glorious Viṣṇu Purāṇa.

19. Yayāti's son Puru

Parāśara:

Puru's son was Janamejaya. His son was Pracinvant. Pracinvant's son was Pravīra. His son was Manasyu. Manasyu's son was Abhayada. His son was Sudyu. Sudyu's son was Bahugava. His son was Saṃyāti. Saṃyāti's son was Ahaṃyāti. His son was Raudrāśva. Raudrāśva had ten sons, named Ṛteyu, Kakṣeyu, Sthaṇḍileyu, Dhṛteyu, Jaleyu, Sthaleyu, Dharmeyu, Sannateyu, Dhaneyu and Vaneyu.

Ṛteyu's son was Rantināra. Rantināra's sons were Sumati, Apratiratha and Dhruva. Apratiratha's son was Kaṇva. His son was Medhātithi, from whom the Kāṇvāyana brahmins were descended. Apratiratha's other son was Ailīna. He had four sons, the eldest of whom was Duṣyanta. Duṣyanta's son was the universal sovereign Bharata. The deities sang this verse to explain his name:

'A mother is but a pouch of skin. The son is indeed his father's, as he is the begetter. Duṣyanta, cherish (*bharasva*) your son, and don't belittle Śakuntalā. *1*

The son, as the bearer of semen, saves his forefathers from destruction wreaked by Yama. You're the maker of this embryo and Śakuntalā spoke the truth, your majesty.'[16] *2*

Bharata had nine sons with his three wives, but because the sons didn't resemble him, their own mothers killed them fearing that Bharata would reject them. No further sons were born to him, but as he still yearned for progeny, he performed a soma sacrifice to the Maruts, the wind gods. When Dīrghatamas was still a foetus in the womb, he kicked out Bṛhaspati's sperm. The Maruts therefore gave Bharata a son, Bharadvāja, with Mammatā, the wife of Utathya. *3* This verse is sung to explain the origin of his name: *4*

15 Karṇa was one of the great warrior heroes of the *Mahābhārata*.

16 *Mahābhārata*, 1.90.30–33. These characters are at the heart of Kālidāsa's great drama, *Abhijñānaśākuntala*.

'Foolish woman, take care of (*bhara*) this child born of two fathers (*dvājam*).' 'No, Bṛhaspati, you take care of him!' So saying, both parents left. That's how Bharadvāja got his name. *5*

Because Bharata's desire for the birth of a son had been in vain (*vitatha*), Bharadvāja, who had been given to him by the Maruts, was also called Vitatha. *6* Vitatha's son was Bhavanmanyu. The sons of Bhavanmanyu were Bṛhatkṣatra, Mahāvīrya, Nara and Garga. Nara's son was Saṃkṛti. Saṃkṛti's sons were Ruciradhī and Rantideva. Garga's son was Śini. Their descendants, known as Gārgyas and Śainyas, were kṣatriyas by birth but later became brahmins. *7* Mahāvīrya had a son called Durukṣaya. He had three sons, Trayyāruṇa, Puṣkarin and Kapi, the last of whom also became a brahmin at a later date. Bṛhatkṣatra's son was Suhotra. Suhotra's son was Hastin, who founded the city of Hastināpura. The three sons of Hastin were Ajamīḍha, Dvimīḍha and Purumīḍha.

Ajamīḍha's first son was Kaṇva. Kaṇva's son was Medhātithi, from whom the Kāṇvāyana brahmins were descended. *8* Ajamīḍha's other son was Bṛhadiṣu. His son was Bṛhaddhanu. His son was Bṛhatkarman. His son was Jayadratha. His son was Viśvajit. His son was Senajit. Senajit's sons were called Rucirāśva, Kāśya, Dṛḍhahanu and Vatsahanu. Rucirāśva's son was Pṛthusena. His son was Pāra. Pāra's son was Nīpa. He had a hundred sons, among whom the foremost was Samara, king of Kāmpilya. *9* Samara had three sons, Pāra, Supāra and Sadaśva. Pāra's son was Pṛthu. Pṛthu's son was Sukṛti. Sukṛti's son was Vibhrāja. His son was Aṇuha, who married Śuka's daughter Kṛtvī. *10* Aṇuha's son was Brahmadatta. His son was Viṣvaksena. His son was Udaksena. His son was Bhallāṭa.

Dvimīḍha's son was called Yavīnara. His son was Dhṛtimant. His son was Satyadhṛti. His son was Dṛḍhanemi. His son was Supārśva. His son was Sumati. His son was Sannatimant. Sannatimant's son was Kṛta, to whom Hiraṇyanābha taught yoga, and who created twenty-four compendiums for brahmins in the east who sang the *Sāma Veda*. *11* Kṛta's son was Ugrāyudha, by whom the Nīpa clan of kṣatriyas was almost annihilated. *12* Ugrāyudha's son was Kṣemya. Kṣemya's son was Suvīra. His son was Ripuṃjaya. His son was Bahuratha. Such were the descendants of Puru, the Pauravas.

Ajamīḍha's wife was named Nalinī and they had a son called Nīla. His son was Śānti. Śānti's son was Suśānti. Suśānti's son was Purujānu. His son was Cakṣus. His son was Haryaśva. Haryaśva's sons were Mudgala, Sṛñjaya, Bṛhadiṣu, Pravīra and Kāmpilya. Their father said, 'My five (*pañca*) sons are able (*alam*) to protect their dominions', hence their epithet, the Pāñcālas. *13* From Mudgala were descended the Maudgalyas, who were born kṣatriyas but later became brahmins. Mudgala's son was Vadhyaśva. Vadhyaśva had twins, a son, Divodāsa, and a daughter, Ahalyā. With Ahalyā, Śaradvat had a son, Śatānanda. Śatānanda's son was Satyadhṛti, who attained perfect knowledge of archery. While spying on the exquisite apsaras Urvaśī, Satyadhṛti ejaculated into a clump of grass. The clump split in half and brought forth two infants, a boy and a girl. One day, King Śāṃtanu was out hunting when he came upon the children and, feeling compassionate (*kṛpā*), he took them in. Accordingly, the boy was named Kṛpa, and the girl, Kṛpī. She later married Droṇa and was Aśvatthāman's mother.

Divodāsa's son was Mitrāyu. Mitrāyu's son was the king called Cyavana. Cyavana's son was Sudāsa. His son was Saudāsa Sahadeva. His son was Somaka. He had one hundred sons, of whom Jantu was the eldest and Pṛṣata the youngest. Pṛṣata's son was Drupada. His son was Dhṛṣṭadyumna. His son was Dhṛṣṭaketu.

Ajamīḍha had another son by the name of Ṛkṣa. Ṛkṣa's son was Saṃvaraṇa. Saṃvaraṇa's son was Kuru, who created the sacred plain of Kurukṣetra. The preeminent sons of Kuru were Sudhanus, Jahnu and Parīkṣit. Sudhanus's son was Suhotra. His son was Cyavana. Cyavana's son was Kṛtaka. His son Uparicara was also known as Vasu. Vasu had seven sons led by Bṛhadratha, Pratyagra, Kuśāmba, Māvella and Matsya. Bṛhadratha's son was Kuśāgra. His son was Ṛṣabha. His son was Puṣpavant. His son was Satyahita. His son was Sudhanvan. His son was Jantu. Bṛhadratha had another son who was born in two halves. These were joined together (*saṃdhita*) by a rākṣasī named Jarā. That's why he was called Jarāsandha, 'Joined by Jarā'. His son was Sahadeva. His son was Somapi. His son was Śrutaśravas. Such were the kings of Magadha. *14*

So ends Chapter Nineteen in Book Four of the glorious Viṣṇu Purāṇa.

20. The lineages of the Kauravas and Pāṇḍavas

The glorious Parāśara:

Parīkṣit had four sons: Janamejaya, Śrutasena, Ugrasena and Bhīmasena. *1* Janhu Janamejaya had a son named Suratha. *2* His son was Vidūratha. Vidūratha's son was Sārvabhauma. Sārvabhauma's son was Jayasena. His son was Ārādhita. His son was Ayutāyu. Ayutāyu's son was Akrodhana.

His son was Devātithi. His son was Ṛkṣa. *3* Ṛkṣa's son was Bhīmasena. His
son was Dilīpa. Dilīpa's son was Pratīpa. He had three sons, called Devāpi,
Śāṃtanu and Bāhlīka. Devāpi retired to the forest while still a child *4* so
Śāṃtanu became the king. In all the world, they sing this verse about him:

'Each old man he touches with his hands grows young again and discovers
perfect peace (*śānti*). That's why he's called Śāṃtanu.' *5*

No rain fell in Śāṃtanu's kingdom for twelve years. *6* Seeing the destruction
of his entire realm, the king asked the brahmins, 'What's caused this drought
in our kingdom? What have I done wrong?' They replied, 'You're enjoying
this earth, which really belongs to your elder brother, as you married before
he did.' Hearing this, the king asked them what he should do. They replied,
'As long as Devāpi doesn't surrender to faults such as heresy, he'll remain
fit to rule. You should therefore abdicate in his favour.' At this, the chief
minister, Aśmasārin, made contact with some ascetics in that same forest
who taught doctrines contrary to Vedic tradition. *7* These ascetics then set
that honest prince's mind on a path that led away from the Vedas. *8*

King Śāṃtanu, smarting at the criticism of his early marriage, sent the brahmins to the forest ahead of him, then proceeded there himself to confer the kingdom on his elder brother. On reaching Devāpi's ashram, they all assembled before the prince. The brahmins then explained to Devāpi that Vedic doctrine required the first-born son to rule the kingdom. Devāpi, however, offered them many rejoinders, but his reasoning was rife with ideas that ran counter to the Vedas. The brahmins then said to Śāṃtanu, 'Come, your majesty. There's no point in persisting with this. The drought will soon be over. This man is an apostate who disparages the timeless Vedic teachings. When an older brother has fallen, it's not unlawful for his younger brother to marry first.' Hearing this, Śāṃtanu returned to the capital and ruled the kingdom. As soon as Devāpi was compromised by uttering words that were inconsistent with the Vedas, the rain god, Parjanya, sent down showers to nourish all the crops.

Bāhlīka's son was Somadatta. *9* Somadatta had three sons, named Bhūri,
Bhūriśravas and Śalya. Śāṃtanu's son with the river goddess Gaṅgā was
Bhīṣma of noble repute, who understood the import of all the scriptures.
Śāṃtanu also had two sons with Satyavatī, Citrāṅgada and Vicitravīrya.
Citrāṅgada was killed while young in battle with a gandharva who had
the same name as himself. Vicitravīrya married two daughters of the king
of Kāśī, Ambikā and Ambālikā. He wore himself out while enjoying
intercourse with them, contracted consumption and died. At the direction
of Satyavatī, her son Kṛṣṇa-Dvaipāyana, believing that a mother's word

must never be disobeyed, had two sons with Vivitravīrya's widow—namely, Dhṛtrāṣṭra and Pāṇḍu. He had another son, Vidura, with a serving-girl who had been thrust upon him. *10*

Dhṛtarāṣṭra had a hundred sons, among the foremost of whom were Duryodhana and Duḥśāsana. Pāṇḍu was unable to sire children himself because he had been cursed by a deer in the forest. His senior wife Kuntī consequently conceived Yudhiṣṭhira, Bhīma and Arjuna with the deities Dharma, Vāyu and Indra, while his younger wife Mādrī conceived Nakula and Sahadeva with the Aśvins, giving Pāṇḍu five sons in all. These five each had a son with Draupadī: Yudhiṣṭhira had Prativindhya, Bhīmasena had Śrutasoma, Arjuna had Śrutakīrti, Nakula had Śatānika and Sahadeva had Śrutakarman.

The Pāṇḍavas also had other sons, as follows: Yudhiṣṭhira had a son, Devaka, with Yaudheyī. Bhīmasena had a son, Ghaṭotkaca, with Hiḍimbā. Bhīmasena had a son, Sarvatraga, with Kāśī. Sahadeva had a son with Vijayā, named Suhotra. Nakula had a son, Niramitra, with Kareṇamatī. *11* Arjuna had a son named Irāvant with Ulūpī, the nāga's daughter. With the daughter of the king of Maṇipura, Arjuna had a son named Babhruvāhana, whom his maternal grandfather adopted as his own son. *12* With Subhadrā, Arjuna had a son, Abhimanyu, who, with his great strength and prowess, destroyed all his enemies' chariots even though he was just a lad. Abhimanyu and Uttarā had a son, Parīkṣit, who, while still in the womb, was burned to ashes by the Brahmāstra weapon loosed by Aśvatthāman after all the Kurus had been annihilated. Parīkṣit was restored to life through the intercession of Lord Kṛṣṇa, whose feet are worshipped by every god and demigod and who took human form of his own volition. It is Parīkṣit who rules all the world today in accord with virtue. *13*

So ends Chapter Twenty in Book Four of the glorious Viṣṇu Purāṇa.

21. The future descendants of Parīkṣit

Parāśara:

I'll now name the kings who will appear in future. The current sovereign, Parīkṣit, will have four sons, Janamejaya, Śrutasena, Ugrasena and Bhīmasena. *1* Parīkṣit's other son, Śatānīka, will study the Vedas under Yājñavalkya. He'll then obtain weapons from Kṛpa but will be disillusioned with worldly pleasures. Under the guidance of Śaunaka, he'll gain knowledge of the Self and will eventually achieve final liberation. *2* Śatānīka's son will be Aśvamedhadatta. His son will be Adhisīmakṛṣṇa. Adhisīmakṛṣṇa's son will be Niścaknu, who'll reside in Kauśambī when Hastināpura is washed away by the Gaṅgā. His son will be Uṣṇa. Uṣṇa's son will be Citraratha. His son will be Śuciratha. His son will be Vṛṣṇimant. His son will be Suṣeṇa. His son will be Sunītha. Sunītha's son will be Ṛca. His son will be Nṛcakṣus. His son will be Sukhibala. His son will be Pariplava. His son will be Sunaya. His son will be Medhāvin. His son will be Nṛpaṃjaya. His son will be Mṛdu. His son will be Tigma. Tigma's son will be Bṛhadratha. His son will be Vasudāna. His son will be another Śatānīka, and his son will be Udayana. Udayana's son will be Ahīnara. His son will be Daṇḍapāṇi. His son will be Niramitra, and his son will be Kṣemaka, about whom there is a verse:

'The lineage, which was the origin of the brahmins and kṣatriyas, and was honoured by sagacious kings, will come to an end in the age of Kali with the king named Kṣemaka.' *3*

So ends Chapter Twenty-One in Book Four of the glorious Viṣṇu Purāṇa.

22. The future descendants of Bṛhadbala

Parāśara:

Now I'll name the future kings in the lineage of Ikṣvāku. Bṛhadbala's son will be Bṛhatkṣaṇa.[17] *1* His son will be Urukṣaya. His son will be Vatsa. Vatsa's son will be Vatsavyūha. His son will be Prativyoma. His son will be Divākara. His son will be Sahadeva. *2* His son will be Bṛhadaśva. His son will be Bhānuratha. His son will be Pratītāśva. His son will be Supratīka. His son will be Marudeva. Marudeva's son will be Sunakṣatra. His son will be Kiṃnara. Kiṃnara's son will be Antarikṣa. His son will be Suvarṇa, and his son will be Amitrajit. His son will be Bṛhadrāja. His son will be Dharmin. Dharmin's son will be Kṛtaṃjaya. Kṛtaṃjaya's son will be Raṇaṃjaya. Raṇaṃjaya's son will be Saṃjaya. His son will be Śākya. Śākya's son will be Śuddhodana. His son will be Rāhula. His son will be Prasenajit. His son will be Kṣudraka. His son will be Kuṇḍaka. His son will be Suratha, and, finally, his son will be Sumitra. These will be the descendants of Bṛhadbala in the lineage of Ikṣvāku. There is a verse about this branch of the family:

17 The forebears of Bṛhadbala in the Ikṣvāku lineage are listed in 4.4.

'This lineage of the Ikṣvākus will finish with Sumitra. With this king, it will come to an end in the age of Kali.' *3*

So ends Chapter Twenty-Two in Book Four of the glorious Viṣṇu Purāṇa.

23. The future descendants of Bṛhadratha

Parāśara:

Now I'll name in order the future descendants of Bṛhadratha, who will be the kings of the Magadhas. In this lineage are mighty men with Jarāsandha as the foremost. *1* Jarāsandha's son was Sahadeva. His son will be Somāpi. His son will be Śrutavant. His son will be Ayutāyu. His son will be Niramitra. His son will be Sukṣatra. His son will be Bṛhatkarman. His son will be Senajit. His son will be Śrutaṃjaya. His son will be Vipra. His son will be Śucināman. His son will be Kṣemya. His son will be Suvrata. Suvrata's son will be Dharma. His son will be Suśrama. His son will be Dṛḍhasena. His son will be Sumati. His son will be Subala. His son will be Sunīta. His son will be Satyajit. Satyajit's son will be Viśvajit. His son will be Ripuṃjaya. These kings, the descendants of Bṛhadratha, will reign for a thousand years. *2*

So ends Chapter Twenty-Three in Book Four of the glorious Viṣṇu Purāṇa.

24. Future kings; The age of Kali

Parāśara:

The last descendant of Bṛhadratha, Ripuṃjaya by name, will have a minister called Munika, who will kill his sovereign and then anoint his own son Pradyota as king. Pradyota's son will be called Pālaka. His son will be Viśākhayūpa. His son will be Janaka, and his son will be Nandivardhana. These five Pradyota dynasts will rule the earth for one hundred and thirty-eight years. *1*

Nandivardhana's son will be Śiśunāga, and his son will be Kākavarṇa. His son will be Kṣemadharman. His son will be Kṣatrojas. His son will be Vidhisāra, and his son will be Ajātaśatru. His son will be Darbhaka, and Darbhaka's son will be Udayana. His son will be Nandivardhana. His son will be Mahānandin. These ten kings in the lineage of Śiśunāga will rule for three hundred and sixty-two years. *2*

Mahānandin's avaricious son, Mahāpadma or Nanda, will be born to a śūdra mother. Like a second Paraśurāma, he will cause the destruction of all the kṣatriyas. *3* From that time on, śūdras will be the rulers of the earth. Having brought the world under one umbrella, Mahāpadma will rule unopposed. *4* He'll have eight sons, beginning with Sumālya, who will reign after him. The sons of Mahāpadma will reign for a hundred years. The brahmin Kauṭilya will eradicate these nine Nandas. *5* After they have passed, the Mauryas will rule the earth. Kauṭilya will anoint Candragupta as king. *6* His son will be Bindusāra. His son will be Aśokavardhana. His son will be Suyaśas. His son will be Daśaratha. His son will be Saṃgata. His son will be Śāliśūka. His son will be Somaśarman. His son will be Śatadhanvan. His son will be called Anubṛhadratha. These ten Maurya kings will reign for one hundred and thirty-seven years.

After them the Śuṅgas will rule the earth. *7* The general Puṣpamitra will kill his sovereign and usurp the kingdom. *8* His son will be Agnimitra. His son will be Sujyeṣṭha. His son will be Vasumitra. His son will be Ārdraka. His son will be Pulindaka. His son will be Ghoṣavasu. His son will be Vajramitra. His son will be Bhāgavata. *9* His son will be Devabhūti. These ten Śuṅgas will rule the earth for one hundred and twelve years. *10*

The dissolute Śuṅga king Devabhūti will be killed by his own minister, a Kaṇva named Vasudeva, who will usurp the kingdom for himself. His son will be Bhūmitra. His son will be Nārāyaṇa. Nārāyaṇa's son will be Suśarman. These four Kāṇvāyana kings will rule for forty-five years.

The Kaṇva Suśarman will be violently overthrown by his own minion, Śipraka of the Andhra clan, who will then rule the earth. Next, Śipraka's brother Kṛṣṇa will become king. His son will be Śrīśātakarṇi. His son will be Pūrṇotsaṅga. His son will be Śātakarṇi, and his son will be Lambodara. His son will be Divīlaka. His son will be Meghasvāti. His son will be Paṭumant, and his son will be Ariṣṭakarman. His son will be Hāla. Hāla's son will be Pattalaka. His son will be Pravillasena. His son will be Sundara Śātakarṇin. His son will be Cakora Śātakarṇin. His son will be Śivasvāti, and his son will be Gomatīputra. His son will be Pulimant. His son will be Śātakarṇin. His son will be Śivaśrī. His son will be Śivaskandha. His son will be Yajñaśrī. His son will be Vijaya. His son will be Candraśrī, and his son will be Pulomāvi. These thirty kings, originally servants of the Andhra clan, will rule the earth for four hundred and fifty-six years. *11*

There will be seven Ābhīra kings and ten Gardabhilas. Then there will be sixteen Śaka kings, then eight Yavanas, fourteen Tuṣāras, thirteen Muṇḍas and eleven Maunas. They'll rule the earth for one thousand three hundred and ninety-nine years. *12* Following this, eleven Paura kings will rule for three hundred years. When they've been overthrown, the Kailika Yavanas will become kings, unanointed—Vindhyaśakti among them. *13* His son will be Puraṃjaya. His son will be Rāmacandra. His son will be Dharma. Dharma's sons will be Vaṅgara, Kṛtanandana, Suṣinandi, his brother Nandiyaśas, Śiśuka and Pravīra. They will rule for one hundred and six years and will have thirteen sons. There will be three Bāhlikas, and thirteen kings, including Puṣyamitra and Paṭumitra, the Mekalas and seven Andhras. There will be nine kings in Kosala, and the same number of Naiṣadhas. *14*

In the land of the Magadhas, a king named Viśvasphaṭika will create new social classes and will give power to Kaivartas, Paṭus, Pulindas and brahmins, having exterminated the entire order of kṣatriyas. Nine Nāgas will reign in the city named Padmāvatī. The Magadha Guptas will rule in Mathurā and along the Gaṅgā as far as Prayāga. Devarakṣita will protect Kosala, Oḍra, Puṇḍra, Tāmralipta and the city by the sea. Kaliṅgas, Māhiṣakas and Māhendras will rule over an earthly refuge.[18] The dynasties of Maṇidhānakas will rule the settlements of the Naiṣadhas, Naimiṣikas and Kālatoyas. Those known as Kanakas will rule the settlements of Trairājya and Mūṣika, Saurāṣṭra, Avanti and Śūdra. The kingdoms of Arbuda and Marubhūmi will be ruled by Vrātyas, brahmins, Abhīras, śūdras and others. The banks of the Sindhu and the realms of Dāvikorvī, Candrabhāga and Kashmir will be ruled by Vrātyas, Mlecchas and other barbarians as well as śūdras.

The end of the age of Kali

These kings will rule the earth at the same time. They'll show little mercy and be subject to intense fury, ever delighting in injustice and immorality. They'll slay women, children and cattle. They'll covet the possessions of others but will remain weak. Most will rise and fall quickly, and they'll be short-lived, having many desires but few morals. *15* Inhabitants of the various settlements will mix with them and ape their behaviour. Encouraged by the support of these kings, and with barbarians as their teachers, the populace will lead immoral lives. As a result, the daily decline and ultimate loss of wealth and virtue will cause the world to decay. *16*

18 This reading as given in the Critical Edition is not very clear. A better reading is found in other editions—for example, 'The Guhas will rule over Kaliṅga, Māhiṣa, Mahendra and Bhauma'.

Riches alone will confer nobility. Wealth will be the sole measure of virtue. Sex will be the only bond between couples. Womanhood will be reason enough for pleasure. Falsehood will be the basis of trade and warfare. The earth will only be valued as a source of gems and copper. The sacred thread will be the only measure of a brahmin. External trappings will be the sole indication of one's stage of life. Dishonesty will count as a profession. *17* Weakness will be the cause of dependence. Pronouncements filled with timidity will be the measure of scholarship. Wealth will be the measure of goodness. *18* A simple bath will count as purification. Donations will be equated with religion. Mutual consent will be the basis for a marriage. Fine clothes will confer respectability. Water from far away will substitute for a sacred ford.

In a world overwhelmed with manifold faults like these, whoever is the strongest, from any of the classes, will be king. Unable to bear the despot's excessive greed, the populace will seek refuge in hidden valleys in the mountains, subsisting on such foods as honey, vegetables, roots, berries, leaves and flowers. Clad only in the bark of trees, they'll endure heat and cold, wind and rain. No-one will live longer than twenty-three years. In this Kali age of unending decadence, humankind will meet its doom. *19*

When the religion of the Vedas and scriptural tradition are in decline and the Kali age nears its end, Lord Vāsudeva—creator of the universe; master of moving and unmoving things; the beginning, end and everything between; the Absolute in the form of the highest self—will manifest an aspect of himself in this world as Kalki in the home of Viṣṇuyaśas, the head brahmin in a village called Śaṃbala. Endowed with eight qualities and perfections, greatness and irresistible power, he will annihilate the Mlecchas and Dasyus, whose thoughts and deeds are evil. Then he will reestablish this whole world in virtue and the minds of those who live at the end of the age, waking when this night has passed, will be stainless, clear and pure. *20* Such people, who are the seeds of all humanity, even though they were begotten and matured at such a time, will bring forth progeny. Their offspring will adhere to the virtues of the Kṛta age. *21* As it's said in this regard:

'When the moon, the sun, the constellation of Tiṣya and Jupiter all gather in one mansion, the age of Kṛta will begin.' *22*

I've now described the kings of the past, present and future in each lineage, best of sages. *23* You should realise that, from the birth of Parīkṣit to the coronation of Nanda, one thousand and fifteen years elapsed. *24*

When the first two stars of the Seven Sages (Ursa Major) are seen to rise in the heavens, and a certain lunar mansion appears at an equal distance between them at night, then the Seven Sages will remain fixed in that position for one hundred years of men.[19] *25*

At the time of Parīkṣit, these two stars were in Maghā, best of brahmins. That marked the start of the Kali age, which endured for twelve hundred years. *26*

When that aspect of Lord Viṣṇu born in the family of Vasudeva returned to heaven, brahmin, the Kali age descended on the world. *27*

But as long as his two feet trod this earth, the Kali age had no effect upon it. *28*

When that aspect of eternal Viṣṇu left the world for heaven, Yudhiṣṭhira, son of Dharma, accompanied by his younger brothers, renounced his kingdom. *29*

Once Lord Kṛṣṇa had departed, the Pāṇḍavas witnessed evil omens and anointed Parīkṣit king. *30*

When the Seven Sages pass beyond Pūrvāṣāḍhā, from Nanda onwards, the influence of Kali will increase. *31*

The day that Kṛṣṇa went to heaven was the very day that Kali started. Now I'll tell you how long it will endure: *32*

Three hundred thousand years, according to the reckoning of men, plus another sixty thousand, brahmin, will be the duration of the age. *33*

When twelve hundred years of gods have passed, the Kṛta age will start again. *34*

Brahmins, kṣatriyas, vaiśyas and śūdras, best of brahmins, all great-souled beings, pass in thousands, from age to age. *35*

As there are so many names and so much repetition, I've not recounted all of them in every lineage. *36*

Puru's scion King Devāpi and Maru, born in Ikṣvāku's family, both possessors of great yogic power, live to this day in the village of Kalāpa. *37*

Having returned to this location in the Kṛta age, these two founders of kṣatriya dynasties will renew the line of Manu. *38*

19 This describes the precession of the equinoxes (Wilson 1961: 390, fn.82).

The sons of Manu each rule the earth in every Kṛta, Tretā and Dvāpara age. *39*

In the age of Kali, some remain on earth to reestablish lineages, just as Devāpi and Maru are doing now. *40*

I've described to you the dynasties in brief, but even lifetimes by the hundred are not enough to do so fully. *41*

These and other kings, blinded by delusion, grew selfish while on earth, even though their bodies perish. *42*

'How may I make this mountain mine? How may my son possess the earth? How may I keep this in my family?' All these kings have met their end while harbouring thoughts like these— *43*

Those who came before them, those who live beside them and others who will follow. *44*

The Earth beholds these sovereigns, distracted from the path of self-control, and laughs, as if she saw spring flowers blooming in the autumn. *45*

Listen to these verses that she sang, Maitreya. They were passed to Janaka, that paragon of virtue, by the sage Asita: *46*

The song of the Earth

The Earth:

How could these kings be so deluded, when they're said to be so wise? Their nature is like the foam on water, yet their hearts are full of confidence. *47*

Before they can control themselves, they wish to overcome their ministers, their servants and their subjects, and then they'll try to overcome their enemies. *48*

'Step by step we'll vanquish all this sea-girt world!' With obsessions such as these, they fail to see that death is near at hand. *49*

To have dominion over me—this whole world with oceans all around—is nothing when compared with self-control, as the reward for self-control is liberation. *50*

Their forebears died but left the world behind them. Their own sires died and did not take it either. Yet these kings falsely think they own the earth and still desire to win it. *51*

Fathers fight with their own sons to conquer me, and brothers fight with brothers on account of this delusion when their hearts are gripped by selfishness. *52*

'The earth is mine', 'All this belongs to me', 'This will always be my family's'. Each foolish king who had such thoughts is dead. *53*

Seeing one whose heart was filled with possessiveness, and who, on leaving me, now walks the path of all who die, how could such an urge to own, which arises on my account, still find a place in their descendants' hearts? *54*

At first, I want to laugh at kings whose ambassadors tell their foe, 'The earth is mine. Give up your claim!', but then I feel compassion for such fools. *55*

Parāśara:

The possessiveness of those who hear these verses that the Earth once sang, Maitreya, will melt away like ice exposed to heat. *56*

I've told you all about the lineage of Manu, the kings of which were aspects of Viṣṇu, preserver of the universe. *57*

One who's pure at heart and listens with devotion, verse by verse, to this account of Manu's line will be absolved of all misdeeds. *58*

Unequalled wealth, good fortune and prosperity are yours and your senses will stay sharp once you've heard the full description of the noble dynasties of the Sun and Moon. The lineage of Raghu who've passed on—Ikṣvāku, Jahnu, Māndhātṛ and Sagara, *59*

As well as Yayāti, Nahuṣa and others who are no more—strong, heroic kings of boundless wealth, *60*

Were all undone by mighty Time. Now all that's left are anecdotes. *61*

Knowing this, and hearing these accounts, a man who is wise will never call his sons or wife, his house or fields, his goods or chattels his own. *62*

Austerities performed by worthy men who hold their arms aloft for many years, and rituals carried out by mighty heroes, are all reduced by Time to tales. *63*

Traversing three worlds unresisted, cleaving enemies with his discus, Pṛthu fell victim to the winds of Time, like cottonwood fibres in a fire. *64*

Kārtavīrya ruled the world; he, too, slayed enemies with his discus, butnowhe's only mentioned in some stories, giving rise to doubt about what's certain. *65*

The sovereignty of Raghu's scion, who slew ten-headed Rāvaṇa, spread out in all directions, but was it not reduced to ashes the instant Yama frowned? Shame on him! *66*

Having heard about Māndhātṛ, once emperor of the world, but now a figure in some story, what wise person, other than a fool, would contemplate possession? *67*

Bhagīratha, Sagara, Kakutstha and Rāvaṇa, Rāma, Lakṣmaṇa, Yudhiṣṭhira and the others—there's no doubt they all existed, but where are they now? We just don't know. *68*

The valiant kings of the present time and those of the future whom I've mentioned, plus all the others we've spoken of, will succumb like those who went before. *69*

The learned man, who knows all this, entertains no sense of ownership towards himself, let alone his son, his wife, his fields or anything, excepting his own body. *70*

So ends Chapter Twenty-Four in Book Four of the glorious Viṣṇu Purāṇa.

End of Book Four.

Book Five: Kṛṣṇa

1. The union of Vasudeva and Devakī

Maitreya:

You've described all the royal lineages in detail and duly recounted the deeds of each. *1*

Now I wish to hear about that aspect of Viṣṇu, holy sage, who came to earth and manifested in the Yadu clan. *2*

Tell me about the acts performed by Lord Kṛṣṇa, the supreme being, sage, after he appeared in the world as an aspect of Viṣṇu's aspect. *3*

Parāśara:

Listen, Maitreya, to this account, about which you've questioned me, concerning the deeds of Kṛṣṇa, who appeared as an aspect of Viṣṇu's aspect to benefit the world. *4*

Long ago, Vasudeva married Devaka's daughter, fortunate Devakī, great sage, who was the equal of a goddess. *5*

After their wedding, Kaṃsa, benefactor of the Bhoja people, served as driver of the couple's bridal carriage. *6*

As they made their way, a loud voice sounded in the sky, rumbling like thunder, and addressed these words to Kaṃsa: *7*

'Fool! The eighth child born of this woman whom you're carrying with her husband in your chariot will end your life.' *8*

Parāśara:

Hearing this, mighty Kaṃsa drew his sword to strike at Devakī, but Vasudeva intervened, *9*

'Don't kill Devakī, great king! I'll give you all the children delivered from her womb.' *10*

Parāśara:

Kaṃsa acceded to this proposal, best of brahmins, and, as he respected Vasudeva, he spared the girl. *11*

The Earth complains of her burden

At that same time, the Earth, oppressed by her great burden, approached the thirteen deities assembled on Mount Meru. *12*

Bowing to the gods with Brahmā at their head, the Earth recounted all her woes, her voice beset with misery: *13*

The Earth:

Just as fire masters gold and the sun is lord of cattle, Nārāyaṇa is my sovereign, as he is of all the worlds. *14*

He is Brahmā, lord of patriarchs, who arose before the earliest beings. He is formless Time composed of seconds, hours and minutes. *15*

Your entire assembly is just his aspect, best of gods. *16*

The Ādityas, Maruts, Sādhyas, Rudras, Vasus, Aśvins, Vahnis and the ancestors led by Atri who made the worlds— *17*

All these are forms of Viṣṇu, the immeasurable heart of greatness. *18*

The yakṣas, rākṣasas and Daityas, the piśācas, nāgas and Dānavas, the gandharvas and apsarases are all but forms of mighty Viṣṇu. *19*

The sky with shining planets, constellations, stars, fire, water, wind, myself the Earth, the objects of the senses and all this world consist of him. *20*

The forms of this many-formed being annul one another day and night, then are themselves annulled, like waves upon the ocean. *21*

At this very moment, Daityas led by Kālanemi have overrun the world of men and continually oppress the populace. *22*

The great demigod Kālanemi, slain by mighty Viṣṇu, has been reborn as Kaṃsa, son of Ugrasena. *23*

Ariṣṭa, Dhenuka, Keśin, Pralamba, Naraka, the demigod Sunda and fearsome Bāṇa, son of Bali— *24*

I cannot count the number of these and other powerful, evil beings who've taken birth in the homes of men. *25*

Many armies of strong and brilliant Daitya kings press down on me, gods of heavenly form. *26*

Suffering beneath the weight of this great burden, I can no longer support myself. That's why I'm telling you, immortal lords. *27*

Relieve me of this load, you fortunate beings, before I sink in misery to the lower realms. *28*

Parāśara:

Having heard the Earth's complaint in full, Brahmā, urged by the thirteen gods, spoke these words to ease the burden that oppressed her. *29*

Brahmā:

All the Earth has said is true, you denizens of heaven. Myself, Śiva, all of you and everything consists of Nārāyaṇa. *30*

Manifestations of his greatness, overcoming one another and being overcome, are at times more powerful, at other times less so. *31*

Come, therefore. Let us proceed to the Milky Ocean. We'll worship Hari on its northern shore and refer all this to him. *32*

That universal being, who is at the heart of everything, always manifests an aspect of himself on earth to uphold virtue and to aid the world. *33*

Brahmā praises Viṣṇu

Parāśara:

So saying, the grandsire of the world set out with all the other gods, and, having gathered his thoughts, he then praised Viṣṇu, whose emblem is Garuḍa. *34*

Brahmā:

You are both kinds of knowledge: that which is handed down in sacred texts and that which isn't. You have two states, formed and formless, Lord. *35*

You are two forms of the Absolute, gross and subtle. You are all and you know all. You are beyond the spiritual power of sound, you are the Absolute and that which consists of the Absolute. *36*

You are the *Ṛg*, *Yajur*, *Sāma* and *Atharva Vedas*. You are the art of Vedic pronunciation, ritual practice, the explanations, metres and the science of the calendar. *37*

You are the histories, myths and grammar, Lord. You are philosophy, logic and the treatises on law, Adhokṣaja. *38*

You are the doctrine that investigates the links between the body, soul and qualities. That doctrine is none other than a form of your highest self, primeval Lord. *39*

You are unmanifest, indescribable, inconceivable, lacking name and colour, hands and feet. You are Viṣṇu, the eternal highest state. *40*

You hear without ears and see without eyes. You are one but have many forms. You move without feet and grasp without hands. You know all but are not to be known by all. *41*

Beholding you as smaller than the smallest and having nonexistent form, one's ignorance will vanish. Nothing else beyond your blissful form supports the wisdom of the wise. You are the highest being. *42*

You are everything, the beginning and the protector of the world. All beings exist in you. You are all that has existed and all that will exist. You are more subtle than the subtlest. You alone are Spirit, which stands apart from primal Nature. *43*

You are one but also fourfold lordly fire, consumer of the sacrifice, which sheds its light and splendour on the world. You are the eye of all. Your forms are endless. You, arranger of the universe, took three steps. *44*

Just as fire, kindled in many ways, is always one, and its essential nature doesn't alter with its changing form, you, Lord, have one all-pervading form, though the forms you animate are many. *45*

You are the single foremost highest state, whom sages see with the eye of knowledge. There is nothing that has been or that will be, supreme spirit, other than your form. *46*

Your form is manifest and unmanifest. You are both totality and individuality, all-knowing and all-seeing, possessor of omnipotence, knowledge, strength and plenitude. *47*

You are not subject to loss or gain. You are independent, beginningless and powerful. You are untouched by fatigue, sloth, fear, anger, desire and other faults. *48*

Blameless, supreme, tranquil, sovereign, your progress is unalterable, you are lord of all, the ultimate foundation of everything, the indestructible abode of all abodes. *49*

Beyond all envelopments, unreached by imagination, the locus of great energy—highest spirit, we bow to you. *50*

Not without a cause, not with a cause, but neither with nor without a cause, you are the highest being, taking human form to uphold virtue. *51*

Parāśara:

Having mentally perceived this song of praise, Hari, the unborn lord at the heart of all, the bearer of universal form, replied to Brahmā. *52*

The Lord:

Greetings, Brahmā. Tell me all that you and the other gods desire from me, and success will be assured. *53*

Parāśara:

Then Brahmā, beholding the divine and universal form of Hari, praised him again, while all the gods bowed down in trepidation. *54*

Brahmā:

We bow to you and bow again, deity of a thousand forms, a thousand arms and many limbs and faces. We bow to you and bow again, boundless cause of creation, preservation and destruction of the world. *55*

Your subtlety is beyond the subtle; your measure beyond measure. You are greater than the greatest. You are at the heart of intellect and senses. You are the supreme heart that lies beyond the root of both. Be merciful to us, Lord. *56*

The Earth, whose ranges are oppressed by mighty demons reborn there, has come to you, Lord, hoping that you'll relieve her burden, as you are the final refuge of all the worlds and your limits are unattainable. *57*

We're all here: this is Indra, slayer of the demon Vṛtra. Here are the Aśvins, Nāsatya and Dasra. This is Varuṇa, and here are the Rudras, Vasus, Suns and others led by Winds and Fires. *58*

These are all the deities, Lord of gods. Tell us all that they and I must do, Lord, as we stand ever ready to follow your commands, faultless deity. *59*

Devakī's eight children

Parāśara:

While they praised him in this manner, the lord, the supreme master, plucked two hairs, great sage, one white, one black. *60*

'Having descended to the world,' he told he gods, 'these two hairs of mine will ease the burden of the Earth. *61*

Manifesting aspects of themselves on earth, let all the gods wage war against the furious and powerful demigods already there. *62*

Then all the Daityas in the world will go to their destruction. There's no doubt that when my gaze falls upon them, they'll be turned to dust. *63*

Vasudeva's wife is Devakī, the equal of a goddess. One of my hairs, you deities, will be her eighth-born child. *64*

Having descended to the earth, this being will slay Kaṃsa, a manifestation of the demon Kālameni.' So saying, Hari withdrew from sight. *65*

The deities bowed before that great unseen being, then returned to the summit of Mount Meru whence they descended to the world. *66*

But Nārada, the lordly sage, told Kaṃsa that Viṣṇu, supporter of the earth, would manifest as Devakī's eighth child. *67*

Hearing this from Nārada, furious Kaṃsa imprisoned Devakī and Vasudeva in his palace. *68*

As he'd promised previously, brahmin, Vasudeva surrendered every child to Kaṃsa as soon as it was born. *69*

It's said that Hiraṇyakaśipu's sons were born as the first six infants. At the command of Viṣṇu, the goddess Nidrā placed them one by one in the womb of Devakī. *70*

Lord Hari spoke to Yoganidrā, a form of his own deceptive power, who veils the world in ignorance. *71*

The Lord:

Nidrā, go at my command and bring six infants from the depths of Pātāla and place them one by one in Devakī's womb. *72*

When they've all been slain by Kaṃsa, an aspect of Śeṣa, and therefore an aspect of an aspect of me, will become the seventh infant in her belly. *73*

Another of Vasudeva's wives, Rohiṇī, resides in the cattle camp of Gokula. Before the child is born, goddess, take him to that woman. *74*

Folk will say that Devakī miscarried the seventh baby because she feared the King of Bhoja and the stress of prison life. *75*

But as he'll be drawn out (*saṃkarṣaṇāt*) from the womb, he'll be called Saṃkarṣaṇa. He'll be a hero as resplendent as the summit of a snowy mountain. *76*

I'll then enter the womb of Devakī, fair one, and you will enter Yaśodā's. *77*

I'll be born on the eighth night of the dark fortnight of the month of Nabhas during the rainy season, and you'll be born just one night later. *78*

With his mind in my control, Vasudeva will bear me to Yaśodā's bed, and he'll take you to Devakī's, blameless goddess. *79*

Kaṃsa will seize you, goddess, and dash you on a rock, but you'll escape into the sky. *80*

On account of his respect for me, hundred-eyed Indra will honour you and, bowing his head, will accept you as his sister. *81*

Once you've defeated Śumbha, Niśumbha and other Daityas by the thousand, you'll adorn the world in many places. *82*

You are prosperity, progeny, fame, patience, heaven and earth, firmness, modesty, nourishment, dawn and every other feminine quality. *83*

Those who address you as Āryā, Durgā, Vedagarbhā, Ambikā, Bhadrā, Bhadrakālī, Kṣemyā and Kṣemakarī, *84*

And who bow down and praise you in the morning and the afternoon, will have all their wishes granted by my grace. *85*

Men will worship you with offerings of liquor, meat and various foods and, if you're satisfied, you may grant them all that they desire. *86*

By my mercy, madam, it's certain that they'll never be in danger. Go now, goddess, and do as I command. *87*

So ends Chapter One in Book Five of the glorious Viṣṇu Purāṇa.

2. The deities praise Devakī

Parāśara:

As besought by Viṣṇu, god of gods, Yoganidrā, nursemaid of the world, then placed six infants one by one in Devakī's womb and bore away the seventh. *1*

When Devakī had borne that seventh child to Rohiṇī, Hari entered her womb to benefit the threefold worlds. *2*

On that very day, Yoganidrā entered Yaśodā's belly, as the highest being had instructed. *3*

When Viṣṇu's aspect came into the world, all the planets proceeded in perfect order through the heavens, brahmin, and the weather was delightful. *4*

None could set their eyes on Devakī because she shone so brightly, and the minds of those who saw her glowing thus were filled with wonder. *5*

By day and night, hosts of gods, unseen by men and women, praised Devakī with Viṣṇu in her womb. *6*

The deities:

You were *prakṛti*, the supreme and subtle natural state, in which Brahmā arose in former times. You were the power of speech of the deity who supports the world, and the womb that held the Vedas, splendid woman. *7*

You are the womb of creation and creation itself, eternal being, the seed of all and womb of the threefold sacrifice. *8*

You are the womb of the outcome, offering, fire and kindling. As Aditi, you are the womb of gods; as Diti, the Daityas's womb. *9*

You are light, the womb of day. You are humility, the womb of knowledge. You are prudence, womb of conduct. You are modesty, origin of respect. *10*

You are desire, the womb of love. You are satisfaction, contentment's womb. You are intelligence, womb of understanding. You are resolve, the womb of firmness. *11*

You are the heavens, womb of planets, stars and lunar mansions. You are the cause of all the world. These are your powers, goddess, and you have others by the thousand. *12*

Similarly, at this moment, within your womb, glorious nursemaid of the universe, rests all the world, resplendent with its countless seas, rivers, lands, forests and cities, replete with hamlets, towns and villages. *13*

All the fires, winds and waters; the sky providing space for everything, adorned with planets, stars and mansions, and filled with airborne chariots by the hundred; *14*

The earthly, aerial and heavenly spheres; the realms of Mahar, Jana, Tapas and Brahmā; and that deity's cosmic egg in full, you splendid woman; *15*

And all the beings who occupy these realms: gods, Daityas, gandharvas, cāraṇas, great serpents, yakṣas, rākṣasas, ghosts and guhyakas, *16*

Humankind, beasts and all other living things, you best of women—all these comprise the everlasting lord of all, and exist within him, creator of the universe. *17*

Viṣṇu, whose every aspect, including forms and deeds, is beyond the realm of comprehension, now lies within your womb. *18*

You are *svāhā*. You are *svadhā*. You are knowledge, nectar and the sky's own light. You came to earth to protect the worlds. *19*

Be merciful, goddess, and bless this world. Bear the lord with fondness, gracious woman, as the world is borne by him. *20*

So ends Chapter Two in Book Five of the glorious Viṣṇu Purāṇa.

3. The advent of Kṛṣṇa

Parāśara:

Thus praised by gods, Devakī bore in her womb heavenly Viṣṇu, the lotus-eyed saviour of the world. *1*

Just as the rising sun at dawn wakes the lotus flower, the great eternal Viṣṇu appeared in the womb of Devakī so that the world might blossom. *2*

The day of his birth spread great joy in all directions, just as moonlight graces the surface of the earth. *3*

Good people experienced deep contentment, cruel winds were stilled and streams flowed with tranquillity when Janārdana was born. *4*

Rivers made sweet music with their murmuring, gandharva lords sang praises, while hosts of apsarases danced. *5*

The deities, coursing through the heavens, showered flowers upon the earth, and fires burned bright and steadily when Janārdana appeared. *6*

At midnight, brahmin, when Janārdana, foundation of the universe, was born, thunderclouds rumbled deeply while shedding flowers like rain. *7*

Beholding the newborn infant, as blue as the petal of a waterlily, in four-armed form with Śrīvatsa on his chest, Vasudeva praised him. *8*

When that wise man had hailed the infant with lofty words, best of brahmins, fearing Kaṃsa, he added this: *9*

Vasudeva:

I recognise you, Lord, god of gods, bearer of the conch, the mace and discus. Be merciful, Lord, and withdraw this heavenly form. *10*

This very day, Lord, Kaṃsa will take revenge on me when he learns that you've appeared in my abode. *11*

Devakī:

May this god of gods—whose forms are boundless and universal, who embraced the worlds within himself while still within my womb, and who, by his own illusory power, assumed this infant form—be merciful. *12*

Withdraw this four-armed form, universal being, so that Diti's grandson Kaṃsa may never learn of your descent. *13*

The Lord:

Since you praised me in former times, hoping for a son, today your wish will be fulfilled, princess, as I've been delivered from your womb. *14*

Parāśara:

After he had spoken, the lord fell silent, best of sages, and Vasudeva picked him up and carried him through the darkness. *15*

The guards at the gates of Mathurā fell under Yoganidrā's spell, and Vasudeva slipped past undetected. *16*

The serpent Śeṣa followed Vasudeva, and with his hoods gave shelter to the infant from the deluge falling from the clouds that night. *17*

As Vasudeva carried Viṣṇu, the Yamunā, profound and swirling with a hundred varied eddies, reached only to his knees. *18*

Nanda and the other cowherd elders assembled on the riverbank with tribute for King Kaṃsa, where Vasudeva saw them. *19*

At that moment Yaśodā delivered Yoganidrā in the form of a baby girl, Maitreya, but she and all the others present succumbed to the goddess's spell. *20*

Vasudeva of boundless splendour laid the boy in Yaśodā's bed and hastened back with that young girl. *21*

When she woke, Yaśodā saw the newborn baby boy, dark as an azure lotus petal, and was filled with greatest joy. *22*

Vasudeva took the girl to his abode, placed her in Devakī's bed and waited by her side. *23*

When they heard the infant's cries, brahmin, the guards leapt up and told the king that Devakī had given birth. *24*

In rushed Kaṃsa to seize the child, but Devakī tried to stop him. 'Let her go! Let her go!' she cried. *25*

He sought to dash the infant on a rock, but as soon as she had left his hand, she rose into the air above and assumed a mighty eight-armed form, a weapon in each hand. *26*

This furious being laughed aloud and said to him, 'Why throw me to the ground, Kaṃsa? The one who'll slay you is already born. *27*

He is the essence of all the gods who caused your death in former times. Consider this, then quickly do what's best for you.' *28*

So saying, the goddess, resplendent in divine garlands and perfumes, departed, while the siddhas in the heavens sang her praises and the king of Bhoja stood and stared. *29*

So ends Chapter Three in Book Five of the glorious Viṣṇu Purāṇa.

4. Kaṃsa plots to kill Kṛṣṇa

Parāśara:

Kaṃsa's mind was troubled, so he summoned all the foremost demons, led by Keśin and Pralamba, and addressed those mighty beings. *1*

Kaṃsa:

'Strong-armed Pralamba, Keśin, Dhenuka, Pūtanā, Ariṣṭa and the rest of you must heed my words. *2*

Those wicked gods, scorched by my prowess, tried to kill me, but I pay them no regard, you heroes. *3*

I scorn that weakling Indra and that lonely yogin Śiva. What can Hari achieve by merely striking at our weaknesses? *4*

I scorn the Ādityas, accompanied by the timid Vasus. I scorn the Agnis and all the other deities defeated by my mighty arms. *5*

Did I not see Indra, king of gods, retreating from the battlefield with arrows in his back? He couldn't take them on the chest. *6*

When Indra stopped the rains from falling on my kingdom, did not the clouds, split asunder by my missiles, release their showers, just as I desired? *7*

Don't all the kings on earth—except my father-in-law, Jarāsandha—fearing the strength of my arms, submit to me? *8*

I despise those gods, you bulls among the Daitya heroes. I mock them as they make their feeble efforts. *9*

Therefore, Daitya kings, I'll strive to worst those base and evil-minded beings. *10*

To these ends, let each ascetic and every sacrificer in the world be put to death to disempower the gods. *11*

The infant girl, brought forth from the womb of Devakī, told me that the being who caused my death in previous lives is born again. *12*

Make every effort, then, to search out all the boys on earth, and be sure to kill those with special powers.' *13*

After Kaṃsa gave this order to the Daityas, he returned to his abode and freed Vasudeva and Devakī from confinement. *14*

Kaṃsa:

I killed your children for no purpose, as the one who's destined to destroy me has escaped. *15*

Forget the woe that you've endured. No other child of yours will die before his natural span expires. *16*

Parāśara:

Reassuring Devakī and Vasudeva with these words and having set them free, best of brahmins, Kaṃsa retreated to the inner chambers, filled with doubt. *17*

So ends Chapter Four in Book Five of the glorious Viṣṇu Purāṇa.

5. Kṛṣṇa slays Pūtanā

Parāśara:

Now free, Vasudeva went to Nanda's wagon, where he saw the joyous herdsman who thought the child was his. *1*

Vasudeva hailed him graciously, saying, 'What a lucky man you are, for even in old age, you have a son! *2*

You've paid in full your annual tribute to the king (the reason that you came), but wealthy people shouldn't tarry here. *3*

When the task that brought you here is done, why stay longer, Nanda? Return as quickly as you can to your own cattle camp. *4*

Rohiṇī has given birth to my own son there. Protect him as you would your own.' *5*

Hearing this, the sturdy cattle-herders led by Nanda, having paid their tribute, set off with fully laden wagons. *6*

Once they'd settled back in camp, the child-killing demon Pūtanā snatched the baby Kṛṣṇa as he slept one night and offered him her breast. *7*

Any child that's suckled by that fiend at night will die at once. *8*

Kṛṣṇa, however, filled with rage, held her breast and squeezed it tight between his hands, then sucked the life right out of her. *9*

Pūtanā screamed, her sinews snapped and that horrid fiend fell dying to the ground. *10*

Startled by the demon's cries, the residents of the camp awoke and found the baby on her lap, but she lay dead already. *11*

Frantic Yaśodā picked up Kṛṣṇa, best of brahmins, and waved a cow-tail whisk with one hand to ward off any evil force that might beset the child. *12*

The cattle-herder Nanda took some powdered dung and sprinkled it on Kṛṣṇa's head to give the child protection, then spoke this benediction: *13*

Nanda:

May Hari, lord of all creation, protect you. From the lotus at his navel came the world. *14*

May Keśava protect you. In the form of a boar, the deity drew the earth up with his tusk. *15*

May Keśava protect you from everything. In the form of Nṛsiṃha—half-man, half-lion—the lord tore apart the chest of his adversary with his claws. *16*

May he protect you always—he, who, as the dwarf, paced out the threefold world with three heroic strides in just one moment, his weapon glinting. *17*

May Govinda protect your head, Keśava your neck, Viṣṇu your genitals and belly and Janārdana your legs and feet. *18*

May eternal and irresistible Nārāyaṇa protect your head, your upper arms and forearms, your mind and all your senses. *19*

May any ghosts, kūṣmāṇḍas or rāksasas who trouble you meet their doom when struck by the blast of the conch sounded by the lordly wielder of the bow, the mace and discus. *20*

May Vaikuṇṭha protect you at the cardinal points, and Madhusūdana at the points between. May Hṛṣīkeśa protect you in the sky, and Mahīdhara on earth.[1] *21*

Parāśara:

After the cattle-herder Nanda blessed the child with this benediction, he laid him in a cot beneath a wagon. *22*

---

1 The commentators do not remark on the apparent incongruity of invoking Viṣṇu in any of the above incarnations to protect Kṛṣṇa—already a form of the deity.

The other herdsmen, staring at the giant form of Pūtanā now lying dead, were filled with horror and amazement. *23*

So ends Chapter Five in Book Five of the glorious Viṣṇu Purāṇa.

6. Kṛṣṇa's childhood

Parāśara:

One day, Madhusūdana, lying beneath the wagon and crying for the breast, kicked his legs about. *1*

But when his feet touched its timbers, the wagon tipped and landed upside down, smashing all the pots and other vessels that it carried. *2*

All the herding men and women cried in anguish, brahmin, and, rushing to him, saw the infant in his cot. *3*

'Who tipped the wagon?' asked the herdsmen. 'That baby,' said some children in reply. *4*

'We heard him crying, then he kicked the wagon with his feet, but no-one else has touched it.' *5*

The herdsmen were all filled with wonder. Most surprised of all was Nanda, who lifted up the child. *6*

Yaśodā then made an offering to the wagon and the broken pots with yoghurt, flowers, fruit and grains. *7*

Without the knowledge of the herdsmen, Vasudeva later sent the priest named Garga to carry out the birth rites for both infants in the camp. *8*

Prudent Garga, foremost of the wise, chose their names and called the elder Balarāma and the other Kṛṣṇa. *9*

Before too long, these two boys were crawling round the cattle camp, brahmin, with scratches on their hands and knees. *10*

They roamed about in dung and ashes, but neither Yaśodā nor Rohiṇī could restrain them. *11*

First, they played in the cowstall and then in the nursery pen, where they amused themselves by pulling the tails of the day-old calves. *12*

Yaśodā couldn't keep those feisty, fun-filled boys in place. *13*

So she tied Kṛṣṇa to a heavy wooden mortar with a rope around his middle, and in frustration scolded the lively child: *14*

'Now let's see if you'll escape,' she said as she resumed her chores. 'You're just too active!' *15*

While Yaśodā was busy with her duties, the lotus-eyed boy dragged the mortar between two *arjuna* trees. *16*

As he pulled the weight along, it lodged between the trunks, whose branches stretched towards the skies. Both trees toppled over! *17*

Hearing the mighty crash, the residents of the camp rushed up and saw the two huge *arjunas*. *18*

Their trunks were broken and branches shattered, lying on the ground. The boy, whose smile was bright with new milk teeth, sat between the fallen trunks, the cord still tied around his middle. *19*

And so they called him Dāmodara, because he had a rope (*dāman*) around his waist (*udara*). *20*

All the elder herdsmen, with Nanda at their head, were troubled and conferred together, fearing some evil presence. *21*

'We can't stay here. Let's find another forest. We've seen many evil omens that portend our doom: *22*

The death of Pūtanā, the upturned wagon, now these trees have fallen without a breath of wind. *23*

Let's move at once from here to Vṛndāvana, before this local evil presence ruins our camp.' *24*

So saying, all the residents of the camp agreed to leave and instructed every family to depart without delay. *25*

A short time later, the herdsmen left with all their cattle and their wagons, with one child per herd to mind the calves. *26*

Before long, the campsite, strewn with disused chattels, brahmin, was left to crows and vultures. *27*

Untiring Lord Kṛṣṇa, wishing only for the increase of the herd, set his joyous mind on Vṛndāvana. *28*

For there, even in the harshest heat, best of brahmins, fresh grass flourishes everywhere, as in the rainy season. *29*

Balarāma and Kṛṣṇa roam the Vṛndāvana forest

In Vṛndāvana, they set up camp and placed the wagons in a crescent round its edge. *30*

Now that Balarāma and Dāmodara were a little older, they tended all the calves together and stayed within the camp itself, intent on childish games. *31*

They added peacock feathers to their wreaths of forest flowers, playing tunes on rustic flutes, homely tambourines and instruments made from leaves. *32*

Their hair was trimmed in 'crow's-wing' style, and they looked like sons of Agni as they roamed and laughed and played in that great forest.[2] *33*

At times they joked together, at times they played with others. Roving with the herdsmen's sons, they led the calves to pasture. *34*

With the passage of time, by the age of seven, these two universal lords ruled the calves in the cattle camp. *35*

When the annual rains arrived, the sky was filled with thunderclouds, binding together all four quarters as if with torrents of rain. *36*

Abounding in fresh green grass and dotted with sturdy herdsmen, the earth resembled an emerald field spread with reddest rubies. *37*

The river waters burst their banks and flowed in all directions, like minds of fickle folk overwhelmed by newfound wealth. *38*

The unstained moon then lost its gleam, concealed by lowering clouds, just like the words of truthful men amid the din of fools. *39*

Indra's bow, although unstrung, still found a place in heaven, like a worthless hanger-on in the court of a feckless king.[3] *40*

Cranes shone in pure formations against the clouds, just as the ways of well-bred folk contrast with those of rogues. *41*

Fickle lightning flashed inconstant in the sky, like the friendship of a scoundrel with a man of virtue. *42*

Paths overgrown with mats of grass were difficult to follow, like the twisted arguments of fools. *43*

2 Monier-Williams (1899): '*kākapakṣa m.*, "crow's wing", sidelocks of hair on the temples of young men (three or five locks on each side left when the head is first shaved and allowed to remain there, especially in persons of the military caste).'

3 There is a nice pun in this verse: *nirguṇa* means both 'unstrung' and 'worthless'.

During that season, in the mighty forest, home to frenzied bees and peacocks, Kṛṣṇa and Balarāma, filled with joy, roamed together with the other lads. *44*

At times those two enjoyed a song while wandering happily with the cows; at others, when the days were cold, they'd shelter beneath the trees. *45*

At times they wore *kadamba* garlands, at others peacock feathers. Sometimes they daubed themselves with coloured minerals brought from distant mountains. *46*

Sometimes, feeling weary, they slept on beds of leaves. At others, on hearing a peal of thunder, they'd cry out in surprise. *47*

Sometimes they praised the cowherds' songs, and played their rustic flutes accompanied by peacocks. *48*

In these varied states and filled with purest joy, the two boys roamed to their hearts' content while playing in the forest. *49*

When dusk approached, these two strong lads returned to camp at leisure together with the herds and other boys. *50*

There, like a pair of deities, they romped amid the cowherd folk. *51*

So ends Chapter Six in Book Five of the glorious Viṣṇu Purāṇa.

7. Kṛṣṇa subdues the serpent Kāliya

Parāśara:

One day, leaving Balarāma in the camp, Kṛṣṇa went to Vṛndāvana. Surrounded by the herding boys and wearing a splendent garland of forest flowers, he roamed about at will. *1*

Now, Kṛṣṇa came to the Yamunā, filled with swirling streams. Its banks lay hidden under drifts of foam, and the laughter of its currents seemed to mock the world around. *2*

There, he beheld the frightful pool where the nāga Kāliya lurked, with flames and poison rising from its horrid depths. *3*

Mighty trees on the riverbank were scorched by fire and venom spewing from the pool. Its waters, whipped up by winds, touched passing birds and scalded them. *4*

Seeing that terrifying pool, gaping like a second maw of Death, Lord Madhusūdana reflected: *5*

'This must be the lair of wicked Kāliya, whose weapon is his poison. Last time I beat this evil beast, it left the sea and disappeared.[4] *6*

He's so defiled the Yamunā, consort queen of Sāgara, that neither thirsty man nor beast can drink from it. *7*

Let me slay this nāga king, so residents of the cattle camp may roam here happily forever. *8*

I descended to the world of men to pacify such wicked beings that take the path of evil. *9*

That *kadamba* tree with its strong limbs is not too far away. I'll climb up it, then dive into the serpent's pool.' *10*

Parāśara:

With this thought, he tightened his waistband, then leapt at once into the watery lair of the nāga king. *11*

That huge lake was set in motion by his dive, and its waters even splashed the trees standing at a distance. *12*

Blasted by the wind and water heated by the energy of the serpent's virulent poison, those trees burst into flame at once, and the conflagration spread to the horizon. *13*

Now Kṛṣṇa was in the nāga's pool, he clapped his hands. On hearing this, the serpent king then rushed towards him. *14*

His raging eyes gleamed like copper, his many hoods ablaze with venom, as other slithering poisonous snakes surrounded him. *15*

Hundreds of his nāga wives, adorned with gorgeous strings of pearls, their loveliness enhanced by the shaking of their earrings, swayed their trembling bodies. *16*

The serpents coiled themselves round Kṛṣṇa and struck him with their fangs that dripped with fiery poison. *17*

4 The commentators explain that this happened during an earlier avatāra when Viṣṇu–Kṛṣṇa appeared as Garuḍa.

When the other cowherds saw that he had dived into the pool and the serpents' coils now held him, they were filled with terror and ran shouting back to camp. *18*

The cowherds:

'Kṛṣṇa's mad! He's jumped into Kāliya's pool! The serpent king has eaten him! Come and see!' *19*

Hearing these cries, which struck them like a thunderbolt, the herding men and women, with Yaśodā in the lead, rushed down towards the pool. *20*

'No, no! Where is he now?' the herdsmen's wives cried out in anguish. Together with Yaśodā, they stumbled forward in a panic. *21*

Nanda, with the other herders and Balarāma of great prowess, rushed towards the Yamunā in the hope of seeing Kṛṣṇa. *22*

There they found him, captive of the nāga king, wrapped within the serpents' coils, yet Kṛṣṇa offered no resistance. *23*

The herdsman Nanda stood quite still and fixed his gaze on Kṛṣṇa's face, best of brahmins, as did Yaśodā, that most fortunate of women. *24*

The other herders' wives looked on and wept in terror, crying out their love for Keśava, their voices choked with fear: *25*

'Let's all jump in the nāga's pool with Yaśodā. There's no point in going back to camp. *26*

What's the day without the sun? What's night without the moon? What are cows without a bull? What's the camp without our Kṛṣṇa? *27*

We won't return to camp without him. Like a lake without its water, the forest has lost its charm. *28*

Hari shines with loveliness like the petal of an azure lily. We're amazed that anyone could savour life without him. *29*

If we poor creatures cannot see him, his eyes as bright and charming as the petal of a fully opened lotus, how will we survive in camp? *30*

We won't go back to Nanda's camp without that lotus-eyed boy who steals the treasure of our hearts with his sweet, sweet words. *31*

See his face, you cowherd women. Even though the nāga king has wrapped him in his coils, he's still smiling in our direction.' *32*

Parāśara:

Hearing the women's words, Balarāma, sturdy son of Rohiṇī, looked with steady gaze upon the herdsmen, who were stiff with fear, *33*

And on Nanda, sunk in deepest misery while staring at his son, and on Yaśodā, who'd fallen in a swoon. Then, conscious of his brother's actual greatness, he spoke these words to Kṛṣṇa. *34*

Balarāma:

Why, lordly god of gods, did you adopt this human form? Don't you know your real self is endless and immortal? *35*

You are the navel of the world, as a hub is to the spokes. You are the threefold creator, preserver and destroyer of the triple realm. *36*

The Ādityas, along with Indra, Rudra, the Aśvins, Vasus and the Winds and Fires, all contemplate you, whose true self is beyond conception, as do all the yogins. *37*

For the benefit of all, universal Lord, you descended here among these mortals, because you wished to ease the burden of the earth, and I, your elder brother, am but an aspect of you. *38*

While you disport yourself as mortal, Lord, all the other deities imitate your pastimes. *39*

First you caused the goddesses to descend here to the cattle camp to join your games, and then you, eternal Lord, appeared. *40*

As we've manifested here, these herdsmen are our relatives, Kṛṣṇa, as are their despairing wives. Why disdain our kinfolk so? *41*

You've shown the marks of a mortal being, and you've had your boyish fun. Now, Kṛṣṇa, you must destroy this wicked sharp-toothed snake. *42*

Parāśara:

Thus reminded of his actual nature, Kṛṣṇa began to smile. He clapped his hands and freed himself from the serpents' coils. *43*

Pressing down upon the centre of Kāliya's hood with his two hands, then climbing on its lowered head, that valiant being began to dance upon it. *44*

Wounds appeared on the serpent's hood where Kṛṣṇa's feet had struck it, but when Kāliya tried to raise his head, Kṛṣṇa forced it down again. *45*

When Kṛṣṇa danced the *recaka*, the nāga swooned and swayed, and when he did the *daṇḍapāta*, the snake began to vomit blood.[5] *46*

Seeing his head and neck both broken as blood streamed from his jaws, Kāliya's women came to Madhusūdana to beg for his protection. *47*

The nāga's wives:

We know you, lordly god of gods. You are the peerless lord of all, the highest god, whose aspect is the finest light beyond imagination. *48*

Even the deities cannot fully praise the lord who arises from no other. How, then, could women like ourselves describe him? *49*

How can we fully praise him, when all the cosmic egg, comprising earth and sky, water, fire and wind, is but one small aspect of one part of him? *50*

We bow to him whose form is endless, the highest goal, smaller than the smallest, larger than the largest, whom feckless beings strive in vain to comprehend. *51*

No-one brought about his birth, and none will bring him to an end. We bow to him as he's the single author of the world. *52*

You are not subject to the slightest anger and are protector of creation. You are the cause of Kāliya's downfall, so listen now to what we say. *53*

Wise men should treat all women gently; even fools are kind to animals. Have mercy, therefore, on this miserable being, as you are the most merciful of all. *54*

You are the foundation of all the world, and this hooded snake is weak. In half a moment he'll breathe his last, trampled by your feet. *55*

What's this poor snake compared to you on whom the world relies? Love and hate are for one's equals or one's betters, eternal Lord. *56*

Show mercy to these desperate beings, master of the universe. This nāga's on the verge of death. We're begging for our husband. Please let him go! *57*

5 There is much inconclusive discussion in the commentaries about these two dance forms.

Kāliya worships Kṛṣṇa

Parāśara:

After they had spoken and, encouraged by their words, the serpent, his body broken, softly begged the lord to spare him. *58*

Kāliya:

Eightfold sovereignty is yours, Lord, self-arisen and supreme. Stripped of my magnificence, how may I presume to praise you? *59*

You are supreme and supreme's beginning, and from you supreme arises. You are supreme beyond supreme. How may I presume to praise you? *60*

From you arose Brahmā, Rudra, the Moon and Indra, the Winds and Aśvins, the Vasus and Ādityas. How may I presume to praise you? *61*

This whole world is but one part of a part of you and is an aspect of just one aspect of your imaginings. How may I presume to praise you? *62*

You whose form is both existent and nonexistent: neither Brahmā nor the other thirteen deities know your highest essence. How may I presume to praise you? *63*

Brahmā and other divine beings honour you with flowers and lotions from Indra's heaven, Nandana. How may I presume to worship you? *64*

Indra, king of gods, always reveres your varied appearances, yet even he knows not your highest form. How may I presume to worship you? *65*

Ascetics who've withdrawn their senses from all external objects worship you with thought. How may I presume to worship you? *66*

They create your image in their hearts and worship you in meditation with offerings of mental states and flowers. Lord, how may I presume to worship you? *67*

I'm unfit to honour or to praise you, blessed god of gods. As your mind is filled with tenderness alone, be merciful to me. *68*

I was born in this cruel class of serpents, Keśava. It's my way, eternal Lord, I've done no wrong. *69*

This whole world was made by you, and you will absorb it. You are the one who fixed the nature of every class of being. *70*

Just as I was made by you, Lord, in this class and form, I was yoked with this same nature and acted as I did. *71*

If my conduct were any different, god of gods, then I'd deserve your punishment, just as you commanded. *72*

I'd happily endure such trials as the universal lord might wreak on me, as I'd wish for nothing else from you. *73*

You've robbed me of my prowess and my venom. You've vanquished me, unfailing Lord. Now spare my life and I shall do your bidding. *74*

The Lord:

You may dwell no longer in the waters of the Yamunā, serpent. Go to the ocean and take your minions and your kinsfolk with you. *75*

Your enemy Garuḍa will not attack you, nāga, when he sees my footprints on your head. *76*

Parāśara:

So saying, Lord Hari freed the serpent king. He bowed to Kṛṣṇa, then set off for the ocean. *77*

With his servants, kin and offspring and all his wives in train, the serpent left his pool behind, while all creation looked on. *78*

After Kāliya had departed, all the herdsmen hugged Govinda as if he had returned from death, anointing his head with teardrops streaming from their eyes. *79*

Amazed to see the waters of the river clear again, the delighted herders all praised Kṛṣṇa, whose actions never tire him. *80*

Eulogised by herding women and praised by herdsmen as they walked along, Kṛṣṇa, whose behaviour tends to kindness, approached the cattle camp. *81*

So ends Chapter Seven in Book Five of the glorious Viṣṇu Purāṇa.

8. Balarāma defeats Dhenuka the Donkey-Demon

Parāśara:

One day while tending cows together, Balarāma and Keśava, wandering in the forest, came to the pleasant grove of Tālavana. *1*

A Dānava named Dhenuka had occupied that grove and, taking on a donkey's form, fed on flesh of man and beast. *2*

Seeing Tālavana filled with masses of ripe coconuts, the hungry herdsmen urged the boys to fetch some down for them. *3*

The herdsmen:

Balarāma! Kṛṣṇa! Because this place is always watched by Dhenuka, the coconuts are ripe. *4*

See the fruit on those palm trees that fill the air with scent? We'd love to get our hands on them. Throw some down for us, if you don't mind. *5*

Parāśara:

Having heard the herding boys' request, Balarāma and Kṛṣṇa threw some coconuts to the ground for them. *6*

But that wicked donkey-demon, dangerous to approach, heard the sound of falling fruit and rushed towards the spot. *7*

With his hind legs, that mighty being kicked Balarāma in the chest, but the lad grabbed hold of them. *8*

Holding tight, he whirled the donkey in the air and spun the life right out of him. With one last heave, he threw the demon up a tree. *9*

Its body struck the palm and caused a shower of coconuts, just as strong winds drive the clouds along. *10*

Other donkey-demons, relatives of Dhenuka, then appeared, but Balarāma and Kṛṣṇa playfully threw them on the palm trees, too. *11*

Soon the ground was spread with fruit, Maitreya, and was resplendent with donkey-demon corpses. *12*

From that day forward, brahmin, the cattle, safe and happy, grazed at Tālavana as they never had before. *13*

So ends Chapter Eight in Book Five of the glorious Viṣṇu Purāṇa.

9. Balarāma destroys Pralamba the Cowherd-Demon

Parāśara:

When that donkey-demon and his ilk were overcome, the pleasant Tālavana grove regained its splendour and was enjoyed by cattle, herding men and women. *1*

Having slain the Daitya Dhenuka, the sons of Vasudeva, filled with joy, next ventured to the banyan tree called Bhāṇḍīra. *2*

There they jumped and sang and explored the tree, while grazing their cattle near and far, calling to each beast by name. *3*

With spare lead ropes on their shoulders and garlands of forest flowers, those two great beings looked wonderful, like two young bulls with new-grown horns. *4*

Their clothes were dusted gold and kohl like a pair of clouds—one white, one black—with a rainbow spread between them. *5*

These two lords of all the gods, appearing on the earth, wandered here and there, enjoying common pastimes. *6*

Delighting in their mortal state and honouring their humanity, they roamed about the forest, indulging in the games that boys enjoy. *7*

These two strong lads exercised by playing on swings, wrestling and heaving boulders. *8*

While they amused themselves like this, a demon named Pralamba, disguised as a herding boy, approached to seize the lads. *9*

That Pralamba, best of Dānavas, inhuman being in human form, fearlessly joined the boys. *10*

He tried to separate the two, but, finding that impossible, decided to kill Kṛṣṇa first and then to kill his brother. *11*

The lads arranged themselves in pairs to play a game called 'Catch the deer', in which one boy chased another. *12*

Govinda took after Śrīdāman, Balarāma chased Pralamba and all the other herding lads joined in. *13*

Kṛṣṇa caught his quarry, as did the son of Rohiṇī, till all the 'deer' were caught by Kṛṣṇa's team. *14*

Then the losers had to bear their captors on their shoulders to the banyan tree and back. *15*

The Dānava quickly lifted Balarāma and put him on his shoulders. Pralamba then ran off, resembling a cloud surmounted by the moon. *16*

Rohiṇī's son was too heavy for that best of Dānavas, so the demon grew in size, like a cloud in the rainy season. *17*

Seeing Pralamba towering like a mountain peak burned black by fire, adorned with swaying garlands and a diadem on his head, *18*

His fearsome eyes as wide as wagon wheels and shaking the earth with every step, Balarāma called to Kṛṣṇa as he was borne away: *19*

'Kṛṣṇa, Kṛṣṇa! I've been captured by some Daitya in a cowherd's guise. He's as lofty as a mountain. Look! *20*

You killed the demon Madhu, now tell me what to do. This wicked creature's running off so fast.' *21*

Kṛṣṇa reminds Balarāma of his divine nature

Parāśara:

Knowing Rohiṇī's son was strong and brave, great Govinda addressed him with a smile. *22*

The Lord:

Why do you—the heart of all creation and hidden secret of every mystery—seem to cling to human form? *23*

Remember, Lord of all the world, that I, the universal cause, and you, my elder brother, are really one, just as everything is merged when the world becomes one ocean. *24*

Don't you know that you and I are the single universal cause, come down to earth to ease its burden? *25*

Your head is sky and your body water. Your feet are earth and your mouth is fire, everlasting being. Your mind is the moon and your breath is wind. The four directions are your arms, eternal god. *26*

You are the great being with a thousand faces, hands, feet and bodies. You are the primal source from which a thousand Brahmās rise, and sages praise you in a thousand forms. *27*

No-one else can know your heavenly form, the appearance praised by all the gods. Don't you know that, in the end, all things will be absorbed by you? *28*

This world, supported by you whose form is endless, bears all things moving and unmoving. In the form of Time, beginning with minutes and divided into Kṛta and other ages, you consume the world. *29*

The fires that burn beneath the waves drive off the ocean's water.[6] This water falls as snow in the Himālaya and melts again beneath the solar rays. *30*

In that same way, this world, absorbed by you at the time of dissolution, inevitably becomes the world again through your creative effort, Lord. *31*

You and I, universal being, are the single cause of all this world and took on separate forms to benefit it. *32*

For this reason, boundless being, remember now your actual self and destroy this Dānava. Lay aside your mortal form and do your kin a favour. *33*

Parāśara:

Thus reminded by great Kṛṣṇa, mighty Balarāma gave a laugh, brahmin, and began to squeeze Pralamba. *34*

His eyes were red with rage as he struck Pralamba on the head, and the demon's eyes popped out. *35*

With his skull cracked open and blood gushing from his mouth, that Daitya hero fell down dead. *36*

Seeing Pralamba slain by Balarāma of wondrous deeds, the delighted herdsmen sang his praises. 'Well done, well done!' they cried. *37*

Now the demon Pralamba had been defeated, Balarāma, praised by herders, returned with Kṛṣṇa to the camp. *38*

So ends Chapter Nine in Book Five of the glorious Viṣṇu Purāṇa.

---

6 Submarine fire, one of the five forms of Agni, remains hidden under the sea and is always ready to destroy the world.

10. Autumn in the cattle camp

Parāśara:

While Kṛṣṇa and Balarāma thus whiled away the time in camp, the rainy season passed and autumn came with lotuses in bloom. *1*

The fishes in the smaller ponds began to feel the heat, like selfish householders concerned about their sons, their fields and all the rest. *2*

Peacocks stood in silence in the forest, their passion spent, like ascetics who've realised the futility of life. *3*

Having shed their showers, pure white clouds then fled the sky, as enlightened beings set out from home. *4*

Warmed by the rays of the autumn sun, the lakes dried up, like hearts of selfish beings beset by many cares. *5*

The autumnal pools proved fit for silver waterlilies, just as hearts of virtuous folk are ready for understanding. *6*

The full moon shone in a star-filled cloudless sky, like an ascetic whose final birth is in a noble family. *7*

The water in the reservoirs receded from the banks, just as the wise inevitably withdraw from selfish attachment to wives and sons and others. *8*

Wild geese returned to lakes they'd previously deserted, just as troubles come again to haunt false ascetics who are beset with obstacles. *9*

The ocean's tranquil waters grew even calmer, like the ascetic's steady heart, which slowly reaches union with the lord. *10*

The waters everywhere grew clear, like wise minds realising Viṣṇu's universal nature. *11*

The sky grew bright when autumn drove away the clouds, like ascetics' hearts when yogic fire has burned all their defilements. *12*

The moon dispelled the sun's hot rays, just as true discernment drives off suffering born of selfishness. *13*

Autumn drew the clouds from the sky, the moisture from the soil and the turbidity from the water, just as the practice of withdrawal retrieves the senses from their objects. *14*

The waters rose, peaked and fell again as if the lakes controlled their breath each day: inhaling, holding and exhaling.[7] *15*

When the constellations reappeared in the cloudless sky above the cattle camp, Kṛṣṇa beheld the residents planning a great festival for Indra. *16*

Seeing the herdsmen keenly preparing for this event, and being curious, that wise being addressed these words to the elders: *17*

'What's this so-called festival of Indra that is causing such excitement?' Nanda the herdsman gave this reply as Kṛṣṇa asked politely: *18*

'Indra is the lord of thunderclouds and rains, the king of gods and deity of a hundred sacrifices. Urged by him, the clouds release the essence of life in the form of showers. *19*

We and other living things subsist on crops brought forth by rain, and it's we who feed the gods. *20*

These dairy cattle and contented cows with calves are satisfied and nourished with the feed the rain provides. *21*

Wherever rain-filled clouds are seen, the earth will not be lacking grain or pasture, nor will people suffer hunger or other woes. *22*

Indra, who gives the rain, draws up water from the earth with the sun's own rays. Parjanya sends it down again as showers to benefit the world. *23*

That's why every joyful king worships the lord of gods with festivals in the rainy season, as do we and other people.' *24*

The herders worship Mount Govardhana

Parāśara:

Hearing the herdsman Nanda praising mighty Indra, Kṛṣṇa then said this to goad the king of thirteen gods: *25*

'We don't plough the earth, nor do we live by trade. Cattle are our deities, dear father, because we're forest nomads. *26*

7 This is a liberal interpretation. The Sanskrit says: 'Breath control, consisting of *pūraka*, *recaka*, *kumbhaka* and the rest, was seemingly practised by the waters of lakes.' *Pūraka* is the filling of the lungs, *kumbhaka* is the holding of the breath and *recaka* is exhalation. Water levels rise during the rains, remain high at the onset of autumn, but fall again as the weather begins to warm up.

Knowledge has four branches: logical, scriptural, political and practical. Listen while I describe the last: *27*

Farming, trade, with herding as the third—these three modes of life comprise the field of practical knowledge, fortunate man. *28*

Agriculture is the life of farming people, as trade is that of merchants, but cattle are our main concern. Such are the three forms of this field of knowledge. *29*

The branch of knowledge by which one lives should be one's first divinity. That branch alone deserves our praise and honour, as only it will succour us. *30*

One who reveres or benefits from a different branch, dear father, will find no prosperity in this world or in the life hereafter. *31*

The margins stretch beyond the fields; beyond the margins lie the forests. Beyond the forests rise the mountains, the furthest limit of our realm. *32*

We don't live behind closed doors, nor do we own fields or houses, but roam freely across the earth. *33*

It's said these mountains can choose any shape at will and, in such forms, disport themselves among the peaks and in this very woodland. *34*

If forest-dwelling folk offend them, mountains take the form of lions or some other beast and kill them. *35*

That's why we should sacrifice to mountains and to cattle. What does mighty Indra mean to us? Cattle and these ranges are our deities! *36*

Brahmins sacrifice with mantras, and farmers worship ploughs. It's natural for folk like us who depend on highlands and forests to worship hills and cattle. *37*

For this reason, having sacrificed a fitting beast, you should praise and honour Mount Govardhana in various ways according to the precepts. *38*

Take the milk produced by this whole herd without delay and offer it to brahmins and others who desire it. *39*

When oblations have been made and brahmins fed, then decorate the herds of cows with wreaths of autumn flowers and circumambulate them. *40*

That's my suggestion, and, if you herdsmen do this gladly, you will please the cattle, mountains and myself.' *41*

Parāśara:

Hearing this, brahmin, Nanda and the other herdsmen in the camp cried, 'Good idea, good idea!', as their faces beamed with joy. *42*

'My dear boy, you've made a wonderful suggestion. We'll do all that you've put forward. Let's conduct a mountain sacrifice!' *43*

Parāśara:

And so the residents of the camp performed a mountain sacrifice and made an offering of yoghurt, milk and meat. *44*

They also offered food to brahmins by the hundreds and the thousands. *45*

Next, they walked around the mountain and the cows that had been worshipped, while all the bulls began to bellow like rain-filled thunderclouds. *46*

On the mountain summit, Kṛṣṇa himself declared, 'I'm this mountain in bodily form', brahmin, and joined the splendid feast offered by the herding women. *47*

In that very form, Kṛṣṇa, accompanied by the herdsmen, ascended to the summit, where he worshipped his second self. *48*

After he withdrew from sight, the herders then received great boons, and, when the festival was over, they all returned to the cattle camp. *49*

So ends Chapter Ten in Book Five of the glorious Viṣṇu Purāṇa.

11. Kṛṣṇa raises Mount Govardhana

Parāśara:

Mighty Indra, furious that his festival had been abandoned, Maitreya, addressed a host of rainclouds called Saṃvartakas. *1*

'Come, come, you clouds, and listen to my words. You must follow my instructions without question or delay. *2*

The herder Nanda is a fool and, along with other herdsmen, has a bloated sense of his importance, protected as he is by Kṛṣṇa, and now he's stopped my festival. *3*

Those cattle are their treasured means of livelihood, and that's what makes them herdsmen. I order you to strike their cattle with a tempest. *4*

Riding on my elephant, towering like a mountain peak, I'll help by bringing wind and rain.' *5*

Parāśara:

Thus commanded by the king of gods, brahmin, the clouds released a dreadful storm to annihilate the cattle. *6*

In an instant, heaven, earth and all between, sage, were beset by a mighty deluge and became as one. *7*

The clouds roared out as if they feared a whipping from the lightning bolts, filling all directions with their thunder and hurling down their torrents. *8*

The earth grew dark as endless showers fell. Above, below and on all sides, this whole world was inundated. *9*

Stricken by the sudden gale that fell on them, the cattle's hips and legs and necks gave way, and some of them then breathed their last. *10*

Others stood in anger with their calves beneath their bellies, sage, yet others lost their young when swept away by floods. *11*

Miserable calves, bellowing piteously and shivering in the wind, seemed to softly cry to Kṛṣṇa, 'Save me, save me!' *12*

Seeing the cattle and the herding men and women of the camp in chaos, Maitreya, Hari was deeply troubled and reflected: *13*

'This must be Indra's doing. He's irked because his festival was abandoned. Now it's up to me to save them all. *14*

I'll raise this mountain steadily, a mass of solid rock, and hold it above the cattle pen like a huge umbrella.' *15*

Parāśara:

With this thought, Lord Kṛṣṇa raised Mount Govardhana with just one finger, holding it aloft with ease. *16*

The lord of all the world, with the mountain above his head, said to the herdsmen: 'Come to the shelter I've provided. *17*

Sit here in comfort. It's not windy. Come in. Don't worry. There's no chance the hill will fall.' *18*

Hearing this, the herders sheltered with their cattle and their laden wagons, as well as all the women who'd been drenched. *19*

Kṛṣṇa held that mountain steadily while all the cattle camp looked on; their eyes were filled with pleasure and amazement. *20*

The joyful herding men and women, thrilled and wide-eyed with affection, praised Kṛṣṇa's efforts as he held that mountain high. *21*

For seven nights, those giant clouds rained down on Nanda's cattle camp to annihilate the herdsmen, brahmin—all at Indra's urging. *22*

But as the camp was safe beneath the lifted mountain, Indra, destroyer of the demon Bala, failing to fulfil his promise, then told the clouds to cease. *23*

When the sky grew clear again and Indra's threat was proven hollow, the whole delighted cattle camp left the shelter of the mountain and returned to their locale. *24*

Kṛṣṇa then placed Govardhana on its old foundations, as the residents of the camp looked on with wonder in their eyes. *25*

So ends Chapter Eleven in Book Five of the glorious Viṣṇu Purāṇa.

12. Indra praises Kṛṣṇa

Parāśara:

After Kṛṣṇa raised the hill and saved the cattle camp, Indra, subduer of the demon Pāka, now desired to see him. *1*

Mounted on Airāvata, his mighty elephant, the lord of thirteen deities and conqueror of his foe found Kṛṣṇa on Govardhana. *2*

There, mighty Kṛṣṇa, herdsman of the universe in the form of a common herding boy, grazed his cows alongside other lads. *3*

Far above, Indra also saw Garuḍa, chief of birds, invisible to mortals, brahmin, shading Hari's head beneath his wings. *4*

Mighty Indra descended from the regal elephant and, standing to one side, smiled as he spoke to Kṛṣṇa, slayer of the demon Madhu, with affection in his eyes. *5*

Indra:

Kṛṣṇa, Kṛṣṇa! Hear why I have come to you. Otherwise, blessed being, you'll never guess the reason. *6*

You alone, foundation of the universe, are lord supreme, come down to earth to ease its burden. *7*

Because my festival was stopped, I sent those clouds to inundate the camp. This calamity was wrought by them. *8*

You raised the mighty mountain up and rescued all the cattle. I was thrilled by your marvellous undertaking, hero. *9*

I believe you satisfied the gods' intention, Kṛṣṇa, as you held aloft this best of mountains with just one hand. *10*

Urged by the very cows you rescued, Kṛṣṇa, I'm here because I want to offer friendly service. *11*

At the cattle's own suggestion, I'll consecrate you, Kṛṣṇa, as Upendra, my younger brother. As lord of cattle, you'll be known as Govinda, 'Finder of the Cows'. *12*

Parāśara:

Taking a vessel of purifying water from the back of Airāvata, Indra then performed the consecration. *13*

As Kṛṣṇa was being anointed, the cattle flooded all the world with streams of wondrous milk. *14*

After Indra, king of gods and Śacī's lord, had consecrated Janārdana at the cows' behest, he spoke with tenderness to Kṛṣṇa, who was bowing with respect: *15*

'I've done as the cows suggested. Now hear what else I have to say, fortunate being, as I also wish to ease the burden of the earth. *16*

An aspect of myself has come into the world, you tiger of a man. His name is Arjuna, and you must always shield him. *17*

He will help you ease the earthly burden, Madhusūdana. Guard this hero as you would yourself.' *18*

The Lord:

I know your aspect has been born as Arjuna in the clan of Bhārata, and I'll protect him for as long as I remain on earth. *19*

While I'm in this world, mighty Indra, none shall vanquish him in battle, victorious king of gods. *20*

A powerful Daitya known as Kaṃsa, one called Ariṣṭa and others such as Keśin, Kuvalayāpīḍa and Naraka— *21*

When all these demons have been slain, king of gods with a thousand eyes, there will be a mighty conflict, during which, you'll understand, the burden of the earth will be relieved. *22*

Go now, worry not about your son. No enemy will prevail while I stand before him. *23*

For the sake of Arjuna, when the Bhārata war is ended, I'll restore to Kuntī all her sons unharmed, with Yudhiṣṭhira at their head. *24*

Parāśara:

Hearing this, Indra, king of gods, embraced Janārdana, mounted his elephant Airāvata and ascended to heaven. *25*

Kṛṣṇa, together with the cows and other herdsmen, then returned to camp along a path rendered pure by the herding women's gaze. *26*

So ends Chapter Twelve in Book Five of the glorious Viṣṇu Purāṇa.

13. Kṛṣṇa delights the herding women

Parāśara:

After mighty Indra had departed, and having witnessed Kṛṣṇa, untouched by deeds, holding Govardhana aloft, the herdsmen addressed him lovingly: *1*

'When you lifted up the mountain, fortunate being, you saved us and our cattle from disaster. *2*

You made it look like child's play, but it was no deed a cowherd boy could do. It was a supernatural feat! You must explain all this to us, dear boy. *3*

Kāliya was killed in the lake, Pralamba was cast down and Mount Govardhana was raised. Our minds are filled with consternation. *4*

Truly, truly, we swear an oath at Hari's feet, since we witnessed your prowess, we no longer consider you, whose courage is immeasurable, to be an ordinary mortal. *5*

This whole camp, including all the women and the children, love you, Keśava. Even the thirteen deities couldn't do what you have done. *6*

When we consider your youth, great strength and glorious birth among us, it makes us worry, Kṛṣṇa. You're beyond all estimation. *7*

Are you a deity, a Dānava, a yakṣa or a gandharva? Why ponder further? You're our kinsman and we bow down to you.' *8*

Parāśara:

After the herdsmen had spoken thus, Kṛṣṇa, slightly peeved, great sage, was silent for a moment, then gave them this reply. *9*

The Lord:

If you herding folk are not ashamed to be my kin, and if my deeds are worthy of your praise, then what's the use of further contemplation? *10*

If you love me and I seem worthy to you, then regard me as the same as other relatives. *11*

I'm no deity, no gandharva, no yakṣa or Dānava. I was born your kinsman. Please don't think of me in any other way. *12*

Parāśara:

Having heard these words of Hari and sensing his displeasure, fortunate sage, the herdsmen all fell silent, then set out for the forest. *13*

Seeing the clear night sky, the splendour of the autumn moon, the lotus forest in full bloom, perfuming the air in all directions, *14*

And wooded paths adorned with wreaths of humming bees, Kṛṣṇa set his heart on making love with the herding women. *15*

In the absence of his brother, Kṛṣṇa began to sing those sweet romantic songs that women love to hear. *16*

Hearing the seductive sound of Kṛṣṇa's voice, the herding girls all left their homes and hastened to Madhu's subduer. *17*

One woman softly joined his melody; another, with fixed attention, drew him to her mind. *18*

One cried out 'Kṛṣṇa, Kṛṣṇa!', but then was overcome with shyness. Another, blind with love, brashly sidled up to him. *19*

One saw her elders outside the house, so, staying indoors, she closed her eyes and contemplated Govinda, as if she were as one with him. *20*

The bliss she felt in doing so released her from the faults that she'd acquired; her anguish at not seeing Kṛṣṇa freed her from her sins. *21*

Contemplating the creator of the world in the form of the highest Absolute, another of the herders' girls won liberation just because she sighed so deeply. *22*

Surrounded by the herding women, Govinda, eager to experience the joy of dancing in a ring, paid homage to the night rendered lovely by the autumn moon. *23*

When Kṛṣṇa had slipped away, groups of women, acting out his movements with their bodies, roamed about the forest of Vṛndavāna. *24*

'I'm Kṛṣṇa, so elegantly am I walking. Watch my gait!' said one, 'and listen to me sing his song.' *25*

'Wicked Kāliya, stay where you are, for I am Kṛṣṇa!' another cried, waving her arms while acting out his encounter with that serpent. *26*

Another said, 'Come, herdsmen, don't be frightened. You stay here. Don't fear the tempest. I'm holding up Govardhana.' *27*

'I've defeated Dhenuka, now graze your cattle where you wish,' said another herding girl while aping Kṛṣṇa's deeds. *28*

Thus, the herding women, intent on Kṛṣṇa's various acts, roamed together through Vṛndavāna's lovely woodlands. *29*

One of the foremost herding girls looked at the ground, then cried aloud, as the hairs on every limb stood up and her lotus eyes grew wide: *30*

'See this line of footprints marked with banner, thunderbolt, goad and lotus? They were made by Kṛṣṇa, his paces rendered lovelier by his games. *31*

Some lucky girl, drunk with passion, has gone with him. Her steps were short and stumbling. *32*

Here's where great Dāmodara picked some flowers while standing on his toes. *33*

She was seated over there when Kṛṣṇa placed the garland on her. In another life she must have worshiped Viṣṇu with all her heart. *34*

Once honoured with the garland, she grew proud. Look! The herder Nanda's son deserted her and set off by another path. *35*

Here a different girl gave up the chase because her hips were heavy. She hurried after him and left behind deep footprints. *36*

This girl placed her fingers in his hand while walking, friend. The mingling of their footprints shows her movements were uncertain. *37*

But as he touched her only with his hand, that cad then let her down. Her footprints show she turned back slowly, disappointed. *38*

Surely, he had said to her, "I'll be back beside you shortly", for here lie Kṛṣṇa's hurried footprints. *39*

As Kṛṣṇa went into this thicket, we can see his tracks no more. We should go back, as the moonlight doesn't reach this far.' *40*

The herding women then turned away, despairing of the sight of Kṛṣṇa, but when they reached the Yamunā, they sang about his exploits. *41*

It's then they saw him drawing near—protector of the worlds, untouched by deeds—his face a full-blown lotus. *42*

One girl was overcome with joy at seeing Govinda there. 'Kṛṣṇa, Kṛṣṇa, Kṛṣṇa,' was all that she could say. *43*

Another knit her brows and, seeing Hari's handsome forehead, drank his lotus features with eyes as black as bees. *44*

One, having glanced at Govinda, closed her eyes and, contemplating him, appeared to be absorbed in yoga. *45*

Then Kṛṣṇa, Madhu's scion, discreetly led some girls with loving words, some with looks and raised eyebrows and others with his hand. *46*

Noble Hari politely pleased those herding women assembled for the circle dance, gladdening their hearts. *47*

But the circle couldn't be completed because the girls, unwilling to leave the side of Kṛṣṇa, were all standing on the spot. *48*

Hari closed the eyes of every girl with his fingertips and, leading them by the hand, arranged them in a ring. *49*

Then the dance began with the jingling of their swaying bracelets, followed by the sound of songs with lyrics suited to the season. *50*

Kṛṣṇa sang about the autumn moon, the moonlight and lotus pools, but the herding girls could only call his name. *51*

Tiring of the circle dance, one herding girl, her bracelets tinkling, laid her slender arm on Madhu's slayer's shoulder. *52*

Another of the herding girls, slyly pretending to sing his praises, grabbed him by one arm and kissed him. *53*

Beads of sweat from Hari's limbs, falling on the cowgirls' faces, caused the down upon their cheeks to rise, just as rain brings forth the crops.[8] *54*

While Kṛṣṇa sang the song of the circle dance in a clear, clear voice, the women cried out twice as loud, 'Well sung, Kṛṣṇa! Well sung!' *55*

When he led, they followed; when he turned, they moved to face him. When he danced to left or right, the women matched his every step. *56*

While Madhu's slayer played among the herding girls, one moment seemed ten million years without him. *57*

Even though their husbands, fathers and brothers forbade it, that night the girls enjoyed themselves with Kṛṣṇa; they all loved making love. *58*

Madhusūdana, a being beyond all limits and descriptions, enjoyed himself without restraint in youthful guise among the cowgirls on those nights. *59*

In his universal form, the lord pervaded them, their husbands and all creation, just as air is everywhere. *60*

This whole world consists of fire and space, earth and air and water. In that same way, he is all-pervading and ubiquitous. *61*

So ends Chapter Thirteen in Book Five of the glorious Viṣṇu Purāṇa.

14. Kṛṣṇa slays Ariṣṭa the Bull-Demon

Parāśara:

As Janārdana enjoyed the circle dance one night, the furious bull-demon Ariṣṭa came to terrorise the camp. *1*

As dark as rain-filled thunderclouds, his horns were sharp, his eyes ablaze like the sun itself and, with his hooves, he rent the earth. *2*

He smacked his tongue against his lips and flicked his tail in fury, his shoulders strongly knit together. *3*

8 This verse required a considerable amount of reworking. The original reads: 'Hari's arms, coming into contact with the girls' cheeks, attained the condition of sweat-rainclouds that bring forth body-hair crops.'

The great hump upon his back was tall beyond any measure, his hind limbs were covered with muck as he terrorised the cows. *4*

His dewlap hung below his mighty jaw and his face was scarred from butting trees. In bovine form, this Daitya caused the cows to cast the young ones from their wombs. *5*

The peerless beast laid waste to forests with his energy as he roamed. *6*

Beholding this creature with such terrifying eyes, the herders and their womenfolk, overcome with fear, cried, 'Kṛṣṇa! Kṛṣṇa!' *7*

Keśava gave his lion's roar and clapped his hands. Hearing this, the beast raced forward to face Dāmodara. *8*

The wicked bull-demon lowered his horns, fixed his eyes on Kṛṣṇa's belly and charged towards him. *9*

Seeing the Daitya bull approaching, mighty Kṛṣṇa stood his ground and smiled at him with playful disrespect. *10*

Madhu's slayer, like a crocodile, seized the bull as he drew near and, holding him steady by the horns, kneed him in the abdomen. *11*

Kṛṣṇa pinned him down, snapped the pride and strength of his two horns, then wrung Ariṣṭa's neck like some wet rag. *12*

Kṛṣṇa then tore out one horn and beat the Daitya with it. The bull fell down and died at once, blood gushing from his mouth. *13*

When this Daitya had been slain, the herdsmen all praised Janārdana, as in former times the hosts of gods praised Indra of a thousand eyes for killing the demon Jambha. *14*

So ends Chapter Fourteen in Book Five of the glorious Viṣṇu Purāṇa.

15. Kaṃsa sends Akrūra to the cattle camp

Parāśara:

After Ariṣṭa the hump-backed bull was slain, Dhenuka overthrown, Pralamba led to death and Mount Govardhana raised, *1*

The nāga Kāliya vanquished, the tall trees felled, Pūtanā killed and the wagon overturned, *2*

Nārada informed Kaṃsa of all of these events in order, and that the infants of Yaśodā and Devakī had been exchanged. *3*

Hearing this from Nārada, the sage with divine perception, wicked Kaṃsa was furious with Vasudeva. *4*

At a meeting of the Yādava clan, filled with fury, he threatened and reproached the clansmen, then pondered his next move: *5*

'I'll kill Balarāma and his brother while they're young and weak, because it won't be possible when they've come of age. *6*

Mighty Cāṇūra and powerful Muṣṭika are here. I'll have them kill those two young fools in a wrestling match. *7*

Under the pretext of some great tournament, I'll invite them from their cattle camp, then I'll do what's needed to send them to their doom. *8*

I'll dispatch Śvaphalka's son Akrūra, that bull among the Yādavas, to their camp to fetch them here. *9*

Then I'll send an order to Keśin, the terrible beast who roams Vṛndāvana. He's strong enough to kill the two boys there. *10*

If those sons of Vasudeva make it here alive, the elephant Kuvalayāpīḍa will trample them to death.' *11*

Parāśara:

With this thought, wicked Kaṃsa resolved to kill Balarāma and Kṛṣṇa. He then addressed heroic Akrūra: *12*

Kaṃsa:

Come, my generous man, and do as I command. You'll be doing me a favour. Take a chariot and ride to Nanda's cattle camp. *13*

Both of Vasudeva's evil sons, Viṣṇu's aspects born for my destruction, are maturing there. *14*

On the fourteenth day this month, I'll hold a tournament here. Go to the camp and invite them to a wrestling match. *15*

My two wrestlers, Cāṇūra and Muṣṭika, are skilled in combat. I want everyone to watch the two boys fight with them. *16*

If they fail, the elephant Kuvalayāpīḍa, urged forward by his driver, will crush Vasudeva's two young wicked sons. *17*

I'll kill them first, then I'll get rid of Vasudeva and that wicked-minded herder Nanda, as well as Ugrasena, my own father, who's just as bad. *18*

Next I'll seize the herders' cattle and all their other property. Those upstarts want me dead. *19*

Except for you, my generous man, all these evil Yādavas detest me, so I'll kill them one by one. *20*

With your assistance, I'll then rule this whole domain, rid of the prickly Yādavas. Your love for me will take you there, brave man. *21*

And tell the herdsmen to bring me all their yoghurt and buffalo butter. *22*

Parāśara:

On hearing this command, Akrūra was filled at once with love for Kṛṣṇa, brahmin, knowing that the next day he would see him. *23*

Akrūra, assenting to the king's request, mounted a splendid chariot. Then that friend of Madhu set out from the city of Mathurā. *24*

So ends Chapter Fifteen in Book Five of the glorious Viṣṇu Purāṇa.

16. Kṛṣṇa slays Keśin the Horse-Demon

Parāśara:

At the urging of a messenger sent by Kaṃsa, mighty Keśin approached Vṛndāvana with the aim of killing Kṛṣṇa. *1*

Rending the surface of the earth with his hooves, scattering the clouds with a flick of his mane, at each leap, he transcended the orbits of the sun and moon as he charged towards the herdsmen. *2*

At the sound of the neighing of that horse-demon, the herders and their womenfolk, filled with terror, fled to Govinda for protection. *3*

Hearing their cries for help, Govinda reassured them with a voice as deep as thunder from a rain-filled cloud. *4*

The Lord:

'Have no fear of Keśin, herdsmen. Have you cattle-folk, overcome with terror, lost your valour? *5*

Enough of this weakling who relies on whinnies, a steed with a Daitya's strength, a wicked prancing pony! *6*

Come here, you wretch. I'm Kṛṣṇa and I'll knock the teeth right out of your jaw, just as Pināka-wielding Śiva did to Pūṣan.' *7*

So saying, Govinda clapped his hands and advanced on Keśin. The horse-demon charged at him, his mouth agape. *8*

Janārdana bent his arm and thrust it down the throat of Keśin, that evil steed. *9*

Kṛṣṇa's arm, now deep inside the horse's mouth, smashed his teeth, which tumbled out like wisps of snowy cloud. *10*

Inside Keśin's body, Kṛṣṇa's arm began to grow, brahmin, like a plague that's in its early stages, in order to destroy the demon. *11*

Keśin's lips were split in two, foaming blood gushed from his mouth, his eyes rolled back and both popped out, and then his ligaments gave way. *12*

Shitting and pissing, he pawed at the earth with his hooves. His limbs were drenched with sweat and, at last, when quite exhausted, he gave up the fight. *13*

That terrible demon, his mouth rent open by Kṛṣṇa's arm, fell to the ground like a tree that's struck by lightning. *14*

Each half of Keśin's body, torn in two, had one pair of legs, half a back, half a tail, one ear, one eye and a single nostril. *15*

After Kṛṣṇa killed the demon, the delighted herdsmen gathered round him as he stood there smiling, unwearied and unscathed. *16*

The herding men and women, amazed at Keśin's death, praised lotus-eyed Kṛṣṇa, whose affection brought them pleasure. *17*

Then spoke the brahmin Nārada, unseen while riding on a cloud. Having seen the death of Keśin, his heart was filled with pleasure. *18*

'It's excellent, excellent indeed, that you, eternal lord of all, slew this Keśin so easily. He brought such woe to denizens of the threefold heavens. *19*

I always love a spectacle, especially a contest between man and horse. Such a match has never taken place before, so I came from heaven just to see it. *20*

I'm amazed by the feats that you've performed since coming down to earth, Madhu's slayer, but this one gave me greatest satisfaction. *21*

Even Indra and the other gods all feared this beast, Kṛṣṇa, when he shook his mane, neighed and looked down from the clouds. *22*

Because you slew this wicked Keśin, Janārdana, you'll be called by the name of Keśava throughout the world. *23*

May all be well with you. I'll be on my way, but we'll meet again when you battle Kaṃsa in two days' time, Keśin's slayer! *24*

When Kaṃsa son of Ugrasena and his ilk have all been killed, you, foundation of the universe, will ease the burden of the earth. *25*

I'll witness many varied contests, Janārdana, between you and other kings. *26*

I'll be going, Govinda. Your great deeds befit the gods, and I am pleased with you. All the best. I really must be off.' *27*

After Nārada had departed, Kṛṣṇa, unsurprised, returned to camp with the other herders—sole object of the cowgirls' gaze. *28*

So ends Chapter Sixteen in Book Five of the glorious Viṣṇu Purāṇa.

17. Akrūra arrives at the cattle camp

Parāśara:

Akrūra set off on his swift chariot for Nanda's camp, eager for the sight of Kṛṣṇa. *1*

'No-one is luckier than I,' he thought, 'as I'll behold this being's face, an aspect of discus-wielding Viṣṇu come to earth. *2*

Today, my life is now worthwhile and night has dawned as day, because I'll see the face of Viṣṇu, whose eyes are like a full-blown lotus petal. *3*

I'll behold the face of Viṣṇu, who dispels the sins of those who call the lotus-eyed being to their hearts. *4*

I'll behold his blessed face, supreme abode of all the gods, from which the Vedas, Vedāṅgas and their supplements arose. *5*

I'll behold the universal lord, who is praised by men as the spirit of every sacrifice, the highest spirit and foundation of the world. *6*

I'll behold Keśava, who has no start or finish, and to whom Indra made a hundred sacrifices and thereby came to rule the gods. *7*

Hari, whose true form is known to neither Brahmā, Indra, Rudra, the Aśvins, Vasus, Ādityas, nor the host of Maruts, will touch my body. *8*

He who is at the heart of all, knows all, is all, abides in all and is extensive, unchanging and pervasive will speak to me. *9*

The birthless being, who took the form of fish, tortoise, boar, horse, lion and the others to preserve the world, will speak to me today.[9] *10*

And now the everlasting master of the universe, who adopts all forms at will, has taken on a mortal body to undertake the duty closest to his heart. *11*

That eternal being, who placed the universe upon his crest, has come to earth to benefit the world and will call on me by name. *12*

I bow to him who appears in forms of father, son, friend, brother, mother and kin—an illusion all the world cannot dispel. *13*

When Viṣṇu fills his heart, the ascetic abandons deepest ignorance and delusion. I bow to the immeasurable being, the heart of knowledge. *14*

I bow to him whom sacrificers call the spirit of the sacrifice; whom devotees call Vāsudeva. Those who know the Vedāntas call him Viṣṇu. *15*

Just as all the world abides in its creator as a refuge, by that same truth, may the existent and nonexistent being be merciful to me. *16*

I take refuge in the birthless, everlasting Hari, the spirit in whom every joy arises when remembered.' *17*

Parāśara:

With these thoughts of Viṣṇu, and bowing in devotion with his heart and soul, Akrūra reached the cattle camp just as the sun was setting. *18*

There he beheld Kṛṣṇa, as the cows were being milked, wandering among the calves, as beautiful as the petal of an azure waterlily in full bloom. *19*

His eyes were unstained lotus petals, his bosom displayed Śrīvatsa, his arms were long, his chest was broad and muscular and his nose was high. *20*

A pleasant smile graced his handsome features, his fingernails were long and rosy, his feet were planted firmly on the ground. *21*

He wore two yellow garments and adorned himself with forest flowers. His arms resembled smooth dark vines, and he wore a circlet of silvery waterlilies. *22*

---

9 This mention of a horse avatāra is curious. Usually the fourth avatāra is said to be Vāmana the dwarf. On the Hayaśīrṣa/Hayagrīva avatāra, see *Bhāgavata Purāṇa* (2.7.11 and 5.18.6).

Akrūra, delighter of the Yadus, saw Balarāma, snowy as a wild goose, jasmine flowers or the moon, brahmin. Clad in blue, he stood at Kṛṣṇa's side. *23*

His arms were long and his shoulders broad, his face like a lotus in full bloom. Balarāma was a second Kailāsa wreathed in clouds. *24*

Seeing these two, wise Akrūra, whose face was like an open lily, spoke, while the hairs on his whole body bristled with excitement, sage: *25*

'This is that supreme abode. This is that highest state. This is the twofold manifestation of Lord Vāsudeva. *26*

Now that they've beheld the foundation of the world, my two eyes are here fulfilled in the highest measure. Would not this body of mine be satisfied, if, by the mercy of the lord, he were to touch me? *27*

Would not this being who appears in endless glorious forms place his lotus-hand upon my back? The touch of his fingers removes all stains and imparts unending perfection. *28*

That hand laid down his cruel and dreadful discus, wreathed with the brilliance of lightning, fire and sun combined, which destroyed the forces of the Daitya lord and robbed the makeup from their women's eyes. *29*

Having made an offering of water to that hand, Bali experienced exquisite pleasures in this world, as well as immortality and sovereignty over thirteen gods, unchallenged, for a whole Manvantara. *30*

But won't this being regard me as an object of contempt, stained with infamy, on account of my relationship with Kaṃsa, even though I'm blameless? A curse on the life of virtuous men unfairly treated! *31*

And yet, what in this world is unknown to him who is knowledge itself, the totality of pure truth, untouched by faults, always manifest and who dwells in all men's minds? *32*

With a heart that's filled with faith, I'll approach the universal lord of lords, Viṣṇu's aspect come to earth, the highest spirit who has no start, no middle or conclusion.' *33*

So ends Chapter Seventeen in Book Five of the glorious Viṣṇu Purāṇa.

18. Kṛṣṇa sets out for Mathurā

Parāśara:

With these thoughts, the Yādava approached Govinda. 'I am Akrūra,' said he, and bowed his head at Hari's feet. *1*

Kṛṣṇa touched Akrūra with his hand marked with banner, thunderbolt and lotus, drew him close with love and hugged him warmly. *2*

Akrūra duly honoured Balarāma and Keśava. The happy youths then led him to their own abode. *3*

Accompanied by the pair, Akrūra received their reverence and accepted food to eat. He then duly spoke with them. *4*

Akrūra told them how their father, Vasudeva, and Princess Devakī had been abused by Kaṃsa, the wicked Dānava, *5*

And how that evil being had mistreated his own father, Ugrasena. Akrūra then explained the reason Kaṃsa sent him. *6*

Having listened carefully to his report, the lord, Keśin's slayer, said, 'All this is known to me already, you generous man. *7*

I'll do what I regard as fitting in this case, you fortunate being. Don't think it could be otherwise. Understand that Kaṃsa is already slain by me. *8*

I'll go with you and Balarāma to Mathurā tomorrow, and the elder herdsmen will follow us with many offerings. *9*

Spend the night here, hero. Do not worry. Within three days, I'll vanquish Kaṃsa and his ilk.' *10*

Parāśara:

Having told the other herdsmen of this plan, Akrūra, Keśava and Balarāma retired to sleep in the home of the herdsman Nanda. *11*

In bright morning light the following day, wise Kṛṣṇa and Balarāma, accompanied by Akrūra, prepared to leave for Mathurā. *12*

Seeing this, the tearful herding women, their bracelets slipping from their arms, with deep sighs and wracked with pain, cried to one another: *13*

'Once Govinda reaches Mathurā, why would he return to camp? His ears will love the city women's sweet and artful talk.' *14*

'Once he's heard the brilliant conversation of the ladies in the town, will his mind return to rustic cowgirls?' *15*

'Robbing us of Hari, the pride of all the camp, accursed Fate has dealt us herding women a cruel blow.' *16*

'The city women's banter is graced with telling smiles, their gait is elegant and charming, and they always make those amorous sidelong glances.' *17*

'Once this Hari, a simple rustic youth, is ensnared by their elegance, what reason would he have to return to us?' *18*

'This—this Keśava has climbed into a chariot to go to Mathurā, deceived by cruel and desperate Akrūra.' *19*

'That callous being is carrying off our Hari, who brings such pleasure to our eyes. Does he not know how much we love him?' *20*

'It's heartless of Govinda to mount this carriage and leave with Balarāma. Quick, let's stop him!' *21*

'We should tell the old folk first.' 'What would you say?' 'We can't do that.' 'What can elders do for us, burning with the pain of separation?' *22*

'The herdsmen led by Nanda are preparing to depart. Not one of them is trying to stop Govinda.' *23*

'This day dawns bright for the womenfolk of Mathurā, as their eyes as black as any row of bees may imbibe the lotus-face of that eternal being.' *24*

'Fortunate are those who follow Kṛṣṇa unhindered on the path. Beholding him, their bodies will bristle with delight.' *25*

'The sight of Govinda's limbs today will provide a feast for the eyes of Mathurā's inhabitants.' *26*

'What dreams will greet those lucky girls when they rest their lovely almond eyes on Kṛṣṇa unimpeded?' *27*

'Sadly, having shown this greatest treasure to the gaze of us cowherd women, hard-hearted Brahmā, arranger of the universe, deprives us of this sight again.' *28*

'Just as Hari's love for us is cooler now that he is leaving, our bangles are slipping from our arms.' *29*

'As cruel Akrūra urges the horses forward, does no-one feel compassion for us women in distress?' *30*

'See the dust thrown up by Kṛṣṇa's chariot wheels.' 'We can't even see the dust. He must be far away.' *31*

Akrūra's vision of Viṣṇu in the river

Parāśara:

So Keśava and Balarāma left the region of the camp, while the broken-hearted herding girls looked on. *32*

Proceeding in the chariot drawn by swiftest horses, Balarāma, Akrūra and Janārdana reached the Yamunā's banks at noon. *33*

There Akrūra said to Kṛṣṇa, 'You two wait while I perform my daily ritual for the river in its waters.' *34*

With their agreement, wise Akrūra bathed and rinsed his mouth, then waded into the Yamunā, brahmin, where he meditated on the highest Absolute. *35*

Below the surface of the waters, Akrūra beheld Balarāma in the form of Śeṣa, circled by a thousand shining hoods, his body white as jasmine and his ruddy eyes like petals of a newly wakened lotus.[10] *36*

Flanked by Vāsuki, Rambha and other powerful serpents, he wore a chaplet of forest flowers, while gandharvas sang his praises. *37*

Clad in two dark garments, a necklace of lovely waterlilies and a pair of gorgeous earrings, he appeared beneath the waters, drunk with joy. *38*

Reclining on the serpent's lap, Akrūra beheld Viṣṇu, dark as thunderclouds, his almond eyes like copper and his noble four-armed form resplendent with his discus and other weapons. *39*

Clad in golden garments and decked with varied garlands, he resembled a cloud adorned with Indra's bow and a diadem of lightning. *40*

With Śrīvatsa on his chest, Kṛṣṇa shone with splendid bracelets, crown and lotus wreaths, as he appeared to be at rest. *41*

Sanandana and other sages, accomplished in yoga and free from faults, their eyes fixed on their noses, stood about him contemplating. *42*

10 Balarāma's ultimate form is the divine serpent Śeṣa, Viṣṇu's attendant. I have added and reordered some phrases for clarity.

Seeing Balarāma and Kṛṣṇa in these forms, Akrūra was astonished and wondered how they got there from the chariot so quickly. *43*

Before he was able to say a word, Janārdana silenced him, so Akrūra left the river and went back to the carriage. *44*

There he beheld Balarāma and Kṛṣṇa in mortal form still seated in the chariot as before. *45*

Akrūra plunged back in the river, where he saw them underwater, still worshipped by the gandharvas, sages, siddhas and mighty serpents. *46*

Realising the actual nature of the everlasting lord, all knowledge's embodiment, generous Akrūra eulogised him: *47*

Akrūra:

I bow to you, whose form is existence alone, whose greatness is beyond conception, the all-pervasive highest spirit, whose forms are one and many. *48*

I bow to you, being beyond all contemplation, in the form of truth and essence of the sacrifice. I bow to you, Lord, whose form is inconceivable, and who lies beyond primeval nature. *49*

You are at the heart of all creation, the senses and primal matter. You are the Self and the highest Self. You are one in fivefold form. *50*

Take pity on me, universal heart of all, the deity who embodies both the permanent and the transient, whether you are addressed as forms of Brahmā, Viṣṇu or Śiva. *51*

Your true form cannot be named, nor can your purpose be described. Your true name cannot be spoken. I bow to you, almighty Lord. *52*

You, Lord, have no name, no birth or other attributes. You are *tat*—'that', the highest Absolute, eternal, unchanging and unborn. *53*

Because we cannot reach our goals without conceptions, you are worshipped with the names of Kṛṣṇa, Acyuta, Viṣṇu and Ananta. *54*

You are every object, birthless deity, of these conceptions. You are the beginning, all the world and everything. The heart of all, you are beyond all changes and existence. There's a part of you in all this world. *55*

You are Brahmā, Śiva, lord of beasts, and Aryaman, arranger, disposer, Indra lord of thirteen gods, Wind and Fire. You are Varuṇa, lord of waters, and Kubera, god of wealth. You alone are Death who brings an end to all. For varied goals, you protect the world with all these different powers. *56*

In the form of a solar ray, you brought forth the universe. This whole world consists of your own qualities, birthless deity. Your highest form is signified by the everlasting syllable *sat*—'existence'. I bow to that being at the heart of knowledge, who exists and is yet beyond existence. *57*

Oṃ! I bow to you as Vāsudeva and as Balarāma. I bow to you as Pradyumna and as Aniruddha.[11] *58*

So ends Chapter Eighteen in Book Five of the glorious Viṣṇu Purāṇa.

19. Kṛṣṇa slays the washerman and blesses the garland-maker

Parāśara:

Having thus praised Viṣṇu appearing in the waters, Akrūra, scion of the Yādavas, made a mental offering to the universal lord with flowers and with incense. *1*

Free from all distractions, his mind set on the deity, he tarried long in the presence of the Absolute, then drew his meditation to a close. *2*

Having done the necessary, that prudent individual rose from the waters of the river and walked back to the chariot. *3*

Seeing Balarāma and Kṛṣṇa seated as before, his eyes filled with astonishment. Kṛṣṇa then said to him, *4*

'You must have seen some prodigy in the waters of the Yamunā, Akrūra, since your eyes are wide with wonder.' *5*

Akrūra:

The prodigy in the waters that I beheld, eternal Lord, I now see standing here before me in mortal form. *6*

Now I've met you, Kṛṣṇa, the greatest prodigy of all, the mighty being whose wondrous form fills all the world. *7*

But enough of this. Let's proceed to Mathurā, Madhusūdana. But I'm afraid of Kaṃsa, as the life of one who lives on charity is cursed. *8*

11 This is the fourfold emanation or *caturvyūha* of Pañcarātra theology (Austin 2019: 14, 27).

Parāśara:

So saying, Akrūra urged the horses forward, faster than the wind, and they reached the city late that very night. *9*

Seeing Mathurā, the Yādava said to them, 'You two brave boys proceed on foot. I'll ride the chariot alone. *10*

But don't approach the home of Vasudeva, as Kaṃsa banished that old man on your account.' *11*

Parāśara:

With these words, Akrūra entered Mathurā, while Balarāma and Kṛṣṇa followed him on foot along the royal road. *12*

Men and women, filled with joy, beheld the heroes as they strode along with ease, entering the city like a pair of youthful elephants. *13*

While wandering, they came upon a washerman dyeing clothes and, with a smile, they asked for something nice to wear. *14*

The startled washerman was arrogant because of Kaṃsa's favour and loudly cursed the lads. *15*

With a single blow, Kṛṣṇa, enraged, struck off that wicked dyer's head, which fell upon the ground. *16*

Having slain him, the two boys helped themselves to clothes. Kṛṣṇa in yellow and Balarāma in blue, filled with joy, then approached a garland-maker's home. *17*

That person's eyes were widened with astonishment as he wondered whose sons they were and whence they came, Maitreya. *18*

Seeing the handsome lads in blue and yellow, he thought that they were deities come down to earth. *19*

When the boys, whose faces shone like blooming lotuses, asked him for some flowers, the garland-maker placed his hands upon the ground and pressed his forehead to the earth. *20*

'I'm fortunate that you two gracious masters have visited my home. I worship you,' said the florist to the boys. *21*

Then, with a cheery smile, to please the boys, he gave them each the finest flowers that they chose. *22*

Again and again, the garland-maker bowed down to those two outstanding beings and gave them garlands, fresh and fragrant. *23*

Kṛṣṇa was pleased with the florist and granted him a boon: 'Prosperity, which flows from me, will never leave you, my good man. *24*

Nor, my friend, will you lack strength or prosperity. As long as one day follows another, your lineage will endure. *25*

After you've indulged in every pleasure and your end is nigh, by my mercy, recalling me, you'll attain a heavenly realm. *26*

Your mind will always dwell on virtue, good fellow, and all your offspring will enjoy long lives. *27*

Those born in your family will not endure disease or other woes, you lucky man, as long as the sun will shine.' *28*

Parāśara:

So saying, Kṛṣṇa, worshipped by the garland-maker, best of sages, left his house with Balarāma. *29*

So ends Chapter Nineteen in Book Five of the glorious Viṣṇu Purāṇa.

20. Kṛṣṇa in Mathurā; The wrestling bout; Kaṃsa's demise

Parāśara:

Approaching on the royal road, Kṛṣṇa then saw a young woman with a crooked spine bearing a jar of massage oil. *1*

'Who are you carrying this lotion for, young girl with lotus eyes? Tell me truly,' Kṛṣṇa asked in fun. *2*

Thus addressed affectionately, the girl warmed to Hari at first sight, and light-heartedly replied, *3*

'Don't you know, you handsome man? I'm called Naikavakrā. I'm employed by Kaṃsa as his masseuse. *4*

He doesn't like the lotion mixed by anybody else, and I've made a lot of money thanks to him.' *5*

Glorious Kṛṣṇa:

This fine and fragrant lotion suits the king, you pretty girl. But it's also good for us, so give us some. *6*

Parāśara:

Hearing this, the girl replied, 'Help yourself', and respectfully gave them enough for two. *7*

Having then applied the oil, these two bulls of men, whose bodies bore the marks of gods, glowed like rain-filled clouds—one white, one black—both graced with rainbows. *8*

Śūra's scion Kṛṣṇa, master of flattery, then took the girl by the chin and lifted her with his two fingertips. *9*

Pressing down her feet with his own, Keśava drew her up, thus stretching out her spine. As soon as her back was straight again, she became the handsomest of women. *10*

With amorous flirtations and languor born of love, she took hold of Govinda's robe and said, 'Come back to my place.' *11*

'Some other time,' replied Hari with a smile, and sent her on her way. Seeing the look on Balarāma's face, Kṛṣṇa laughed aloud. *12*

With marks of godhood on their bodies and wearing garments of blue and gold, still adorned with finest garlands, the two young men next reached the hall of archery. *13*

There they asked the guards about a mighty bow called Āyogava, the 'Iron Cow'. On being told about it, Kṛṣṇa then raised the bow and drew it to its full extent. *14*

On account of his great strength, when he did so, the bow snapped in two and that retort filled all of Mathurā. *15*

The guards reproached the boys for what they'd done, but ignoring them, the two youths left the hall behind. *16*

Kṛṣṇa defeats the elephant and the wrestlers

When Kaṃsa heard that Akrūra had returned and learned the bow was broken, he summoned his two wrestlers, Cāṇūra and Muṣṭika. *17*

Kaṃsa:

'The cattle-herder's sons are here. I want them killed in a match before my eyes, as they're my mortal enemies. *18*

I'd be pleased if you can kill them in a contest. I'll give you anything you want, you mighty wrestlers, but not otherwise. *19*

Destroy those enemies of mine, by any means foul or fair, and, when they're dead, I'll share this realm with you.' *20*

After he'd given this order to the wrestlers, he summoned his elephant-driver and shouted this instruction, 'Take the elephant to the entrance of the wrestling arena. *21*

When the two herding boys reach the gate for the contest, I want Kuvalayāpīḍa to trample them to death.' *22*

Having given this command, and seeing all the seating was in place, Kaṃsa, whose death was near at hand, now waited for the sun to rise. *23*

The residents of the city filled the stands, and the king and his ministers took the dais reserved for them. *24*

Kaṃsa sent the referees to the middle of the arena, while he himself sat high on the viewing platform. *25*

Separate seating was arranged for palace women, for courtesans and townsmen's wives. *26*

Nanda and the herders were given other seats, while Akrūra and Vasudeva sat at the end of the benches. *27*

Among the townsmen's wives sat Devakī, who yearned for Kṛṣṇa: 'Even if he's killed, I'll see my son's fair face again.' *28*

When the music first began and Cāṇūra leapt up, the crowd let out a roar as Muṣṭika clapped his hands. *29*

The mahout drove Kuvalayāpīḍa towards the boys, but they slew the beast. With limbs now smeared in musth and blood, they armed themselves with tusks. *30*

Balarāma and Janārdana then strode into that arena, looking round with proud and jaunty glances, like a pair of lions amid a herd of deer. *31*

The astonished crowds in all the stalls at once let out a mighty cry: 'That's Kṛṣṇa, and that's Balarāma!' *32*

The onlookers:

'He's the one who killed that fearsome night-ranging Pūtanā, overturned the wagon and snapped the *arjuna* trees. 33

He's the boy who danced on the serpent Kāliya and held up Mount Govardhana for seven nights. 34

He's the great being who easily slew wicked Ariṣṭa, Dhenuka and Keśin. Look! He's Acyuta, the imperishable deity. 35

And that's strong-armed Balarāma, his elder brother, proceeding with ease in front of him, delighting the hearts and eyes of all the girls. 36

The wise who know the gist of ancient texts say the herdsman Kṛṣṇa will raise the declining clan of Yādava once more. 37

He's Viṣṇu's aspect, the ultimate origin of all creation, descended to the world to ease the burden of the earth.' 38

When people spoke of Balarāma and Kṛṣṇa in this way, Devakī's bosom swelled with pride and her two breasts flowed with milk brought forth by love. 39

For Vasudeva, seeing the faces of his sons was cause for celebration and, shrugging off the years, he grew young once more. 40

The palace women couldn't draw their eyes from Kṛṣṇa, nor could the crowd of townsmen's wives: 41

'Look at Kṛṣṇa, friends, whose eyes are red, whose face is flecked with beads of sweat from the effort of fighting off the elephant. 42

It's like a blooming autumn lotus, bejewelled with drops of dew. Give your present life some meaning and look at him!' 43

'Look, my dear, at that young man's broad chest marked with Śrīvatsa, and those two arms with which he crushed his enemies.' 44

'Can't you see Balarāma approaching, dressed in blue, his face as white as jasmine, the moon or fibres of a lotus stalk?' 45

'See, my friend, how Balarāma laughs in the face of prancing Muṣṭika and Cāṇūra.' 46

'Look, friends, Hari approaches Cāṇūra for a fight. Are no elders here to referee the match? 47

On one side is Hari, whose tender form is on the verge of youth, while on the other is this mighty demon, with a muscled body, hard as diamonds.' *48*

'These two lovely lads are already on the field, and the demon wrestlers led by Cāṇūra will show no mercy. *49*

The judges of the spectacle have made a big mistake in permitting referees to oversee this match between an adult and a child.' *50*

Parāśara:

While the palace women and townsmen's wives were saying this, Lord Hari tightened his waistband and jumped upon the ground, causing it to tremble. *51*

When Balarāma clapped his hands and leapt about in play, it was a miracle the earth didn't crack beneath his feet. *52*

Then Kṛṣṇa, whose prowess was immeasurable, fought Cāṇūra, while the demon Muṣṭika, himself a skilful wrestler, battled Balarāma. *53*

Hari and Cāṇūra fought together, each seizing then releasing the other, with throws and blows of elbows, fists and forearms. *54*

Dire indeed was the bout between them, kicking one another, their bodies intertwined. *55*

That terrible hand-to-hand combat was vicious and, as the excited crowd looked on, both life and strength were jeopardised. *56*

The longer Cāṇūra fought with Hari, the more his initial strength began to ebb. *57*

But Kṛṣṇa, the essence of the world, wrestled him as if in play. The wreath on Cāṇūra's head began to slip as weariness set in, yet still he fought. *58*

Seeing Cāṇūra weaken as Kṛṣṇa grew ever stronger, furious Kaṃsa brought the music to a stop. *59*

The instant that the drums and other instruments fell silent, all kinds of heavenly music sounded in the sky. *60*

'Victory to Govinda! Defeat the demon Cāṇūra, Keśava!' cried the joyous gods unseen. *61*

Having toyed with Cāṇūra for a while, Madhu's subduer raised him in the air, spun him round and prepared to end his life. *62*

Victorious Kṛṣṇa whirled the demon wrestler round a hundred times then dashed him to the ground, and Cāṇūra's life force ascended to the sky. *63*

The demon's body, cast down by Kṛṣṇa, broke into a hundred pieces and made the earth a red and bloody mire. *64*

Balarāma, at that same time, fought the mighty demon wrestler Muṣṭika, just as Hari wrestled Cāṇūra. *65*

Balarāma struck his rival on the head, kneed him in the chest, threw him to the ground, then crushed the life right out of him. *66*

Next, with a blow of his left hand, Kṛṣṇa struck mighty Tośalaka, king of wrestlers, felling him to the ground. *67*

When Cāṇūra had been slain, Muṣṭika overthrown and Tośalaka put to death, all the other wrestlers fled. *68*

Kṛṣṇa and Balarāma then pulled other boys their age on to the field, where they danced for joy. *69*

Kaṃsa is overthrown

Kaṃsa's eyes were red with rage as he shouted to his lackeys, 'Take those herding boys away where the public cannot see them, using force if necessary. *70*

Bring that wicked Nanda here in iron chains and put Vasudeva to death—a fate too good for that old man. *71*

Confiscate the cows and any other property belonging to the herders who are dancing here with Kṛṣṇa.' *72*

As Kaṃsa was issuing these commands, Madhu's subduer gave a laugh, leapt up on the dais and smartly seized the king. *73*

Kṛṣṇa knocked the crown from Kaṃsa's head, dragged him by the hair, then threw him to the ground and jumped on top of him. *74*

When Kṛṣṇa leapt on Kaṃsa with the weight of the universe, Ugrasena's royal son gave up the ghost. *75*

Mighty Madhusūdana then took Kaṃsa's body by the hair and dragged it to the middle of the field. *76*

Because of its great weight, the corpse, when drawn along by Kṛṣṇa, left behind a channel as if cut by the current of a mighty river. *77*

When Kṛṣṇa first seized Kaṃsa, his brother Sunāman rushed forward angrily, but was dispatched with ease by Balarāma. *78*

Seeing the king of Mathurā killed with such contempt by Kṛṣṇa, everyone in the arena let out a cry of anguish. *79*

Strong-armed Kṛṣṇa, accompanied by Balarāma, immediately touched the feet of Vasudeva and of Devakī. *80*

Lifting up Janārdana, his parents recalled what he had said to them at birth and bowed before him. *81*

Vasudeva:

Lord, be merciful. You grant the wishes of the gods when they're despondent, Lord. So, too, through your mercy for us, Keśava, you became upholder of the world. *82*

Because the blessed lord appeared for the destruction of the wicked in my home, our family has been purified. *83*

You are at the heart of every creature and abide in them. Both past and future emanate from you, the heart of everything. *84*

You are always honoured with the sacrifice and embody all the deities, eternal being. You alone are the sacrifice and sacrificer, highest lord of sacrifices. *85*

My mind was playing tricks when Devakī and I loved you like a son—a grave misjudgement. *86*

How improper that my mortal tongue might call you, creator of all creatures with neither start nor finish, 'son'. *87*

How can it be fitting, other than by illusion, that he from whom this world arises, the universal lord, was born to us? *88*

How can he, in whom this world of moving and unmoving things abides, first lying in a womb, then be born to mortals? *89*

Be merciful, highest Lord. Protect the world by manifesting aspects of yourself. You're no son of mine. Why delude this whole world, from Brahmā down to the merest tree, Lord, when it comes from you, heart of the highest spirit? *90*

Because my eyes were clouded by illusion, I regarded you as my own son. Fearing Kaṃsa, and overcome by dread, I took you to the safety of the cattle camp where you grew up. Lord, I no longer claim you as my own. *91*

The deeds of yours we witnessed could not be done by Rudra, the Maruts, the Aśvins or by Indra, for you are Viṣṇu, Lord, come for the benefit of the worlds. Now we understand this, our delusions are dispelled. *92*

So ends Chapter Twenty in Book Five of the glorious Viṣṇu Purāṇa.

21. Ugrasena is reinstated

Parāśara:

Now that Devakī and Vasudeva's insight had been wakened, having seen the exploits of the lord, Hari covered them again with his illusion to deceive the Yadu clan. *1*

'Dearest mother, dearest father,' said he, 'Balarāma and I have always looked on you with love, but we were fearful of Kaṃsa. *2*

Decent folk regard the lives of those who live without respect for parents as deficient and in vain. *3*

But, father, the lives of those who respect their guru, gods, the twice-born orders and their parents are fulfilled. *4*

Forgive us, therefore, for all that we have done in error, father, as we were subject to Kaṃsa's will on account of his temper and his power.' *5*

Parāśara:

So saying, both Kṛṣṇa and Balarāma duly honoured the Yadu elders according to their station, then paid respects to all the other townsfolk. *6*

Kaṃsa's wives, surrounding his corpse upon the ground, bewailed him, and pain and grief overwhelmed his mothers. *7*

Hari, filled with deep regret, sought to comfort them, as tears were streaming from his eyes. *8*

Madhu's subduer then set Ugrasena free, and, now that his son Kaṃsa was no more, he was anointed sovereign of the realm again by Kṛṣṇa. *9*

After Kṛṣṇa had enthroned him, the lion of the Yadu clan then held funerals for his own son and the others who'd been slain. *10*

When the rites had been completed and Ugrasena returned to his lion throne, Hari said to him, 'Your majesty, surely you should tell us what to do. *11*

Because of Yayāti's curse, this clan deserves no sovereignty, but while I'm at your service, you may rule the gods, not to mention other kings.'[12] *12*

Parāśara:

After he had spoken, Kṛṣṇa summoned Vāyu with a thought, and the wind god came at once. Lord Keśava in human guise addressed him: *13*

'Go to Indra, Vāyu, and tell that chief of Vasus to set aside his pride. He should give his assembly hall that's known as Sudharmā to Ugrasena. *14*

Tell him Kṛṣṇa says Sudharmā is a peerless gem that suits a king. It's fitting that the hall becomes the Yadu clan's.' *15*

Parāśara:

Hearing this, the wind god went to Indra, Śacī's husband, and relayed to him the message. Accordingly, Indra, destroyer of his rivals' cities, gave the hall to Vāyu. *16*

Vāyu then delivered it, sparkling with jewels of every kind, to the Yadu heroes, who enjoyed it, thanks to the might of Govinda's arms. *17*

Sāndīpani's son is rescued

Those two peerless heroes of the Yādavas, who grasped each branch of knowledge and possessed all wisdom, wished to demonstrate the bond between the teacher and his pupil. *18*

Accordingly, Balarāma and Janārdana called on Sāndīpani—born in Kāśī, but now residing in the city of Avantī—to learn the use of weapons. *19*

Those two heroes became disciples and, intent upon the service of their guru, displayed the finest conduct in the presence of everyone. *20*

Brahmin, it was a marvel that they mastered secret weapons, the science of archery and its use in battle in four and sixty days. *21*

Sāndīpani, who thought such superhuman feats impossible, felt as if the sun and moon had come to him. *22*

As they mastered every class of weapon as soon as they'd been taught, they asked what fee their guru might expect. *23*

12 Yayāti's son Yadu refused to exchange his youth for his father's old age, so Yayāti cursed him that his descendants, the Yādavas, would never achieve sovereignty (4.10.7).

That wise man, having seen their supernatural feats, asked for his son who'd drowned at Prabhāsa in the ocean. *24*

The heroes took up their weapons, but the mighty Ocean, greeting them hospitably with water for their feet, said, 'It wasn't I who took the son of Sāndīpani. *25*

A Daitya named Pañcajana, appearing as a conch, has seized the boy. He still resides below my waters, demon slayer.' *26*

Parāśara:

Hearing this, Kṛṣṇa dived into the ocean, slew Pañcajana and seized his wondrous shell, as hard as bone. *27*

(When that conch is sounded, Daityas lose their strength, the ardour of the gods increases and evil is destroyed.) *28*

Hari blew a note on Pāñcajana, then, entering the city of the dead, accompanied by mighty Balarāma, defeated Yama, the Sun's own son. *29*

Kṛṣṇa and Balarāma, foremost of mighty warriors, saved the boy from that place of torment and gave him to his father in his original body. *30*

To the delight of Mathurā's men and women, they returned to that very city, now ruled by Ugrasena. *31*

So ends Chapter Twenty-One in Book Five of the glorious Viṣṇu Purāṇa.

22. Kṛṣṇa battles Jarāsandha

Parāśara:

Mighty Kaṃsa married two of Jarāsandha's daughters, Maitreya: Asti and Prāpti. *1*

Jarāsandha, the powerful king of Magadha, was furious when Hari slew his daughters' husband, and set out with a mighty force to slay that scion of Yadu. *2*

Reaching Mathurā, the lord of Magadha besieged the city with a force of twenty-three divisions.[13] *3*

13 One division or *akṣauhiṇī* consists of 21,870 elephants, 21,870 chariots, 65,610 cavalry and 109,350 foot soldiers (Monier-Williams 1899).

Powerful Balarāma and Janārdana set out with a retinue to confront the force of Jarāsandha. *4*

Balarāma and Kṛṣṇa made the wise decision to deploy their ancient weapons, best of sages. *5*

That instant, Hari's bow, Śārṅga, and two inexhaustible quivers descended from the heavens, brahmin, as did his mace, Kaumodakī. *6*

As soon as Balarāma called his blazing plough to mind, it, too, descended from the sky, brahmin, with his mace, Saunanda. *7*

The pair of heroes overcame the king of Magadha and his army in that battle, then returned to Mathurā. *8*

Wicked Jarāsandha had been vanquished, sage, but as he had escaped alive, Kṛṣṇa did not consider him defeated. *9*

In fact, Jarāsandha returned with another force, best of brahmins, but was overcome again by Balarāma and Kṛṣṇa and escaped once more. *10*

The doughty king of Magadha fought eighteen such battles with the Yadus led by Kṛṣṇa. *11*

In each encounter, Jarāsandha was beaten by a smaller force of Yādavas, even though outnumbering them, but he always managed to escape. *12*

The army of the Yādavas, unconquered by Jarāsandha in every clash, relied on Kṛṣṇa's greatness—an aspect of discus-wielding Viṣṇu. *13*

To launch his varied weapons at a foe was just a game for the universal lord in mortal form. *14*

How little effort is the conquest of an enemy for one who brings about creation and destruction of the universe through thought alone? *15*

Nevertheless, he followed the usual practices of mortals, such as allying with the strong and waging war against the weak. *16*

He also practised conciliation, bribery, punishment and subversion, and sometimes even took to flight.[14] *17*

Adopting all these strategies of mortal men, the universal lord engaged in games like these at will. *18*

So ends Chapter Twenty-Two in Book Five of the glorious Viṣṇu Purāṇa.

14 These are seven traditional forms of warcraft described in works such as the *Artha Śāstra*.

23. Kṛṣṇa leads the Yādavas to Dvārakā

Parāśara:

At a public gathering one day, in the presence of the Yadu clan, the brahmin Gārgya's brother-in-law accused the man of impotence, and everybody mocked him, brahmin. *1*

Gārgya was filled with rage and journeyed to the southern lands, where, desiring a son who could wreak revenge on the Yādavas, he undertook austerities. *2*

To propitiate Lord Śiva, he lived on iron filings for a dozen years. That great god, being gratified, then granted him a boon. *3*

The king of Yavanas, who also had no children, received Gārgya hospitably. The latter had intercourse with the king's own consort and she gave birth to a son as black as a bee. *4*

Kālayavana or 'Black Yavana' was that child's name, and his chest was as hard as the tip of a thunderbolt. The Yavana lord anointed his son as king of the realm and then retired to the forest. *5*

Maddened by pride in his own prowess, Kālayavana asked Nārada which were the mightiest kings on earth. 'The Yādavas,' was his reply. *6*

Flanked by barbarians in the thousands of millions, in train with elephants, horses and chariots, and sparing no effort, *7*

He advanced each day on Mathurā—tiring his transport, but not himself—indignant on the Yādavas's account, Maitreya. *8*

Kṛṣṇa feared that if the Yādava force were weakened by the Yavanas in battle, they might then be defeated by the Magadha king. *9*

But if the Yādavas were reduced by the Māgadhas, then the powerful Kālayavana might defeat them. Thus, the Yādavas faced a twofold threat. *10*

'I'll build a stronghold for the Yadus that's difficult for their enemies to attack. It will be defensible by womenfolk alone, to say nothing of the heroic Vṛṣṇi tribe. *11*

If I'm careless, asleep, abroad or drunk, even a mighty horde of wicked enemies won't be able to defeat them.' *12*

With this in mind, Govinda asked the Ocean for twelve leagues of land, on which he built the city known as Dvārakā. *13*

With extensive parks and lofty ramparts, it shone with a hundred reservoirs. Filled with residences and courtyards, it resembled Indra's city Amarāvatī. *14*

Janārdana led the residents of Mathurā to Dvārakā, then returned to Mathurā, just as Kālayavana drew near. *15*

When the latter's army was camped outside the city, Govinda came forth unarmed and saw the Yavana king. *16*

The strong-armed monarch recognised Vāsudeva and pursued him, but Kṛṣṇa travelled faster than the greatest yogins' thoughts. *17*

With the Yavana in pursuit, Kṛṣṇa entered a deep cavern where Mucukunda, that powerful hero and king of men, was sleeping. *18*

The wicked Yavana entered the cave and saw the sleeping figure. Mistaking him for Kṛṣṇa, he gave the man a kick. *19*

As soon as Mucukunda set eyes on him, the Yavana was burned by fire born of fury, Maitreya, and was reduced at once to ashes. *20*

(Long ago, Mucukunda had helped the gods defeat the mighty demigods in battle and, being fatigued, he asked the gods for the boon of a long repose. *21*

The gods then promised that anyone who disturbed his rest would be burned at once to ashes by fire from his body.) *22*

After the wicked king was consumed by flames, Mucukunda beheld Madhu's subduer and asked him who he was. 'I was born in the Lunar Dynasty, as the son of Vasudeva, in the lineage of Yadu,' he replied. *23*

King Mucukunda worships Hari

Mucukunda then recalled an ancient prophesy of Garga.[15] *24*

With that recollection, he threw himself upon the ground and addressed these words to Hari, the universal lord of all: 'I know that you're an aspect of Viṣṇu, highest Lord. *25*

Long ago, Garga foretold that Hari would be born in Yadu's lineage at the end of the twenty-eighth Dvāpara age. *26*

You are the one who's come, no doubt, for the benefit of all mortal beings. *27*

15 A Garga was also the *purohita* or family priest of Vasudeva (5.6.8).

That's why I can't withstand your brilliance. That's why your voice is deeper than the rumbling of a rain-filled thundercloud. That's why the earth subsides when pressed beneath your feet. *28*

In the great war between the gods and demigods, the mighty warriors of the Daitya army could not withstand my ardour, but even I'm unable to withstand yours. *29*

You alone are the highest refuge for every being who has come into this world. Be merciful, ease the pain we suffer and deliver us from evil. *30*

You are the oceans, mountains and the rivers. You are forests, earth and sky, wind and fire and water. You are mind. *31*

You are intellect, the primal substance of the universe. You are breath and lord of life, the spirit and that which lies beyond, all-pervading, unchanging and unborn. *32*

You transcend sensations such as sound, undecaying, immeasurable, imperishable, ageless and indestructible. You are that which is the Absolute, without a start or finish. *33*

From you arise immortals, ancestors, yakṣas, gandharvas, kiṃnaras, siddhas and apsarases. From you arise humanity, birds and animals. *34*

From you arise the serpents and other wild creatures, all the plants that grow upon the earth, all that has existed and all that's yet to come and everything in this world, both moving and unmoving. *35*

Formed and formless, gross and subtle—all this is you, creator of the world. Nothing lies beyond you. *36*

Always wandering in the cycle of existence, Lord, overwhelmed by threefold suffering, I cannot find release. *37*

Mistaking pain for pleasure, like thirsty deer confused by a mirage, I grasp at indulgences, Lord, but they only bring me further pain. *38*

A kingdom, lands, power, wealth, allies, children, wives, servants, pleasant sounds and other sensations, Lord— *39*

I acquired all these, thinking they would bring me joy, changeless deity. But in the end, Lord, they only brought me misery. *40*

Even hosts of gods in heaven wanted help from me, Lord. Whence comes eternal liberation? *41*

Without worshipping you, the cause of the existence of all the worlds, highest Lord, who can achieve lasting freedom? *42*

Their minds are clouded by your illusory power and, having felt the pain of birth, old age and death and so on, people then face Yama. *43*

They meet with terrifying tortures in the realms of hell as wages for their former deeds, because they failed to recognise your actual form. *44*

Hooked on sensual pleasures and beguiled by your illusion, highest Lord, I stagger round the pit of pride created by my sense of self. *45*

I come to you for refuge—limitless, praiseworthy Lord, the highest state beyond which there's nought. My heart is wearied by the travails of life and I yearn for nirvāṇa, the perfect rest.' *46*

So ends Chapter Twenty-Three in Book Five of the glorious Viṣṇu Purāṇa.

24. Balarāma returns to the cattle camp

Parāśara:

Thus eulogised by prudent Mucukunda, Lord Hari, beginningless master of all creation, replied, *1*

'You'll proceed to the heavenly realms you wish for, king. Your sovereignty will not be challenged by another, and you'll be nourished by my mercy. *2*

After you've tasted the delights of heaven, you'll be born in a noble family and, remembering your former lives, you'll win liberation through my grace.' *3*

Parāśara:

Hearing this, the king bowed down before the unfailing universal lord. When Mucukunda emerged from the mouth of the cave, he noticed that the people were much shorter than they were before. *4*

Realising that the age of Kali had begun, the king set out for Mount Gandhamādana to undertake austerities in the ashram of Nara and Nārāyaṇa. *5*

Kṛṣṇa, meanwhile, destroyed his rival with a stratagem, then returned to Mathurā, where he seized his rival's army with its splendid elephants, chariots and steeds. *6*

He led all these to Ugrasena in Dvārakā, and there informed the Yadu clan that they need no longer fear defeat. *7*

Now that the war was over, Balarāma wished to see his family again, Maitreya, and so set out for Nanda's cattle camp. *8*

The victorious warrior met the herdsmen and their women as before with love and great respect. *9*

Some hugged him and he hugged others, while he and the herding people laughed together. *10*

The herdsmen had many kind words for Balarāma, the wielder of the plough, but some of the women spoke sulkily because of their affection, while others expressed their envy. *11*

Yet other herding women said, 'I hope the darling of the city girls is happy. But Kṛṣṇa's fickle love will only last for half a second.' *12*

'I hope he doesn't mock our manners with the women of Mathurā. He'll make them feel so special, but he'll only love them for a minute.' *13*

'I hope that Kṛṣṇa remembers how we used to sing so softly with him. Will he come back just once to see his mother?' *14*

'Why bother mentioning him? It's a different story now we live without him, and he no longer lives with us.' *15*

'Didn't we leave our fathers, mothers, brothers, husbands and relations to be with him? That man is the standard-bearer of ingratitude.' *16*

'I hope that Kṛṣṇa spoke of coming back. Tell us truly, Balarāma.' *17*

'Govinda is still Dāmodara, the toddler with the cord tied round his middle.' 'The city girls will set their hearts on him. He doesn't love us anymore. I doubt we'll see him further.' *18*

Parāśara:

The herding women even called Balarāma 'Kṛṣṇa' and 'Dāmodara' as they wept aloud, since Hari stole their hearts. *19*

Balarāma comforted them with kind, sweet, affectionate, modest and charming messages from Kṛṣṇa. *20*

He also swapped amusing tales of interest with the herdsmen as before and enjoyed himself in their company in the lands around the camp. *21*

So ends Chapter Twenty-Four in Book Five of the glorious Viṣṇu Purāṇa.

25. Balarāma diverts the Yamunā River

Parāśara:

While the mighty serpent Śeṣa, upholder of the world, in the mortal form of Balarāma roamed the forest with the herding men, *1*

And achieved great deeds through his actions as he wandered through the world, Varuṇa, most anxious for amusement, addressed his consort: *2*

'You, Madirā, liquor goddess, pleasant and delightful, are always agreeable to mighty Śeṣa, so go now and amuse him.' *3*

Thus addressed, Varuṇa's consort hid in the hollow of a *kadamba* tree that stood in the forest at Vṛndāvana. *4*

Balarāma, wandering nearby, caught a tempting whiff of liquor and his old hankering for wine returned. *5*

When the bearer of the plough saw the stream of liquor trickling from the tree, Maitreya, he was as happy as can be. *6*

The herding men and women gathered round while Balarāma drank his fill, and those who were skilled in song and music entertained him sweetly. *7*

Drunk and moody, Balarāma, agleam with pearls of perspiration, said to the river, 'Come here, Yamunā. I want a bath.' *8*

Because he was drunk, the river ignored him, but when she failed to do his bidding, furious Balarāma grabbed his plough. *9*

Addled by wine, he caught the riverbank with his weapon and dragged her towards him, saying, 'You wicked river! You won't come? You won't come? Now try to get away!' *10*

Dragged with force by Balarāma, the river left her usual course and flowed into the forest where he sat. *11*

Appearing to him in human form, Yamunā came to Balarāma with terror in her eyes and begged the wielder of the plough to be merciful and let her go. *12*

'You disrespect my courage and my strength, you river, so I'll dash you into a thousand pieces with my plough!' *13*

Parāśara:

Yamunā was terrified by these threats, but convinced Balarāma to show her mercy and, after the river gave her waters to all the land, he released her. *14*

Mighty Balarāma took a bath, and Lakṣmī, goddess of beauty, then appeared with a lovely azure waterlily as an ornament for one of his ears and an earring for the other. *15*

She also gave him gifts from Varuṇa: a garland of fresh lotuses and a pair of sea-blue garments. *16*

With the lily and the earring, clad in blue and wearing flowers, Balarāma shone like loveliness itself. *17*

Thus adorned, he amused himself in the cattle camp for the next two months, then returned to Dvārakā. *18*

There he married Revatī, daughter of King Raivata, who bore him two sons, Niśaṭha and Ulmuka. *19*

So ends Chapter Twenty-Five in Book Five of the glorious Viṣṇu Purāṇa.

26. Kṛṣṇa abducts Rukmiṇī

Parāśara:

Bhīṣmaka, king of the Vidarbha lands, who lived in Kuṇḍina, had a son named Rukmin and a beautiful daughter, Rukmiṇī.[16] *1*

Kṛṣṇa fell in love with Rukmiṇī, and that sweetly smiling maiden loved him in return. But her brother loathed the discus-wielder and wouldn't let her go to Kṛṣṇa as requested. *2*

Brave Bhīṣmaka, urged on by Jarāsandha and with Rukmin's agreement, gave Rukmiṇī instead to Śiśupāla. *3*

All the monarchs led by Jarāsandha, desiring Śiśupāla's felicity, assembled in Bhīṣmaka's capital for his daughter's wedding. *4*

Kṛṣṇa also came to Kuṇḍina to see the nuptials of the Cedi king, surrounded by a host of Yādavas including Balarāma. *5*

16 For more on Rukmiṇī, see Austin (2014).

But the day before the wedding, Hari carried the girl away, leaving Balarāma and his other kin to fight against their enemies. *6*

Pauṇḍraka, Śrīmant, Dantavakra, Vidūratha, Śiśupāla, Jarāsandha, Śālva and the other kings were furious. *7*

They made every effort to conquer Hari but were overcome in battle by Balarāma and the other Yadu heroes. *8*

Rukmin swore he'd not return to Kuṇḍina until he'd vanquished Keśava and set off in pursuit to do so. *9*

But the bearer of the discus had no trouble in defeating Rukmin's army with its elephants, horses, infantry and chariots; then he struck Rukmin to the ground. *10*

After Madhu's subduer had completely vanquished Rukmin, he married Rukmiṇī, whom he'd forcefully abducted. *11*

She bore him the hero Pradyumna, an aspect of Madana, god of love. The demon Śambara abducted Pradyumna, but Pradyumna slew him in the end. *12*

So ends Chapter Twenty-Six in Book Five of the glorious Viṣṇu Purāṇa.

27. Kṛṣṇa's son Pradyumna is taken by a demon

Maitreya:

How was this hero Pradyumna taken by Śambara, sage, and how did Pradyumna kill that fearless being? *1*

Parāśara:

Śambara snatched Pradyumna from his nursery, sage, when the child was only six days old, because that demon, as terrible as Death, believed the infant would one day slay him.[17] *2*

After Śambara seized Pradyumna, he threw him into the frightful salty sea, the crocodiles' abode, with its terrifying monsters and whirlpools whipped up by waves. *3*

17 For a full account of the cycle of Pradyumna narratives, see Austin (2019).

As he fell into the water, the child was swallowed by a fish, but, warmed by the fire in the fish's belly, the baby didn't die. *4*

That fish, along with its kin and others, brahmin, were caught in time and delivered to the demon. *5*

Śambara's blameless wife, Māyāvatī, was mistress of all his household and supervised the cooks. *6*

When the fish's belly was opened, she beheld the lovely baby boy, like a fresh green shoot on the once charred tree of love. *7*

That slender woman was filled with wonder about the child's identity and how he came to be there, till Nārada enlightened her: *8*

'This is the son of Viṣṇu, creator and destroyer of the universe, taken from his nursery by the demon Śambara. *9*

He was cast into the ocean and swallowed by this fish. Now this treasure of humanity is in your care, and you, fair-browed and fearless woman, must nurture him.' *10*

Parāśara:

After Nārada gave Māyāvatī this explanation, she cared for the child from the time he was young with deep affection, beguiled by his wondrous beauty. *11*

When he acquired the handsomeness of youth, great sage, Māyāvatī, her gait as stately as a she-elephant's, began to desire him. *12*

Blind with love, she conferred all her illusionary powers on Pradyumna, sage, her heart and eyes set on him alone. *13*

Pradyumna, son of Kṛṣṇa, rebuked that lotus-eyed woman who lusted after him, 'You've abandoned normal motherly affection. Why are you acting differently with me?' *14*

'You're not my son,' she said, 'but are the son of Viṣṇu. Śambara, as terrible as Death, abducted you. *15*

He threw you in the ocean and I saved you from the belly of a fish. Your natural mother weeps for you because she loves you deeply.' *16*

Parāśara:

Hearing this, mighty Pradyumna challenged Śambara to battle and, with fury in his heart, waged war against his foe. *17*

Madhu's scion destroyed the Daitya's army, leaving nothing, and seven times foiled the phantoms conjured by that demon. *18*

He tamed the eighth and sent it back to kill the Daitya Śambara, as terrible as Death. With the aid of that same being, a form of Māyāvatī, Pradyumna rose up in the air and flew to the residence of Kṛṣṇa, his natural father. *19*

When the women saw Pradyumna descending to the inner chambers with Māyāvatī, they mistook him for his father. *20*

The eyes of blameless Rukmiṇī were filled with tears as she said tenderly, 'Any woman would be glad to have a son like you on the threshold of maturity. *21*

Pradyumna, my own son, would be about your age, if he were still alive. Some lucky mother has you as an ornament, dear boy. *22*

And yet, such is the love I feel for you and such is your own beauty, my dear, you must be Hari's son.' *23*

Parāśara:

At that very moment, Nārada appeared, accompanied by Kṛṣṇa, and addressed the princess Rukmiṇī, resident of the inner chambers, gladdening her heart: *24*

'This is indeed your son, you fair-browed woman. He was taken as a child from his nursery by Śambara, but Pradyumna slew that demon and now he has returned. *25*

This good woman is Māyāvatī, the wife of your own son, not Śambara. Listen while I explain: *26*

After Manmatha, the god of love, had been destroyed,[18] the goddess of beauty, Rati, intent on seeing him reborn, took illusory form and enchanted Śambara. *27*

She appeared to the Daitya as a seductive phantom, her eyes as intoxicating as wine, and they enjoyed themselves in many ways together. *28*

The god of love has been reborn as your son Pradyumna, and Māyāvatī is his beloved Rati. Have no doubt that she's your splendid daughter-in-law.' *29*

Both Rukmiṇī and Keśava were filled with joy, and all the city cried in jubilation. *30*

18 Manmatha disturbed Śiva's meditation and the deity burned him to ashes.

The denizens of Dvārakā were all amazed to see her reunited with her long-lost son. *31*

So ends Chapter Twenty-Seven in Book Five of the glorious Viṣṇu Purāṇa.

28. Pradyumna's son Aniruddha; Balarāma slays Rukmin

Parāśara:

Cārudeṣṇa, Sudeṣṇa, brave Cārudeha, Suṣeṇa, Cārugupta, Bhadracāru, *1*

Cāruvinda, Sucāru and Cāru, strongest of the strong, were the sons of Rukmiṇī. She also bore a daughter, Cārumatī. *2*

Kṛṣṇa had seven other splendid wives: Kālindī, Mitravindā, Nagnajit's daughter Satyā, *3*

Divine Jāmbavatī, shape-changing Rohiṇī, the king of Madra's decorous daughter Suśīlā and Satrājita's daughter Satyabhāmā. *4*

The discus-wielder also wedded sweetly smiling Lakṣmaṇā and sixteen thousand other women. *5*

Mighty Pradyumna fell for Rukmin's lovely daughter at her *svayaṃvara*, the tournament for suitors, and she chose that son of Hari as her husband. *6*

She and Pradyumna had a son named Aniruddha, brave and strong, a sea of courage when met in battle, a destroyer of his enemies. *7*

Keśava chose Rukmin's granddaughter for his grandson Aniruddha, even though Rukmin advised against it. *8*

On the occasion of their wedding, Hari, Balarāma and the other Yādavas came to Rukmin's city, brahmin, Bhojakaṭa by name. *9*

After the marriage of Pradyumna's powerful son, several monarchs led by the king of Kaliṅga gave this advice to Rukmin: *10*

'Plough-wielding Balarāma is a gambling addict but doesn't have much skill. Why don't we beat him in a game of dice, your majesty?' *11*

Parāśara:

Mighty Rukmin agreed to this, and a match with Balarāma was held in the assembly hall. *12*

In the first round, Rukmin won a thousand pieces of gold from Balarāma and, in the second, another thousand. *13*

Balarāma then staked ten thousand pieces, but Rukmin, an expert gambler, won that as well. *14*

The king of Kaliṅga laughed so loud that you could see his teeth, brahmin, and unwise Rukmin, puffed up with excitement, said, *15*

'I've beaten foolish Balarāma in this match. Blind with pride in gambling, he vainly insulted all the experts.' *16*

When the wielder of the plough saw the monarch's teeth and heard Rukmin's slander, he was filled with rage. *17*

Balarāma, mad with fury, then staked ten million pieces, and Rukmin rolled the dice. *18*

Balarāma won the throw and called, 'It's mine!', but Rukmin cried aloud, 'No, it's mine, Balarāma. Don't lie! *19*

It's true you staked the bet, but I did not accept it. If you won like this, then am I not a winner, too?' *20*

Parāśara:

At that moment, a deep voice sounded in the heavens, further stirring mighty Balarāma's wrath: *21*

'Balarāma won this fairly. What Rukmin said is wrong. Even though he didn't accept the challenge with his words, he accepted with his actions.' *22*

That mighty warrior Balarāma leapt up; his eyes were red with rage. He struck Rukmin with the game-board, killing him. *23*

Furious Balarāma then seized the trembling king of Kaliṅga and smashed the very teeth that he'd revealed before. *24*

He grabbed a massive golden pillar and slew the other royals who sided with the Kaliṅgan king. *25*

All the monarchs cried aloud, brahmin, as they tried to flee from Balarāma's fury. *26*

When Madhu's subduer heard that Balarāma had slain Rukmin, Maitreya, he said nothing as he feared both Rukmiṇī and his brother. *27*

Keśava then led newly married Aniruddha and the Yadu clansmen back to Dvārakā, best of brahmins. *28*

So ends Chapter Twenty-Eight in Book Five of the glorious Viṣṇu Purāṇa.

29. Kṛṣṇa slays the demon Naraka and retrieves Aditi's earrings

Parāśara:

Maitreya, in Dvārakā, mighty Indra, lord of threefold worlds, came to Kṛṣṇa, Śūra's grandson, riding on his raging elephant Airāvata. *1*

Entering the city, he met Hari and told him of the Daitya Naraka's wicked deeds: *2*

'Subduer of Madhu and leader of the gods, even though you've appeared in human form, you bring all suffering to an end. *3*

You slew Ariṣṭa, Dhenuka and Keśin and all those who tried to harm ascetics. *4*

Kaṃsa, Kuvalayāpīḍa, child-killing Pūtanā and all the other blights on earth were led to their doom by you. *5*

When the threefold worlds are protected by your prowess and your wisdom, the denizens of heaven are nourished by the portions of the sacrifice received from worshippers. *6*

When you've heard the reason for my present visit, Janārdana, you must try to help me. *7*

The son of Earth named Naraka, lord of the city of Prāgjyotiṣa, is wreaking havoc on all creation, slayer of your enemies. *8*

This demon carried off the daughters of the gods and siddhas, demigods and kings and locked them in his palace. *9*

He stole wise Varuṇa's umbrella from which the waters flow, and carried off the gem-laden peak of Mount Mandara. *10*

That demon stole the heavenly earrings, source of nectar, from my mother, Aditi, Kṛṣṇa, and now he wants my elephant Airāvata. *11*

Now I've told you of his mischief, Govinda, you must think of retribution.' *12*

Parāśara:

Hearing this, the lord, son of Devakī, smiled, took Indra by the hand and rose from his splendid throne. *13*

Kṛṣṇa mounted sky-ranging Garuḍa, whom he summoned with just a thought, and, helping Satyabhāmā up, flew to the city of Prāgjyotiṣa. *14*

Mighty Indra then set out on Airāvata for the thirteen gods' abode, Maitreya, while the residents of Dvārakā looked on. *15*

The land around Prāgjyotiṣa for a hundred leagues was filled with razor-nooses laid by the demon Muru, best of brahmins. *16*

With one blow of his discus, Sudarśana, Hari cut them all. Muru then sprang forward, but Keśava killed him, too. *17*

With his flaming weapon, Hari burned Muru's seven thousand sons like so many moths. *18*

After he had slain the demons Muru, Hayagrīva and Pañcajana, brahmin, wise Hari swiftly marched on Prāgjyotiṣa. *19*

There he battled Naraka and his great army, and Govinda slew the Daityas by the thousands. *20*

The Earth's son Naraka sent forth showers of missiles and other weapons, but the mighty discus-wielder and destroyer of demon hordes cast Sudarśana at the Daitya, cutting him in two. *21*

When Naraka had been slain, the Earth brought forth Aditi's earrings. She approached the universal lord and said: *22*

'After you lifted me, Lord, in the form of a boar, I produced this son, arising from your touch. *23*

You presented him to me, but now you've killed him, so take these earrings and guard his children. *24*

Your aspect, Lord, beneficent and handsome, has come into this world to ease my burden. *25*

You are creator, transformer and destroyer, the origin and dissolution of the world. You are the world's own form. What's praise to you, eternal Lord? *26*

You, Lord, are pervader and pervaded; action, act and agent. You are at the heart of all creation. What, then, is praise to you? *27*

As you are the highest spirit, the very spirit, creation's heart, eternal Lord, what, then, is praise to you? *28*

Be merciful, heart of all creation. Pardon Naraka for his deeds. He died, but may your son be free from sin.' *29*

Parāśara:

The lord, cause of creation, granted all the Earth's requests, best of sages, and recovered various treasures from the realm of Naraka. *30*

In the women's quarters, Kṛṣṇa of unequalled prowess found sixteen thousand girls, great sage, and one hundred more. *31*

He also saw six thousand awesome four-tusked elephants and twenty-one million Kambojan steeds. *32*

Govinda sent the girls, the elephants and the horses to Dvārakā at once, along with Naraka's servants. *33*

Hari also found the umbrella of Varuṇa and the jewelled peak of Mount Mandara and placed them on Garuḍa. *34*

Mounting the king of birds himself, Kṛṣṇa then flew with Satyabhāmā to the thirteen gods' abode to return Aditi's earrings. *35*

So ends Chapter Twenty-Nine in Book Five of the glorious Viṣṇu Purāṇa.

30. Aditi praises Kṛṣṇa

Parāśara:

Garuḍa flew easily with Hṛṣīkeśa and his consort, the umbrella of Varuṇa and the jewelled mountain peak. *1*

When Hari reached the gates of heaven, he blew his conch. The deities then welcomed him with bowls of water to wash his feet. *2*

Honoured by the gods, Kṛṣṇa entered their mother's residence, resembling the summit of a snowy cloud, and there beheld Aditi. *3*

In company with mighty Indra, Janārdana bowed to her, handed her the splendid earrings and informed her of the death of Naraka. *4*

Aditi, mother of the world, was pleased with Hari, foundation of the universe, and, setting her heart on him, lauded him without distraction: *5*

Aditi:

I bow to you, lotus-eyed protector of devotees, eternal, universal, essence of creation and origin of the world. *6*

Author of the intellect, the mind and senses, you are the heart of all three qualities, yet lie beyond them. You are pure and free from all dualities, abiding in every heart. *7*

You are beyond all conceptions such as appearance and dimension, untouched by birth and other processes, free from sleep and other limitations. *8*

You are twilight, day and night, earth and sky, wind and water, fire and mind, intellect and all the rest, Acyuta. *9*

You are the agent of creation, preservation and destruction, and the master of creators, in three forms known as Brahmā, Viṣṇu and Śiva, Lord. *10*

The deities, yakṣas, Daityas, rākṣasas, siddhas, nāgas, kūṣmāṇḍas, piśācas, gandharvas and humans, *11*

Wild and domestic animals, birds, insects, snakes, trees, shrubs, vines, creepers and every kind of herb— *12*

You are every individual entity, large, medium and small, and smaller than the smallest, as well as everything that takes a concrete form. *13*

This, your illusion, beguiles all those who do not know your true condition. The deluded person is restrained by this, misplacing recognition of the spirit on to something that it's not. *14*

Conceptions such as 'I' and 'mine' that arise in folk from this illusion, Lord, which is itself the mother of the world, are all your doing. *15*

Those men intent on their own duties while praising you, Lord, transcend all this illusion and liberate themselves. *16*

Brahmā and the other gods, humankind and animals are all enveloped by this darkness and blinded by this error in the whirlpool of Vaiṣṇava illusion. *17*

Having worshipped you, some desire to fulfil their wishes and bring their own existence to an end—this is simply your illusion, Lord. *18*

Others worship you as they want a son or desire to conquer enemies, but not for liberation—this, too, is just the play of your illusion. *19*

Like asking for a humble loincloth from a wish-fulfilling tree, to do so is an error made by those who have no merit; it arises from their own deficiencies. *20*

Be merciful, therefore, eternal cause of this illusion that seduces all the world, Lord of creation, and destroy that ignorance masquerading as true knowledge. *21*

I bow to you, wielder of the discus. I bow to you, bearer of Śārṅga. I bow to you, Viṣṇu, holding mace and conch. *22*

I see your form that's marked with signs, but your highest form still lies beyond my comprehension. Show us your mercy, highest Lord. *23*

Parāśara:

Thus praised by the deities' mother, Aditi, Viṣṇu laughed and said, 'Mother goddess, may *you* be merciful to *us* and grant a boon.' *24*

Aditi:

So be it. As you wish. You will never be defeated by god or demon in the mortal world, you tiger of a man. *25*

Parāśara:

Satyabhāmā, with Śacī, wife of mighty Indra, at her side, bowed at once to Aditi and asked repeatedly for her blessing. *26*

Aditi:

By my mercy, fair-browed woman, you'll be never old or ugly, always retaining your flawless form. *27*

Satyabhāmā desires the Pārijāta tree

Parāśara:

With the permission of Aditi, Indra, king of gods, first honoured Janārdana, then duly praised him. *28*

Then Kṛṣṇa, accompanied by Satyabhāmā, visited the other lovely pleasure gardens of Nandana and the deities, best of sages. *29*

There, Keśava, universal lord and Keśin's slayer, beheld the Pārijāta tree, richly scented, bearing flowery masses, bestowing pleasant coolness and resplendent with reddish sprouts. *30*

The Pārijāta, which first appeared when the ocean was churned for nectar, had bark that shone like gold. *31*

When Satyabhāmā saw it, best of brahmins, she said to Govinda, 'Kṛṣṇa, why don't we take it back to Dvārakā? *32*

If what you say to me is true and you really love me, let's take it for the pleasure grove at my residence. *33*

Kṛṣṇa, you've often said with fondness, "Neither Jāmbavatī nor Rukmiṇī are as dear to me as you are, Satyā." *34*

If that's true, Govinda, not mere flattery on your part, then this Pārijāta tree should become a feature in my residence. *35*

With its flowers in my hair, I want to shine amid the other queens.' *36*

Parāśara:

Hearing this, Hari smiled at Satyabhāmā and put the Pārijāta on Garuḍa's back. But the keepers of the grove admonished him: *37*

'Excuse me, sir, but that belongs to Śacī, consort of the king of gods. You can't just take the Pārijāta tree, Govinda. *38*

Brought forth for decorative flowers for Śacī when the gods first churned the ocean, it cannot be removed! *39*

It belongs to Śacī, whose face the king of gods delights to see. It's folly to desire it. Who could ever take it? *40*

The king of gods will surely want revenge for this, Kṛṣṇa, and the other gods will side with mighty Indra with his thunderbolt in hand. *41*

Don't provoke these deities, Acyuta. The wise do not commend an act that leads to bitterness.' *42*

Parāśara:

After they had spoken, furious Satyabhāmā then replied, 'What does Śacī have to do with the Pārijāta tree? And who's this Indra, king of gods? *43*

The tree was brought forth at the churning of the nectar as the property in common for all the worlds, you gods, so why should Indra keep it for himself? *44*

Like the nectar, moon and Śrī, you keepers of the grove, this tree belongs to all the peoples of the world. *45*

Śacī's very proud of her husband's mighty arms, and so she wants to keep it. Tell her she need no longer look for it, as Satyā's had it taken somewhere else. *46*

Go at once and give this weighty message to Puloman's daughter, and say to her that Satyabhāmā sent it: *47*

"If your husband loves you and obeys you, then let him try to stop *my* husband carrying the tree away. *48*

I know your husband, Indra, and I know he's lord of thirteen gods. All the same, I, a mortal woman, am taking this Pārijāta away from you."' *49*

Parāśara:

Hearing this, the keepers went to Śacī and delivered Satyā's message. Śacī spurred into action her husband, that lord of thirteen deities. *50*

Accordingly, he set out to battle Hari for the tree, brahmin, flanked by armies of all the gods. *51*

The thirteen deities, armed with finest weapons, such as bludgeons, swords, clubs and spears, prepared themselves, while mighty Indra stood with thunderbolt in hand. *52*

When Govinda saw Indra mounted on the king of elephants and advancing with his retinue of deities to do battle, *53*

He blew his conch, filling all directions with its sound, and loosed a flight of arrows numbering tens of millions. *54*

Seeing each direction and the sky itself beset with arrows by the hundreds, all thirteen gods unleashed their varied weaponry and missiles. *55*

But Madhu's subduer, lord of worlds, easily reduced to a thousand fragments each weapon and each missile the deities released. *56*

Garuḍa, serpents' devourer, dragged aside the noose that Varuṇa, king of oceans, cast, and, like the body of a tender snake, ripped it with his bill. *57*

With a blow of his mace, Lord Kṛṣṇa, son of Devakī, broke Yama's staff and knocked it to the ground. *58*

Next, the lord, Śūra's scion, shattered Kubera's weapon, Śibikā, with his discus and, with a glance of just one eye, robbed the Sun of brilliance. *59*

He cut Agni, god of fire, into hundreds with his arrows, and caused the Vasus to flee in all directions. He felled the Rudras to the ground, their lance blades shattered by his discus. *60*

With arrows loosed from his bow, Śārṅga, he scattered the Sādhyas, Viśvas, Maruts and gandharvas in the air, like fluff that blows from cottonwood trees. *61*

Garuḍa tore the deities with his bill, beat them with his wings and ripped them with his blade-like talons. *62*

The king of gods and Madhu's slayer showered arrows on each other by the thousand, like a pair of rain clouds shedding torrents. *63*

Garuḍa took on Airāvata in that battle, and mighty Indra, with all the gods, engaged Janārdana. *64*

When all their arrows, missiles and other weapons had been cut down, the Vasus' leader, Indra, swiftly seized his thunderbolt as Kṛṣṇa raised his discus. *65*

Seeing the king of gods and Janārdana with their weapons, best of brahmins, the threefold worlds cried out in anguish. *66*

But Lord Hari caught the thunderbolt hurled by Indra and, holding back his discus, called on Indra to desist. *67*

Now the king of gods had lost his weapon, his elephant was wounded by Garuḍa and he was on the point of fleeing, Satyabhāmā said to Indra, that heroic god: *68*

'It ill befits you, lord of all three worlds and Śacī's husband, to run away. May Śacī approach you with a wreath of Pārijāta flowers. *69*

What's the good of your heavenly kingdom if you can't see Śacī with such a garland, and if she doesn't love you as before? *70*

Let's stop this battle, Indra. Don't be ashamed. Keep this Pārijāta tree and tell the deities not to worry. *71*

Śacī's proud of her husband and didn't show me courtesy or look on me hospitably when I came to visit her. *72*

As a woman, I'm no deep thinker. My husband's reputation is my only care. That's why, Indra, I began this war with you. *73*

I've had enough of this Pārijāta. It's someone else's property, yet we tried to take it. Śacī's proud of her good looks, and what woman isn't proud of her own husband?' *74*

Parāśara:

Hearing this, the king of gods turned and said, 'Enough of these upsetting words, my ardent friend. *75*

I feel no shame in being beaten by the god of universal form, the agent of creation, destruction and preservation of all the world, *76*

In whom this universe abides, who has no middle or beginning, from whom the world arises, the universal being who'll bring it to an end. How can one who is defeated by the cause of the origin, dissolution and preservation of the world feel shame, good woman? *77*

He takes the form of the origin of the world, as subtle as an atom, which only those who understand all things can understand, and no-one else. Who could defeat the birthless, uncreated, eternal lord, who appears in mortal form of his own accord to benefit the world?' *78*

So ends Chapter Thirty in Book Five of the glorious Viṣṇu Purāṇa.

31. Kṛṣṇa plants the Pārijāta tree in Dvārakā

Parāśara:

Lord Keśava, thus praised by Indra, best of brahmins, smiled and made this profound reply: *1*

The Lord:

You are Indra, king of gods, and we're mere mortals, universal lord. Forgive us our transgression. *2*

The Pārijāta should be returned to its proper place. I only took it, mighty Indra, because Satyā told me to. *3*

Here's the thunderbolt I took when you hurled it at me. Please accept your rival-slaying weapon, mighty god. *4*

Indra:

Why do you deceive me, Lord, claiming to be mortal? We're fortunate that we recognise you, even though we cannot grasp your subtlety. *5*

You are who you are, Lord, bent on the task of universal liberation. You, demon slayer, remove all thorns from the flesh of the world. *6*

Take this Pārijāta to the city of Dvārakā, Kṛṣṇa, where it should remain till you leave the mortal realm. *7*

Parāśara:

'So be it,' said Hari to the king of gods. He then returned to earth, while attendant siddhas, gandharvas and sages sang his praises. *8*

Arriving over Dvārakā, Kṛṣṇa blew his conch, brahmin, delighting the city's residents. *9*

He alighted from Garuḍa and, with Satyabhāmā's help, planted the mighty Pārijāta in her pleasure garden. *10*

All who approached that tree recalled their previous existences, and the scent of its flowers perfumed the world for three leagues all around. *11*

Then all the Yādavas, showing their faces to the tree, beheld the original heavenly forms that each of them embodied.[19] *12*

Kṛṣṇa then took possession of the booty that he'd seized from Naraka: elephants, horses and other valuables, as well as women, all carried thither by the demon's servants. *13*

At an auspicious season, Janārdana married all the girls whom Naraka had abducted from elsewhere. *14*

At one and the same moment, Govinda duly took the hand of every girl in marriage with proper rites, great sage, each in her own residence. *15*

The lord then manifested one form of himself for each of the sixteen thousand and one hundred women. *16*

Every girl believed that she alone had married Madhu's subduer. *17*

Keśava, creator of the world, spent the nights in all of their abodes, brahmin, as he may take on many forms at will. *18*

So ends Chapter Thirty-One in Book Five of the glorious Viṣṇu Purāṇa.

32. Uṣā dreams of Aniruddha

Parāśara:

I've mentioned Pradyumna and the other sons of Rukmiṇī and Hari. Satyabhāmā bore Bhānu and Bhaimarika. *1*

Rohiṇī's sons with Hari included Dīptimanta and Prayakṣa. Jāmbavatī had Sāmba and others who relied on their own strong arms. *2*

Nāgnajitī's mighty sons included Bhadravinda. Chief among Śaibyā's sons was Saṃgrāmajit. *3*

19 The gods descended to earth to become the hundred and one branches of the Yadu clan (4.15.24).

Mādrī had Vṛka and other sons. First among the sons of Lakṣmaṇā was Gātravant. Kālindī had Śruta and others. *4*

The bearer of the discus had one hundred and eighty thousand sons with his other wives. *5*

Rukmiṇī's son Pradyumna was the eldest of them all. His son was Aniruddha. His son was Vajra. *6*

Mighty Aniruddha, victorious in battle, won Uṣā, daughter of Bāṇa and granddaughter of Bali, best of brahmins.[20] *7*

On that occasion, there was a great and terrible contest between Hari and Śiva, in which Hari severed Bāṇa's thousand arms with his discus. *8*

Maitreya:

How did this battle over Uṣā come about, brahmin, and how did Hari cut off Bāṇa's limbs? *9*

Please describe all this to me, fortunate sage, as I'm very keen to hear this narrative of Hari. *10*

Parāśara:

Bāṇa's daughter Uṣā saw Pārvatī and Śiva making love one day, brahmin, and conceived a great desire to do the same. *11*

Fair Pārvatī, who could read the minds of all, said to that lovely woman, 'Why torment yourself? Just find a husband.' *12*

Hearing this, Uṣā wondered when this might happen and who might be her husband. Pārvatī continued: *13*

'The man who sweeps you away in a dream on the twelfth night of the bright fortnight in the month of Vaiśākha, princess, will be your husband.' *14*

Parāśara:

Just as the goddess had foretold, a man appeared in a dream that night and Uṣā fell in love with him. *15*

But when she woke, she couldn't see him anymore, Maitreya, and within hearing of her companion anxiously cried out, 'Where have you gone?' *16*

20 Both forms, Ūṣā and Uṣā, are used interchangeably in the following verses. I have standardised on Uṣā.

Now, this companion, Citralekhā, daughter of Bāna's minister Kumbhāṇḍa, asked Uṣā whom she was addressing. *17*

Thrown into confusion, Uṣā at first said nothing, but after Citralekhā reassured her, she explained it all. *18*

Now that Citralekhā understood the matter, Uṣā asked her to find a way to fulfil the goddess's prediction. *19*

Parāśara:

Accordingly, Citralekhā painted on a canvas the portraits of the foremost deities, Daityas, gandharvas and men, and showed them to her friend.[21] *20*

Uṣā passed over the gandharvas, nāgas, gods and demons, but her eyes were drawn to the men of the Andhaka and Vṛṣṇi clans. *21*

Seeing Kṛṣṇa and Balarāma, that fair-browed woman was overcome with shyness, brahmin, and, at the sight of Pradyumna, she modestly dropped her gaze. *22*

The moment she saw Pradyumna's lovely son, brahmin, that wanton woman cast off all restraint. *23*

'That's him!' she cried, 'That's him!' Citralekhā reassured her friend and, as she possessed the yogic power of flight, she set off for Dvārakā. *24*

So ends Chapter Thirty-Two in Book Five of the glorious Viṣṇu Purāṇa.

33. Aniruddha is bound by Bāṇa and freed by Kṛṣṇa

Parāśara:

Some time earlier, the Daitya Bāṇa bowed to three-eyed Śiva, Maitreya, and spoke these words to him, 'Lord, in the absence of a war, my thousand arms are an embarrassment. *1*

I hope there'll be a battle to afford these limbs some use, as, without a fight, they're just a burden. What purpose do they serve?' *2*

21 The apsaras Citralekhā's name, which itself means 'portrait', suggests her artistic talents.

Śiva:

When your peacock banner breaks, Bāṇa, you shall have a war to delight flesh-eating ghouls. *3*

Parāśara:

Filled with glee, Bāṇa bowed to Śiva and went back home, where, seeing his broken banner, his excitement was redoubled. *4*

At that very time, the exquisite apsaras Citralekhā, employing the power of her yogic knowledge, returned from Dvārakā, bringing Aniruddha with her. *5*

When the palace guards found Aniruddha making love with Uṣā in the inner chambers, they went to the Daitya king to report the matter. *6*

That mighty being sent his servant army, but Aniruddha, destroyer of his doughty foes, seized an iron bar and killed them. *7*

After they had been subdued, Bāṇa himself, mounted on his chariot, resolved to kill the interloper. Bāṇa battled Aniruddha with all his might, but was driven back by his rival's heroism. *8*

At the urging of his ministers, he set on Aniruddha a second time and, deploying his magic powers, bound the Yadus' hero with a serpent-weapon. *9*

The Yādavas in Dvārakā asked where Aniruddha was, and Nārada informed them that he was Bāṇa's captive. *10*

When they heard that he'd been taken to the city of Śoṇita by a woman with yogic powers, they were reassured he hadn't been abducted by the gods. *11*

Hari, mounted on Garuḍa, whom he summoned with a single thought, advanced on Bāṇa's city with Balarāma and Pradyumna. *12*

Coming to that city, Hari battled the Pramathas, Śiva's demon minions, and, having overcome them all, he entered Bāṇa's capital. *13*

There, a mighty Fever, in the form of a three-legged, three-headed emanation of Śiva, fought valiantly with Hari, Śārṅga's wielder, in defence of Bāṇa. *14*

Scorched by contact with the Fever's embers, Balarāma closed his eyes and hid behind his brother. *15*

While fighting the divine wielder of Śārṅga, the Śaiva Fever was quickly driven off by a Vaiṣṇava Fever that rose from Kṛṣṇa's body. *16*

When divine Brahmā, grandsire of the world, saw the Śaiva Fever enduring the blows of Nārāyaṇa's arms, he begged the god to pardon him. *17*

Lord Madhusūdana duly forgave the Śaiva Fever and withdrew the Vaiṣṇava sickness to himself. *18*

'Those who recall the battle I fought with you will never suffer our disease,' the Śaiva Fever declared to Kṛṣṇa as he left. *19*

Lord Viṣṇu then overcame and crushed the fivefold Fires and broke with ease the army of the Dānavas. *20*

All the Daitya forces, Bāṇa, son of Bali, Śiva and his scion Kārttikeya then fought with Kṛṣṇa, Śūra's offspring. *21*

The battle Hari fought with Śiva was terrible indeed, and all the worlds were trembling as the deities' flaming weapons scorched them. *22*

As that awful conflict raged, the thirteen gods all feared the world would surely be destroyed. *23*

With the weapon known as Jṛmbhaṇa, Govinda made Śiva yawn, then destroyed the Daityas and Pramathas on all sides. *24*

Yawning uncontrollably, Śiva sank down on the chariot seat, unable to fight Kṛṣṇa, the being untouched by deeds. *25*

Kārttikeya's mount was downed by Garuḍa, as Pradyumna's missiles pierced him. His strength undone by Kṛṣṇa's thundering bow, Kārttikeya fled. *26*

Kṛṣṇa fights the demon Bāṇa

With Śiva yawning, the Daitya army vanquished, Kārttikeya beaten and the Pramatha forces destroyed by Śārṅga's wielder, *27*

Bāṇa mounted his great chariot, to which Śiva's bull, Nandīśa, had been harnessed in place of steeds, and advanced to fight with Kṛṣṇa, his son Pradyumna and Balarāma. *28*

The mighty hero Balarāma tormented Bāṇa's army with his arrows repeatedly and, having stripped it of its honour, forced it to retreat. *29*

Bāṇa saw his army dragged away on the tip of Balarāma's plough and beaten with his hammer, while discus-wielding Kṛṣṇa showered it with arrows. *30*

Thus, the battle between Kṛṣṇa and Bāṇa unfolded on all sides. *31*

Each warrior split the other's brilliant armour-piercing arrows with missiles of his own. Bāṇa split each of Keśava's, and the bearer of the discus did the same to Bāṇa's. *32*

Bāṇa and Kṛṣṇa, both impulsive warriors, striving for the upper hand, intent upon destruction, brahmin, then loosed their shafts at one another. *33*

When all their arrows had been cut down and their missiles almost spent, Hari turned his mind in full to Bāṇa's annihilation. *34*

Hari, bane of the Daitya host, raised his discus, Sudarśana, whose brilliance equals that of a hundred blazing suns. *35*

That enemy of Madhu cast his discus to fell Bāṇa, but the naked demoness Koṭavī, conjured by the Daitya's secret knowledge, appeared in front of Kṛṣṇa. *36*

Seeing her before him, unblinking Kṛṣṇa loosed his discus to fell his rival Bāṇa's forest of arms. *37*

Cast by Acyuta and famed for its destruction of the demons' serried weapons, it severed one by one the limbs of Bāṇa. *38*

When Bāṇa's mass of arms had all been amputated, Śiva, assailant of Tripura city, knew that Madhusūdana would launch the discus in his hand for Bāṇa's final doom. *39*

Seeing Bāṇa bleeding freely from the wounds where his limbs were missing, Umā's husband came with words to soothe Govinda: *40*

Śiva:

Kṛṣṇa, Kṛṣṇa, universal Lord! I know you as the highest spirit, highest lord, highest Self and highest being with neither start nor finish. *41*

Appearing in this bodily form among the gods and beasts and mortals is just a game for you, universal being, and is but a minor mark of your activity. *42*

Be merciful, therefore. I've vouched for Bāṇa's safety, Lord. Don't let my word prove hollow. *43*

He grew up under my protection and hasn't wronged you, eternal god. I granted him a boon, now I beg you to forgive him. *44*

Parāśara:

Hearing this, Govinda's visage softened. He shed his anger with the Daitya and spoke to Umā's husband, who held a trident in his hand: *45*

The Lord:

As Bāṇa received a boon from you, Śiva, I'll spare him and, because I respect your words, I'll recall my discus. *46*

I'll uphold in full the guarantee you gave him, Śiva. Regard yourself as being one with me. *47*

I'm all the world, including mortals, gods and demigods, and so are you. Only those confused by ignorance see a difference between us. *48*

Parāśara:

So saying, Kṛṣṇa proceeded to the place where Pradyumna's son was held. There, the serpents binding Aniruddha were blasted by Garuḍa's breath and fled. *49*

Placing Aniruddha and his wife on Garuḍa's back, Balarāma, Kṛṣṇa's son Pradyumna and Dāmodara himself returned to the city of Dvārakā. *50*

So ends Chapter Thirty-Three in Book Five of the glorious Viṣṇu Purāṇa.

34. Kṛṣṇa burns Vārāṇasī

Maitreya:

Performing mighty deeds in mortal form, Śūra's scion defeated Indra, Śiva and all the other gods with ease. *1*

Tell me what other deeds were done by that being capable of supernatural feats, fortunate sage, as I'm very curious. *2*

Parāśara:

Listen closely, brahmin sage, while I recount how Kṛṣṇa in mortal form burned the city of Vārāṇasī. *3*

There was once a man named Pauṇḍraka Vāsudeva. Folk misled by ignorance told him he was the actual Vāsudeva, Viṣṇu's avatāra in this world. *4*

He began to think he was indeed that being come down to earth. Forgetting his own true nature, he made himself a set of Vaiṣṇava insignia. *5*

He sent an emissary to mighty Kṛṣṇa, saying, 'Give up your discus and other emblems, and renounce the name of Vāsudeva, *6*

Shed your pride and come to pay me homage, fool, if you value life.' *7*

Hearing this, Janārdana gave a laugh and said, 'Take this message back to Pauṇḍraka: "I'll surely send my discus-emblem to you. *8*

I understand the import of your words: what must be done will indeed occur. *9*

With my emblem in my hand, I'll come to your city and present it to you without a doubt. *10*

Just say the word, and I'll appear to you on time tomorrow. *11*

Once I receive your protection, sire, I'll do what's needed so I need not fear you."' *12*

Parāśara:

Hearing this, the emissary departed. Hari then mounted Garuḍa, whom he summoned with a thought, and proceeded swiftly to the city where Pauṇḍraka resided. *13*

When the king of Kāśī learned of Keśava's intention, he set out to act as Pauṇḍraka's rearguard with all his troops.[22] *14*

Pauṇḍraka Vāsudeva advanced to counter Keśava with his own extensive force accompanied by the royal army. *15*

Hari saw Pauṇḍraka in the distance, riding in a splendid chariot, with discus, mace, sword and lotus in his hands. *16*

He wore a garland, held a bow like Śārṅga and his banner showed Garuḍa. Hari noticed that he even had a mark like Śrīvatsa on his chest. *17*

Seeing Pauṇḍraka clad in yellow garments with a diadem and earrings, the Garuḍa-banner's rightful owner laughed aloud. *18*

Kṛṣṇa battled Pauṇḍraka's army with its elephants, cavalry and foot soldiers, brahmin, armed with swords and lances, clubs and pikes, spears and bows. *19*

In a trice, he routed it with enemy-cleaving arrows loosed from Śārṅga and blows of mace and discus. *20*

Janārdana sent the king of Kāśī's army to its doom, then spoke to foolish Pauṇḍraka, who still displayed his Vaiṣṇava insignia. *21*

22 Kāśī is an alternative name for Vārāṇasī, a famous centre of Śaiva worship.

The Lord:

Pauṇḍraka, your emissary said I must renounce my emblems, so now I'll let you have them. *22*

I'll send this discus and this mace, and here's Garuḍa. Put him on your standard! *23*

Parāśara:

So saying, Hari cast his discus, cutting Pauṇḍraka to pieces. He struck him with his mace, while Garuḍa downed the bogus emblem on his standard. *24*

People cried in anguish as the mighty king of Kāśī fought with Vāsudeva to avenge his ally. *25*

With shafts he loosed from Śārṅga, Hari severed the royal head and flung it into Kāśī, spreading panic among the populace. *26*

After slaying Pauṇḍraka, the king of Kāśī and his followers, the scion of Śūra returned to Dvārakā, where he indulged in heavenly pleasures. *27*

Seeing the king of Kāśī's head that landed in the city, the bewildered residents wondered what had happened and who had done the deed. *28*

When the prince learned that his father had been killed by Vāsudeva, guided by his family priest, he propitiated Śiva. *29*

At the sacred site of Avimukta, the royal scion gratified that deity, who then offered him a boon. *30*

The prince replied: 'By your grace, Lord Śiva, let a phantom rise to bring about the death of Kṛṣṇa, my father's murderer.' *31*

Parāśara:

'It will be so,' replied the god, and from the fire in the southernmost of the prince's sacrificial hearths arose at once a monstrous phantom. *32*

Her gaping maw blazed with fire; her hair was a mass of flames. Crying Kṛṣṇa's name repeatedly, the raging ghoul set out for Dvārakā. *33*

When the people saw her, sage, their eyes began to dart with terror and they fled for protection to Madhu's subduer, the refuge of the world. *34*

The discus-wielder understood that this great spectre had been conjured forth by bull-bannered Śiva when the king of Kāśī's son had worshipped him. *35*

In the middle of a game of dice, Kṛṣṇa casually released his discus with the order to destroy the frightful apparition whose locks were a mass of blazing fire. *36*

Viṣṇu's weapon Sudarśana set off at once towards the dreadful fire-belching spectre, her hair a fiery garland. *37*

Confounded by the discus's blow, that phantom born of mighty Śiva fled as quickly as she could, but the weapon in pursuit was just as fast. *38*

As she hastened into Vārāṇasī, best of sages, Viṣṇu's discus sapped her strength. *39*

The king of Kāśī's army, with a mighty force of Pramathas, armed with every kind of weapon and with missiles, met Sudarśana. *40*

Hari's discus burned the armies with its energy, even though they knew the use of weapons. Then it burned down all of Vārāṇasī, source of the apparition, *41*

Along with its king, his minions, subjects, horses, elephants, men and all its stores and granaries such as even deities rarely see. *42*

Until every residence, square and rampart was engulfed by flames, Hari's discus burned it all. *43*

Sudarśana, ablaze with splendour, then returned to Viṣṇu's hand with undiminished energy and a thirst for further missions so easily accomplished. *44*

So ends Chapter Thirty-Four in Book Five of the glorious Viṣṇu Purāṇa.

35. Balarāma threatens Hastināpura

Maitreya:

I'd like to hear some more about wise Balarāma's prowess. Kindly tell me, brahmin. *1*

I've heard how he dragged the Yamunā and other feats, master, but tell me, fortunate sage, what other things he did. *2*

Parāśara:

Listen, Maitreya, to this feat performed by Balarāma, who in truth is Śeṣa, the eternal, immeasurable upholder of the earth. *3*

Jāmbavatī's son, the hero Sāmba, seized the daughter of Duryodhana as she was preparing for her *svayaṃvara*. *4*

The mighty warriors Karṇa, Duryodhana, Bhīṣma, Droṇa and the rest were furious. They worsted Sāmba in battle and imprisoned him. *5*

Hearing this, the Yādavas were all enraged by Duryodhana and his friends, Maitreya, and devised a scheme to slay them. *6*

But Balarāma butted in and, slurring his words in drunkenness, exclaimed, 'I'll go alone to the Kauravas and make them set him free.' *7*

When he reached Hastināpura, the city named for elephants, he didn't enter, but waited on its outskirts in a grove. *8*

When Duryodhana and the other princes heard that he'd arrived, they presented him with cattle and some water as a gift. *9*

Balarāma duly accepted these, but then addressed the Kauravas: 'Ugrasena orders you: set Sāmba free at once.' *10*

Bhīṣma, Droṇa, Karṇa, Duryodhana and the others heard his words, best of brahmins, and flew into a rage. *11*

All the furious Kauravas, Bālhīkas and the rest, who considered Yadu's lineage unworthy of a kingdom, said to the wielder of the plough: *12*

'Hey! Hey! What's this you say, Balarāma? Who among the Yādavas gives orders to Kuru clansmen? *13*

If Ugrasena commands the Kauravas, we might as well give up our white umbrellas, the symbols of our sovereignty. *14*

Go or stay, Balarāma, but we won't release ill-mannered Sāmba just as you or Ugrasena wish it. *15*

You Kukuras and Andhakas have never shown the respect that we deserve, but what's this order from a servant to a master? *16*

Just because you sit and eat with us, you've grown arrogant. We didn't think it wrong to show you kindness, because of our affection. *17*

We sent you gifts of welcome because we liked you, Balarāma, but it doesn't really suit your clan to receive a gift from ours.' *18*

Parāśara:

So saying, the Kauravas refused to release Sāmba, son of Hari, and, being in agreement, they returned at once to the city named for elephants. *19*

Mad with fury at this insult, plough-wielding Balarāma spun around, leapt up and kicked the earth. *20*

The earth, struck by that mighty being, split asunder, and the sound of the fracture spread in all directions. *21*

With reddened eyes and knitted brows, he shouted, 'Ha! Such is the haughty arrogance of these worthless, wicked people. *22*

The sovereignty of the Kauravas and ours is the gift of fate, as is the fact they think today they can ignore the command of Ugrasena. *23*

Śacī's husband and other gods duly follow Ugrasena's orders, and he holds court in Sudharmā, Indra's assembly hall. *24*

I curse their pride in a royal throne that has been occupied by a hundred men! Is not Ugrasena, whose servants' wives wear garlands from the Pārijāta tree, lord of the earth? *25*

May Ugrasena remain the master of every monarch. Before I enter his city today, I'll rid this world of Kauravas. *26*

This very day, I'll kill Karṇa, Duryodhana, Droṇa, Bhīṣma, Bāhlika, Duḥśāsana and his brothers, Bhūri, Bhūriśravas, *27*

Somadatta, Śala, Bhīma, Arjuna, Yudhiṣṭhira and the twins Sahadeva and Nakula, as well as the other Kauravas, along with their horses, chariots and elephants. *28*

Then I'll rescue brave Sāmba and his wife, and bring them back to Dvārakā, where I'll see Ugrasena and my other kin once more. *29*

Better still, I'll take the Kauravas' capital, the city named for elephants, along with the Kurus themselves, and throw them in the Gaṅgā River.' *30*

Parāśara:

So saying, his eyes still red with drunkenness, plough-wielding Balarāma laid his weapon, blade down, upon the city wall and pulled. *31*

Seeing Hastināpura abruptly start to topple, the Kauravas' hearts all trembled and they cried aloud, *32*

'Balarāma, Balarāma! Forgive us, mighty warrior, forgive us. Don't be angry. Be gracious, plough-wielding hero. *33*

Here are Sāmba and his wife. We'll set them free for you, Balarāma. We didn't know how strong you were. Forgive us our offence.' *34*

Parāśara:

The Kauravas immediately came out of the city, best of sages, and handed over Sāmba and his wife. *35*

Balarāma, bowing, spoke to Bhīṣma, Droṇa, Kṛpa and the other Kauravas as they tried to calm him. 'I forgive you,' said that best of heroes. *36*

Even to this very day, brahmin, Hastināpura seems to list, such was the power of Balarāma, as shown by his strength and courage. *37*

The Kauravas then paid respects to Balarāma and sent off Sāmba and his wife with wedding gifts. *38*

So ends Chapter Thirty-Five in Book Five of the glorious Viṣṇu Purāṇa.

36. Balarāma defeats the giant monkey Dvivida

Parāśara:

Listen, Maitreya. Now you'll hear about another feat performed by mighty Balarāma. *1*

There was a monkey, Dvivida by name, a powerful warrior and ally of Naraka the demon king and rival of the deities. *2*

After Kṛṣṇa, at Indra's urging, had slain Naraka, that mighty beast then became the gods' sworn enemy, saying: *3*

'Because of this, I'll take revenge on all the gods by disrupting every sacrifice and destroying the world of men.' *4*

Accordingly, misled by ignorance, he prevented acts of worship, overstepped the limits of the wise and wrought destruction on living beings. *5*

That wanton creature burned the land, the cities, towns and everything between them. Here and there he crushed the villages and other settlements by hurling mountains down on them. *6*

He picked up massifs and dropped them in the seas and rivers, and churned the ocean while standing in its waters. *7*

Stirred by Dvivida, brahmin, the ocean broke its banks and swiftly flooded towns and cities and other places on its shores. *8*

That monkey, who could take on any shape at will, appeared in monstrous form and ruined all the crops by rolling, roaming and trampling on them. *9*

This whole world, ravaged by that evil beast and deprived of Vedic recitation with ritual cries of *vaṣaṭ*, Maitreya, was filled with misery. *10*

One day, plough-wielding Balarāma was drinking in the garden of Raivata with fortunate Revatī and some other lovely women. *11*

While they sang his praises, that foremost of the Yadu clan enjoyed himself, surrounded by a splendid throng of girls, like Kubera on Mount Mandara. *12*

But then Dvivida appeared and, snatching Balarāma's plough and club, he mocked the Yādava to his face. *13*

That monkey laughed at Balarāma in front of all the women and kicked the wine-filled vessels over, smashing all of them. *14*

Furious Balarāma cursed the monkey, but Dvivida, ignoring him, just chattered back. *15*

Balarāma leapt up and seized his club in fury, but the magic monkey grabbed a boulder of enormous size and hurled it. *16*

The hero of the Yādavas smashed that rock into a thousand pieces with his club and brought it to the ground. *17*

The monkey flew up in the air, dodged the club and, rushing forward, beat his paws against his chest in anger. *18*

Raging Balarāma struck Dvivida on the head; the monkey dropped down to the ground, spewing blood, his life force spent. *19*

Dvivida's body fell on a mountain and smashed its peak in a hundred pieces, Maitreya, as if struck by Indra's thunderbolt. *20*

The deities caused flowers to fall like rain on Balarāma and, descending from the heavens, praised him, saying, 'Excellent indeed is this feat that you've accomplished. *21*

All the world was troubled by this wicked monkey doing favours for the Daityas, hero. Luckily he's dead.' *22*

Parāśara:

Many peerless deeds like this were done by prudent Balarāma, who was really Śeṣa, supporter of the earth. *23*

So ends Chapter Thirty-Six in Book Five of the glorious Viṣṇu Purāṇa.

37. The destruction of the Yādavas

Parāśara:

Thus Kṛṣṇa, helped by Balarāma, destroyed the Daityas and the evil kings to benefit the world. *1*

With Arjuna's assistance, Lord Hari eased the burden of the earth by destroying many armies.[23] *2*

After he'd accomplished this and brought down all the monarchs, he then annihilated his own clan, the Yādavas, owing to a brahmin's curse. *3*

Kṛṣṇa then abandoned Dvārakā and left his mortal body. This self-born being, with all his manifested aspects, then resumed his natural state as Viṣṇu. *4*

Maitreya:

Why did he destroy his clan owing to the brahmin's curse, and how did Janārdana leave his mortal form? *5*

Parāśara:

One day, at the sacred site of Piṇḍāraka, some young boys of the Yadu clan spied Viśvāmitra, Kaṇva and the great sage Nārada. *6*

These fine lads, impelled by fate, dressed Sāmba, son of Jāmbavatī, as a woman. *7*

They then approached the sages and, bowing with respect, said, 'This is Babhru's wife, and she desires a son. Will her baby be a boy or girl?' *8*

Parāśara:

The sages, endowed with divine perception, felt insulted by the boys and angrily declared, 'She will bear a pestle, which will end the clan of Yādavas!' *9*

Thus addressed by the sages, the youths told Ugrasena what they'd done, and Sāmba later brought forth a pestle from his belly. *10*

Ugrasena had that iron pestle ground to dust. This was thrown into the ocean, where it grew as reeds. *11*

23 This is a reference to the Mahābhārata war.

When the Andhaka clansmen destroyed the pestle, brahmin, there remained one blade-like splinter they couldn't crush. *12*

This they also cast into the sea, where it was swallowed by a fish. The fish was caught by fishermen, and a hunter known as Jaras found the fragment in its belly. *13*

Although the slayer of Madhu foresaw the final outcome, the lord had no desire to change the course of fate. *14*

The gods dispatched a messenger to Keśava, who bowed before him, saying, 'Lord, I'm an envoy sent in secret by the deities. *15*

Mighty Indra with the Vasus, Aśvins, Maruts, Ādityas, Rudras, Sādhyas and the others wish to tell you this, so listen carefully, Lord. *16*

It's more than a hundred years since you, Lord, propitiated by the thirteen gods, descended to the earth to ease her burden. *17*

The wicked Daityas have been destroyed and the burden of the earth relieved. May we thirteen deities in threefold heavens always have you as our leader. *18*

More than a hundred years have passed, universal Lord. Now, if it pleases you, return to heaven. *19*

The deities also said that, if you're happy here, then you should remain as long as your dependants need you.' *20*

The Lord:

All you've said is known to me, messenger, and I've already begun the Yādavas' destruction. *21*

Even now, the burden of the earth will not be eased until the Yādavas are destroyed. Before I leave, I'll annihilate them all in seven short nights. *22*

When the ocean has reclaimed the land I took for Dvārakā, and I've destroyed the clan, I'll then return to the abode of the thirteen deities. *23*

Tell the king of gods and others that, when I've left this mortal form, I'll come back with Balarāma. *24*

Jarāsandha and the other kings who were a burden on the earth have all been killed, yet even a single Yādava boy is no less a load than they. *25*

Tell the gods that I'll return to guard their realm when I've removed this weighty burden from the earth. *26*

Parāśara:

Thus addressed by Vāsudeva, the heavenly envoy bowed to him, Maitreya, and, with the speed of the deities, returned to Indra's presence. *27*

By day and night, the lord observed bad omens in the sky, on the ground and in the air, portending the ruin of Dvārakā. *28*

Noting these, he then addressed the Yādavas, 'Behold these dreadful portents! We'll go at once to Prabhāsa to ward them off.' *29*

Parāśara:

Uddhava, his foremost devotee, said to Hari with a bow, 'Tell me, Lord, what I must do, as I suspect you'll reabsorb the clan. *30*

Signs portending its destruction have been seen, eternal Lord.' *31*

The Lord:

Go with the speed of deities, which you'll acquire through my mercy, to the auspicious ashram of Badarīka on Mount Gandhamādana, residence of Nara and Nārāyaṇa, whose existence purifies the world. *32*

Contemplate me there and, with my blessing, you'll achieve perfection. I'll return to heaven when I've reabsorbed the clan. *33*

The moment I depart from Dvārakā, the ocean will reclaim it. *34*

Parāśara:

Hearing this, Uddhava bowed to Hari and left for Nara and Nārāyaṇa's abode as suggested. *35*

Mounted on swift chariots, the Yādavas then all set out for Prabhāsa, brahmin, with Kṛṣṇa, Balarāma and the rest. *36*

On reaching that location, the Kukura and Andhaka clansmen bathed and then, encouraged by Vāsudeva, began to drink in earnest. *37*

Friction rose among them as they drank. This friction sparked an argument, and a fight flared up, which led to their destruction. *38*

Victims of their destiny, they struck each other with weapons and, when the weapons were exhausted, they seized the reeds that grew nearby. *39*

The reeds were thunderbolts in their hands, with which they slew each other in that terrible affray. *40*

Led by Pradyumna and Sāmba, Kṛtavarman, Sātyaki, Aniruddha, Pṛthu and Vipṛthu, *41*

Cāruvarman, Cāruka, Akrūra and many others, brahmin, they fought with bolts of lightning in the form of reeds. *42*

Hari tried to stop them, but the Yādavas all thought he'd come to their assistance, so battled on regardless. *43*

Furious Kṛṣṇa grabbed some reeds, which became a club of iron for the Yādavas' destruction. *44*

Wielding this weapon, he slew the murderous clansmen, leaving none alive, while others clashed together and slaughtered one another. *45*

Jaitra, the discus-wielder's chariot, best of brahmins, was swept into the ocean with its steeds as its driver, Dāruka, looked on. *46*

Hari's discus, club and bow, his quivers, conch and sword all circled him respectfully, then departed by the solar path. *47*

Soon, great sage, not one Yādava remained alive, except for mighty Kṛṣṇa himself and Dāruka. *48*

Balarāma and Kṛṣṇa abandon their mortal forms

As they wandered, Dāruka and Kṛṣṇa saw Balarāma seated by a tree with a giant serpent coming from his mouth. *49*

That massive coiling creature emerged from Balarāma and set off for the ocean, worshipped by the siddhas and other nāgas. *50*

The Ocean came to welcome him with gifts of hospitality, and he slid into its waters while foremost serpents sang his praises. *51*

Seeing Balarāma had withdrawn, Keśava said to Dāruka, 'Report all this to Vasudeva and to Ugrasena: *52*

Balarāma has departed and the Yādavas are no more. I'll repose in yoga, then I'll leave my mortal form. *53*

Tell Āhuka and Dvārakā's inhabitants that the ocean will soon reclaim their city. *54*

They should prepare for Arjuna's arrival, as they cannot stay in Dvārakā. When the son of Pāṇḍu leaves, *55*

They must follow that Kuru scion wherever he may lead. *56*

Go and repeat my words to Arjuna, son of Kuntī: he must protect these folk, my kin, with all his might. *57*

Accompanied by Arjuna, you must lead them all from Dvārakā, and Vajra will become the Yadus' king.' *58*

Parāśara:

Hearing this, Dāruka bowed to Kṛṣṇa many times, circled him respectfully, then set out as instructed. *59*

When the prudent driver had departed, he did as Kṛṣṇa ordered him in Dvārakā, leading Arjuna to the city and setting Vajra on the throne. *60*

Lord Govinda, who maintained the highest form of Vāsudeva among the living, now merged into the Absolute.[24] *61*

Respecting the words of the brahmin Durvāsas, Kṛṣṇa engaged in yoga, best of sages, seated with one foot upon his knee.[25] *62*

The hunter known as Jaras appeared at that location. His arrow bore the remnant shard of iron from the pestle at its tip. *63*

Standing at a distance, he mistook the foot of Kṛṣṇa for a deer, best of brahmins, and, with that very missile, he shot him in the sole. *64*

Drawing closer, Jaras saw the four-armed being. He threw himself upon the ground and begged repeatedly for mercy: *65*

'I didn't know what I was doing and mistook you for a deer. Forgive me. I'm consumed by shame, so please don't punish me anymore.' *66*

Parāśara:

'Have no fear,' the Lord replied. 'Go with my blessing, hunter, to the heavens where gods reside.' *67*

Parāśara:

As soon as he had spoken, a celestial chariot appeared. The hunter climbed aboard and departed for the heavenly realms, with Kṛṣṇa's blessing. *68*

---

24 The commentators and my fellow translators have all struggled to make sense of this verse. This is the clearest version I can offer.

25 According to the *Mahābhārata* (CE 13.144), the sage Durvāsas was once a guest in Kṛṣṇa's abode. The sage told Kṛṣṇa to smear himself with leftover rice porridge, while Durvāsas applied it to Rukmiṇī. Kṛṣṇa's soles were left uncovered and so became vulnerable.

After Jaras had set off, the lord merged with the highest, eternal, inconceivable, purest form of Vāsudeva, *69*

Which is birthless, ageless, indestructible, immeasurable and universal. He then transcended the threefold state and abandoned his mortal form. *70*

So ends Chapter Thirty-Seven in Book Five of the glorious Viṣṇu Purāṇa.

38. Arjuna leads the women from Dvārakā

Parāśara:

On finding the remains of Kṛṣṇa and Balarāma, Arjuna performed the rites for them and the other Yādavas in turn. *1*

Kṛṣṇa's eight consorts, whom I mentioned, led by Rukmiṇī, embraced the corpse of Hari and ascended his funerary pyre. *2*

Revatī embraced Balarāma's body, best of sages, and entered the blazing fire, which seemed cool to her on account of her joyous union with her husband. *3*

Hearing of this, Ugrasena, Vasudeva, Devakī and Rohiṇī also entered the flames. *4*

After Arjuna had duly carried out rituals for them all, he led the people, including Vajra, from the city. *5*

Watching over Kṛṣṇa's myriad consorts, with Vajra and the others as they abandoned Dvārakā, the son of Kuntī set forth slowly. *6*

When Kṛṣṇa left this mortal realm, Maitreya, the assembly hall Sudharmā and the Pārijāta tree both rose to heaven. *7*

On the very day that Hari left the earth for heaven, this dark and potent Kali age descended on the world. *8*

The mighty ocean flooded empty Dvārakā, sparing just the Yadu god's abode. *9*

Even now, the ocean cannot take it, brahmin, as Lord Keśava always dwells there. *10*

Having seen that place of great good fortune, where Viṣṇu, who removes all wickedness, disports himself, one is freed from sin. *11*

In the land that's watered by five rivers and abounds in grain, Arjuna, son of Pṛthā, made a home for all the people, best of sages. *12*

Seeing women bereft of husbands, led by the archer Arjuna alone, the cupidity of certain bandits was aroused. *13*

Those wicked men whose hearts were filled with avarice met with fierce Ābhīra tribesmen and conferred with them: *14*

'Here, the single archer Arjuna, having overrun us, is leading widowed women through our lands. Shame upon your army! *15*

Slaying Bhīṣma, Droṇa, Jayadratha, Karṇa and the others, Arjuna grew proud, but he doesn't know how strong we villagers can be. *16*

Come! Come! Take up your staves! This fool looks down on us. What use are your strong arms?' *17*

Parāśara:

Thousands of plundering bandits armed with staves then fell on the defenceless throng. *18*

The son of Kuntī checked the tribes and, with a laugh, he said, 'Retreat now—ignorant of virtue—if you do not want to die.' *19*

But they ignored his warning and seized the women—once the wives of mighty Kṛṣṇa—Maitreya, along with their possessions. *20*

When that hero Arjuna tried to string Gāṇḍīva, his heavenly bow that never failed in battle, he found it was impossible. *21*

He strove to tighten up the string, but it came undone again. The son of Pāṇḍu tried to summon magic weapons, but his memory also failed him. *22*

Impatient Arjuna, wielder of Gāṇḍīva, loosed arrows at his foes, but they barely scratched their skin. *23*

Arjuna's unfailing shafts, gifts from Agni, were destroyed in battle with the herdsmen, and now his very life was threatened. *24*

The son of Kuntī recalled how Kṛṣṇa's power had let him vanquish hosts of earthly kings with showers of arrows. *25*

While Pāṇḍu's son looked on, some splendid women were seized by Ābhīras, while other women ran towards them lustily. *26*

When all his arrows were exhausted, Dhanaṃjaya struck the brigands with his bow, sage, but they merely mocked his blows. *27*

While Arjuna was watching, the tribesmen all set off, best of sages, taking those lovely Vṛṣṇi and Andhaka women with them. *28*

Broken-hearted and lamenting, Arjuna cried out, 'Alas, alas! I've been forsaken by the lord. *29*

This bow, these weapons, this chariot with its steeds—all is wasted in an instant, like donations to a brahmin who's unworthy. *30*

Alas! Powerful indeed is destiny. Without great Kṛṣṇa by my side, Fate awarded victory to the lesser party, even though they're weak. *31*

These are my arms, this is my fist, here is my place and I am Arjuna! But without auspicious Kṛṣṇa, it's all in vain. *32*

The Arjuna-ness of Arjuna and Bhīma's Bhīma-ness were doubtless due to Kṛṣṇa. Without him, I've been defeated by mere tribesmen. How otherwise could this happen?' *33*

Parāśara:

So saying, Arjuna departed for the wondrous city known as Mathurā. There he enthroned Vajra, delighter of the Yādavas. *34*

In Mathurā, Arjuna found Vyāsa living in a forest ashram and, approaching that blessed seer, he greeted him respectfully. *35*

The sage looked long at Arjuna lying at his feet and asked, 'What's the reason for your lacklustre appearance? *36*

Have you had sex with a menstruating woman? Have you killed a brahmin? You're so pale you've surely endured some tragedy. *37*

Have your prayers for a son or something else all failed? Have you had sex with a woman who shouldn't be approached? Is that why you look so jaded? *38*

Have you been eating delicacies alone, not offering them to brahmins first? Have you stolen a poor man's goods, Arjuna? *39*

Were you downwind from a winnowing fan, Arjuna, or has the evil eye befallen you? Why else would you look so pale? *40*

Were you touched by water from someone's fingernails, or splashed with water from a pitcher? Does that explain your pale complexion? Or have you lost a battle to inferior opponents?'[26] *41*

---

26 A person standing downwind from a winnowing fan may be covered with dust, but none of the commentators or earlier translators can explain how water from the fingernails or a pitcher causes pallor.

Parāśara:

Arjuna, son of Pṛthā, sighed and said, 'Listen', then explained to Vyāsa how he'd been defeated. *42*

Arjuna:

Hari, who was our strength, energy, courage, prowess, glory and lustre, has abandoned us and gone away. *43*

Without that great being, sage, who was one of us and always addressed us with a smile, we're merely men of straw. *44*

The highest spirit, who was the power invested in my missiles, arrows and my bow, Gāṇḍīva, has left. *45*

As long as we could see him, our glory, victory, fortune and prosperity never failed, but Lord Govinda has deserted us and gone away. *46*

Kṛṣṇa—by whose prowess Bhīṣma, Droṇa, Karṇa, king of Aṅga, Duryodhana and the other Kauravas were consumed—has left this world. *47*

The earth, like me, has lost its youth, deprived of glory, robbed of beauty. Neither I nor the rest of the world, dear Vyāsa, will shine again without that discus-wielding Kṛṣṇa. *48*

Because of my faith in him, Bhīṣma and the others were drawn like moths to my flame, but, in Kṛṣṇa's absence, I've been beaten by some cattle-herders. *49*

With my faith in Kṛṣṇa, Gāṇḍīva, my bow, was famed in all three worlds, but, without him, it's no match for tribal staves. *50*

Despite my efforts, mighty sage, the women in my charge were carried off in thousands by brigands armed with sticks. *51*

All of Kṛṣṇa's dependants have been seized by Ābhīras, who defeated me with blows of staves and robbed me of my strength, Vyāsa. *52*

It's no surprise that I am pale—it's amazing that I'm still alive! Heaped with abuse by inferior men, grandsire, I've no shame left. *53*

Arjuna and the other Pāṇḍavas retire to the forest

Vyāsa:

That's enough of modesty, Arjuna. Grieving doesn't suit you. You need to understand no being is immune from the vagaries of Time. *54*

Time brings all things into being, son of Pāṇḍu, then destroys them. Once you understand the world is ruled by Time, Arjuna, hold on to strength while it endures. *55*

The rivers, oceans, mountains and all the world with gods and mortals, animals, trees, insects and reptiles were all brought forth by Time. *56*

And Time will bring them to an end again. When you see that Time is at the heart of this, you'll find peace. *57*

Kṛṣṇa's greatness is just as you've described it, Dhanaṃjaya. He came to earth to ease the burden of the world. *58*

In former times, the Earth, oppressed by weight, approached the assembly of the gods, and Janārdana, who also takes the form of Time, descended to the world on her behalf. *59*

That task has been accomplished, Arjuna, as all the kings are slain and the race of Andhakas and Vṛṣṇis is no more. *60*

In this world, the lord has nothing more to do and, hence, his task completed, he has departed in accordance with his desire. *61*

At the moment of creation, the god of gods brings forth the world; while it exists, he keeps it and, in the end, he is capable of its destruction, as he has shown just now. *62*

Don't dwell on being beaten, Arjuna, as men have prowess only for a fraction of their lives. *63*

Bhīṣma, Droṇa, Karṇa and the other kings were slain by you alone, but their death was really brought about by Time. Wasn't your defeat by lesser men the same? *64*

Just as you defeated them with your faith in Viṣṇu, your defeat by bandits is, in the end, attributable to Time. *65*

That deity, master of the universe, assuming different forms, preserves the world and finally destroys creation. *66*

During your own lifetime Janārdana was your ally, son of Kuntī, but now your life is drawing to a close, your enemies are overseen by Keśava. *67*

Who'd believe that you would slay the Kauravas, including Bhīṣma, son of Gaṅgā? And who'd believe the Ābhīras defeated you? *68*

That you, the son of Pṛthā, beat the Kauravas but were yourself defeated by Ābhīras is just the playful sport of Hari, the universal being. *69*

You're grieving for the women seized by bandits, Arjuna, but I'll tell you why this happened. *70*

Long ago, a brahmin known as Aṣṭāvakra vowed to live in water, son of Pṛthā, and he spent many years in worship of the everlasting Absolute. *71*

When the armies of the demigods had been defeated, a great celebration was held on the foothills of Mount Meru. Some heavenly womenfolk saw that brahmin as they journeyed to the festival. *72*

Hundreds and thousands of apsarases, Rambhā and Tilottamā among them, son of Pāṇḍu, extolled that great ascetic and sang his praises. *73*

Intent upon their eulogies, they reverently bowed before the sage as he stood neck-deep in water, with his matted locks piled upon his head. *74*

All those apsarases, best of Kauravas, sang the praises that they thought would please that foremost brahmin. *75*

Aṣṭāvakra:

'You've pleased me, blessed women. Ask for anything you desire, and I shall grant it, even if it's hard to come by.' *76*

Rambhā, Tilottamā and other apsarases, celebrated in the Vedas, replied to him, 'Isn't it sufficient, brahmin, that you're pleased with us?' *77*

But some among them said, 'Brahmin, if indeed you're gratified, we'd like to have the best of mankind for our husband.' *78*

Vyāsa:

'As you wish,' the sage replied, emerging from the waters, but then the apsarases saw that he was very ugly, as his body was deformed (*vakra*) in eight respects (*aṣṭa*). *79*

Seeing this, some tried to hide their mirth, but others burst out laughing, joy of Kurus, and the sage in fury cursed them: *80*

'Because you think I'm ugly and you mock me, I pronounce this curse on you: *81*

Through my blessing, Kṛṣṇa, the best of men, will be your husband, but cursed by me, you'll all be ruined and fall into the hands of bandits.' *82*

Vyāsa:

Hearing this, the apsarases soothed the sage to some extent, so he promised in the end that they'd attain the realm of Indra, king of gods. *83*

That's why, on account of Aṣṭāvakra's curse, those splendid women first had Keśava as their husband, but were later seized by brigands. *84*

For this reason, son of Pāṇḍu, you shouldn't grieve for them at all. All this ruin was brought about by the universal lord. *85*

And now your own demise is near at hand, as he has withdrawn your strength and glory, your courage and your greatness. *86*

Death is certain for every being that's born, just as falling is assured for those who've risen. Union ends in separation, and all that's gathered will be scattered. *87*

Knowing this, wise people neither grieve nor cheer, and others who learn their habits become like them. *88*

For this reason, knowing this, you should leave behind this tangled life, outstanding man, and retire to the forest with your brothers to undertake austerities. *89*

Go and give my orders to Yudhiṣṭhira, king of virtue, and prepare to set out with your brothers—not tomorrow, but the following day. *90*

Parāśara:

Hearing this, Arjuna met the other sons of Pṛthu, Yudhiṣṭhira and Bhīma, and the twins Nakula and Sahadeva, and told them all he'd seen and done. *91*

Hearing Vyāsa's words conveyed by Arjuna, the five sons of Pāṇḍu set Parīkṣit on the throne and departed for the forest. *92*

Thus, Maitreya, I've described for you at length the deeds of Vāsudeva when he was born in Yadu's lineage. *93*

So ends Chapter Thirty-Eight in Book Five of the glorious Viṣṇu Purāṇa.

End of Book Five.

Book Six: Dissolution

1. The decline of virtue in the age of Kali

Maitreya:

You've described in detail the creation of the world, great sage, the lineages of patriarchs, the duration of the Manvantaras and the deeds of the dynasties. *1*

Now I wish to hear about the destruction of the world, known as the 'great dissolution', and annihilation at the end of every era, foremost sage. *2*

Parāśara:

I'll now describe precisely how dissolution happens at the era's end, Maitreya, and explain how primal nature is absorbed. *3*

One day and night for ancestors are a month for mortals. One year for mortals is a day and night for gods. Two sets of a thousand cycles of four ages are a day and night for Brahmā, best of brahmins. *4*

Kṛta, Tretā, Dvāpara and Kali are the ages, and each fourfold cycle takes twelve thousand years of gods. *5*

Every cycle is the same, Maitreya, as they start with Kṛta and end with Kali. *6*

In the beginning, Brahmā creates the world in the Kṛta age, and he brings about its dissolution in the age of Kali. *7*

Maitreya:

Please describe in detail the nature of this age of Kali, master, during which fourfold virtue is corrupted. *8*

Parāśara:

You want to ask about the nature of the Kali age, Maitreya, so listen, sage, because that age is now upon us. *9*

At this time, folk no longer follow the provisions for their orders or stage of life, nor do they perform the rites determined by the *Sāma*, *Ṛg* and *Yajur Vedas*. *10*

Marriage in the Kali age is no longer moral, nor do students live in their gurus' homes. The customs governing husbands and their wives will be ignored, as will rituals for the sacred fires and deities. *11*

In this age, a powerful lord, irrespective of his natal clan, will feel entitled to procure a woman of any order. *12*

In the age of Kali, a twice-born man may be initiated into any spiritual tradition, but, irrespective of his choice, Maitreya, it will merely be atonement. *13*

Anything said to be a scripture will be thus regarded in the Kali age, brahmin; anything may be worshipped as a god and anyone may follow each stage of life. *14*

Fasting, austerities and donations made by those who feel the need will amount to virtue at this time. *15*

Pride in small amounts of wealth will count as riches in the age of Kali, and women will be proud of their appearance, merely thinking of their hair. *16*

In the Kali age, when garments have no gold or gems, jewels or other ornaments, women's only source of beauty will be coiffure. *17*

Wives will abandon husbands when they lose their wealth, but will marry any man with money in this age. *18*

One who pays the biggest bribes gains mastery over men, and positions of nobility will derive from one's connections, not one's birth. *19*

One's concerns will be limited to one's home, one's wealth and chattels, and money will be squandered on amusements in the age of Kali. *20*

Women will be free and yoked to pleasure, while men will hanker after ill-gotten gains. *21*

Even when requested by a friend, a person will not give up one-eighth part of a farthing, brahmin.[1] *22*

Commoners regard themselves as equal to the brahmins in this age, and cows are only valued for their milk. *23*

All will live in fear of drought—the cause of famine—always looking at the sky. *24*

Wracked by drought and other troubles, they will starve themselves to death, eating roots and leaves and berries like ascetics. *25*

Always hungry, troubled and unprotected, they'll find no ease or pleasure in the age of Kali. *26*

They'll eat before they wash; sacred fires and gods and guests will not be tended; nor will they offer water to the ancestors when this age arrives. *27*

Women will be greedy, short and gluttonous, having few resources but many mouths to feed. *28*

Scratching their heads with both their hands, surly women will ignore the orders of their elders and their husbands. *29*

They'll be selfish, sullen, slovenly, abusive and untruthful in the Kali age. *30*

Even well-born women, drawn to wicked men, will be vulgar and depraved. *31*

Boys and the uninitiated will receive instruction in the Vedas, and householders will neither sacrifice nor make suitable donations. *32*

Ascetics in the forests will take the food of villagers, and mendicants will be bound by bonds of sentiment to family and friends. *33*

Kings will not protect their subjects, but, under the pretext of levying taxes, will plunder them like bandits when the age of Kali comes. *34*

Anyone rich in horses, chariots and elephants will be a monarch, and the weak will be their subjects at this time. *35*

Vaiśyas will leave their natural occupations in trade and farming and will take on roles of śūdras and live as artisans. *36*

The lowliest śūdras will take the vows of mendicants and, bearing outward signs of wandering monkhood, will lead a life of heresy, being unordained. *37*

1 *Paṇa*, or farthing, is the copper coin of least value.

Miserable people, gravely oppressed by the weight of tax and famine, will flee to lands still rich in wheat and barley. *38*

When the Vedic path has been abandoned and folk devote themselves to heresy, with the spread of vice, the people's lifespan will decrease. *39*

Folk will practise awesome penance not sanctioned by the scriptures, and infants will perish on account of the sovereign's sins. *40*

Girls will bear children at the age of five or six or seven with boys aged eight or nine or ten in the Kali age. *41*

The hair of youths will turn grey at twelve, and none will live past twenty. *42*

Since men are foolish, false and mean, they'll all die young in the age of Kali. *43*

Whenever a rise in heresy is noted, Maitreya, the wise infer the spread of Kali. *44*

Whenever pious men on the Vedic path grow fewer, the wise perceive the growth of Kali. *45*

When the endeavours of men who practise virtue vanish, then the rise of the age of Kali is inferred by the learned. *46*

When the lord of sacrifice, foremost being, is no longer honoured by men with offerings, the influence of this age can be discerned. *47*

When people find no joy in Vedic recitation but delight in heresy, best of brahmins, the wise infer the spread of Kali. *48*

During this period, Maitreya, people are seduced by heresies and no longer worship Viṣṇu, the universal lord, the master and creator of the world. *49*

Brahmin, those seduced by heresies exclaim, 'What do we care for gods or brahmins, the Vedas or ritual baths!' *50*

Parjanya will release few showers, brahmin, the crops will yield but little grain and fruit will have no substance when the Kali age begins. *51*

Most clothes will be made of flax, most trees will be *śamīs* and the people mostly śūdras. *52*

Most grain will be millet, most milk will come from goats when the age of Kali comes and massage oil will be made from *uśīra*-grass. *53*

One's in-laws will be honoured in preference to one's parents in the age of Kali, best of sages. One will befriend the brothers of one's wife, her kin and men with pretty wives. *54*

'What's a mother and what's a father, when one's role is shown by actions?' Such will be the view of those who regard their parents-in-law as their own. *55*

Constantly beset by sins of body, voice and mind, foolish folk will err each day. *56*

All that causes pain to false, impure and shameless men will flourish in the age of Kali. *57*

When Vedic recitation ceases and the cries of *vaṣaṭ*, *svadhā* and *svāhā* are heard no more, the world will be as if alone. *58*

In that world, one may, with little effort, earn a peerless store of merit, which, in the Kṛta age, would require much more austerity. *59*

So ends Chapter One in Book Six of the glorious Viṣṇu Purāṇa.

2. Vyāsa reveals the single virtue of the Kali age

Parāśara:

Hear me, fortunate sage, while I truthfully relate wise Vyāsa's words in this regard. *1*

There was once a debate among the seers about the age in which the smallest virtue gave the most reward, and by whom this could be achieved most easily. *2*

To put forward their uncertainties and dispel their doubts, the leading sages called on Vyāsa, the greatest seer and arranger of the Vedas. *3*

They saw my son, the blessed sage Veda-vyāsa, in the waters of the Gaṅgā, brahmin, performing his ablutions. *4*

Those great seers waited on the bank of that mighty river in a shady grove while Vyāsa finished washing. *5*

Rising from the waters of the river where he'd been bathing, my son Vyāsa cried, 'This age of Kali is the best! The very best!' Those sages heard his cry as he dived back underwater. *6*

When he emerged a second time, he shouted, 'Śūdra, you're the best. The very best! How fortunate you are!' *7*

Once more the sage immersed himself and, coming up again, he cried, 'Women are the best and luckiest. Who's luckier than them?' *8*

When my son had finished washing, duly rinsed his mouth and completed all the rites, those holy seers approached him with respect. *9*

They offered salutations and found themselves a seat. Vyāsa, son of Satyavatī, then asked them why they'd come. *10*

'We came to ask about some doubts,' they said, 'but let's forget all that. Now we want you to explain another matter. *11*

You just said the Kali age, a śūdra and a woman are the best, and stated that they're fortunate. *12*

We want to hear about this, sage, as long as it's not secret. Then we'll ask about the other thing that's on our mind.' *13*

Thus questioned by the sages, Vyāsa gave a laugh and said, 'Listen, best of seers, to why I said that they're the best. *14*

Merit that takes ten years to earn in the Kṛta age takes but a single year in the Tretā, a month in the Dvāpara and just a day in this age of Kali. *15*

The same applies to the rewards of austerity, the student's life of chastity, the recitation of mantras and so on, brahmins. That's why I said the Kali age is best. *16*

The rewards for meditating in the Kṛta, sacrificing in the Tretā and worshipping in the Dvāpara may all be won by merely adoring Keśava in the age of Kali. *17*

A person may experience a great increase in his merit with little effort in this age. That's why I delight in it, you sages who know virtue. *18*

The Vedas are adopted by the twice-born orders who've taken vows. They then perform the sacrifice with wealth acquired through communal duty as ordained by custom. *19*

Recitation, sacrificial feasts and offerings don't benefit those communities, and are always undertaken by self-restrained practitioners to their detriment.[2] *20*

2 This is a strange statement as it stands. The commentator explains that this is the case if the practices do not include the worship of Kṛṣṇa–Viṣṇu.

If these rites are not performed correctly, the doers incur iniquity from them all. Merely eating and drinking, brahmins, will not confer the outcome they desire. *21*

In all their undertakings, they're subject to the will of others, brahmins, and attain the realms ordained for them with difficulty. *22*

By serving the twice-born orders, a śūdra who oversees the offerings of food attains the realms ordained for him and is therefore luckier. *23*

Since there's no restriction for such a person on what he may or may not eat or drink, you tigers among sages, I say that he's the best.[3] *24*

The wealth that's won by men through constant obedience to communal duty should be placed in worthy hands or spent on sacrifice, as prescribed by custom. *25*

Great pains are undergone in earning and retaining wealth, you best of brahmins, and similarly, men know pain from its improper use. *26*

Enduring these and other challenges, men attain their proper realms, best of brahmins, such as that of Prajāpati and others, in order of their merit. *27*

A woman may attain the same realm as her husband, brahmins, merely by attending him with body, voice and mind. *28*

She's unlike the man who only wins such realms through great travails. That's the reason for my third remark, that women are the best. *29*

Now that I've explained all this to you, brahmins, feel free to ask the question that brought you here, and I'll duly answer.' *30*

Parāśara:

'The matter that we came to ask about,' the sages said, 'has been addressed most adequately in your response to our second question, sage.' *31*

Vyāsa Kṛṣṇa-Dvaipāyana the seer then laughed and addressed the gathered ascetics, whose eyes were wide with astonishment. *32*

'With divine insight, I perceived your question. That's why I said, "The best, the very best!" to you in that regard. *33*

Merit is achieved in the Kali age with little effort by those whose faults are washed away by the water of their own virtues: *34*

3 The idea seems to be that śūdras, who are not subject to dietary restrictions, can never be faulted for breaking dietary rules. This makes it easier for them to reach the heavenly realms designated for them.

By śūdras intent on serving the twice-born orders, best of sages, and similarly, by women with the simple task of waiting on their husbands. *35*

Hence, I regard these three as fortunate, as it's fraught for twice-born folk to win such merit in the Kṛta age and others. *36*

I've told you all you wished to hear, even before you brahmins who know virtue asked. What further may I do for you?' *37*

Parāśara:

The sages worshipped Vyāsa and praised him repeatedly, then departed as they'd come, their doubts dispelled by him. *38*

I've revealed to you this secret, lucky sage, the sole great virtue of the terrifying age of Kali. *39*

I'll now describe the destruction of the world you asked about, and the periodic breakdown of the elements. *40*

So ends Chapter Two in Book Six of the glorious Viṣṇu Purāṇa.

3. The causal dissolution at the end of every aeon

Parāśara:

It's thought that dissolution of creation is threefold: causal, elemental and final. *1*

Causal or Brāhma dissolution occurs at the end of every aeon. Elemental dissolution occurs after two *parārdhas*, and final dissolution is liberation from existence.[4] *2*

Maitreya:

Describe for me the duration of a *parārdha*, master, after two of which, elemental dissolution then occurs. *3*

4 A *kalpa* or aeon is one of Brahmā's days and two *parārdhas* constitute his entire lifespan. Liberation from existence, or *mokṣa*, is the highest goal of spiritual practice.

Parāśara:

Counting from one place to the next in the decimal system, brahmin, a *parārdha* is said to occupy the eighteenth place.[5] *4*

The dissolution that occurs after two *parārdhas* is elemental, brahmin. At that time, the Seen is absorbed into the Unseen, which is its ultimate cause. *5*

A *nimeṣa*—a blinking of the eye—is the length of a short syllable in the Sanskrit language. Fifteen *nimeṣas* make one *kāṣṭhā*, and thirty *kāṣṭhās* make a *kalā*.[6] *6*

A *nāḍikā* lasts for fifteen *kalās*. *7*

Measured with a water clock, a *nāḍikā* is also the time taken to fill a vessel made of twelve and a half *palas* of copper, having the capacity of one *prastha* of water (following the Magadhan system of measurement), with a hole in the bottom into which is inserted a tube made of four *māṣas* of gold, as long as four fingers are wide.[7] *8*

Two *nāḍikās* make one *muhūrta*, best of brahmins. There are thirty *muhūrtas* in one day and night, and thirty days in a month. *9*

There are twelve months in a year, which is one day and night for gods. Three hundred and sixty mortal years are one year for gods, the rivals of the demigods. *10*

One cycle of four ages takes twelve thousand divine years, and a thousand such cycles are said to be a day for Brahmā. *11*

One such day is one aeon or *kalpa*, during which fourteen Manus preside, great sage. At the end of each aeon, the causal or Brāhma dissolution of the world takes place, Maitreya. *12*

The nature of elemental dissolution is terrifying, Maitreya; now listen while I describe it for you. *13*

5 That is, 10^{18} or one million million million years.

6 The verses on units of time are virtually a repeat of verses 1.3.8 ff.

7 The root text is incomprehensible. My rendering—more an attempt at explanation than a translation—is a synthesis of a number of sources, including the two very lengthy Sanskrit commentaries and the prior attempts by my two brother translators and their respective footnotes. It seems that an empty vessel of known weight and volume with a tube of known weight and length inserted into its base is set in a larger container of water. The time taken for such a vessel to fill and sink is one *nāḍikā*. See also Fleet (1915).

At the end of a thousand cycles, when the earth is generally exhausted, there'll be a dreadful drought that lasts a hundred years. *14*

As a result, all living things on earth, lacking nourishment, proceed to their destruction, best of sages, driven by their suffering. *15*

Next, Kṛṣṇa, the eternal lord, appearing in the form of Rudra, will strive for the dissolution of all beings that abide within himself. *16*

Lord Viṣṇu, occupying seven solar rays, then imbibes the waters, best of sages. *17*

By absorbing all the moisture from the earth and living things, Maitreya, he desiccates the world. *18*

He'll destroy the oceans and the rivers, the mountains and their streams and the water found in Pātāla and other lower realms. *19*

Next, with his power, those seven rays, strengthened by the added water, give rise to seven suns. *20*

Blazing up and down, brahmin, those suns will burn the threefold worlds and all the lower realms. *21*

The threefold worlds, with mountains, seas and rivers, brahmin, being scorched by those blazing suns, will lose their moisture. *22*

When all the world is robbed of plants and water, brahmin, it resembles a tortoise shell. *23*

All-consuming Hari, appearing in the form of Rudra and the conflagration at the end of time, then becomes the serpent Śeṣa's scorching breath and burns the lower realms of Pātāla. *24*

When that blaze has burned those realms, it spreads up here and destroys all things upon the surface of the earth. *25*

A great, cruel whirling wreath of flames consumes the world, the atmospheric realms and heavens. *26*

All threefold worlds then glow like a griddle, ringed by swirling flames, deprived of lifeforms, mobile and immobile. *27*

Beset by heat, the residents of the upper realms, great sage, who are privileged to do so, then retreat to Maharloka. *28*

But when that realm becomes too hot for them, its denizens, fleeing for their lives and seeking somewhere higher, withdraw to Janaloka. *29*

When Janārdana in Rudra's form has burned the world, best of sages, the breath emerging from his mouth gives rise to clouds. *30*

These terrifying clouds, called Saṃvartakas, resembling herds of elephants, shedding bolts of lightning and roaring thunderously, arise above. *31*

Some are blue like *utpala* lilies, some glow white like *kumuda* flowers, some are grey as smoke and others yellow. *32*

Some are dun like donkeys, some are red as *lodh*-tree sap, some are blue as lazuli, others are green as emerald. *33*

Some are white as conch or jasmine flowers, some are black as kohl, some glow like fireflies and others are as red as arsenic. *34*

Some arise like mounds the hue of blue-jay feathers, some resemble splendid cities, others tower like mountains. *35*

Some rise up like roof-top dwellings, while others appear flat. Huge and rumbling, they fill the sky. *36*

Shedding mighty torrents, brahmin, they quell the dreadful fires that swept across the threefold worlds. *37*

They douse the flames, then pour down rain for a hundred years or more, best of sages, inundating this whole world. *38*

When all the earth is filled with raindrops as big as dice, the waters flood the atmospheric realm and then the heavens, brahmin. *39*

And when this whole dark universe with all things moving and unmoving has disappeared, those great clouds rain for yet another century. *40*

So ends Chapter Three in Book Six of the glorious Viṣṇu Purāṇa.

4. The elemental dissolution

Parāśara:

When they reach the dwelling of the Seven Sages, the waters cease to rise, great seer, and all this threefold universe becomes a single ocean. *1*

Wind born as breath from Viṣṇu's mouth dispels the clouds, Maitreya, and blows for yet another hundred years. *2*

The lord, who is all things, beyond all thought, creation's source, beginningless yet the origin of all, then absorbs the wind in its entirety. *3*

In the middle of that ocean, Lord Viṣṇu rests on Śeṣa as on a couch, then Hari, source of all, in Brahmā's form, reposes. *4*

Adored by Sanaka and other siddhas who withdrew to Janaloka, and contemplated by those who rose to Brahmaloka seeking liberation, *5*

Firm in heavenly *yoganidrā*, which emanates from his own illusion, the highest lord contemplates himself in the form called Vāsudeva. *6*

This is known as causal dissolution, Maitreya, because it's caused by Hari reposing in the form of Brahmā. *7*

When that universal being awakes, the world begins to stir and, when the everlasting god reclines upon his own bed of illusion, the whole world shuts its eyes. *8*

Just as one day for lotus-born Brahmā is a thousand cycles of ages, the night, when the world is submerged beneath the universal ocean, is of the same duration. *9*

When he wakes at the end of the night, Viṣṇu, the unborn being in the form of Brahmā, creates the world again, as I explained to you before. *10*

I've thus described the causal dissolution at the end of every aeon, brahmin. Now listen while I describe the elemental dissolution. *11*

After the onslaught of drought and fire, sage, when everything in all the worlds and the lower realms of Pātāla is under water, *12*

The elemental dissolution starts, in which the permutations of *mahat* and all the other basic elements are destroyed in accordance with the will of Kṛṣṇa. *13*

The waters swallow up the quality previously possessed by earth, the phenomenon of scent, and, when the element of earth is robbed of scent, it is destroyed. *14*

The earth without its fragrance is united with the waters. The rushing, roaring waters then increase. *15*

Filling all the world, the billowing floods spread fitfully across each realm on every side. *16*

The quality of taste imbuing water is then absorbed by the element of fire and, when that quality is lost, water is no more. *17*

When the waters lose their taste, they become one with fire and, when this happens, fire overtakes the world. *18*

When fire spreads in all directions, it consumes the waters, and this whole world is slowly filled with flames. *19*

When the universe above, below and on all sides is burned by fire, the element of air then swallows form, the ultimate quality of fire. *20*

When fire has been entirely reduced to air and the element of form destroyed, then light is deprived of form. *21*

Light grows dim and the element of air begins to tremble when the world is dark, and fire and air are one. *22*

Air, having reached the root that is its origin, shakes violently in all directions: above, below and on each side. *23*

Space then swallows touch, the property of air. Air grows still, and limitless space alone abides. *24*

Lacking form, taste, touch, scent and shape, space appears in pure immensity and fills the universe. *25*

Vacant and ubiquitous, it's characterised by the quality of sound. Consisting of sound alone, space is all-pervading. *26*

When the elements with sound and other qualities have been absorbed together, they're characterised by pride and dullness, it is thought. *27*

The elements and all the rest are swallowed by *mahat*, the element of Greatness, which is characterised by intellect. *28*

The earth and *mahat* form the inner and outer limits of the universe. *29*

Thus, the seven natural elements that arise from *mahābuddhi*, 'great intellect', all re-enter one another at the time of elemental dissolution. *30*

The cosmic egg is dissolved in the waters that surround it, along with the seven continents and oceans, the realms and mountain ranges. *31*

This sheath of water is then absorbed by fire; fire by air, and air by space. *32*

Mahat and other elements swallow space and the elemental state, *prakṛti*, absorbs *mahat*, along with all the elements, brahmin. *33*

When the qualities are in balance, neither too little nor too much, sage, it's called the elemental state, *prakṛti*, the origin, primal Nature, the highest cause. *34*

Thus, this entire elemental state is both Seen and Unseen, and the first is absorbed into the second, Maitreya. *35*

The singular, pure, immutable, eternal, ubiquitous primal Spirit, *puṃs*, is also an aspect of the universal highest Self, Maitreya. *36*

Concepts such as name and station don't apply to the universal lord, who should be understood as pure existence and who consists in knowledge and transcends the Self. *37*

This is *brahman*. This is the Absolute. This is the abode, the highest Self, the lord. This whole world is Viṣṇu, from whom the perfect sage does not return. *38*

Primal Nature, *prakṛti*, which I've described, manifest and unmanifest in form, and primal Spirit, *puruṣa*, are absorbed by the highest Self. *39*

This highest Self, foundation of the universe and highest lord, is hymned by name as Viṣṇu in the Vedas and their supplements. *40*

Sacrifice and renunciation are two forms of pious acts prescribed in Vedic texts. Through these two paths, men worship Viṣṇu in universal form. *41*

Following the paths of the *Ṛg*, *Yajur* and *Sāma Vedas*, the lord and spirit of the sacrifice, the highest spirit, is adored by men with sacrifices. *42*

Viṣṇu, who confers rewards of liberation and is at the heart of knowledge, is worshipped in the form of knowledge through the yoga of knowledge by ascetics on the path of renunciation. *43*

All that's named with short, long or extended syllables, and all that's beyond the reach of words, is eternal Viṣṇu.[8] *44*

He is Seen, Unseen, eternal Spirit, highest Self, universal Self and Hari of universal form. *45*

Primal Nature, consisting of the Seen and Unseen, and primal Spirit, Maitreya, are absorbed into that all-pervasive, unimpeded state. *46*

The period of two *parārdhas* that I described to you, Maitreya, is said to be a single day for Viṣṇu. *47*

When the Seen is absorbed into primal Nature, and Nature is absorbed in Spirit, and Spirit is absorbed in that supreme being, then there is another period, a night, which is of the same duration as one of Viṣṇu's days, great sage. *48*

8 Syllables in Sanskrit are short, long or, very rarely, 'prolated', and are held for one, two or three beats, respectively.

There is, in fact, no day or night for the everlasting highest being, brahmin. It's just a way of speaking of the lord. *49*

Thus, I've described the dissolution of the elements for you, Maitreya. Now you'll hear about the final dissolution, brahmin. *50*

So ends Chapter Four in Book Six of the glorious Viṣṇu Purāṇa.

5. The final dissolution and the nature of suffering

Parāśara:

The wise person who understands three kinds of worldly suffering, including pain arising from within, Maitreya, and in whom spiritual knowledge and dispassion have arisen, will attain the final dissolution. *1*

Pain arising internally is of two kinds, affecting both the body and the mind. Bodily afflictions are divided into many classes. Listen to these: *2*

Headaches, colds, fever, gout, fistula, spleen, haemorrhoids, asthma, tumours, vomiting and many others. *3*

There are also diseases of the eye, dysentery and leprosy. This is how bodily afflictions are classified. Now hear about afflictions of the mind. *4*

Desire, anger, fear, hatred, greed, delusion, depression, grief, envy, contempt, jealousy, selfishness and other emotions— *5*

There are many such mental afflictions, best of brahmins. These are the classes of suffering arising from within. *6*

Wild animals, birds and other people, flesh-eating piśāca demons, serpents and rākṣasas, as well as snakes and insects—these living things may bring harm to people. *7*

I shall also mention suffering inflicted by natural forces, including cold, heat, wind, rain, floods and lightning, most excellent of brahmins. *8*

The sufferings arising in pregnancy, birth, old age, ignorance, death and hell are divided into myriad classes, best of sages. *9*

The tender-bodied embryo in the womb is surrounded by filth, wrapped in a caul, with its back, neck and bones hunched over. *10*

The suffering of the growing foetus is heightened by discomfort caused by acidic, pungent, sharp, hot and salty foods eaten by its mother. *11*

Unable to stretch or bend its limbs and lying in a mire of excrement and urine, it's afflicted on all sides. *12*

It cannot breathe but is conscious and, recalling earlier births by the hundred, it waits in the womb amid great suffering, bound by deeds performed in previous lives. *13*

As it's being born, its face is smeared with faeces, urine, blood and semen, and its bones and sinews wracked by labour pains. *14*

Upside down, it's squeezed from the womb by strong and painful contractions and is beset by woe. *15*

The infant is deprived of earlier memories when it breathes the air outside, best of brahmins, and is born in ignorance. *16*

As if its limbs are pricked by thorns or hacked with saws, it falls to the ground like a maggot from a foetid wound. *17*

Unable even to scratch itself, the infant lies in a helpless state, dependent on the will of others for washing, food and drink. *18*

Lying on a dirty rug, the babe is bitten by mosquitoes, bugs and other pests, and cannot fend them off. *19*

Many are the earthly pains attending birth, and many are those which follow them in childhood. *20*

Shrouded in ignorance and dullness, and filled with delusion, the individual knows not whence he came, who he is, whither he will go or his own nature. *21*

He knows not the bonds that bind him, what's a cause and what is not, what's to be done and what is not, what's to be said and what is not, *22*

What is virtue and what is not, where virtue exists and why, what is duty and what is not and what is good and what is not. *23*

Thus, deluded individuals, obsessed with their own penis and their stomach, are no better than the animals and endure great suffering born of ignorance. *24*

Ignorance is a state of dullness, brahmin, because of which unknowing beings, who should engage in sacrifice, neglect such acts. *25*

Great sages have declared that hell is the consequence of neglected worship. As a result, the ignorant suffer greatly in this life and the next. *26*

When a man's body is old and frail, his limbs grow weak, his teeth are loose or missing and sinews, veins and wrinkles cover him, *27*

He can't see far but stares blankly, hairs sprout from his nostrils and he's wracked by tremors. *28*

His bones stick out, his back is bent, his joints are swollen, he eats little as digestion fails and he hardly moves at all. *29*

It's hard for him to walk or rise, lie or sit or move; his eyes and ears grow weak; he dribbles down his chin. *30*

All his senses fail as he approaches death, and he forgets events as soon as they have happened. *31*

When he has to repeat himself, he's overcome with weariness, but the dreadful strain of drawing breath and coughing robs him of his sleep. *32*

When a man is old, others must help him up, and others dress him, but his servants, sons and wife all mock him. *33*

He cannot clean himself, yet still craves food and other pleasures. His attendants laugh at him and all his kin ignore him. *34*

Recalling exploits of his younger days as if they happened in another lifetime, he sighs deeply and is troubled. *35*

Having endured the woes of dotage, now hear about the torments met in death. *36*

His neck, fingers and hands hang loose and his body begins to twitch. One minute, he lies limp and tired, the next, he seems to wake a little. *37*

Remembering the things he owns, he frets about his gold, stores, sons, wives, servants, houses and all the rest. *38*

His bones and joints are wracked by stabbing pains of Death's sharp arrows, which rip his vital organs like cruel saws. *39*

His eyes roll back, his hands and feet convulse, his palate, lips and tongue are dry, then the rattle of death is heard. *40*

His throat is blocked by floods of morbid humours and breath is laboured. Afflicted by great suffering, thirst and hunger torment him. *41*

Overwhelmed by pain as Yama's minions goad him, he dies, only then to receive another body to be tortured in the realms of hell. *42*

The living endure these and other frightful pains at the time of death. Now listen to the torments that the dead will meet there. *43*

Caught in the noose of Yama's servants and struck with rods, they must bear the fearful sight of the Lord of Death as they face the terrible road to hell. *44*

In that realm of frightful burning sands, fires, machines, weapons and the rest are found each kind of hellish torment, brahmin, so difficult to endure. *45*

Hacked with saws, cooked in pots, chopped with axes, buried in the ground, *46*

Impaled on stakes, eaten by tigers, torn by vultures, devoured by leopards, *47*

Boiled in oil, drowned in slime, dropped from heights, thrown from catapults— *48*

The torments they endure in hell, arising from their own misdeeds and administered by the denizens of that realm, brahmin, are innumerable. *49*

But hell is not the only place of pain, best of brahmins. In heaven, too, a being is never free from the fear of falling to a lower realm. *50*

There he will be conceived, only to be born once more. Leaving the womb and entering the world again, he's destined for another death. *51*

He may die an infant or in childhood, as a youth or adult or in his dotage, but death is certain. *52*

While he lives, he's beset by varied troubles, like a cotton seed amid a mass of fibres before they're spun as thread. *53*

Winning, keeping and losing wealth all bring woe to men, as do the pains of those we love. *54*

Each thing that brings us joy, Maitreya, becomes the seed of a tree of pain. *55*

Wives, sons, friends, possessions, houses, fields, wealth and all the rest cause more trouble than the joy they yield. *56*

Vāsudeva as the antidote to suffering

Where may those whose hearts are thus tormented by scorching rays of worldly pain seek shelter, other than the shade of the tree of liberation? *57*

The wise therefore hold that the antidote for this threefold suffering arising in the womb—birth, old age and the other states of life— *58*

Is complete and final union with the lord, which alone is marked by a state of bliss and eclipses every other joy. *59*

That's why the wise should strive for him. Knowledge and sacrifice are said to be the means for doing so, great sage. *60*

They say that knowledge is twofold, arising from scripture and from reflection. Scripture consists of the Absolute in the form of the Word, but the highest form of the Absolute is born of meditation. *61*

Just as the sun dispels the deepest darkness, wise brahmin, so, too, does knowledge gained through the senses and born of meditation shine like a lamp on ignorance. *62*

Manu himself relayed the import of the Vedas as he recalled it, best of sages. Now listen as I repeat what he said in this regard. *63*

Two forms of the Absolute are to be recognised: the Word and the Supreme. One well versed in the former may reach the highest state of the latter. *64*

The *Atharva Veda* also describes two forms of knowledge. By means of the higher, one attains the imperishable state, while the other consists of the *Ṛg* and other Vedas. *65*

That which is unmanifest, unageing, inconceivable, unborn, undecaying, indescribable, formless, lacking hands and feet and other features *66*

Is the universal, eternal lord, the uncaused source of all creation, the all-pervading but unpervaded origin of everything—it's this the sages see. *67*

This is the Absolute, Supreme, the abode to be contemplated by those who yearn for liberation. Subtle, but alluded to by words of sacred scripture, it's the highest state of Viṣṇu. *68*

The word 'blessed'—*bhagavant*—is also a form of the Supreme, and is the means of expressing the primal, eternal being.[9] *69*

9 The word *bhagavat* literally means 'possessing fortune'. It is a common epithet used for Viṣṇu–Kṛṣṇa in the *Viṣṇu Purāṇa* and for other major deities and sages. I have consistently but reluctantly translated it as 'lord' or occasionally as 'blessed'. The following verses only become intelligible if this word is left untranslated.

One who truly grasps the import of this expression will comprehend the other form of knowledge embodied in the Vedas. *70*

The term *bhagavat* is used to worship that form of the Absolute, brahmin, which lies beyond the reach of words. *71*

Therefore, Maitreya, it's used to express the pure, supreme Absolute, known as the almighty, the cause of the cause of everything. *72*

The syllable *bha* implies the two meanings of maintainer (*saṃbhartṛ*) and protector (*bhartṛ*), sage, while the syllable *ga* signifies the leader, driver (*gamayitṛ*) and creator. *73*

The syllables *bha* and *ga* express six qualities: supremacy over all, power, glory, majesty, knowledge and asceticism. *74*

Va implies all creatures dwell (*vasanti*) in the universal being at the heart of all creation, and that the everlasting deity dwells in all. *75*

Thus, this great word *bhagavat* applies to the highest Absolute, Vāsudeva and nothing else, you peerless sage. *76*

In this context, the term implies a state of reverence. It has a special expressive function and is not figurative, but in other contexts, it may be so. *77*

One who understands the beginning of creation and its end, the right way and its opposite and knowledge and its absence may be called a *bhagavat*, a blessed one. *78*

In the former instance, the term denotes wisdom, energy, strength, supremacy, power and brilliance without remainder, and the absence of any negative traits. *79*

As all beings dwell in the highest being and the universal being dwells in them, he is known as Vāsudeva. *80*

This is how in former times Keśidhvaja, when asked about eternal Vāsudeva's name, accurately explained it to Khāṇḍikya Janaka: *81*

Because he abides in beings and they abide in him, the creator and disposer of the worlds is Lord Vāsudeva. *82*

He transcends the nature of all creation, sage, its transformations and all its qualities, good and bad. He's beyond all limits and is at the heart of everything. All space in the world is filled by him. *83*

He is at the heart of all blessings and goodness, and accomplishes the creation of all beings with a mere fraction of his ability. He assumes an expansive form at will, and showers benefits on all the world. *84*

He is the sole store of energy, power, supremacy, perception, might, strength and other qualities. Higher than the highest, no faults exist in the all-inclusive lord. *85*

He is sovereign, one but many, unmanifest yet visible, lord of all, all-seeing, all-knowing, all-powerful and is called the highest master. *86*

That by which he's known, beheld or understood is faultless, pure, supreme, unsullied, uniform spiritual knowledge. All else is ignorance. *87*

So ends Chapter Five in Book Six of the glorious Viṣṇu Purāṇa.

6. Khāṇḍikya and his cousin Keśidhvaja

Parāśara:

The highest spirit may be perceived through Vedic recitation and through yoga. That's why the Absolute, the means of attaining that state, is described by the formula 'It is this—*tad etat*'. *1*

After recitation, one should practise yoga, and, after yoga, recitation. Through excellence in both, the highest spirit manifests. *2*

Vedic recitation is one eye with which to see the lord, and yoga is the other, as the Absolute lies beyond the bodily eye. *3*

Maitreya:

Speak on yoga, master, as I wish to understand it. When I comprehend that, I may be able to perceive the highest lord, foundation of the universe. *4*

Parāśara:

I'll describe yoga to you, great sage, just as Keśidhvaja explained it to Khāṇḍikya Janaka in former times. *5*

Maitreya:

Who was Khāṇḍikya, brahmin, and who was Keśidhvaja? How did their talk of yoga come about? *6*

Parāśara:

Janaka Dharmadhvaja had one son, Amitadhvaja, and another named Kṛtadhvaja, a king who constantly found joy in the highest spirit. *7*

Kṛtadhvaja had a son named Keśidhvaja, brahmin. Amitadhvaja's son was Khāṇḍikya Janaka. *8*

Khāṇḍikya excelled on the path of ritual action and was skilled in worldly matters, but Keśidhvaja was an expert in spiritual knowledge. *9*

These two, however, both wished to usurp the other, and Keśidhvaja deprived Khāṇḍikya of his kingdom. *10*

Driven from his realm, Khāṇḍikya wandered in the jungle, where travel is not easy, accompanied by his priest and ministers but taking little else. *11*

He still conducted sacrifices, but, lacking true spiritual insight, he hoped in his ignorance to gain knowledge of the Absolute and escape from death thereby. *12*

One day, Keśidhvaja was engaged in yoga when a fearsome tiger killed his dairy-cow in a trackless forest, you yoga expert. *13*

Hearing that his cow was dead, the king then asked his priests about atonement. *14*

'We don't know,' they said, 'but you should question Kaśeru.' The king then asked that sage, who gave the scion of Bhṛgu the same reply: *15*

'I don't know, your majesty, but ask Śunaka. He's an expert in such things.' The king then went to Śunaka and asked him, sage, and Śunaka replied, 'Listen: *16*

Neither Kaśeru, nor I, nor any other man on earth at present knows the answer. The only one who truly knows is your rival Khāṇḍikya whom you've vanquished.' *17*

The king replied to Śunaka, 'I'll go and ask my enemy, sage, and even if he kills me, I'll obtain the reward of sacrifice. *18*

On the other hand, if I ask him and he tells me how to make amends, then my yoga practice will be unimpaired, best of sages.' *19*

Parāśara:

So saying, the king, dressed like an ascetic in a black antelope hide, mounted his chariot and entered the forest where wise Khāṇḍikya camped. *20*

When Khāṇḍikya saw his enemy approaching, his eyes grew red with fury and, nocking an arrow to his bow, he said, *21*

Khāṇḍikya:

You attack me with a deer skin as protection, and you think I won't fight back because I'm wearing the same thing! *22*

But tell me, fool, isn't this the hide from the back of an antelope that you and I both killed with our deadly sharpened arrows? *23*

I'm going to kill you now. You'll not escape alive. You, the foolish thief who stole my realm, are now my enemy! *24*

Keśidhvaja:

I've come to ask a question, Khāṇḍikya, not to fight you, so set aside your anger. Put down that arrow. *25*

Parāśara:

Wise Khāṇḍikya then consulted all his ministers and priests in private. *26*

'Now your rival's in your power you should kill him,' his advisors said. 'If you do so this whole world is yours.' *27*

'It's surely true,' Khāṇḍikya said, 'that once he's dead the world is mine. *28*

But victory in the next world will be his, even if this world belongs to me. If I forbear to kill him, I'll win in the afterlife, and he can have this mundane realm. *29*

Victory in the next world is eternal, but victory here is fleeting. I'll therefore spare the man and listen to his question.' *30*

Parāśara:

Khāṇḍikya Janaka approached his adversary and said, 'Ask me all you wish to say, and I'll reply.' *31*

Keśidhvaja told him that his cow had died, brahmin, and asked how he should make amends. *32*

Khāṇḍikya then described to Keśidhvaja the atonement to be performed in full, brahmin, according to the law. *33*

Now that great Khāṇḍikya understood Keśidhvaja's intention, he granted him permission to proceed to the sacrificial ground, where he duly undertook the rites. *34*

When King Keśidhvaja had carried out the rituals in the proper order and according to the law, and performed the requisite purification afterwards, he'd done his duty, but then he thought, *35*

'I've worshipped all the priests and honoured the assembled officiants. Similarly, I've satisfied the desires of all who wanted something. *36*

I've behaved appropriately towards everybody here, so why's my heart not satisfied with this sacrifice?' *37*

Reflecting thus, he realised that he hadn't paid Khāṇḍikya his sacrificial fee, the *guru-dakṣiṇā*. *38*

Mounted on his chariot, the king returned to the trackless wood, Maitreya, where Khāṇḍikya resided. *39*

When Khāṇḍikya saw the king returning, he raised his bow and stood intent on killing him, but Keśidhvaja spoke again: *40*

'I haven't come to fight, Khāṇḍikya, so don't be angry. Understand I'm here to make the payment due to you as guru. *41*

I've completed all the rituals as instructed, and I wish to compensate you, so name your fee.' *42*

Parāśara:

King Khāṇḍikya consulted with his ministers once more, saying, 'He wants to pay a fee, so how much should I ask for?' *43*

'You should ask for your whole realm back again,' the ministers replied. 'Skilful men win sovereignty without deploying arms.' *44*

Wise King Khāṇḍikya laughed at them and said, 'Why would such a man as me request a fleeting earthly kingdom? *45*

You provide advice for handling mundane matters but know nothing of the highest truth or how it may be reached.' *46*

Parāśara:

Having spoken thus, Khāṇḍikya went to King Keśidhvaja, asking, 'Do you truly wish to pay the *guru-dakṣiṇā*?' *47*

'Indeed, I do,' was his reply. Khāṇḍikya then said, 'You're well-versed in spiritual knowledge and highest truth. *48*

If you wish to pay my fee, then say what acts are able to dispel my misery?' *48*

So ends Chapter Six in Book Six of the glorious Viṣṇu Purāṇa.

7. Keśidhvaja instructs Khāṇḍikya in yoga

Keśidhvaja:

Why didn't you demand my kingdom, free from impositions? Nothing is dearer to kṣatriyas than winning sovereignty. *1*

Khāṇḍikya:

Understand, Keśidhvaja, why I didn't request your realm, which an unwise person might desire. *2*

It's the duty of all kṣatriyas to defend their subjects and to slay in righteous battles those who challenge their authority. *3*

It wasn't wrong of you to seize the kingdom from me, when I was unable to defend it. I've now set aside such ignorance that merely tied me down. *4*

My desire for sovereignty was the product of my birth, my lust and greed, not the fault of another man, and was a bar to virtue. *5*

Wise men think it's wrong for kṣatriyas to ask for gifts. That's why I didn't foolishly request the realm. *6*

Unwise men whose hearts are carried off by a sense of self, drunk with pride, crave sovereignty—not men like me! *7*

Parāśara:

King Keśidhvaja was delighted. 'Excellent!' he cried and said to Khāṇḍikya Janaka with affection: 'Listen to what I say. *8*

On account of ignorance, I wanted to escape from death, so I ruled the kingdom and undertook many sacrifices, but I squandered merit in enjoyments. *9*

You're lucky that your heart was drawn to the power of contemplation. Now listen, pride of our family, to the nature of ignorance. *10*

The error that the self consists in something that's not the self, and what is not one's own is indeed one's own, is the twofold seed from which grows the tree of ignorance. *11*

The ignorant embodied being, who occupies a body composed of fivefold elements, bewildered by the darkness of delusion, stridently proclaims this view: "I am this body." *12*

The self is different from space, air, fire, water and earth, so who'd maintain that it exists within the body? *13*

As the self is not an aspect of the body, what wise person thinks he owns his house, his fields and other things, when these can only be enjoyed through bodily means? *14*

Similarly, as the self is not an aspect of the body, what thoughtful man regards his sons and grandsons arising from his body as his own? *15*

Every act a person undertakes is to satisfy the body, but if the spirit and the body are distinct, then everything that he regards as vital will further bind him. *16*

Just as a house that's built of clay is plastered with a mix of clay and water, in that same way, the body, which consists of earth, is kept alive with earth and water.[10] *17*

If a person's body, consisting of five elements, is sustained by food of these same elements, then what has that person to be proud of? *18*

Trudging on the worldly path of a thousand births, he's wearied by delusion and cloaked in the dust of yearning. *19*

Washing off that dust in the warming bath of knowledge, he sheds the weariness of delusion gathered on saṃsāra's roads. *20*

When fatigue is at an end, his heart grows light and he attains supreme nirvāṇa, matchless and transcending pain. *21*

The self entails the pure state of nirvāṇa and embodies wisdom. The blemishes of suffering and ignorance mark the natural world, but not the self. *22*

Water in a pot takes heat from the fire beneath it, without contact with the flames, even as it boils and bubbles, sage. *23*

Similarly, the self, interacting with the natural world and corrupted by egoism and pride, manifests properties of that world, even though it's separate and unchanging. *24*

That's why I say that it is the seed of ignorance and, apart from yoga, there is no antidote for suffering.[11] *25*

10 One of the commentators suggests that 'earth' and 'water' stand for food and drink.

11 As will become apparent in the following verses, yoga in this context refers to spiritual union with the divine accomplished through meditation.

Khāṇḍikya:

Then describe that yoga, fortunate king. In the lineage of Nimi, you're thought to be an expert on the subject, as you grasp the sense of all the relevant treatises. *26*

Keśidhvaja:

Listen, Khāṇḍikya, and I'll explain the reality of yoga. A sage established in this practice, having reached the state of the Absolute, will never fall from it again. *27*

A man's mind is the cause of both his bondage and his liberation. Attachment to the objects of the senses causes bondage, while freedom from attachment leads to liberation. *28*

Having withdrawn the mind from the objects of the senses, the knowledgeable sage should contemplate the highest lord, the Absolute, to accomplish liberation. *29*

The Absolute attracts the being who shares its nature and contemplates that state, sage, just as a magnet, made of iron, has the power to attract the same material. *30*

The particular mental exercise, undertaken through one's own endeavour, and during which the union with the Absolute is felt, is known as 'yoga'. *31*

A practitioner whose yoga is marked by performance of the highest excellence in this regard is said to occupy the cusp of liberation. *32*

A practitioner who begins to master himself in this way is said to be disciplined through yoga, and one who has attained the supreme Absolute is said to have accomplished *samādhi*, or perfect union. *33*

If the heart of the former has been sullied by faults, then he will experience liberation after practising yoga during further lifetimes. *34*

A practitioner who has accomplished *samādhi* will achieve liberation in his own lifetime, as his accumulated karma is soon consumed in the fire of yoga. *35*

The practitioner should embrace chastity, nonviolence, truth, honesty and poverty, while remaining free from desire and directing his mind towards its proper object. *36*

The self-restrained individual should undertake study, purity, contentment and austerity, while bending his mind towards the highest Absolute. *37*

These five, known as the major and minor observances, respectively, offer great rewards to those who want them, but result in liberation for those who are free from yearning. *38*

Imbued with these qualities, and adopting a posture such as *bhadrāsana*,[12] the self-restrained practitioner should discipline himself by means of the ten previously mentioned observances. *39*

After repeated practice, he supresses the flow of air called *prāṇa* with breath control or *prāṇāyāma*, either with a seed or without one. *40*

By means of the twofold practice of alternately controlling the airflows of *prāṇa* and *apāna*—inhalation and exhalation—a third form of control arises from the suppression of both of these. *41*

The foundation for most individuals is gross form, best of brahmins, but for one who practises yoga, the foundation is the infinite deity. *42*

Having withdrawn the sense organs from sensations such as sound to which they are attracted, one who knows yoga should focus on mental activities, intent on curbing senses. *43*

By this practice, a state of supreme control arises even for those whose minds are fickle, but if the senses are untamed, the practitioner will remain unable to reach union. *44*

With breath controlled through *prāṇāyāma*, and senses curbed by the practice of withdrawal, one may set one's steadied mind on the perfect refuge. *45*

Khāṇḍikya:

Tell me, fortunate king, what's the perfect refuge for the mind, on which basis every source of blemish is destroyed? *46*

Keśidhvaja:

The refuge of the mind is the Absolute, and it's twofold, sire: formed and formless, or primary and secondary. *47*

Realisation of this refuge is threefold, your majesty. You must understand all this: that which is called the Absolute, that which is known as action and that which consists of both. *48*

12 Authorities disagree on the definitions of this posture, but all are variations on sitting cross-legged.

Realisation in the form of action is one; that marked by the Absolute is another; and that marked by both is the third. Hence, realisation is threefold. *49*

Sanandana and other sages reached realisation of the refuge marked by the Absolute. The deities and other beings, both mobile and immobile, achieved realisation marked by action. *50*

For Brahmā, born of the golden egg, and other deities, knowing their responsibilities, realisation is twofold and is marked by both Absolute and action. *51*

Until all knowledge and action directed towards differentiation have ceased, for those who see distinctions, all the world is one thing and spirit is another, your majesty. *52*

Realisation that is free from differentiation is pure existence, is beyond the reach of words and is to be comprehended as the Self; this is called the Absolute. *53*

This is the supreme, unborn, unchanging form of formless Viṣṇu, the highest spirit, marked by ubiquity and diversity. *54*

Since the practitioner cannot contemplate that form, your majesty, one should meditate on the physical form of Hari that lies within the reach of all. *55*

Lord Brahmā, Indra, chief of Vasus and protector of his subjects, the Maruts, Vasus, Rudras, the suns, the stars and planets, *56*

Gandharvas, yakṣas, Daityas and all other creatures of divine origin, humans, animals, mountains, oceans, trees and rivers, *57*

All beings, your majesty, and those which are the cause of beings, beginning with primal Matter and ending with differentiated entities, sentient and insentient, *58*

One-footed, two-footed, many-footed and footless—all these are manifest forms of Hari to be apprehended by three kinds of realisation. *59*

All this, the entire world of mobile and immobile things, is filled with Viṣṇu's energy in the form of the highest Absolute. *60*

This energy of Viṣṇu is said to be primary. That energy which is called consciousness, *kṣetrajña*, is secondary. That which is known as ignorance or action is called energy of the third kind. *61*

On account of the all-embracing and omnipresent energy of consciousness, your majesty, one undergoes all kinds of worldly sufferings in succession. *62*

And because it's obscured by that third force, the energy known as consciousness is observed to a greater or lesser degree in creatures, sire. *63*

In unliving things, it's very weak. In living things that do not move, it's a little stronger. In those that creep or slither it's stronger still, and stronger yet again in those with wings. *64*

It's stronger in wild animals than in birds, and stronger again in domesticated beasts. It's stronger yet in humans than in animals. That's why we have mastery over them. *65*

It's stronger in nāgas, gandharvas, yakṣas and other divine beings than in humans, sire. *66*

In mighty Indra, protector of his subjects, it's stronger than in all the other deities. Brahmā is also set apart by a greater share of energy than mortal men. *67*

All these are forms of Viṣṇu, sire, since they're pervaded by his energy, as by ether. *68*

The second state of the being known as Viṣṇu on which practitioners of yoga meditate, great sage, is the shapeless form of the Absolute, called by the wise 'the existent'. *69*

All those energies are established in it, sire; it's a form of the universal being and is the other great form of Hari. *70*

It brings forth, as if in sport, deities, animals, humans and other living things, all of which are forms of his energy, your majesty. *71*

This all-pervading, uninterrupted activity of the immeasurable deity is for the benefit of the worlds and does not arise for the sake of action. *72*

One disciplined through yoga should contemplate that form of the universal being, sire, to purify himself, as it expunges all iniquity. *73*

Just as fire with leaping flames burns a dried-out thicket when fanned by wind, so does Viṣṇu abiding in ascetics' hearts destroy their sins. *74*

One should therefore fix one's mind on the basis of all forms of energy, a technique known as pure *dhāraṇā*, or 'holding'. *75*

It's the perfect place for one's own mind and for the universal being. It lies beyond the three modes of realisation and is attained by ascetics for their liberation, sire. *76*

The minds of others find no refuge, tiger of a man. The deities and all other imperfect beings come into existence as the result of actions. *77*

The manifest form of the lord has no desire for any other refuge. This meditation is called 'holding' because the mind retains this very image. *78*

Now you'll hear about the form of Hari to contemplate, your majesty. In the absence of such a basis, holding is impossible: *79*

A lovely, pleasing face, eyes like lotus petals, smooth cheeks, a broad and brilliant forehead, *80*

His well-matched ears with finest earrings hanging from their lobes, a neck as white as conch-shell, while his broad chest bears Śrīvatsa. *81*

His belly with its deep navel is crossed by three graceful folds. His long arms are either four or eight in number. *82*

His strong legs are well-formed, and his lotus-like feet and hands are shapely. One should meditate on this form of Viṣṇu, the Absolute being, clad in garments of pure yellow. *83*

Adorned with diadem, lovely armlets, bracelets and other jewellery, *84*

Holding bow and conch, mace and sword, prayer beads and discus—the ascetic, who himself consists of Viṣṇu, should contemplate this form with a focused mind. *85*

As long as he maintains the practice of *dhāraṇā*, your majesty, while walking, standing or doing anything he likes, if this image never leaves his heart, he may regard the practice as perfected. *86*

Next, the wise person may meditate on the lord in tranquil form, without the conch or sword, bow or discus or other items, holding only prayer beads. *87*

When this state of *dhāraṇā* is stable, he should visualise the image without the diadem, armlets and other ornaments. *88*

Then the wise man should set his mind on the deity with a single limb. Next he should meditate on the body to which that limb belongs. *89*

A single mental image of Viṣṇu's form, stable and unbroken, is known as *dhyāna*, or 'meditation', and is reached in six initial stages, sire. *90*

When this heavenly form is borne in mind, free from other thoughts, as a result of meditation, that state is known as *samādhi*. *91*

If the highest Absolute is to be achieved, your majesty, then knowledge will enable it. Similarly, the Self is reached when all other forms of realisation are exhausted. *92*

Consciousness *has* the means, while knowledge *is* the means by which one reaches liberation. When liberation has been reached, the role of knowledge has been fulfilled and is no more. *93*

When the individual self reaches the realisation of its true nature, then it becomes one with the supreme Absolute, no longer divided from it. The separation of the two is caused by ignorance. *94*

When ignorance that gives rise to difference is finally transcended, who would distinguish between the Absolute and the self, when such distinction does not exist? *95*

I've described yoga to you, Khāṇḍikya, as requested, part in brief and part in full. What else may I do for you? *96*

Khāṇḍikya:

Now that the reality of yoga has been explained, you've done everything for me. All impurities in my mind have been removed through your instruction. *97*

The word 'mine', which I've used so often, is a lie. Those who know what must be known can't say otherwise, your majesty. *98*

'I' and 'mine' are forms of ignorance that dictate daily conduct. The highest goal can't be described, as it's beyond the scope of words. *99*

Go now, for all you've done is for my benefit, Keśidhvaja, as you've described eternal yoga, which leads to liberation. *100*

Parāśara:

King Keśidhvaja received due homage from Khāṇḍikya, brahmin, then returned to his own capital. *101*

Khāṇḍikya gave his kingdom to his son and retreated to the forest with his heart set on Govinda to perfect his yoga practice. *102*

There, delighting in this single quest and purified by virtues such as self-restraint, the king achieved absorption in the purest Absolute in the form that's known as Viṣṇu. *103*

Keśidhvaja turned his back on his responsibilities and indulged his senses, but still performed the rituals without attachment to the outcome to accomplish liberation. *104*

In spite of worldly pleasures, he was cleansed of all his sins and, being purified, brahmin, achieved that perfection which results in the destruction of all suffering. *105*

So ends Chapter Seven in Book Six of the glorious Viṣṇu Purāṇa.

8. The benefits of listening to the *Viṣṇu Purāṇa*

Parāśara:

I've thus described in full the third and final kind of dissolution: liberation as absorption in the everlasting Absolute. *1*

I've told you all about the first and subsequent creations, the lineages of the patriarchs, the periods of the Manus and the deeds of the royal dynasties. *2*

This imperishable Vaiṣṇava purāṇa, which sweeps away all sins, is the first among all sacred texts as a path to reach the goals of human life. *3*

I've duly related this everlasting scripture to you, Maitreya, as you wished to hear it. What else should I speak about? Ask me now, and I'll respond. *4*

Maitreya:

Master, you've told me all I asked about. I've listened with devotion, sage, and have no further questions. *5*

All my doubts have been dispelled and now my mind is clear. Through your kindness, I understand the origin, state and conclusion of the world. *6*

I understand Viṣṇu's fourfold nature and his threefold energy, guru, and I comprehend completely the threefold nature of realisation. *7*

I understand all this as the product of your kindness. What use is further knowledge, brahmin, when the universe and Viṣṇu are but one? *8*

I've reached my goal and have no further doubts, thanks to your mercy, sage, as now I fully understand the duties of all four orders and other practices. *9*

I understand completely the sacrificial and meditative modes of pious life. Be merciful, best of brahmins. I have nothing more to ask. *10*

Forgive me for troubling you to relate all this, guru, but the wise make no distinction between a student and a son. *11*

Parāśara:

This purāṇa which I've relayed to you is the equal of the Vedas. By hearing it, the sins amassed from faults of every kind will be dispelled. *12*

I've told you all about the first and subsequent creations of the world, the lineages, Manvantaras and dynastic histories. *13*

I've spoken of the deities, Daityas, gandharvas, nāgas, rākṣasas, yakṣas, vidyādharas, siddhas and apsarases. *14*

I've described the purest sages imbued with ascetic energy, the fourfold social system, men of uncommon feats, *15*

Hallowed places on this fertile earth, holy seas and rivers, sacred mountains and the exploits of the wise, *16*

Traditions such as those that govern the four communities and all about the schools of Vedic learning. Hearing this, one is freed at once from all misdeeds. *17*

I've described Lord Hari, the universal everlasting cause of creation, preservation and destruction of the world, who abides at the heart of everything. *18*

By calling his name, even unintentionally, all one's sins are scattered in an instant, like frightened deer fleeing from a lion. *19*

When a person speaks his name with faith, he is completely purified, Maitreya, just as fire refines the ores of minerals. *20*

The moment Viṣṇu is called to mind, the awful faults of the Kali age, which lead folk to infernal grief, are ended. *21*

Brahmā, born of the golden egg, Indra king of gods, Rudra, Āditya, the Aśvins, Vāyu, the Fires, the Vasus, the Sādhyas, the Viśvedevas and other gods, *22*

The yakṣas, rākṣasas, nāgas, siddhas, Daityas, gandharvas, Dānavas, apsarases, stars, constellations and all the planets, *23*

The Seven Sages, the quarters of the sky and their protectors, brahmins and other mortals, animals of farm and forest, *24*

Those that creep and crawl, those that course the sky, *palāśa* trees and other plants that grow upon the earth, forests, mountains, oceans, rivers, the lower realms and all that underlies them, *25*

Together with sound and other objects of the senses, and the universe entirely in the form of the cosmic egg, brahmin—all this consists of Viṣṇu, yet is no more to him than an atom is to Meru, best of brahmins. *26*

He is all and is all-knowing. He takes all forms, and yet is formless. He is the lord who is praised as Viṣṇu, destroyer of all worldly sin. *27*

The entire reward that's won by a man who has finished his ablutions at the end of an Aśvamedha, best of sages, may be gained by hearing this account. *28*

The reward that's won by a man who has fasted at Prayāga, Puṣkara, Kurukṣetra or Arbuda may be gained by hearing this. *29*

The highly meritorious reward achieved from a well-conducted year-long Agnihotra sacrifice, brahmin, may be gained at once by hearing this purāṇa. *30*

After bathing in the waters of the Yamunā at Mathurā on the twelfth day of the bright fortnight in the month of Jyeṣṭha, and having beheld Hari, one attains the highest state. *31*

But that same reward is gained when one recites this narrative, sagacious brahmin, with perfect concentration and one's mind on Keśava. *32*

One who bathes in the Yamunā, best of sages, on the twelfth day of the bright fortnight in Jyeṣṭhāmūla, after fasting, *33*

And who has worshipped Acyuta correctly at Mathurā with a focused mind, achieves the full reward of an Aśvamedha sacrifice. *34*

Seeing the felicity enjoyed by ancestral spirits who'd been redeemed by their descendants, other spirits uttered this complaint: *35*

'If only someone in *our* family would bathe in the waters of the Yamunā and praise Govinda at Mathurā after fasting, *36*

In the bright fortnight of Jyeṣṭhāmūla, we, too, might enjoy such felicity and be redeemed by our descendants.' *37*

After worshipping Janārdana in the bright fortnight of Jyeṣṭhāmula, one born in an upright family may make food offerings of *piṇḍa* to his ancestors by the Yamunā. *38*

After praising Kṛṣṇa with devotion at that time and place, and offering *piṇḍa* to his ancestors and bathing in the waters of the Yamunā, *39*

The auspicious reward he receives while redeeming his own forefathers is the same as a devotee receives from hearing just one chapter of this purāṇa. *40*

This is the peerless means of salvation for those who fear saṃsāra. It dispels all nightmares and sets folk free from all defilements. *41*

This sage discourse was related in former times by lotus-born Brahmā to Ṛbhu. He relayed it to Priyavrata, and Priyavrata to Bhāguri. *42*

Bhāguri passed it to Stambhamitra, and he related it to Dadhīca. Dadhīca passed it to Sārasvata, and Bhṛgu heard it from him. *43*

Bhṛgu passed it to Purukutsa, and he repeated it to the river Narmadā. Narmadā passed it to the nāgas Dhṛtarāṣṭra and Āpūraṇa. *44*

They related it to the nāga king Vāsuki, brahmin, and he passed it to Vatsa, who repeated it to Aśvatara. *45*

He passed it on to Kambala, from whom it came to Elāpatra. *46*

When the sage Vedaśiras visited the lower realm of Pātāla, he heard this purāṇa and related it to Pramati. *47*

Pramati passed it on to wise Jātūkarṇa, and Jātūkarṇa repeated it for other beings of worthy conduct. *48*

With the boon Pulastya granted me, I acquired this sacred text and now I've given it to you, Maitreya. *49*

At the end of the Kali age, you'll narrate it to Śinīka. *50*

One who hears this—the closely guarded means of removing the stains of Kali—brahmin, will be freed from all misdeeds. *51*

One who hears it daily thereby praises all the gods with more effect than may ancestors, yakṣas and other mortals. *52*

The hard-won merit gained by giving a tawny milk cow to a brahmin is certainly achieved by hearing just ten chapters of this discourse. *53*

One who hears this whole purāṇa with his mind on Acyuta, the universal, all-embracing foundation of all the worlds, the refuge of the Self, who is both knowledge and its object, who has neither start nor finish, the benefactor of all immortals—such a one will surely win the whole reward of an Aśvamedha sacrifice. *54*

The lord, master of moving and unmoving things, who consists of knowledge of the Absolute, infallible Acyuta, overseer of creation, preservation and destruction of all the world, is present at the beginning, end and middle of this purāṇa. Those who hear it, read it or hold it in their hearts with faith will win the highest state of purity existing nowhere else in all the worlds: Hari, the singular state of perfection. *55*

Those who set their minds on Hari never go to hell, but heaven also makes it hard to contemplate him. When Hari fills a person's heart and mind, even Brahmā's realm will count for little. Since you are the eternal being abiding in people's stainless minds, the bestower of liberation, then is it any wonder that misdeeds are dispelled when you, Acyuta, are praised? *56*

Those who understand and offer sacrifices worship Hari as the everlasting lord of sacrifice with the offerings that they make. The knowledgeable contemplate him as consisting of the Absolute, the highest and higher than the highest. Having attained his state, one is no longer subject to birth or death, gain or loss. He is not existent or nonexistent—what more can be said about Hari? *57*

In the form of the ancestors, the lord enjoys correctly made oblations. In the form of a deity, he has neither start nor finish and is invoked with cries of *svāhā* and *svadhā*. In the form of the Absolute, all power abides in him. The measures by which other things are quantified cannot be applied to him. When Hari enters through your ear, he destroys all sins. *58*

I bow to the highest spirit, praiseworthy lord, who has neither start nor finish, who is not subject to decay or gain or loss, whose substance is untouched by change. *59*

I bow to the everlasting, changeless spirit who assumes all qualities, both one and many, pure but seeming not so, as he appears in different forms, imbued with knowledge and the source of every being's power. *60*

I praise him, the single essence of all knowledge, sacrifice and ascetic practice, who skilfully provides enjoyments for individuals, who is at the heart of all three qualities, who is the changeless cause of the cause of existence, the source of every form, who never ages. *61*

I always bow to him, who arranges space and air, fire and earth and water, who gifts the sound and other sensations experienced by the senses, who benefits humanity with all his actions and who is manifest, pure and subtle. *62*

Thus may Hari, the eternal unborn lord, whose form is manifold and embodies both Spirit and Nature, bestow on all humanity supreme beatitude beyond the reach of birth, decay and other woes. *63*

So ends Chapter Eight in Book Six of the glorious Viṣṇu Purāṇa.

End of Book Six.

End of the glorious Viṣṇu Purāṇa.

Appendix

Errors in the Baroda Critical Edition of the *Viṣṇu Purāṇa*

1.4.32	for payū-, read yūpa-
1.5.29	for kṛrvataḥ, read kurvataḥ
1.9.16	for maddatā, read maddattā
1.9.110	for trivipaṣṭam, read triviṣṭapam
1.9.118	for vārtā, read vārttā
1.12.76	for tapaphasastalaṃ, read tapastatphalaṃ
1.12.80	for durlabha, read durlabham
1.12.83	for bhavā, read bhavān
1.13.52	for mahāyajño, read mahāyajñe
1.13.52	for jajño, read jajne
1.13.54	for jñāāyate, read jñāyate
1.13.55	for jñāāyante, read jñāyante
1.13.69	for śarām̐śca, read śarāṃśca
1.14.39	for ananvagyram, read ananvagryam
1.15.30	for pranty-, read praty-
1.15.36	for hyto, read hṛto
1.15.78	for tapoviśaiṣair, read tapoviśesair
1.15.98	for pṛthvyāśca, read pṛthivyāśca

1.18.25	for ukṛṣṭa, read utkṛṣṭa
1.20.1	for agyraṃ, read agryaṃ
1.21.16	for gṛdhyrapi, read gṛdhryapi
1.22.68	for ahakāra, read ahaṃkāra
1.22.87	for kārtikyāṃ, read kārttikyāṃ
2.1.33	for sālagrāme, read śālagrāme
2.1.40	for viṣvagjyotiḥ, read viśvagjyothiḥ
2.2.28	for savairḍya, read savaiḍūrya
2.4.24	should read śālmalena samudro 'sau
2.4.84	for dhātakīṣaṇḍa, read dhātakīkhaṇḍa
2.5.2	for agyraṃ, read agryaṃ
2.7.28	for vyāpi, read vyāpī
2.7.43	for kiṃcivdyatiriktam, read kiṃcidvyatiriktam
2.8.16	for vikarṇau dvau vikarṇasthas, read vikoṇau dvau vikoṇasthas
2.13.33	for tatkālakṛtā, read tatkālakṛtāṃ
2.14.18	for punaś, read putraś
2.16.23	for vāsti, read nāsti
3.1.10	for Maitraya, read Maitreya
3.3.30	for ṛṅmyaḥ, read ṛṅmayaḥ
3.4.5	for prabham, read prabhum
3.4.6	for matputraṇa, read matputreṇa
3.5.18	for paramājñararūpiṇe, read paramākṣararūpiṇe
3.8.27	for śahmājīvo, read śāstrajīvo
3.9.23	for doṣāṣṭhayel, read doṣañjayel
3.10.16	for nātikheśām akheśāṃ, read nātikeśām akeśāṃ
3.10.18	for śmaśruvyaṣṭhanavatīṃ, read śmaśruvyañjanavatīṃ

3.10.23	for padṛamīṃ, read pañcamīṃ
3.11.9	for naiṛtyām, read nairṛtyām
3.11.22	for ādarśāṣṭhana, read ādarśāñjana
3.11.62	for bhuṣṭhan, read bhuñjan
3.11.64	for pādṛyajñikam, read pāñcayajñikam
3.11.69	for bhuṣṭhante, read bhuñjante
3.11.72	for bhuṣṭhan, read bhuñjan
3.11.74	for bhuṣṭhīta, read bhuñjīta; for bhuṣṭhataś, read bhuñjataś
3.11.81	for bhuṣṭhīta, read bhuñjīta
3.11.87	for mudṛta, read muñcati
3.11.88	for padṛgrāsaṃ, read pañcagrāsaṃ
4.4.49	for tasmā dapyajaḥ, read tasmādapyajaḥ
4.6.4	for -śila ceṣṭāvadbhir, read śīlaceṣṭāvadbhir
4.7.18	for akṣvāku, read ikṣvāku
4.13.38	for upadrāvā, read upadravā
4.13.45	for cāsyā saṃśayam, read cāsyāsaṃśayam
4.13.51	for pragaṭīkṛtavān, read prakaṭīkṛtavān
4.15.9	for atipauḍha-, read atiprauḍha-
4.20.12	for arjunasyā–pyulūpyāṃ, read arjunasyāpyulūpyāṃ
4.23.2	for chṛtavāṃs, read chrutavāṃs
4.24.16	for -vdyavaccheda-, read -vyavaccheda-
4.24.38	for -vaṃśa bīja-, read -vaṃśabīja-
4.24.63	for -amekān, read anekān
5.2.6	for jājjvalyamānāṃ, read jājvalymānāṃ
5.7.27	for vinā candreṇa ko vrajaḥ, read vinā kṛṣṇena ko vrajaḥ
5.9.5	for ruṣita-, read rūṣita

5.13.53	for parabhya, read parirabhya
5.17.12	for akūreti, read akrūreti
5.29.17	for guru, read muru
5.32.8	for dhoraṃ, read ghoraṃ
5.37.20	for cedama thātraiva, read cedamathātraiva
5.37.21	for vedmyatad, read vedmyetad
6.3.9	for muhūrtto, read muhūrto

Selective index

Note: This index provides book, chapter and verse numbers.

www.ingramcontent.com/pod-product-compliance
Lightning Source LLC
Chambersburg PA
CBHW061112100726
47911CB00013B/510

9781760464400